THE CARCERAL CITY

THE CARCERAL CITY

Slavery and
the Making of
Mass Incarceration
in New Orleans,
1803–1930

JOHN K. BARDES

The University of North Carolina Press
Chapel Hill

Designed by April Leidig
Set in Miller by Copperline Book Services

Manufactured in the United States of America

Cover art: *Photographs:* Glass plate negatives from the New Orleans
Police Mugshot Collection, City Archives and Special Collections, New
Orleans Public Library. *Background:* Henry Möellhausen and Benjamin
Moore Norman, *Norman's plan of New Orleans and environs*, 1845,
Geography and Map Division, Library of Congress, Washington, DC.

Library of Congress Cataloging-in-Publication Data
Names: Bardes, John K., author.
Title: The carceral city : slavery and the making of mass
    incarceration in New Orleans, 1803–1930 / John K. Bardes.
Description: Chapel Hill : The University of North Carolina Press,
    [2024] | Includes bibliographical references and index.
Identifiers: LCCN 2023045910 | ISBN 9781469678177 (cloth) |
    ISBN 9781469678184 (paperback) | ISBN 9781469678191 (epub) |
    ISBN 9798890886972 (pdf)
Subjects: LCSH: Imprisonment—Louisiana—New Orleans—History. |
    Prisons—Louisiana—New Orleans—History. | Mass incarceration—
    Louisiana—New Orleans—History. | Slavery—Louisiana—New
    Orleans—History. | Criminal justice, Administration of—Louisiana—
    New Orleans—History. | Discrimination in criminal justice
    administration—Louisiana—New Orleans—History. | New Orleans
    (La.)—Race relations. | BISAC: HISTORY / African American & Black |
    SOCIAL SCIENCE / Penology
Classification: LCC HV9481.N33 B38 2024 | DDC 364.9763/35—
    dc23/eng/20231122
LC record available at https://lccn.loc.gov/2023045910

This book will be made open access within three years of publication
thanks to Path to Open, a program developed in partnership between
JSTOR, the American Council of Learned Societies (ACLS), the University
of Michigan Press, and the University of North Carolina Press to bring
about equitable access and impact for the entire scholarly community,
including authors, researchers, libraries, and university presses around
the world. Learn more at https://about.jstor.org/path-to-open/.

For Lindsay, with all my love

CONTENTS

ILLUSTRATIONS

Figures

Graphs

Map

THE CARCERAL CITY

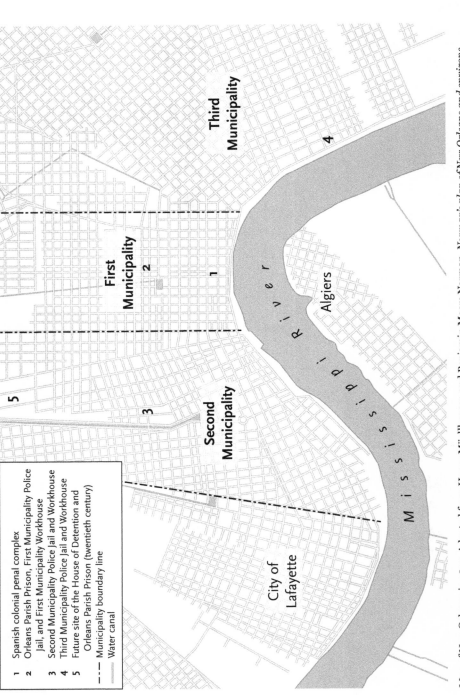

1   Spanish colonial penal complex
2   Orleans Parish Prison, First Municipality Police Jail, and First Municipality Workhouse
3   Second Municipality Police Jail and Workhouse
4   Third Municipality Police Jail and Workhouse
5   Future site of the House of Detention and Orleans Parish Prison (twentieth century)
– · – Municipality boundary line
        Water canal

Map of New Orleans in 1845. Adapted from Henry Möellhausen and Benjamin Moore Norman, *Norman's plan of New Orleans and environs, 1845*, Geography and Map Division, Library of Congress, Washington, DC.

INTRODUCTION

On the night of August 18, 1943, after several unsolved robberies sparked fears of a new crime wave and as the nation waged unrelenting war on tyranny overseas, New Orleans's police chief ordered the arrest of all the "vagrant negroes."

Police began sweeping street corners, dance halls, and barrooms for Black men, charging them all with vagrancy: the crime of appearing idle and unemployed. By August 20, police had arrested nearly 100 "vagrant" Black men; after another two days, more than 400. By then, suspects in the robberies had been found and charged. Yet the arrests continued. Citing Louisiana's patriotic duty to maximize war production, New Orleans mayor Robert Maestri vowed to prosecute the "wholesale arrests" of Black vagrants until all the jobless "loiterers" had been driven "to jail or to work." In court, virtually every detainee protested that he in fact already had a job. On August 27, the number of vagrancy arrests surpassed 600. By September 4, their number neared 1,000—equivalent to roughly 2 percent of all adult Black men in New Orleans.[1]

The prisoners were herded into an infamous New Orleans prison known as the House of Detention. After several days, as the first detentions were set to expire, a fleet of trucks pulled up, provided by the American Sugarcane League. The prisoners were released but given a choice. Either they boarded the trucks—bound for rural plantations, where they would be forced to accept jobs harvesting sugarcane at fixed wages—or they would be immediately rearrested, reconvicted, and reincarcerated for vagrancy. Daniel Byrd, president of the New Orleans chapter of the NAACP, called it "nothing short of peonage."[2]

That summer, similar mass arrests of Black workers on vagrancy charges erupted in Birmingham, Jackson, Miami, Dallas, Wilmington, and other cities throughout the South. The governors of Alabama, Mississippi, and North Carolina declared statewide wars on vagrancy. "Idleness can not, and will not, be tolerated," Mississippi governor Paul Johnson declared on August 31, "while our sons are fighting and dying for the principles we hold so dear."[3]

Americans familiar with the history of Jim Crow have encountered similar stories: mass arrests and confinements, targeting Black Americans arbitrarily, often in the service of elite white economic interests. Yet beginning here erases the first half of the story. In fact, the policing and carceral practices on display in 1943 date to the early nineteenth century.

Consider, for a moment, the New Orleans House of Detention itself. Once known as Louisiana's "slave penitentiary," the prison had been founded in 1805 for the confinement and torture of resistant and fugitive enslaved people before their return to their owners. By 1943, this institution had been in the continuous business of conveying Black people to sugar plantations for 138 years. Before Emancipation, police brought enslaved people to this prison as "runaway" slaves. After Emancipation, police brought free people to this prison as "vagrant" wageworkers. In other words, antebellum coercive tactics directly informed the design of postbellum coercive tactics. The ways that New Orleans policed, imprisoned, and forcibly redeployed Black Americans in the twentieth century derived from the ways that New Orleans had policed, imprisoned, and forcibly redeployed enslaved people in the early nineteenth century.

For most of the late twentieth and early twenty-first centuries, New Orleans has been the world's carceral capital: the city that incarcerates people at the highest rate of any American city, within the state that incarcerates people at the highest rate of any American state, within the country that incarcerates more people than any other nation on the globe. New Orleans is the epicenter of what scholars have termed "mass incarceration": the explosive growth of imprisoned populations, disproportionately Black, since the 1970s.[4] No country on earth has ever caged a higher percentage of its own people or of the human race. Black Americans account for 13 percent of the US population but nearly 40 percent of the US prison population, raising fundamental questions regarding American identity, race, violence, inequality, the legacy of slavery, and the meaning of freedom.[5] Scholars of mass incarceration often point to proximate causes: labor dislocations during the 1970s, the nation's ill-conceived "wars" on drugs and crime, "broken windows" policing, and backlash against the civil rights movement, to name a few.[6] Other scholars locate mass incarceration on a longer historical timeline that stretches as far back as the late nineteenth century, when police and prisons were bastardized into appendages of white power in the aftermath of slave emancipation and during the codification of Jim Crow.[7] Yet as this book shows, the features associated with mass incarceration—astronomical incarceration rates, state violence on a vast scale, the targeted internment of entire populations—began in New Orleans long before the late twentieth century, or Jim Crow. Indeed, by the 1820s, New Orleans incarcerated enslaved residents at higher rates than the city, state, or nation incarcerates Black Americans today.[8]

This book examines the rise of state coercion in the world's carceral capital, from the Louisiana Purchase in 1803 through to the nadir of Jim Crow in the early twentieth century. In legal parlance, public officials' ability to coerce peoples falls under the umbrella of *state police power*: generally defined as the power of governments to regulate and restrain populations and property for the public good, though restricted here to the coercion of laboring people through the threat or use of imprisonment. State police power is an old concept: rooted in early modern European law, it predates the modern connotations of the word "police," today referring to the municipal agents tasked with maintaining order. In US constitutional law, state police power derives from the Tenth Amendment to the Constitution, which reserves to the states all powers not delegated to the federal government.[9]

Whereas previous scholars have argued that slavery stymied coercive state power, the central argument of this book is that many antebellum slaveholders were fiercely committed to, and deeply reliant upon, the use of police and prisons to coerce enslaved *and* free labor. Decades before the Civil War, southern port cities created the first municipal police forces in the United States, jailed Black *and* white workers at astronomical rates, and contrived massive slave prisons and specialized slave penal labor systems to maintain control and maximize profit. Emancipation disrupted, but did not destroy, the publicly managed policing and penal systems developed within cities: rather than starting anew, southern authorities adjusted, adapted, and refined the prisons and policing practices already at their disposal—including prisons and policing practices originally devised for the subjugation of the enslaved—into the brutal coercive machinery of Jim Crow. In other words, the histories of racialized policing and imprisonment in the United States begin in the early antebellum urban South, with the very origins of prisons and municipal police. To peer within New Orleans's "slave penitentiary" is to witness the roots of Jim Crow and our nation's current carceral crisis.

Prison and Plantation

Before the 1990s, the field of prison history had far less to say about slavery, race, or the American South. Historians of the prison have traced its origins to the actions of social reformers, working in the northeastern United States and northern Europe, during the late eighteenth and early nineteenth centuries. These reformers resolved to abolish public spectacles of corporal punishment, which seemed out of step with the changing economic and ideological needs of liberalizing and industrializing post-Enlightenment society. In place of degrading public rituals, reformers envisioned cloistered and controlled institutions where deviants could be transformed into law-abiding citizens and "restored" to society. Thus was the prison born; gradually, these institutions spread throughout the world.[10] Historians of organized policing have generally traced a similar, northern-focused narrative.[11] Slave societies, which have never fit neatly into this story, have largely been left out.

Yet the explosive growth in American incarceration rates during the late twentieth century and the wildly disproportionate confinement of Black Americans sparked new and intense interest in the relations among slavery, race, and the prison. Scholars have demonstrated that after Emancipation, former slaveholders created new systems of bonded labor through the penal system.[12] Prominent studies have traced the underlying social origins of racialized policing and imprisonment back to this postbellum moment, when slaveholders' power to punish had to leap from plantation to prison. Whether explicitly or tacitly, these studies often imagine the modern prison as the confluence of two "ancestral lines": the original "rehabilitative penology" developed by reformers in the post-Enlightenment North and a "subjugationist discipline," assembled from the residues of slavery, in the post-Emancipation South. Over time, a new popular narrative has seeped into the national consciousness—popularized by acclaimed best-sellers such as Michelle Alexander's *The New Jim Crow*, award-winning documentaries such as Netflix's *13th*, and the 1619 Project of the *New York Times Magazine*—constructing a direct genealogical link between slavery and present-day mass incarceration by positioning the postbellum prison as slavery's "replacement."[13]

This scholarship relies on the assumption that enslaved people themselves were rarely or never incarcerated. Indeed, most historians have long accepted that slavery and expansive state power were incompatible, that plantation and prison were redundant systems of social control, and that the antebellum South lacked a fully articulated penal tradition or expansive carceral infrastructure before Emancipation. In this view, insofar as enslaved people were ever incarcerated, it was only fleetingly—following a fugitive's recapture or immediately before an enslaved person's sale—reflecting neither deliberate forethought nor the influence of global developments in rehabilitative penology. The "South already possessed total institutions containing those perceived as inherently criminal," one historian writes. "A penitentiary would have been redundant." "The very idea of imprisonment as a punishment for crimes committed by slaves was a contradiction," echoes another. "The criminal justice system which emerged prior to the Civil War was for whites only."[14]

Theories of modernity and power, if not common sense, suggest the fundamental incompatibility of "modern" forms of state power with slavery's "premodern" reliance on privately inflicted corporal violence.[15] The two most influential approaches within the field of prison history, pioneered respectively by scholars working in the Marxist tradition and by Michel Foucault, both suggest the impossibility of prisons for the enslaved: the Marxist approach because it links the rise of prisons to the rise of wage-labor relations, and Foucault's approach because it explains the rise of prisons in terms of a broader societal shift away from corporal violence and toward subtler forms of disciplinary power.[16] Traditional treatments of the southern planter class as categorically opposed to concentrated state power—committed to Jeffersonian republicanism, fiscal conservatism, and honor culture—further preclude the South's development of expansive policing and penal systems.[17]

Admittedly, scholars of urban slavery, going as far back as Richard C. Wade's book *Slavery in the Cities* in 1964, have noted distinctive patterns of state surveillance and punishment within southern cities.[18] Yet the general tendency within urban slavery scholarship has been to emphasize the relative freedoms that enslaved people accessed within cities, rather than the particular policing and carceral systems that cities developed to counteract those freedoms.[19] Perhaps because cities themselves have often seemed somehow "inauthentically" southern, the broader literatures of American police, prison, and state development have tended to overlook the antebellum urban South entirely.[20] With few exceptions, past works have focused on the nineteenth-century cities of Europe and the American Northeast, especially Paris, London, Philadelphia, and New York: a scholarly lacuna that reaffirms the assumption that modern forms of institutional power developed first in free societies, then later trickled South. Most syntheses omit the antebellum South entirely or relegate its summation to a single sentence, paragraph, or page. No monograph on prison development in the urban South has ever been published. Only one quantitative analysis of slave prison records from anywhere in the South—Betty Wood's article of 1987 on Savannah's slave workhouse, based on a single existent jail book spanning only six years—exists.[21]

And yet, the long-forgotten ledgers of New Orleans's police and prisons, containing hundreds of thousands of arrest and imprisonment records for free and enslaved persons, plainly reveal that antebellum New Orleans was a police state. Arrest rates, incarceration rates, police-to-population ratios, the degree to which the city relied on penal labor: each was far higher than what existed in major antebellum US cities outside the South and rivals or exceeds contemporary figures of major US cities.[22] Surviving records from Charleston, Savannah, Richmond, and Memphis suggest similar trends.[23] Municipal authorities exercised an extreme level of control over the activities and choices of menial workers, free and enslaved. Enslaved people grew to expect, and slaveholders grew to depend on, persistently repressive government action.

Two forms of human captivity—slavery and the prison—have played profound roles in shaping the meaning of American freedom. We can sense that these two institutions, each defining freedom's limits, are somehow interconnected. Because it excludes slave societies, the traditional, northern-focused paradigm of American prison development has done little to untangle the historical interplay of race, slavery, and the growth of state power and thus has little to say with regards to the extreme inequity and racialized state violence that characterizes prisons today. The "plantation-to-prison" narrative offers a much-needed solution to this impasse by providing a framework by which to consider the historical connections among race, slavery, and imprisonment.

Yet as an explanatory framework, the plantation-to-prison narrative is limited. It conjures unsophisticated configurations of continuity and change. It relies on and reproduces traditional assumptions regarding the "Old South"—that it was premodern, protocapitalist, anti-statist, and authentically rural—to which fewer and fewer historians of the antebellum South ascribe.[24] It effectively excludes Black Americans from the first century of American prison development while framing as "premodern" the institutions through which postbellum Black Americans were policed and punished, as though ideas about Black criminality and punishment "had not been shaped by modern ideas or modern agencies."[25] It struggles to account for the presence of white prisoners. It typifies as "southern" all prison violence, racism, neglect, and economic exploitation, blinding us to other histories of racial violence and exploitation that emerge from the prisons of the American Midwest, Far West, and North.[26] It assigns a singular, metaphysical, essential nature to the postbellum southern prison, by suggesting that postbellum southern criminal justice *only* pursued the re-creation of a captive and racialized labor force: foregrounding southern elites' narrow pursuit of profit and racial control while neglecting the far more complex ways that economic pressures, state interests, competing community values, theories of crime, fear of social upheaval, and legal tradition all coalesce in the formation of punitive practice. Most vitally, the plantation-to-prison narrative simply doesn't match the clear documentary record left behind by slaveholding cities.

Here, I take a different approach. Rather than presupposing that slavery and the development of coercive state power were incompatible, I examine the sorts of coercive state institutions and legal strategies that slave societies *did* generate. Instead of assuming that Emancipation was the pivot point on which southern state violence hinged, I consider how Louisiana lawmakers continually developed, adapted, and refined state coercive tactics in response to multiple historic transformations, including the cotton and sugar revolutions, the late antebellum growth of immigrant wage labor, Emancipation, Reconstruction, and the rise of Jim Crow. Throughout, I try to resist the temptation to reduce southern criminal justice to a simplistic caricature or to suggest that any singular subtext or motivation constitutes the essential nature or pursuit of Louisiana's penal and policing systems, discernable from the moment of birth and historically constant throughout time. Always, prisons and police are complex social institutions that perform multiple societal functions, including (but not limited to) the expression of power relations, acculturation of values, service of economic interests, regulation of behavior, affirmation of state authority and legitimacy, and organization of people's ideas surrounding good and evil, order and disorder, conformist and deviant, just and unfair.[27]

This approach renders visible distinct patterns that the plantation-to-prison narrative obscures or omits. The South's first major transition from privately inflicted violence to state-managed punishments occurred more than a half-century before Emancipation, as waves of revolutionary upheavals, propagated in part by the slave revolution in Saint-Domingue (present-day Haiti), spurred southern port cities to develop new municipal police forces, slave prison systems, and coercive legal strategies. The South's coercive tactics never developed in isolation: urban slave societies exchanged carceral technologies and policing strategies between one another, adapted technologies and strategies from the North and Europe, and exported innovations to free labor societies. Over time, several slaveholding cities came to coerce labor through two parallel legal frameworks: Black workers were primarily policed and imprisoned through regulations governing illicit slave mobility, which slaveholders called "marronage," while vagrancy laws provided the primary legal mechanism by which antebellum authorities regulated white wageworkers. With Emancipation, former slaveholders endeavored to collapse together these two legal frameworks by reshaping vagrancy law to include powers that antebellum law enforcement had exercised over maroons. In the name of suppressing Black vagrancy, former slave prisons and their practices were restructured and relaunched, providing a physical infrastructure and institutional knowledge that would help structure the coercive state tactics deployed under Jim Crow.

Still, Jim Crow–era lawmakers were unable to entirely re-create the level of coercive control exercised by their antebellum predecessors. Contrary to prevailing wisdom, arrest and incarceration rates in Jim Crow New Orleans were considerably *lower* than those endured by the city's enslaved residents before Emancipation. Put another way, the antebellum slave city established degrees of state coercion and surveillance not reproduced until the "age of mass incarceration" in the late twentieth century.

Slavery and the State

New Orleans offers an exceptional setting to study the growth of state police power within slave society. Founded by French colonists near the mouth of the Mississippi River in 1718 and acquired by the Spanish Empire in 1762, the city was incorporated into the United States in 1803, coinciding with a total revolution in the Deep South's economy, demography, and environment. The cotton revolution and the simultaneous discovery of a sugarcane variety that could be produced in southern Louisiana at a commercial scale transmuted the rich alluvial soils of the Lower Mississippi River valley into some of the most sought-after agricultural land on the continent. Within a generation, spaces that had been overwhelmingly Choctaw, Chitimacha, Caddo, Bayogoula, Chickasaw, Houma, Natchez, Tunica, and Creek were violently rearranged into a new heartland for the wealthiest slave society in the Americas. By 1860, the narrow stretch of slave plantations running along the Mississippi River from New Orleans to Natchez, Mississippi, were home to most of the nation's millionaires and the greatest concentration of per capita wealth in the entire country. New Orleans's strategic location near the Mississippi River's mouth meant that all the region's consumer goods, peoples, and wealth were funneled through the city's port. New Orleans became the nation's largest slave market. Every winter, half of all the cotton and virtually all the sugar produced in the South passed through the city's port. By 1840, New Orleans had also become the Deep South's largest city, the third largest and the wealthiest city in the country, the second most active immigration port of entry in the United States, and the fourth busiest commercial port in the entire world.[28]

The slaveholders of the Lower Mississippi River valley thrived, in part, because they could rely on the state to assist them in the coercion of labor. During the past quarter-century, scholars of early American economic development have endeavored to "bring the state back in," stressing the importance of nineteenth-century governance to the creation and regulation of new markets. Rejecting what he terms "the Myth of the 'Weak' American State," historian William Novak traces the emergence of expansive American governance back to nineteenth-century cities, documenting local governments' commitment to regulating social life and economy and exploring the "convergence of public and private power" that sustained early American economic development. Expansive state intervention, Novak suggests, was not a twentieth-century phenomenon, though antebellum state police power was typically decentralized, exercised at the municipal level, and existed alongside (sometimes in partnership, sometimes in rivalry with) private power.[29]

A related literature has revived debates over the relation between American slavery and the development of American capitalism. In drawing connections between slavery and capitalism, scholars have developed a variety of approaches. Some have stressed how the wealth generated by slavery accelerated global economic development. Others have suggested that slaveholders themselves were deeply "capitalistic," particularly in their managerial styles, financing methods, and quest for maximized returns. Others still have challenged the classical interpretation, suggested by Karl Marx and Max Weber, of capitalism and slavery as incompatible modes of production: by examining mixed labor markets that depended on both enslaved workers and wageworkers, practices of slave hiring, or the ways that enslavers stored, invested, transported, and inherited wealth through the persons whom they held as property.[30]

This book sits at the convergence of these two literatures by examining how the state harnessed enslaved, free, and freed laborers in the service of both private wealth accumulation and public economic development.[31] Just as slaveholders of the Mississippi River valley relied on banks to finance their purchase of plantations and slaves and steamboats to carry their cotton and sugar to markets, so they relied on municipal and state governments to help quash laborers' resistance, squeeze greater labor from underperforming workers, build and maintain penal facilities for the storage and subjugation of human property, and deploy penal laborers in the construction and maintenance of the essential public infrastructure—roads, canals, wharves, levees, highways, bridges, water supply systems, and sewers—that promoted economic development and made large-scale cash-crop agriculture possible.

In debates over capitalism's boundaries, penal labor often looms large. Marxist approaches to the study of the prison, pioneered by Georg Rusche and Otto Kirchheimer in the 1930s, attribute penal developments to changes in political economy, emphasizing correlations between a society's punishments and its dominant modes of production.[32] That southern criminal justice underwent a complete transformation following Emancipation has long seemed to affirm the Rusche-Kirchheimer thesis: suggesting a fundamental jump from one mode of production to another and substantiating the broader tendency to depict capitalism and slavery as incompatible systems.[33]

Yet in designing state coercive systems, public officials in New Orleans did not observe strict theoretical delineations between wageworkers and slaves.[34] Penal technologies developed for imprisoned wageworkers were often adapted and redeployed for use on imprisoned slaves, and vice-versa. In constructing public infrastructure, authorities deployed various configurations of rented slaves, hired wageworkers, white penal laborers, enslaved penal laborers, and free Black wageworkers seized on the legal fiction that they might be fugitive enslaved people. Even when segregated by race and legal status, white prisoners and imprisoned enslaved people often toiled as interconnected cogs within the same municipal machinery: white prisoners carved the cobblestones that enslaved prisoners paved into the streets, white prisoners manufactured the brooms that enslaved prisoners used to sweep sidewalks. Nor did Emancipation mark a complete departure from preexisting state coercive systems: into the twenty-first century, New Orleans's municipal economy continued to rely on networks of prisons, penal labor crews, and police patrols first established to control enslaved populations in 1805.

Prison development in New Orleans also poses a conceptual challenge to the main alternative to the Marxist approach, pioneered by Michel Foucault, David Rothman, and Michael Ignatieff in the 1970s. Foucault, in particular, famously identified the period between the late eighteenth and early nineteenth centuries as the age of "the birth of the prison," when the dominant approach to state punishment within Western societies metaphorized from public rituals of corporal violence into rehabilitative confinement within totalizing institutions. Breaking from a previous tradition that had explained this transformation in terms of humanitarian progress, these scholars developed a "revisionist" framework that identified the development of prisons with the rise of disciplinary power and a broader societal shift toward subtler forms of control. In Foucault's configuration, this shift demarcated the arrival of "modernity" itself.[35]

Scholarship patterned after this revisionist framework has long struggled to explain prison development in slave and colonial societies, where corporal violence and public shaming remained integral long after the arrival of the prison. If, as Foucault suggested, the decline of public shaming and physical torture parallels the transition to modernity, then the endurance of shame and torture would seem to suggest an insufficient or incomplete transition.[36] One response, proposed by scholars of African American history, has been to suggest that Foucauldian "modernity" was simply never extended toward Black Americans and other colonized peoples: toward them, prisons have aimed "not so much to transform" but instead to "torture" and "eliminate."[37] Another explanation suggests that slave and colonial societies only made partial progress toward modernity, developing disorganized and chaotic prisons and law enforcement agencies that reflected a "transitional type" or "hybrid form" between the premodern and modern.[38] Both of these interpretations uphold essentialist constructs of a "premodern" South. They bolster the revisionist paradigm—and Foucault's work, in particular—as the exemplar against which their subjects fall short.

Yet records from New Orleans's slave prisons suggest that administrators *did* seek to effect reformative transformations within enslaved prisoners: though rather than seeking to "uplift" prisoners for society, authorities sought to violently brutalize resistant Black workers into idealized slaves who accepted the terms of their subjugation.[39] And although many southern prisons were disorganized and chaotic places, visitors and prisoners often described the slave prisons of the South's largest and wealthiest slave cities in starkly different terms—"grand and imposing," "magnificent," "well arranged," "scientifically" designed, "massive," and, "in every respect, successful"—that bespeak substan-

tial public investment, advanced bureaucratization, and thoughtful intentionality. Urban slave prisons were "the only clean, well organized and thoroughly
administered institutions which I have seen in the South," wrote one of the
most influential social reformers of his age, Samuel Gridley Howe, during a
regional tour in 1841. "Every part is kept scrupulously clean; everything is well
adapted to its purpose; every officer is active and energetic."[40]

Slavery did not prohibit the sort of prison development associated with tran-
sitions to capitalism and "modern" forms of institutionalized power, though
slavery *did* mean that southern prison development pursued distinctive priorities down a unique path.[41] From New Orleans, three distinctive trends emerge.

First, prisons played significant roles in the production of "race" itself. In
every society, prisons serve as important sites of state categorization and codification, regulating populations, and the reproduction of difference.[42] Yet prisons played particularly important functions within slave ports such as New
Orleans, swirling tumultuously with enslaved, free, and freed workers, locally
born and immigrant, of various African, European, Indigenous, and multiracial ancestries. Through punishments, the slave state tried to fabricate racial
logic from this human medley by sorting, categorizing, and racializing bodies;
deploying punitive rituals through which social hierarchies and power relationships were enacted and performed; and attaching ideas of innate biological
difference and rights to certain bodies (while withholding those ideas from
other bodies) through the regulation of permissible and impermissible bodily
treatments.[43]

Prisons were not only places where *static* social categories were *reinforced*:
through prisons, authorities actively reworked and adjusted power relations
and social hierarchies. Sometimes, jailors deliberately *transgressed* the very
social hierarchies that they were tasked with upholding: by ordering Black
men to whip white women or by assigning enslaved women to tasks restricted
to enslaved men. At times, public authorities used prisons to rewrite an entire
population's social status: such as when nativists sought to punish European
immigrants together with enslaved prisoners or when Confederates jailed well-
to-do freeborn Black landowners together with fugitive enslaved people. Race
was neither static nor self-reproducing: inside the prison, power relations and
social hierarchies were continuously reworked and remade.

Second, among the many regulatory functions performed by Louisiana's police and prisons, none was more important than the suppression of workers'
mobility. New Orleans's coercive tactics evolved in response to the specific resistance strategies that both enslaved and free workers deployed.[44] Chief among
those resistance strategies, and common across enslaved, free, and freed labor,
was the withholding of labor and the assertion of autonomy by running away:

vagabondage, marronage, flight, migration, tramping, deserting, violating curfew, stealing time, jumping ship. Workers fled for a variety of economic, political, psychological, and physiological reasons. Some workers absconded to escape intolerable working conditions, either by hiding temporarily or by seeking better conditions elsewhere. Others fled to supplement their insufficient caloric intake or income by scavenging, peddling, foraging, prostituting, or circulating stolen goods with the local "shadow economy." Workers fled to participate in prohibited social and cultural events or to reconnect with friends and family. Sometimes they fled simply to gain feelings of control over their bodies, lives, and labor.[45]

More than any other single factor, efforts to regulate workers' mobility shaped the development of state police power in early New Orleans. Lawmakers identified "maroon" slaves, poor white "vagrants," and free Black transient workers as the three greatest threats to public order. They developed prison systems and policing routines that prioritized the pursuit and subjugation of these three resistantly mobile criminalized castes.

Third, elite Louisianians' understandings of crime, race, and coercion were structured by a theory of master-servant relations derived from early modern European law. This theory of social order held that a white man's mastery derived not from his race or gender per se but from his status as the manager of his household. Here, "household" referred not only to the familial relatives of the household head but to everyone who worked for him, worked on his land, or owed allegiance to him, including all subordinate wageworkers, servants, apprentices, and enslaved people. Unskilled, landless hirelings who sold their labor for a wage—much like wives, children, apprentices, servants, and slaves—were classified as *dependent* persons, incapable of managing their own lives and labor, who rightfully deferred decision-making to their master or employer. Within this logic, societal well-being and prosperity depended on the master's ability to control his dependents' lives and labor. This system of thought rationalized the submission of slaves to their owners, of women and children to their husbands, and of wageworkers to their employers. It naturalized racial, gender, and class hierarchies; justified white male householders' exclusive claim to political rights; and attached a powerful "taint of dependency" to women, Black Americans, and menial wageworkers, particularly if they did not own land.[46] Although often identified as derivative of British common law, analogous ideas were present in French civil law.[47] Louisiana's Civil Code of 1808, informed by both legal traditions, devoted the entirety of its first book, "Of Persons," to defining these dependent hierarchies between "husband and wife," "father and child," and "master and servant"—with "servant" further divided into four subclasses consisting of slaves, wageworkers, indentured servants, and apprentices.[48]

State police power derived from this theory of social order: just as the patriarch bore responsibility for managing his dependents' lives and labor, so the state was duty bound to police the industry and orderliness of persons within its jurisdiction, especially if they were wayward dependents without firm attachments to any master.[49] Critically, this logic did not recognize meaningful distinction between coercing labor to prevent crime and coercing labor to maximize profit: the key to protecting economy *and* public safety lay in asserting control over autonomous dependents.

Similar ideas had structured labor relations in the colonial North. Yet the rise of wage labor relations during the first half of the nineteenth century, and the concurrent maturation of proslavery thought in the South, resulted in a deepening ideological commitment to the master-servant relationship in the South, at the same time that the master-servant relationship was losing sway in the North. While the antebellum North transitioned toward a "free labor ideology" that celebrated the individual wageworker's ability to climb the economic ladder through hard work and self-reliance, elite antebellum southerners grew increasingly convinced that the maintenance of statically hierarchical relations between master and servant provided the foundation of both social order and economic prosperity.[50] To antebellum slaveholders, this way of configuring social relations suggested that innately dependent persons who violated the sacred covenant between master and dependent—enslaved people who fled their masters, women who defied their husbands, children who opposed their parents, landless wageworkers who abandoned their employers—posed the gravest of hazards to social stability, public safety, and economy. They were uncontrolled yet incapable of controlling themselves. They were beyond the reach of traditional governmentality. The state had an interest and duty in reasserting control over these dangerously rebellious persons.

This logic further suggested conceptual connections among enslaved fugitives, poor white vagrants, and free Black migrants. This perception of connection facilitated the transference of coercive tactics between these groups and across categories of legal and racial difference and informed how former slaveholders approached the coercion of labor following slavery's collapse. To be clear, this study does not find evidence of collective class consciousness across enslaved and free labor: quite the opposite, incarcerated laborers often clung tenaciously to the racial, legal, and caste differences that distinguished themselves from one another. Nor does this study mean to equate white wageworkers with enslaved people; to minimize the significance of race, legal status, and gender in shaping people's lived experiences; or to reproduce the pernicious article of slavery apologia which holds that white wageworkers and enslaved people were exploited, dominated, or brutalized to comparable degrees. Always, whiteness provided poor white workers with legal and social protections—what

W. E. B. Du Bois famously likened to "a sort of public and psychological wage"—
totally unavailable to either enslaved people or poor free Black Americans.[51]
Rather, my contention here is that slaveholders' commitment to white power
and racial caste obscured a subtler and contradictory conviction that *all* menial
labor was a commodity that the state should help make available to capital.[52]
Several dividing lines—between wage labor and slave labor, white persons and
Black persons, antebellum and postbellum—shaped public application of coercive power. Yet above these divisions hovered elite Louisianans' supreme conviction that landless menial laborers were dependent persons who worked best
if coerced, threatened public safety if permitted to roam freely, and required
the disciplinary hand of a public or private master.

The chapters that follow trace the development of state coercion in New Orleans across enslaved, free, and freed labor. Chapter 1 uncovers the origins of
Louisiana's modern correctional systems, beginning in the immediate aftermath of the Louisiana Purchase. In May 1805, fearing the slave rebellion that
had recently destroyed the nearby colony of Saint-Domingue and perceiving
that slaveholders' privately inflicted punishments were becoming less effective,
authorities in New Orleans launched two concurrent reforms: they created one
of the first municipal police forces in the United States, and they constructed
a slave prison for the "correction" of fugitive and resistant enslaved people. In
designing their new slave penal system, authorities adopted ideas and practices
from preexisting slave penal institutions scattered about the Caribbean while
also incorporating recent developments in mainstream penal theory from the
American Northeast and Europe. From this first slave prison emerged a theory and practice of slave penology that gradually spread to cities and towns
throughout the Mississippi River valley.

Chapter 2 charts the incarceration of enslaved convicts at the state level. In
the 1820s, a new reform movement swept the nation, leading to the construction of the first state penitentiaries. As Louisiana's peer states built penitentiaries, slaveholders in Louisiana debated if and how this reform movement
should reshape the punishment of the enslaved. Some civic leaders proposed
the creation of more "humane" slave prisons or the construction of a specialized
state penitentiary for enslaved convicts. Others feared that such reforms raised
deeply destabilizing questions regarding the nature of bodily difference that
ultimately threatened the racial order on which Louisiana's economy relied.
These fraught discussions produced a series of experiments in state penal systems for enslaved convicts, each of which grappled with the relation between
imprisonment and race.

Chapters 3 and 4 examine the coercion of free labor in New Orleans. Chapter 3 explores the coercive strategies that New Orleans deployed toward
transient free Black laborers—in particular, sailors and steamboat workers—

who entered the city in search of work. In examining state violence toward free Black workers, past scholarship has focused on the South's infamous "Negro Seamen Acts," first passed by South Carolina in 1822, which sought to "quarantine" free Black sailors by imprisoning them while their ships were docked in port. Records of New Orleans's prisons reveal an alternate approach to mobile free Black labor, which predated the Negro Seamen Acts: there, police systematically seized free Black sailors and steamboat workers on the legal fiction that they were fugitive enslaved people, condemning them to torture and forced labor within slave prisons while denying them the ability to sue for redress or release. Instead of "quarantining," this practice sought to equate free Black sailors with the enslaved and their mobility with enslaved people's marronage: underscoring the role that police and prisons played in the management of legal status and race.

Chapter 4 explores the coercion of poor white workers through vagrancy law. As late antebellum cities grew increasingly reliant on hired immigrant labor, New Orleans joined other southern cities in launching secondary penal labor systems for the punishment of white workers convicted of vagrancy. Through vagrancy law, authorities sought to control immigration and seasonal migration patterns, to criminalize wageworkers' efforts to withhold labor or renegotiate wages, to suppress behaviors considered disruptive, and to affirm landless workers' dependency on propertied mastery. These antebellum efforts to coerce white labor through vagrancy law built atop prior efforts to police and imprison fugitive enslaved people and provided key precursors to the coercion of Black labor after Emancipation.

Chapters 5 and 6 chart the transformation of these various coercive strategies through the Civil War, Emancipation, and Reconstruction. Chapter 5 traces events in southeastern Louisiana following the region's surrender to the Union army in 1862. Initially, local and Federal authorities worked together to maintain the region's preexisting infrastructure for arresting, confining, and redeploying resistant enslaved people. Yet as slavery's imminent collapse became clear, locals and Federals began arresting freedpeople as vagrants, using vagrancy laws to legitimate freedpeople's continued seizure and coercion without violating the dictates of Federal antislavery policy. From these coercive experiments emerged a "Louisiana Plan" for post-Emancipation labor that Federal troops gradually imposed throughout the occupied South.

During the Reconstruction era, freedpeople, freeborn Black Louisianians, and former slaveholders battled over the future of the city's police and prisons. These struggles are the focus of chapter 6. Freedpeople demanded greater protections from arbitrary arrest and imprisonment, arguing that freedom was meaningless if the state had the power to summarily seize them at will. Meanwhile, former slaveholders envisioned the reorganization of the state's prewar slave prison system, perceiving in vagrancy law the re-creation of their broad antebellum powers to punish resistant enslaved people. These struggles would climax with the ratification of Louisiana's radical State Constitution of 1868, which established expansive due process rights, restricted penal labor, and nullified all state vagrancy laws.

Chapter 7 explores labor coercion in New Orleans during Jim Crow. Following the collapse of Reconstruction, New Orleans joined several peer cities in reopening its former slave prison—now repurposed for the confinement of Black and white wageworkers charged with vagrancy. Vagrancy arrest rates soared: throughout the early twentieth century, New Orleans police performed more vagrancy arrests than the police departments of New York City, Chicago, Philadelphia, and Detroit *combined*. For Black New Orleanians of the Jim Crow era, the omnipresent threat of vagrancy arrest and the subjection to a humiliating penal regime that traced its origins to the disciplining of resistant enslaved people hung over their lives like a dark pall. Yet as horrific as this coercive regime was, arrest rates, imprisonment rates, and police-to-population ratios in Jim Crow New Orleans were actually *lower* than rates previously endured by enslaved New Orleanians.

The epilogue traces the history of New Orleans's jail system through the rise of mass incarceration in the late twentieth century, Hurricane Katrina in 2005, and ultimately the closure of the House of Detention in 2012. Throughout the late twentieth century, federal observers repeatedly identified the House of Detention as the single worst prison in the nation; and yet, no one alive knew that this jail traced its parentage to a slave prison founded in 1805 for the torture of fugitive and resistant enslaved people. New Orleans had the highest incarceration rates of any American city: still, those rates were no higher than incarceration rates endured by enslaved New Orleanians nearly two centuries earlier. Mass incarceration is an acute crisis, but its practices and structures have evolved over more than 200 years. To trace its origins and development is critical not only for our understanding of the relation between race and state violence but for our comprehension of the very meaning of American freedom.

A note on terminology: racial categories in New Orleans, as throughout the Americas, have always been malleable, subjective, and fluid. The French, Spanish, and American legal regimes each imposed different systems of racial designation, packing terms like "negro," "person of color," "mulatto," "griffe," "mestizo," and "quadroon" with social and legal connotations that shifted across time, context, and legal system. When assigning racial and legal categories to persons, antebellum authorities often evaluated subjective factors unrelated to presumed ancestry or legal status, such as the person's perceived social standing, occupation, nativity, and habits. Complicating matters further,

Louisiana's antebellum court system recognized legal and racial distinctions, not formalized elsewhere in the United States, between Louisiana's indigenous population of "free persons of color" and "free negroes" who were not considered members of that population—though that distinction, too, was subjective and malleable. Paradoxically, New Orleans's prison system and police have only ever sorted inmates into two racial groupings—"white" and "negro" (updated to "black" or "African American" in the late twentieth century)—disregarding the indigenous legal distinction between "person of color" and "negro" while at the same time shoehorning inmates who might otherwise be considered Native American, Asian, or multiracial into a bipartite racial order. To simplify matters, I employ the inclusive term "Black" to refer to people of perceived African ancestry and "free Black" to refer to people of perceived African ancestry who self-identified as free persons and were not claimed as chattel by a legally recognized owner. When referring to persons who disputed their perceived racial ancestry, I discuss the contours of that dispute on a case-by-case basis.

CHAPTER 1

The Problem of Incarceration
in the Age of Slavery

The incarceration of enslaved people seems at once paradoxical and redundant: slaves were already prisoners, without any freedoms left to revoke. Penal labor seems all too similar to the enslaved person's normal routine. Incarceration withheld the enslaved from labor and encroached on slaveholders' unassailable power to privately punish those whom they held as property. Early American prison development was predicated on the premise of "uplifting" deviant citizens and "restoring" them for society: yet proslavery thought held that the enslaved were incapable of uplift and unqualified for citizenship, with no social identities to restore.[1] In 1858, the Georgia jurist and proslavery theorist Thomas R. R. Cobb concluded that imprisonment could have no effect on the slave, who "can be reached only through his body . . . the extremes, death and whipping, being the only available punishments." "Imprisonment is no punishment to the negro," agreed Louisiana congressman and sugar baron William Pugh. "With a sufficiency to satisfy the cravings of his appetite and a life of idleness, you have before you the embodiment of a negro's paradise."[2]

And yet, Louisiana developed expansive slave prison systems for the purported transformation of resistant enslaved people into subjugated servants through specialized and standardized penal routines. Two years after the Louisiana Purchase, the governing elite of New Orleans launched a slave prison where masters and civic authorities could send fugitive and resistant enslaved people for state-managed "correction." Hardly disorganized or assembled thoughtlessly, this facility copied features of slave penal systems previously deployed in South Carolina, the British Caribbean, and the former colony of Saint-Domingue while incorporating adjusted aspects of mainstream American and European penal theory. Louisianians called their new slave prison the "Police Jail" (*Geôle de police*), a name that predates the modern connotations of the word "police."[3] By 1850, Louisiana had multiple police jails, Mississippi and Tennessee had created derivative institutions, and the New Orleans "police jail system" had inspired the formation of a state-level penal system for enslaved state convicts.[4]

The police jail system thrived, not *in spite of* the inherent contradictions that the incarceration of enslaved people raised, but *because of* the solutions to those contradictions that authorities reached. Creation of the first Police Jail coincided with the "birth of the prison," when cities in the northeastern United States and Europe suppressed public corporal punishments and created bureaucratic institutions for the rehabilitation of deviants through cloistered reflection and hard labor. Louisiana's slaveholders observed these developments closely, as did their Caribbean peers. They concluded that if cloistered penal labor within prisons could elevate white convicts into uplifted citizens prepared for the rigors of republican civic participation, then humiliating outdoor penal labor before the public gaze could debase enslaved prisoners into degraded subjects fit for abject subservience. These slaveholders devised a mixed system of indoor captivity with outdoor penal labor that was economical, humiliating, more physically exhausting than typical slave labor, and intended to reach the enslaved prisoner through both body and mind. French speakers in New Orleans called their new public penal labor system the "*nègres de chaîne*," a term borrowed from the slave prisons of Saint-Domingue. By the 1820s, English speakers in New Orleans had anglicized nègres de chaîne into "chain gang" in the first use of that expression anywhere in the United States.[5]

In the American imagination, the dreaded southern chain gang has long represented the thoughtless brutality of incarceration during Jim Crow—a ruthlessly exploitative system, devoid of any penological theory or rehabilitative intent.[6] Yet chain gangs were not born in the Jim Crow era, divorced from either antecedent practice or intelligible penological theory. Nor were twentieth-century reformers speaking hyperbolically when they charged that chain gangs seemed somehow "worse" than slavery: indeed, creating an effective penal deterrent for enslaved people was foundational to the institution's design.[7] Rather, the architects of the South's first chain gangs exchanged ideas and strategies across oceans and seas. They created specialized slave penal systems, first deployed in cities, that encoded a fully realized slave penology, developed through the thoughtful adaptation and adjustment of global developments in penal theory for the particular economic and political needs of slave society. These are the origins of the southern penal tradition.

The Birth of the Chain Gang

In 1791, Saint-Domingue—the jewel of France's colonial empire, the world's leading producer of sugar, and among the richest slave societies in the world—erupted in revolution. By 1804, the former slaves had liberated themselves, abolished slavery, massacred or expelled any remaining white residents, and proclaimed themselves citizens of the sovereign state of Haiti. A total of 200,000 Black revolutionaries and more than 100,000 European soldiers and white colonists lay dead. Bruised by so great a loss, Napoléon Bonaparte resolved to divest himself of the Western Hemisphere, selling the Louisiana Territory to the United States in 1803.[8]

As they watched revolution consume their neighbor, horrified slaveholders in Louisiana worried that Black radicalism, propagated from Saint-Domingue, had infected the local enslaved population.[9] They described growing numbers of maroons, constant illicit mobility, widespread refusal to work, and what territorial governor William Claiborne called "A general Spirit of Insubordination." "The negroes are in a shameful state of Idleness, and want of subordination," New Orleans's future mayor John Watkins warned in February 1804. "They are suffered to wander about at night without passports, stealing, drinking and rioting." Enslaved people seemed "less subject to authority and more able to move around without supervision," echoed Jacques Pitot, another future mayor of the city. "The anxious owner lives in a state of war with his slaves." In June 1804, a coalition of the region's wealthiest slaveholders reported to New Orleans's municipal council that marronage rates were skyrocketing. "The danger is growing more and more," the councilmen agreed. "The larger part of the population of the Colony appears to be alarmed over its symptoms."[10]

The men who sat on this municipal council were members of an elite oligarchic clique, predominantly French-speaking and Catholic, that had controlled Louisiana's government and economy throughout much of the eighteenth century. Most members were locally born "Creoles" whose families had lived in Louisiana for generations, though a few European transplants and some wealthy evacuees from Saint-Domingue had also been incorporated into this privileged circle. By profession, the male members of this clique were astute businessmen, engaged in commerce, plantation agriculture, and usually some combination of both enterprises. The councilmembers represented the uppermost tier of this clique: men such as Étienne de Boré, Pierre Bertonnière, and Jacques Pitot, who owned large plantation estates, and dozens of enslaved people, on the outskirts of town. By temperament, this ruling oligarchy was hierarchical, authoritarian, conservative, and status conscious: fiercely committed to protecting its power and prestige and the slave-labor system from which that power and prestige derived.[11]

These men recognized that the marronage crisis threatened not only their personal livelihoods but public safety and economy, if not the colony's very survival. They reported that maroons survived by "robbing and plundering," spreading "disorders" and sowing social upheaval. Maroons often raided plantations, sometimes (the councilmen suspected) with the help of Indigenous peoples and neighboring white indigents in a terrifying breakdown of racial order that hinted at the possibility of broader, multiracial revolt. To the slave-holder, the maroon encampment represented a frightening, disorderly alter-native to planter patriarchy, a possible source of inspiration for slaves still held in bondage, and a potent illustration of the possibility of Black self-rule.[12] That bands of maroons had initially precipitated the revolution in Saint-Domingue a decade earlier was doubtless lost on no one. These slaveholders would also have recalled the harrowing crises of 1795—the Caribbean "planters' darkest hour," in the words of one historian—when events in Saint-Domingue had helped inspire slave uprisings in Jamaica, Dutch Guiana, St. Vincent, Curaçao, Vene-zuela, and just upriver from New Orleans at Pointe Coupée, Louisiana.[13]

Yet 1795 had marked another dramatic revolution for Louisiana: Étienne de Boré's production, under the guidance of experienced technicians from Saint-Domingue, of Louisiana's first commercial crop of granulated sugar. Boré's innovation, coupled with Saint-Domingue's removal from the global sugar market and the expansion of cotton production into the Mississippi River valley, had ignited furious commercial activity and rapid economic growth. By 1804, the plantations surrounding New Orleans were producing 6 million pounds of sugar annually. The yearly value of gross exports from New Orleans approached $5 million, nearly four times what it had been a decade earlier.[14] Ambitious American entrepreneurs, seeking to harness this new economic opportunity, had begun flocking to New Orleans in droves, riding dreams of future wealth, power, and prestige. In contrast to the old Creole oligarchy, these "Yankee" émigrés tended to be young, Protestant, educated professionals: law-yers, doctors, engineers, merchants, and prospective planters eager to establish sugar plantations, marry into the families of local elites, and leverage their trading contacts in Boston, Philadelphia, Baltimore, New York, and London.[15]

For the moment, the city these newcomers encountered was little more than a muddy, underdeveloped, fledgling frontier outpost. Home to barely 8,000 souls, New Orleans had no paved streets or sidewalks, few public buildings, and public works that "would provoke the risibility of an engineer." Émigrés com-pared city streets to "a common sewer," reeking "of nastiness, dirt, and corrup-tion." Most of the town's drainage ditches were "caved in or filled in," creating "pools of stagnant and fetid water in all sections of town." "Garbage and dead animals" lay strewn everywhere. The settlement's main canal, vital to shipping and drainage, was "choked" with mud and "ruined." "The mind can, I think, scarcely image to itself a more disagreeable place," one émigré apprehended in 1802. Still, with its favorable location near the mouth of the Mississippi River, New Orleans seemed "destined" to "become one of the principal cities of North America, and perhaps the most important place of commerce in the new world.

. . . The most sanguine mind cannot but predict its future greatness, wealth and prosperity."[16]

All the dreams and ambitions of elite Creoles and American newcomers—of titanic wealth accumulated, a mighty metropolis risen from the swamps, a wilderness annexed for sugar and cotton cultivation—would require colossal quantities of human labor. Thus even as they feared imminent death at the hands of maroons, slaveholders demanded the importation of more African slaves. In March 1804, a coalition of Louisiana's wealthiest francophone Creoles and Yankee transplants petitioned the US Congress to reopen the international importation of enslaved people into the Louisiana Purchase, which Congress had prohibited. To draft the petition, the coalition selected one of the colony's most prestigious American newcomers, Edward Livingston, a lawyer and the former mayor of New York City. To some, Livingston may have seemed an odd selection as spokesman, for he had arrived in New Orleans from New York only a few days prior, seeking a fresh start in the nation's newest entrepôt following his shameful involvement in a ruinous financial scandal. The planters and merchants knew, however, that the Livingston name carried powerful symbolic weight: his older brother, Robert Livingston, had served on the Continental Congress during the Revolutionary War and had been part of the Committee of Five tasked with drafting the Declaration of Independence in 1776. "African labourers," Livingston declared to Congress, were vital "to the very existence of our country." Without the importation of more enslaved Africans, "cultivation must cease, the improvements of a century be destroyed, and the great river resume its empire over our ruined fields and demolished habitations."[17] Well aware that Louisiana hovered on the edge of slave revolution, many in Washington were shocked by the petition's demands, including Thomas Paine. "You speak in your memorial, as if *you* were the *only* people who were to live in Louisiana, and as if the territory was purchased that *you* exclusively might govern it," Paine replied, incredulously. "*Do you want to renew in Louisiana the horrors of [Santo] Domingo?*"[18]

Louisiana's ruling elites felt trapped within a contradiction, bounded by their insatiable demand for more enslaved laborers and their implacable fear of imminent slave revolt. They sought to escape that trap: to re-create Saint-Domingue's sugar economy while avoiding Saint-Domingue's fate. "The impression is general among the Inhabitants of the City, that they are in eminent Danger," Governor Claiborne informed President Thomas Jefferson in September 1804. And yet, there was "but one sentiment throughout the Province," Claiborne added that November: "*They must import more Slaves.*"[19]

The municipal council attributed the marronage crisis to the "daily influx" of refugees from Saint-Domingue, many of whom seemed tainted by the rebels' "revolutionary principles." "One cannot pause but shudder," councilmembers warned, "at the thought that these men with their hands still reddened with the blood of our unfortunate fellow countrymen are arriving daily in great number in our midst and that perhaps tomorrow their smoking torches will be lighted again to set fire to our peaceful homes." To curb this revolutionary contamination, the council proposed a ban on the entry of Black people, enslaved or free, from the Caribbean.[20] Still, refugees from Saint-Domingue, Black and white, continued pouring into the colony: ultimately, more than 10,000 Saint-Domingue refugees would flee to Louisiana by 1810, doubling the population of New Orleans.[21]

The ruling elite also attributed the marronage crisis to the colony's growing number of poor transients from upriver and overseas. Elites feared that they were becoming victims of their own successes—that the region's explosive economic growth had attracted, alongside well-to-do entrepreneurs such as Livingston, an unsavory caste of disreputable "vagabonds" who owned neither slaves nor land, lodged in taverns or boardinghouses, fraternized with the enslaved, and seemed to inspire slave resistance by their chaotic presence. The city had become awash in these loafers, complained one merchant: "untractable sailors, drunken Indians, and Kentuckey boatmen" who required "energetic" surveillance. The newly appointed territorial secretary, James Brown, was particularly alarmed by these miscreants' tendency to "drink with free negroes or slaves, who appear to be their principal associates." In August 1804, the municipal council declared that the number of transient strangers in the territory was fast becoming a second crisis. Soon the council resolved to preemptively arrest all propertyless strangers until their character could be ascertained.[22]

Fears that these vagabond hordes encouraged marronage and circulated dangerous Caribbean radicalism would seem confirmed in September 1805, when authorities uncovered a plot, orchestrated by a migratory white laborer variously identified as Le Grand and Grand-Jean, "to produce an insurrection among the Negroes, Massacre the Whites and make themselves masters of the city." A former French soldier who had deserted, resettled in Saint-Domingue, fled the revolution for Baltimore, and crisscrossed Kentucky before finally relocating to New Orleans, Le Grand seemed the archetypal transient, further contaminated because he had witnessed the "massacre of the whites" in Saint-Domingue firsthand. To New Orleans mayor John Watkins, the lesson of Le Grand's plot was obvious: the municipal council needed to overcome its fiscal conservatism and fund a permanent police force. Watkins acknowledged the council's opposition to constant surveillance and militarization but argued that the imminent dangers faced by the colony were too great: "I am not a friend to standing Armies in a free country but we are in a country of Slaves."[23]

While the municipal council indicted disorderly transients and radicalized refugees, demographic changes occurring within Louisiana's enslaved communities point toward another explanation for rising rates of marronage. At this moment, Louisiana slave society was particularly fractured, unacculturated, and desperate. During the narrow window between Louisiana's sugar revolution in 1795 and the Louisiana Purchase in 1803, slaveholders had financed an unusually large and rapid influx of newly enslaved people, overwhelmingly African-born and male, into the colony. The largest share had come from the Kingdom of the Kongo, along with significant populations from the Angola and Bight of Benin regions. As a result, a profound "re-Africanization"—or, perhaps more accurately, a "Kongolization"—of Louisiana slave society was underway. The rapid influx of first-generation enslaved people would have been socially disruptive, while the shared cultural and linguistic background of the Kongo immigrant population would also have provided a foundation for organized, collective resistance. Tellingly, fugitive slave advertisements from the period identify two-thirds of runaways as African-born; of those, half were identified as Kongo natives. Louisiana's transfer to the United States had also eliminated enslaved people's access to the legal mechanisms for obtaining freedom that had existed under the previous regime, increasing incentives for flight.[24]

In the aftermath of the Louisiana Purchase, the colony seemed poised on the precipice of violent transformations, be they lucrative or destructive. Slaveholders foresaw opportunity to accumulate unprecedented wealth. At the same time, they felt haunted by autonomous nomads—fugitives from slavery, suspicious strangers from upriver, radicalized refugees from the Caribbean—poised to unite in revolution. Louisiana's ruling elite sought a solution that would allow them to expand the plantation system and evade destruction.

Several piecemeal responses were tried: raids on maroon settlements, new pass and curfew regulations, civilian patrols, militia reorganization, a declaration of general amnesty for maroons who returned voluntarily. Each effort failed to alleviate the mounting marronage crisis.[25]

Then in May 1805, the municipal council arrived on an organized, state-managed solution: the simultaneous creations of one of the first municipal police departments in the United States and a standardized penal system for the transformation of captured maroons into dutifully submissive slaves. Although the police department was also tasked with monitoring the city's suspicious strangers, its primary mandates would be the pursuit of maroons, the examination of slave passes, and the dissolution of slave gatherings.[26] Maroon capture fees, moneys confiscated from captured maroons, and a one-dollar-per-slave tax on slaveholders would finance the expensive experiment. Once arrested, captured maroons would be brought to a preexisting wing within the city's old colonial prison, called the Police Jail, where jailors would oversee the captives' "correction" by inflicting standardized corporal punishment before organizing them into shackled penal labor crews ("nègres de chaîne") for employment on public works.[27]

Similar developments were unfolding in port cities across the South. The revolution in Saint-Domingue and the subsequent influxes of refugees triggered slave revolution panics in Charleston, Savannah, Richmond, and elsewhere.[28] In response, these southern port cities transformed their city guards, civilian patrols, and state militias into the nation's first professionalized, full-time, bureaucratized, publicly funded, and salaried municipal police forces: Richmond in 1801, New Orleans in 1805, Charleston and Savannah in 1806. Such metropolises as Philadelphia, New York, Boston, and London would not follow suit for another generation.[29]

One year later, on June 7, 1806, Governor Claiborne signed three interrelated policing bills into law. A new slave code, drawn both from the French colonial Code Noir of 1724 and US slave law, laid the groundwork for a statewide network of police jails by mandating that every jailed maroon held anywhere in the state "be condemned . . . to hard labour" on public works by local authorities. A new vagrancy law authorized the preemptive seizure of poor, suspicious strangers, described as "idle and disorderly persons" without "any property wherewith to maintain themselves" who "frequent grog shops, gaming houses, and other disorderly places." A new immigration law empowered judicial authorities to seize any free Black refugee from Saint-Domingue, disregard their free status, incarcerate them as "fugitive slave[s]," and redeploy them as penal laborers on public works.[30] With this trifecta, the governor cemented an enduring legal framework for policing the state's dangerous populations: fugitive enslaved people through the police jail system, propertyless poor white migrants through vagrancy law, and free Black migrants on the pretense that they were fugitive enslaved people.

Theorizing Slave Penology

In its new slave penal system, Louisiana's ruling elite envisioned public institutions that would simultaneously produce docile slaves and facilitate economic growth. The problem with preexisting approaches to slave punishment, city leaders agreed, was that slaveholders' privately inflicted violence had grown ineffective. Slaveholders were too erratic in administering the lash: indeed, councilman Pierre Bertonnière argued, "The slaves who see him performing this kind of punishment, and who dread what their master may do to them, seeing no other means of avoiding it than escape," appeared even likelier to "engage in marronage."[31] Simply to imprison captured maroons, without instituting a reformative penal labor program, established a "state of idleness" that "contributes to their degeneration and is very detrimental to their masters," other councilmembers argued. In contrast, forced labor for the public's benefit—ceaseless work, Monday through Saturday, from sunrise to sundown—would expunge maroons' proclivity toward laziness and reassert Black bodily commitment to continual toil. Prisoners on the nègres de chaîne would also suffer the profound "shame and humiliation" of public display: "a greater punishment," argued New Orleans mayor Nicholas Girod, "more keenly felt" than "the lash." Moreover the system would be financially lucrative, providing the fast-growing city with a cheap labor force.[32]

These ideas drew from recent developments in penal theory. Beginning in the 1780s, reformers in the Americas and Europe had conducted several experiments in public penal labor, predicated on the belief that humiliating outdoor work would inspire moral discipline in prisoners and spectators alike. Cesare Beccaria, the most influential criminologist of the late eighteenth century, proposed that public penal labor was the ideal punishment because it inflicted little permanent bodily damage on the criminal while establishing a public spectacle that deterred crime by creating a visible, omnipresent illustration of the state's justice: "the strongest and most lasting impression on the minds of men" with "the least torment on the body of the criminal." In 1776, Thomas Jefferson proposed a public penal labor system for Virginia (though he specified the exclusion of the enslaved, for whom forced public labor "would be no punishment or change of condition"). A decade later, Pennsylvania established a public penal labor system made up of convicts known as wheelbarrow men because they were sometimes chained to their wheelbarrows. Officials throughout New York, Maryland, France, and Great Britain implemented or debated similar systems.[33]

By the 1790s, faith in the rehabilitative power of public penal labor had soured. Too often, the spectacle seemed to foment disorder, engender public sympathy for convicts, and deepen prisoners' degradation. "Instead of reforming," wrote Jefferson, public labor "plunged" convicts "into the most desperate and hardened depravity," producing an even deeper "prostration of character" and "abandonment of self-respect." Benjamin Rush, another signer of the Declaration of Independence and the young nation's leading penologist, agreed: instead of inspiring public virtue, public penal labor seemed to "harden the hearts of spectators, and thereby lessen the natural horror which all crimes at first excite in the human mind." Furthermore, both Jefferson and Rush expressed discomfort with the conspicuous resemblance that shackled outdoor labor bore to chattel slavery. In London, Paris, New York, and Philadelphia, penology pivoted from humiliating outdoor labor to cloistered indoor labor within controlled environments, a turn that soon led to the creation of the world's first penitentiaries.[34]

Historians have explored how the failure of public penal labor led to the birth of the penitentiary in the northeastern United States and Europe but have overlooked how many southern and Caribbean slave societies conducted simultaneous experiments in public penal labor, often drawing far more favorable conclusions. In particular, authorities in New Orleans almost certainly drew inspiration from another public penal labor system made up of captured and chained fugitive slaves, the nègres de chaîne, created in Cap-Français, Saint-Domingue's largest city, in 1787. Many of Louisiana's leading residents in 1805, including New Orleans mayor Jacques Pitot, were former Cap-Français residents who would have been familiar with the nègres de chaîne.[35] Cap-Français had first explored public penal labor for chronic maroons as an alternative to their execution in 1741. That experiment had proven a failure, according to the Saint-Domingue resident and chronicler Médéric Louis Élie Moreau de Saint-Méry, because colonial administrators had typically assigned prisoners to relatively light domestic work within their own households. This was an egregiously defective mode of punishment, Moreau de Saint-Méry argued, because it was neither publicly visible nor strenuous enough to deter the enslaved. Saint-Domingue's attorney general Nicolas-Louis François de Neufchâteau expressed similar frustrations: "The chained Negroes are a loss to their masters while they remain there, and are also a loss to the public. They remain in idleness, corrupt one another, and exit the prison much more perverted." Moreover, "the Negroes are not afraid of it."[36]

Like his latter peers in New Orleans, François de Neufchâteau sought an effective deterrent for enslaved people amid rising marronage rates. Yet he feared that public sentiment had turned against bloody bodily mutilations and public executions and also opined that the enslaved rarely feared death. As a solution, and one year after Pennsylvania's creation of the wheelbarrow men, François de Neufchâteau resolved in 1787 to restructure the nègres de chaîne by sentencing captured maroons to "the most painful and dangerous" public works projects: "draining swamps, moving earth, digging canals, building or maintaining roads." In such work, they would suffer experiences far worse than the slave's normal routine while creating a "continual spectacle" for the terror of enslaved onlookers. The attorney general predicted that "this new kind of torture would leave on the minds of Negroes a deeper impression than gallows and wheels."[37] His decision to replace corporal torture with penal labor and establish public spectacle indicates the obvious influence of contemporary carceral theory and may have been directly inspired by the creation of the wheelbarrow men in Philadelphia, a city with which Cap-Français had exceptionally close trading ties.[38]

In perceiving that institutionalization could discipline resistant workers, slaveholders also drew inspiration from the well-established practice of sentencing rebellious laborers to workhouses. An early precursor to the modern prison, workhouses first emerged in sixteenth-century Europe, amid the disintegration of feudalism and resulting growth of urban pauperism, as places for the confinement and forced labor of vagrants, beggars, prostitutes, and other "disorderly" members of the urban poor. Colonists brought workhouses with them to the Americas: Boston had one by 1660.[39] Initially, New World workhouses disciplined white indigents, rebellious indentured servants, and resistant enslaved people alike, often without distinction.[40] Yet as racial categories calcified in the eighteenth century, slave societies began segregating their workhouses. The Georgia legislature proposed a workhouse exclusively "for the Custody and Punishment of Negroes" in 1763. South Carolina segregated its workhouse in stages between 1768 and 1787. Jamaica constructed several workhouses throughout the 1770s and 1780s, initially for both the "great number of White Vagrants" and "all idle and runaway slaves" but soon restricted to the enslaved.[41] British Caribbean slave workhouses began issuing "workhouse gangs," similar in design to the nègres de chaîne of Saint-Domingue, for labor on public works.[42] In 1808, the Tobago legislature referred to its workhouse gang as a "chain gang"—alluding, possibly, to gang-system slave labor, performed by captured maroons hobbled with chains—in that phrase's earliest known recorded use anywhere in the Americas.[43]

Just as the prison was born through collaboration between reformers in Europe and the Americas, so the administrators of slave workhouses also communicated with one another, exchanging ideas and best practices across oceans and between empires. In 1807, New Orleans mayor James Mather explicitly cited "the custom in existence in Jamaica" as the basis for proposed adjustments to New Orleans's nègres de chaîne.[44] In 1817, new regulations for New Orleans's Police Jail included provisions directly copied from the regulations of Charleston's slave workhouse dating to 1807.[45]

Initially, English speakers in New Orleans referred to the "chain negroes," employing a direct translation of the "nègres de chaîne." Officials also spoke of the "city gang."[46] Yet during the 1820s, anglophone residents began colloquially referring to the nègres de chaîne as the "chain gang," a term likely imported from the British Caribbean. By 1829, "chain gang" had transitioned into formal use in New Orleans, though it would remain an unfamiliar term outside the Mississippi River valley into the 1840s.

By the 1830s, a cogent slave penology had spread throughout the Caribbean and Latin America. Specialized slave prisons existed in most major cities. Gangs of incarcerated fugitive slaves labored on the public works of Rio de Janeiro, Port of Spain, Havana, Kingston, and other French, British, Portuguese, and Spanish colonial centers.[47] From New Orleans, the practice of organizing resistant and fugitive slaves into municipal chain gangs spread to communities throughout Louisiana, then up the Mississippi River to Natchez (in around 1824), Baton Rouge (1826), Vicksburg (1829), Nashville (1831), and Louisville (1835). In Memphis, authorities petitioned for legislative permission to adapt the system in 1841, received that permission, but apparently never followed through. Richmond also created a slave chain gang in 1855. The Mississippi legislature authorized the creation of slave chain gangs in every town and county in 1824; Tennessee's legislature did the same in 1844.[48] Thus was this racialized penal practice, born of Caribbean experimentation, introduced by New Orleans to the American South.

Building the Slave State

The transformations of May 1805 marked a new stage in Louisiana's governing capacity. The prior French and Spanish regimes had tried repeatedly, with limited success, to track marronage and standardize punishments. Louisiana's Code Noir of 1724 had prescribed a progressive sequence of bodily mutilations for each runaway attempt—first ear cropping, then branding, and finally hamstring severing—partly so that enslaved people's physical bodies served as chronicles of their criminal records. After assuming control of Louisiana, Spanish authorities had tried to standardize the weapons and number of lashes with which maroons could be tortured. New regulations in 1795 and 1798 had required that slaveholders promptly report both missing slaves and any instance of anyone shooting at maroons. In part, efforts to document marronage reflected a unique feature of Louisiana law, called redhibitory law, which enabled slave buyers to sue sellers for failure to disclose the purchased person's "habit of running away."[49] Efforts to standardize punishments also reflected lawmakers' perceptions that erratic, unpredictable penalties encouraged slave rebellion. In practice, documenting marronage proved a perpetual challenge, and both regimes had routinely violated the dictates of their own slave codes by condemning enslaved prisoners to diverse medleys of bodily mutilations: colonial court records refer to amputations, brandings, the severing of hamstrings and wrist tendons, the rack, the giblet, the wheel, and "torture boots."[50]

The creation of a police and slave prison encouraged the broader trend toward standardized slave punishments and created a new municipal bureaucracy tasked with documenting enslaved people's criminal records and penalties. Now a lengthy paper trail, maintained by professionalized clerks, followed every enslaved New Orleanian, chronicling their arrests, prison sentences, and penal labor details. In effect, the marronage crisis birthed a modern administrative apparatus.[51]

The innovations of 1805 also resolved a long-standing internal crisis pertaining to the maintenance of vital public works. The dilapidated state of the city's public infrastructure described by newcomers—leaking levees, canals "choked with mud," roads devolved "into swamps"—reflected an ongoing political feud, between slaveholders and colonial officials, over the state's conscription of enslaved laborers for the maintenance of public infrastructure.[52] The French colonial regime had built public works through the *corvée* system, under which slaveholders had been required to loan their enslaved workers to the state for a certain number of days each year. After France ceded Louisiana to Spain in 1762, the new regime had tried a similar system of slave conscription while also experimenting with renting enslaved laborers from their owners, deploying convict laborers, and requiring that all landowners privately maintain any gutters, levees, and roads that bordered their property. All these strategies had failed to meet the colony's mounting labor needs while engendering endless conflicts between slaveholders and the state. Wary of any infringement on their private powers and pocketbooks, slaveholders had refused to commit their labor resources to public works, and colonial authorities had lacked the strength to compel them.[53] The new police jail system sidestepped these old battles: in slave penal labor, the state found a stable and cost-effective public works force without eliciting slaveholder resistance.

Tensions between slaveholders and the state over which party controlled the enslaved prisoner's labor persisted throughout the Police Jail's early years.[54] Slaveholders appreciated the publicly managed system for capturing and confining maroons but resisted the state's efforts to punish and forcibly work enslaved prisoners, which seemed to infringe on slaveholders' absolute power over their property. By 1813, the Police Jail was perilously overcrowded, but slaveholders refused to let jailors employ their prisoners on public works. Mayor Girod grumbled that slaveholders constantly "abuse" the system, "contrary to the interests of the City," by treating the Police Jail as little more than a convenient storage facility. Councilman Bertonnière complained that slaveholders' misuse of the system failed to curb marronage and depleted city coffers by forcing the hire of additional laborers. To incentivize slaveholders, the council agreed to partially subsidize slaveholders' daily jail fees on condition that they permit the deployment of their incarcerated property on the nègres de chaîne, a practice that Mayor Girod attributed to Jamaican slave workhouses.[55] The arrangement remained contentious. In 1815, slaveholder Joseph Chardon was enraged to learn not only that the city had claimed the labor of the imprisoned woman whom he claimed as property, Phibie, throughout her two-year confinement for "correction" but that the jail had charged him $103.25 in food, medical expenses, and jail fees for the privilege.[56]

A series of municipal ordinances and court decisions gradually navigated these competing public-private claims to the enslaved prisoner. Far from enshrining slaveholders' absolutism, control over the incarcerated enslaved person steadily shifted from slaveholder to state. New jail regulations in 1817 forbade slaveholders from withholding their incarcerated property from the chain gang if the prisoner was to be held for longer than three days; capped the number of lashes that slaveholders could command jailors to inflict; and ordered jailors to ignore slaveholders' requests for alternative punishments. In 1821, after considerable debate, the council affirmed jailors' power to transfer sick prisoners to the hospital. In 1836, the Louisiana Supreme Court sustained the city's right to work prisoners without their owners' consent and ruled that the city was not liable for inmate escapes.[57] After 1836, courts considered it settled jurisprudence that slaveholders' authority did not fully extend beyond prison walls. When slaveholder George Lewis sued New Orleans following the death of the incarcerated slave Jessie, the state supreme court ruled that Lewis's claim rested on a fundament misunderstanding of the relation between slaveholder and prison: the Police Jail existed for "public purposes" and not for the "private advantage or profit" of any individual slaveholder.[58]

From New Orleans and its environs emerged a model of economic development wherein slaveholder and state were deeply involved in one another's affairs. Through police and prisons, public authorities used state power to help slaveholders compel enslaved labor. In exchange, the state claimed a right of access to slaveholders' enslaved labor force, which the state dispatched toward the development of the vital public infrastructure that made governance and economic growth possible. This arrangement was not entirely without conflict, given that the interests of slaveholders and the state did not always perfectly align. Yet in general, this public-private partnership provided a mutually beneficial framework that sustained both personal wealth accrual and growing state power.

Policing the Slave City

Most historical syntheses of American policing identify the nation's first "publicly funded, organized" municipal police force as that of either Boston (established in 1838) or New York City (established in 1845). If mentioned at all, law enforcement agencies within the antebellum South are typically equated with slave patrols, which in turn are characterized as a primitive, "transitional stage" preceding the advent of "modern" policing.[59]

Yet wealthy slaveholding ports such as New Orleans, Mobile, Savannah, Charleston, and Richmond were pioneers, not stragglers, in the development of organized policing and the growth of the surveillance state. Antebellum visitors to these cities expressed shock at the extent of the police presence, unparalleled in either size or level of militarization to the cities of the Northeast and Europe. "In the appearance of an armed police, Charleston and New Orleans do not resemble the free cities of America," concluded one British traveler after a tour in 1830, "but the great number of the black population, and the way in which they are treated by the whites, render this precaution, I have no doubt, indispensably necessary." A traveler from New York compared Charleston at sunset—when the "streets become forthwith alive with patrolling parties"—to "a great military garrison" under "a general siege." Frederick Law Olmsted likened Richmond to "a prison or fortress," Charleston to a city "in a state of siege."[60] Not every white landowner approved of this omnipresent standing army. Tension between republicanism and omnipresent police presence was palpable to the *Louisiana Advertiser*, which charged in 1834 that a standing police force seemed characteristic of "ancient despotic governments," not a young republic. "In what free country? In what enlightened city?," asked the paper, "Save New Orleans, do we see a 'watch,' a *civil* police forsooth, parading the streets at noon day in all the panoply of war, 'armed to the teeth,' like the body guard of an eastern despot?" Perpetual surveillance was a "blot on the face of a free country, an ancient barbarism in a great commercial and REPUBLICAN city . . . a glaring remnant of despotism in a land of LIBERTY."[61]

Though a civil institution, New Orleans's early police force was decidedly martial in character. Patrols consisted of four-man squads, marching through thoroughfares at regular intervals. They carried pistols and swords: in emergencies, muskets were available from the police armory. They wore blue uniforms and enlisted for six-month terms.[62] The police-to-population ratio was high, comparable to that of major US cities in the twenty-first century.[63] Pay was low, and complaints of excessive force were frequent.[64] Initially, most policemen were recruited among the poorer Saint-Domingue refugees: dispossessed men with few other employment options.[65] Their understanding of police service was doubtless informed by their memories and observations of Saint-Domingue's colonial militias, some of which had also been tasked with hunting maroons.[66] In its early years, the force also included a small number of free Black officers, drawn from both the refugee community and Louisiana's native-born free Black population, though the municipal council specified that white applicants should receive hiring preference and that only white officers should occupy command positions. As Saint-Domingue refugees aged out of the force, other marginalized immigrants, predominantly German and Irish, replaced them.[67] Critics railed against the investment of such expansive policing powers into the hands of "St. Domingo cut-throats" and veterans of "the wars of enslaved Europe." The police were little better than "AN ARMED BAND OF FOREIGN MERCENARIES," complained the *Louisiana Advertiser*: "ignorant, irresponsible, and too often brutal hirelings" who "create disturbances," "frighten freemen," and seemed incapable of "rendering any really beneficial services, beyond dragging disorderly slaves to prison."[68]

For the enslaved of New Orleans, pervasive police surveillance characterized urban life. Each night, the firing of a cannon activated the city's slave curfew, after which any slave found outdoors without a pass would be arrested, imprisoned within the Police Jail, and issued twenty-five lashes.[69] A witness to Charleston's version of this ritual described nightly panic: "negroes scouring the streets in all directions, to get to their places of abode, many of them in great trepidation, uttering ejaculations of terror as they ran." In Louisiana, a proverb "Après yé tiré cannon, Nègue sans passe c'est nègue-marron" (After the cannon is fired, a Black without a pass is a maroon) passed into Creole dialect. Sometime in the late 1830s, a fugitive from slavery named John Brown slipped off a steamboat and onto the New Orleans wharf, hoping to find passage to England. Quickly identifying him as a fugitive, Black dockworkers warned Brown that he had no hope of evading the New Orleans police: "[They] told me I should be certain to be taken up before night, and put into the calaboose or prison; and that I should be flogged every morning until I told the name of my master." Convinced that he would be arrested but determined to evade his master, Brown surrendered himself to a local slave trader for illegal sale to a new owner.[70]

Carceral Patterns in the Slave City

Between 1800 and 1840, New Orleans grew faster than any other US city, from roughly 8,000 residents to more than 100,000. Plantation slavery flourished: from about 18,000 cotton bales and 5,000 hogsheads of sugar in 1802, exports from New Orleans leapt to roughly 1 million bales and 100,000 hogsheads during the season of 1844–45. To feed this economic behemoth, by 1840, slave traders had carried some 70,000 enslaved people to New Orleans from the Upper South, reshuffling the demography of the region's enslaved communities while mutating New Orleans into the nation's largest slave market. "This country has changed much," wrote one Saint-Domingue refugee who had lived in New Orleans since 1809. "Foreigners of all calibers" were daily "vomited" onto the docks. Ambitious Anglo-American entrepreneurs continued pouring into the city, building townhouses and neighborhoods "without respite." Neighborhoods were "no longer recognizable."[71]

Tensions simmered among the old Creole elite, wealthy Anglo-American transplants, and burgeoning foreign-born immigrant population. In 1836, a coalition of Anglo-Americans, frustrated by their underrepresentation on the municipal council, successfully petitioned the state legislature to divide the city into three autonomous municipalities, each with its own public institutions, laws, police force, and governing body. The old francophone elite dominated the city's old quarter, which became the First Municipality. Immediately upriver, Anglo-Americans controlled the wealthy "American Sector," now redubbed the Second Municipality. A diverse mixture of new immigrants from Europe, Saint-Domingue refugees, and Black and white Creoles dominated the downriver Third Municipality, by far the poorest of the three.

By then, New Orleans had long outgrown its old colonial prison and original Police Jail. Between 1830 and 1833, city surveyor (and Saint-Domingue refugee) Joseph Pilié drafted at least four sets of architectural plans for a new penal complex.[72] The municipal council eventually approved a design that consisted of two adjacent buildings, built to identical specifications—a "Parish Prison" for "free" prisoners and an abutting Police Jail for enslaved prisoners. Completed in 1835 at an estimated cost of $200,000, this new penal complex was massive: occupying a full city block, each prison three stories in height, and boasting a cumulative capacity of roughly 600 prisoners (larger than the capacity of many contemporary state prisons).[73] When the city splintered into three municipalities in 1836, the Second and Third Municipalities constructed their own police jails while the First Municipality retained use of the centralized police jail designed by Pilié, which also received most enslaved prisoners committed from outside the city. All three municipalities shared use of Pilié's Parish Prison.[74]

Throughout, the city incarcerated enslaved people at rates that surpass local, state, and national incarceration rates in the twenty-first century.[75] In 1820, enslaved people were committed to the Police Jail at a rate of 19.0 imprisonments for every hundred enslaved residents. By 1830, that admittance rate had climbed to 32.2 per hundred. On any given day between 1820 and 1830, the Police Jail held between 1 and 2 percent of the city's enslaved population. Between 1830 and 1840, the city's enslaved population more than doubled. After 1836, existent records of the city's three police jails, though not synchronous, show that the overall number of prison committals climbed, though not at pace with the burgeoning slave population, resulting in a decline of the cumulative imprisonment rate to roughly 14 per hundred.[76] At such rates, incarceration would have been a regular part of every enslaved city dweller's life (graph 1.1).[77]

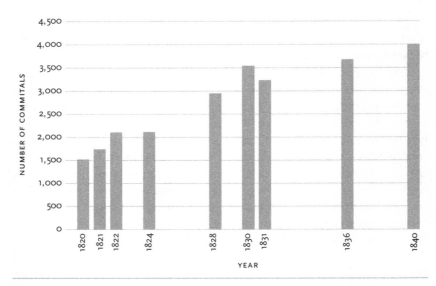

Graph 1.1. Estimated (1820–1824, 1840) and actual (1828–1836) Police Jail committals.

These figures exclude all legally free persons jailed on suspicion that they were enslaved and all infants jailed with their parents. Although New Orleans was a destination for fugitives from throughout the South, who often sought freedom by stowing away aboard outgoing ships, the overwhelming majority of prisoners belonged to local slaveholders.[78]

Existent records from other slaveholding cities, though not nearly as comprehensive as those of New Orleans, suggest comparable incarceration rates. A single surviving register from Savannah's prison reveals an average annual commitment rate of 26.4 per hundred between 1810 and 1814.[79] Monthly statistical reports from Charleston's slave workhouse indicate roughly 15 imprisonments per hundred enslaved residents during the 1840s and 1850s.[80] Richmond police committed enslaved people to the prison at an average rate of 9.3 per hundred between 1854 and 1859: the overall imprisonment rate, including enslaved prisoners committed by slave patrols, courts, and their owners, would have been significantly higher.[81] A single surviving arrest book from Memphis shows that police arrested enslaved people at an average rate of 15.6 per hundred in 1859 and 1860: again, the overall imprisonment rate would have been higher.[82]

New Orleans's police jail system provided several distinct services. The institutions offered critical infrastructure for the suppression of Black mobility and detention of captured maroons, who accounted for roughly three-fourths of all committals.[83] Slaveholders also committed enslaved people to police jails as a form of punishment and alternative to the private infliction of corporal pain. When committing enslaved people for punishment, owners were empowered to choose the sentence length, select between solitary and group confinement, decide the number of lashes to be inflicted (capped at twenty-five per day, with three-day intervals between whippings), and choose the instrument of torture (generally either a wooden paddle, flat leather strap, or heavy horse-skin whip). Records of these punishment instructions do not survive from New Orleans's police jails but do survive from Charleston's slave workhouse:

> The master of the Work House will receive the boy Sam, + give him twenty paddles + confine him in solitary confinement subject to my orders.
>
> [Place] the servant woman into solitary confinement until Monday next + then order her given 10 or 15 stripes.
>
> Please put the two Boys Henry + Peaton in solitary confinement until Monday morning, And then have Henry paddled to the extent of the law, and Peaton half the amt.

Some slaveholders chafed against the regulation and standardization of corporal violence within the workhouse, as indicated by instructions that jailors should administer the paddle to the fullest "extent of the law" or that strikes should be especially "*well laid on*."[84]

Police jails also held enslaved people who had been formally convicted by local or distant courts, though these accounted for 3 percent or less of all slave commitments. Some were sentenced for months and years; others had seen their death sentences commuted to life imprisonment as a "humane" reprieve. For larceny of goods valued at $900, Jim received six months in the Police Jail. For plotting insurrection, one Ascension Parish court sent an enslaved man to the New Orleans Police Jail for twenty-one years. For stabbing an abusive slave trader through the hand in self-defense, Church received a life sentence. For striking her mistress, an enslaved woman in West Feliciana Parish was sentenced to hang—but the mistress pleaded for leniency, so the court "shipped her for N. Orleans to be confined for life, either in the dungeon or put to the ball and chain."[85]

Not every commitment was intended as punishment: slaveholders also relied on police jails for the temporary warehousing of enslaved people, a practice known as "safekeeping." Motives behind "safekeeping" were diverse. Slaveholders relied on this secure storage system when they traveled abroad, during legal disputes over the person's ownership, to preempt an imminent escape attempt, or to resolve marital strife by temporarily removing the victim of master-on-slave sexual violence from the household.[86]

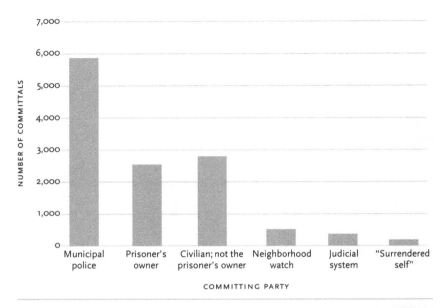

Graph 1.2. Identities of persons who committed enslaved people to the City/First Municipality Police Jail, November 1835–August 1841.

Police jails also operated public whipping stations, where slaveholders could purchase corporal torture without confinement. No record attesting to the extent of the practice survives, though the ex-slave William J. Anderson, who spent three months in the Police Jail following a botched escape attempt, described "ninety or a hundred" whippings daily.[87]

The system blurred boundaries between public and private power. The City Police Jail, which became the First Municipality Police Jail after the city's partition, received 12,297 commitments of enslaved people between November 1, 1835, and August 18, 1841 (graph 1.2). Roughly half were performed by professional law enforcement: 5,869 commitments (47.7 percent) by municipal police or rural sheriffs and 514 commitments (4.2 percent) by a private neighborhood watch. Prisoners' owners performed 2,546 commitments (20.7 percent), whether as punishment or for "safekeeping." Court officers or their agents performed 401 commitments (3.0 percent). Civilians not listed as the prisoners' owner—many of them slave catchers, who received a small bounty for committing suspected maroons—performed 2,804 commitments (22.8 percent). An additional 33 infants and small children were carried into the prison with their jailed parents.[88]

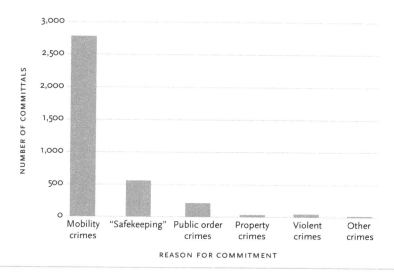

Graph 1.3. Reasons for which enslaved people were committed to the Third Municipality Police Jail, May 1846–March 1851.

Regardless of who committed them, the vast majority of prisoners were jailed for illicit movement. A surviving ledger of the Third Municipality Police Jail includes reasons for 3,656 of the commitments of enslaved people made between May 13, 1846, and March 27, 1851 (graph 1.3). Of these, 2,780 commitments (76.0 percent) were made for mobility crimes: "runaway," "no pass," and violating curfew. All property, violent, and other public order crimes accounted for only 296 commitments (8.1 percent). These figures are somewhat misleading, however, as jailors applied "maroon" and "runaway" to a wide variety of unauthorized and autonomous activities: for example, when police arrested Anaïse for being "utterly drunk," jailors logged Anaïse as a "runaway."[89] "Safekeeping" accounted for 561 commitments (15.3 percent).[90]

For most inmates, prison terms were brief: measured in days and timed to facilitate enslaved people's prompt return to their owners. Roughly one-third of enslaved prisoners were released within two days, while roughly two-thirds were released within one week (graph 1.4). Brevity was hardly the rule, however: while captured maroons constantly cycled through prison gates, police jails gradually accrued long-term and permanent populations, made of both captured maroons whose owners had intentionally left them in the prison and prisoners who had been committed for penal labor by their owners or by courts. On any given day, roughly one-fifth of all incarcerated enslaved people in New Orleans had been imprisoned for at least one year. Of the 128 enslaved people

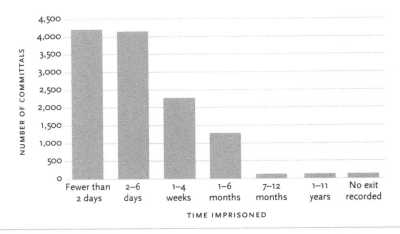

Graph 1.4. Jail times for enslaved people committed to the City/First Municipality Police Jail, November 1835–August 1841.

within the First Municipality Police Jail on June 1, 1840, 26 (20.3 percent) had been confined for at least one year. Of the 58 enslaved people confined within the Second Municipality Police Jail on October 1, 1843, 15 (25.9 percent) had been imprisoned for at least one year. Of the 11 enslaved people held in the Third Municipality Police Jail on May 11, 1846, 2 men had been imprisoned for more than one year while a third man, committed by his owner for "correction," had already been imprisoned for 5 months.[91] The most physically grueling penal labor was overseen by the city surveyor, and inmates assigned to the surveyor's chain gang typically endured the longest prison terms. Among 288 prisoners worked by the city surveyor in 1821, the average term at labor was more than 100 days, with another 30 days, on average, spent confined without labor.[92]

Every major slaveholding city in the United States developed a comparable prison system for the confinement of runaways, torture of the resistant, and "safekeeping" of the warehoused. Arrangements varied. Charleston and Savannah joined New Orleans in building distinctive slave prisons.[93] Other cities, including St. Louis, Louisville, Nashville, and Augusta, built amalgamated workhouses for resistant enslaved people, "vagrant" poor white people, and "suspicious" free Black travelers, confining these populations together, much as colonial workhouses once had.[94] Natchez, Washington, DC, and Baltimore relegated enslaved prisoners to segregated departments within their main city jails.[95] Slaveholders in Richmond, a central hub of the domestic slave trade, often outsourced punishments to the city's uncommonly large network of privately owned slave pens, an early experiment in prison privatization.[96]

Outside the reach of major cities, a patchwork of county prisons, town jails, private plantation dungeons, state penitentiaries, and public whipping stations provided slaveholders with many of the same services.[97] The Kentucky and Missouri state penitentiaries rented cells to slaveholders.[98] Harriet Ann Jacobs, enslaved near Edenton, North Carolina, recalled that her master regularly threatened slaves with incarceration in the local county jail (which Jacobs knew as the Edenton "work house"). As punishment for an escape attempt, Frederick Douglass's master left him in the Easton, Maryland, jail for about ten days. William J. Anderson claimed to have been jailed nearly sixty times before successfully escaping slavery in 1836.[99] Routine imprisonment was hardly universal, however, since many enslaved people lived in regions without access to significant penal infrastructure. "They waren't no such place as a jail whar we was," freedman James Bolton of Athens, Georgia, recalled in the 1930s. Before Emancipation, Black workers received the "lash," after Emancipation, "I seed 'em on the chain gangs."[100]

The authors of Louisiana's slave code of 1806, in mandating penal labor for every incarcerated enslaved person in the state, clearly envisioned a statewide network of police jails akin to the diffuse workhouse systems maintained by many British and French Caribbean colonies. That dream was never fully realized. Some rural parishes constructed police jails—or, at least, assigned that title to jails designated for the confinement of enslaved people.[101] Yet when deciding where to have enslaved people imprisoned, Louisiana planters clearly preferred the more developed slave prisons of New Orleans, Baton Rouge, and Natchez over their local jails, which they often described as insecure, disorderly, and unsanitary. Indeed, elite Mississippi River valley planters were sometimes willing to incur considerable expenses in transportation costs, jail fees, and lost labor to have enslaved people brought to the New Orleans, Baton Rouge, or Natchez slave prisons. Before Natchez created its own slave chain gang, at least one of its residents sent an enslaved person to New Orleans for punishment. On three occasions between 1833 and 1836, Rachel O'Connor of West Feliciana Parish described how her neighbors sent enslaved offenders "to N. Orleans to be put to the ball and chain," 200 miles away by river.[102]

In the 1820s, the Louisiana legislature abandoned its aspirations of a statewide police jail network, transitioning to what would become known as the "slave depot system." Seven centralized jails, strategically dispersed throughout the state, would confine captured runaways left unclaimed in local jails for longer than sixty days.[103] Each slave depot was authorized to deploy chain gangs, and at least some did so, although only that of Baton Rouge grew to such a scale that local authorities saw fit to hire a full-time chain gang overseer.[104] In 1855, the Louisiana legislature further centralized the slave depot system, designating the Baton Rouge facility the exclusive slave depot for the entire state.[105]

Smaller towns deployed slave chain gangs on an ad hoc basis. In Lafayette, the seat of Jefferson Parish, public infrastructure was built and maintained by four hired hands, under the direction of a municipal surveyor, throughout the 1830s. Yet after the unusually rainy winter of 1840–41 rendered Lafayette's streets "completely cut up and destroyed," Lafayette's council refused the surveyor's pleas for the hiring of additional hands but granted him provisional access to the jailed fugitive slaves. Thereafter, between two and six imprisoned slaves worked alongside the four hired hands at no additional cost to the town. Enslaved penal laborers and wageworkers were paired together, perhaps to minimize the risk of the former escaping in the absence of full-time overseers.[106]

Life inside the Police Jail

In 1842, one of the nation's preeminent social reformers, Samuel Gridley Howe of Boston, inspected New Orleans's First Municipality Police Jail while touring the South to promote the construction of public asylums for the blind. In a letter to a young Charles Sumner, Howe recalled a scene that "absolutely chilled me to the marrow of my bones." Howe described three flights of galleries, lined by cells "filled with slaves of all ages, sexes and colors," overlooking a paved courtyard. In the center of that courtyard "there lay a black girl, flat upon her face on a board, her two thumbs tied and fastened to one end, her feet tied and drawn tightly to the other end. . . . She was entirely naked." As the woman "writhed and shrieked," an enslaved man applied "a long whip" with "dreadful power and wonderful precision. . . . Every stroke brought away a strip of skin." Howe was particularly disturbed by the "entirely indifferent" expressions on the faces of the imprisoned onlookers, who seemed desensitized to the torture unfolding beneath them. They "hardly noticed it," Howe observed with revulsion: chatting, "laughing," and engaging in "childish pursuits" while the naked woman begged for reprieve.[107]

To this noted reformer, the scene seemed a perverse parody of modern penology. Every tenet of contemporary carceral theory—proportionality, seclusion, judicial procedure, the elimination of corporal pain, prisoners' segregation by gender and age—seemed deliberately violated. Rather than uplifting offenders "in God's image," the Police Jail seemed intent on debasement, rendering prisoners "sunk," "degrad[ed]," and "low."[108] At the same time, there was much that Howe could recognize as familiar. Jail clerks kept diligent records. The inmates wore uniforms. The bureaucratization and standardization of punishments, the use of captivity to effect a behavioral transformation, and faith in the redemptive power of penal labor, each reflected the influence of contemporary penal theory.[109]

Howe's perception that the Police Jail practiced a distorted variant of mainstream penology, adapted to the priorities of slave society, was apt. This divergence between the public institutions with which Howe was familiar, and the slave prisons of the South, lay in their dissimilar missions. He was accustomed to institutions that promised to uplift lost souls in preparation for full citizenship. The Police Jail, by contrast, sought strategically to debase resistant persons into submissive servants. One sought to create perfect citizens; the other, shattered slaves.[110]

Public humiliation was central to the police jail system. Whether by accident or strategy, the prison designed by Joseph Pilié resembled a panopticon: inward-facing galleries and cells flanking the open-air courtyard where jailors administered corporal punishments, a design that pressured each inmate to watch every whipping. The city's other police jails mimicked this design.[111] The goal was debasement: as one resident put it, police jails existed for the purpose of "degrading" the slave who "is getting too damned smart."[112] Administrators consciously debated ways of accentuating this degradation. In 1848, the Second Municipality Council discussed the merits of replacing prisoners' unicolor uniforms with a "ridiculous . . . parti-colored dress," theorizing that such garb would be even more "humiliating" and that "as a mark of punishment the ridicule it will create will be experienced with much more severity by the slaves . . . humiliating [them] without violating the dictates of humanity." These proposals recalled the prediction of Mayor Nicholas Girod, made three decades earlier, that the "shame and humiliation" of public penal labor would be "more keenly felt" than "the lash."[113]

The first police jail had initially relied on a simple whipping post mounted into the ground, but by the 1830s, every police jail employed a whipping rack like the one observed by Howe: resembling a gurney, with straps and fasteners for pinning nude victims facedown and with their limbs extended. William J. Anderson suffered a version of this device:

> I will now try to describe the scenes in the calaboose whipping room. They have a large, strong ladder, with ropes at each end and one in the middle. The subject to be whipped is divested of wearing apparel, and made to lay down; if he refuses to do so he is knocked down, and by the time he recovers he is stretched out and tied fast to the ladder, with the rope tight across the middle of the body. Then the fourth man lays on with the whip, paddle, or whatever he chooses. In this way perhaps ninety or a hundred are whipped every day.

The ex-slave and famed abolitionist William Wells Brown, who lived in New Orleans while hired out to a local slave trader, recalled that jailors colloquially referred to this device as "the stretcher." Baltimore's slave prison employed a similar device.[114] Charleston's workhouse used a system of weights and wall-mounted pullies to stretch and elevate prisoners for their beatings, as though floating in midair. In each institution, prisoners were stripped entirely nude for whippings.[115] Former prisoners and witnesses described these devices as "so well arranged for whipping," seemingly "scientifically" designed, a vehicle on which one was "whipped according to modern science," the "*ne plus ultra* of their kind," a "torture . . . such as I never experienced either before or since."[116]

Jailors mastered a synchronized, routinized, bureaucratized infliction of corporal pain. Former prisoners described strictly regimented routines, beginning with a predawn roll call. Jailors next called forward prisoners consigned to whipping and ordered them to strip. Bodies were strapped down, lashed, and released with such rapid efficiency that William Wells Brown expressed "surprise and astonishment at the quickness with which the whole thing had been accomplished." After the whipping, skin ointments were applied to ensure speedy recovery and reduce scarring.[117]

After the morning whippings, prisoners were assigned to their penal labor details. Although justified as a tool of behavioral correction, the labor exerted by the city's chain gangs grew so indispensable to New Orleans's development that the number of imprisoned enslaved people directly determined the pace of urban improvements.[118] Each day, the city surveyor employed a main force of between 20 and 120 prisoners on massive public works projects: most commonly street, bridge, levee, and wharf construction. These prisoners worked alongside white and free Black hired laborers and hired enslaved people, though workers were divided into squads based on their race and legal condition.[119] Penal laborers were restrained by a chain running up the body from ankle to waist and linked into pairs by heavy hog chain, roughly ten feet long, which dragged behind them as they worked. An enslaved driver set the pace while white guards maintained discipline.[120]

While the surveyor's main force labored on large-scale public works, smaller squads toiled in virtually every city department and institution. They assisted at the public hospital, orphanages, police stations, and fire stations. They bore exclusive responsibility for all the least desirable daily custodial projects: collecting trash, sweeping streets, scrubbing marketplaces, cleaning parks, clearing obstructions from gutters and sewage lines, removing dead pack animals, dredging canals, interring paupers, planting trees, operating the public ambulance service, and disposing of corpses during epidemics.[121] After a cholera epidemic in 1832, the chain gang burned stacks of putrefied corpses abandoned to an overwhelmed hospital. During one particularly brutal yellow fever outbreak in 1853, the chain gang worked for more than twenty-four consecutive hours, without rest and beyond the point of exhaustion, interring a literal mound of

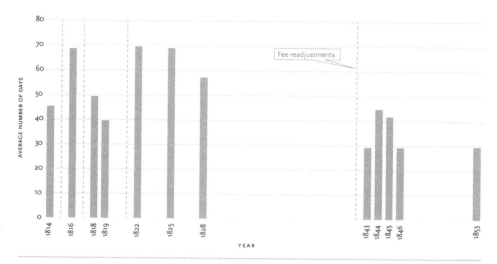

Graph 1.5. Average times on the chain gang, 1814–1853.

"swollen and bursting" bodies "enveloped in swarms of flies."[122] They managed, in short, the city's feces, putridity, decaying flesh, and death.

From employers' standpoint, a significant advantage of wage labor over slave labor is the ability to promptly adjust workforce size, in response to labor demand fluctuations, by hiring and firing workers. To Karl Marx, this elastic ability to draw from or add to the "surplus labouring population" was an essential "condition of existence of the capitalist mode of production."[123] City leaders in New Orleans found a different means of adjusting workforce size. As the city's labor needs rose and fell, the municipal council calibrated the size of the city's penal workforce by adjusting the rate at which the city subsidized prisoners' jail fees. When the city lowered the effective cost of slave incarceration, slaveholders committed enslaved people in greater numbers and for longer periods. When the city raised the effective cost, commitment rates and average prison terms fell. City leaders recalibrated jail fees in 1815, 1817, 1821, and sometime in the early 1840s, often explicitly timing these adjustments with the start or completion of major public works projects (graph 1.5).[124]

Chain gang labor exacted extreme physical and psychological tolls. John and Charlotte Callis, husband and wife chained together, described how hunger and overwork reduced them "to mere skeletons." Survivors experienced intense animalization: they felt "chained together as brutes," and "driven like oxen."[125] They described the severe humiliation, shame, "ignominy" and "contempt" attached to the chain gang: "I never felt so degraded in my life," one former inmate remembered.[126] Witnesses recalled bowed heads and distressed faces: "sullen and dogged," "straggling," "tattered," "wearied," "bending."[127] Suicides were not uncommon.[128] Some prisoners suffered debilitating nervous breakdowns. One jailor complained of how Fanny, an imprisoned runaway, made the "night hideous with her howling." A traveler witnessed an acute psychological crisis on the chain gang, describing how one woman flung herself into the gutter, writhing and scratching open partially healed wounds as jailors whipped her and ordered that she stand: "She roars, rolls in the mud yelling, tears open her wound, rips into shreds the cloth bandage barely covering it, and remains, mute with rage and pain, at the feet of the prison officer."[129] Constance Bique Perrine, a pregnant free woman jailed after police mistook her for a slave, suffered a miscarriage after she was stripped naked, strapped to the whipping rack, and lashed in the Police Jail courtyard. For several weeks thereafter, Perrine refused to leave her bedroom: symptoms of traumatic "retentions," her physician believed, that would have "serious consequences for a life time."[130] The sounds of the chain gang unsettled the city's visitors. The architect Benjamin Latrobe described a "clanking . . . distressing sound." A traveler from Maine recalled noises that "startled our horses." A recent émigré compared the "combination of discordant sound" emanating as the chain gang passed her window to the noises of hell. Before the abandonment of the old Police Jail building, distracted legislators in the adjacent statehouse complained that all the screaming rendered concentration impossible.[131]

In theory, penal labor details were divided by sex, with jail regulations restricting female prisoners to street cleaning, trash removal, and other comparatively light custodial tasks.[132] In practice, jailors regularly assigned select women to grueling public works projects on all-male construction crews, perhaps employing defeminization as an added punishment. Over time, the number of women assigned to all-male construction crews steadily increased. In the 1820s, only one or two women per day were assigned to construction crews. By the 1840s, dozens of women labored aside men on large-scale construction projects, even as all-female gangs continued performing the city's custodial work. For example, on September 3, 1842, the First Municipality surveyor assigned twelve women to cleaning marketplaces, five men to assisting at police stations and jails, twelve men to cemetery maintenance, and forty-eight men and thirty-six women to building public works.[133]

Public and Private Violence

Despite early civic authorities' intentions, police jails complemented but never supplanted slaveholders' private inflictions of violence. Indeed, some prisoners arrived at police jails bearing visible marks of recent violence: one nine-year-old inmate arrived having "been beaten, cut with a knife, her thumbs mashed into jelly, her person burnt by the application of lighted paper, and her entire body scarred and mangled by cruel blows." Slaveholders often used state violence and private violence in ways interchangeable and complementary. William Johnson, a free Black barber in Natchez, employed a combination of privately inflicted corporal punishments and publicly administered penal labor on Steven, a heavy drinker and frequent runaway. Johnson committed Steven to the Natchez slave chain gang in October 1840. Between 1836 and Johnson's decision to sell Steven in 1844, Johnson also inflicted both "genteel" and "severe" whippings on Steven, asked others to whip the man, chained him, and locked him in a corncrib.[134] Bennet Barrow of West Feliciana Parish, one of the wealthiest cotton planters of the Lower Mississippi River valley, recorded a diverse litany of punishments in his diary, including whippings, beatings, sessions in his plantation stocks, dunking people underwater, "hand-sawing," staking people to the ground, withholding food, and forcing men to wear women's clothing. Yet Barrow also believed that imprisonment played an important role in the management of enslaved labor. In November 1839, he debated whether to have the fugitive slave Dennis committed to the New Orleans Police Jail "'til spring," a term that would have removed the valued field hand during the labor-intensive harvest season. Instead, Barrow decided to construct his own plantation jail.[135]

Elite planters such as Barrow tended to rely on urban slave prisons as an ancillary punishment, useful when privately inflicted violence proved insufficient. The overseer of Tally-Ho Plantation in St. Mary Parish, while growing increasingly frustrated that the fugitive slave Lew had repeatedly eluded recapture, resolved that "when he is caught, it will be best to put [him] in a chain gang. . . . Let the yellow fever kill him if it can." While watching bloodhounds tear into a chronic fugitive, one exasperated Mississippi slaveholder conceded that he had already "tried every species of punishment . . . without effect." "If he lives," the planter resolved, "I intend to send him to Natchez or to New Orleans to work with the ball and chain."[136] Commitments from rural regions represented a minor share of overall commitments, however. In Savannah, 1,100 commitments were made by prisoners' owners or their owners' agents between April 30, 1809, and May 16, 1815, but only 59 of those commitments (5.4 percent) were of persons who had been brought from outside Savannah.[137]

Compared to their rural peers, urban slaveholders relegated a far higher proportion of punishments to slave prisons. For urban elites, reliance on institutionalized violence connoted social status. It established distance between the slaveholder and the infliction of pain, enabling maintenance of a culture of domesticity—emphasizing sentimentality, self-control, and the tranquility of the domestic sphere—in conflict with the gruesome bodily violence that slavery's sustenance required. In the countryside, elite slaveholders could rely on drivers and overseers to inflict pain on their behalf: this distancing strategy was unavailable to slaveholders in cities, where overseers and drivers were rarely employed. Slave prisons also provided urban and urbane slaveholders with a strategy for legitimating their reliance on violence, at a time when penal reform ideology and shifting cultural mores were rapidly delegitimating the private infliction of bodily pain, by reframing that violence as structured and state-sanctioned justice.[138]

Urban slaveholders also imagined that slave prisons were essential to maintaining domestic tranquility within the townhouse, where masters and enslaved domestic workers lived close at hand.[139] "Slavery dislikes a dense population," perceived abolitionist Frederick Douglass. "Very few in the city are willing to incur the odium of being cruel masters." New Orleans slaveholders relied on police jails because they were "averse to correcting their slaves in a rigorous manner at home," one traveler observed. Outsourcing violence to prisons redirected the victim's anger from owner to jailor, one resident explained, shielding the owner from "the indignation of the slave, which would naturally become aroused if the punishment was inflicted by the hand of the master himself." A visitor to Charleston perceived that slaveholders there relied on slave prisons to avoid the "disagreeable nature" of whippings. Richmond's public whipping post insulated slaveholders from "a slight wear and tear of feeling," explained ex-slave Louis Hughes. Mistresses were often particularly reliant on the state to enact violence on their behalf. One well-to-do mistress explained that "most ladies" in New Orleans relegated all corporal punishments to police jails—though she herself disapproved of how harshly jailors administered whippings and preferred to "flog her servants herself." "If your cook is bad, better have him put in jail, & get your former one back," sugar planter Jacques Telesphore Roman advised his wife, Célina, during her sojourn in their New Orleans townhouse.[140]

For both rural and urban slaveholders, outsourcing punishments to prisons also fulfilled slaveholders' conviction that the ideal punishments were those that were administered methodically and dispassionately, establishing a sense of emotional distance between master and slave. Depersonalized punishments, suggested sugar baron William Minor, "impress [on] the culprit that he is punished for his bad conduct only and not for revenge or passion." "Never display yourself before them in a passion," advised a popular slave management handbook: punishments inflicted "in a mild, cool manner" will "produce a tenfold effect."[141]

Prisons played a particularly complex role in navigating the acute cultural anxieties prompted by the infliction of violence on enslaved women. Women tended to represent a third of all slave commitments but a disproportionately higher share—greater than 40 percent—of all inmates directly committed by their owners, whether for "safekeeping" or "correction." Women also tended to endure longer prison sentences: among 12,297 commitments made to the First Municipality Police Jail, the average prison term of enslaved women was 34 percent longer than that of enslaved men.[142]

Several factors underlie these trends. First, the intimate infliction of physical violence within the household on women may have aroused greater anxiety from slaveholders than the infliction of violence on men, as torturing women may have seemed a greater violation of antebellum sentimentality and domestic culture. Second, several formerly enslaved people noted that women were regularly incarcerated as an instrument of sexual coercion. William J. Anderson noted that many of the "women and girls" in the Police Jail had been sent by "white gentlemen" for refusing to "gratify their hellish passions." John Brown recalled a slave trader threatening a woman with Police Jail incarceration for refusing his sexual advances, believing that she would submit "to escape the ignominy of working in the public streets, in what is called 'the chain-gang.'" Harriet Ann Jacobs was also regularly threatened with incarceration for refusing her owner's sexual advances.[143] Sexual coercion through prisons allowed slaveholding men to wield intense power over enslaved women while maintaining the illusion of their gentility and of the women's sexual consent: allowing the slaveholder to imagine, perhaps, that he was not engaged in torture and rape. Third, mistresses may have relied on police jails to block their husbands' infidelity by temporarily removing enslaved targets of sexual violence from the household.[144]

Women also constituted a disproportionate share of prisoners abandoned to police jails by their owners for life. To simply sell such persons would have been the more rational economic choice, suggesting a sadism that transcended purely financial motivations. In 1815, George Roussel gifted the enslaved woman Nina to the city of New Orleans, "on condition that she be put in chains and made to work on public works for the rest of her life." Slaveholder John Brown committed Sophie in September 1825; she remained incarcerated until the First Municipality sold her in August 1845. Anna, a fugitive from Mobile, carried her one-year-old baby, Precillia, with her into the First Municipality Police Jail in 1838. Though Anna identified her owner by name, the owner neglected to reclaim either mother or daughter. Anna died in the prison in 1841, leaving authorities confounded as to the child's fate. It was not until August 1845 that the municipality resolved to sell the girl, by then about eight years old. The Police Jail would have been the only world that she had ever known.[145]

City of Voyeurs

It would have been virtually impossible, before the Civil War, to find a single city street, park, or pipe in New Orleans that had not been manufactured, repaired, or cleaned by slave penal labor. Incarcerated enslaved people also built the public infrastructure of Baton Rouge, Natchez, Vicksburg, Nashville, Louisville, Richmond, and innumerable smaller towns.

Yet the "work" performed by slave chain gangs cannot be measured by economic output alone. Omnipresent and highly visible, these roving spectacles of Black humiliation performed a series of deceptively complex acculturative functions, leaving deep impressions on witnesses and participants alike. In addition to all else, chain gangs were public street performances—Michel Foucault famously compared chain gangs to a "festival" and "saturnalia of punishment"—communicating powerful meanings to the enslaved prisoners forced to participate, the enslaved bystanders forced to watch, and the white passersby.[146] For prisoners, these performances were intended to humiliate; for enslaved observers, to terrorize. City officials noticed that chain gangs visibly distressed the enslaved passersby "who daily witness it." The passing chain gang "strikes terror in the negro mind," observed an English traveler, adding that "the threat" of incarceration was "often sufficient to tame the most incorrigible."[147] To white audiences, these spectacles affirmed Black inferiority and Otherness. As they strolled about their city—to work, home, marketplace, church, opera, park, brothel, business, bank, barroom—they were surrounded by these mobile theaters of Black humiliation. These staged rituals of white dominance and Black degradation saturated the urban landscape.

Yet efforts to maximize the mental anguish, visibility, and humiliation of the enslaved encoded a tension, emblematic of the broader contradictions that slave incarceration engendered. Humiliation was predicated on the exploitation, not denial, of Black humanity. The slave chain gang's logic was rooted not in white authorities' perceptions of Black insusceptibility to emotional suffering and internal transformation, but rather in attentiveness to the universal human capacity for mental anguish. In seeking to degrade enslaved people's social identities and private senses of self-worth, the police jail system's public shaming rituals tacitly acknowledged the existence of enslaved people's social and internal lives.[148] The New York abolitionist William Goodell once noted that "the slave, who is but 'a chattel' on all other occasions . . . becomes 'a person' whenever he is to be punished."[149] Goodell's observation, made in reference to slave criminal law, encapsulates the underlying theoretical tenet of slave penology. In incorporating precisely regimented routines of shame and spectacle, authorities acknowledged slaves' capacity for physical and psychological torment while attempting to dominate body and soul.

CHAPTER 2

A Line of Demarcation in Punishments

Slavery and the Penitentiary
Movement, 1820–1861

Penitentiary development in the slave South confronted a paradox. In that imprisonment entailed forced labor, loss of personal freedom, and submission to authority, it closely resembled slavery.[1] But penitentiaries emerged during an age of calcifying racial boundaries in the United States, when lawmakers throughout the nation—though especially in the South—tried to manufacture absolute distinctions between white freedom and Black servitude.[2] How then could the state imprison white offenders without assigning them the roles of slaves? This paradox is embodied in the person of Edward Livingston, the scion of a prestigious New York family turned Louisiana statesman, sugar planter, and penal theorist.

In 1822, Livingston released the preliminary outline of his much-anticipated plans for the total redesign of Louisiana's criminal laws, state punishments, and public institutions. Ultimately published in stages between 1826 and 1833, Livingston's magnum opus would receive approbation throughout Europe and the Americas, influence the development of the world's first penitentiaries, and thrust Louisiana into the center of the international movement to ameliorate and rework criminal penalties for the enlightened, rational, modern age.[3] Livingston called for the elimination of outdoor penal labor, corporal punishment, capital punishment, and punitive shaming: these punishments, he argued, destroyed men's bodies without reforming men's souls. In place of such degradations, Livingston envisioned the diffusion of power throughout an intricate, omnipresent network of public institutions—juvenile reformatories, workhouses, public schools, lockups, prisons, and penitentiaries—that would inculcate obedience without inflicting bodily harm, molding deviants into upright citizens through constant, institutionalized pressure, expressed from cradle to grave. Livingston's vast blueprint contained one critical caveat: nothing he wrote should be misconstrued as applicable to the enslaved.[4]

Livingston was a leader within the penitentiary movement, the successor to the prison reform movement of the late eighteenth century, which began sweeping the nation in the 1820s with the promise of culminating the broad societal transformation initiated by its predecessor. In creating penitentiaries, reformers imagined totally controlled penal environments, characterized by constant labor, solitary reflection, and spiritual atonement. These new institutions would counteract the nation's growing immorality by manufacturing disciplined and industrious citizens. The advent of penitentiaries paved the way for a broader societal shift toward institutionalization. On the heels of the penitentiary movement came public school systems, state insane asylums, almshouses, state hospitals, and juvenile reformatories, all embodying common themes: isolation from the moral contaminants of the outside world, the inculcation of industrious habits through constant work, and faith in the power of totalizing institutions to transform.[5]

While Livingston envisioned a fundamental revolution in the organization of society and the technologies of power, the New Orleans Police Jail regularly tortured people whom Livingston held as property. Between 1820 and 1822 alone, as Livingston drafted his plans, jailors recorded twenty-three admittances of people enslaved by Edward Livingston. Some may have been maroons captured by police, but on at least one occasion, Livingston (or his agent) purposefully sentenced an enslaved person to penal labor, condemning Charles to the chain gang for ten months, from January 13, 1821, until his jailors registered him as too enfeebled to work on November 13, 1821.[6] Despite the remarkable breadth and volume of Livingston's writings, the theorist chose to omit entirely any mention of slave prisons, the only feature of Louisiana's carceral landscape on which Livingston personally and regularly relied.

Livingston's contribution to the global history of the prison disrupts how that history has been told. Scholarship has tended to construct essentialist distinctions between southern and northern penal histories: whereas northern prison development often is framed as a modernizing project that evolved in pursuit of reformers' rehabilitative ideal, treatments of southern prison development often emphasize a violent backwardness that is attributed to slavery's brutal legacy.[7] Livingston, by contrast, shows that Louisiana was fully integrated into the global circulation of penal practices and discourses, not only as a consumer of ideas from without but also as a contributor. A New Yorker by birth and a Louisiana slaveholder by choice, Livingston drafted a penology that incorporated lessons gleamed from the social reformers of the North, the plantations of the South, and the slave chain gangs of New Orleans. His influential writings, prepared in the shadow of the Police Jail, directly shaped the development of the world's first penitentiaries: connecting the histories of the penitentiary and the slave prison while suggesting that the development of penitentiaries owes something to the Police Jail.

Livingston's writings also force us to reconsider the relation between slavery and penitentiary development in the South. Prior histories have argued that antebellum penitentiaries—and by extension, the wave of public institutions that followed in their wake—"simply were not for slaves."[8] Yet clearly, Livingston *did* believe that institutionalization could have a remedial impact on the enslaved and that slave and prison were not irreconcilably incompatible. He was intimately familiar with cost-effective slave penal systems. These are the prior explanations offered for why southern penitentiaries excluded enslaved people, yet here they seem not to apply. Why, then, did Livingston erase enslaved people from his plans for the modern prison system?

Livingston himself alluded to his reasons. Livingston's anxiety was not that slave and prison were incompatible but rather that slave and convict already appeared too *similar*. He feared that any penal procedure that drew attention to these similarities risked the complete destruction not only of the penitentiary experiment but, moreover, of southern society itself. "There is a line of demarcation," concluded Livingston, "which it would be rash in the extreme to destroy even in punishments; and the sight of a freeman performing the forced labour, or suffering under the stripes usually inflicted on the slave, must give rise to ideas of the most insubordinate nature. A false economy only could suggest the repetition of an experiment which has every where failed, every where produced increase of misery, degradation and crime; and here might be the cause of evils worse than all these combined."[9]

Livingston perceived that state punishments and the fabrication of race were inexorably intertwined in antebellum America. By punishments, the state attaches or detaches ideas of rights and protections to certain bodies; encodes and enforces assumptions regarding the nature of people's bodies, stations, and societal functions; and propagates societal values.[10] Having intuited the connection between race-making and punishment, Livingston concluded that punishments which evoked parallels between Black slave and white convict were profoundly dangerous: they blurred the very parameters of racial difference, encouraged abolitionism, and might even unleash a revolution like the one that had destroyed Saint-Domingue (a cataclysm that Livingston's own wife, a Saint-Domingue native, had narrowly survived but that had claimed the lives of her brothers and grandmother).[11] To protect slavery and prevent revolution, punishments' racial subtexts required rigorous management. The parallels between slave and convict needed to be suppressed, a "line of demarcation" in punishments carefully maintained.

Livingston's anxieties underscore how penitentiary development and the reification of racial boundaries were intertwined and codependent movements in Jacksonian America. Put another way, Louisiana lawmakers conceived of their state penitentiary as a race-making technology: a tool for naturalizing the biological essentialism of race, elevating whiteness, and demarcating white bodies as bearing rights. Authorities endeavored to exclude Black people from these new penal institutions not because they believed that incarceration would not "work" on Black prisoners or because they were opposed to encroaching on slaveholders' autonomy: rather, by excluding Black prisoners from the scope of penal reform, authorities sought to demarcate Black bodies as profane, unprotected, and vulgar. During Louisiana's penitentiary movement, lawmakers tried to uphold Livingston's "line of demarcation" by diligently suppressing penal practices that appeared to blur boundaries between white convict and Black slave. They worked toward the creation of two parallel penal systems that reproduced distinctions between white and Black bodies, minds, and societal functions: cloistered indoor penal labor for uplifting white prisoners and humiliating outdoor penal labor for debasing Black prisoners.

Paradoxically, even as lawmakers sought to reify race through prisons, prisons were also sites where racial differences were regularly undermined or blurred. Lawmakers could not always control prison administrators' actions or how the uncontrolled diffusion of penal reform ideology reshaped public attitudes toward slave punishments.[12] Jailors undermined Livingston's "line of demarcation" by subjecting rebellious white convicts to tortures associated with the enslaved as a means of racial humiliation. Reformist-minded slaveholders undermined the "line of demarcation" by promoting police jail reform, arguing that brutal conditions within police jails were out of step with the penitentiary movement's humanist aims. By the late antebellum era, as public interest in the penitentiary movement waned, cynical prison administrators disregarded racial segregation entirely, condemning both white and Black convicts to lucrative penal labor systems that pursued profit over all else. In such moments, the "line of demarcation" proved unmaintainable. The power of punishments to reinforce racial difference was a double-edged sword: what the prison could create, it also could destroy.

"The Great End of Punishment"

In the 1820s, Louisiana lawmakers grew concerned that the state lagged in the implementation of modern carceral technologies. A second wave of prison reform was starting to sweep the nation. Frustrated with the perceived failures of the preceding prison reform movement, the nation's lawmakers had begun drafting and debating plans for various new penal systems. Between 1819 and

1823, agents at Auburn Prison in New York State suppressed the use of stocks, floggings, and irons, built a new cellhouse where the most "hardened" convicts could be kept silent in solitary confinement, and launched a new penal labor system for the remaining prisoners: creating, in essence, the nation's first penitentiary. By 1833, ten states had replicated the Auburn model.[13]

As Louisiana's peers began constructing totalizing institutions that promised decreased costs, lower crime rates, and the humane transformation of deviants into productive citizens, Louisianians perceived disorder, barbarism, and ineffectiveness within their own prisons. The Police Jail was the only specialized penal institution in the state. Most other facilities indiscriminately lumped offenders together, regardless of age, race, social standing, or crime—a practice that "contaminated" light offenders and children by forcing their "association with veteran[s] in vice." The state prison, located in New Orleans's main square, had been built during the Spanish colonial era to house fifty prisoners; now, it routinely held three times that number. Moreover, the building was "falling to pieces." Escapes were regular. Instead of rehabilitating criminals, the institution seemed "a kind of school" in vice.[14] Little brought greater embarrassment than the indictment of noted French intellectuals Gustave de Beaumont and Alexis de Tocqueville, sent by King Louis-Philippe to study America's great experiment in penology, who after inspecting Louisiana's state prison declared it "a horrid sink" where prisoners "are put in chains like ferocious beasts; and instead of being corrected, they are rendered brutal."[15]

Most alarmingly, Louisiana's overcrowded state prison was incapable of implementing a rehabilitative penal labor program for the reformation of Louisiana's convicts. Instead of fostering virtue and rendering offenders "elevated in dignity" through hard labor, convicts were "kept in idleness" within congested cells: a deficient "mode of punishment," complained New Orleans mayor Denis Prieur, that "produced no salutary effect on the offenders." As impoverished European immigrants and domestic migrants settled in Louisiana in ever-growing numbers, authorities perceived rising crime rates and feared that these strangers were unproductive and ill-prepared for republican citizenship. Only some system of "constant labor and solitary confinement" could remedy the state's growing evils, complained Governor Thomas Robertson in 1820. "There is no object of greater importance to the state," agreed Robertson's successor, Governor Henry Johnson, in 1826.[16]

To modernize Louisiana's penal system, the legislature turned to Edward Livingston, the same well-regarded lawyer and statesman who had drafted the petition to Congress, on behalf of Louisiana's planters, in 1804. Born in 1764, Livingston came from a prestigious New York family. After practicing law in New York City, Livingston was elected to the US House of Representatives, where he promoted penal reform. In 1801, Livingston was appointed US attorney for the District of New York and mayor of New York City. He served in both capacities—simultaneously—until 1803, when Treasury Department inspectors uncovered the embezzlement of public funds by someone within Livingston's office. Disgraced, Livingston relinquished his property to cover the debt and fled to New Orleans, seeking to rebuild his reputation and wealth. On arrival, Livingston immediately reopened his law practice, engaged in rampant land speculation, and organized a bank. In 1805, he married Louise Moreau de Lassy, a refugee from Saint-Domingue whose father had been among that colony's wealthiest sugar planters. In January 1815, he served as Major General Andrew Jackson's adviser and aide-de-camp in the Battle of New Orleans, amid the War of 1812. The following year, Livingston purchased two sugar plantations in Plaquemines Parish, immediately downriver of New Orleans, and dozens of enslaved people. In 1820, Plaquemines Parish elected Livingston to the Louisiana legislature.[17]

In 1821, the legislature commissioned Livingston to draft a new state penal code, but in 1822 Livingston returned with a tentative proposal that greatly exceeded the scope of his original mandate. Livingston envisioned an integrated network of workhouses, penitentiaries, prisons, lockups, public schools, and juvenile reformatories: a totalizing system, bent on reform rather than retribution, molding and upholding disciplined republican citizens from cradle to grave. Each institution would scientifically classify offenders by age, gender, and offense. Although each institution would be specialized for a particular category of person or type of offense, each institution would strive toward the same overarching goal of indoctrinating restraint, productivity, and lawfulness—what Livingston called "habits of industrious obedience" and "the duties of a citizen towards the state"—through carefully regimented routines and ceaseless labor.[18]

Many of the features of Livingston's plan resembled other leading penological proposals of the age. Prevalent social theory identified idleness as both the root cause of deviance and the prevailing characteristic of a deviant person. It was a foregone conclusion that an idler was too lazy to perform honest labor and would thus resort to crime; idleness also signified that the person lacked the self-discipline to properly manage him- or herself. Like most contemporary penal proposals, Livingston's plan embraced hard labor as a way of purging convicts of vice, inducing them to embrace industrious habits and forcing them to contribute something toward the cost of their correction.[19]

Yet what distinguished Livingston's plan from competing penal proposals was his vision for coercing convicts into accepting *voluntary* penal labor.

Livingston observed that convicts resisted the imposition of their redemptive penal regime. To keep convicts employed and to maintain discipline, jailors in even the most progressive penal institutions resorted to whips, chains, and violent threats—the very coercive and corporal tools that the reform movement sought to eliminate. Despite the penitentiary movement's lofty goals, Livingston feared that the experiment was simply shifting bodily torture out of the public square and into the hands of jailors, who were coming to wield an "illegal . . . cruel . . . [and] tyrannical" power over their wards. In a republic, Livingston argued, it was natural for "the patriot to resist civil tyranny." This natural republican resistance to coercion "goads on the convict" into opposing the virtue and discipline that penal labor attempted to instill, "with an obstinacy in exact proportion to the severity of the punishment." Livingston concluded that "labour forced by stripes [of the whip] must always produce" resistance and is never "calculated to produce reformation." For the penitentiary movement to succeed in its mission of training free citizens in the proper exercise of their liberty, deviants would need to be persuaded to embrace their own rehabilitation voluntarily.[20]

Livingston's solution was to reconceptualize penal labor as a reward earned by convicts through good behavior. At first, all convicts would be confined to solitary confinement without labor, consuming a "coarse diet" and suffering "the tedium arising from want of society and of occupation." Eventually, Livingston predicted, the torturously bored convict—trapped in isolation, facing near-total sensory deprivation, and as dead to the world as a body within a coffin—would plead for the right to work, yearning for an opportunity to be reborn. As they grew more productive, laboring convicts would be offered additional rewards—pay, extra rations, time in the courtyard, books, educational opportunities—thereby creating "lasting habits of industry and virtuous pursuit" and ultimately releasing each man "a better, a wiser, and a happier man than he entered."[21]

While penitentiaries would transform hardened criminals, an expansive network of institutions would preempt the creation of criminals by establishing the same habits of industry and discipline in children, immigrants, and paupers before their vices could fester into full-blown criminality. Public schools would instill "habits of industrious obedience" in children. Workhouses and juvenile reformatories would establish these habits in wayward immigrants while they were still in the "earliest stages of their profligacy." Livingston took particular interest in the rehabilitation of vagrants, who embodied the very idleness that was the root origin of deviance. Vagrants, Livingston recognized, had yet to actually commit a crime. But while "not absolutely criminals," they were "so generally the nursery for criminals of every description, that preventive justice is forced." By arresting the idling poor for vagrancy and by instilling in them industrious habits through workhouses and juvenile reformatories, "the moral maladies of society" could be corrected "before their profligacy assumes the shape of crime."[22]

Livingston's voluminous plans pointedly omitted any mention of slave punishments or slave prisons. While mapping an intricate and comprehensive network of penal institutions for Louisiana, his writings never once mention police jails. Indeed, even when denouncing forced penal labor as tyrannical, Livingston refused "to call it by a harsher name," evading the word "slavery" as though the word itself were taboo.[23]

Yet the shadow of the Police Jail pervades Livingston's work. Livingston was intimately familiar with slave chain gangs that sought to construct idealized slaves, and fabricate racial meanings, through public agony and strategic humiliation. Livingston's familiarity with these slave chain gangs and his experiences as a slaveholder undoubtedly underlay his conviction that "public labour" and corporal punishment could never be inflicted on white convicts "without danger of the most serious kind."[24] Slave chain gangs were also doubtless on Livingston's mind when he concluded that forced penal labor only produced slavish subjects and that the production of self-disciplined republican citizens required an entirely different penal project. In envisioning a penal labor system without compulsion—"labour not coerced, but granted as a favour"—Livingston was trying to devise a penal labor program for white prisoners that was as far removed from slavery and from the Police Jail as conceivably possible.[25]

In part, Livingston may have evaded explicit mention of slave punishments and slave prisons to broaden his work's appeal with penal reformers in the North, among whom the penitentiary movement was in the process of stimulating new critiques of slavery. There was considerable organizational overlap in such cities as Philadelphia, New York, and Boston between the movement for punishment's reform and the movement for slavery's abolition. Philadelphia's most prominent champion of prison reform, Roberts Vaux, was also a leading member of the Pennsylvania Society for Promoting the Abolition of Slavery (as well as Livingston's friend and regular correspondent). Louis Dwight, founder of Boston's Prison Discipline Society and the nation's leading advocate of the Auburn prison system, was also involved in antislavery politics. For penitentiary advocates such as these, who imagined themselves as proponents of humanitarian progress and as adversaries of despotic power, the rehabilitation of convicts and the uplift of enslaved people seemed like aligned missions. Livingston may well have recognized that discussion of slave prisons could discredit his ideas among a core contingent of his audience.[26]

Yet Livingston's effort to widen distinctions between penal labor and slave labor also spoke to the concerns of southern slaveholders, many of whom shared Livingston's anxiety that penitentiaries produced conditions dangerously similar to chattel slavery. "Under the Penitentiary system, the freeborn citizen is made to labor directly under the lash as a slave," charged one North Carolinian opponent of the institutions. "Is not this worse than death?" "What is the difference," asked another proslavery critic, "between selling a white man into slavery, and confining him in a penitentiary, where he is made to labor?" Some similarities were obvious: both slavery and the penitentiary relied on forced labor, regimentation, total submission to an authority, loss of freedom, social death, and the violent suppression of resistance. Yet the connections went beyond the superficial. Citing John Locke's social contract theory, some southern social theorists identified imprisonment as a form of justified, temporary enslavement. There was no fundamental theoretical distinction, argued prominent proslavery theorist George Sawyer, between slavery and penitentiary confinement: "both alike" were "in violation of the natural rights of man" but rendered "necessary" for the broader "peace, prosperity, and safety of society." Sawyer charged the northern penal reformers who dabbled in abolitionism with hypocrisy, as "the same principles that would abolish the relation of master and slave ... would also, if carried out to their necessary results, abolish all restraint imposed by penal codes, prison discipline, and poor laws."[27]

Livingston's plan resolved these northern and southern anxieties by simultaneously erasing the slave prison and broadening the gulf between slavery and penitentiary imprisonment. Penal labor "enforced by chains or stripes" produced debased subjects fit only for despotic rule. Voluntary penal labor, incentivized through an escalating hierarchy of rewards, produced obedient republican citizens.[28]

The reaction to the publication of Livingston's system was ecstatic. "No American book has ever attracted such attention from the civilized world or been so universally and so highly praised," proclaimed one penologist a century later. British jurist Sir Henry Maine declared Livingston "the first legal genius of modern times." Victor Hugo called it "a beautiful book, a useful book, a model book." The French politician and writer Abel-François Villemain declared that nothing "in the arts, in the literature, and in science . . . reflects more credit upon our modern times." Thomas Jefferson, James Madison, Alexis de Tocqueville, Gustave de Beaumont, New York legislator and legal scholar James Kent, Chief Justice John Marshall, German jurist Carl Joseph Anton Mittermaier, the czar of Russia, the kings of Sweden and the Netherlands, and members of the US Senate all lauded Livingston's triumph. England's leading penal theorist, Jeremy Bentham, encouraged Parliament to consider a British adaptation of Livingston's system. The French jurist and politician Alphonse-Honoré

Taillandier predicted that Louisiana would soon be "endowed with the noblest body of penal laws which any nation has hitherto possessed."[29] Livingston had thrust Louisiana into the center of the penitentiary movement. The slave state seemed poised to lead the world into an age of enlightened, rational, republican discipline.

For a brief moment, it even seemed probable that Livingston's plan for Louisiana would be adopted throughout the United States. In 1823, Livingston was elected to the US House of Representatives, where he began revising his Louisiana plan into a national penal code. Congressman Daniel Webster introduced a resolution in 1826 that called for government publication of Livingston's national penal code. That same year, Livingston was appointed to the US Senate, where he introduced a bill for the national adaptation of his code. These efforts were abandoned only days later when Livingston was appointed secretary of state by President Andrew Jackson, sixteen years after his service as Jackson's aide-de-camp.[30]

Livingston's ideas had a far more direct influence on the development of a new penitentiary system in Pennsylvania, first implemented at Philadelphia's Eastern State Penitentiary in 1829, that quickly became the leading rival to New York's Auburn model. In contrast to Auburn's "congregate system," wherein prisoners performed factorylike labor in large (albeit silent) groups before retreating to their cells at night, Philadelphia reformers developed a "separate system," wherein prisoners suffered a period of total isolation before gradually earning the right to perform solitary penal labor within their cells.[31] Though often overlooked today, the direct influence of Livingston's ideas on Pennsylvania's development of the separate system was widely recognized by contemporary penologists.[32] Livingston's published writings, as well as his unpublished manuscript drafts, were in the hands of Philadelphia penologists as they devised the separate system, between 1826 and 1829. Roberts Vaux, the leading commissioner charged with designing Eastern State Penitentiary's rehabilitative program, explicitly identified Edward Livingston's plan for Louisiana as his source of inspiration. In March 1826, the Philadelphia *National Gazette* began publishing regular excerpts from Livingston's unpublished manuscript at the behest of an unidentified local penologist (perhaps Vaux himself) who encouraged Pennsylvania to consider an adaptation of Livingston's penal system. In 1833, Beaumont and Tocqueville also attributed Pennsylvania's separate system to Livingston's "profound theories" in their study of America's penitentiary movement (the first English-language translation of which was dedicated to Livingston and Vaux).[33]

Governments around the world began building prisons modeled on Pennsylvania's separate system and Livingston's principles. Guatemala formally adopted Livingston's penal code, in its entirety, in 1837 (the only nation to do so). An Australian penal colony imposed a point system based on Livingston's theory of coercion into voluntary penal labor. England, Prussia, France, Belgium, Holland, Sweden, Denmark, Hungary, Norway, Poland, and Switzerland each build separate-system prisons, often identifying Livingston's ideas as the key catalyst.[34] Many of these countries deployed the separate system well into the twentieth century.

Derbigny's Chain Gang Crisis

Even as the separate system flourished in Europe, praise for Livingston's ideas quickly yielded to financial considerations in the United States. State governments recognized that prisons built to Auburn's congregate system were considerably less expensive to construct and administer than Pennsylvania's separate system, let alone Livingston's sprawling carceral network.[35] Citing costs, the Louisiana legislature refused to take any action. Meanwhile, the state convicts in New Orleans's prison remained deleteriously idle. Frustrated by the legislature's inaction, New Orleans's municipal council proposed a radical interim solution to the convicts' idleness: the creation of a convict chain gang system, to be worked in tandem with New Orleans's slave chain gangs. In October 1827, a "considerable crowd" assembled to watch as the state convicts—"dressed in red from head to foot" and bearing "a considerable weight of chains"—joined the slave chain gang on New Orleans's streets.[36]

The creation of a chain gang for state convicts harkened back to an earlier period in Louisiana's penal history, when French colonial officials had deliberately fostered racial ambiguity in punishments as a means of symbolically equating poor white offenders to enslaved people and thereby deepening their humiliating degradation.[37] Yet the move also violated the spirit of Livingston's plan, flouting his explicit warning that deploying white convicts at "public labour" endangered the stability of slave society.[38] Clearly aware of these concerns, New Orleans mayor Louis Philippe de Roffignac proposed to limit the penal system's racial ambiguities by dressing white and Black prisoners in differently colored uniforms and by keeping them engaged at separate tasks, "to distinguish [Black convicts] from white." One year later, the employment of free Black men as chain gang guards was prohibited. For their part, members of the legislature demanded the urgent construction of a state penitentiary.[39]

State convicts and enslaved prisoners labored side by side until April 1829, when Governor Pierre Derbigny prohibited the public employment of white convicts after a court sentenced Louis Gayarre, member of a prosperous planter family and Derbigny's distant cousin, to hard labor for murdering his mother-in-law. For Derbigny, the reduction of an affluent peer to the symbolic status on an enslaved prisoner seemed too perverse a disruption of racial and class hierarchies to bear. Still, Derbigny's obvious nepotism outraged many citizens, who rallied to "express the public indignation."[40] Defensively, Derbigny explained that he was merely an advocate of penal reform and the studious racial management of punishments. Public exposition of white convicts was "improper and impolitic in a country like ours," Derbigny argued. Invoking the language of the penitentiary movement, Derbigny asserted that public humiliation merely hardened white convicts, placing them "beyond the possibility of reformation."[41] Some slaveholders agreed with Derbigny's arguments even as they doubted the governor's motives. "Whatever Governor Derbigny's motives may be," one planter wrote, "his sentiments, with regard to the public exposition of convicts, are consonant. . . . [The chain gang] is a retrograde step in the science of criminal jurisprudence. It is at variance with all that is taught us by the Beccarias, the Benthams, and the Livingstons." White chain gangs were an offense to all Americans, though particularly "impolitic and improper . . . amongst us," the writer continued, due to "the influence of slavery."[42] Derbigny and the municipal council eventually reached a compromise whereby white convicts would be returned to the streets, but on the condition that Gayarre wear civilian dress: a tacit signal that Gayarre retained a degree of class privilege, partially shielding him from total debasement. On April 11, Gayarre's return to the chain gang—dressed in a "blue roundabout, [and] a common hat" and chained "to a particularly huge robust fellow"—generated jeering crowds.[43]

The political crisis seemed to affirm Livingston's observation that race-making and state punishments were inseparably intertwined and that the maintenance of social order required the strict ideological management of racially differentiated punishments. Yet the popular anger directed at Derbigny also indicated the limits of authorities' control over popular sentiment: members of the public did not necessarily share civic authorities' preoccupation with suppressing punishments that seemed to undermine racial boundaries.

New Orleans Reconstructed

In the aftermath of Derbigny's chain gang fiasco, New Orleans entered into an extraordinary penal building spree, constructing each and every institution that Livingston had prescribed. Joseph Pilié's new Parish Prison and adjacent Police Jail were completed in 1834 and 1835. Simultaneously, the state convicts were removed from New Orleans's old prison to a new state penitentiary, built in Baton Rouge.[44] In 1837, two additional police jails were built for the Second and Third Municipalities, following the city's division into three autonomous governing bodies.[45] The city launched a public school system for white children in 1841.[46] Between 1842 and 1843, the city added three workhouses for the reformation of white paupers convicted of vagrancy, lewd behavior, public intoxication, and other petty misdemeanors: here, the disorderly poor would be transformed into industrious citizens, before their immorality could fester into full-blown criminality, through constant penal labor, performed in silence, from sunrise to sundown.[47] A juvenile reformatory, called the House of Refuge and completed in 1845, promised to instill a parallel transformation in the young by seizing the children of "inefficient, vicious, or criminal parents" and converting them into "respectable, orderly and industrious citizens."[48] By 1847, a new state insane asylum had been completed, and New Orleans boasted a citywide network of neighborhood lockups for the confinement of arrestees before their arraignment.[49] With the exception of the city's three police jails, every new institution restricted or prohibited corporal punishments and public shaming—practices designed to degrade—and promised to uplift citizens humanely through rational, modern, scientific systems of instruction, silent reflection, and labor. The extent and rapidity of the city's transformation was nothing short of remarkable. In the span of a decade, the exercise of state violence had been dramatically restructured, establishing a basic network of public institutions that would survive into the twenty-first century.

Similar transformations were underway throughout the nation. "In the history of the world," concluded Ralph Waldo Emerson in 1841, "the doctrine of Reform had never such scope as at the present hour."[50] By 1850, virtually every state in the country, including every southern state except for the Carolinas and Florida, had built a state penitentiary. In the wake of state penitentiaries, cities throughout the nation constructed juvenile reformatories, workhouses, poorhouses, public school systems, public hospitals, and insane asylums with dizzying speed. Massachusetts opened sixty new poorhouses between 1820 and 1840. Before 1810, only Virginia boasted a public insane asylum; by 1851, most states had one. Juvenile prisons did not exist before 1825: within three decades, houses of refuge had built in New York, Boston, Philadelphia, Rochester, Cincinnati, Providence, Baltimore, Chicago, Pittsburgh, and St. Louis.[51]

New Orleanians proclaimed that they were participating in a great social revolution, leaving a primitive era defined by violent torture for an "enlightened age" governed by "human benevolence and philanthropy." "In no respect has the wisdom of American ideas on the subject of the Government of men been more signally manifested," lauded one grand jury in 1835. "[We] are proud . . . that all the improvements for the reclaiming of the reprobate are in train of application." It was "one of the most decisive improvements ever made" in human history, declared one New Orleans newspaper, the *Daily Picayune*: the creation of penal institutions set on *"reforming* instead of *degrading."* Crime and vengeance would soon fade away, superseded by rehabilitation and prevention. Governor André Roman declared it "the great end of punishment" in the state of Louisiana.[52] Livingston would not live to see it: after serving as President Jackson's secretary of state and later as minister to France, Livingston retired to a family estate in Upstate New York, where he died in 1836.[53]

Louisiana's revolution in governance went hand in hand with the reification of racial difference. Whereas cells in the old state prison had often been integrated, each new facility was strictly segregated by presumptive race and legal status.[54] Practices that evoked parallels between convicts and slaves were suppressed. Newspapers stopped printing advertisements for escaped convicts next to advertisements for fugitive enslaved people.[55] The legislature forbade the chaining of penitentiary prisoners, and inspectors suppressed the use of chains to restrain rebellious poor white prisoners within workhouses.[56] In short, anything that suggested parallels between convict and slave grew objectionable and was expunged.

During this age of reform and racialization, New Orleans's police force was simultaneously demilitarized and purged of all free Black members. Both Louisiana and prerevolutionary Saint-Domingue had long traditions of free Black militia service: indeed, in prerevolutionary Saint-Domingue, the task of policing enslaved people had primarily fallen on a *maréchaussée*, or rural militia, composed entirely of Black enlistees.[57] Between 1805 and 1830, a small number of Black policemen had served on the New Orleans force: after 1830, Black policemen disappeared entirely from police rolls. The Louisiana legislature subsequently disbanded Louisiana's free Black militia in 1834.[58] In 1836, New Orleans's police force was restructured to divest the institution of its resemblance to a standing army and better align it with the spirit of republican civil society. Patrolmen surrendered their swords and pistols and took up truncheons and spontoons (though in practice, policemen simply transitioned to carrying personal handguns and knives). The former patrol system of four-man squad sweeps was replaced with individual patrolmen walking territorial "beats." Leather caps, emblazoned with the wearer's unique roll number, replaced the force's blue uniforms (blue uniforms would be reinstated in 1855).[59]

Echoing Livingston's proscriptions, nothing assumed weightier racial subtexts during this era of racial bifurcation than whether penal labor was performed indoors or outside. Both the state legislature and the New Orleans municipal government strictly forbade any outdoors employment of white convicts, as well as the public display of white prisoners in foot stocks or pillories. Even the employment of white convicts at perfunctory tasks, such as fetching water from a well or removing trash from their prisons, became deeply taboo.

In 1840, the rumor that penitentiary convicts had cut timber outside of the penitentiary's walls provoked public outcry in Baton Rouge: in response, the legislature reiterated its policy that white convicts "should never, without weighty reasons, be employed outside." Even when faced with catastrophic river flooding in 1847, New Orleans authorities rushed the slave chain gangs to reinforce faltering levees but refused to deploy any white convicts from the parish prison or workhouses.[60] In short, the racial distinction between white convicts and Black slaves had been firmly transmuted onto the division between indoor and outdoor penal labor.

The Limits of Racial Differentiation

Behind the weightily racial symbolism attached to penal labor's visibility, distinctions between white prisoners' indoor labor and Black prisoners' outdoor labor were often tenuous. Theoretically, New Orleans's new Parish Prison, workhouses, and House of Refuge prepared white inmates for industrious citizenship by training them in marketable trades. Yet the city refused to purchase manufacturing equipment, citing costs. To the frustration of prison agents, inmates within the new Parish Prison remained entirely idle while inmates within the city's workhouses and House of Refuge could only ever be assigned to tedious tasks—breaking rocks, sorting trash, picking oakum—that did not require investment in expensive manufacturing machinery and that made no pretense of developing marketable skills. Blacksmith shops, shoe shops, carpentry shops, tin shops, and bakeries were slowly added to these institutions through the late 1840s and 1850s, though these workstations were always too small to accommodate more than a handful of inmates at a time.[61]

In practice, poor white prisoners and enslaved prisoners labored as two meshed cogs within the same municipal penal labor machine. From their indoor workshops inside the city's workhouses, poor white prisoners fitted and fixed the chain gang slaves' shovels and picks. They built the paupers' coffins that chain gang slaves later buried in potter's fields. They smashed the rocks and carved the flagstones with which chain gang slaves graded and paved city streets, and they manufactured the brooms with which chain gang slaves swept marketplaces, sidewalks, and gutters. In the workhouse's blacksmith shop, poor white prisoners manufactured the chain gang slaves' chains.[62] Commitment to the symbolic distinction between indoor and outdoor labor obscured the city's efforts to fully leverage inmates' laboring capacity.

Racial differentiation was further undermined by jailors' enduring reliance on the whip to maximize production and crush rebellion. Overconfident city leaders had assumed that workhouse inmates would become partners in their rehabilitation, readily embracing their penal labor routine. Yet only one month after the city's first workhouse opened, the inmates rebelled, violently attacking their overseers.[63] Escape attempts and work stoppages became regular.[64] In reaction, jailors quietly revived the whip, violently forcing workhouse inmates into submission whenever they refused to work. The city government repeatedly tried, without success, to suppress jailors' reliance on the whip. Periodic scandals, precipitated by accounts of particularly brutal workhouse whippings, plagued New Orleans's workhouse system for years.[65]

Jailors were cognizant of the whip's powerful racial connotations, deploying the instrument's mighty symbolism with thoughtful intentionality. Within New Orleans's workhouses, jailors typically had rebellious white inmates whipped by imprisoned enslaved people borrowed from adjacent police jails, a practice that repeatedly provoked public outcry. The state penitentiary warden also manipulated the whip's racial subtexts, writing in 1839 that while whipping white convicts, he tried to encourage "the sense of degradation attached" to the whip by reminding the prisoners that they were receiving "the same treatment as our slaves." He advised frugal application of the whip on white convicts so as not to dilute the punishment's racial connotations.[66] Soon thereafter, the state penitentiary constructed a whipping rack virtually identical in design to that of New Orleans's police jails. A state convict who experienced this rack firsthand described procedures reminiscent of the Police Jail: he was "ordered to strip," strapped down, and "drawn by both extremes until I cried out, lest they should part my body." A physician observed each penitentiary whipping to ensure that inmates survived.[67]

Debating Police Jail Reform

Racial differentiation in punishments was further complicated by public debates over police jail reform. Civic authorities clearly identified the modernization of New Orleans's police jail system with the city's broader penal transformation.[68] Yet as New Orleans celebrated its ascension into penal modernity, the constant visage of slave chain gangs provoked public discomfort and dissonance. Discussions over how best to reform the police jail system provoked more anxiety as authorities attempted the impossible task of reconciling a penal reform ideology that rejected corporal pain and shame with a slave penal system dependent on the routine infliction of violence, humiliation, and terror. Livingston's fear— that the inclusion of enslaved people within the scope of penal reform might undermine the concept of racial caste itself—seemed realized.

Since its inauguration in 1805, the police jail system had avoided meaningful entanglement in public controversy. That changed in the 1840s when a series of notorious scandals rocked the city's slave prisons, hinting at the mounting anxieties that the institutions engendered. In May 1845, white New Orleanians were conspicuously outraged when an enslaved child named Sylveste collapsed in the gutter after leaving the First Municipality Police Jail, his back having been reduced to what one reporter described as a mass of "raw, trembling, skinless, parti-putrid, lacerated flesh." New Orleanians were no strangers to the mutilated backs of enslaved people, and yet, the image of Sylveste's back seemed to refute convictions that police jails meted out proportional and measured punishments, in conformity with the spirit of the penitentiary movement. An investigation revealed that Sylveste's owner, Clément Philippe de Neufbourg, enraged by a missing pocket watch, had deceived an inexperienced jailor into administering lashes beyond the regulated allotment. A media frenzy ensued. The *Daily Picayune* denounced de Neufbourg's subversion of the police jail "into a house of torture." Public anger at de Neufbourg grew so great that some predicted his imminent lynching. A subsequent grand jury investigation demanded police jail reforms, including stricter regulations governing the infliction of violence upon enslaved children. New Orleans's attorney general refused petitions to indict de Neufbourg, though legal battles precipitated by the scandal dragged on for months.[69]

Three years later, concerned slaveholders launched a movement to abolish New Orleans's slave chain gangs, arguing that the labor system reflected an outdated and barbaric approach to penal discipline. Calling "the spectacle of these slaves in chains" a "bad commentary on the spirit of republicanism," councilmember John W. Smith of the Second Municipality Council introduced a bill to eradicate the institution. Proponents of Smith's bill denounced slave chain gangs as "antiquated," "revolting," opposed by "nine-tenths" of the city, "outraging [to] the public sight," and out of touch with the "ameliorating spirit of the age." The *New-Orleans Commercial Times* endorsed abolition: too often, and instead of reclaiming maroons for the public's benefit, police jails seemed governed "by a spirit of vengeance" and the whims of "a vindictive or rancorous owner." Public penal labor was simply too outdated and ineffectual, even if the prisoners were enslaved: "In every penal system, in the present enlightened age, as an abstract principle, shackles, in our opinion, should always be accompanied by seclusion. . . . The delinquent should be withdrawn from society . . . within the walls of a prison, where the best means may be devised for his speedy reformation." Lest any mistake their critiques for latent antislavery sentiment, the chain gang's opponents carefully avowed their proslavery credentials, arguing that northern abolitionists secretly loved New Orleans's chain gang because its brutality "furnishes an argument" legitimating their "fanatical interference with our rights." As a compromise, some proposed alternative penal labor systems—perhaps dressing the enslaved prisoners in "ridiculous" costumes rather than hindering their movement with chains—that would increase both the productivity of their labor and the "severity" of their suffering, "without violating the dictates of humanity." When the vote came, the majority of the Second Municipality Council deemed the institution too critical to the city's economy, and the abolition bill was rejected. The city's general assembly refused to take on the issue.[70]

In denouncing the slave chain gang as insufficiently "republican" and by protesting the Police Jail's subversion "into a house of torture," reformers highlighted the cognitive dissonance and ideological confusion that lay at the intersection of slave prisons and penal reform. What was the Police Jail if not "a house of torture"? What system of slave punishment, aligned to "the spirit of republicanism," did reformers envision? In such moments, Livingston's fears would seem validated: the intermingling of penal reform and slavery was engendering impossible ideological incongruities.

Ultimately, pressure for slave prison reform came to naught. Police jails were simply too central to slave control and the municipal economy to be tampered with. No significant changes to work routines, disciplinary procedures, or living conditions were instituted. Bodily torment, overwork, and violent spectacle remained constant. In 1847, an enslaved prisoner named Ned died after the chain gang left him "so emaciated and feeble as then to be unable to get up on his knees without assistance." In 1848, an enslaved prisoner named Jane died after being found "covered with her own excrements . . . which had been permitted to harden."[71]

The reformist pressure led to tangible changes, however, with regard to slave executions. Louisiana's slave code of 1806 mandated death for a broad variety of crimes, including the malicious destruction of grain, produce, or buildings; poisoning; murder; rape of a white woman; and any act that encouraged or supported "insurrection." The code also required the execution of any enslaved person convicted of a third offense of striking any white person or convicted of a first offense of striking or otherwise drawing blood from his or her owner or owner's family.[72] Public slave executions, as well as the public display of condemned enslaved people's body parts, were intensely meaningful rituals in slave society, deeply ingrained within the local social fabric.[73] For enslaved viewers, these rituals were meant to deter resistance through terror. For example, following a major slave uprising in 1811, the rebels' decapitated heads were displayed on pikes on the road leading to New Orleans. In 1837, some 2,000 to 3,000 enslaved people were forced to view the mangled corpse of a longtime maroon who had gained a folkloric following among the enslaved, "for the sake of example" and in hopes that "it would have a salutary effect [upon the slaves] to let them gaze upon the outlaw and murderer as he lay bleeding and weltering in his gore." For white viewers, slave executions and dismemberments were carnivalesque affairs, attracting massive crowds: "a sort of cheap amusement for the people," described the *Daily Picayune*, "jovial and jocose." The execution in 1846 of Pauline, sentenced to death for striking her mistress, drew some 5,000 spectators. Witnesses described streets "thronged" with "men and boys, and women, too, with infants in arms. . . . There were carriages filled with female spectators, and all were stretching their necks, standing on tip-toe, pushing and jostling each other that they might get a good sight."[74]

Yet with Louisiana's penal revolution, a growing chorus of critics began complaining that the rituals had grown vulgar, provoked disorder, no longer roused respect for the law, and degraded "public morals." "Instead of inspiring people with a terror of eternity and awe of death," said the *Daily Picayune* in 1842, public slave executions "seem to furnish a theme for coarse humor and ribald wit." Similar anxieties emerged from Louisiana's rural regions: "We are more than ever convicted that Public Executions have a deleterious effect upon morality," proclaimed the *St. Landry Whig* following the execution of the slave Nat in 1845.[75]

In 1843, the Louisiana legislature amended Louisiana's slave code, curtailing the number of slave capital offenses and formally authorizing the incarceration of enslaved people convicted of capital crimes as an alternative to their execution. In 1845, authorities moved New Orleans's gallows from the central town square to the concealed alleyway between Parish Prison and the adjacent First Municipality Police Jail.[76] In 1846, the Louisiana legislature banned public slave executions altogether, except as punishment for insurrection. Two years later, the Louisiana Supreme Court cited the "growing opinion opposed to capital punishment" in a judgment affirming an enslaved man's twenty-year sentence to hard labor. When the legislature debated the reinstatement of public slave executions in 1852, opposition was strong. "No good effect could result from the public execution of a slave," argued Representative Michael Ryan. Representative J. G. Sever called the rituals "morbid and sickly." Representative C. C. Lathrop insisted that public slave executions had "not answered the ends desired by their advocates, instead of inspiring terror, they had tended to render those criminally disposed more hardened and callous."[77]

Economic factors doubtless played into the decision to curtail slave executions. For slaveholders, slave executions were tantamount to property condemnations, and the market value of enslaved people climbed precipitously during the 1830s. Louisiana law provided for the compensation of executed slaves' masters but capped that compensation at $500, lowered to $300 in 1846—far below a healthy enslaved adult's typical market value.[78] With incarceration, the state could at least retain use of the enslaved prisoner's labor, and the slave-holder stood a small chance of eventually regaining ownership through gubernatorial pardon.[79]

Yet critics of public slave executions also cited the dangerous ways that condemned enslaved people resisted their performative function within the rituals. From their gallows, condemned enslaved people were expected to profess guilt and show repentance. Yet with a captive audience and nothing to lose, enslaved people felt free—perhaps for the first time—to speak their minds. Too often, warned one state legislator, condemned slaves hurled "obscenities" from the gallows, openly mocked the legitimacy of the proceedings, and "seize[d] the opportunity to make confessions on the scaffold detrimental to the character of white persons."[80] During George's execution in 1838, George said something—newspapers refused to print it, referring only to "one continued stream of blasphemy and pollution"—that so electrified audiences that a public disturbance, also too scandalous to describe in print, was provoked. At the execution of Jackson two weeks later, police sent "a strong force of guards . . . with fixed bayonets" to prevent any recurrent unrest, while the *Daily Picayune* expressed relief that Jackson had remained silent.[81] Pauline's execution in 1846 haunted viewers, implanting powerful memories that circulated for decades—in part because Pauline had seemed unapologetically dignified on the gallows and in part because the first attempt to end Pauline's life had been delayed at the eleventh hour, after Pauline had revealed that she was pregnant with her enslaver's biological child, so that Pauline could give birth before she was executed.[82]

Louisiana's movement to restrict slave executions mirrored transatlantic trends. A similar movement to limit or abolish capital punishment, closely aligned to the penitentiary movement, was sweeping the United States and Europe at precisely the same time. Pennsylvania abolished public executions in 1834, Massachusetts and New York followed suit in 1835, Maine virtually abolished the death penalty in 1837, and Michigan abolished the death penalty entirely in 1847. In each of these states, reformers invoked Edward Livingston's writings, which provided the intellectual foundation for the American anti-death penalty movement.[83] In condemning slave executions, Louisiana reformers parroted many of the same ideas as reformers elsewhere: that the rituals had fallen out of step with changing public sensibilities, failed to inspire public virtue, and provoked disorders. What is striking about Louisiana's reformist impulse is not when it emerged or the discourse with which it was clothed but that slaveholders were applying the language of humanist reform upon the bodies of the enslaved. Slavery and Enlightenment humanitarianism would seem

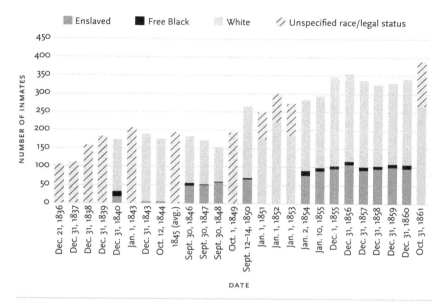

Graph 2.1. Louisiana State Penitentiary inmates, 1836–1861.

irreconcilable. Edward Livingston had feared that their intersection would prove slavery's downfall. Yet slaveholders could not simply divorce their ideas regarding penal reform from ideas regarding slave punishment.[84] The line of demarcation was failing.

"Calculated to Defeat the Ends of Punishment": Integrating the State Penitentiary

Faced with mounting opposition to slave execution, Louisiana courts began sentencing condemned enslaved people to the Louisiana State Penitentiary for life. The state penitentiary's creators seemed not to have foreseen this possibility: although no law or regulation explicitly forbade the penitentiary confinement of enslaved people, the institution had been designed exclusively with white convicts in mind and lacked the physical infrastructure to enforce racial segregation.[85] By 1841—two years before the Louisiana legislature would formally condone the sentencing of enslaved people to the penitentiary—enslaved people accounted for 10 percent of the penitentiary population (graph 2.1).[86] By the eve of the Civil War, nearly a third of the penitentiary's inmates were enslaved. Virtually all enslaved inmates had been convicted of violent crimes: arson, poisoning, murder and attempted murder, and striking or injuring white persons. Virtually all had been sentenced to life imprisonment.

Historians of the penitentiary movement have contended, as a general rule, that penitentiaries did not imprison slaves. The presence of enslaved convicts within the Louisiana State Penitentiary, insofar as it has been acknowledged, has been described as an anomalous exception to that general rule. Yet a close reading of penitentiary records from other southern states reveals that the intertwining of slavery and penitentiary, though often controversial, was hardly unique to Louisiana. Every southern state penitentiary, excepting those of Alabama, Tennessee, and Georgia, tinkered with the confinement of enslaved people. The state penitentiaries of Kentucky and Missouri rented spaces to slaveholders. The state penitentiaries of Arkansas (beginning in 1849) and Texas (beginning in 1861) sent all unclaimed runaway slaves to the penitentiary; both states required that "such slave[s] be put to labor as other prisoners." Before 1858, Arkansas also allowed for the penitentiary confinement of enslaved people convicted of second-degree murder and manslaughter. The Maryland legislature wavered back and forth, barring enslaved prisoners from the penitentiary between 1818 and 1845, and again immediately before the Civil War, and barring free Black prisoners between 1825 and 1826. Virginia's penitentiary prohibited slave incarceration as punishment for a crime but allowed the temporary housing of convict slaves while they awaited out-of-state deportation. The Mississippi legislature refused to authorize the penitentiary confinement of unclaimed fugitive slaves: penitentiary budget reports disclose that the penitentiary confined unclaimed fugitives anyway.[87] South Carolina did not build a penitentiary until after the Civil War. But after a revolt within Charleston's slave workhouse in 1849, the old slave workhouse building was replaced with a massive fortified structure, frequently referred to as South Carolina's "slave penitentiary," that held slaves sentenced to life imprisonment, as well as slaves committed by their owners. A visitor in 1854 described this "penitentiary for slaves" as a "massive building, capable of accommodating nearly 300 prisoners, and containing work-shops, tread-mills, places where the most unskillful negro could be employed, [and] cells for the solitary confinement of prisoners . . . in every respect, completely successful."[88] In *theory*, penitentiaries were not for slaves; in *practice*, slaves were a regular presence in southern penitentiaries.

Though not as anomalous as it may seem, the incorporation of enslaved people into Louisiana's state penitentiary deeply alarmed lawmakers. In his annual address of 1841, Governor André Roman decried the "indiscriminate" cohabitation of white and enslaved convicts. State legislators declared penitentiary integration to be "entirely inconsistent" with the aims of the penitentiary movement, "repugnant to the spirit of southern institutions," and "calculated to defeat the ends of punishment" by placing the white convicts beyond the reach of uplift. The penitentiary lacked the infrastructure to work enslaved people under specialized penal labor regimes: "Detention in an establishment of this kind," protested Roman, was "hardly such a punishment as will deter a slave from crime."[89]

Several solutions, each seeking to redraw Livingston's line of demarcation, were proposed. Some state officials considered the construction of a state penitentiary for slaves, perhaps modeled on the New Orleans police jail system. Others recommended the transfer of all convict slaves to New Orleans's First Municipality Police Jail, where they could "be better supported, employed, and guarded . . . than anywhere else"—a measure heartily endorsed by New Orleans mayor William Freret, who cited the city's preexisting "facility," "organized means of surveillance," and well-established experience in working with imprisoned enslaved people. Freret invited New Orleans's municipal council members to imagine what they might accomplish with so large an addition to their public works force: an unprecedented investment in infrastructure, the total drainage of all the swamplands bordering the city. Still others raised well-trodden objections to the very concept of slave incarceration. "The doom of bodily labor though of the most humiliating nature, can scarcely be deemed a matter of great terror to a slave," complained one legislator.[90]

Instead of allowing New Orleans to monopolize the financial boons of convict slave labor, in 1842, the legislature created a statewide facsimile of the New Orleans chain gang system by transferring all male penitentiary slaves (later extended to include "free" Black male convicts) to Louisiana's Board of Public Works for chain gang labor on state infrastructure projects. These Black male convicts joined a preexisting force of state-owned enslaved people whose numbers had been decimated by disease and overwork in Louisiana's alluvial backcountry. Under the direction of the state engineer, the Black male convicts and surviving state-owned slaves dug canals, strengthened levees, laid railroad track, cleared river obstructions, and connected Louisiana towns by new roads.[91] Initially, the state engineer praised the new system, announcing within three months that "over 125,000 acres of valuable lands have been entirely reclaimed." Empowered by such "a proper, economical and judicious system of internal improvement," the engineer prophesized Louisiana's transformation into "by far the wealthiest State of our Union," with "hundreds of fine canals," bustling highways conveying "valuable products to market," and rich floodplains opened for cultivation.[92]

Toward Prison Privatization

In the transfer of the Black male convicts to the Board of Public Works, one sees both the continuing contribution of slave penal labor to southern state-building and economic development and a clear predecessor to Louisiana's postbellum convict labor systems. The creation of the state slave chain gang also represented the ultimate realization of an indigenous approach to slave penology that had been in production in Louisiana since 1805. The reallocation of the Black convicts from the penitentiary to public works created an ironclad racial division between indoor and outdoor penal labor. Louisiana had achieved two separate and fully realized state penal systems: an indoor system of "skilled" manufacturing tasks designed to prepare white convicts for industrious citizenship and an outdoor system of "unskilled" menial work designed to reinforce Black submission and servitude.

Yet Louisiana's experiment in two racially differentiated state penal systems would prove short-lived. The energetic optimism that had characterized the penitentiary movement's early years was beginning to fade, in Louisiana and throughout the nation. Penitentiary advocates had predicted that the institutions would eliminate crime and turn a profit. In reality, penitentiaries proved incredibly expensive, and crime persisted. Lawmakers and the public grew disillusioned, then frustrated. Eager to render penitentiaries profitable, state governments throughout the nation, north and south, began leasing convicts to private corporations as forced laborers. Penitentiary buildings were reconceived as factories, where far greater emphasis was placed on maximizing revenue than on reforming behavior. By 1850, the vast majority of the nation's convicts, on both sides of the Mason-Dixon Line, worked for private contractors.[93] In 1844, disenchanted with the penitentiary movement and plagued by mounting penitentiary debts, the Louisiana legislature joined the trend by leasing the state penitentiary to two Baton Rouge planters and businessmen from Kentucky, James McHatton and William Pratt.[94]

Critics of convict lease called it convict slavery. "In a State like Louisiana, white convicts ought not to be traded, and put to the mercy of speculators," protested the *Baton Rouge Gazette*. One state representative put the issue more crassly: "How would we like to be hired out like n——s?" he asked the legislature.[95] Yet apathy and fiscal conservativism eclipsed concern over the proper racial management of punishments.

Concurrently, Louisiana lawmakers grew disillusioned with the state slave chain gang. The state engineer reported that the costs of guarding and transporting the prisoners exceeded the value of their labor. Planters vigorously opposed the employment of Black convicts in their neighborhoods, fearing "corrupting communication with their slaves." In 1845, a legislative committee concluded that the system was simply not worth the trouble.[96] In that year, the legislature returned the Black male convicts to the penitentiary, on condition that they "be worked separate and apart from the white convicts."[97] Ignoring this condition, the lessees found it more economical to simply work, house, and feed all enslaved, white, and free Black convicts together. Segregation was "impracticable," the lessees explained, given "the present arrangement of work shops."[98] For those lessees, that arrangement was also profoundly lucrative. Between December 1850 and May 1854, the lessees recorded net profits of $69,302. In 1854 alone, penitentiary workshops churned out 1,018,058 yards of cloth, 1,659,000 bricks, 3,013 cotton bales, and 3,994 pounds of thread, yard, and warp.[99] A former inmate testified that those who refused to work were savagely beaten, whipped to the edge of death, or shot dead in their cells: lessees "instated the most cruel tyranny, to eke out the dollars and cents of human misery."[100] To the Louisiana legislature, the penitentiary was out of sight, out of mind. Hidden behind high walls, the lessees had created the unimaginable: a racially integrated factory, employing a mixed labor force of white, enslaved, and "free" Black convict labor.

Limited racial segregation was imposed, gradually. By the 1850s, white male convicts usually worked in indoor textile workshops, while Black male convicts usually manufactured bricks in the outdoor brickyard.[101] White and Black women lived together in "two large unfinished rooms," where they performed domestic chores and laundered clothes. In 1856, the construction of new "apartments for female prisoners" imposed gender separation and perhaps a greater degree of racial segregation. A separate dining hall for white male convicts, constructed by 1857, provided for segregated dining.[102]

One racial taboo was always inviolable: only Black convicts could ever be assigned to public penal labor outside of the penitentiary's walls. When supplies needed to the hauled from the river, or trees cut for lumber, Black convicts performed the labor.[103] It was also a poorly kept secret in Baton Rouge that the lessees often worked the Black convicts on their private plantations and hired them out to private industries throughout town, in direct violation of state law. James McHatton brought in his brother, Charles McHatton, as co-lessee, and together the brothers used the profits of convict labor to purchase two sugar plantations, named Gartness and Arlington, less than four miles from the penitentiary. Baton Rouge residents began decrying the continual back-and-forth stream of Black convicts between penitentiary and plantation. "What punishment is it, to one of these fellows, to be sent to a Penitentiary when he works all the time as he has been doing before he went there?" complained the *Baton Rouge Gazette*. In 1857, another resident denounced the practice of hiring out

Black convicts: "You must understand that these negro convicts (a hundred or two of them) have heretofore been, and now daily are, worked at all sorts of mechanical employments outside of the Penitentiary, all over the city of Baton Rouge." Knowledge of the McHattons' exploitative practices reached New Orleans's Parish Prison, where terrified free Black inmates whispered to one another that if they were transferred to the state penitentiary, they would be worked as slaves on a "farm at Baton Rouge."[104]

During this age of cynicism, corruption, and prison privatization, New Orleans's municipal government also resolved to lease the City Workhouse to private contractors, citing frustrations that the inmates' labor failed to turn a profit. In 1852, the three municipalities were reunified into one single city government, and the Second Municipality Workhouse was designated the exclusive workhouse for the entire city. In 1856, one Robert Brown purchased a five-year lease to that workhouse, for $115 per annum.[105] Unable to turn a profit, Brown began summarily releasing workhouse inmates who were too lame or enfeebled to work, to the outrage of the city's government, before abandoning the lease prematurely in January 1857.[106] Under the terms of a new ten-year lease issued to one Gardner Johnson, the city agreed to pay Johnson $11,000 per annum—slightly less than what the institution's annual expenses had been under public management—and Johnson was permitted to keep whatever profits he was able to eke from the prisoners' labor.[107] Baton Rouge took a different route: after debating whether to build a workhouse for the city's growing number of poor white paupers, the city resolved to turn any white prisoners convicted of vagrancy over to the overseer of the city's slave chain gang so that they, too, might labor on public works.[108]

Simultaneously, the state pursued ways to better use the labor of incarcerated fugitives from slavery held in local parish jails. In 1855, the legislature revived the practice of resupplying the state engineer's state-owned labor force with enslaved penal laborers. This time, instead of using Black convicts from the state penitentiary, the state engineer was given access to all incarcerated fugitives left unclaimed in jail for longer than twelve months.[109] Thereafter, a force of ninety unclaimed enslaved fugitives and state-owned enslaved people were distributed among an armada of state-owned snag boats. Moving throughout the state, they opened Louisiana's waterways for trade and travel by removing river obstructions. Eager to retain access to enslaved prisoners' labor, New Orleans brazenly defied the legislature by refusing to send unclaimed enslaved prisoners to the state engineer, prompting state congressional investigations.[110]

The state also made the reproductive labor of incarcerated Black women available for public use. At least twelve children were born of the enslaved women in the state penitentiary. The identities of the children's fathers, and circumstances surrounding their conception, are unknown. The children's legal ownership posed a conceptual conundrum for the legislature. By law, their mothers had become state property on receiving a life sentence, but custom held that enslaved convicts' prior owners still retained some meaningful, if unwritten, claim (for example, an enslaved convict who received a gubernatorial pardon was automatically returned to his or her prior master, even though that prior master no longer had any legal property claim to the enslaved person).[111] In 1848, the legislature resolved this lingering uncertainty by declaring that children born in the state penitentiary of enslaved mothers were state property, to be sold on their tenth birthday, with the proceeds going to Louisiana's public school fund for white pupils. Most of the dozen children were purchased by penitentiary lessees and employees.[112]

By the eve of the Civil War, Louisiana was close to leveraging the full laboring capacity of all the state's prisoners. In New Orleans's City Workhouse, poor white prisoners toiled for private contractors. On the streets of New Orleans, slave chain gangs continued building the public infrastructure that enabled the city's ongoing growth and extraordinary prosperity. Under the direction of the state engineer, snag boats of state-owned enslaved people and unclaimed fugitive enslaved people cruised the state's waterways. In Baton Rouge, public works were built by chain gangs of enslaved prisoners, unclaimed fugitive enslaved people from the Baton Rouge Slave Depot, and poor white laborers convicted of vagrancy. In the Louisiana State Penitentiary, white convicts labored within indoor workshops; Black convicts labored in the penitentiary yard and on the plantations of the penitentiary lessees or were hired out; and Black female convicts birthed the children whose sale funded the education of white schoolchildren.

All of this must have made Edward Livingston roll over in his grave. Most of the state's white prisoners worked for private corporations under threat of the whip. Racial segregation in the state penitentiary was inconsistent and lackluster. The studious racial management of punishments, designed to sanctify white bodies and vulgarize Black bodies, had taken a back seat to private profit and public infrastructural development.

Historian Heather Ann Thompson observes that representations of American criminal justice are often "blinded by a 'barbaric' South." The tendency is to emphasize the "exceptional" nature of southern prison history, obscuring the extent to which the North and South participated in the same patterns and trends. The tendency is also to essentialize both regions' carceral histories, equating northern prison development with progressive reformers' rehabilitative penology while typifying as "southern" all prison violence, racism, neglect, and economic exploitation.[113] Yet rehabilitative penology and racial violence were intertwined, not incompatible, in Louisiana. Although Louisiana's commitment to slavery shaped every aspect of Louisiana's penal development, that commitment did not preclude the state's full engagement with national and transnational developments in penal practice and theory. Slavery often led Louisiana's penitentiary development down a distinctive path: and yet, that path cannot be typified as any more simplistic or unidimensional than the route taken by penitentiary development in the North. The manifold factors that forged Louisiana's state penal systems—racism, greed, Enlightenment humanitarianism, fiscal conservatism, fear, bloodlust, legal tradition, and slavery's shadow—were national, not local, in nature.

Within Louisiana, these various driving forces were often in tension. Edward Livingston had predicted that these tensions, if not carefully managed, might destroy slavery and southern society itself. Ultimately, Livingston underestimated slaveholders' ability to reconcile irreconcilable ideological inconsistencies.[114] State penitentiaries *could not* hold slaves: and yet, they held slaves. Southern criminal law construed the enslaved as persons exercising free will during questions of criminal guilt but as nonpersons incapable of autonomous free will in all other legal matters. Efforts to humiliate incarcerated enslaved people were rooted in recognition of their full emotional range and sense of social identity—the human capacity to experience emotional, physical, and psychological suffering—even as these systems strove to naturalize and assert their lack of personhood and humanity. Contradictions abounded, yet the revolution that Livingston feared never came. With the reintegration of the penitentiary and waning public faith in the transformative power of imprisonment, Louisianians resolved to ignore these paradoxes.

CHAPTER 3

Soi-Disant Libre

Travelers of Color, Free Status,
and the Slave Prison

O n Christmas Eve in 1840, the night before Rufus Kinsman's ship was to return him to his home and family in Boston, New Orleans police arrested the free Black sailor as a fugitive slave. Kinsman presented legal documentation of his free status, known as freedom papers, which the policemen ignored. Thrust into the Second Municipality Police Jail, Kinsman was shocked to encounter scores of other free Black women and men, all held as fugitive slaves, from free communities scattered throughout the Black Atlantic: Philadelphia, New York, Annapolis, Baltimore, Canada, Great Britain, Jamaica, Bermuda, Tortola, Saint Barthélemy, Mexico, and Venezuela. "We are stowed away hear like smugled goods," Kinsman surreptitiously wrote from the prison that June: "We may Die for a friend or healp. . . . I have Lain in this Prison 6 mounth. . . . Release me from Hell."[1]

Kinsman's seizure as a slave was neither anomalous nor accidental: New Orleans imprisoned and tortured hundreds of free Black sailors and migrant workers each year on the pretext that they were captured runaway slaves. Indeed, the seizure of free Black travelers as fugitive slaves was pervasive throughout the antebellum South. Understanding this practice, and what southern law enforcement hoped to accomplish, takes us deep into the mission of slave prisons and the dynamics of racialized policing in antebellum America.

Mariners such as Rufus Kinsman were central to the economies of free Black neighborhoods, the circulation of antislavery thought, and the forging of collective identity between Afro-descendant communities dispersed throughout the Black Atlantic world. Several distinguished Black antislavery activists, including Olaudah Equiano, Paul Cuffe, Denmark Vesey, and William Wells Brown, were former sailors or riverboat workers.[2] Their ability to travel provided more than opportunity for economic activity and cultural exchange: in journeying between states and nations, free Black sailors also laid implicit claim to citizenship, human rights, and their capacity to subsist independent of white management.[3]

But free Black sailors and migrant workers deeply alarmed southern lawmakers, who equated their presence with crime, the instigation of slave rebellion, and the potential disintegration of southern social order. In exploring stories such as that of Rufus Kinsman, scholarship has focused on the Negro Seamen Acts: US laws, first passed by South Carolina in 1822 following the Denmark Vesey Conspiracy but eventually replicated by every coastal slave state, that tried to "quarantine" free Black sailors to prevent their contaminating influence on the enslaved by requiring their incarceration while their ships remained in port.[4] That Louisiana did not pass a Negro Seamen Act until 1842, decades after Atlantic Seaboard states, has been attributed to Louisiana's relative racial permissiveness and laxity.[5] Other scholars have explored jails' role in the "kidnapping" of vulnerable free Black Americans for their illegal sale into slavery.[6]

Neither "quarantining" nor "kidnapping" explains what happened to Rufus Kinsman. Kinsman was not quarantined: for thirteen months, he was literally shackled to enslaved people while cleaning sewers, scrubbing marketplace stalls, and building New Orleans's levees, streets, and canals. Nor was Kinsman seized for sale into permanent slavery: after a year of being whipped and worked as a state-owned slave, chained to those who had never experienced freedom, this sailor from Boston was unceremoniously released into the custody of a ship captain bound for Liverpool.

Rather, New Orleans's public officials used prisons to obscure distinctions between free Black workers and enslaved workers, and between free Black mobility and enslaved workers' marronage, by deliberately subjecting mobile free Black workers to punishments designed for the subjugation of enslaved fugitives. Antebellum authorities interpreted Kinsman's mobility and autonomy as an unnatural breakdown in racial dependency and thus a threat to southern social order. They perceived that the disciplinary practices designed for the subjugation of maroons who had abandoned their owners were equally applicable to the reassertion of white mastery over dangerously masterless and independent free Black travelers. Through whips, chains, and ritualized public humiliation, police jails used bodily violence to assign itinerant free Black workers the social status of "slave" and to bolster a stark dichotomization between landed residents deemed free and transient strangers deemed unworthy of freedom. The practice sought to impress on people such as Kinsman that they had no rights worthy of recognition and no hope of claiming autotomy or personhood; their obligations were to constant labor and perpetual dependency on white authority. Jailors sought not to "quarantine" or "kidnap" Kinsman but to "rehabilitate" him, in the sense that they sought to use the prison to effect a corrective transformation within this criminally mobile Black worker, and thus restore him to his proper societal role. For jailors operating within a slave society, to "rehabilitate" this man of the world was to render him slavish, deferential toward white power, and readied for economic redeployment.[7]

New Orleans's policemen did not indiscriminately seize all free persons of African ancestry. Free Black Louisiana natives and well-to-do free Black travelers were not systematically seized as slaves. Nor, for that matter, was every prisoner confined as a slave a person of African ancestry. Police jails routinely confined mobile workers of Native American or South Asian ancestry on the pretense that they were runaway slaves. Police jail committals were "not always confined to those of the African race," one British subject complained, noting that New Orleans policemen routinely "pounced upon Hindoos and natives of Bengal": indeed, Kinsman's prison mates in 1841 included natives of Bombay and Calcutta.[8]

In practice, the line that defined the segregation of New Orleans's criminal justice system was not between white or Black or between enslaved and free but rather a far more nuanced division between *presumptive slavery* and *presumptive freedom*. In creating that boundary, policemen assessed visual and auditory cues such as dress, accent, and mannerism that encoded financial stability, social station, nativity, employment status, and thus the degree to which a person appeared unqualified for self-rule. The practice tells us something about the nature of "slave" status itself. Through state torture and imprisonment, Louisiana assigned the rank of "slave" to persons who appeared undeserving of freedom even while recognizing that no slaveholder claimed them as property. Their "property-ness" derived not from webs of deeds or titles but from perceptions of their innate dependency.[9] Slavery and freedom are usually framed as opposites, each defined in relation to the other. Prisons allowed for the creation of liminal spaces between slavery and freedom: places to warehouse and subjugate those who were deemed neither chattel nor capable of owning themselves.

The Numbers Game

In 1846, a Black New Yorker, abolitionist, and former sailor named William Powell resolved to calculate the number of free Black mariners seized annually by southern ports. Powell operated New York City's Colored Sailor's Home, a boardinghouse for Black seamen. Through his boardinghouse, Powell regularly quartered fugitives from slavery and provided free shelter, food, clothing, and medical care to destitute mariners, many of whom shared harrowing stories of the abuses they had endured in southern jails. Powell resolved to draw public attention to these sailors' plight. In a pathbreaking multipart series published in the *National Anti-Slavery Standard*, Powell charged that Charleston incarcerated 240 free Black sailors annually, Savannah and Mobile more than 200 each, Cuba 100, and New Orleans around 420.[10]

Present-day studies have rejected Powell's figure for New Orleans as impossibly high.[11] Ledgers from New Orleans's police jails, however, show that Powell's figure for New Orleans was remarkably accurate: throughout the 1830s, New Orleans's police jails received some 500 free Black detainees each year, of whom about 85 percent (or, roughly 420 persons annually) were sailors and steamboat workers. Of the tens of thousands of prisoners thrust into New Orleans's slave prisons between 1820 and 1840, more than one in ten identified as free.

Such precise figures are ascertainable because Louisiana's jailors inscribed the initialism "SDL" beside the names of all free travelers seized as slaves. Though sometimes extended to "*se dit libre*" or "*se disant libre*" (claims to be free), SDL probably derived from *soi-disant libre* (so-called free), a little-known French colonial legal category describing emancipated persons who had obtained their freedom from foreign jurisdictions with laxer manumission policies.[12] In a sampling of 34,895 police jail commitments made between 1820 and 1845, jailors identified 4,642 of the nominal slaves as soi-disant libres: 13.3 percent (graph 3.1).[13] The development of vernacular legal categories for demarcating free Black travelers held as slaves was not unique to Louisiana. Analogous designations for free persons held as slaves—"pretends to be free," "claims to be free," "runaway [committed] for want of his free papers," "he is informed that he is a slave"—littered jail registers throughout the South.[14]

When pressed, authorities in New Orleans emphatically denied that police jails knowingly held any free people.[15] Yet jailors' record-keeping practices and statistical analysis of committals clearly indicate that SDL signified an established category that connoted persons who would be jailed *as though* they were slaves even while law enforcement officers did not believe them to be property. Jailors recorded surnames for virtually all prisoners listed as SDL, though for virtually none of the prisoners claimed by owners.[16] Jailors were strikingly consistent in their notation, unfailingly labeling certain prisoners as SDL even across documents and decades. Jailors often used different notation for free persons mistaken for enslaved people.[17] Errors were rare: among 13,921 admittances recorded in one jail inventory, only 31 prisoners—0.2 percent—were initially registered as SDL but subsequently identified as property and released into their owners' custody.[18] SDL prisoners were also far likelier to die in captivity and to attempt escape.[19]

The overwhelming majority of SDL prisoners were sailors, steamboat employees, and migrant workers from out of state. SDL committals correlate to port activity, peaking in December as sugar and cotton shipments left port

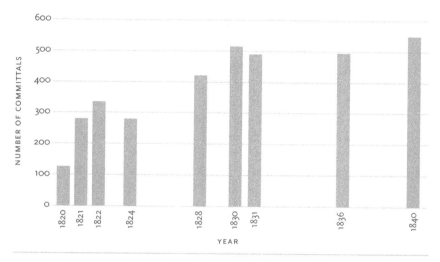

Graph 3.1. Estimated (1820-1824, 1840) and actual (1828-1836) SDL Police Jail committals.

and plummeting during the commercially inactive summer season.[20] Although about one-third of enslaved commitments were of women, only one out of ten SDL commitments were of women (comparable to the share of women among transient white wageworkers imprisoned for vagrancy in the city's work-houses).[21] Records from the Second Municipality Police Jail include the names of the ships on which prisoners were employed and explicitly delineate which legally free prisoners were not sailors or steamboat workers, indicating that 84.2 percent were employed by riverboats or oceangoing ships.[22] It is also clear that the seizure of out-of-state wageworkers as slaves was a coordinated police practice: whereas a mix of police, slaveholders, and private individuals acting as slave catchers were responsible for committing enslaved prisoners, virtually all SDL prisoners were committed by law enforcement.[23]

The Contours of Racial Persecution

All free Black people in the antebellum South faced intense legal and social persecution. At the same time, white southerners typically manufactured distinctions between trusted "free colored" neighbors—framed as gainfully employed, financially stable, and industrious—and the aggregate "free Negro" population characterized as dangerous, itinerant, and disruptive. Discriminatory laws and practices, though nominally aimed at all free Black persons, were often selectively enforced on the ground, targeting persons whom white elites perceived as transient and disreputable while exempting persons whom white elites perceived as local and reputable.[24]

In Louisiana, these manufactured distinctions between reputable free Black tradespeople and disreputable free Black transients were layered atop indigenous laws and customs, rooted in French and Spanish colonial law, directed toward the state's large and unusually prosperous free Black community. Some members of this population were the descendants of Louisianians emancipated in the eighteenth century; others, refugees from Saint-Domingue and their descendants. Either way, members of Louisiana's free Black community often traced their ancestry to eighteenth-century unions between enslaved Africans and European colonial settlers: as such, they tended to be Catholic, francophone, and have a high proportion of European ancestry. As a legacy of Louisiana's French and Spanish legal heritage, free Black Louisianians enjoyed rights and levels of social acceptance unequaled elsewhere in the South. Though denied the right to vote, sit on juries, or send their children to public schools, they could sue and be sued, testify in court against white persons, and freely buy and sell property, and they were not required to register with local officials. They were a socioeconomically diverse population, with poor and rich members. Taken as a whole, however, New Orleans's free Black population was the wealthiest in the nation, counting among their ranks skilled artisans, craftsmen, shopkeepers, merchants, and, in 1850, more than a quarter of all skilled professionals, managers, artists, clerks, and scientists of African ancestry in the fifteen largest cities in the United States.[25]

In part to rationalize this population's particular rights and protections, Louisiana's courts manufactured a distinction between "negro" and "person of color." Within this context, "person of color" (alongside subcategories including "mulatto," "griffe," "quadroon," and "yellow") referred to persons whose light complexion suggested mixed European African ancestry and thus implied membership within Louisiana's indigenous free Black community of colonial ancestry. "Negro" referred to persons whose dark complexion suggested unmixed African ancestry. According to an established body of state case law, "negroes" were presumed enslaved unless they could provide documentary evidence of freedom. "Colored" persons were presumed free under the law, meaning that they did not carry the legal burden of providing evidence of their freedom and could freely travel without fear of police molestation.[26]

Thus when state authorities pronounced, as the Louisiana Supreme Court did in 1849, that free "colored" Louisianians were "a different class of persons" from those "unworthy" and "degraded" free "negroes . . . of the slave States generally," they channeled two overlapping racial logics: a local legal doctrine that constructed a racial distinction between American "negroes" and "colored" Louisianians and a regional if unformalized tradition of framing well-reputed free Black neighbors as superior to the nation's aggregate free Black population.[27]

This complex theoretical taxonomy did not accurately reflect actual groupings on the ground. In practice, New Orleans was a multiethnic port city, home to peoples of diverse Anglo-American, Caribbean, Latin American, European, Asian, and Native American heritage whose families had emigrated to the city at various times and from various places. Free people's complexions ran the full spectrum of skin tones. Some free Black residents were transplants from elsewhere in the United States, or their descendants. Despite enduring social and cultural divisions between free Black transplants and free Black Louisianians of French or Spanish colonial ancestry, these two communities occasionally intermarried, cohabitated, and reproduced together. Louisiana's lawmakers imagined that free Black Louisianians constituted a homogenous community and that membership was both hereditary and visually discernable by skin tone. Complexion, nativity, and ancestry never aligned so tidily as Louisiana's lawmakers would have liked.[28]

Origins

New Orleans's practice of seizing nonwhite travelers as maroons emerged from the same confluence of fear, greed, and revolutionary upheaval that produced the city's first police jail and police force in May 1805. Amid that crisis, New Orleans's municipal council feared that the influx of disreputable and impoverished "strangers"—white and Black—threatened social upheaval. New ordinances mandated the surveillance, registration, and preemptive arrest of these "strangers." One such ordinance, passed in July 1805, addressed the lawlessness of Black strangers, particularly those from Saint-Domingue, who "call themselves free without proof." It ordered that they "be considered as slaves and treated as such." One year later, the territorial legislature empowered judicial authorities to selectively disregard the legal documentation of free Black refugees from Saint-Domingue and employ them on public works as though they were captured maroons.[29]

In invoking the soi-disant libre framework, the municipal council adopted a regulatory legal mechanism already circulating throughout the French Caribbean. Soi-disant libre was one of several legal expressions—alongside *"libre de fait"* (free in practice), *"libre de savane"* (unofficially set free), and *"patronné"* (living as free under another's patronage)—generated in the eighteenth-century French Antilles to designate individuals who enjoyed de facto freedom but whose legal claim to free status was shaky under French colonial law. French colonial law placed significant barriers to manumission, relative to other empires' legal systems, prompting some French colonial residents to travel overseas to obtain manumission records. Though sometimes used as a generic descriptor for anyone who lacked valid documentation of their freedom, soi-disant libre often connoted persons who had obtained their freedom papers abroad: in other words, persons recognized as free by foreign jurisdictions, though not by French colonial law.[30]

In the late eighteenth century, as revolutionary rumors and anxieties swept the Americas in waves, French colonial authorities viewed these ambiguous populations with increasing hostility and began orchestrating arrests, enslavements, and expulsions of the soi-disant libres.[31] Saint-Domingue authorities repeatedly ordered arrests of soi-disant libre residents during the tumultuous decades leading to that colony's revolution. Both Guadalupe and Martinique ordered the arrest of all soi-disant libre persons in September 1789, as news of the storming of the Bastille arrived from Paris. Martinique again ordered all soi-disant libre persons arrested and expelled, as refugees poured in from Saint-Domingue, in 1803—only months before New Orleans's adaptation of the regulatory category.[32]

Louisiana's intention was not to expel or seize *all* nonwhite strangers but rather to regulate *which* nonwhite strangers were to be recognized as enjoying the legal protections and privileges of free status. A telling moment occurred in May 1809, when thousands of refugees from Saint-Domingue, expelled from their original haven in Cuba following the outbreak of war between France and Spain, arrived off the Louisiana coast. Among the flotilla were refugees who had been classified as white, as free people of color, and as slaves in prerevolutionary Saint-Domingue: though *everyone* from Saint-Domingue had been declared legally free by the French Empire in 1794 and 1795. As the refugees disembarked in New Orleans, authorities made new and subjective assessments— based on appearance, negotiation, and whatever legal documentation the refugees carried—as to who would be considered white, who would *not* be considered white, and who would be designated "slave." Atop New Orleans's levee, some 3,000 refugees were designated free colored persons, tripling the size of the city's free Black population. More than 3,000 refugees, many of them legally free since 1794, were assigned the status of "slave" by the stroke of a pen.[33]

In deliberating whether to admit the refugees, Louisiana's leaders distinguished between propertyless dependents whose freedom posed a danger to the colony and propertied masters who could be trusted to exercise their freedom properly. The territorial governor, William Claiborne, acknowledged that he technically possessed "the power" to expel the entire "Body of Strangers" but felt that his policing powers should pertain only to "worthless" refugees "who had no property to loose" and not to men of property. "Industrious planters and mechanics" who had "some property on [Saint-Domingue]" deserved the full "hospitality and indulgence which humanity and courtesy require." New Orleans mayor James Mather expressed similar sentiments: exclusionary "law relative to free people of Color" should not be applied to those who "possess property," nor to "faithful slaves who had fled with their masters."[34] The proper subjects of exclusionary law, Claiborne and Mather understood, were property-less Black transients without owners. Of course, few refugees possessed property in any literal sense: what they had owned in Saint-Domingue had been destroyed, seized, or emancipated by Haitian revolutionaries. In identifying certain refugees as property owners, Mather and Claiborne voiced their perception that those refugees were *capable* of managing property: they had the capacity for mastery and thus should not be categorized as dependent persons.

Thus the soi-disant libre category must be read in the context of a society in which race and legal status could be contestable and malleable, particularly amid dealings with strangers and during border crossings, and the status of "slave" was informed by subjective assessments of a person's capacity for self-rule. It is unknown whether "soi-disant libre" was assigned to any refugees in May 1809. The earliest chain gang records, dating from 1814, show only two soi-disant libre prisoners among the hundreds who entered the Police Jail that year.[35] Their numbers gradually increased: by 1820, jailors recorded the admittance of about ten soi-disant libre prisoners monthly.[36] Significantly, New Orleans's first widespread use of the soi-disant libre category emerged one year *before* the Denmark Vesey Conspiracy, the event commonly cited as the parent of the Negro Seamen Acts. In 1821, rumors of ample employment opportunities constructing Mississippi River fortifications prompted a massive influx of white and Black migrant laborers into southeastern Louisiana. As the labor supply outstripped demand, surplus workers congregated haplessly in New Orleans's streets, where in July 1821, Mayor Louis Philippe de Roffignac declared a vagrancy crisis.[37] As police seized white transient workers as vagrants, the number of soi-disant libre committals to the Police Jail tripled.[38] Their numbers remained high through the Vesey Conspiracy panic and never subsided.

The roots of this policing practice underscore the conceptual connections that slaveholders forged among race, dependency, and crime. Slaveholders construed free Black itinerants as innately criminal not only because of their race and their mobility but also because their race and their menial station connoted their dependent status—and thus, their incapacity for self-rule—while their mobility and their autonomy suggested their dangerous detachment from propertied mastery. In this sense, the criminal danger posed by free Black itineracy was analogous to the criminal danger posed by other itinerant dependents, including fugitive enslaved people and vagrant poor white people.[39] Slave-holders did not equate these three categories of masterless dependent person, nor did they perceive that all masterless menial workers posed equal degrees of danger, but they did perceive that the same legal rationales that justified the preventative seizure of vagrants and maroons also justified the preventative seizure of free Black itinerants. Tellingly, when southern jurists felt pressed to defend the summarily seizure of free Black sailors, they often did so by citing the states' established legal right to seize maroons and vagrants. Jurists argued that all three preventative policing practices derived from the same state regulatory powers guaranteed by the Tenth Amendment to the Constitution, as reaffirmed by two US Supreme Court cases—*New York v. Miln* (1837) and *Prigg v. Pennsylvania* (1842)—wherein the court upheld the right of states to police dangerous populations in part by reasoning that laws governing vagrants, maroons, and itinerant free Black persons were analogous.[40] When Great Britain and Massachusetts protested the South's summary seizure of their free Black citizens, the New Orleans *Daily Picayune* charged hypocrisy, because both those societies were reputed to enforce the "most stringent regulations" against vagrants. If Massachusetts would reject Louisiana's right to seize free Black sailors, Louisiana should deport all its vagrants there, the *Daily Picayune* proposed sarcastically, where the vagrants "could not be rightfully subjected to restraint or imprisonment."[41]

Yet while all masterless menial workers posed some degree of criminal danger, the threat posed by free Black mobile workers seemed unmatched, since their Blackness accentuated perceptions of their innate dependency and dangerous uncontrollability.[42] "Every foreign free negro who comes into our state is regarded as a suspicious character," asserted the *New-Orleans Commercial Bulletin*. "The law makes it the duty of all police officers to watch persons of that class with the strictest vigilances." Just "as a tame negro, trained to work, is one of the most useful of creatures," echoed the Baton Rouge *Daily Advocate*, "so a wild one, turned loose to thieve and starve, is one of the most intolerable nuisances." They were "a dangerous body of incendiaries," a class "most dangerous to our institutions," inculcating "insurrection and massacre." Sailors and steamboat employees, capable of fluidly penetrating the boundaries between slave and free societies, seemed particularly threatening. After 1833, many free Black sailors heralded from the emancipated British Caribbean and thus seemed tainted by radical abolitionism.[43]

While their categorization as soi-disant libres was particular to Louisiana, the broader seizure of mobile free Black laborers as fugitive slaves was pervasive. Abolitionists warned free Black workers against traveling in the South, where they were "liable to be taken up, in every town and district, on suspicion as runaway slaves, thrust into prison, confined sixty days or more, and sometimes sold into bondage for their jail fees."[44] The practice "is common all over," delegates to one antislavery convention in 1834 alleged, "and prevails to an extent of which few are aware."[45] The escaped slave and former steamboat worker William Wells Brown identified New Orleans as a particularly egregious offender but noted that the custom also existed "in many other American ports."[46] William Powell identified Havana, Mobile, Charleston, Savannah, and New Orleans as the worst offenders. Arrests were also widespread in Rio de Janeiro.[47] "If any of you wish to know how FREE you are, let one of you start and go through the southern and western States of this country," abolitionist David Walker chided darkly in his *Appeal to the Coloured Citizens of the World* (1829). "[They will] put you in jail, and if you cannot give good evidence of your freedom, sell you into eternal slavery."[48]

Though few survive, existent ledgers from other cities' slave prisons also often indicate the presence of nonwhite transient workers. Among the 87 prisoners entered into the "Runaway Book" of the Richmond, Virginia, jail between March 13, 1841, and March 14, 1842, 37 (42.5 percent) appear to be free Black travelers, listed with surnames, and arrested "for the want of his [or her] free papers" and for entering Richmond "Contrary to Law."[49] The "Runaway Docket" of the Baltimore County jail, 1836–37, contains 205 names; 14 (6.8 percent) were listed as "proven free."[50] In the "Runaway Slave Book" of the Washington, DC, jail, 96 of the 1,216 committals (7.9 percent) made between April 6, 1848, and December 31, 1860, are listed as "free."[51] Many cities' slave workhouse regulations provided explicit guidelines for the confinement of nonwhite travelers as slaves.[52]

Newspaper descriptions of jailed runaways, typically required by law, also suggest regular seizures of free Black mobile wageworkers. In 1807, the Washington, DC, jail held John Clemmons "as a runaway," who wore "sailors clothes" and claimed to be a free seaman from Lancaster, Pennsylvania.[53] Also in 1807, one Maryland jail committed David Jones, a "runaway negro" who "Says he is a free man" and "a cook on board the frigate Chesapeake."[54] The Alexandria jail held "as a Runaway" James White, who "says that he is free, and was born in Wilmington . . . came to this place in the Schr. Talma . . . from the island of Cuba."[55] Charleston's slave workhouse held William Gale, who claimed to be a freeborn sailor and Boston native, "brought into the state in a British vessel from Liverpool."[56] A North Carolina jail held John Cary, who "says that he is free" and a railroad worker, detained while "migrating into the State" in search of employment.[57] A Georgia jail held "George McLane . . . [who] says that he is free, that his father lives in Cincinnati."[58] The Natchez jail held Nancy Smith, who claimed to be a free milliner, a New Yorker by birth, and a recent émigré from Nova Scotia.[59] Although these prisoners' stories are unverifiable, sheriffs' inclusions of their stories and surnames suggest that authorities gave credence to these prisoners' claims. Sometimes, these prisoners were auctioned into permanent slavery.[60]

Despite the enormous risks, free Black workers regularly sought employment as seafarers or hired laborers, joining the seasonal labor flows that cycled through antebellum port cities. Discriminatory hiring practices and restricted opportunities for vocational training and advancement pushed free Black workers into industries that offered lower wages and minimal job security. By the early nineteenth century, free Black workers accounted for about one-fifth of all employees onboard American ships. With exceptional risks came uncommon opportunities: international travel, consistent wages, and the possibility of individual achievement within a maritime work culture that, while at sea, sometimes downplayed the calcifying boundaries of race.[61]

Fears that free Black sailors disrupted southern social order were not entirely misplaced. Some free Black sailors *did* regularly aid fugitives from slavery—particularly those living in the Deep South, for whom waterways offered the best hope of escape—by concealing them among crates, dressing them as well-to-do free passengers, or disguising them as longtime ship employees. "There was a fascination about the river that I could not resist," recalled John Parker, who escaped New Orleans aboard the steamboat *Magnolia*, "because I knew that was my only avenue of escape from my bondage." Nor were slaveholders entirely irrational in suspecting that some Black workers merely pretended to be free. The demand for maritime labor was often so high that some employers made only a cursory glance at laborers' free papers or accepted verbal assurances, sometimes inadvertently aiding fugitives' escapes. Famed fugitives Henry Bibb, Harriet Ann Jacobs, and Frederick Douglass each escaped slavery by posing as free sailors or ship passengers: Bibb by confidently boarding a steamboat as though a passenger, Jacobs by dressing and "walk[ing] ricketty" like a sailor, and Douglass by borrowing a sailor's clothing and seaman's protection certificate.[62]

Policing Presumptive Freedom

Soi-disant libre prisoners often explained that police had seized them on identifying them as "strangers" through subjective assessments of dress, accent, and mannerism.[63] Tellingly, one imprisoned Bostonian sailor attributed his Police Jail release to his ability to speak French: a false indicator, to jailors, that he was no "stranger" but rather a member of New Orleans's francophone free community.[64] Others were arrested after having initially attracted police attention through various disorderly behaviors: sleeping outside, gambling, fighting, prostitution, interracial revelry, loitering about the levee.[65] Black migrants were particularly vulnerable to arrest after dark when they sought New Orleans's nightlife but unwittingly violated the city's slave curfew.[66]

While being masterless, menial, and mobile marked free Black migrants as dangerous, it was their *strangeness*—the recognition that they lacked attachment to local community networks—that made their freedom violable. Legal protections in the antebellum South were often bounded by social relationships, community networks, and reputation. Free Black southerners guarded their freedom by garnering the approbation and recognition of their white neighbors. If ever they needed to avail themselves of the legal system, free Black southerners turned to these white neighbors to testify or to enter suits on their behalf.[67]

Yet if community networks provided limited protections, *strangeness* stripped those protections away. Transient workers had no reputable neighbors to vouch for them: "no one," Rufus Kinsman observed, "who can swear that they know them and where they were born."[68] Soi-disant libre prisoners were "detained from inability to prove their alleged freedom, being foreigners," recognized one sympathetic grand jury; they lacked access to "persons of respectability . . . who can furnish proof of their being free."[69]

Separated from kinship and community networks, nonwhite transient workers were wholly dependent on legal documentation of their freedom, known as freedom papers—which New Orleans's police, judges, and jailors regularly destroyed, seized, and voided. Steamboat worker William Freeman recalled watching his free papers "taken from him and torn in pieces before his eyes" in a New Orleans court.[70] Others relied on state-issued seamen's protection certificates, learning too late that New Orleans authorities considered the certificates invalid.[71] Many never learned precisely why authorities had voided their papers. Between 1839 and 1841, Jim Allen was incarcerated as a runaway slave in three river ports—New Orleans, Louisville, and Baton Rouge—despite holding his freedom papers throughout.[72]

In transit, papers also became lost or damaged. Prisoner Mathias Freeman, a freeborn sailor from Hudson, New York, confessed to having "casually lost his certificate of Freedom."[73] Free papers were so valuable that travelers often secured them within trunks, incorrectly assuming that, if arrested, police would permit their retrieval. Louis Polony, a Guadeloupian sailor incarcerated for over two years in the Second Municipality Police Jail, complained that he was never permitted to fetch his baptismal records from his trunk aboard the brig *Lucy*. Polony's prison mate, Henry Goings of Virginia, explained that his papers were safely stowed in a nearby grog shop.[74] Others had entrusted their papers to reputable white persons: Thomas Lloyd, a white merchant, sheepishly admitted to losing the papers of Westley Moody, from Kentucky.[75] Ship captains commonly retained sailors' free papers to prevent their jumping ship.[76]

Some sailors were aware of the dangers but had entered New Orleans involuntarily, either seeking medical treatment or when their captain unexpectedly dismissed his crew.[77] Some were young, freeborn, and perhaps naive, raised in northern communities where their freedom was so ubiquitously recognized that they hadn't understood free papers' necessity. John Shelby of Springfield, Illinois, didn't carry any documentation during his first journey away from home, working aboard a Mississippi River steamboat in 1856, because back home the Shelbys "were always believed to be free—no one doubted it."[78] After nearly a year within the Police Jail, Shelby used an intermediary to contact a hometown lawyer and former congressman whom he had heard express sympathy for Black Americans: Abraham Lincoln. Lincoln informed Shelby's mother that her missing son had been found, contacted Illinois's governor, raised money for Shelby's jail fees, and orchestrated Shelby's release.[79]

Infrequently, soi-disant libre prisoners were longtime or semiregular Louisiana residents: either adopted members of the city's transient poor or sailors who had grown to consider New Orleans their hometown in between deployments. Charles Clark, a sailor and transplant from New York, protested in court that police took him to the Police Jail regularly. Benjamin Savage, a sailor from Germantown, Pennsylvania, employed onboard a British ship, and who claimed to have lived in New Orleans since 1825, was imprisoned for at least nine months in 1840–41, after police found three contradictory sets of free papers and four abolitionist pamphlets in his pockets.[80]

An Afro-Venezuelan sailor living under the anglicized name Augustus Smith also claimed to be a longtime New Orleans resident while relaying his biography to a sympathetic lawyer who visited the Police Jail in March 1841. Smith claimed to have been born in Angostura, a remote riverport deep within the Venezuelan countryside. He would still have been a child in 1817 when Simón Bolívar conquered Angostura, using the city as a base of operations from which to denounce slavery and racial caste and wage guerrilla warfare against the Spanish Empire. As a young man, Smith found work as a sailor, visiting New Orleans for the first time in around 1830 aboard the Baltimore-based schooner *Dutch Chest*. Later, Smith found work aboard the Boston-based brig *Cordelia*, running a regular circuit between New England and the Caribbean. He claimed that his father still lived in Angostura, suggesting that he visited or remained in contact with the city, perhaps through his work aboard the *Cordelia*. By March 1841, Smith had already sat in the Police Jail for seven months. Moreover, this was not Smith's first time in the Police Jail: he had been arrested as a fugitive slave twice before, in 1836 and 1838. Remarkably mobile, with transatlantic connections, and a firsthand witness to antislavery and anti-colonial revolution, Smith embodied slaveholders' worst fears: no surprise, then, that New Orleans police seemed so committed to his captivity.[81]

There were always exceptions: unusual circumstances or police errors by which native-born free Louisianians were committed to the Police Jail as soi-disant libres, though such persons almost always appear to have been released within hours of their arrest. A short-lived private security force, hired to patrol a wealthy neighborhood in July 1835 and terminated in August 1836, deliberately targeted free Black resident property owners for harassment, arresting them after dark for violating the city's slave curfew and committing them to the slave prison as soi-disant libres. Among those seized was one Jean Baptiste Roudanez, a francophone Louisiana native whose appearance, language, and name would have made his status and heritage obvious. In 1840, police raided an "amateur circus" attended by "a bevy of blacks, free and slaves," bringing several children to the Second Municipality Police Jail, including a teenager named Paul Trévigne, also a native-born free resident, perhaps rounded up in error. In 1848, police brought to the Third Municipality Police Jail a Louisiana-born carpenter, born into slavery, named Oscar Dunn. Dunn's father was from Virginia, and perhaps Dunn's Anglo-American heritage, dark complexion, and former-slave status called his membership within the local free community into question. These three committals are noteworthy because Roudanez, Trévigne, and Dunn would each become leading civil rights activists and Republican Party leaders during postwar Reconstruction. In 1862, Roudanez and Trévigne would cofound the South's first Black-owned and -operated newspaper. In 1868, Dunn would become the first Black lieutenant governor of any US state. These men's lives are well documented, though their arrests are heretofore unknown. However brief, their terrifying moments within police jails doubtless shaped their perspectives on unrestrained police power.[82]

Punishing Freedom

Once arrested, soi-disant libre prisoners were subjected to penal routines designed to brutalize and degrade insubordinate and noncompliant Africans into submissive slaves. Alongside jailed fugitives from slavery, soi-disant libre prisoners were stripped naked, strapped to whipping racks, and deployed on slave chain gangs. Many recognized jailors' purposeful efforts to debase and humiliate them. In a letter secreted from the Second Municipality Police Jail, six imprisoned sailors decried the "infamie" of the chain gang, which seemed deliberately calculated to "degrade the feeling and honor of a true honest man."[83]

John Hatfield, a Pennsylvanian who barbered aboard a river steamboat, considered his twenty-three hours in the Police Jail to be the most dehumanizing experience of his life. To Hatfield, his arrest as a runaway resembled a public performance, calculated "to degrade me" before bystanders. This strategic degradation continued within the prison: "They measured me, and recorded my name. . . . In the morning the whip was cracking, starting out the chain-gang, just as one would start up horses. . . . I had committed no crime. I never felt so degraded in my life. If I had murdered a man or stolen a horse, I could not have been treated with more contempt."[84] The noted Boston abolitionist James Barbadoes described how his brother, Robert, endured similar routines of subjugation during a five-month Police Jail term: "He was often severely flogged to be made submissive, and deny that he was free born."[85]

These efforts to "degrade" sailors, by subjecting them to punishments associated with the enslaved, was also a feature of South Carolina's Negro Seamen Act. Sailors seized under the act were held in Charleston's slave workhouse, tortured in the workhouse punishment room, and assigned to penal labor tasks that were otherwise restricted to incarcerated slaves, even though the law recognized them as legally free persons.[86] Sailors were also prominently "manacled and marched through the streets" while en route to the slave workhouse, a practice that onlookers likened to "parading" and that seemed intent on attracting "attention to the coloured seamen."[87] Such punishments, one British critic noted, appeared calculated to "turn our freemen into slaves"—bent on "not only the imprisoning, but converting."[88]

When pressed to defend the Negro Seamen Act in federal court, lawyers for South Carolina developed the legal argument that the act was analogous to a "quarantine," aimed at preventing radicalized sailors from "infecting" the enslaved with dangerous antislavery ideologies. This rationale has diverted attention from the law's implicit aim of equating free Black sailors with slaves and reasserting their subjugation through humiliation and penal violence. Indeed, some South Carolina slaveholders opposed the Negro Seamen Act because it patently failed to establish a quarantine. Why parade sailors through city streets, jail them with rebellious slaves, and authorize their sale into slavery, if the purpose was to prevent interactions between sailors and the enslaved? By "confining these coloured seamen from Northern and West-Indian ports in the same jail, under the same rules, with slaves confined therein for crimes and misdemeanors, there is afforded every opportunity to corrupt them," one South Carolina lawmaker protested. In a federal circuit court ruling in 1823, Supreme Court Justice (and Charleston native) William Johnson charged that South Carolina's Negro Seamen Act seemed "to defeat its own ends" by placing sailors "into the very situation in which they would enjoy the best opportunities of pursuing their designs." If the true purpose were to establish a quarantine, would it not make far greater sense, Johnson reasoned, for the sailors to be "confined to their ships"? Johnson deduced that the state's equivalence of the act to a "quarantine" was little more than a legal ploy, designed by the lawyers representing South Carolina to circumvent any interpretation of the law as a commercial regulation, and thus a clear violation of the Constitution's commerce clause, which prohibits states from regulating interstate and international commerce. The law's true aim, Johnson intuited, was to render Black sailors "domesticated."[89]

In smuggled letters written in blood or contraband ink, soi-disant libre prisoners described their mental exhaustion and mounting despair.[90] "We are free men & have done nothing to merit this punishment," fifteen imprisoned men wrote from the Second Municipality Police Jail in 1841. "We are deprived of the privilege of having any of our friends to give us something to eat or some clean clothes to wear, we are deprived of the privilege of having something to write with." They pondered the fortunes of their "families in different parts of the world. . . . [We] dont know what has become of them, & they may be in a state of starvation for all we know."[91] In another letter smuggled from the same jail, six sailors described feelings of invisibility, their suffering "unbeknownst to anyone except those who are here." Yet they vowed to resist such extreme dehumanization, writing that as freemen who had "been suckled with that sweet milk of Liberty and freedom," they would rather "Lay ourself Down and die like men" than submit to such "arbitrayre power on us."[92]

Releases and the Reassertion of White Mastery

Louisiana law permitted the sale of unclaimed runaway slaves at auction, a looming terror for every imprisoned sailor.[93] Yet selling sailors into slavery was not Louisiana authorities' primary aim. Rather, jailors and judges readily released soi-disant libre prisoners into the custody of virtually any white employer who claimed wardship over their labor, paid their jail fees, and removed them from the state.[94] In effect, release was predicated on the establishment of white mastery over free Black labor, even while the practice of summarily handing these nominal slaves over to men who were not their owners represented authorities' tacit concession that they knew these prisoners to be legally free.

Conversely, prisoners found that it was virtually impossible to win release into their own recognizance. "It seme to us who are shut up that the recorder is affraid to have us put at Liberty," the six imprisoned sailors noted, "the reason we cannot imagine."[95] When prisoners' hometowns transmitted free papers, Louisiana's judges often demanded Sisyphean verifications: that the governor

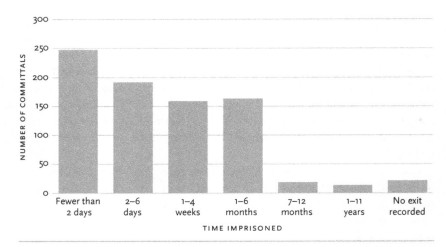

Graph 3.2. Jail times for SDL prisoners committed to the City/First Municipality Police Jail, January 1837–August 1841.

of the freeperson's native state confirm the documents' validity, that the judge who had originally penned the papers transmit proof that he was licensed to practice law.[96] Even after these requirements were fulfilled, prisoners remained incarcerated until an employer paid their jail fees and claimed their labor: effectively, they waited until a reputable master purchased them.[97] Two sailors who had proved their freedom in 1836 still awaited release, pending payment of jail fees, in 1841.[98] One sympathetic lawyer noted that it took him over twenty trips to the prison and court to gain the release of Baltimore-based ship's cook Ephraim Larkin. The judge finally conceded that Larkin was a free person but refused to waive $29.89 worth of jail fees or even the cost of Larkin's runaway slave advertisements.[99]

The demand for maritime labor was high enough that roughly half of all prisoners were released within one week, likely into the custody of their original captains, with jail fees under two dollars (graph 3.2).[100] Often captains docked these jail fees from sailors' future wages, binding employee to employer until the loan was repaid.[101]

Others were not so lucky: roughly one prisoner in five remained imprisoned for months and years. These long-term inmates were often less-appealing hires: women, the disabled, migrant laborers with no captain to vouch for them, and prisoners who had accrued massive jail fees. Charles Beckett, a Delaware sailor, endured three years; John H. Slate, of Connecticut, suffered four years and six months, the chain gang shackle having chafed the flesh of his ankle down to the bone.[102] To regain their freedom, desperate prisoners often agreed to unfavorable contract terms, and captains learned to rely on police jails as a source of inexpensive labor and contract coercion.[103]

Though rare, some long-term soi-disant libre prisoners were sold into permanent slavery. After police arrested George McDowell, a New York sailor, in January 1838, frostbite contracted in his unheated cell necessitated the amputation of his leg. Incapable of labor, McDowell began accumulating massive jail fees. In 1841, a judge rejected appeals from McDowell's New York friends. In August 1845, having accumulated over $500 in jail fees, the First Municipality sold McDowell and nine other prisoners for $2,360. One month later, the Second Municipality sold Mary Abrams and Alexis, both of whom also claimed to be free. Throughout his tenure, jailors consistently inscribed "SDL" aside McDowell's name. Auction advertisements marketed him as "a runaway . . . owner unknown."[104]

Resistance and Mariner Networks

Impossibly ensnared, denied any legal rights, and threatened with the possibility of permanent enslavement, soi-disant libre prisoners' best resources were the social ties and informal communication networks among mariners: far from their hometowns, sailors created their own communities.[105] Sailors regularly spotted old friends and familiar faces within police jails; on release, former prisoners contacted the families and employers of those still confined.[106] Some sailors were rescued after former shipmates recognized them on the slave chain gang. The only boon of chain gang labor was that it routinely placed prisoners on the city's wharves, where manacled sailors could surreptitiously flag down former colleagues. This was how Captain William Hess and his free Black mate, George Cain, discovered imprisoned fellow Philadelphian Joseph Kim.[107] Lieutenant Carpenter spotted John Callis, a former shipmate on the USS *Constitution*, shackled to his wife, Charlotte Callis, a ship's stewardess.[108] A white traveler named Rueben Bunker was incredulous when a chain gang slave furtively whispered that the two had been childhood playmates in Hudson, New York—until the prisoner, Mathias Freeman, accurately described members of Bunker's family. Bunker subsequently contacted Hudson's mayor and Freeman's parents.[109]

Prisoners' letters suggest a sense of mariner community that transcended national boundaries. One letter included signatures of men from Pennsylvania, Jamaica, and Venezuela. Another included signatories from the United States, British Caribbean, Swedish Caribbean, and Indian subcontinent.[110] Conspicuously, no surviving letters mention or describe the enslaved cellmates of soi-disant libre prisoners—though the writings of formerly imprisoned enslaved people make clear that they were very aware of their legally free cellmates—suggesting that soi-disant libre prisoners tried to differentiate themselves from the enslaved.[111]

Mariners of color also circulated cautionary tales regarding the most dangerous slaveholding ports. In 1835, one former sailor identified New Orleans's Police Jail as "famous" among "all seamen."[112] When the abolitionist and former steamboat worker William Wells Brown toured Britain with twenty-four painted panoramas depicting American slavery, he devoted two panels to the Police Jail: one portraying the institution's interior and another depicting its chain gang, "partly made up of Free coloured persons who are found in the city without Free papers."[113]

Foreign-born mariners sometimes appealed to their governments for intervention. The British, French, and Mexican consuls tried freeing their subjects from police jails.[114] In 1840, New Orleans mayor William Freret instructed police to reject any freedom documentation issued by the British consul, following accusations that the consul regularly furnished freedom papers to any Black sailor employed on a British ship, regardless of the sailor's nationality.[115] In 1859, New Orleans police sparked a diplomatic crisis by arresting the French consul after he refused to deliver Pierre Redmond, a free Black French subject, whom police had chased into the consulate after arresting all his Black shipmates.[116]

In the North, mariners pressured abolitionist societies to confront the "continual stream" of free Black sailors seized in southern ports.[117] In Boston, mariners and abolitionists began holding regular meetings, petitioning their state government and Congress for intervention. These efforts culminated in state hearings in Massachusetts in 1843, leading the commonwealth to send commissioners to Charleston and New Orleans in 1844 and 1845. Both commissioners were chased away by lynch mobs. The South Carolina legislature subsequently passed a law barring any such future commissioners, while the Louisiana legislature passed a resolution condemning Massachusetts's inflammatory interference.[118]

Few did more in service of imprisoned sailors than William Powell. Following their release, many former prisoners headed straight for Powell's Colored Sailor's Home in New York, where Powell provided much-needed medical aid and financial support. As word of his services spread, Powell began receiving a steady stream of desperate letters from southern prisons. From sailors' letters and testimonials, Powell constructed his pathbreaking study of the history, commercial impact, and persecution of free Black sailors, published in the *National Anti-Slavery Standard* in 1846. Powell's study was the first of its type, arming sailors and abolitionists throughout the nation with much-needed information regarding southern policing practices (during Senate hearings in 1850, proslavery legislators mocked abolitionists' total reliance on the research performed by some disreputable "keeper of a *negro hotel*").[119]

Sailors also turned to collective action, by mutinying, striking, or jumping ship. In 1857, eighteen sailors mutinied after learning that their ship was bound not for New York but rather for Mobile.[120] Yet this was the age of cotton: for sailors, southern port cities could not be avoided. Indeed, many soi-disant libre prisoners reported multiple confinements in New Orleans, over several years.[121] Some conceded to the inevitability of incarceration, resorting to pressuring their captains into guaranteeing immediate payment of their jail fees.[122]

Facing mounting resistance, some captains began concealing southern destinations from their crews. Marianne Edwards, wife of captain Guy Edwards, witnessed her husband's deceptions firsthand. Though bound for New Orleans, "Guy does not say so on board for . . . all coulored people coming there will have to go to jail while the ship is in port, and all on board know it." When rumors of their next destination arose, four crewmembers jumped ship in Rio de Janeiro, forfeiting their wages. The six remaining Black crewmembers "all asked for there discharge, [but] Guy . . . would not give it to any of them." On reaching New Orleans, Edwards reported, "all our coloured people go to jail."[123]

Not all white captains shared Guy Edward's callousness toward Black shipmates. In 1821 and again in 1824, Captain Theophilus Adams of Massachusetts discovered former employees languishing in the Police Jail, demanding their release both times.[124] Captain Smith of the *Sea Bird* failed to win Edwin Matthews's release in April 1845 but tried again, and succeeded, during their steamer's return in August.[125] For some, mariner loyalties ran deep.

From Soi-Disant Libre to the Negro Seamen Acts

Ultimately, these mariner loyalties contributed to Louisiana's decision in 1842 to curtail the seizure of sailors as soi-disant libres and pass a Negro Seamen Act. When fashioning himself as a populist or recalling his Nantucket childhood, Jacob Barker described himself as a former sailor. In truth, Barker had spent far more time owning shipping interests than working aboard ships. A Quaker who once had been one of New York's wealthiest financiers, Barker had relocated to New Orleans after a ruinous scandal in 1834. Like Edward Livingston before him, Barker purchased a sugar plantation and launched a successful law practice.[126] Publicly, Barker advanced proslavery arguments.[127] Yet even as he rebuilt his wealth and reputation, Barker's affection for sailors persisted.

In 1837, Barker heard rumors that the Third Municipality Police Jail held a Baltimore sailor as a fugitive slave. Intrigued, Barker investigated, upon which three other prisoners approached him, also claiming to be free, including a man from Nantucket who identified himself as the grandson of Barker's childhood neighbor. Shortly thereafter, as Barker attended an inquest at the Second Municipality Workhouse, Henry Tier, a former employee of Barker's from New York, called out through the bars of the adjacent Police Jail. Alarmed, Barker penned an urgent letter to Nantucket newspapers, warning Black mariners "not to come here on any consideration whatever" as "the laws of Louisiana presume all blacks to be slaves."[128]

In 1841, Rowland Hazard, a Rhode Island Quaker and distant cousin of Barker who traveled South each winter to hawk the raw "negro cloth" manufactured by his family's mill, also spotted a hometown acquaintance on the slave chain gang. Barker and Hazard resolved to win the release of all sailors held in police jails.[129]

To win prisoners' freedom, Hazard and Barker needed to establish that reputable white persons considered them free. In March 1841, the pair interviewed nearly 100 soi-disant libre prisoners, transcribing lists of names of "respectable" white persons—former employers, hometown civic leaders, and childhood neighbors—capable of vouching for each prisoner's identity.[130] Shorthand notes from these interviews survive:

> Rufus Kinsman, Born in Lisbon Connt.
> Capt. David Drinkwater[,] Jacob Knight,
> Asa Clapp, Ezekiel Kinston all
> of Portland + Capt Lewis Henchman
> Henry Harris, Cob, Amasa Hunt
> All of Boston know him—been
> in 2 months—no money [to pay jail fees].[131]

The prisoners interviewed by Barker and Hazard hailed from at least four continents, fourteen US states, seven Caribbean islands, and ten modern-day countries. Many had been confined for days or weeks, others for the better part of a decade. At least fifteen prisoners claimed that they had already been determined free in a New Orleans court but either owed jail fees or had been subsequently rearrested. Hazard returned North to collect freedom papers, affidavits, and donations for jail fees while Barker began suing for each prisoner's release.[132]

Authorities refused to concede that police jails held free persons, battling Barker at every step. Rufus Kinsman's case is illustrative. The recorder rejected the affidavits and free papers sent from Kinsman's Connecticut birthplace because the documents lacked the seal of Connecticut's governor. When Governor William Ellsworth personally avowed the documents' legitimacy, the judge determined that New Orleans held another man because Kinsman's original arrest record listed his surname as *Parsman*. Returned to the chain gang, Kinsman grew despondent: "Now [I] am sick. . . . I am a Stranger here. . . . I belong to Connecticut. . . . I Pray you in the Name of God. . . . Send me an answer."[133] After thirteen months, Kinsman was released, whereupon he immediately boarded a ship bound for Liverpool.[134]

Barker's efforts underscore the protections that mariner brotherhood provided but also the limitations of that brotherhood, for he entirely ignored all imprisoned free women. In the First Municipality Police Jail, Barker overlooked free Black women Mary Ann Martin (imprisoned since February 1836) and Suzanne Jackson (imprisoned since February 1840). In the Second Municipality, Barker ignored a group of unnamed free women, described by a grand jury in 1842 as held "from one to four years."[135] Though proportionately few in number, women were particularly susceptible to longer prison terms; they were likelier to be excluded from the limited protections of informal mariner networks and employers were less likely to claim their labor. Tellingly, among free Black prisoners released from the Second Municipality Police Jail between 1843 and 1845, the average prison term among men was twenty-six days— among women, eighty-two days.[136]

Barker's litigating also exposes the hidden complexities and contradictions of how race and legal status operated within Louisiana. In theory, New Orleans police were permitted to summarily seize only persons whom they racialized as "negro." Persons racialized as "colored" were presumed free, under the law. Persons perceived as not having *any* maternal African ancestry could not be legally enslaved. Yet Barker found that many imprisoned sailors were of very light complexion and did not appear classifiable as "negro." As a test case, Barker sued on behalf of six of the lightest-complexioned prisoners. Forced to admit that the confinement of such persons violated established legal doctrine, the judge summarily released five as presumptive free persons.[137] Another judge released William Augustus, a Nova Scotia native, solely based on "his complexion, without any other testimony."[138] Augustus and another light-complexioned former prisoner subsequently sued their arresting officer for wrongful arrest.[139]

Barker also encountered prisoners who did not appear to have any African ancestry whatsoever. Barker uncovered multiple Native American prisoners, including Solomon Jones, a Philadelphia native held for at least eighteen months who "cannot be mistaken" for a person of African ancestry "as his hair and features plainly indicate him to be an Indian."[140] Barker also met two British subjects, John Colington and Munwell Wegg, identified as natives of Calcutta and Bombay. Jean Le Corez Coro told Barker that he had been born in northern Mexico but "came from Texas [and] was a priest there," a story suggesting Indigenous Latino ancestry.[141] In an editorial, Barker denounced police disregard for established case law, arguing that their actions threatened the rights of *white* persons. To "allow the police-men to usurp the power" of drafting laws, Barker warned, was to permit the establishment of a tyranny wherein "the white population of every grade in society becomes more abject slaves than those who are of black skin."[142]

Police seizures of light-complexioned and non-Black persons indicate how subjective perceptions of dependency, localism, and marginality informed the murky boundaries between presumptive slavery and presumptive freedom. In determining who should be assigned the status of "slave," police were supposed to assess freedom papers and presumptive racial ancestry. In practice, and particularly amid dealings with low-status transient workers living along the port city's margins, law enforcement routinely disregarded complexion and documentation, instead assessing such factors as clothing, accent, mannerism, nativity, social station, apparent wealth, and employment status that encoded the degree to which a person appeared unworthy of self-rule. Within this racial logic, all gradients of nonwhiteness—and not simply Blackness—connoted some degree of dependency. Seizures of Native American, Indian, and Southeast Asian sailors indicate police efforts to construct a de facto racial order within which full freedom was limited to whiteness and many nonwhite, migratory, and dependent outsiders, whether legally enslaved or not, were either bound to masters or controlled by the state.

Barker's actions divided slaveholders. Some attacked the Quaker lawyer for verifying abolitionist hearsay. "He is making himself very obnoxious to every citizen, by this course of his," observed one paper. "Does he suppose that he can come southward with impunity, and act as the counsel for every black vagabond who may land on our shores?"[143] Others joined Barker in decrying officials' obvious disregard for the legal documents issued by other states and for Louisiana's own case law. "[We] do not know whether [we] should find fault with the *Laws* under which slaves, and those suspected of being runaway slaves are confined in this Jail or with the manner in which these laws are executed," one grand jury complained. "But certain it is that there is something very wrong."[144]

Yet slaveholders' worst fears seemed realized in July 1841 when planters near the town of Bayou Sara, the second largest steamboat port along the Lower Mississippi, reported their discovery of an imminent slave uprising, stretching from New Orleans to Natchez and coordinated by an underground network of free Black steamboat workers, fugitive enslaved people, and poor white vagrants. The panic was sparked by a single plantation overseer who while conducting his nightly rounds had overheard enslaved people discuss secret plans for an unspecified event, slated for August 1. Word traveled upriver to the town of Pointe Coupée, where one slaveholder reported that he, too, had overheard enslaved people discussing vague plans for an imminent date. Full-blown panic erupted. Firearms flew off the shelves of New Orleans's gun stores, hundreds of enslaved people were seized and packed into rural parish jails, and communities throughout the river valley joined together in demanding a total prohibition on "the employment of free persons of color on board our steamboats."[145] Amid the panic, a committee of New Orleans residents informed Jacob Barker that if he did not immediately cease all legal efforts on behalf of free Black sailors, he would be lynched.[146] Fearing for his life, Barker yielded.[147]

Though slaveholders eventually dismissed the conspiracy as a "humbug," the coordination among sailors and enslaved people may have been very real. The date that the overseer had overheard slaves discuss—August 1—marked the anniversary of the abolition of slavery in the British Empire in 1834 and was a day of festivity among free Black communities throughout the British Caribbean. By the 1840s, August First celebrations had begun spreading, by way of British Afro-Caribbean sailors, into free Black communities in the North.[148] Black British steamboat workers also traveled the Mississippi River: only three months earlier, one New Orleans newspaper had decried the employment of "British free negroes" aboard river steamboats.[149] That enslaved people along the Mississippi River were aware of August First and evidently planning their own commemoration provides tantalizing evidence that the free Black steamboat workers were indeed circulating illicit information, forging ties among dispersed Black Atlantic communities and spreading word of Black liberation.

Faced with Barker's litigating and the August First panic, lawmakers resolved to redesign Louisiana's approach to policing nonwhite transient labor. During the summer of 1841, as Barker began winning releases, police curtailed soi-disant libre arrests, relying instead on an underenforced law of 1830 that barred the immigration of free Black migrants from out of state and established procedures for the expulsion of any free Black resident who had immigrated to Louisiana after 1825. Violation of an expulsion order resulted in a one-year prison sentence; a second offense resulted in imprisonment for life.[150] The press noted the sudden change, commending police for their "extremely active" enforcement of this underenforced law. Mass arrests of free Black migrants who contravened this law, dubbed "contraventionists," became regular.[151]

Many of the prisoners interviewed by Barker were either swept up in these mass arrests of "contraventionists" or were directly transferred from the prison to the court for expulsion. Benjamin Savage, the Pennsylvania native and long-time Louisiana resident who had been arrested in possession of multiple sets of freedom papers and abolitionist pamphlets, was interviewed by Barker in March, convicted of contravention in July, and condemned to the penitentiary in August for failing to leave the state.[152] William Wilson of Annapolis,

Maryland, and Simon Brown of Newport, Rhode Island, were also released from the Police Jail, charged with contravention, and sentenced to the penitentiary for their failure to emigrate. Their refusal to leave suggests that they, like Savage, were longtime residents with inseverable ties to the city. Brown was particularly unlucky. In March 1843, he was among the free Black penitentiary inmates to be transferred to the Board of Public Works to supplement the state's dwindling force of state-owned slaves: for the second time, he was condemned to a Louisiana slave chain gang.[153]

In March 1842, Louisiana's governor signed into law "An Act More Effectually to Prevent Free Persons of Color from Entering into This State, and for Other Purposes." The new law adapted the approach of South Carolina's Negro Seamen Act, mandating the incarceration in New Orleans's Parish Prison of any free Black sailors, riverboat workers, or passengers transported by sea or river from out of state until the ship on which they had arrived could remove them. The legislature next revised Louisiana's "contravention" rules: now, free Black residents who had moved to Louisiana before 1838 could remain only if they registered their residency, posted bond, formally petitioned for permission to remain, and provided evidence of their good moral character. Similar state laws, expelling or restricting the in-state entry of free Black migrants, were passed by six other southern state legislatures—those of Mississippi, Arkansas, Tennessee, Missouri, Alabama, and Florida—in the months following the August First panic. Of the slave states bordering the Mississippi River, only Kentucky failed to act.[154]

After 1842, New Orleans policed nonnative free Black migrants through three parallel and occasionally overlapping legal frameworks: negro seaman, contraventionist, and soi-disant libre. Sailors and riverboat workers who submitted themselves at New Orleans's docks were jailed under the act of 1842. Out-of-state workers who skirted past port authorities and were arrested from city streets continued to be confined in police jails as fugitive enslaved people. Longer-term nonnative residents who garnered police attention were charged with "contravention" and expelled.

Thus Louisiana's passage of a Negro Seamen Act reflected not an escalation in the state's war on free Black travelers so much as a refinement, legitimating the continued seizure of nonwhite transient workers without so blatantly running afoul of the state's legal doctrine that "colored" persons enjoyed presumptive freedom. For many imprisoned sailors, the new legal regime had the ironic effect of lessening their suffering: the First and Third Municipalities acknowledged the free status of persons seized under the act of 1842, sparing those prisoners from the Police Jail, whipping rack, and chain gang. In the chain gang ledger of the First Municipality surveyor, maintained between June 1840 and April 1851, the share of "free" prisoners plummeted after the act's passage from 12.9 percent to 1.3 percent.[155] Their numbers in the Third Municipality Police Jail also fell sharply, from about 160 committals in 1839 to about 30 in 1847.[156] For others, the new legal regime changed little. Ignoring the requirement that they be considered free persons and confined in Parish Prison, the Second Municipality continued condemning sailors and steamboat workers to the Police Jail and slave chain gang—allegedly, to funnel sailors' lucrative jail fees into the Second Municipality's coffers—triggering protracted legal battles between the municipalities.[157]

Though "contravention" was generally applied to longer-term residents, virtually everyone thus charged after 1842 was poor, marginalized, and poorly integrated into the wage labor market: sex workers, beggars, drunks, purveyors in stolen goods, and other persons whose disorderliness, landlessness, and poverty connoted their innate dependency and incapacity for self-rule. The *Daily Picayune* called them "the suspicious portion of the colored population," persons whose "habits and character" suggested that they were not "qualified for freedom," in contrast to "the old families of free colored persons, who own property and form a respectable class."[158] Sex workers were targeted with particular vigor.[159] The state initiated expulsion proceedings against Julia Arbuckle, a formerly enslaved brothel keeper from Kentucky, three times between 1849 and 1860.[160] The state ordered the expulsion of Sarah Conner, a "not at all reputable" Virginia native, after she was seen "dancing in company with some sixteen colored girls, mostly slaves, and about ten or twelve white men."[161] Many had lived in New Orleans for years. Faced with expulsion, a Baltimore native named Henry Williams protested that he had resided in New Orleans for nearly a decade.[162] Hannah Cornelius, an Arkansas native who had lived in New Orleans for four years, pleaded for recognition as a southerner: "I have never been in any free state. . . . I know nothing about the North. . . . I have been Born and raised in a slave state. . . . Let me have a chance." The next day, Cornelius received a one-year penitentiary sentence for violating her expulsion order.[163]

"Slavery" and "freedom" were never absolute and oppositional states of being among the city's poor, marginal, and transient free Black residents. Indeed, many members of the city's transient poor were jailed as soi-disant libres and as "contraventionists," multiple times, throughout their lives. Mary Ann Martin, one of the women overlooked by Barker in 1841, was ultimately imprisoned as soi-disant libre for more than eight years, from February 1836 to June 1844. She sued the city on her release, winning an abysmal $119 in damages. The very same day as her release, Martin was convicted of contravention. She violated her court order to emigrate, for which police rearrested her in 1846. Pleading guilty, she received a one-year penitentiary sentence.[164]

The tribulations of Augustus Smith, the longtime New Orleans resident from Angostura, Venezuela, were similar. Barker failed to win Smith's release in 1841. He was still in the Police Jail in February 1842 when sympathetic grand jurors appealed for his release on the logic that he looked "mulatto" and therefore could not legally be presumed enslaved. By August 1843, Smith had been released—only to be arrested for contravention and jailed in Parish Prison in March 1845. Unlike Mary Ann Martin, Smith beat the charge, presumably by proving that he had emigrated to Louisiana before the cutoff in 1838. One year later, in March 1846, police rearrested Smith for contravention. He assembled the money to hire a lawyer, who entered a plea of "autrefois acquit"— previously acquitted of the same crime. Smith was released, only to be re-arrested for contravention one month later, in April 1846. Again, Smith beat the charge. Shortly after midnight on June 3, 1846, police arrested Smith *again*— this time as a fugitive slave. He was released from the Third Municipality Police Jail, only to be arrested for contravention *yet again*, in May 1848. For the fourth time, Smith survived his expulsion hearing, asserting his right to remain within the state: in his lawyer's words, Smith should be considered "a Citizen of the State of Louisiana, and not in the State in contravention of the Law." Undeterred, police received in 1852 a warrant for Smith's arrest as a "dangerous and suspicious" vagrant, describing him as "in the habit of prowling about at late hours of the night, and frequenting grog-shops and other disorderly places." The warrant was never served, and perhaps Smith fled the state. In all, the Afro-Venezuelan faced imprisonment in New Orleans at least nine times between 1836 and 1852: four times as a fugitive slave, four times as a free Black resident alien, and once as a vagrant.[165]

Mobile free Black workers developed new strategies to cope with Louisiana's revised policing regime. Because the act of 1842 made it easier for enslaved people to enter Louisiana than for free Black persons, free Black workers began "smuggling" themselves into Louisiana by forging slave passes and posing as enslaved. In 1847, police detained Mary Carter as she disembarked from the steamer *Little Missouri*. A search revealed two sets of documents: freedom papers and slave self-hiring papers. Under the headline "A New Way of Smuggling Free Negroes," the *Daily Picayune* noted the dangerous potential of this new strategy, which "would, if not detected, cut its way through almost every legal ordinance." A subsequent search of all Black travelers aboard the *Little Missouri* led to the detention of eight other persons "claiming to be slaves, but who were arrested, supposing them to be free": a striking inversion.[166] Two years later Phoebe Black, a white woman and notorious grifter, smuggled Kentucky freewoman Sarah Lucas into the state by disguising her as her slave (police uncovered the scheme after Black attempted to mortgage Lucas).[167] In 1859, police raided the steamship *Northern Light*, arresting "twenty blacks and mulattoes" who "represented themselves as being slaves" but whom police identified as free.[168] Others purchased forged birth records stating that they were Louisiana natives.[169]

The Crises of the 1850s

In the 1850s, as the nation's sectional schism intensified, free Black Americans faced renewed persecution throughout the South. A fresh spate of expulsion laws, voluntary enslavement laws, prohibitions on slave manumission, and free Black head taxes sought to suppress the growth of free Black populations, if not eliminate those populations entirely. The Louisiana legislature banned assemblies of free Black persons with slaves, the possession of liquor licenses by free Black persons, and the creation of any free Black "religious, charitable, scientific or literary society."[170] Dropping pretenses, officials in New Orleans began openly acknowledging that some Police Jail prisoners were out-of-state free persons.[171] A revised contravention law in 1859 provided a ten-dollar bounty for the arrest of any free Black contraventionist, reduced the time for contraventionists to emigrate from sixty days to five, and established a process for free Black voluntary enslavement.[172] In parishes west of New Orleans, white militias launched armed attacks on their free Black neighbors and white allies, massacring dozens. "*We lay it down as an incontrovertible proposition, that slave labor and free negroes are incompatible and can not exist together*," proclaimed one local newspaper, amid the carnage: "Remove the internal cancer."[173]

As the South hovered over a genocidal precipice, affluent white residents in New Orleans debated whether the state should pursue the removal of *all* free Black persons or whether certain segments of the population—reputable tradespeople, the well-to-do, or perhaps only the native-born—should be permitted to remain. Publicly, officials continued distinguishing suspicious "free negroes" from Louisiana's respectable "free colored" population. In 1856, Louisiana's supreme court reiterated that "a free man of color" in Louisiana was as distinct from a slave as "a white man" was from a slave. In 1857, when Louisiana's attorney general denounced free Black people as "prolific" criminals, "uneducated, ignorant and debauched," and petitioned for "stringent measures to diminish their number," he dutifully added that his words were "not applicable to the free colored native population, many of whom are respectable and useful men." Expulsions should not "be enforced indiscriminately against all persons, without regard to character or habits," the *Daily Picayune* concurred, in September 1859. The "true meaning and spirit" of Louisiana's exclusionary laws were "to rid this city" of free Black residents "whose known licentiousness of life, or impudence of character, or busy mischief making, works untold injury to slaveholders," and not to remove "the better portion."[174]

The climate changed after John Brown's raid on Harpers Ferry in October 1859. Contravention arrests surged.[175] Panicked free Black residents rushed to register their residency with the state.[176] The *Daily Picayune*, which until recently had pleaded restraint, began advocating the total and immediate expulsion of all free persons of African ancestry, regardless of their repute, social station, landownership, or birthplace: "Their place is not among us. . . . We cannot but rejoice at a means of getting rid of a population that cannot be classed socially."[177]

To the heedful it was becoming clear that the total expulsion of all free Black southerners—nonlocal and local, poor and landowning, transient and financially stable—was imminent. Arkansas expelled all free Black residents, effective January 1, 1860. Other state legislatures debated similar measures.[178] New vagrancy laws in Georgia and Maryland equated free Black residents with vagrants as a means of rationalizing their expulsion.[179] From Charleston in August 1860, James Marsh Johnson, a free Black property owner, described mounting despair. "It is too late," Johnson realized. "The next session [of the state legislature] will wind up the affairs of every free col[ore]d man & they will be made to leave. Those who are now hunted down have divined what is to be done with them & . . . are wisely leaving by every Steamer & Railroad. . . . The time is at hand when none may remain but them [white persons] & their slaves."[180]

Still, in New Orleans, the social, familial, and professional ties between white and free Black professionals ran deep. The harassment of Dr. Thomas Jennings, a Harvard-educated dentist and dealer in dental supplies from New York City, and his wife, Angelina Jennings, also from New York, highlight the straining protections that wealth, property ownership, repute, and community ties still provided. Thomas and Angelina Jennings had lived in New Orleans for decades. When registering their residency, Dr. Jennings had been racialized as "griffe," while his wife had been racialized as "copper colored." Widely celebrated for his dental skill and business acumen, Dr. Jennings had a personal estate valued at $5,000 in 1860. Even the virulently racist *New Orleans Daily Crescent* considered Dr. Jennings "a genius." The couple enjoyed social recognition and broad community acceptance, though neither were native-born Louisianians nor persons of local colonial ancestry. Yet in November 1860, a white dentist named Dr. James Knapp, apparently seeking to eliminate his nonwhite competitors, pressed a litany of criminal charges against three of his nonwhite rivals: Dr. Jennings, a free Black cupper and bleeder named Stephen Rogers, and an *enslaved* dentist named Charles Johnson. In court, several of the city's leading white dentists denounced Thomas and Angelina Jennings. Dr. Knapp testified that Dr. Jennings was "a dangerous person in our city," that he had heard Angelina Jennings confide that "she was entirely opposed to slavery," and that both were "engaged in the work of propagating abolition sentiment among the other free negroes and the slaves of this city." Other white dentists testified that Dr. Jennings was "dangerous" and "extremely cunning, tricky and shrewd." Yet several "gentlemen of high social standing" also testified on behalf of the couple. A prominent white cotton merchant, James Greenleaf, volunteered to post Thomas Jennings's bond. Ultimately, the court declined to expel the couple or convict them of spreading abolitionist sentiment. Four days after these charges were dismissed, Dr. Jennings was arraigned for receiving mail on another person's behalf: a bizarre charge, suggesting close police scrutiny. In May 1861, Dr. Knapp again demanded Dr. Jennings's expulsion from Louisiana, after the dentist and his wife accepted the invitation of a white hostess to a benefit gala, where the couple had "promenaded around," eaten "ice cream and cake," bid in the charity auction, consumed "refreshments, and otherwise [put] themselves on a par with the white people." Several prominent white socialites, including the mayor's wife, testified in this second trial, both for and against the Jennings. Noting that they taught Sunday school classes where "free colored children and slaves mixed," the *New Orleans Daily Crescent* assured readers that this time, Dr. Jennings's expulsion was all but guaranteed. Once again, the court demurred. Two months later, police arrested Dr. Jennings for disturbing the peace. He died of consumption in January 1862, upon which Angelina Jennings assumed control of the dentistry supply business.[181]

What in the twenty-first century might be called "racial profiling" was bounded, during the first half of the nineteenth century, by layered perceptions of dependency, reputability, transience, class, color, landownership, nativity, and community embeddedness. Angelina and Thomas Jennings's racial categorization and status as émigrés heightened their vulnerability to state violence. Their prosperity, social repute, landownership, and relationships with affluent white residents each provided degrees of protection. On the eve of the Civil War, white New Orleans was not unanimous on the status of the city's free Black residents, though it was clear to prosperous free Black residents such as Angelina and Thomas Jennings that the protections of class, reputation, and social standing were being stripped away. A new racial order was taking form, one in which free Black tradespeople and landowners would be subjected to the same police powers as vagrants, dishonorable seamen, and fugitive slaves.

CHAPTER 4

Idle and Dangerous

Poor White Workers, Freedom's Limits, and Vagrancy Law

During the 1830s, the elite merchants, planters, and businessmen of New Orleans increasingly perceived that they were incessantly swarmed by hordes of unruly vagrants. As one grand jury proclaimed in 1852, vagrants were "one of the greatest evils with which New Orleans is afflicted." The city was plagued, wrote one resident in 1831, by "a heap of vagrants of all nations who ooze crime!" It became axiomatic that vagrants promised the apocalyptic ruin of southern social order and economy. They were incapable of Christian salvation, unqualified for American citizenship, and "like the wandering Jew . . . spread consternation, death and destruction at every step." Although considered primarily an urban problem, vagrants also polluted the countryside: "Often do we see," complained the Plaquemine *Southern Sentinel*, these "destitute and ragged objects of humanity, with no apparent aim or desire, wandering along the highway."[1]

At face value, the vagrant refers to any homeless wanderer who refuses to work.[2] In practice, the category's meanings are elastic across time, place, and context. What did the crime represent to the members of Louisiana's elite landowning classes? Who were these vagrants who seemed to pollute the region? Why did their presence incite slaveholders' passionate ire?

Labor law historians have paid particular attention to vagrancy law, the most powerful and widely used legal tool for coercing free labor in nineteenth-century America.[3] Prior studies have tended to focus on the North while excluding the South, assuming that slave societies were uninterested in, or dogmatically opposed to, the coercive regulation of white labor.[4]

Yet determination to quash the vagrant was not merely rhetorical in Louisiana. Comparative examination of annual arrest data shows that between 1849 and 1861, New Orleans police maintained the highest vagrancy arrest rate of any major American city: a rate more than four times that of New York

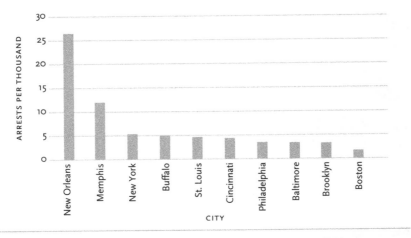

Graph 4.1. Average vagrancy arrest rates in select cities, 1849–1860.

City, nearly ten times that of Philadelphia, at least fifteen times that of Boston (graph 4.1).[5] Not even London, the city perhaps most closely associated with coercive poor law in today's popular imagination, seized vagrants at anything approaching New Orleans's rate.[6] New Orleans's exceptionally high vagrancy arrest rate was not simply a product of New Orleans's overall arrest rate, though that, too, was exceptionally high (graph 4.2); vagrancy constituted 15 percent of all arrests in New Orleans, compared to roughly 7 percent, on average, across the major cities of the Northeast.[7] Of the South's other large cities, disaggregated arrest data are available only from New Orleans and Memphis, though in Memphis, too, the vagrancy arrest rate was more than twice that of any major city in the North. Southern authorities were *not* opposed to coercing white labor through vagrancy law—quite the opposite, southern cities would seem *far more* preoccupied with the coercive regulation of poor white persons than their northern peers.

Louisiana slaveholders believed that the state had a vital part to play in the coercion of *all* menial labor: white *and* Black, free *and* enslaved. Their ideological commitments to Black servitude and to white freedom were not incompatible—at least, not irreconcilably so—with the compulsion of poor white persons who appeared criminally underproductive and dangerously rebellious. It would be difficult to overstate how important vagrancy law was to the resident slaveholders of late antebellum New Orleans or how much attention Louisiana lawmakers paid toward vagrancy policy. In vagrancy law, authorities saw a multipurpose tool for regulating flows of immigrants and

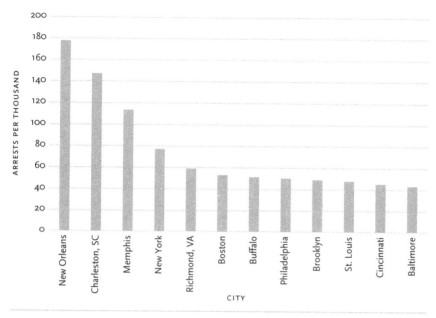

Graph 4.2. Average arrest rates for all crimes in select cities, 1849–1860.

migrants into and out of the city, criminalizing behaviors deemed deviant among the urban poor, driving down wages and disrupting workers' efforts to seek better working conditions by withholding their labor, guaranteeing a steady labor supply, and asserting control over landless peoples who seemed dangerously independent and autonomous.

Slaveholders' deep hatred of the vagrant also reflected a particular way of configuring relations among economy, freedom, and social order. Labor relations in the nineteenth-century South derived from a theory of household governance, rooted in early modern European law, which contended that social order depended on the ability of household heads to manage the lives and labor of subordinate household members. The ability of landowning white men to vote, run for public office, or make other rational managerial decisions derived from their ability to command their households: by definition, persons who could not supervise households were considered incapable of supervising themselves or of participating in civic life. Law and custom classified certain subsets of society—women, children, slaves, and hired wageworkers—as subservient members of the household and as *dependent* persons, incapable of managing their own lives and labor, who rightfully deferred control to their master or employer.[8] Critically, within this ethos, public safety and economic development were codependent. By controlling dependents' lives and labor, masters prevented disorder *and* created favorable conditions for economic prosperity. State police power also derived from this theory of social order: just as the master was obliged to regulate his household, so the state was duty bound to regulate public order within its borders. Above all else, the state was obligated to police itinerant dependents who had absconded from their masters and households entirely.[9]

When elite Louisianians denounced vagrants, they imagined white indigents of dependent status who had rebelled against this vital relationship between master and subordinate: wives who had left their husbands, children who had fled their parents, and migratory menial hirelings who worked only when they pleased and refused to commit themselves to any single employer. As innately dependent persons, vagrants lacked the capacity for self-management. It was a foregone conclusion that they would idle their time and resort to petty crime if not compelled to work. More than a source of crime and economic disfunction, vagrants seemed to undermine societal structure itself. By seeking an independence for which they were not qualified and by mismanaging their lives and labor in the process, vagrants desecrated the web of relations and restraints that propped up the entire social order. It was akin to promoting anarchy. Vagrants were autonomous, untethered, and mobile. They were unbothered by the obligations—to community, family, master—that structured southern life.

Scholarship has traditionally overlooked southern fixation on the vagrant because that fixation is at odds with how scholars have traditionally portrayed white interclass relations within the antebellum South. Before the 1990s, historians tended to emphasize how the South's commitment to white supremacy promoted interclass white solidarity and precluded the persecution of the white poor. This interpretation often relied on underestimating the number of landless white people in the South or overlooking their existence entirely.[10] In his landmark study from 1949 of southern yeomen, Frank L. Owsley argued that white southerners were "not class conscious," that southern yeomen "admired" the planter class "as a rule" and that the truly poor—the chronically impoverished, landless, and migratory—were exceedingly few in number.[11] In 1971, George Fredrickson characterized the South as a "herrenvolk democracy" where white supremacy ensured white interclass solidarity.[12] Only in recent years has a new paradigm emerged, one that emphasizes the unremitting hostility between elite southerners and the very lowest rungs of white society: the landless, itinerant, and marginalized poor who sold their labor on the open market, migrated repeatedly in search of work, and likely constituted 30–50 percent of the overall southern white population.[13]

Understanding how and why slaveholders decried, policed, and punished the vagrant is also critical to understanding how former slaveholders would approach the policing of Black labor after slavery's destruction. In no small measure, the shift from policing enslaved people as maroons to policing wage-workers through vagrancy law was already well underway decades before Emancipation in the cities of the South. Two decades before the Civil War, New Orleans led the nation in the development of prisons, policing systems, and criminal laws aimed at the coercion of free wageworkers. These late antebellum reforms provided key blueprints for the subsequent readjustment of criminal justice systems following the Civil War.

Defining the Vagrant

Vagrancy laws have a long history. The laws first emerged in late medieval Europe as rising labor demand, in the aftermath of the Black Death, created a growing class of landless, migratory, "masterless" farmhands who appeared removed from their traditional feudal restraints.[14] These laws were imported to the colonial Americas, where they continued to regulate persons of dependent status—unruly women, runaway indentured servants, itinerant paupers—who appeared to have absconded from their rightful masters. Because they did not own land, dependent poor white persons were considered not economically autonomous and thus incapable of making rational decisions. Alexander Hamilton called them "persons of indigent fortunes" who "have no will of their own" and belonged "under the immediate dominion of others."[15]

Vagrancy arrests are *preemptive*, executed on the logic that vagrants *will* commit crimes, even if they have yet to do so. Vagrants' future criminality was a foregone conclusion: "Preventive justice is forced," Edward Livingston realized in 1824.[16] As one New Orleans judge explained in 1850, it was "better to check the evil in its bed than to wait for its blooming . . . [better] to prevent the commission of great crimes, than to punish them after they were committed."[17] In 1866, legal scholar Christopher Tiedeman summarized this logic: "The vagrant has been very appropriately described as the chrysalis of every species of criminal. A wanderer through the land, without home ties, idle, and without apparent means of support, what but criminality is to be expected from such a person? If vagrancy could be successfully combatted, if every one was engaged in some lawful calling, the infractions of the law would be reduced to a surprisingly small number; and it is not to be wondered at that an effort is so generally made to suppress vagrancy." Yet the danger with this line of reasoning, Tiedeman recognized, was that the category's vagueness armed police with incredible discretionary power. Police needed merely to suspect vagrancy, or perceive "lines of criminality upon the face," to warrant arrest. There were no consistent criteria for evaluating vagrancy; as the Ohio Supreme Court ruled in 1881, "The offense does not consist in particular acts but in the mode of life, the habits and practices of the accused." The appearance of poverty, unemployment, homelessness, itinerancy, raggedness, or suspiciousness each *strongly indicated* vagrancy, but proof of employment, property, or respectability did not refute vagrancy.[18]

Louisiana's use of vagrancy law to coerce undesirable populations was as old as the colony itself. The French colonial attorney general had ordered the expulsion of vagrants, citing their habit of socializing with the enslaved, in 1763. The territory's congressional delegate had reported that patrols used vagrancy law to harass Ouachita people in 1808. New Orleans police had used vagrancy law to eject flatboatmen migrating from Kentucky to Texas in 1820. Ironically, some of Louisiana's oldest families descended from convicted vagrants, expelled from France to the New World between 1717 and 1720.[19]

Yet preoccupation with vagrancy surged throughout the United States during the early nineteenth century, as a series of profound social, demographic, and economic transformations undermined the system of household governance upon which social order had relied. Advancements in agricultural production and transportation infrastructure, the decline of apprenticeship and indentured servitude in the aftermath of the American Revolution, and the growth of industrial manufacturing had produced a growing number of mobile wageworkers who sold their labor on the market, traveled between communities in search of work, and seemed divorced from the management of any natural master. Exploding rates of international immigration further added to the growing ranks of migratory, masterless peoples who worked for wages. These changes brought urbanization and mounting economic inequality. To many, it seemed that the bonds that structured society—the duties of child to parent, worker to employer, neighbor to community, and dependent to master—were unraveling. The "ties which connect society have been relaxed," realized a committee of Philadelphia social reformers in 1827: "The incentives to industry have been weakened." From the ashes of traditional household governance emerged a "world of strangers," cities and towns crowded with mobile wageworkers who seemed untethered from their natural allegiances and restraints.[20]

Even though the South as a whole remained overwhelmingly rural and reliant on slave labor, by the 1850s, much of the urban South had transitioned from near-exclusive reliance on enslaved labor to primary reliance on hired wage labor.[21] This upheaval triggered a unique set of anxieties in the urban South. "We are losing a valuable, manageable, and healthy population for one, in every sense the reverse," warned one Charleston resident in 1853, "the submissive, acclimated, non-voting negro pushed aside by the turbulent, feverish, naturalized foreigner." "It will soon be rare to see a black [*sic*] acting coachmen, carmen, or even porters," fretted an anxious Richmond resident in 1847.[22] These transformations were particularly dramatic in Louisiana, where by 1860, 43 percent of white residents lived in urban areas, over four-fifths of whom worked as unskilled or semiskilled wageworkers. In New Orleans the enslaved share of the population fell from 24 percent to 6 percent between 1830 and 1860, while the share of white persons skyrocketed from 43 percent to 85 percent.[23]

The composition of New Orleans's ruling elite was also changing. For a century, elite plantation owners, predominantly of French ancestry, had controlled the city's politics and economy. Now, a new caste of bankers, merchants, and businessmen were ascendant. Abdiel Crossman, elected mayor in 1846, was a shopkeeper and banker from Maine; Charles Waterman, elected in 1856, was a hardware merchant from New York; his successor, Virginia native Gerald Stith, was a printer and the de facto editor of the New Orleans *Daily Picayune*. None of these men were Louisiana born, whereas all their elected predecessors had been natives of either Louisiana or France. They were slaveholders in the sense that they held small handfuls of men and women in bondage, mostly as house servants, but their wealth did not derive—at least, not directly—from the toil of dozens of enslaved plantation hands.[24]

Throughout the nation, the vagrant came to embody the powerful anxieties wrought by the transition to wage labor and disruption of traditional household governance. North and South, law enforcement agents relied on vagrancy law to target poor, alienated populations—beggars, prostitutes, charlatans, tramps—who seemed to embody, and were themselves produced by, these profound economic and social upheavals. In enforcing vagrancy law, antebellum authorities were bound by few constitutional limitations or due process rights. When a Portland woman challenged her summary seizure without the benefit of trial in 1834, Maine's state supreme court ruled that vagrants, like "idiots and insane persons," cannot "exercise the rights of citizens" and "have no just right to complain."[25] Summary roundups were standard and routine. When New York City's mayor ordered a crackdown on street prostitutes in 1855, police summarily seized hundreds of unaccompanied poor women as vagrants, denying them due process on the logic that vagrants "had no rights."[26]

Yet while summary arrest and conviction were features of vagrancy laws' enforcement throughout the nation, the meanings and anxieties that southerners and northerners attached to the vagrant increasingly diverged during the antebellum period. In the North, the rise of wage labor relations drove the growth of a free labor ideology that celebrated the wageworker's ability to achieve economic independence though thrift, self-reliance, and industriousness. There the vagrant came to be imagined as an "able-bodied beggar"—a person who appeared physically capable of work yet was jobless and homeless—whose voluntary choice to reject honest employment and rely on poor relief seemed to reflect a dangerous refutation of the qualities necessary for economic uplift. In the North, social reformers increasingly justified vagrancy laws as necessary tools for drilling the free labor ethos into the deviant poor: compulsion, in other words, designed to teach paupers how to be free.[27] Yet while the North drifted toward a free labor ideal, the South remained wedded to household governance and the theory of master-servant relations embedded therein. The growing abolitionist movement only deepened southern slaveholders' reactionary conviction that certain members of society—women, children, slaves, hirelings—were innately dependent persons who required their masters' guidance. Southern and northern ideas surrounding vagrancy always bore far more similarity than difference; furthermore, every community's understanding of vagrancy bore the stamp of local market conditions. But if northern societal reformers tended to imagine the vagrant as an able-bodied beggar who rejected the free labor ideal, the southerner tended to imagine a masterless and migratory dependent whose autonomy, transience, and lack of attachments threatened the web of hierarchical relationships on which social order relied.[28]

This was a divergence in emphasis, not in fundamental doctrine. North and South, landowners regularly denounced vagrants in harsh terms, decried their apparent refusal to work, and suggested that vagrants should be excised from public life. Yet this divergence was clearly manifest in dissimilar systems of poor relief. Scholars of northern poor relief have noted welfare agents' deep preoccupation with distinguishing able-bodied beggars from the "deserving poor." Scholars of southern poor relief have found a different pattern: there, the distinction between "worthy" and "unworthy" poor was "transmuted," Michael Katz writes, "into a division between neighbors and strangers." Similarly, Barbara Bellows finds that a "dichotomy" between "familiar faces" and "threatening . . . strangers" structured the distribution of charity in antebellum Charleston, Richmond, and Savannah: "Fear of strangers, vagrants, and vagabonds better describes the antipathy aimed at some indigents of the city." While northern communities constructed almshouses, southern communities tended to continue to rely on the "outdoor" poor relief model, dolling out aid directly to families who were recognized members of the community. Tellingly, antebellum New Orleans refused to build an almshouse—rare, for an antebellum city of its size—for fear of provisioning vagrants.[29]

As the white wageworker displaced the slave within New Orleans's labor market, the vagrant eclipsed the maroon within the nightmares of Louisiana's propertied classes. By the 1840s it was the vagrant—not the maroon—whom authorities identified as the primary threat to social order. New Orleans joined other southern cities in building new workhouse systems for the correction of "vagrant" white persons. Workhouse systems for white vagrants were built in Louisville (ca. 1830), New Orleans (1841), St. Louis (1843), Baton Rouge (ca. 1852), Baltimore (1854), Richmond (1855), Charleston (1856), Memphis (1857), Nashville (1858), and Augusta and Lynchburg (both under construction by 1861, though not completed until after the Civil War). These joined preexisting workhouse systems in Alexandria and Mobile.[30] The incarceration rate in New Orleans's workhouse system was high, though far lower than incarceration rates of enslaved people within the city's police jail system. In 1844, New Orleans's three workhouses received roughly 2,300 admittances, virtually all of whom were white—equivalent to 3.2 imprisonments for every hundred white residents. Between June 1856 and June 1857, the City Workhouse reported 4,469 admittances, equivalent to 3.6 imprisonments per every hundred white residents, and higher than the present-day jail admission rates of New York City, Los Angeles, or Chicago.[31]

The summary seizure of white indigents as vagrants was not without controversy in Louisiana. This was the age of Jacksonian Democracy, when American popular culture and politics celebrated the social and political equality of all white men, and some Jacksonian Democrats protested that vagrancy laws violated the inalienable liberties of the white worker. Vagrancy law trampled "the rights, the freedom, and the constitutional and personal liberty of the whole laboring people of the great valley of the Mississippi," one impassioned attorney argued during a four-hour oration in 1842. A grand jury denounced Louisiana's vagrancy law in 1846 as an "unjust, partial, and tyrannical exercise of power," opposed "to the spirit of our institutions, and repugnant to the established and fundamental principle that for every offence there shall be a defined and specific punishment"—a fiery rebuke that prompted the resignation of New Orleans's attorney general, but not before he, too, denounced vagrancy law as "the most tyrannous of laws," by which virtually any laborer at any time might suffer the "misfortune to have fallen under the notice of the police as a vagabond." In 1850, several New Orleans judges released nearly all vagrants from the city's workhouses, ruling that their confinement without jury trial was unconstitutional.[32]

Yet the laws' supporters countered that the preemptive seizure of vagrants was simply too essential to public safety. They cited a growing body of higher court rulings that affirmed the states' right to prevent future crimes by preemptively seizing dangerous populations. The US Supreme Court affirmed the principle of preventative seizure in 1837, ruling that states had a fundamental obligation to "provide precautionary measures against the moral pestilence of paupers, vagabonds, and possibly convicts." In 1842, the court affirmed the

Fugitive Slave Act by reasoning that the power to arrest fugitive slaves, even if they had yet to break local law, was analogous to the states' unquestionable right to seize "idlers, vagabonds, and paupers," whose "depredations and evil example. . . . may endanger the peace and good order of society."[33]

After 1850, Louisiana's summary seizure of vagrants was no longer subject to serious debate. In 1851, the Louisiana Supreme Court refused to hear a challenge to the state's vagrancy law, arguing that the summary seizure of vagrants was simply beyond question. A new crime law in 1855 made it illegal to knowingly harbor a vagrant, increased the maximum penalty for vagrancy to three years at hard labor, and further expanded the category's subjectivity by establishing that a person was vagrant if he or she *appeared* vagrant in the eyes of the arresting officer.[34] In 1856, a New Orleans judge nullified vagrants' right to habeas corpus (with the exception of cases involving juveniles), as under the law of 1855, police *perception* of vagrancy constituted inarguable proof of the crime.[35] Persons convicted of vagrancy would not regain access to habeas corpus in Louisiana until 1868.[36]

Policing the Vagrant

New Orleans's criminal justice system classified vagrants into four types: "loafers," the "lewd and abandoned," "juvenile vagrants," and the "dangerous and suspicious" (graph 4.3).[37] What united these seemingly unrelated forms of deviance was the presumption of their dangerous disconnect from customary power relationships and rejection of their natural master. "Loafers" were understood to be transients who refused to work and lacked an employer's supervision. The "lewd and abandoned" were perceived to be sexually depraved women who rejected their obligations to husbands and home. "Juvenile vagrants" had defied parental authority. The "dangerous and suspicious" were perceived to be traveling conmen, forgers, counterfeiters, pickpockets, and gamblers. There was some disagreement over whether this final group truly qualified as vagrant, because not all of them were impoverished. Yet it was also understood that these tricksters were vagrant in the sense that they relied on dishonest intimacies—false sincerity, deceptive charisma, and self-misrepresentation—establishing illegitimate social relationships that usurped legitimate forms of public authority and power.[38] All four types were perceived as wanderers, further disrupting normative power relations by rejecting allegiance to their natural kin network or community.

"Loafing" men and "lewd and abandoned" women further disrupted social relations by violating normative gender roles. In refusing to work, loafers failed to support their families while rejecting the industriousness and economic

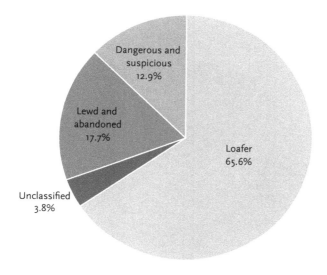

Graph 4.3. Classification of convicted vagrants committed to the Third Munici-pality Workhouse, January 1850–April 1851.

self-reliance integral to nineteenth-century masculinity. By wandering provoc-atively in public, "lewd" women rejected domesticity and, it was presumed, yielded to vulgar sexual passions. Tellingly, antebellum police forces commonly used vagrancy law to police prostitution (legal in most communities) and ha-rass persons who might today self-identify as gay, nonbinary, or transgender.[39]

In New Orleans, accused vagrants were summarily tried by municipal jus-tices of the peace, known as recorders. During the trials of men, recorders challenged the prisoner to produce evidence of steady employment under a consistent employer.[40] During the trials of women, recorders challenged the prisoner to produce evidence of her virtue and domestic respectability.[41] No evidence of vagrancy, beyond the arresting officer's visual discernment, was relevant. Only the testimony of a reputable employer, husband, or parent guar-anteed exoneration.[42] Unsurprisingly, the conviction rate was high.

On conviction, adult vagrants were committed to New Orleans's workhouse system, typically for one to six months, while juvenile vagrants were sentenced to the House of Refuge until their apprenticeship, their twenty-first birthday, or the house's managing board determined that they were reformed. Within both institutions, inmates performed hard labor: breaking rocks, picking oakum, manufacturing simple tools, cutting and carving paving stones.[43] Forced work was seen as both rehabilitative and retributive, a means of teaching vagrants

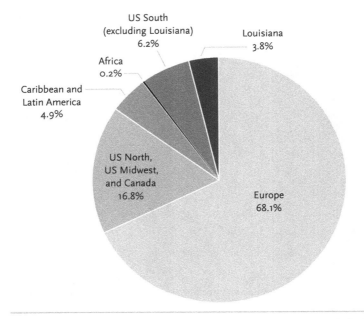

Graph 4.4. Birthplaces of convicted vagrants committed to the Third Municipality Workhouse, March 1846–April 1851.

how to be industrious and a strategy for deterring the further immigration of vagrants, since it was axiomatic that vagrants hated nothing more than work. By performing forced labor, vagrants would also directly repay the financial debt they had accrued by withholding their labor and parasitically leeching resources from society.[44]

Louisiana slaveholders described vagrants in uniform terms: all vagrants were outcasts, impoverished, dirty, unemployed, lazy, transient, untrustworthy, parasitic. Yet actual records of persons charged with vagrancy paint a far less coherent picture. For example, court reporters often commented on the socioeconomic diversity of persons charged with vagrancy: they were a "motley throng" of "great variety," showcasing "all kinds of mechanics and working men." There was no "uniformity of appearance among them," one courtroom reporter observed. "The dress of some of them might be called respectable."[45]

There was some truth to the perception that all vagrants were outsiders: indeed, workhouse records reveal that virtually everyone jailed for vagrancy in New Orleans had come from someplace else. In the Third Municipality Workhouse, only 10.0 percent of vagrants were native-born southerners, and only 3.8 percent were native-born Louisianians (graph 4.4).[46] Of those locally born prisoners, nearly half were free Black Louisianians, though those were almost the only Black prisoners. Put another way, police applied the vagrant category toward nonnative white persons; very rarely, police also extended the category to free Black Louisiana natives, perhaps to distinguish them from the free Black travelers held in police jails.[47]

Yet while practically all vagrants were nonnative, not all vagrants considered themselves nonlocal: many arrestees protested that they were longtime New Orleans residents who considered the city their permanent home.[48] In seizing vagrants, police relied on subjective cues in accent, dress, or behavior that encoded impoverished Otherness. Manuel Perez, a native of Panama, was arrested at least twice for vagrancy; his "exterior," "countenance," and "mothertongue" all "bore a suspicious quality that instantly attracted the policeman's optics." Public records identify Perez as a cigar maker and longtime local resident who would eventually marry and raise a family in the city.[49] The "countenance" of Henry Lewis, an Irish immigrant arrested for loafing suspiciously along the levee, also suggested vagrancy. Census records suggest that Lewis, another married resident with a family, only "loafed" along the levee because he worked as a levee "warehouseman."[50] Police arrested Marianne Prudhomme, the French-born wife of a common laborer and a "well known and troublesome character," for vagrancy at least four times between 1848 and 1856. The Prudhommes were poor and mobile: after immigrating from France to New Orleans in 1841, they initially moved to Missouri, only to return to New Orleans by 1846.[51] Yet like Perez and Lewis, Marianne Prudhomme was not precisely a homeless transient, as the law implied.

Slaveholders tended to view the mobility of poor people such as the Prudhommes as indicative of intrinsic moral failing. It was understood that vagrants traveled to evade their responsibilities to their families, neighbors, and employers. Vagrants were "strangers . . . who live by preying on the honest portion of the community," explained the Daily Picayune. "No man can be a good citizen without a home," decried the Baton Rouge Daily Comet amid a diatribe against vagrants, "for a floating attachment is no attachment."[52]

These incriminations masked the reality that among the South's landless poor, regular migration, like that of the Prudhommes, was the norm by the late antebellum period. As prices for arable farmland and enslaved people boomed, the dream of landownership was becoming increasingly out of reach with each passing year for poor white southerners. Among the 30 to 50 percent of white southerners who owned no land, virtually none appears in the same neighborhood on consecutive censuses, suggesting that poor white residents almost never stayed put for very long. For the landless, packing up and seeking better terms elsewhere was one of the only available strategies for improving livelihood: a possible path for escaping low wages, exploitative working conditions, abuse, and perhaps even poverty itself.[53]

The Vagrant "Loafer" and New Orleans's
Seasonal Economic Cycle

Most people charged with vagrancy in New Orleans were arrested while "loafing," and more than 90 percent of these vagrant "loafers" were men.[54] Police patrolled the city's streets, parks, and wharfs for men who looked poor but idle, demanding that they provide proof of their employment by producing a contract, paystub, or employment voucher.[55] Inactivity was evidence of guilt; as one policeman testified, he had arrested a suspected vagrant "because he wasn't sayin or doin anything at all." Certain behaviors or appearances attracted more police attention than others: in particular, police detained laborers found gambling, drinking, lounging, or sleeping in public parks during normal working hours, as well as idling persons who somehow appeared unsavory, disruptive, alien, foreign, disheveled, suspicious, or rude. The *Daily Picayune* referred to "that indescribable air of vagrancy," impossible to precisely define but "readily perceive[d]" by "those at all familiar with the looks of that class."[56]

If the arresting officer was uncertain, a search of the suspect's pockets typically confirmed vagrancy. Playing cards, dice, and suspicious instruments were considered incontestable proof of loaferdom. Frederick Delorme's vagrancy was confirmed after a search revealed "two packs of cards, a counterfeit dollar, and seven pieces of dice." A search of Michael Burns's pockets proved his vagrancy by revealing "an ugly carving knife, a silver spoon, and two suspicious keys."[57]

Most convicted vagrants protested that they were not, strictly speaking, idle and unemployed (graph 4.5).[58] Rather, they shifted between several short-term, unstable economic activities—day laboring, unlicensed peddling, washing, sowing, scavenging, pawning secondhand goods—that lacked written contracts, reliable hours, or consistent employers. Matt Collins, arrested for vagrancy while beating dust from carpets, explained that he sometimes performed household tasks for hire, endured periodic bouts of unemployment, and "sometimes steamboated it, and sometimes went to sea." Irish immigrant Michael Daffy described similar rhythms of short-term, intermittent employment: "I am a laboring man. Sometimes I work on the Levee, sometimes in the cotton yard, sometimes steamboating." Maritime workers were particularly vulnerable to vagrancy arrest, since they were nominally unemployed, or forced to find various odd jobs, in between their deployments; in the Third Municipality Workhouse, 25.5 percent of vagrants claimed to be sailors or steamboat workers.[59]

Whether a person's employment status was stable enough to preclude vagrancy was subjective and imprecise. One vagrancy trial, involving a property-less New Orleans renter who sold oysters and worked as a pimp, prompted

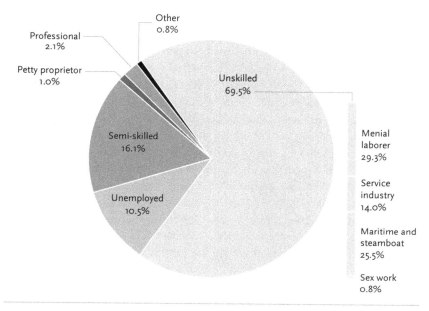

Graph 4.5. Occupations of convicted vagrants committed to the Third Municipality Workhouse, March 1846–April 1851.

courtroom debate over "what constitutes a vagrant?" The arresting policeman argued that the man was vagrant because his "source of revenue" was the sinful behavior of vagrant women, rationalizing that financial dependency on vagrants, ipso facto, qualified one as vagrant. The prisoner countered that he was not a vagrant because he also sold oysters and thus qualified as a "proprietor." The judge chose a third definition: the prisoner was not a vagrant because the regularity with which he paid rent suggested economic stability.[60]

As with constant mobility, this reliance on multiple income streams was criminalized by landed elites but was an essential survival strategy among the antebellum landless poor. Labor demand in nineteenth-century America was extremely prone to seasonal variation. By 1850, perhaps two-thirds of all American laborers were "seasonally and involuntarily idle for about four months each year." During off-seasons, survival depended on thrift, judicious budgeting, and flexibility. Many workers turned to unstable, episodic, and illegal sources of revenue—scavenging, pawning, gambling, prostitution, performing odd jobs, petty crime—to make it through the months when full-time work dried up.[61]

New Orleans's labor market was especially prone to seasonal fluctuation and short-term, uncontracted employment. By 1850, New Orleans had the smallest manufacturing workforce of any major American city. Two-thirds of all free men worked in transportation and shipping: the port *was* the city's economy, with seasonal fluctuations in port activity impacting virtually every other economic sector. Yet despite a negligible industrial sector and high seasonal fluctuation, New Orleans boasted a massive population of free menial laborers— about 41,000, in 1860—because when the port was active, wages were among the highest in the nation, with unskilled menial laborers earning between $1 and $1.50 per day.[62]

New Orleans's business season stretched from November to July, cresting in December and January as sugar, cotton, and agricultural products from the Midwest—what *Frank Leslie's Illustrated Newspaper* called "the immense agricultural wealth of half the Union"—moved through the port en route to domestic and international markets. During these months, New Orleans was a vibrant center of speculation, entertainment, trade, and frenetic economic activity. Bankers, merchants, planters, speculators, wholesalers, and shoppers flooded into the city to buy, sell, trade, and haggle in every imaginable trade good, luxury item, and currency. A witness to the annual event described flatboats loaded with "pork, bacon, potatoes, onions, turnips and Ceres only knows what else" from the midwestern United States; schooners bringing manufactured goods "from the ports of the north and east"; steamers "burthened with foreign articles of luxury" from Europe. The docks burst with feverish energy: "Such forests of masts!" one December visitor exclaimed. "Such flaunting colours and flags, of every hue and of every country!" The entire city assumed an "air of briskness." A "confused medley of sounds" filled the streets. Everywhere was "life and activity . . . excitement and turmoil."[63] By the 1840s, estimates of the size of the "floating population" drawn into the city each winter ranged from 30,000 to 50,000.[64] According to one contemporary source, this influx included some 20,000 to 30,000 white migrant laborers, drawn to the city "by high rates of wages."[65] Charleston, also a major cotton export center, experienced similar seasonal population growth.[66]

Preparations for the annual influx began as early as August with the refurbishing of billiard halls, saloons, curiosity shops, arcades, theaters, boardinghouses, and brothels that serviced the mass of young, unaccompanied men from out of state. Typically, the city hired temporary policemen to handle this seasonal influx. As the first waves of strangers began to arrive, runners employed by the cheapest boardinghouses choked the docks in their search for customers.[67]

Vagrancy arrest rates mirrored the rhythms of this economic cycle, albeit in surprising ways. Typically, studies find direct correlation between vagrancy arrest rates and unemployment rates: when work was plentiful, vagrancy arrests

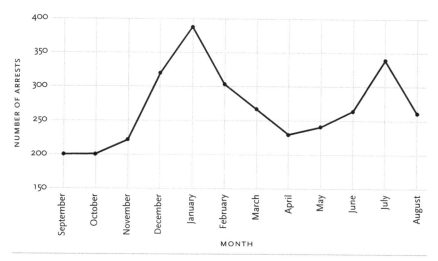

Graph 4.6. Monthly averages of vagrancy arrests, 1852–1861.

were rare, suggesting that police targeted homelessness, panhandling, and other behaviors associated with seasonal poverty.[68] The opposite was true in New Orleans: when work was plentiful, vagrancy arrests surged (graph 4.6).[69] This counterintuitive seasonal pattern points to the particular way that local slaveholders conceptualized vagrancy. Rather than targeting the seasonally impoverished, New Orleans used vagrancy law to regulate flows of migrant labor.

Even as they celebrated the wealth that business season generated, slaveholding Louisianians feared that the season attracted a tidal wave of vagrants—freeloading parasites who refused to work, driven from the North and Midwest—who sowed disorder, economic inefficiency, and crime. "This State, and particularly this city," one judge grumbled, "receives every winter a large accession of these criminally idle persons—of men who can and will not work—who have no means of livelihood, and who, if left to remain here and run at large, are almost certain to endanger the lives and property of our citizens." A "horde of desperate villains," echoed the *New Orleans Daily Crescent*, "prey on the community for a few months, and then return to the northern cities, where they belong." "The vicious, the idle, the dishonest and the depraved, all flock hither, thinking that New Orleans, in its season of business and bustle, is a favorable theatre on which to practice their wiles and their villainy," warned the *Daily Picayune*. "*Look Out!*" the same paper cautioned in November: "Vagrants from every where are flocking in upon us. We earnestly recommend caution."[70]

There doubtless were many career criminals, charlatans, and confidence men among the laboring masses that visited New Orleans every winter. James Seward, a free Black man born in Oneida County, New York, recounted from a St. Louis jail cell how he had played the Mississippi River valley's economic cycle to his advantage. During the business season of 1836–37, Seward sold counterfeit bills in Kentucky before retreating to New Orleans for the winter to work as a waiter as wages there surged. During the season of 1837–38, Seward used money robbed from a store in Galena, Illinois, to buy stolen groceries in New Orleans, which he resold in St. Louis, all while eliminating his shipping and travel expenses by working as a riverboat hand. Seward resolved to repeat the cycle every year: "By purchasing from smugglers and by saving the freights, which we could, by shipping as steward, cook or cabin boy, and by investing the proceeds in fresh butter, eggs, &c., we could soon realize a handsome sum."[71] Swindlers such as Seward, who fluidly shifted between licit and illicit economies, learned to ride the river valley's seasonal economic rhythms like surfers atop a wave.

Yet the bulk of the vagrant armada that terrorized the minds of Louisiana's well-to-do every winter were not so much drawn to the city by lust for crime as they were pushed and pulled into the city by structural economic factors. In the North and Midwest, seasonal economic activity peaked between July and September, when crops were harvested. Work slowed to a complete standstill in the winter, when, as one New York newspaper put it, laborers were left "to beg, steal, or go to the poorhouse." Thousands turned to urban panhandling and thus risked vagrancy arrest.[72] Yet at the precise moment that unemployment rates spiked in the North and Midwest, employment opportunities abounded, and wages were high, in New Orleans and other southern export centers.

The rise of inexpensive transportation made possible seasonal migration between the North and South, particularly among young, unmarried men. By the 1850s, the average price of a steamboat deck ticket from Louisville to New Orleans was three dollars. The average price from Pittsburgh to New Orleans was six dollars. Steamboats charged even lower rates for menial laborers willing to work for their transport, as many did, by hauling wood for the engine's boilers.[73] Once in New Orleans, an unskilled laborer from the Northeast could reasonably expect to recoup his travel expenses within a week.

The seasonal labor influx taxed the local housing supply.[74] Census records show that many of the persons convicted of vagrancy in New Orleans were not homeless in the literal sense of sleeping outside: rather, they often pooled their resources, renting rooms from the local poor and congregating in majority male, nonfamily groups. Antonio Lopez, a native of Mexico and convicted vagrant, appears on the 1850 census as a renter cohabitating with Irish-born and German-born laborers in the household of a German-born butcher. Thomas

Hearn, an Irish immigrant and another convicted vagrant, shared a house with ten other immigrants from Ireland, most of them listed as laborers.[75]

Thus Louisiana's slaveholders were correct in perceiving a mass migration of poor, propertyless people every winter.[76] Yet to criminalize this population en masse was to obscure the realities of an interdependent economic ecosystem that slaveholders themselves had created. In much the same way that slaveholders relied on enslaved people to grow and harvest crops, and bankers to finance the purchase of land, machinery, and slaves, slaveholders depended on "vagrant" migrant labor to operate the steamships that carried their crops downriver, to unload and reload all that sugar and cotton at New Orleans's port, and to operate the oceangoing ships that carried their products to overseas markets.

The beginning of New Orleans's business season also coincided with the period of peak international immigration through New Orleans, because the same ships that arrived to collect cotton had relatively little cargo to bring from Europe and thus offered exceptionally inexpensive passenger fares. Some cotton ships completed a second transatlantic crossing, resulting in a second, smaller wave of immigrants in May. By 1840, these low fares had propelled New Orleans into the second busiest immigrant port of entry in the United States, after New York City. The New Orleans route offered the cheaper path to the American West, though also the more dangerous route, due to the longer transatlantic journey and prevalence of yellow fever in Louisiana. Unlike New York, New Orleans had no formal immigrant screening mechanism: as a result, this route was also favored by the poorest, disabled, sickly, or infirm who doubted their ability to pass close inspection.[77]

Timing was everything for immigrants passing through New Orleans. Often unable to pay for their entire journey in one lump sum, the poorest immigrants traveled in stages, scheduling their stopovers in different port cities to coincide with each city's peak economic season. Joseph and Rosina Eder, Bavarian immigrants who reached New Orleans during the winter of 1853–54, had first stopped in Bremen, where "during the summer there is always much work." Reaching New Orleans in winter, the Eders were awestruck by the ample employment opportunities: "There are no poor people here. . . . We have not seen a single man begging. . . . [Joseph] found work at once. . . . Every one can earn enough in a short time to acquire a pleasant estate and to have a carefree life."[78] That spring, the Eders moved onward to Texas. This multistage immigration strategy required judicious budgeting and timing. Any miscalculation, injury, sickness, or arrest could drain funds entirely, trapping travelers in New Orleans past the period of readily available employment. One British philanthropist warned Irish immigrants of the dangers of poor timing: "Unless New Orleans itself be your destination, go at once to the interior of the country and scatter. . . . Do not loiter until your money is spent, luggage held by boardinghouse and you are thrown out on the street as beggars."[79]

In addition to policing migrants, police used vagrancy law as a de facto immigrant regulatory mechanism, seizing certain persons—the disabled, suspicious, and particularly unkempt—shortly after their arrival. In 1843, one grand jury described how "people wholly unknown to the police and who have landed on our shore but a few days previous, are lodged in the work house, for six, eight, ten months" on the basis of their suspicious appearance. Tellingly, the closest thing Louisiana had to formal immigration regulations was a section of the state's vagrancy law of 1818, which required that vessels post security— capped at $300 per passenger—to protect against the event that any "become a vagrant" or commit a crime within two years.[80]

If ever convicted of vagrancy, migrants often had little choice but to leave. One British tourist was awed by the lengths the New Orleans police would go to harass persons previously detained as vagrants. "There is a strong body of police here, and some of their powers are autocratically autocratic: thus, a person once committed as a vagrant is liable to be re-imprisoned by them if met in the street unemployed." He recounted how a poor workingman had begged a shopkeeper for permission "to lie concealed in his store during the day, lest the police should re-imprison him before he could get on board one of the steamers to take him up the river." It was ironic and perhaps "cruelly arbitrary," the Brit felt, that policemen had made it impossible for the man to search for work.[81] Indeed, most "loafers" appear to have fled the city: in the Third Municipality Workhouse, the recidivism rate was only 3.4 percent among men jailed for vagrant "loafing" but well over 20 percent among other inmates.[82]

The frenetic economic activity slowed to a crawl in the late spring and early summer as the city emptied in preparation for the arrival of yellow fever. Summer was the season of economic "paralysis" and "business torpidity." These was an air of "uncertainty . . . mental anxiety" and "failure" among those few hapless immigrants and migrants still trapped in the city, the *Daily Picayune* noted. They lingered nervously in bars, clinging to the "illusion that something will 'turn up' for them." According to the paper, their vagrancy arrest was inevitable.[83] Indeed, a second surge in the vagrancy arrest rate occurred every July, suggesting that police used vagrancy law to drive out surplus laborers— foreign-born immigrants and domestic migrants alike—as the business season ended.

Threatening poor workers with arrest for vagrant "loafing" served different functions at various stages of New Orleans's economic cycle. Through vagrancy law, police regulated the flow of migrants and immigrants into New Orleans, excluding certain persons from participating in the economic frenzy while po-licing poor strangers' behaviors as they remained within the city. The threat of vagrancy arrest also established and enforced an intense normative pressure on these guest workers: communicating that they could remain in the city only insofar as they worked, only insofar as they behaved themselves, and only so long as their work was needed. At the end of the economic cycle, police used vagrancy law to push surplus migrant and immigrant workers back out of the city. Throughout the year, police simultaneously used vagrancy law to regulate the behaviors and working habits of the city's long-term poor residents, primar-ily by criminalizing their reliance on short-term, unstable economic activities during the economic off-season. This entire coercive system was rationalized by the criminalization of poor hirelings as innately dependent persons: chron-ically lazy, criminally dangerous, and characteristically incapable of properly managing themselves without coercive state pressure.

An irony of this system was that policemen were themselves recruited from the same populations that vagrancy arrests targeted. Most New Orleans police-men were young, unmarried, and foreign-born. Annual turnover was high: during the 1840s, one officer in four had lived in New Orleans for less than one year.[84] For these itinerant white men, service on the police force provided a steady wage, a degree of status, protection from state violence, and feelings of power over the city's dispossessed masses.

Policing Other Vagrant Types: The Lewd, Juvenile, and Suspicious

Seizing "loafing" men was only part—though the largest part—of how police used vagrancy law to manage the city's working poor. New Orleans's police also used vagrancy law to suppress behaviors among women who seemed to threaten hierarchical gender relations. Between 15 and 20 percent of all va-grancy arrests were of women; of those, roughly two-thirds were categorized as "lewd and abandoned."[85] Many were sex workers, though technically, pros-titution was legal in New Orleans. By policing sex work through vagrancy law, police delineated prostitution's geography and visibility, regulated publicly im-permissible licentious behavior, and perhaps extracted a small "sin tax" in fines and bribes.[86] Daytime vagrancy raids on the red-light district were common, indicating enforcement of a de facto prostitution curfew.[87]

Poor white women accused of living or sleeping with enslaved men—and thus subverting southern racial and sexual hierarchies simultaneously—were also policed through vagrancy law. Policemen charged Eliza Norman with "lewd and abandoned" vagrancy after she was "found in a room sleeping with a slave negro." Mary West was charged with "lewd and abandoned" vagrancy after being discovered "in close companionship" with "a slave named Aaron." Alice Crawford was convicted of vagrancy for her "amalgamationist" bedroom habits. Catherine Rutledge, an Irish immigrant, was convicted for refusing to "hide away" her "disgraceful" multiracial newborn. Policemen charged sex workers Elizabeth Carr and Susan Daily with vagrancy on discovering that their brothel keeper was an enslaved man living as though free.[88]

While "lewd and abandoned" clearly implied sexual impropriety, many "lewd" women had violated various other rules of feminine domesticity, unrelated to their sexual habits: cursing in public, creating public spectacles, drinking with men in grogshops. Police charged Maria Basecala with "lewd" vagrancy for "sitting [on a doorstep] in an unseemly manner." They arrested Julia Wilson in a coffeehouse, "where she was playing cards, and drinking whiskey with a crowd of sailors." Mary Lynch was convicted of vagrancy for wearing men's clothes, Eliza Terry for "running about the streets in her chemise."[89]

Just as vagrancy law policed women who seemed to subvert normative gender relations, so the category of "juvenile vagrancy" criminalized children who subverted child-parent relations: teen runaways, homeless orphans, rebellious adolescents, and young malcontents whose delinquency was attributed to parental neglect. Between 1847 and 1857, the New Orleans House of Refuge received 629 boys and 148 girls, as young as four years old and as old as twenty-one. The average inmate was imprisoned for one to two years. Virtually all were either born overseas or the children of immigrants.[90]

Perhaps no policing practice inspired such continual, enthusiastic resistance from the city's poor than the seizure of their children as juvenile vagrants. The House of Refuge never informed parents of their children's arrest: from the parents' perspective, their children simply disappeared. On discovering that their children had been taken to the House of Refuge, parents fought bitterly for their return: lambasting the house's managers, relentlessly petitioning the courts for their children's release, orchestrating jailbreaks.[91] The children themselves rebelled continually. In 1849, they burned the House of Refuge to its foundations, resulting in the escape of all but thirty inmates. The city rebuilt the institution, only for the children to reignite it, albeit less successfully, in 1850.[92] In 1858, the children "conspired together for a general brake out," in the exasperated warden's words, orchestrating continual revolts from March to July. Prearranged squads sawed secret passageways, rushed guards en masse, picked dormitory locks, fabricated rope ladders from bedsheets, and pried jail bars from windows. A particularly determined boy swam to freedom through the privy vault.[93] Sometimes, the repairmen and washerwomen employed by the House of Refuge helped children escape, suggesting some level of broad class opposition to the institution.[94]

The "dangerous and suspicious" tested the parameters of the vagrant category. Often, these were professional petty criminals: conmen, counterfeiters, hucksters, and swindlers. Not all were poor and landless: some owned property, while others had the resources to hire lawyers for their defense.[95] Though acknowledging that not everyone might consider such men vagrant, the *New Orleans Daily Crescent* defended their vagrancy arrest as "invaluable," since only the "continual arrest" of these professional criminals could pressure them into leaving the city, absent any "specific charge against them."[96]

Seth Place, a New Orleans resident repeatedly arrested as a "dangerous and suspicious" vagrant, was emblematic. The *New Orleans Daily Crescent* described Place as a "degraded" man and "disgrace to his race" who "hangs around cabarets and other disorderly 'holes in the wall,' in company with negroes, drinking at their expense and writing passes for them." Between 1846 and 1861, Place was arrested on a near-continual basis for larceny, burglary, forging slave passes, and "dangerous and suspicious" vagrancy. Although the law considered Place a habitual vagrant, he was also a fixed resident and family man, listed on the 1850 census as a sailor living with his parents and siblings.[97]

Vagrancy was a nebulous crime. Some vagrants were career criminals. Some were alien immigrants and migrants, chasing seasonal fluctuations in labor demand. Some were members of New Orleans's local poor. The definition of the crime was so broad that virtually any poor person in the city was vulnerable to arrest.

Yet vagrancy was not so arbitrary, broad, and vague a category as to be completely devoid of any articulable meaning. Nearly all persons charged with vagrancy were white, nonnative, landless, poor, and of perceived dependent status. Moreover, Louisiana's deep preoccupation with suppressing vagrancy encoded a series of well-defined and delineable apprehensions over wage labor, human migration, economic inequality, power, and the disruption of hierarchical relations between dependent and master. By tasking police with seizing vagrants, authorities chased the unobtainable ideal of a well-ordered urban society where every poor hireling was static, industrious, and controlled, whether by an employer or by the power of the state.

The Political Language of Vagrancy in the Antebellum South

Throughout the 1850s, no major city in the nation—perhaps even the world—arrested vagrants on New Orleans's scale. Yet preoccupation with vagrancy was hardly exclusive to the city: across the South, many smaller towns and villages also used vagrancy law to orchestrate expulsions of undesirable populations, though typically on a far more episodic basis. In 1856, after residents of

Chester, South Carolina, complained that their town had grown "infested by a swarm of Irish Pedlars"—itinerant, debauched, and without "visible means of support"—twenty peddlers were arrested for vagrancy and sentenced to be sold for one year or, "if there be no purchaser . . . thirty-nine lashes" and expulsion.[98] In 1851, following the immigration of Polish Jewish peddlers into Abbeville, South Carolina, residents there demanded the removal of that "worthless clan" through vagrancy law.[99] During a moral panic in 1835 known as the Murrell Excitement—sparked by rumors that a "Mystic Clan" of white highwaymen were planning to incite slave rebellions in every southern state—towns across the South expelled suspicious poor white strangers and neighbors as vagrants. Nashville alone announced the arrest of "more than four hundred persons, for the most part idle vagrants," during the panic.[100] "Let Council meet and have all idle fellows (who are filling our streets as vagrants,) arrested," demanded one Savannah resident in 1839: "Such measures have cleared our city before."[101]

Slaveholders were well versed in the idea that vagrants were loathsome parasites who should be forced to work or face expulsion. Writing in 1851, a slaveholder in South Carolina called vagrants "a nefarious clan of miscreants" who should be "ejected unceremoniously" from society. Writing in 1840, one Georgian compared vagrants to insect infestations and wished for their extermination, or at least their expulsion: "If such a one cannot be killed, he should at least be thrown out of the hive." In 1844, the grand jury of Meriwether County, Georgia, declared that vagrants "cannot be viewed in any other light than a general disturber of society, and as a common burthen upon the good citizens of our country . . . always consuming and never, by honest employment, contributing." In 1859, the vigilance committee of Napoleon, Arkansas, warned that vagrants entered their community "at their own peril." During his tour of the southern states, Frederick Law Olmsted encountered countless complaints regarding the prevalence of poor white vagrancy. One Mississippi political candidate vowed to have all unemployed white men transported to the penitentiary "to make 'em work and earn something to support their families." Olmsted believed that southerners themselves were unaware of how "universal" such sentiment was because so few southern writers were willing to acknowledge the existence of prevalent white poverty in the South.[102]

Despite the pervasiveness of this vehemence, proslavery theorists denied the existence of southern vagrancy. The South had no class conflict, proclaimed Georgia proslavery theorist Thomas R. R. Cobb, because no white southerner was engaged in a "menial occupation" and every white freeman "stands on the same social platform." "The mass of laborers not being recognized among citizens, every citizen feels that he belongs to an elevated class," Cobb explained: "The poorest meets the richest as an equal." The presence of slavery guaranteed "freedom from crime" and "freedom from pauperism," echoed Georgia senator John Forsyth. "We have but few in our jails, and fewer in our poor houses," agreed the region's leading proslavery polemicist, George Fitzhugh. "There is no starvation, no begging, no want of employment among our people, and not too much employment either," asserted Senator James Henry Hammond of South Carolina. In the North, the "hireling class of manual laborers . . . are essentially slaves," Hammond contended. "Our slaves are black . . . hired for life and well compensated."[103]

In developing the proslavery retort to northern free labor ideology, southern labor theorists formulated several arguments, some of them mutually exclusive. One central line of reasoning held that the subordination of labor to capital was natural and that the preservation of static, hierarchical relations between dependents and masters provided society's best means of preventing poverty, unemployment, social dysfunction, and crime. The problem with free labor systems, Fitzhugh argued, was that workers grew estranged from their masters and the humane services that masters provided. Whereas the southern laborer was protected by the mutual obligations built into the master-servant relation, the northern laborer became "the slave of society," alienated from their masters and prone to abuse. The responses to crime and poverty developed by free labor economies—systems of impersonal and bureaucratic almshouses and charities—exacerbated the problem by further disrupting the intimate bonds between master and dependent. In contrast, the southern system corrected societal dysfunctions quickly and efficiently by empowering every master to directly respond to his dependents' needs. "We have no loafers," Fitzhugh explained, because "the poor relative or friend who borrows our horse, or spends a week under our roof, is a welcome guest."[104]

This line of thinking failed to acknowledge—yet paradoxically, would seem to amplify the threat posed by—the existence in the South of migratory wageworkers who had neither fixed community nor static master. If the preservation of social order depended on the maintenance of intimate relations between dependent and master, then the wandering hireling without any master posed a profound danger. Indeed, even as proslavery theorists publicly denied the existence of southern vagrancy, many of the same theorists demanded aggressive measures against dependents who resisted submission to capital. "Guardians are provided for children, masters for apprentices, captains for sailors," argued Fitzhugh. "No one doubts that it is as well the right as the duty to make these provisions, and abridge or take away the liberty from all white citizens who are not qualified to enjoy it." In Fitzhugh's worldview, society was broadly divisible into two groups: landowning "men born to command" and the "masses" of "mediocrity" suited only for submission. The ideal society was one in which

the landowning elite achieved a complete stranglehold over *all* laboring dependents, whether they be white wageworkers or slaves: "To secure true progress,
we must unfetter genius, and chain down mediocrity. Liberty for the few—
Slavery, in every form, for the mass!" The Mississippi sociologist Henry Hughes
also divided all societies into two broad classes: property-owning "warrantors"
and dependent "warrantees." Warrantors could be trusted to fulfill their economic obligations because fear of economic failure provided intrinsic motivation. Yet menial laborers, whether wageworkers or slaves, could not be trusted
to perform their economic obligations voluntarily since they had no property to
lose and lacked the mental capacity for internal motivation. Thus warrantees
needed to be "ordered to be industrious," either by their masters or by the penal
sanctions of an authoritarian state: "This is the method of warranteeism. This,
its expedient to execute the law of public industry. Warranteeism is vagrancy
organized; mendicancy orderly and productive. Its idlers are industrialized.
There are no beggars, or vagabonds. There are no rags in warranteeism. All
work; none are idle. There are no loiterers. Capitalists idle, under penalty of
loss of capital. Skilled-laborers are a thinking class. Thinking men are not
vagrants."[105]

In championing the total subjugation of white menial labor, Fitzhugh and
Hughes drove a system of proslavery thought to its logical conclusion. Few
southern slaveholders dared join Fitzhugh and Hughes, at least not in such
explicit terms. More commonly, southern labor theorists dodged the question
of poor white subjugation entirely by simply denying the existence of poor white
southerners altogether.[106] Yet there was broad understanding among southern
slaveholders that unpropertied hirelings, whatever their race and legal status,
were unqualified for true freedom and worked best when coerced. "Pity it is,"
bemoaned proslavery intellectual William Gilmore Simms, "that the lousy and
lounging lazzaroni" and *"unlaboring* people of Europe" cannot "be made to
labor in the fields, under the whip of a severe taskmaster." "Man is naturally a
vagrant animal," explained the Plaquemine *Southern Sentinel.* "Not one out of
five loves work, in the first place, for work's sake merely." One Massachusetts
traveler recalled a South Carolina planter's shock on learning that Massachusetts did not coerce free laborers through penal sanctions. "How can you get
work out of a man," the incredulous planter asked, "unless you *compel* him in
some way?"[107]

This vision of societal order fashioned connections between the different
dependent members of the household: within this worldview, vagrant workers, rebellious slaves, unfaithful wives, wayward children, and itinerant free
Black hirelings were similar problems in that the existence of each represented
a rebellion against mastery. "Slaves, wives and children" must be made "the

subjects of family government," demanded Fitzhugh. "Each planter in fact is a Patriarch," echoed a future member of the Confederate cabinet, Christopher Memminger. "His position compels him to be a ruler in his household." Leonidas Spratt of South Carolina, a leading advocate of southern secession, conflated the emancipation of slaves from their masters, the revolt of wives from their husbands, and the autonomy of wageworkers from capital in his assertion that a disruption of any one of these relations threatened the fundamental "props of social order." Free labor societies were moving toward a "carnival" of excessive democracy, Spratt declared, wherein labor was no longer subservient to capital. Next, women would assume "the places and habiliments of men," the "sexes shall consort without the restraints of marriage," and "youths and maidens, drunk at noon day, and half naked, shall reel about the market place." Only the South, with its clear and inviolable relations between masters and dependents, was protected from sexual, social, and economic anarchy: the slave "restrained by power, the master by the trusts of a superior position."[108]

Slaveholders' ideological commitments to household governance, and to universal white power, were in direct conflict. In a sense, southern slaveholders were the inheritors of two incompatible ways of rationalizing societal relations: a legacy of the American Revolution that insisted that all white men were equally free and an older legal tradition of household governance that suggested that every dependent, regardless of his or her race, required domination and compulsion.[109] Faced with this paradox, the idea of the vagrant— an outsider parasitizing the body politic, requiring correction and coercion— offered an invaluable means of reconciling their contradictory commitments to universal white supremacy and intraracial class hierarchy. Slaveholders could pledge unfailing commitment to white unity, white equality, and universal white freedom from coercion, provided that they continually carved out a broad but self-evident exception for the white vagrant.

This reliance on vagrancy law as a tool for navigating interclass divisions between white people was on display during debates in Louisiana over whether to extend universal political and civil rights to all white men. Even as they expanded the suffrage to most white adult men, most states, North and South, prohibited vagrants from voting.[110] In Louisiana, debates over universal white male suffrage provoked repeated arguments over how best to "withhold the right to vote from the vagrant." Louisiana state congressman Thomas Wadsworth declared vagrant suffrage even more offensive than the enfranchisement of women. During Louisiana's state constitutional convention in 1844–45, there was broad agreement that property requirements on white male suffrage could be struck down only if new restrictions on vagrant suffrage were added. When one delegate questioned the convention's opposition to vagrant suffrage, he was overwhelmingly shouted down by opponents calling vagrant suffrage "madness," "ignorance and folly," a grave threat to "our well-being," and "liberality . . . at the expense of our safety."[111] As Louisiana state senator Charles Conrad argued, certain classes of white persons were simply incapable of self-governance and required their master's management. "The same principle" that would *entirely* disregard distinctions between different classes of white men, argued Conrad, would likewise reject the obedience that "women and children, free persons of color and negroes" owed to their natural patriarchs.[112]

The virulently xenophobic Know-Nothing Party, following its meteoric rise throughout the South and the nation in 1854 and 1855, wielded the idea of the vagrant with particular agility and venom.[113] In Louisiana, the rise of Know-Nothingism corresponded with increasingly violent and hyperbolic language toward vagrants: they were "a drag and a tax," "the curse of the nation," and "mottled, bloated, characterless specimens of 'moral black vomit.'"[114] Nativist newspapers charged that vagrants committed regular voter fraud, calling on local citizens to "guard the ballot-box from pollution" while fanning anti-immigrant riots.[115] Draconian measures, aimed at vagrants, were proposed. Charging that vagrants had infiltrated New Orleans's municipal government, the *Daily Picayune* proposed the creation of an antivagrancy police task force, a registry of gainfully employed local laborers, and tougher restrictions on vagrant suffrage, each to "rid our city government of the drones and vermin."[116] For their part, city councilmembers proposed the creation of a 200-man antivagrancy task force and the automatic dismissal of any patrolman who neglected to arrest a passing vagrant. After Know-Nothings seized control of New Orleans's municipal government during municipal elections in March 1855, the party immediately purged the New Orleans police force of foreign-born men.[117] Amid that purge, vagrancy arrests surged: police reported 1,516 vagrancy arrests from April to June, more than twice the seasonal average. Louisiana Know-Nothings also used vagrancy to deflect accusations of anti-immigrant prejudice. "When we raise objections to foreigners . . . we should be distinctly understood," explained one nativist paper, "that we are alluding to this dominant class of emigration in that country, which is wholly composed of poor vagrants, criminals and other waste." It was not the party's aim "to prevent foreigners from settling in our midst to engage in the industrious pursuits," agreed another nativist outlet, merely "to prevent Europe from sending her vagrants."[118]

The exclusion of vagrants from the customary legal protections of whiteness was reinforced by representations of vagrants as less than fully human, and perhaps not entirely white. While considered a choice or a consequence of environmental inducements, paradoxically, vagrancy was often framed as congenital. Vagrants were members of that "certain percentage of the human family," argued the *Daily Picayune*, who "appear to be corrupt from their very cradles." Frances Kemble, the British wife of a Georgia planter, described "abjectly poor" Georgians who "will not work" as members of a "degraded race," merely "claiming an Anglo-Saxon origin . . . filthy, lazy, ignorant, brutal, proud, penniless savages." In *Social Relations in Our Southern States*, Alabamian Daniel Hundley suggested the congenital nature of southern class stations. There were "natural causes" for "the existence in the South of a class of lazy vagabonds known as Poor Whites," Hundley argued. "Everywhere they are just alike, possess pretty much the same characteristics, the same vernacular, the same boorishness, and the same habits. . . . every where, Poor White Trash."[119]

Some theorized that vagrancy was the last vestige of a more primitive stage in human evolution: a remnant of prehistoric hunter-gatherers, concentrated among the modern-day poor. British journalist Henry Mayhew proposed the existence of "two distinct and broadly marked races, viz., the wanderers and the settlers—the vagabond and the citizens—the nomadic and the civilized tribes."[120] This vestigial trace of prehistoric nomadism linked the white vagrant to the world's uncivilized races, who shared the defective, genetic predisposition to nomadism and idleness. Indigenous peoples were often cast as chronically, instinctively vagrant. In 1857, the commissioner of Indian affairs James W. Denver argued that rations and annuity payments incentivized "idleness" and "dependence" and therefore delayed Native Americans' evolutionary transition from vagrancy into sedentary civilization. Denver requested judicial authority to establish a network of prison forts and arrest and incarcerate all "worthless idlers and vagrants of their own tribes, whose wild habits and roving disposition preclude them from settling down quietly or orderly."[121]

Vagrancy also featured prominently in national debates surrounding slave emancipation. During British emancipation in the 1830s, proslavery detractors predicted that without slavery's paternalistic guidance, the formerly enslaved people of the Caribbean would devolve into their primordial, vagrant state. Later US proslavery thinkers inherited this argument, invoking the apparent disorganization of labor in the West Indies as evidence that emancipations yielded mass vagrancy. "Witness the miserable experiment made by the English and French in the West Indies," one *DeBow's Review* contributor proclaimed: "Vagrant labor stalking through a desolate land, with hungry and brutal ferocity." "Vagrancy is the curse of nearly all the English West India Islands," another proslavery theorist argued.[122] Not all abolitionists entirely disagreed with this reading of Caribbean history: although radical abolitionists rejected this characterization of West Indian emancipation, antislavery moderates, who endorsed a program of gradual emancipation, suggested that West Indian history demonstrated the necessity of coupling emancipation with stringent antivagrancy measures to guide the formerly enslaved toward industrious hab-its. "Vagrancy is a crime," British abolitionist Marshall Hall advised his Ameri-can counterparts: "If any, after the discipline of self-emancipation, be found idle and thriftless, let *severe* measures be adopted."[123]

Some antebellum states orchestrated expulsions of Native Americans and free Black Americans through vagrancy law. While the tendency within the Deep South states was to equate vagrancy with whiteness, the Upper South states of Virginia, Maryland, and Delaware had vagrancy laws on the books aimed explicitly toward free Black residents.[124] In 1859, Georgia bucked this trend, passing new laws that equated Blackness with vagrancy to legitimate the complete expulsion or enslavement of all free Black persons within the state.[125]

White Vagrants, Enslaved Fugitives, and Free Black Travelers

Within the slaveholder psyche, poor white vagrants, itinerant free Black hire-lings, and fugitives from slavery—resistantly mobile dependents, each—shared something in common. To be clear, slaveholders did not perceive that the dan-gers posed by these three criminal classes were equal, and whiteness always provided white laborers with legal rights, social protections, and employment opportunities—including opportunities to join police forces—totally unavail-able to Black workers. Yet while never conflating these three criminal castes, the logic of master-servant relations implied that these three categories of crim-inally autonomous worker were each guilty of an analogous rebellion against elite white mastery. This latent perception of connection was deeply imbed-ded within southern police power and reflected in the region's penal sanctions, carceral institutions, and policing regulations.

Galveston's curfew regulations subjected "Free Negroes, Mulattoes and Slaves" to "the penalties prescribed for vagrants."[126] A Maryland law of 1831 barred compulsory penal labor, with the exception of enslaved people, free Black persons, and vagrants.[127] In South Carolina, special magistrates and freeholders courts exercised jurisdiction over cases involving enslaved people, free Black persons, and vagrants.[128] In 1839, a joint resolution of the Texas legislature instructed all state law enforcement officers to begin arresting "all vagrants and idle persons," whip them, and assign them to public works.[129] Though controversial, communities with limited penal infrastructure some-times sold white convicted vagrants into indenture at auction.[130]

The development of New Orleans's workhouse system also reflected this per-ception of connection between poor white vagrancy, slave marronage, and free Black itineracy. In 1842, the First Municipality removed enslaved prisoners from the First Municipality Police Jail, which was repurposed into the municipality's workhouse for "vagrant" white prisoners. The Police Jail keeper was reappointed the workhouse warden. The Second Municipality promptly followed suit by transforming its police jail into a subordinate department within its workhouse. The Second Municipality subsequently constructed a new facility, serving as both workhouse and police jail, and partitioned into three segregated wards: one walled enclosure each for white male vagrants, white female vagrants, and free or enslaved Black persons of either sex. By 1848, both the First and Third Municipalities had similarly brought their workhouse and police jail under joint management. Normally, enslaved prisoners and imprisoned vagrants were segregated from one another, though they were confined together whenever their facilities underwent repairs. After the reunification of the three municipalities in 1852, this Second Municipality's penal compound was designated the workhouse and police jail for the entire city: a single, amalgamated complex for transforming deviant dependents into diligent laborers.[131] In 1854 and 1855, as Know-Nothing sentiment raged, New Orleans also briefly flirted with the abolition of its slave chain gang and the institution's replacement with a vagrant chain gang. The general council voted to approve the change, though it was never implemented, and the approval was almost immediately repealed.[132]

Other southern cities tested the coincarceration of resistant enslaved people and "vagrant" poor white detainees. The workhouse systems of Baton Rouge, Nashville, St. Louis, Louisville, Richmond, and Alexandria imprisoned and worked both resistant enslaved people and white vagrants to varying degrees of segregation. Augusta's workhouse, though not completed until after the Civil War, was also initially conceived for both "[enslaved] negroes confined for punishment, and idle and profligate whites," according to that city's mayor.[133] Recalling his time in the Louisville workhouse, the abolitionist and ex-slave Henry Bibb reflected on how "astonishing" it was "to see so many whites as well as colored men loaded down with irons, at hard labor, under the supervision of overseers."[134]

Slave patrols were often tasked with policing white vagrants. The charter of the Jefferson Parish, Louisiana, slave patrol mandated the arrest of maroons, suspicious free Black persons, and "all vagrants." In 1835, an Ascension Parish slave patrol reported the arrest of "five vagrants" after local planters accused them of intending "to create an insurrection among the slaves." In describing patrol duties, South Carolina's governor Robert Allston identified the policing of white vagrants as more vital than the policing of the enslaved.[135]

Slaveholders were haunted by fears that fugitive enslaved people and vagrant poor white people would conspire together in resistance to slaveocracy. One Louisiana sugar planter told Frederick Law Olmsted that he objected to the presence of poor white vagrants because "it was best that [slaves] should not see" any autonomous menial laborers, regardless of their race, whom the planter "did not command." This slaveholder believed "that the contrast between the habits of the former—most of the time idle, and when working, working only for their own benefit and without a master—constantly offered suggestions and temptations to the slaves to neglect their duty, to run away and live a vagabond life, as these poor whites were seen to do."[136] Other slaveholders echoed this impression that the presence of poor white vagrants inspired slave resistance. The *Daily Picayune* advised against permitting interactions between vagrants and the enslaved, noting that vagrants inspired "an air of insolence and disrespect" in enslaved people, rendering them "worthless," demoralized, and "debauched by the associations they form." Slaveholders often accused vagrants of being abolitionist agents. Vagrants were "spies" for "*Garrison and Douglas[s]*," charged one South Carolinian, who "would glory in the downfall of slavery, and the entire overthrow of the whole institution." In 1859, residents of Lafayette County, Mississippi, petitioned for the expulsion of itinerant peddlers as vagrants, asserting that as wanderers "having no interest in any locality," vagrants "corrupt the slaves" and were "fruitful source and the *trunk of the underground railroad traffic.*" Vagrants "debauch our slaves" and "deprave their morals," complained the *New Orleans Daily Crescent*: "Worse than worthless trash, [they] should be put in the chain gang."[137]

Perhaps there was some truth to these fears. Migratory laborers threatened slaveholders' ability to control the dissemination of information. Often, they came from societies that had outlawed slavery. As strangers of unknowable reputations, vagrants were an unpredictable variable within the slaveholder's well-ordered world. Kidnapped from Washington, DC, and illegally sold into slavery in Louisiana, Solomon Northup regained his freedom through the help of an itinerant Canadian-born carpenter named Samuel Bass. Northrup described Bass as somewhat peculiar, "liberal to a fault," "wandering from one state to another" without permanent abode: the precise sort that Louisiana officials charged with vagrancy. Bass illustrates the real threats that mobile laborers posed to closed societies. Mobile travelers were often well traveled, flexible, experienced in working alongside many different peoples, and had themselves endured prejudice and criminalization. The danger that such persons might aid or empathize with the enslaved were real.[138]

It is revealing that during four of antebellum Louisiana's largest slave rebellion panics—in 1805, 1835, 1841, and 1856—fearful slaveholders imagined elaborate alliances among poor white vagrants, resistant enslaved people, and itinerant free Black hirelings, denouncing these three embodiments of their threatened mastery within the same breath. It was fears of vagrants, maroons, and free Black émigrés from Saint-Domingue that led to the creation of New Orleans's first police force and police jail system, in 1805. During the Murrell Excitement in 1835, panicked slaveholders demanded tougher laws governing vagrant white people and itinerant free Black workers to protect themselves from slave insurrection.[139] During the August First panic in 1841, vigilance committees up and down the Mississippi River again demanded harsher laws "against free persons of color, vagrants and loafers."[140] Vagrant white workers and itinerant free Black workers were again identified as the puppet masters behind a perceived slave insurrection plot in 1856: as the *New Orleans Daily Crescent* concluded in that panic's aftermath, slavery's survival would depend on "new white laws as well as new black laws."[141]

During the final months of the Civil War, as Louisiana's former slaveholders lost hope that slavery might endure, many saw clearly what needed to be done. Rebuilding the South's economy, suppressing crime, and reestablishing social order from the chaos of free labor would require stringent enforcement of vagrancy law. Louisiana already had vagrancy laws that were robust and broad. These laws provided a familiar and legitimate framework for coercing wage labor and a way to discriminate the deserving from the undeserving, community members from parasitic outsiders, men entitled to political rights from unqualified dependents. Vagrancy law would be the South's salvation.

CHAPTER 5

From Marronage to Vagrancy

Policing Freedom in Wartime
Louisiana, 1862–1865

In April 1862, as the Civil War entered its second year, a Union navy flotilla dashed past the Confederate forts guarding the mouth of the Mississippi River and sailed, unopposed, toward New Orleans. On May 1, Major General Benjamin F. Butler of Massachusetts occupied the Confederacy's largest city with 15,000 Union troops.[1]

Three months later, some thirty women and men, enslaved by Thomas Morgan of Plaquemines Parish, resolved to run the twenty-eight miles to the Union army in New Orleans and to freedom. They began their marathon at sunset. Some of the fugitives carried cane knives: "to resist," as a reporter for the *New York Herald* would later write, "any attempt on the road to return them to slavery." Jogging down the path that ran along the ridge of the Mississippi River levee, they reached the city's outskirts with the dawn. A squad of New Orleans policemen awaited them. The policemen demanded that the fugitives submit to arrest. Instead, the fugitives declared their intention to fight their way to the Union army and to freedom. Barricading themselves behind cargo freight, they hurled ballast stones and slashed at the officers with their cane knives. To the fugitives' relief, a detachment of Union soldiers appeared. To the fugitives' horror, the Union soldiers opened fire. Nine fugitives were shot; one man lay dying. The Federal soldiers arrested fourteen enslaved men. Perhaps an equal number of fugitives managed to escape into the city amid the chaos.[2]

Word of "insurrectionary negroes" battling policemen along the levee spread far and wide, sending shockwaves of terror to slaveholders throughout the South.[3] Initial newspaper accounts described an insurrectionary slave army: heavily armed, numbering in the hundreds, marching on New Orleans in co-ordinated "semi-military style." The event triggered deeply ingrained nightmares of slave insurrection. It would have seemed that the feared uprising of the maroons—that day of reckoning imagined and dreaded since the Saint-Domingue Revolution—had arrived at long last.[4]

Federal authorities debated the fate of the fourteen prisoners. Thomas Morgan's estate petitioned for their return. Panicked slaveholders demanded their blood. When news of the skirmish reached the North, abolitionists demanded the slaves' immediate emancipation and release. In an open letter to Abraham Lincoln, the New York newspaper editor and publisher Horace Greeley asked why Union troops had helped traitors recapture freedom seekers. "They sought their liberty," Greeley protested, and "were butchered or reënslaved for so doing by the help of Union soldiers." President Lincoln replied that his objective was not to free slaves but to "save the Union."[5]

Months later, as the fourteen men languished in a military prison, the Union army realized that the solution to this legal, ethical, and political quagmire was to reconceive of the fourteen "fugitives" as "vagrants." In February 1863, Thomas Morgan's attorney again petitioned for the fugitives' return—this time, not as captured maroons, but under Union army labor policies governing the forced repatriation of criminal vagrants. This arrangement must have satisfied the Union army because the prisoners' names soon reappeared on Thomas Morgan's plantation rolls.[6]

Southeastern Louisiana was the first sizable region of the Deep South to be liberated by the Federal army and was liberated months before the Federal government had embraced emancipation as a military objective. For the remainder of the war, occupied Louisiana would provide the Federal government and the nation with a critical testing ground from which to develop policy toward enslaved people, emancipation, and the postwar labor system. As the abolitionist Wendell Phillips succinctly discerned in 1864, "Mr. Lincoln's model of reconstruction is the experiment in Louisiana."[7]

The rebellion of the men and women enslaved by Thomas Morgan, their dramatic flight to New Orleans, and the reimagining of their marronage as vagrancy capture in microcosm the course of the wartime battle over freedom's meaning within the occupied state. Initially, the Federal government hoped to coax support from slaveholders in occupied Louisiana by protecting their claims to persons held as property. Local policemen worked hand in hand with Federal military police, known as provost marshals, using Louisiana's pre-existing police jail system to facilitate the capture, incarceration, and return of rebellious enslaved people. Yet by continuously seeking their freedom within Union army lines, fugitive enslaved people destabilized slavery to the point of its collapse, forcing the Union army and the Federal government to reckon with the war's implications for the institution's future. As slavery's downfall became clear, Federal authorities turned to vagrancy law as a way of steering emancipation's trajectory and restraining freedom's implications. Under the auspices of suppressing Black vagrancy, the Union army arrested and imprisoned tens of thousands of self-emancipated Louisianians, forcibly transporting them to former slave plantations. This reimagining of marronage as vagrancy conceded slavery's de facto destruction while simultaneously legitimating ongoing efforts to coerce Black labor.

In recruiting vagrancy law as the primary legal mechanism by which to regulate emancipation, Federal authorities fashioned a critical stepping stone on the road to Jim Crow. Yet the ambiguities of vagrancy law beset local and Federal efforts to coerce freedpeople's labor and lives. By what criteria would police differentiate "idling" Black vagrants from gainfully employed Black residents? What sorts of employment would exempt freedpeople from vagrancy arrest? Would Black women, children, the elderly, and the disabled be considered vagrant if they declined wage labor? Would Black veterans of the Union army be considered vagrant on their honorable discharge? What would freedom mean for freedpeople if they were to be perpetually subject to the threat of summary seizure? As the nation debated the significance and shape of Black liberation, battles between policemen, soldiers, and fugitive enslaved people in the streets of New Orleans would have lasting repercussions for the nation, the postwar labor system, and the evolution of state police power in the American South.[8]

Escape to New Orleans

One month after New Orleans's surrender, in June 1862, Union army major Frank Peck, stationed immediately upriver of the city, reported an alarmingly "large and constantly increasing number of blacks" moving toward Union lines. Peck described fugitives "of all ages and physical conditions—a number of infants in arms, many young children, robust men and women, and a large number of lame, old and infirm." Many had "eaten nothing for days." Peck requested clarification: did his orders to turn away all civilians include fugitive human property?[9]

Similar reports soon materialized up and down Union army lines. "Darkies come flocking in here," Colonel Edward Jones, commander of the two forts at the Mississippi River's mouth, also reported in June. "They have heard all sorts of stories . . . all tending to implant the notion that if they can only get to the forts they are free." "They swarm in, whole plantations of them at a time," one Connecticut soldier wrote his mother. "The jails have become full, and I have no means of feeding them," reported Captain Charles Conant from St. Bernard Parish. "What shall I do about the negroes?" asked General Godfrey Weitzel. "I have no rations to issue to them. I have a great many more negroes in my camp now than I have whites. These negroes are a perfect nuisance."[10]

The enslaved of Louisiana recognized what many in the Union army did not:

that the arrival of an invading army provided a possible pathway to freedom. As word of New Orleans's surrender spread deep into the countryside, thousands of enslaved people emancipated themselves and began fleeing toward the occupied city.[11] Over the subsequent decade, upward of 30,000 Black Americans would flee into New Orleans.[12] Initially they sought de facto emancipation, protection from white violence, escape from white surveillance, and the possibility of reassembling divided family, later, the higher earning potential, and greater opportunity for social life, that urban life provided.[13] They traveled by foot, horse, mule, plantation cart, and skiff. Many migrated with their belongings: clothing, food, "boxes, bedding, and luggage of all sorts," in one witness's words. Others came in "scarred, wounded, and some with iron collars round their necks," as another officer recalled: starving, virtually naked, and carrying nothing at all.[14]

For Major General Benjamin Butler, commander of the newly created Department of the Gulf, this unanticipated exodus created an immense political, economic, and humanitarian crisis. Louisiana was home to many "Unionist" slaveholders who championed slavery but had opposed secession. Hoping to maintain their loyalty and recruit broader local support, Butler had vowed to safeguard the region's economy, suppress "every species of disorder," respect surrendered planters' "rights of property," and "restore order out of chaos." He was also bound by the terms of the Second Confiscation Act, passed in July 1862, which prohibited the use of military power to return fugitives to rebel slaveholders who had sided with the Confederacy. Yet as the general wrote Secretary of War Edwin Stanton, his troops could not tell apart the fugitive slaves of "loyal and disloyal masters." As makeshift camps grew along Union army lines, so, too, did the costs of provisioning the fugitives with clothing and rations, as well as death rates from hunger, insufficient sanitation, and disease.[15]

Among both Federal troops and southern slaveholders, the exodus stoked deep anxieties regarding migration, idleness, and the deleterious effects of superfluous dependence on public charity.[16] Butler shared the common theory of a direct causal link between idleness and criminality: as such, he predicted that the congregation of unemployed persons would fuel disorders. His reactions toward the fugitives also reflected the precepts of northern free labor ideology, which attributed itinerancy and unnecessary reliance on charity to individual moral failing. "Those that come early to us are by no means the best men and women," Butler wrote Stanton. "With them as with the whites it is the worse class that rebel against and evade the laws that govern them . . . the adventurers, the shiftless, and wicked, to the exclusion of the good and quiet." Meanwhile, the exodus terrified and angered proslavery southerners, undermining Federal efforts to recruit their support. "The conduct of the negroes in New-Orleans is intolerable to their owners," observed one paroled Confederate soldier. "They laugh and talk and walk together up the streets in the most disgusting style, showing very little indications to make way on the banquette for ladies or gentlemen. . . . A more idle, filthy, lazy, degraded looking set of wretches never were seen." "The Negroes will commit all kinds of depredations . . . [he will be] totally spoiled for the future whatever his condition may be," one slaveholder predicted. "Free or slave . . . [the negro] must be controlled."[17]

To "save" the fugitives "from idle and vicious habits," Butler ordered that they be impressed as military laborers, turned over to Unionist slaveholders, or expelled from Union army lines.[18] Butler further resolved to leave Louisiana's preexisting policing and carceral infrastructure in place, instructing his troops to leave fugitive slaves "subject to the ordinary laws of the community."[19] The New Orleans Police Department was placed under the command of one of Butler's provost marshals, a colonel and veteran of Boston's city guard named Jonas French. Under French's direction, police began enthusiastically arresting and imprisoning fugitives. The Police Jail announced the resumption of whippings. Some slaveholders reclaimed custody of their fugitive property on condition that they first pledge loyalty to the Union.[20]

When impressing the fugitives of rebel slaveholders, Butler relied on the legal rationale that they had become confiscated war "contraband" on reaching Union army lines. A lawyer by training, Butler had first conjured this "contraband" category in early 1861 while in command of Fort Monroe in Virginia, as enslaved people began journeying to the fort in search of asylum. This legal and conceptual maneuver legitimated the quartering of Confederate masters' slaves without violating the Fugitive Slave Act of 1850 or challenging the legal principle of chattel slavery.[21]

Yet dissidents among Butler's troops secretly undermined or defiantly refused to follow Butler's orders to impress, return, or expel fugitives. "I cannot and will not assist in any way in returning slaves to their masters," Captain Edward Page boldly wrote his superior.[22] General Neal Dow, stationed downriver of New Orleans, began issuing freedom certificates to anyone who reached his lines.[23] Brigadier General John Phelps, commander of a Union camp immediately upriver of New Orleans, openly encouraged the exodus to his lines and ordered emancipation raids into the countryside. The number of fugitives in Phelps's camp rapidly swelled into the thousands. When Butler ordered Phelps to compel the fugitives to strengthen camp defenses, Phelps rejoined, "I am not willing to become the mere Slave-driver," and resigned.[24]

Desperate to reassert control over their rebellious property, slaveholders turned to the police jail system as never before. "I have three of them in prison for now. This costs $36 a month," complained one mistress to her son, adding that she had many others who might soon need to be "caged up right fast." To preempt escapes, slaveholders ordered enslaved people's incarceration for "safe-keeping" in record numbers. By November, the New Orleans Police Jail held nearly 300 persons—the prison's approximate maximum capacity—two-thirds of whom were held for "safekeeping." To alleviate the overcrowding, Butler or-dered the removal of all able-bodied men and boys from the Police Jail and their impressment as military laborers. Soon, every neighborhood lockup and parish jail, inside the city and throughout its environs, was also egregiously overcrowded.[25]

Slaveholders began offering policemen hefty bounties for fugitives' capture and return. Although paying policemen to search for fugitives had been routine before the war, the size of these payments soared, while the issuance of private moneys to police smacked of bribery and corruption to northern soldiers un-familiar with the practice. As the fall harvest season approached and demand for labor mounted, police and provost marshals realized that fortunes could be made by smuggling captured fugitives to rebel slaveholders, in violation of the Second Confiscation Act. A lucrative human trafficking scheme developed, and persistent rumors alleged that none other than Colonel Jonas French, Butler's chief of police, was at the helm. One police informant communicated to the Federals that New Orleans's Fourth District Police Station had become the main way station for smuggling captured fugitives from city to countryside. Another informant alleged that his colleagues skirted all other policing duties, devoting their entire shifts to hunting fugitives for profit.[26] Some planters were content to receive *any* prisoner, regardless of their identity or the identity of their legal owner, and several fugitives found themselves furtively "returned" to plantations where they had never previously been enslaved. Dr. Frederick Knapp—son of Dr. James Knapp, the dentist who had previously sought the ex-pulsion of Dr. Thomas Jennings, in 1860 and 1861—was identified as a leading coordinator of this trafficking ring among planters, providing himself and his neighbors with incarcerated maroons smuggled from New Orleans's streets.[27]

Hounded by police and provost marshals, fugitives began building strategic relationships with sympathetic Union army soldiers, exchanging their labor and services for protection from arrest.[28] After fleeing her mistress, a fugitive named Malissa "sought the protection of Capt. [Joseph] Bromley," quarter-master of the Thirteenth Connecticut Volunteers. Malissa's mistress com-plained that when police found and arrested Malissa, Captain Bromley imme-diately "procured her release" from the Police Jail. In response to her petition, Colonel French issued an order for Malissa's arrest, which Captain Bromley refused to honor. Malissa "has since remained in the Service of Capt. Broml[e]y, who screens her from Punishment, and deprives me of her services," the mistress protested. Similar complaints flooded in from slaveholders throughout the city.[29]

As fugitives forged strategic alliances with Federals, their descriptions of New Orleans's police jail system tended to radicalize some Union army troops. The hire of policemen as slave catchers and the incarceration of prisoners at their owners' whim violated northerners' notions of the proper boundaries between public and private power. William Gray was an army surgeon from Massachusetts dishonorably discharged for refusing to expel the fugitives who had taken shelter within his field hospital. Rendered jobless, Gray began drafting a steady stream of petitions on behalf of Police Jail prisoners. The prisoners are "not charged with crime," Gray seethed in disbelief. They are confined *"without any form of trial, and for an indefinite period of time."*[30] Other Union officers began summarily paroling prisoners who had been committed only for "safekeeping." To prevent this Federal interference, some jailors began coding persons confined for "safekeeping" as "larcenist" in prison ledgers.[31] Even Butler was baffled by Louisiana's penal practices, particularly after he ordered the impressment of 122 able-bodied Police Jail prisoners and received, to his astonishment and outrage, a bill for $2,527.35 in jail fees. Rationalizing that the Police Jail's billing system was analogous to that "taken in all countries with debtors confined by creditors," Butler declared that thereafter, slaveholders would be required to pay for the incarceration of their slaves in advance.[32] The use of military resources to capture and imprison fugitives in New Orleans was also becoming a growing political liability in the North. "Is not this a shame that the agents and employees of the Great Republic should be engaged constantly in the business of slave-hounds?" asked Horace Greeley's *New-York Tribune.*[33]

As the fall sugar harvest approached in 1862, it was becoming clear that the state's machinery for policing and jailing fugitive enslaved people was incapable of the task, mired in corruption, a threat to the political legitimacy of Butler's regime, and a drain on Union army morale. Slaveholders manipulated the system; Union soldiers refused to enforce it; northern abolitionists denounced it. Nor could the police jail system keep pace with the general uprising of enslaved people unfolding all around.

As cracks in the police jail system emerged, some free Black residents saw opportunity to pry those cracks into fissures. Louisiana's free Black residents were hardly united in their opinions regarding slavery. Some were themselves slaveholders; a few were wealthy members of the planter class. Yet others recognized that the racial persecution to which they were subjected was directly tied to slavery—that they could never escape discrimination so long as racialized slavery endured. In July, a committee of freeborn Black residents petitioned

Butler for permission to create a free Black Union army regiment but was rebuffed. Free Black community leaders began holding pro-Union assemblies, while rumors swirled of secretive free Black abolitionist societies. Some free Black radicals began furtively aiding fugitives. On August 14, police arrested Lucien Jean-Pierre Capla, a prominent freeborn shoe merchant, for quietly opening his gate so that a fugitive named Charlie could evade perusing policemen.[34] Cyprian Clamorgan, a freeborn barber from St. Louis of very light complexion, began representing Police Jail prisoners in court, adapting the alias of a white attorney named C. C. Morgan, with the aim of establishing precedents to chip away at the police jail system's legality.[35]

Meanwhile, between August 1862 and January 1863, the political situation in Louisiana evolved rapidly. In August, facing a chronic manpower shortage, Butler authorized the formation of one of the first Black military regiments of the war, the First Louisiana Native Guard, paving the way for the broader enlistment of Black soldiers into the Union army. In theory, the native guard was to consist only of free Black Louisianians. In practice, hundreds of fugitives lied about their legal status and enlisted.[36]

In November, as the harvest loomed, Butler negotiated a new arrangement with planters. The army would supply plantations with "contraband" laborers, maintain order on plantations, and suspend rations for all "idle and worthless" fugitives who had found refuge within Union army lines. In exchange, planters would swear loyalty to the Union, promise to pay their workforce, and forgo corporal punishment. The population of the contraband camps surrounding New Orleans fell from the thousands to the hundreds.[37]

These orders would be among the general's last in Louisiana. In December, President Lincoln recalled Butler, ruling him a diplomatic liability after a series of scuffles between the general and foreign consuls in New Orleans. Major General Nathaniel P. Banks, a former governor of Massachusetts, was sent to Louisiana as Butler's replacement.

On January 1, 1863, President Lincoln issued the final Emancipation Proclamation, declaring freedom for everyone enslaved within regions still in active rebellion. Although the proclamation did not formally apply to regions already under Federal control, it affirmed the Federal government's commitment to eliminating slavery. The proclamation thrust the status of New Orleans's enslaved residents, and of the thousands of fugitives who had found quarter within the city, into a state of ambiguity. Some remained bonded to their legal owners, though those bonds were fraying. Others had escaped their owners' reach but could be seized and forcibly returned at any moment. Still chattel by law, they occupied a hazy status between slavery and freedom.

General Orders 12

On January 29, 1863, General Banks tried to resolve these mounting ambiguities and refine his predecessor's labor system by reconceiving all remaining "contrabands" as "vagrants." General Orders 12 prescribed "constant occupation and employment" as the best remedy for fugitives' "vagrancy and crime." The order established a system of one-year paid agricultural labor contracts. Enslaved people who refused to contract, or who absconded before their contract's expiration, would be "arrested as vagrants" and "compelled" to labor in chain gangs on public works. A Bureau of Negro Labor would be created to coordinate fugitives' arrest, assignment, and labor. Banks promised that the labor system would save the agricultural economy and prevent the descent of the self-emancipated into disorder and destitution.[38]

With General Orders 12, Banks envisioned a new system of compulsory plantation labor that seemed aligned with the letter—if not the spirit—of the Emancipation Proclamation. Under the rationale of suppressing vagrancy, the order essentially criminalized Black liberation from plantations. The order legitimated the forced impressment of fugitives and their involuntary relocation to plantations by framing compulsory labor as an essential policing action and racially neutral penalty for criminal "idleness." The text of the order acknowledged that "the forcible seizure of fugitives" for plantation labor was "inconsistent" with the Confiscation Acts and the spirit of the Emancipation Proclamation. Yet none could deny, the order countered, that all states had a duty to seize and compel vagrants: "the public interest peremptorily demands" it. What reasonable person could object to enforcement of so universal a police power? Revised labor regulations issued in February 1864 were even more explicit: "Labor is a public duty, and idleness and vagrancy a crime. . . . Every enlightened community has enforced it upon all classes of people by the severest penalties. . . . No [one] . . . is exempt from the operation of this universal rule."[39]

General Orders 12 established the basic contours of a government-managed labor system that would endure in Louisiana for the remainder of the war, inspire labor programs imposed by other occupation forces throughout the South, and lay elements of the groundwork for the South's postwar labor system.[40] In recruiting the concept of vagrancy as both the labor system's justification and its coercive mechanism, Banks may have been inspired by Louisiana's slaveholders themselves, a coalition of whom had made labor recommendations to Banks in early January.[41] Banks's understanding of vagrancy law and how the accusation of vagrancy could be used to legitimate coercive state action were also doubtless informed by his prewar experiences as Massachusetts's

Know-Nothing governor, during which time he had overseen the stringent applications of vagrancy and pauper laws as means of expelling European immigrants.[42]

Louisiana slaveholders received Banks's plan with cautious optimism. "To place these now idle hordes back upon the plantation is a work of great humanity," ruled the *Daily Picayune*. Though imperfect, this "exceedingly practical" compromise would ensure planters' economic survival while alleviating the "curse" of idle Black transients who would otherwise be "allowed to wander," spreading the "evils of hunger and crime." Many northerners also responded favorably. This was the "only solution," wrote one Boston banker and confidant of General Banks: "carrying out the principles of our vagrant laws" to create "something like a serfdom." The *New York Times* agreed, declaring Banks's plan "eminently just": freedpeople "must not be turned over to idleness . . . must not be left to choose for themselves whether they will work or not." President Lincoln also expressed approval, though on the condition that this was a "temporary arrangement" preceding "permanent freedom." Privately, Banks was ecstatic, writing his wife that General Orders 12 was "the best act of my life" and predicting that it would "within three months solve all the troubles here about Slavery."[43]

Despite regional differences in how northerners and southerners conceptualized vagrancy, dependency, and free labor, their divergent understandings shared enough common ground that both sides could project their own assumptions and cultural anxieties into Banks's labor plan.[44] Louisiana slaveholders could see in Banks's recruitment of vagrancy an altogether familiar effort to prevent disorder and maximize economic production by firmly binding menial workers to their natural masters. The plan would have seemed aligned with the antebellum labor theories of proslavery thinkers such as George Fitzhugh and Henry Hughes, who had argued that "free" labor was essentially a myth, that most people were incapable of self-regulation, and that all menial laborers required compulsion. The difference between arresting resistant enslaved people as maroons and arresting resistant wageworkers as vagrants needn't be more than superficial.

Northerners who supported Banks's plan came in two stripes. Some white northerners, including many who opposed slavery, still held the racist view that all Black persons were congenitally prone to idleness, lacked the self-discipline necessary for free labor, and would require external coercion to participate successfully within free society. Other white northerners rejected congenital Black laziness but argued that slavery's degradations had crushed the moral character and work ethic of its victims. By forcing enslaved people into a condition of total dependence on their owners, slaveholders had destroyed the qualities—self-reliance, industriousness, perseverance—essential for success-ful participation within a free labor society. Proponents of this view cited histo-ries of Caribbean emancipations as evidence that immediate and unregulated emancipation produced mass vagrancy. For decades, these antislavery mod-erates had long called for a program of gradual emancipation, consisting of a temporary system of inducements and penalties designed to coercively train freedpeople in the proper exercise of freedom.[45]

Northern antislavery moderatism, in other words, was not irreconcilable with endorsement of Black coercion. Regardless of whether they considered Black laziness to be congenital or acculturated or envisioned a system of tem-porary or permanent coercion, Banks's northern supporters read Black eman-cipation through a combination of racial prejudice and free labor ideology. Thrown out onto the world and left to their own devices, former slaves would devolve into idleness, grow unjustly reliant on charity, and become burdensome pests on society: examples of those "unworthy poor" whose alleged refusal to work piqued northern anxieties. They argued that Banks's antivagrancy poli-cies merely replicated the coercive strictures of northern poor law. "Every State has its laws concerning vagrants," asserted the *New York Times*, in an article praising Banks's labor regulations. "The same principle must regulate legisla-tion concerning the enfranchised slaves." "Every civilized nation in the world has vagrant laws," echoed *Harper's Weekly*. Linking Black emancipation to the reformation of white paupers into dutiful wageworkers, the magazine reasoned that vagrant laws were essential to economic uplift. "Time was when our ances-tors needed the gentle stimulus of the law to compel them to earn their living": by the same token, Banks's "salutary and humane" regulations would teach the freedman to embrace "his responsibilities as a free man."[46]

Banks's labor plan, in essence, appealed at once to the South's master-servant ideology, the North's free labor ideology, and the gradual emancipation propos-als of many white antislavery moderates. The plan did meet with criticism, how-ever. Radical abolitionists had long rejected the gradual emancipation programs of antislavery moderates, charging that such schemes smacked of paternalism, replaced slavery with serfdom, and reproduced the proslavery precept that Black Americans were unprepared for freedom. In the past, a faction of radical abolitionists had gone so far as to condemn all coercive state power, includ-ing poor laws and prisons (though their New England Non-Resistance Society, founded by William Lloyd Garrison in 1838, had collapsed by 1849).[47] Demand-ing immediate and unconditional freedom, radical outlets like the *Liberator* and *National Anti-Slavery Standard* were quick to denounce Banks's program as state-sponsored slavery.[48] Predicting Banks's plan by several months, Fred-erick Douglass had already begun condemning any future coercive government program designed to instill proper work ethic in freedpeople as early as February 1862. Posing the rhetorical question "'What shall be done with the four million slaves if emancipated?'" Douglass had answered, "Do nothing with them. . . . Please to mind your business and leave us to mind ours. If we cannot stand up, then let us fall down. We ask nothing at the hands of the American people but simple justice, and an equal chance to live."[49]

Initially, the transition from policing marronage to policing vagrancy looked much like a change in name only. Colonel French instituted an evening curfew for Black vagrants that transparently reproduced the city's antebellum slave curfew. Police continued the fervent hunt for fugitives in the name of suppressing Black vagrancy. In January, New Orleans resident Moses Townsley lodged a complaint after four policemen burst into his home, seizing the Black woman whom he sheltered. Townsley argued that the Federal government had nullified the state's fugitive slave laws. Colonel French conceded the point but rejoined that police *were* authorized to arrest and return a "slave as a Vagrant." Later that week, Cyprian Clamorgan demanded to know why the Police Jail still imprisoned enslaved people for "safekeeping." Again, French retorted that masters could still purchase jail time for their workers, provided that the worker was "vagrant." When William Gray drafted a similar letter of protest, he, too, was told that jailing a Black woman for "safekeeping" was "perfectly proper . . . to prevent her from being a vagrant about the streets." Former slaveholders quickly recognized that they could regain control over their resistant property by manipulating the Union army's preoccupation with suppressing Black crime. One Black woman reported that her mistress threatened that "she can do what she likes with her servants by saying [to the army] they were disturbing the peace."[50]

For those seeking refuge in New Orleans, the distinction between their antebellum policing as fugitive slaves and their wartime policing as Black vagrants doubtless felt nearly meaningless. Nathan McKinney, his wife, Harriett, and their young sons, John and Nathan Jr., had escaped into New Orleans after their owner had fled the Union army's approach. The couple found employment within the city, earning sufficient wages to rent a room. In January 1863, after the family had rented in New Orleans for three weeks, Nathan McKinney learned that police had arrested and imprisoned Harriett, separating "the mother from hire suckling Child." Nathan McKinney assumed that police intended to return Harriett to their owner, but as the anxious husband and father wrote in a desperate letter to his government, "I and my wife . . . [are] not willing To go Back."[51]

With each passing day, more and more fugitives and Black New Orleanians, though still enslaved by law, insisted that something *had* changed: that even if the Emancipation Proclamation did not apply to occupied Louisiana, their de facto status was something different from "slave," entitling them to protections from arbitrary arrest and confinement. Writing from the City Workhouse in February 1863, eight imprisoned Black men declared themselves "unjustly confined" in a letter to General Banks. Legally the men were the property of the New Orleans Gas Light Company, though their supervisors had expelled them that previous November. Ever since, they had lived and worked as free persons, until January, when they had been arrested by police while leaving their workplace for dinner, "for no cause, but that we had no passes." The men had found gainful employment and thus demonstrated their ability to rule themselves. They asserted that they should have the legal rights to a hearing before "judge or court," to face specific charges, and to testify in their defense. One of the men noted the irony that by leaving his infirm wife and child without any support, his arrest had caused the very destitution and dependency on charity that vagrancy statutes were nominally intended to suppress. Writing on behalf of her friend Rosanna, Nancy Young expressed similar sentiments. Rosanna had also been expelled by her master and subsequently lived as though free. Yet "After leaveing her in Charge of her Self," Rosanna's master returned and "Put her in prisin," condemning Rosanna to "conseel[ed] Ponishment" and separating her from her three children, including "her baby Not two months old." Young asserted that Rosanna was entitled to her children and to due process. Having already lived "in Charge of her self," Rosanna had demonstrated her capacity for self-rule: why did the state presume that Rosanna's autonomy posed a public menace?[52]

In protesting their arbitrary confinement, Louisianians who were still enslaved laid claim to legal rights. In and of itself, this was revolutionary. For the time being, these petitions often fell on deaf ears. Tentatively, the Union army had come to support slavery's destruction. Yet supporting emancipation had not relieved Federal authorities of their deep anxieties regarding Black freedom.

"The Privileges of Free Men"

While enslaved Louisianians rebelled against slaveholders and state, a parallel rebellion against racial caste was coalescing within New Orleans's free Black population. Within this population, few families were more prosperous, or held in higher regard, than the Bonseigneurs. The family patriarch, Jean Baptiste Deterville Bonseigneur, was a respected community elder, having lived in New Orleans since his evacuation from revolutionary Saint-Domingue as a baby. As a teenager, Jean Baptiste had fought under General Andrew Jackson in the Battle of New Orleans, during the War of 1812. Later he had opened a grocery, which flourished. He purchased several properties about the city and claimed ownership of at least one slave. His sons and nephews were all accomplished tradesmen, artisans, and businessmen.[53]

Yet since the 1850s, all the Bonseigneurs had faced mounting harassment. In 1858, as white New Orleans debated the complete expulsion of all free Black residents, two of Jean Baptiste's sons—Virgil Bonseigneur, a plasterer, and Henri Bonseigneur, a cigar store clerk—had been charged with illegal residency and "contravention" at the behest of their late uncle's estranged widow, Marie-Thérèse Blanchard, following an intrafamily dispute. Though Virgil and Henri Bonseigneur were both Louisiana natives and prominent men within their community, the brothers had been humiliatingly summoned to court, compelled to post a $1,000 bond, and forced to face the fearsome possibility of expulsion from their homeland.[54]

In April 1861, immediately on the outbreak of war—as policemen rounded up "contraventionists" en masse and as the expulsion of all free Black Louisianians seemed imminent—a coalition of free Black businessmen had endeavored to protect their community and demonstrate their southern belonging by organizing a free Black Confederate militia unit. Perhaps recalling his expulsion hearing of two years before, Virgil Bonseigneur resolved to enlist in this unit and was assigned the rank of captain. State Confederate leadership never felt comfortable with the idea of Black militiamen, however, and refused to provision the unit with uniforms or arms. The state legislature outlawed nonwhite military enlistment in January 1862, and the unit was disbanded.[55]

Now the Federals controlled New Orleans, and the city's free Black residents debated their next course of action. When General Butler had authorized the formation of a free Black Union army regiment, many of the Bonseigneurs' peers had enlisted, eliciting howls of betrayal from their white neighbors. Catholic clergy had denied the sacrament to free Black enlistees and expelled them from their church services. White landlords had evicted and harassed the families of Black enlistees, while white pedestrians heckled and hooted at passing Black troops. Remaining social ties between white and Black colleagues and neighbors were severed, and fights between police and Black soldiers regularly erupted in the streets.[56] Virgil and Henri Bonseigneur would have recognized that enlistment within the Union army posed new opportunities and renewed risks. Should they try to court the esteem of their white peers or abandon any remaining hope of that esteem by committing themselves to the Federal cause?

In many ways, that decision was made for the Bonseigneurs, and the city's other free Black residents, by the actions of policemen on the night of January 21, 1863.

Under the pretense of enforcing Banks's labor system, Colonel French had scheduled for that night a coordinated citywide roundup of all Black persons found outdoors after the vagrant curfew without passes or free papers. The unannounced roundup netted between 300 and 600 people, among them dozens of freeborn Black professionals and property owners deliberately targeted by policemen who knew them to be free.[57] For New Orleans's free Black residents, the nocturnal raid on "vagrants" amounted to the threat of a pogrom.

Two northern newspapermen—Albert Hills of the *Boston Evening Traveller* and Francis Schell of *Frank Leslie's Illustrated Newspaper*—happened to take a stroll that evening in the affluent neighborhood surrounding their hotel. A well-dressed young woman and an older woman whom they presumed to be her mother came running down the avenue, tearful and terrified, begging Schell and Hills for protection from their pursuers. The newspapermen watched as policemen overtook the women, seizing them "for being out without passes." "The women begged, with tears in their eyes, for their liberty," Hills later described. Schell's sketch of the incident would appear in the subsequent issue of *Frank Leslie's Illustrated Newspaper*. Hills resolved to follow the women to the jail.[58]

"The scene at the jail," a third reporter, John Hamilton of the *New York Times*, would later write, "was something that will not easily be forgotten by those who saw it." In the First District lockup, Hills witnessed some fifty weeping Black women, "packed like so many cattle" in a cell built to hold no more than eight prisoners. In an opposite cell stood their "fathers, husbands and brothers. . . . Over one hundred colored men and boys." Everyone was "weeping, imploring, and almost scared to death." Many of the free Black prisoners may have believed that, like soi-disant libre prisoners before them, they were being transformed into slaves through the prison. Yet the imprisoned enslaved people looked particularly distraught, according to Hamilton, since they had inferred from their arrest that the Emancipation Proclamation had been revoked. Husbands and wives reached for one another through the bars. Into the night, the crowd of enslaved and free Black detainees sang "John Brown's Body" and hymns.[59]

That night, similar scenes replayed throughout all of New Orleans's lockups and jails. Even to outsiders it was obvious that police were deliberately disregarding the customary class and caste distinctions between presumptive free persons and presumptive slaves by intentionally comingling the enslaved and free, young and old, rich and poor, laborer and landowner, on the pretense that all were vagrant. This purposeful erasure of social distinctions seemed a gross violation to the white northerners who witnessed it. Schell called it a "promiscuous heap" and "revolting." Hamilton deplored how "respectably dressed

females and children—some as fair as the fairest Caucasians—were piled ig-
nominiously and promiscuously with the lowest of both sexes." Hills also fixated on how many of the prisoners appeared well dressed or were of such light
complexion that they "would pass for white . . . in New York or Boston." The
next day, Colonel French was relieved of duty. The military transferred some
prisoners to the Bureau of Negro Labor, releasing others to their masters for
$1.25 each in jail fees. The legally free prisoners were required to purchase their
liberty for $1.50.[60]

Propertied white residents applauded the arrests. "Nothing has given such
unbound satisfaction as this order," an informant reported to Banks. "Citizens
say they are now passing the first peaceful evenings for many months." "Col.
French, our indefatigable Chief of Police, is beginning to take the contraband
bull by the horns, with a view of teaching him a salutary lesson," lauded the
Daily Picayune. "Now the old rule of legal restraint is to be enforced."[61]

Yet for the free Black community of New Orleans, the ordeal of January
21 was a profound collective trauma and a galvanizing moment. Their worst
fears of the 1850s—that policing powers governing maroons, vagrants, and free
Black transients would be extended to include them and used to erase their
customary legal protections—seemed realized.[62]

In response, 487 free Black New Orleanians—nearly 1 of every 5 of the city's
free Black men—signed a petition protesting police disregard for the state's
legal doctrine that "colored" individuals could travel within Louisiana free of
police harassment. "The undersigned respectfully represents [*sic*]," read the
document, "that they are free colored persons, and natives of this State and
city." "All of them born free, as well as their parents before them . . . all of them
owners of movable property" and "engaged in trade and commercial occupations" or "mechanical and industrial pursuits." "By the laws of Louisiana," the
petitioners explained, "persons of color are presumed to be free" and "entitled
to the privileges of free men." The petitioners rejected the "frivolous, vexatious
and unjust" notion that they needed to provide proof of their freedom, arguing
that "having been free for several generations," the requirement was not only
insulting but that, in many cases, such documentation no longer existed. Recognizing that the theory of preventative policing was being broadly redeployed
as a weapon of racial harassment, they requested "that henceforth they may be
delivered from vexatious and illegal arrest and confinement, and directions issued to the police and all in authority to respect the presumption of law in favor
of their freedom, and to make no arrests except in cases of violation of law."[63]

The sheer logistics of collecting nearly 500 signatures, performed within
eight days of the arrests, is a noteworthy accomplishment in community organization. Yet the petition is remarkable in other ways. In it, the petitioners

showcased various discursive strategies that New Orleans's free Black community had developed in their multigenerational struggle for citizenship rights. The petitioners set forth the legal basis for the presumption of their free status, citing a chain of state judicial rulings stretching back to 1810. Although New Orleans's free Black population was socioeconomically diverse, with both freeborn and formerly enslaved members from Louisiana and elsewhere, virtually all the petition's signers came from a relatively privileged upper echelon of native, freeborn, and francophone businessmen, skilled artisans, professionals, and landowners. Atop the petition's first page, the petition's organizers prominently clustered the names of seventeen surviving veterans of the War of 1812, including Jean Baptiste Deterville Bonseigneur: a reminder to audiences, in an age when citizenship and military service were closely linked, of the community's proud tradition of military service. Next appeared signatures representing fourteen men who presumably had organized the petition: Eugène Rillieux, Lucien Lamanière, the "Dumas Brothers" (Joseph Dumas and Julien Clovis), Étienne Dubois, François Lacroix, the "Tinchant Bros" (Joseph, Pierre, and Jules), Dr. Louis Charles Roudanez, Jean Baptiste Roudanez, Georges Alces, and the Bonseigneur brothers, Virgil and Henri. These organizers included some of the city's most respected and prosperous freeborn businessmen and community leaders: Georges Alces's cigar factory was said to employ 200 workers, Dr. Roudanez had medical degrees from Dartmouth College and the Faculté de Médecine de Paris, and François Lacroix was among the city's wealthiest landowners.[64] Of the hundreds of proceeding signatures, each one suggests a degree of literacy and education.[65] Many signatories proudly self-identified as property owners, merchants, and Union army officers, underscoring their respectability while tacitly emphasizing the absurdity of seizing members of their community for vagrancy. Five women signed, four of whom were members of the Tinchant-Gonzales family, each proudly identifying herself as a *"propriétaire"* (property owner).[66]

In no small measure, the petition of January 1863 marked the beginning of a new civil rights struggle: a step onto a road leading to the political mobilization of Black Louisianans; Reconstruction-era battles for Black political, suffrage, and labor rights; and, eventually, a campaign against racial segregation that would be stifled by the landmark Supreme Court case *Plessy v. Ferguson* in 1896.[67] Several of the petition's organizers and dozens of other signatories would fast become influential figures and important political leaders within state and national Reconstruction politics. Two of the petition's organizers, brothers Louis Charles and Jean Baptiste Roudanez, had recently founded the first general circulation Black newspaper in the South, *L'Union,* in September 1862, along with fellow signatory Paul Trévigne (both Jean Baptiste

Roudanez and Paul Trévigne had spent nights in the Police Jail as young men). In 1864, after *L'Union* had been driven out of business, these men would found a second newspaper, the *New Orleans Tribune*, which would fast cultivate a national and international readership, becoming a powerful forum for Black radical politics.[68] Other petition organizers and signatories included the future leadership of Louisiana's Republican Party: delegates to the state constitutional convention of 1868 Henri Bonseigneur, Édouard Tinchant, Arnold Bertonneau, Jean Baptiste Esnard, William Vigers, and Pierre Deslondes (who also would serve as Louisiana secretary of state); Reconstruction-era state legislators Victor-Eugène Macarty, Joseph Mansion, Octave Belot, and Jean Baptiste Jourdain; Louisiana governor P. B. S. Pinchback; and innumerable leaders of Republican Party ward clubs and neighborhood associations. The petitioners' claim that persons of African ancestry were entitled to public dignity and unencumbered movement within the public sphere also suggests an emergent assertion of "public rights" that would underpin subsequent civil rights battles over the integration of transit, schools, and public spaces.[69]

The arrests and protests of January 1863 also coincided with the collapse of New Orleans's police jail system. In March 1863, the military barred the exchange of moneys for fugitives' return and transferred all prisoners confined for "safekeeping" from the Police Jail to the Bureau of Negro Labor. In July, New Orleans's Police Jail—by then, virtually empty—was closed entirely and converted into a military prison.[70] Thereafter, Black persons arrested for vagrancy were either incarcerated in the City Workhouse alongside white inmates or immediately removed to a requisitioned cotton press that the Bureau of Negro Labor had repurposed as a temporary internment facility.

"We Are Hunted Up in the Streets"

Fears that police were cementing a new racial regime, under the guise of suppressing vagrancy, would soon seem confirmed. For French's replacement as chief of police, Banks selected Brigadier General James Bowen, a former police commissioner from New York City, who ordered in March another coordinated roundup of all "vagrant negroes having no regular habitation or employment . . . in order that they may be placed at work upon plantations or upon government works." Bowen's orders neglected to define vagrancy, and perhaps the general assumed that police would only target fugitives who appeared able-bodied, homeless, and unemployed. Instead, police and provost marshals again seized any person of African descent found outdoors, including the employed and freeborn. To rectify the confusion, Bowen instituted a new vagrant pass system, instructing police and provost marshals to arrest *only* Black persons who lacked passes signed by their employers. This solution outraged free Black property owners, many of whom protested that they had no employers or were employers themselves. The legally free and fugitive alike thronged the office of the provost marshal general to obtain coveted exemptions.[71] It mattered little: police disregarded Bowen's pass system, continuing to arrest any person of African descent. "Owners passes are utterly disregarded and the documents of free persons of Color entirely ignored," Colonel George Hanks, the super-intendent of the Bureau of Negro Labor, complained. Concluding that "the order for the arrest of vagrants is made an instrument of oppression rather than a correction of an evil," Bowen halted the arrests, pending a clearer defi-nition of crime. Two days later, Bowen resumed the arrests, on condition that police and provost marshals "be careful" to seize *only* unemployed Black per-sons who had abandoned their owners, were "loafing about the streets without passes," and whose "appearance" incontrovertibly indicated itinerant poverty.[72]

It had become clear to Bowen that Federal authorities and southern police-men, while all declaring their intention to suppress Black vagrancy, did not all mean the same thing. Bowen appears to have assumed that police and provost marshals would target the homeless, itinerate, and unemployed: enforcing, in other words, a definition of vagrancy aligned to northern free labor ideology. In practice, many provost marshals grabbed Black pedestrians indiscriminately, while local law enforcement policed vagrancy in ways similar to the ways by which the crime had been policed in antebellum New Orleans, by seizing per-sons who seemed innately dependent and unqualified for total freedom, re-gardless of their actual employment status. Simultaneously, local police used the arrests as a pretext to harass New Orleans's free Black population and erase that population's customary legal protections.

In August, New Orleans's free Black community was thrust into turmoil a third time—this time, by squads of Black soldiers as well as local police, em-powered by Union army recruitment officers to seize Black vagrants for im-pressment into the army. The scale of these arrests was considerable: the *Daily Picayune* described "several hundreds" arrested on the night of August 7 alone. Once again, police "exceeded their instructions," in the words of one recruit-ment officer, by indiscriminately seizing freeborn and fugitive, employed and unemployed, landless and landed. The hunt for vagrants extended to Baton Rouge, where some three dozen free Black residents petitioned for remon-strance: "We are hunted up in the streets, in the market house, and other places whilst engaged in our daily vocations, and marched off to the Peniten-tiary, whence we are placed with contrabands, and forced into the service. . . . We were born free, have lived free, and wish to be treated as freemen." Ironi-cally, this search for criminally homeless vagrants extended into many private residences. Among the homes entered was that of freeborn man of color William Bourgeois, ransacked late at night by six police officers, who brutally beat and removed his young son, Peter, when the adolescent refused military service. *L'Union* expressed particular vexation at the seizure of Drauzin Gabriel, a freeborn Black veteran of the recent Battle of Port Hudson, arrested only days after his honorable discharge from Union service.[73]

These sequential waves of arrests demonstrated to Louisiana's free Black community that their long-standing protected legal status was moot. Previously, antebellum police had tended to assess multiple factors in determining whom should be summarily seized, including a person's presumed race, ancestry, class, employment, social station, or place of birth. Wartime policemen cast these complex calculations aside. Under the auspices of suppressing Black vagrancy, police enforced a new racial order, in which the protections of class were diminished, and African ancestry—irrespective of social station—became a marker of presumed criminal vagrancy.

"To Announce Their Freedom Is Not to Make Them Free"

Across the South, as the Federal army advanced, occupation forces imposed coercive labor systems that resembled, and were often directly modeled on, the Louisiana contract system developed by Butler and Banks. People fleeing plantations and into occupied towns were arrested by provost marshals and local law enforcement—initially as contrabands, later as vagrants—and compelled to sign one-year plantation contracts, build public works, or labor in government-managed plantations and workcamps. Declaring that "labor is a public duty and idleness and vagrancy a crime," Major General Ulysses S. Grant's army imposed labor regulations, modeled on "the rules adopted by Maj. Gen. N. P. Banks," in March 1864. "Treat [them] as vagabonds," advised a provost marshal general stationed in South Carolina that August: "Keep all the people possible on the farms or plantations at *honest steady* labor" while sending anyone who fled their plantation or who refused to work to "a place where they *must work*—a work house or chain gang." Federals in Memphis began arresting "all idlers, vagrants and persons without lawfully occupation or means of support" in June 1863. Federals in Natchez expelled all *"idle* negroes . . . not employed by some *responsible white person"* in March 1864. As in New Orleans, these mass arrests encoded assumptions, common to many white southerners and northerners, regarding the relation between idleness and crime, the dangers of unwarranted dependency on public support, and freedpeople's unpreparedness or unworthiness for freedom.[74]

Some Federals recognized that the creation of a compulsory labor system, maintained through the omnipresent threat of vagrancy arrest, fell far short of true freedom. "I have grown satisfied that there is, and can be, no such thing as the actual immediate emancipation of a large mass of plantation slaves," one lieutenant colonel confessed from Mississippi. "To announce their freedom is not to make them free, and the continuous rigors of necessity and restraints of authority . . . constitutes essentially the substance of slavery still." Faced with "black masses" of "vagrants," the officer concluded that "the thorough, careful policing of the entire area of the slave States" combined with an "intimate, close-fitting system of prescriptions" would be necessary to compel "every able-bodied negro to work." To a Confederate propagandist stationed in London, these mass arrests of freedpeople revealed the Federals' true intentions. In slavery's place, they would "substitute a 'workhouse system' which retains all the worst characteristics [of slavery] without any of the compensating advantages."[75]

Within New Orleans, as the newly emancipated began the arduous work of building new lives in freedom for themselves and their families, the constant threat of seizure, family separation, and forced transport to the countryside sowed unremitting terror. Arrests were "so general all over the City" that Black residents were afraid to leave their homes, Colonel Hanks reported in July 1863, "lest they should be picked up in the Streets." Other Federals described how vagrancy arrests triggered "excitement," anxiety, distrust, "a state of the upmost uneasiness and excitement," and "the greatest consternation" among Black residents. Julia Le Grand, the headmistress of school for white girls, noted in her diary how one servant, Mary, grew visibly anxious whenever her daughter, Emma, left for work: Mary was terrified that "the Yankees will take her [daughter] off." Le Grand expressed satisfaction at how the arrests had cowed New Orleans's Black population: "The insolent negroes who have been boasting of Yankee support are very much crest-fallen and ashamed."[76]

Mass roundups struck without warning. "To-day from forty to fifty colored women, picked up without notification on the streets, were driven at the point of Yankee bayonets on a boat and taken to a plantation," Le Grand noted in her diary on March 30, 1863. Newspapers alluded to mass arrests on a weekly, and sometimes daily, basis:

March 27, 1864: "Several contrabands were brought up and sent to [the army] in order that they might purge themselves of the charge of vagrancy."

March 29, 1864: "A number of vagrant negroes . . . were sent to Col. Hanks."

July 1, 1864: "Nearly a regiment of colored individuals were brought up by the police on the charge of being vagrant contrabands."

July 7, 1864: "More than the usual number of vagrant and homeless negroes were forwarded to Government agents for disposal."

July 8, 1864: "A number of vagrant negroes were turned over to
government agents for proper disposal."

In addition to conducting street arrests, provost marshals regularly emptied
the City Workhouse of Black prisoners, categorizing everyone as "vagrant" regardless of the actual crime for which they had been committed. In April 1864,
one officer counted 1,100 persons, seized in both countryside and city, imprisoned within a requisitioned cotton press, awaiting their rural relocation.[77]
Black residents learned to scatter at the approach of Union troops. Writing
his wife from a New Orleans suburb, a New Hampshire soldier described the
process of arresting Black vagrants and forcing them onto transports: "Part of
the company went down to an old brickyard this morning, and surrounded a
lot of n——s, and put them on a boat. . . . [You] have to drive them to the boat
at the point of the bayonet; when they see you coming they run like a flock of
sheep, but draw your gun up to your shoulder and tell them to halt, and they
will stop as quick as if they were shot. They're as afraid of a soldier as they
are of the devil."[78] Soldiers were authorized to use deadly force when arresting
"vagrant negroes." For two months in 1863, New Orleans newspapers closely
followed the trial of a Black army sergeant named Pete Johnson, charged with
murder for shooting dead a fleeing suspected vagrant. Ultimately the judge
ruled that although the "deceased was not a vagrant," sergeant Johnson had
believed him to be one and therefore was "guilty of a crime less than murder."[79]
Meanwhile, in the Union-occupied countryside, provost marshals tasked
with maintaining plantation discipline used vagrancy arrests to quash strikes,
detain plantation workers who broke their contracts, and dismantle independent farming collectives. "The Provost Marshal tells the negro what they
must do," explained one officer: "Either work faithfully under this Contract,
for wages, or for Govt without wages."[80] Initially, provost marshals had relied
on corporal violence to subdue resistant workers: freedpeople were whipped,
locked in stocks, and restrained with ropes. Throughout 1863, the Department
of the Gulf endeavored to suppress provost marshals' use of corporal violence,
deepening their reliance on the threat of vagrancy arrest, imprisonment, and
penal labor.[81] Provost Marshal William Bragg, tasked with maintaining order
on plantations throughout St. Bernard and Plaquemines Parishes, reported
the issuance of fifteen punishments on plantation field hands between July 15
and July 30, 1864. For crimes that included "indolence," "feigning sickness,"
"interfering with policeman," "disobedience of orders," "abusive language,"
"fighting," "stealing," and "running away," Bragg docked workers' wages, had
workers jailed, sentenced workers to the chain gang, and forced one woman to
stand atop a barrel.[82]

Provost marshals grumbled that these punitive measures were poorly designed for the task at hand. "They will not work," complained Edward Page, an exasperated provost marshal overseeing some thirty plantations, in February 1863. "To prevent in ordinary times negroes from running away was difficult, now, tis simply impossible." Page estimated that he had already declared 300 plantation workers to be vagrant that week alone, sending them all to the Bureau of Negro Labor's requisitioned cotton press in New Orleans. He predicted that he would send another 300 before the week's end.[83] Black Louisianians, it was becoming clear, would not readily submit to a new system of bonded labor.

Redefining Racial Dependency

In January 1864, General Banks declared that Louisiana's state constitutional provisions regarding slavery were "inoperative and void." Two months later, and acting under President Lincoln's instructions, Banks called for the creation of a new state constitution that would officially abolish slavery in Louisiana. With ratification of the new state constitution in September, slavery was formally outlawed in the state.[84]

Slavery's formal abolition did little to resolve Louisiana's disputes over vagrancy policy. At its core, conflicts over vagrancy reflected subtler deliberations over the nature of Black dependency and the relation of race to criminality. Federals who held the racist conviction that Black Americans were congenitally dependent—a "people identified with the cultivation of the soil," in Banks's words, destined for serfdom and perpetually incapable of self-governance— tended to equate *any* autonomous Black economic activity, or nonagricultural employ, with criminal vagrancy. Proponents of this racial logic sought to bind every freedperson to a white master, performing vagrancy arrests in ways aligned to the vision of former slaveholders.[85] Federals who rejected the assumption of innate Black inferiority but believed that slavery had crippled Black work ethic and self-sufficiency perceived that the government's antivagrancy policies were temporary measures, designed to relieve freedpeople of their dependency by instilling industrious habits. In policing vagrancy, proponents of this logic strove to distinguish freedpeople who already were "industrious" and "self-supporting" from those whom they presumed to be reliant on thievery or public charity.

Freedpeople, radical abolitionists, and a growing camp of dissidents within the Union army rejected the coercion of freedpeople outright. They argued that former slaves knew the meaning of hard work better than anyone and that to charge a gainfully employed or economically self-sufficient freedperson with vagrancy was patently absurd. To proponents of this view, arrests seemed cruelly arbitrary and racially biased. Police summarily seized freedpeople "for *fear* they might become a public charge," argued William Gray, while "in ninety cases out of a hundred . . . the vagrants about the streets . . . belonged to the white race."[86]

Efforts to police vagrancy in New Orleans forced Union army soldiers to confront their own assumptions regarding the relation of race and crime. The arrests of honorably discharged Black veterans of the Union army, and of the families of active servicemen, proved particularly contentious. "I respectfully request information," one confused provost marshal wrote. "Is a contraband, (who has enlisted in the Army or Navy of the United States, and been honorably discharged thereupon)—to all intents and purposes, a free man? And can he go where he will, without molestation, on showing his discharge papers?"[87] Active servicemen were both distraught and incensed to learn that their wives and children were not exempt from seizure. "Nearly every day the wife of some Soldier is spirited away," protested the commander of one Black regiment. The soldiers had believed that their military service afforded them the status of household heads and their wives and children the protections of dependent household wards. Banks disagreed: the families of Black soldiers "will not be relieved from the necessity of labor, any more than families of men in the white regiments."[88]

The criminalization of freedwomen proved no less vexing. With freedom, many freedwomen resisted full-time wage work, asserting a right to allocate the bulk of their labor to maintaining their households and rearing their children.[89] "The female laborers give me the most trouble," one provost marshal complained from St. John the Baptist Parish. "With their freedom, came the idea that they should attend exclusively to domestic duties."[90] Similar questions applied to freedchildren who withdrew from wage labor to attend school. Colonel Hanks, superintendent of the Bureau of Negro Labor, complained that his office was "daily" besieged by parents seeking to regain custody of their children. "Are not the Parents[,] being free[,] entitled to the Custody of their offspring[?]" Hanks asked his superior. "If not, of what benefit is their freedom[?]"[91]

In practice, each provost marshal enforced his own definition of the crime. In Jefferson Parish, Colonel Robert Brown instructed troops under his command to arrest any freedperson "not regularly employed by some Planter, or other person who has a permanent residence." In St. Mary Parish, Captain Albert Stearns defined vagrancy as the appearance of idleness while also instructing troops under his command to exempt from arrest all women "whose *husbands* or *fathers* are employed," any servant employed by the army or a private household, and any self-employed worker whose labor he considered essential to the Union army (in particular, laundresses).[92]

Other officers ordered the indiscriminate arrest of any self-employed freed-person. In August 1864, as another harvest season loomed, a cabal of former slaveholders informed the army of four autonomous communities of freed-people, spread throughout various swamps beyond city limits, where an estimated 10,000 freedpeople survived by hunting, farming, and selling lumber while remaining "in idleness part of the time." The planters conceded that these freedpeople "work enough to exist" but defined them as vagrant because they lacked white management. Soldiers under the command of Brigadier General Thomas Sherman "scoured" the swamps, later reporting that all the vagrants had been arrested for labor reassignment—though Sherman conceded that many of the prisoners looked neither idle nor unemployed. "How is a party of soldiers to ascertain exactly whether a stray negro is employed or not, other than his own word for it[?]" Sherman mulled. "If their words are to be taken—none, or fewer negroes could be obtained."[93]

Freedpeople protested that in the name of discouraging Black dependency, the military was actively suppressing Black self-sufficiency. A group of roughly sixty freedpeople in Terrebonne Parish addressed this irony as they tried to hold onto the independent farming collective that they had established on the abandoned plantation of their former owner. In April 1863, the government resolved to transfer the plantation to a white lessee. The freedpeople dissented, declaring that they embodied the Black self-reliance that the government professed to desire. "We have succeeded in making ourselves in a measure independent," the freedpeople protested. "We think it but just that we should be allowed to work the land" and not be forced to hand "it all over to someone else." A provost marshal confirmed that these "neat, thrifty & industrious laborers" had "supported themselves creditably by their own exertions & labor" while receiving "no aid from the government."[94] The freedpeople persevered until that following March, when another provost marshal ruled that the farm must be placed "under the superintendence of some white Man" because the existence of independent Black farmers inspired dissent among workers on neighboring plantations. The plantation was turned over to a white lessee, and the residents were made into subordinate wage laborers.[95]

The conflict in Terrebonne Parish laid bare the core paradox undergirding Federal labor policy: criminalization of Black dependence, coupled with deep fear of Black autonomy. Federal antivagrancy policies assumed that Black reliance on government handouts would have a morally deleterious influence on freedpeople's work ethic. At the same time, these policies reflected racial fears that Black Americans were chronically prone to idleness, were incapable of self-sufficiency, and threatened public order if not coerced. For many within the army, the objective of Banks's labor arrangement was not the suppression of Black dependency so much as the enforcement of Black dependency on white employers.

To sort through these quagmires, in April 1864, Colonel Hanks created an "Inspector of Vagrants," charged with distinguishing idlers from the industrious. To the post, Hanks appointed an army chaplain from New York, already well known among freedpeople through his massive, 1,000-pupil Sunday school classes, named Thomas Conway. On assuming the post, Conway launched a thorough investigation of New Orleans's prisons, finding and releasing "large numbers" of freedpeople incarcerated on flimsy or nonexistent charges concocted by their former owners. He began siding with freedpeople when former owners petitioned for their arrest. Not long after Conway's appointment, Henriette Cougot petitioned for the arrest of a "vagrant" freedwoman who lurked menacingly near Cougot's home. Interviewing the alleged vagrant, Conway learned that she lurked because Cougot held the freedwoman's daughter, Coucotte, in bondage. Furthermore, Conway felt persuaded that the freedwoman was "industrious," lived "in a way entirely creditable and honorable," took "excellent care" of her daughter, and was married to a discharged soldier. Ruling that the freedwoman was not a vagrant, Conway ordered that Coucotte be returned to her mother.[96]

"To Choose One's Own Employment"

Throughout 1863 and 1864, radical abolitionists in the North were unrelenting in their denunciation of Banks's coercive labor program. "'Banks's freedom' . . . is no freedom to me," decried Wendell Phillips, a regular critic of the Louisiana plan. "The idea of Northern liberty is, a man competent to sell his own toil, to select his own work," and who had the "right to quit" and to negotiate wages.[97] Frederick Douglass was another persistent critic, declaring "Gen. Banks' policy" to be the "chief danger" facing Black Americans "at the present moment. . . . It practically enslaves the Negro, and makes the Proclamation of 1863 a mockery and delusion." If freedom "means anything," Douglass continued, "it is the right to choose one's own employment."[98] Implicit in these radicals' denunciations lay a conceptualization of freedom district from that enshrined by northern free labor ideology: true freedom, these radicals suggested, was incompatible with coercive poor law and expansive state police power.

By late 1864, northern support for Banks's labor policies was waning as radical abolitionists' critiques begun resonating with broader audiences. Banks had created "a police system" bent on creating "serfs," not "freedmen," charged Brigadier General James S. Wadsworth following a tour of Louisiana in 1864.[99]

In 1863, the preliminary report of the American Freedmen's Inquiry Commission had endorsed "a scheme of guardianship or protection" for freedpeople, perhaps modeled on "the system of apprenticeship in the English West Indies": only one year later, the final report denounced all racialized labor controls, including those "relative to vagrancy," citing "experience in the West Indies" as proof that "emancipation, when it takes place, should be unconditional and absolute."[100] James McKaye, a member of that commission, accused Banks's labor program of inhibiting Black "self control" and "self reliance." "If the only object to be accomplished was simply 'to compel the negro to labor' in a condition of perpetual subordination and subjection, this arrangement would be appropriate enough," McKaye argued. "But if the object be to make the colored man a self-supporting and self-defending member of the community, then he must . . . be left to take the responsibilities of his on existence and well being, as well as that of his family."[101] For their part, northern conservatives continued defending Banks's plan as an essential albeit temporary expediency, designed to instill habits of autonomy and industry in a people unready for total freedom.[102]

Faced with mounting resistance from within and outside Louisiana, Banks endeavored to rebrand his antivagrancy policies as temporary charitable interventions, rather than punitively coercive and permanent measures, aligned to the northern poor relief model. Launching a goodwill tour of the North, the general argued that he had always intended for his regulations to be short-lived. At a speech in Boston, Banks insisted that assuaging freedpeople's "suffering, disease and death"—and not the protection of the plantation economy, the suppression of Black autonomy, and the seduction of Unionist slaveholders—had always been his labor program's primary aim. Back in Louisiana, Colonel Hanks proposed a system of industrial farms modeled on the "pauper farms in New England . . . where the indigent infirm and aged can be cared for, and the vagrant and insubordinate be disciplined." Four former plantations were transformed into government-managed "home colonies" where elderly and disabled freedpeople could receive medical care while working "as much as they are able." In circulars posted in Black churches, Hanks tried to appease freedpeople's fears. Vagrancy policing was an act of "benevolence and mercy, for the benefit of the Colored People," aimed at alleviating urban crowding, disease, unemployment, and pauperism. The industrious and self-supporting "need have no fears of being arrested," Hanks promised.[103]

In August 1864, Hanks was removed from the Bureau of Negro Labor, following accusations that he received bribes from planters in exchange for workers. The Reverend Thomas Conway, the city's "Inspector of Vagrants," was appointed Hanks's successor.[104] After renaming the department the Bureau of Free Labor, Conway restricted the definition of vagrancy to male household

heads who refused to work and to support their dependents. Conway's definition affirmed that Black men were to be considered legitimate household
heads, that Black women were entitled to restrict their labor to the domestic
sphere, and that Black children were entitled to attend school.[105]

As Conway assumed control of the department, provost marshals launched
a fourth and final attack on New Orleans's freeborn and formerly freed Black
residents. This final wave of arrests was particularly painful: several children and distinguished veterans of the War of 1812 were among those seized.
Arrestees were marched from the city at the point of bayonet and imprisoned
for days. The *New Orleans Tribune*, successor to *L'Union*, declared it a week
of "gloom and sorrow." Six leading freeborn Black property holders, including
L'Union and *Tribune* editors (and Police Jail veterans) Jean Baptiste Roudanez
and Paul Trévigne, petitioned for an end to the "arbitrary" seizure of members
"of our population . . . as if they were felons or criminals."[106]

By then, two years of intrusive police action within New Orleans had had
major ramifications for the city, region, and nation. Labor programs modeled
on Banks's "Louisiana Plan" were fast spreading throughout the occupied
South. The nation was deeply emmeshed in a debate over the relation of race,
dependency, and crime. Among New Orleans's freeborn and formerly freed
Black residents, two years of targeted police harassment had galvanized an
increasingly radical politics. For the tens of thousands of freedpeople seeking
refuge in the South's occupied cities, Emancipation had been a fraught and
fitful process mediated by private and state violence.

Yet with this final wave of arrests and Conway's ascension, vagrancy seizures
within New Orleans ground to a halt. In March 1865, as the Confederacy crum-
bled, Congress established the Bureau of Refugees, Freedmen, and Abandoned
Lands for the care, provisioning, and direction of freedpeople. Conway's Bureau of Free Labor was subsumed into this new agency.[107] From his new post
as superintendent of the Louisiana Freedmen's Bureau, Conway declared that
there were no longer any true vagrants left in the city. Every freedman was employed, he argued, generally under satisfactory terms. Freedwomen were free
to choose between wage work and the maintenance of domestic households.
Freed children were free to attend school. Since the arrival of the Union army,
"the main question" had been between "employment on the one hand or idleness and vagrancy on the other." That question, Conway declared, "is settled."
Arbitrary arrests had been stopped, the basic contours of a postwar labor system laid out. Prophetically, Conway foresaw two potential sources of future
disunion: the machinations of the city's "discontented" freeborn and formerly
freed Black activists, many of whom clamored for full civil and political rights,
and the "prejudice" of the "old slave-holder class," who plotted the resurrection
of slaveholder power.[108]

Bird's-eye view of New Orleans. By 1840, New Orleans was the wealthiest city in the South, the third largest city in the nation, the second most active immigration port of entry in the United States, and the fourth busiest commercial port in the world. Historic New Orleans Collection, New Orleans, LA.

Vue d'une rue du Faubourg Ste. Marie, Nelle. Orléans (Louisiane) by Félix Achille Beaupoil de Saint-Aulaire, 1821. This street scene shows a group of enslaved penal laborers clearing gutter obstructions. The prisoners wear color-coded uniforms—blue for men, red for women—typical of New Orleans's slave chain gangs. The woman in this image also wears a neck collar, while the men are restrained by waist and ankle chains. L. Kemper and Leila Moore Williams Founders Collection, Historic New Orleans Collection, New Orleans, LA.

Orleans Parish Prison and Police Jail, ca. 1863. Built to identical specifications, these two adjacent prisons were completed in 1834 and 1835, respectively. Marshall Dunham Photograph Album, Special Collections, Louisiana State University Libraries, Baton Rouge.

Before the Civil War, rebellious and resistant enslaved people were brought to this prison courtyard, stripped naked, strapped to a whipping rack, and tortured in full view of other prisoners. A survivor of this ordeal described witnessing "ninety or a hundred" whippings daily. Historic New Orleans Collection, New Orleans, LA.

Statesman and Louisiana sugar planter Edward Livingston (1764–1836), portrait by Anson Dickinson, ca. 1827. Livingston's influential writings shaped the development of the world's first penitentiaries. While articulating his theories, Livingston regularly had enslaved people committed to the Police Jail. Metropolitan Museum of Art, New York.

Revival of the Old Slave Laws of Louisiana, 1863. Under the auspices of arresting enslaved fugitives from the countryside, New Orleans police seized Black pedestrians indiscriminately, including the well-to-do and freeborn. Library of Congress, Washington, DC.

Chain-Gang at Richmond by W. S. Sheppard, *Harper's Weekly*, December 5, 1868. Richmond Nineteenth-Century Print Collection, Virginia Commonwealth University Libraries, Richmond.

Dr. Louis Charles Roudanez (1823–90) photograph, ca. 1857. During Reconstruction, Roudanez was a leader within New Orleans's radical community of civil rights activists. In 1864, Roudanez cofounded the nation's first Black-owned daily newspaper, the *New Orleans Tribune*, with his brother Jean Baptiste Roudanez and Paul Trévigne. As young men both Trévigne and Jean Baptiste Roudanez had been arrested as presumptive fugitive slaves and imprisoned in the Police Jail. Gift of Mark Charles Roudané, Historic New Orleans Collection, New Orleans, LA.

Oscar Dunn (1822–71), the nation's first Black lieutenant governor. Twenty years before this photograph was taken, Dunn had been imprisoned in the Police Jail as a presumptive fugitive slave. As lieutenant governor of Louisiana (1868–71), he worked to curtail the power of police to perform arbitrary arrests. Mathew Brady Photographs of Civil War–Era Personalities and Scenes, National Archives at College Park, MD.

Taken in Newport News, Virginia, in 1901, this photograph shows a typical chain gang of the Jim Crow era. These penal laborers would have been arrested for minor misdemeanors—in particular, vagrancy. Alamy Stock Photo.

Completed in 1904, the New Orleans House of Detention replaced the former Police Jail. Photograph ca. 1910, Historic New Orleans Collection, New Orleans, LA.

Orleans Parish Prison inmates held on a highway overpass after Hurricane Katrina in 2005. During the storm, inmates spent up to four days in flooded cells without access to food, drinking water, air conditioning, or medical care. Reuters, Alamy Stock Photo.

CHAPTER 6

We Are All Vagrants

Reconstructing Police Power, 1865–1877

"I have no prejudices to overcome, I would do the blacks all the good in my power," sugar baron Tobias Gibson explained in December 1864, but Louisiana's reconstruction would require "a manly, masculine, vigorous exercise of executive power." The problem, in Gibson's view, was that by nullifying slaveholders' power to punish, the military had disrupted the web of "wholesome restraints" that maintained social order by binding worker and master together. "How, then," the incredulous planter asked, "can good order, good morals, and honest industry be maintained, when immunity from punishment is patent?" Gibson's only solution was to recreate the "stimulus of *corporal punishment*" within "the admonitions of the law": the state needed to assume full responsibility for coercing Black labor. To those who would suggest that freedom and omnipresent state coercion were incompatible, Gibson retorted that freedom was a fantasy concocted by "namby-pamby" idealists and "professional philanthropists." "Nobody is absolutely free, white or black. I have been a slave all my life," the planter, whose net worth had been estimated at $2.5 million in 1863, contended: "all of us . . . must continue to be subject to wholesome restraints."[1]

That June, and a mere ten weeks after General Robert E. Lee's surrender, a man formerly enslaved by Tobias Gibson named John Martin was arrested for vagrancy while selling chickens in New Orleans's Jackson Square. "I told [the policeman] that they were my own property, and raised by me," Martin later recalled, but the policeman "told me that they were stolen chickens, and that I must go with him." That very morning, Martin had fled into New Orleans from Tobias Gibson's Live Oak Plantation, in Terrebonne Parish, where the levees had failed and floodwaters had enveloped the land. To both the policeman and judge, Martin's vagrancy was self-evident: plainly manifest in the freedman's mobility, ragged dress, alienation from his employer, and itinerant peddling. Once coded as a vagrant, the vagrant's criminal emblems—laziness, shiftlessness, intemperance, lustfulness, thievery—could be assumed. It didn't matter that Martin had been displaced by natural disaster, that Gibson had authorized Martin's journey to New Orleans, or that Martin had raised the chickens from the egg: he was convicted of vagrancy and sentenced to six months' hard labor in the New Orleans Workhouse. "Hundreds of similar cases" occurred "every week," noted the organ of New Orleans's freeborn Black residents, the *New Orleans Tribune*: "We are all vagrants when we are black or colored, and do not work for a white man."[2]

In the aftermath of the Civil War, former slaveholders saw in vagrancy law the centerpiece of a new criminal justice system in which the state's power to punish criminals would supplant the slaveholder's power to punish slaves.[3] For Tobias Gibson and his peers, this would not be a revolution in relations between state and private power so much as a shift in emphasis. State and private violence had complemented one another before the war and would continue to do so afterward. Louisiana already had robust vagrancy laws; an established prison tradition; and an ideological system that suggested that slaves and wageworkers, maroons and vagrants, were variations on common themes. Certainly, much would have to change. Planters such as Tobias Gibson would need to grow less reliant on the whip, more reliant on the workhouse. The state would need to expand its network of prisons and police forces dramatically, particularly in rural regions. The coercive powers that the antebellum state had wielded when policing marronage would need to be reworked and subsumed into vagrancy law. But they needn't reinvent coercive state power. In 1865, the former slaveholders of Louisiana believed that they could continue to rely on the same penal institutions, legal paradigms, and policing systems to which they were accustomed.

In sketching the transformation of southern criminal justice after Emancipation, histories of Reconstruction usually invoke the infamous postbellum Black Codes as shorthand. These state legislative packages, passed in virtually every former Confederate state (and some border states) between 1865 and 1866, used vagrancy laws and other criminal penalties to reassert planter control over labor. The Black Codes are significant primarily because they outraged many in the North, contributing to a radical shift in Reconstruction politics. Yet relying on the Black Codes to narrate the transformation of southern police power paints a misleading picture. Because they were so inflammatory, the Black Codes were almost immediately nullified and were rarely enforced: these short-lived and underenforced laws do little to illuminate freedpeople's actual experiences with law enforcement or the battles over the coercive powers of the state that emerged on the ground. Moreover, invoking the Black Codes as the exemplar of postbellum law enforcement suggests a rapidly improvised system, lacking substantive indigenous precedent, seeking only to harass and redeploy Black labor under the flimsiest of veils. Framing postbellum practices within the longer intellectual history of southern state police power yields a more accurate picture of the transformation afoot.[4] Louisiana's former slaveholders sought to expand and revise, not reinvent. Neither underdeveloped nor parochial, their vision for postbellum labor coercion drew inspiration from both indigenous precedent and earlier reforms enacted by their Caribbean peers, tapping into a longer history of post-emancipation police power that stretched all the way back to the abolition of slavery in Saint-Domingue.[5] Guided by these Caribbean antecedents, Louisiana slaveholders did not pursue an unprecedented transition from the "private" coercion of Black workers on plantations to their "public" coercion through prisons—that transition, however lumpy and incomplete, had been underway since 1805—so much as they shifted from coercing Black workers as maroons to coercing them as vagrants. In essence, Louisiana's former slaveholders aspired to fuse the two dominant legal paradigms by which they and their forebearers had coerced labor—marronage and vagrancy—into a single legal paradigm that would sustain their continued prosperity.

As John Martin's story demonstrates, nothing in 1865 posed so direct and immediate a threat to freedom's possibilities than this incorporation of marronage law into vagrancy law. In the name of suppressing vagrancy, the state could summarily seize, convict, forcibly work, hire out, expel, and deny suffrage and due process rights to just about any economically autonomous freedperson at any time. Perhaps just as dangerously, the dense cultural package surrounding vagrancy provided a language for construing freedpeople as deviant. The discourse surrounding vagrancy armed former slaveholders with a powerful tool for rationalizing and legitimating forced labor, forced resettlement, confinement, and violence by framing Black laborers as future criminals incapable of self-management.[6] For these reasons, vagrancy law would be a central flashpoint in Reconstruction-era debates within New Orleans over labor, equal rights, and the future meaning of Black freedom.

"Total Disruption"

As the Civil War ended, it seemed to many as though the entire South were on the move. James McKaye, investigating local conditions as a member of the Freedmen's Inquiry Commission, described "a state of total disruption. Either the master or the slave, or both, had become fugitives." A Union officer outside of Jackson, Mississippi, reported roads choked with "hungry, naked, footsore" people "wandering up and down" the road: "aliens in their native land, homeless, and friendless." "Starving people are coming in from every direction," complained General Edward Hatch from Eastport, Mississippi. "I would rather face an old-fashioned war-time skirmish line any time."[7]

The migrating multitudes included Confederate army deserters and camp followers, refugees displaced by invasion and retreat, and war orphans and widows. Yet it was the tens of thousands of freedpeople arriving in cities whose movement most captivated and alarmed authorities. Between 1860 and 1870, the Black population of New Orleans grew by 30,000 persons: an increase of nearly 110 percent. Other cities and towns, large and small, experienced similar mass migrations. In Norfolk, Virginia; Charlotte, North Carolina; Nashville, Tennessee; Louisville and Lexington, Kentucky; Natchez, Mississippi; Pine Bluff, Arkansas; and Galveston, Texas, the numbers of Black residents more than doubled. The Black populations of Houston and San Antonio, Texas, more than tripled, while those of Memphis, Tennessee; Vicksburg, Mississippi; and Jacksonville, Florida, quadrupled. In Atlanta, Georgia; St. Louis, Missouri; and Little Rock, Arkansas, the numbers of Black residents increased by fivefold or more. Meanwhile, these cities' white populations stagnated or decreased.[8]

Freedpeople moved to cities for a variety of reasons. For many, urban migration represented the rational economic choice. Plantation regulations in Louisiana of March 1865 capped monthly wages for field hands at five dollars for women and ten dollars for men, half of which the employer could withhold until the end of the year. Laborers in New Orleans, by contrast, could expect to earn between one and two dollars per *day* and receive full payment immediately. Cities were also safer, offering proximity to military posts and protection from the gangs of discharged Confederate veterans who roamed the countryside. Many vital institutions and public services—schools, churches, professional clubs, and Freedmen's Bureau offices—were clustered in towns and cities. Cities offered a higher likelihood of locating loved ones stolen away by the domestic slave trade. Many freedpeople also perceived that urban life was more liberating, exciting, and engaging. As one enslaved plantation worker told a traveler immediately before the war, he "would rather live in New Orleans" than anywhere because life was "gayer there" and "had more society."[9]

The act of migrating itself had particularly powerful meanings for freedpeople. As one Florida planter perceived, "The negroes don't seem to feel free unless they leave their old homes." By migrating, freedpeople claimed self-ownership of their bodies and created space to reconstruct identity away from geographies controlled by their former owners. Because marronage had provided a central lens through which enslaved people had conceptualized freedom's meaning, freedom and mobility were also closely intertwined within Black vernacular political thought.[10] After resolving to walk two dozen miles from his enslaver's plantation to Shreveport, Henry Adams refused to bring his former owner's pass so that he could "see whether I am free by going without a pass." Freedman Felix Haywood, enslaved in Texas, perceived that through migrating, freedpeople "seemed to want to get closer to freedom, so they'd know what it was—like it was a place or a city." One North Carolina freedwoman explained her reason for migrating: "I have never been free and I am goin' to try it." To these freedpeople, the ability to leave was not merely a right achieved because of freedom: migration *was* freedom made manifest.[11]

Yet urban migration posed distinct challenges. Urban housing markets were overwhelmed, forcing freedpeople to construct makeshift structures or cluster, often in multifamily groups, in overcrowded and dilapidated apartments. Most freedpeople lived in "filthy" homes and "miserable holes," one New Orleans provost marshal complained in 1865: "crowded rooms in much plenty and want." New Orleans's newspapers described "rotten and stinking" shantytowns hastily constructed atop marginal swampland along the city's outskirts.[12]

Job markets were overwhelmed, forcing freedpeople to survive through perilous combinations of peddling, scavenging, and short-term, uncontracted day labor. In New Orleans, freedmen typically found work in construction and longshoring, freedwomen as launderesses or domestic workers. Mary Johnson, who fled with her family from Mississippi to New Orleans as a child, remembered the varied economic activities—construction, longshoring, fishing, growing a little cotton, selling a few eggs—by which her parents eked out family survival in the new city. "My daddy [was] a workin' man and he help build the big custom house in New Orleans and help pull the rope to pull the boats up," Johnson recalled with pride. This sort of mixed, short-term employment offered flexibility but was also prone to seasonal fluctuation and extremely vulnerable to fraud. According to one New Orleans Freedmen's Bureau agent, employers quickly made habit of "hiring freed people at a dollar a day, by the day, and then discharging them before the work is done, with half pay, and without reason." Thousands of claims against employers for nonpayment of wages, filed with the New Orleans Freedmen's Bureau—"$10.00 for 10 days wages," "$2.75 for washing," "$4.00 for services," "$1.15 [for] 1 day's work," "$2.50 [for] 1 week's wages"—testify to the ubiquity of both fraud and short-term, uncontracted labor.[13]

To former slaveholders, the concentration of so many masterless Black people seemed nothing short of apocalyptic. Migrating freedpeople "fill every white Southerner with anger," one northerner observed. Society was under direct attack, one candidate for Louisiana senate proclaimed, by "the thousands of idle, vicious, vagrant freedmen who swarm through the land in all the insolence of a mistaken freedom." "Is this a white man's country?" the *New-Orleans Times* asked: "Negroes and vagrants accumulate. . . . Nuisances and encumbrances which appear every day to be increasing. . . . Idle and apparently worthless *citizens* . . . as thick as the leaves of Vallambrosa." Former slaveholders concluded that freedpeople's preference for "odd jobs" and "makeshift existence" in cities, instead of the "regular employment" that awaited them on plantations, was clearly irrational and evidence of their immoral predilection for idleness. Social order derived from the submission of dependents to their natural masters; it was thus a foregone conclusion that the clustering of so many unattended dependents, "who cannot be restrained from habits of vice and crime," would yield chaos, delinquency, and ruin. The "evils" of nomadic dependents were "patent to all," declared Mississippi governor Benjamin Humphreys: "vagrancy and pauperism, and their inevitable concomitant crime and misery, hang like a dark pall over a once prosperous and happy, but now desolated land."[14]

Caribbean Blueprints for Postbellum Law and Order

Faced with these crises, Louisiana's former slaveholders looked to state power to supplant their waning private powers. They identified vagrancy law as the best available tool for reclaiming control over labor and one that would be readily accepted by Union army occupiers, who had themselves imposed such stringent antivagrancy policies. As early as 1863, Louisiana planters had debated how vagrancy laws might be remade for a postslavery world.

These conversations were guided by former slaveholders' readings of Caribbean history. Just as their forebears had looked to their Caribbean peers amid mounting marronage rates in 1805, borrowing and implementing policing and penal mechanisms while conceding the transfer of some coercive powers from slaveholder to state, so elite Louisianians again looked southward in 1865, perceiving that policies implemented during prior British, French, and Dutch emancipations offered blueprints for the revitalization of coercion in the postwar South. To former slaveholders, the lesson of these Caribbean antecedents was clear: a powerful police and workhouse system, empowered by a broad mandate to suppress vagrancy, could supplant their antebellum reliance on privately inflicted corporal violence and re-create the state's pre-Emancipation powers to coerce Black workers as maroons.

In looking to the Caribbean, Louisiana planters invoked a legal history of post-emancipation police power that stretched as far back as liberated Haiti, where one of the freed nation's earliest leaders, Henri Christophe, had tried revitalizing cash crop production by enlisting vagrancy law to bind freed agricultural workers to plantations. Christophe's labor plan assigned each laborer to a plantation; absconding laborers were to be arrested for vagrancy and formed into chain gangs for labor on public works. Christophe's successor, Jean-Pierre Boyer, included similar antivagrancy provisions within his Code Rural, passed in 1826. Though it severely curtailed the freedoms for which Haiti's self-emancipated subjects had so bitterly fought, the Code Rural was widely circulated throughout the Atlantic world by both abolitionists and pro-slavery theorists as a possible model for future emancipations. Slaveholders saw in the Code Rural a means of maintaining the plantation system in the unwelcome event of emancipation. As early as 1827, and anticipating emancipation within the British Empire, Jamaican slaveholder Alexander Barclay included sections of the Code Rural, its regulations "necessary for the purpose of regenerating agricultural labour," within his own proslavery treatise. The Code Rural was also favorably circulated within antislavery circles, particularly amid contentious debates between activists over whether US Emancipation should be gradual or immediate. The New York abolitionist Elizur Wright, for example, argued in 1836 that the Code Rural "exhibits a wise adaptation" by establishing a "coercive power . . . well adapted to correct individual cases of idleness or vagrancy which might be expected to abound."[15]

In 1833, Parliament had passed the Slavery Abolition Act, providing for the gradual abolition of slavery throughout the British Empire. The act established a transitory period during which formerly enslaved people would be "apprentices," bound to their former owners and supervised by crown-appointed "special magistrates." In response to the act, every British Caribbean colonial legislature immediately passed a new vagrancy law with the aim of ensuring that "order might be maintained more or less imperfectly," as one civil servant explained, and "the Negroes [withheld] from running wild." In practice, these new vagrancy laws were virtually never enforced, because planters preferred to rely on special magistrates' extensive powers to condemn apprentices summarily to chain gangs and workhouses. Antislavery parliamentarians concluded that the colonial legislatures were laying the groundwork for a new system of serfdom to be imposed after the apprenticeship period's expiration. "There is no vagrancy at present in the Island of Jamaica," one member of the House of Lords noted. "*Nil.* Not a single prosecution—not a single case of vagrancy. . . . What necessity is there to pass an immediate law to prevent vagrancy?" Parliament forced the repeal of these laws, though weaker vagrancy laws followed.[16]

To southern slaveholders, Parliament's interference served as a dire warning. Louisiana planters held far more favorable opinions of the antivagrancy policies enacted in the French Caribbean following slavery's abolition throughout the French Empire in 1848. When debating the procedures by which slavery would be abolished, the architects of French emancipation had recommended new vagrancy laws and the organization of "national workhouses" and chain gangs throughout the French colonies to prevent freedpeople from leaving their former owners' plantations and to instill industrious habits.[17] Authorities in Martinique and Guadeloupe quickly passed broad vagrancy laws and established or expanded colonial police forces, which were specifically instructed to target vagrants. In 1852, those colonies added an antivagrancy pass system.[18] Louisiana planters were particularly intrigued by the policies instituted by Louis Henri de Gueydon, governor of Martinique from 1853 to 1856. Gueydon required all agricultural laborers older than sixteen to carry passports signed by their employers, without which police could arrest them for vagrancy. To ensure that prisoners faced harsher work conditions than they would have encountered on plantations, Gueydon invested in the construction of new workhouses, chain gangs, and penal treadmills. He instituted a tax on Black Martinicans to force greater dependency on wage labor. Observers, including many American slaveholders, perceived that these policies had been successful: one British traveler, for example, described Black vagrancy as "prevalent" throughout the British Caribbean but invisible in the French Antilles.[19]

"Look at the West Indies, the English and French Antilles, look at Hayti," directed one delegate to Louisiana's constitutional convention of 1864: unless Louisiana began to "prosecute idleness and vagrancy to the utmost limit," emancipation would beget "idleness, idleness would become misery, and misery degenerate into crime." "We have before us the warning of French and English legislation in the West Indies on the question of emancipation," another planter echoed. "The negro should not be allowed to wander from his home in vagrancy." At a convention of Louisiana planters in October 1864, a pamphlet summarizing Gueydon's reforms was circulated; his efforts to "reduce the number of vagrants" were thoroughly scrutinized. The *New Orleans Bee* subsequently published a multipart series on Gueydon's reforms, and other newspapers and agricultural journals began publishing comparative studies of Caribbean antivagrancy policies. Writing from Guadeloupe in 1865, one Louisiana-born transplant made two advisements to his kindred, derived from "freed labor under the French system": import "Asiatic laborers" and adopt "a rigid police and vagrant system, which places the negro between the alternatives of laboring on the plantations or on the public works." The establishment of new "criminal penalties" was "the great question of the day," the French consul in New Orleans reported home to his superiors in 1865. "Laws adopted in our French colonies regarding vagrancy, apprenticeship, etc. . . . serve as a model."[20]

Amid these discussions, Louisiana planters were often despondent. "Henceforth I have nothing to look forward to but a life of drudgery," wrote one. "All is dark and dreary in the future," confided another.[21]

Yet there were also those who saw opportunity in calamity: if the South constructed a sufficiently taut web of workhouses and police patrols, production might actually be increased at lower cost to the planter. "The Law which freed the negro, at the same time freed the master," the *Southern Cultivator* opined in July 1865: Emancipation had released planters from the burden of provisioning, feeding, and housing workers and of retaining those too young, old, or infirm to work. Through regular articles in *DeBow's Review*, proslavery polemicist George Fitzhugh reminded readers that distinctions between slave labor and wage labor were somewhat superficial. "It makes no difference whether the laborers be (so-called) free, or slaves," Fitzhugh emphasized in 1866. "All laborers are alike slaves." Nor had Emancipation negated that "first and most incumbent duty of all governments[:] to compel all men to work." Should the South construct "a strong police, and jails, &c., to punish the vagrant and vicious negroes," the "liberated negroes" might even be "compelled to work harder, and to produce more, after liberation than when slaves."[22]

As former slaveholders sketched their impenetrable carceral network, they debated whether it should target *only* freedpeople or forever bind *all* wayward laborers—Black and white alike—to capital. When former slaveholders denounced the vagrant menace, it was frequently understood, as one Alabama politician remarked, that "the vagrant contemplated was the plantation negro." Yet other voices cautioned that preoccupation with Black vagrancy would obscure the ongoing dangers posed by vagrant white people. There "are white as well as black people" who "insist on becoming vagrants" and must "be properly punished by a term of labor under legal coercion," cautioned one New Orleanian in July 1865. "Let the [vagrant] act, too, extend to worthless white men," echoed the Shreveport *South-Western*. The sentiment was not exclusive to Louisiana. Future antivagrancy measures should harness "all the LABOR that there now IS in the Southern States . . . both the white and black," advised the *Memphis Bulletin*. It was "vain" to "disguise the fact that the industry of the white man, too, is greatly unnerved and demoralized, and like evil consequences are ready to follow," suggested one North Carolina legislative committee. "We conceive it to be among the first of legislative duties . . . [to] direct the energies of the entire population in appropriate channels of honest labor."[23]

That former slaveholders in 1865 remained preoccupied with the coercion of white labor underscores the sincerity of their conviction that *all* menial hirelings posed an economic and criminal danger if left unattended and uncoerced. Far more than a disingenuous legal ploy, their commitment to vagrancy law reflected established legal precedent, time-tested policing practice, and a fully developed and articulated theory of public order, affirmed by their Caribbean peers.

"Hunted Down like Brutes"

In March 1865, James Madison Wells, a Unionist and former member of Louisiana's slaveholding elite, assumed the governor's office following his predecessor's election to the US Senate. Immediately, Wells purged municipal and state offices of General Banks's appointees, replacing moderate and radical Republicans with conservative Unionists and former Confederates. Wells appointed Hugh Kennedy, a staunch political ally, as mayor of New Orleans. Kennedy, in turn, launched a similar purge of New Orleans's police department. General Banks nullified Wells's appointments, perceiving that the governor was trying to "re-establish in power men of the old slavery system."[24]

Immediately following President Lincoln's assassination in April, Wells and Kennedy traveled to Washington to ingratiate themselves with Lincoln's successor, President Andrew Johnson. During their meeting, the three men realized that they agreed on much: the Union occupation of the South should be brief, the states of the former Confederacy should be quickly restored into the Union, and the extension of Black civil and political rights should be minimal. Immediately after this meeting, Johnson removed Banks from command, confirmed Wells's appointments, and proclaimed the return of suffrage rights to virtually all former Confederate soldiers and officials. Louisiana, one contemporary recognized, was now firmly controlled by "the disloyal and proslavery element."[25]

Wells and Kennedy had not yet returned from Washington when, on June 12, New Orleans's acting mayor ordered police to begin vigorously enforcing the antivagrancy articles of Louisiana's crime law of 1855. Policemen began seizing freedpeople by the "dozens." Thomas Conway, now acting in his new capacity of superintendent of the Louisiana Freedmen's Bureau, accused police of indiscriminately arresting "all colored laborers who were found on the streets . . . not employed just at the moment when the police saw them." Newspapers alluded to mass roundups: a "posse of negroes" arrested on July 31, and another twenty-five vagrants, "of various names and colors," on August 12. Police raided nighttime church services, arresting congregants for violating the vagrancy curfew. In New Orleans's suburbs, local law enforcement raided private homes in search of vagrants and arrested any freedperson found outside after 5:00 p.m.[26]

As during the antebellum era, arrestees were not necessarily unemployed, though they typically were landless, poor, and uncontracted. In particular, policemen targeted longshoremen found resting along the levee between loading and unloading shiploads. Provost Marshal General Andrew Morse, tasked with overseeing these prisoners' rural relocation, was flabbergasted by how many "vagrants" still carried cotton hooks: proof incarnate of "the nature of their occupation." To Conway, the arrest of laborers who were still dressed "in their working garments," with "their cotton hooks hanging to their belts," after they had "worked all day long in the burning sun, loading or unloading ships," seemed cruelly farcical.[27] Conway's outrage obscured his ongoing role in enforcing coercive policies under General Banks's labor plan. After Mayor Kennedy requested the removal of 241 incarcerated freedpeople from the City Workhouse to plantations on July 22, Conway's bureau complied on August 12, removing 137 men and boys and 37 women and girls. With bureau authorization, some planters visited the workhouse to select workers personally.[28]

Meanwhile, in Louisiana's rural parishes, local authorities accelerated the transformation of antebellum machinery for policing fugitive and resistant enslaved people into post-Emancipation machinery for policing Black "vagrants." Former slave patrols were reconceived as antivagrancy patrols and reestablished across the state. Revised patrol regulations in Bossier Parish targeted "all idle and vagrant persons"; those of East Baton Rouge Parish targeted "all suspicious persons and vagrants." In Jefferson Parish, where antebellum patrol regulations had already targeted both vagrant wageworkers and fugitive slaves, authorities simply struck antebellum clauses mentioning the enslaved.[29] Simultaneously, Louisiana towns crafted ordinances that sentenced freedpeople to chain gangs if they entered town, violated curfew, or engaged in virtually any community or economic activity without their employers' permission.[30]

Similar mass arrests of "vagrant" freedpeople erupted in cities and towns throughout the occupied South. In Mobile, Alabama, one witness estimated that police arrested fifty Black vagrants daily. In Nashville, Tennessee, an estimated 2,000 "vagrant Negroes" were arrested in one single, coordinated sweep. Municipal chain gangs for "vagrant" freedpeople were organized in virtually every hamlet and town, large and small, with ferocious rapidity. In July, the San Antonio *Herald* announced that "all the vagrant negroes who have been here loitering about the city" had been driven into chain gangs. In Alabama, the creation of chain gangs was announced by Huntsville, Selma, Mobile, Grove Hill, Troy, Union Springs, Tuskegee, Jacksonville, and Montgomery, where the institution was said to be "composed of sixty vagrant negroes."[31] In Georgia, chain gangs were formed in Columbus, Macon, Augusta, Atlanta, Milledgeville, and Savannah. "In every village and city one can see negroes in the chain-gang, and see negroes whipped," one correspondent reported from that state.[32]

Federal troops, tasked with implementing contract labor systems modeled on General Banks's "Louisiana Plan," often worked hand in hand with local authorities. "It is not the southerners we dread but the federal soldiers," a group of Black residents of Mobile declared in a petition to the Freedmen's Bureau. In Memphis, where the Freedmen's Bureau superintendent characterized freedpeople as "lazy, worthless vagrants who will never be induced to leave the life they are now leading, except, by use of force," provost marshals were offered a five-dollar bounty for every Black vagrant arrested, encouraging indiscriminate seizures of freed and freeborn alike. Freedpeople in Richmond reported that "the military and police authorities will not allow us to walk the streets by day or night, in the regular pursuit of our business or on our way to church, without a pass. . . . [Their] business is the hunting of the colored people." If not organized into chain gangs, arrestees were forcibly transported to plantations, typically without opportunity to contact family or friends, precipitating frantic searches for disappeared husbands, wives, and children. A resident of Montgomery, Alabama, described the removal of "ten wagon loads of freedmen" from the city: "It would please us to see a hundred or two hundred loads going off daily till our city was found almost rid of the surplus negro population. Let the good work go on."[33]

In the major cities that had previously deployed slave chain gangs, these postbellum chain gangs for vagrants were explicitly framed as the "revival" or "reestablishment" of the antebellum institution. Nashville completed this transition first, redeploying its municipal slave chain gang as a "contraband negroes" chain gang in February 1863. Richmond's mayor announced the "reestablishment" of the city's antebellum chain gang, previously designated for fugitive enslaved people and vagrant poor white people, in 1866.[34] New Orleans was a relative latecomer, launching a chain gang for convicted vagrants in 1867.[35] The "old chain gang" was being "revived" according to the *Daily Picayune*, "re-established" according to the *New-Orleans Times*.[36]

Previously, chain gangs had been exclusive to large towns; now, virtually every hamlet had one. The rapid proliferation of chain gangs reflected several factors. Most small southern towns lacked the infrastructure to confine and forcibly work large prisoner populations. That the chain gang was uniquely well suited for the vagrant—who had robbed his or her labor from the community, could be redeemed only through hard work, and was an outsider unentitled to the protections of community members—was already axiomatic. Throughout the war-torn South, public infrastructure was in tatters; chain gangs provided a cheap and fast way to rebuild.

The proliferation of chain gangs also reflected public authorities' awareness of how the institutions could be used to manage racial meanings and assert community boundaries. More than a technology for extracting labor, the chain gang was a tool for rearranging social hierarchies. By these humiliating rituals, authorities hoped to reaffirm total Black subjugation, terrorize Black communities, and reclaim white control over contested urban space. Chain gangs seemed engineered to "strengthen the impression that the colored people are naturally vicious," Black residents of Mobile observed. "Colored women are put on the streets to work," one resident protested. "It is, in my opinion, done to intimidate [us]." "We have endeavored to reach them with boots, brick-bats, empty bottles, and pistol shots, but thus far have signally failed," a white resident of Alton, Louisiana, wrote. Now a chain gang was necessary to put freedpeople back in their "proper place."[37]

Use of public punishments to reassert Black subjugation was particularly pronounced within the punitive rituals administered to freedman Ned Scott of Richmond, Virginia, in June 1865. Scott and his wife, Jenny Scott, had been walking hand in hand down Richmond's Main Street when two paroled Confederate veterans deliberately collided into the couple, groping Jenny Scott's breasts before flinging the freedwoman from sidewalk to gutter. When Scott chased the men away, three off-duty provost marshals, enraged by reports that white men had been "insulted by a damned n———," ran to the scene and began beating Scott. Scott drew a pocketknife, cutting two of the provost marshals. A military tribunal sentenced Scott to a series of public humiliations, culminating with the chain gang. First, Scott was bound and rolled back and forth in the muddy Main Street gutter. Black passersby were seized and ordered to whip him. Next, Scott was forced to march down Main Street while wearing a placard reading, "I stabbed two of the provost guard." Then the provost marshals choreographed Scott's living funeral. After whitening Scott's face with flour so that he would resemble a corpse and rubbing his body with cornmeal to attract flies, the provost marshals nailed Scott shut inside a pine coffin "with all the gravity which would accompany the preliminaries for burying a man alive." Provost marshals paraded the coffin throughout Richmond, escorted by a marching band. A Black Baptist preacher was forced to deliver Scott's eulogy before massive crowds. "Hundreds of persons . . . enjoyed the spectacle hugely," the *Richmond Times* reported. "We never saw a more ludicrous or amusing scene." Only after this carnivalesque celebration of Black social and biological death was Scott committed to prison, where he remained for three months.[38]

As New Orleans policemen had throughout 1863 and 1864, police in several southern cities deliberately targeted prosperous Black artisans and landowners who were known to be free before the Civil War as a way of debasing their community standing and asserting their social equivalency with the formerly enslaved, in response to their perceived support for the Union occupation. Albert Brooks, owner of a profitable livery stable with four employees, described himself as an "old and well known resident of Richmond" of "good character." In June 1865, Brooks reported that "old policemen, who had known all about me and my business for many years[,] called at my stable," arresting Brooks for his inability to produce papers, signed by a white employer, demonstrating that he was not a vagrant. Later, the jailor, who also "knew all about me and my business," told Brooks that to cure him of his vagrancy, he would be hired out "for $5.00 a month." When Brooks asked why he would be hired out for so meager an amount when he was a landowner with four employees, whom he paid thirty-five dollars a month, the jailor retorted, "[Ask] your Yankee friends." "I have lived here 40 years, have never received a stripe, and was never before arrested for any cause whatever," Brooks testified. Now, police "stop [me] on nearly every corner of the street, and make it nearly impossible for me to carry on my business." Other freeborn and formerly freed Black artisans and proprietors described similar humiliations. "I was well known by the police to be a respectable man," reported Edward Davenport, a boardinghouse keeper. "They disregarded all my papers, and I was obliged to submit to arrest." "The oldest citizens of collor in this city are hunted down like brutes," Anthony Motley, a Memphis barber, reported, "and taken to a corall like beasts." "Well didn't I tell you so, you damned fool, that when the Yankees came here you'd be a damned sight worse off," one policeman told another formerly free detainee.[39]

The condition within the urban South was fast approaching former slaveholders' vision of postbellum criminal justice: an impenetrable policing web, maintained at public expense, with vagrancy law as its centerpiece. "Our present condition is, in many respects, worse than when we were slaves, and living under slave law," a committee of Richmond freedpeople wrote the president in June 1865. "Under the old system, we had the *protection* of our masters, who were financially interested in our physical welfare. That protection is now withdrawn." "We are in danger now, with the Freedmen's Bureau and the troops here to protect us," echoed freedman William McLaurin of North Carolina. "It would be better if we had been left in slavery and never brought out than to be left in the hands of our enemies."[40]

"We Regard All Black and Colored Men as Brothers and Fellow Sufferers"

Urban Black communities mobilized. In Nashville, after bureau agents transported some fifty convicted vagrants from the workhouse to Arkansas plantations, Black churches held mass meetings, and rumors swirled that Black residents were on the verge of rioting, raiding the workhouse, and liberating all prisoners. To defuse the crisis, bureau agents rushed to Arkansas to recover the Nashville vagrants, only to find that virtually everyone had already escaped.[41] In Richmond, chain gang prisoners organized a protracted inmate strike, demanding the removal of their humiliating chains.[42] In Mobile, Sam Gaillard, a Black preacher assigned to the chain gang, defiantly refused to work. The chain gang overseer shot Gaillard dead, a "salutatory" lesson, according to the Mobile *Daily Times*, for the city's Black residents. Five months later, some 200 armed Black men marched on the Mobile chain gang, demanding the release of all prisoners.[43]

In petitions and public addresses, freedpeople challenged the presumption of Black predilection for idleness. "We scorn and treat with contempt the allegation made against us that we understand Freedom to mean idleness," wrote freedpeople in Petersburg, Virginia. "We are charged with being unproductive. They say we will not work. He who makes that assertion asserts an untruth," argued freedman George Cook of Norfolk, Virginia. "We have been working all our lives, not only supporting ourselves, but we have supported our masters, many of them in idleness." "We used to support ourselves and our masters too when we were slaves and I reckon we can take care of ourselves now," one Alabama freedman remarked.[44] To these freedpeople, that former slaveholders would accuse former slaves of dependency and laziness seemed painfully ironic.

In New Orleans, propertyless freedpeople and freeborn Black property holders, recognizing that power lay in numbers, began realizing the necessity of a broad grassroots alliance that crossed class and caste lines to unite all persons of African ancestry. Since long before the Union army's arrival, the upper echelon of New Orleans's free Black community had debated the nature of their relationship to the enslaved. After the Union army's arrival, some community leaders had advocated a conservative approach. They sought to protect the traditional legal and social divisions that had distinguished them from the enslaved, fearing—not without reason—that to voice support for freedpeople would be to imperil their own struggle for citizenship rights. Other freeborn New Orleanians, including the editors of *L'Union* and the *New Orleans Tribune*, endorsed a more radical approach. Arguing that slavery and race prejudice were inexorably linked, these radicals denounced slavery unequivocally, condemned Banks's labor program and demanded full suffrage rights for all Black men.[45]

Events under Union occupation pushed New Orleans's freeborn Black residents decisively toward the more radical approach. Police harassment in 1863 and 1864 and the deliberate seizure of freeborn professionals and skilled artisans as vagrant plantation hands communicated that their traditional legal and social protections were moot. The Louisiana Democratic Party platform of 1865 declared full support for the perpetual disenfranchisement of all persons of any African ancestry: "We hold this to be a Government of white people, made and to be perpetuated for the exclusive benefit of the white race. . . . People of African descent cannot be considered as citizens of the United States." By 1865, there was growing agreement among New Orleans's freeborn Black activists that unanimity with the formerly enslaved was essential. "We see now that our future is indissolubly bound up with that of the negro race in this country; and we have resolved to make common cause," one formerly free Black New Orleanian told a northern reporter in 1865. "We have no rights which we can reckon safe while the same are denied to the field hands on the sugar plantations."[46]

Earnest coalition-building, transcending long-standing class, caste, color, cultural, language, and legal distinctions, began during the winter of 1864–65. At a mass meeting in December 1864, Oscar Dunn, born enslaved but emancipated before the war, initiated the proceedings by declaring, "We regard all black and colored men as brothers and fellow sufferers." The second speaker that night, physician Paschal Randolph of New York, proclaimed that he no longer represented "mulattos" but now stood proudly as an "African." After another such assembly that January, the *New Orleans Tribune* celebrated the radical transcendence of old divisions. "There were seated side by side the rich and the poor, the literate and educated man, and the country laborer, hardly released from bondage. . . . All the classes of society were represented, and united in a common thought: the actual liberation from social and political bondage."[47]

As this alliance matured, activists from within New Orleans's freeborn Black community began advancing increasingly radical critiques of state police power. Although the *New Orleans Tribune* had long opposed Banks's labor plan, the paper had tended to support the basic principles that undergirded vagrancy law, objecting primarily to those laws' prejudicial enforcement. "A good law on vagrancy, equally applicable to the whole population," suggested the paper in February 1865, "giving power to set to work the man who has no honest means of existence, will effectively protect the general interests of society." The paper even attempted to claim the legacy of Gueydon's antivagrancy reforms in Martinique, suggesting (falsely) that those policies had been colorblind. Yet as channels of communication developed between freeborn and formerly enslaved, freeborn leaders began rejecting the concept of state-managed labor coercion itself. In June, the paper mulled over the subjectivity of vagrancy law: "What is meant by a life of idleness? This will be constructed in many different ways." "Let the laborer alone," the paper emphatically demanded in April. "We denounce every plan calculated to keep him from moving about, in order to compel him to work for low wages."[48]

In February 1865, a coalition of white and Black Republicans launched the Freedmen's Aid Association, conceived of as a radical joint venture in corporative economics and an alternative to the Federal government's coercive labor program. To facilitate further collaboration and communication between labor and capital, the association began hosting open forums where freedpeople might express priorities and air grievances. It came as something of a surprise to the association's board that freedpeople seized these forums as a chance to attack constant police and provost marshal harassment. "Whenever a new Provost Marshal comes he gives us justice for a fortnight or so," one freedman testified, "then he becomes acquainted with the planters, takes dinners with them, receives presents; and then we no longer have any rights."[49] On July 18, discussion of vagrancy law dominated the forum. Black longshoremen described how police regularly raided the levee. A group of freedpeople from Live Oak Plantation, formerly enslaved by Tobias Gibson, described their unsuccessful struggle over the previous three weeks to obtain the release of their friend and compatriot, freedman John Martin. Moved, the association selected three men—white Unionists William Crane and Henry Train, and freeborn Black activist Clément Camp—to petition Thomas Conway for intervention.[50]

Their meeting with Conway would precipitate a chain of events with national repercussions. Conway was no friend of the city's freeborn Black activists, who had vocally condemned Conway for his role in enforcing Banks's labor system and for his statements in support of the resettlement of Black Americans in Africa. Conway, in turn, had charged the activists with exploiting freedpeople for political purposes and had even lobbied for the suppression of the *New Orleans Tribune*. Placing enmity aside, both sides recognized that the number of powerful allies in Louisiana was fast dwindling: unity between radical and moderate factions was essential if either was to survive politically. Moreover, as General Banks's "Inspector of Vagrants" and as superintendent of the Louisiana Freedmen's Bureau, Conway had grown increasingly disturbed by freedpeople's stories of police harassment, arbitrary confinement, and family separation. Indeed, only days earlier, Conway had met with the Live Oak Planation freedpeople in their effort to win John Martin's release. Realigning himself with the city's radicals, Conway resolved to deviate from government policy by denouncing racially discriminatory enforcement of vagrancy law.[51]

Following their meeting, Conway barred any further vagrancy arrests of freedpeople in Louisiana, ordered John Martin's immediate release, and instructed all Louisiana Freedmen's Bureau agents that henceforth freedpeople were "entirely free to work where and for whom they please." In an editorial to the conservative *New-Orleans Times*, Conway dismissed the specter of Black vagrancy as racist fantasy. "Numerous men, in writing about the freedmen, put all down as vagrants whom they see unemployed at the moment they look upon them," Conway charged; in reality, there were not "five hundred vagrant negroes in all of Louisiana." Under the guise of suppressing vagrancy, policemen had been seizing "industrious and self-supporting" freedpeople, an "injustice inflicted upon the freedmen at the hands of the New Orleans police" that "can hardly find its equal in the history of any city in Christendom."[52]

Governor Wells reported Conway's endorsement of Black lawlessness directly to President Johnson. Conway "thinks the black better than the white man," Wells wrote the president. The superintendent had rejected the truism "that freedom meant work" and was "allowing the negroes to go where they please and to work for whom they please."[53]

President Johnson agreed with Wells's assessment. When asked to share his own thoughts on vagrancy law, Johnson often recounted how, as a child, he had been apprenticed to a master in Virginia and how by the wholesome restraints of that master-servant relation, laziness and improvidence had been beaten out of him. "All men by nature are lazy; I know I am myself," Johnson joked. "There must be vagrant laws for the negroes, as there are for whites. . . . I was a regular indentured apprentice myself, and I don't think it would hurt them at all." Johnson's storytelling omitted critical details: he had *hated* his apprenticeship and had fled his master, who had posted a ten-dollar reward for the future president's capture. It was only by chance, luck, and guile that while running home to Tennessee, young Andrew Johnson had not been arrested as a vagrant.[54] In response to Wells's letter, Johnson pressured the commissioner of the Freedmen's Bureau, Otis Howard, into firing Conway and sending the president's own ally within the bureau, Brigadier General Joseph Fullerton, to Louisiana to reverse Conway's reforms.[55]

Arriving in New Orleans on October 16, Fullerton abruptly closed Louisiana's home colonies, accelerated the return of confiscated Confederate property, forbade bureau interference in civil courts, and ordered the immediate arrest of all vagrant freedpeople congregated within the city. Police responded so enthusiastically that Fullerton later estimated "nearly all of the vagrant blacks, and many who were not vagrants," seized within two days. Roving groups of policemen arrested "squads of colored men" en masse. At a farewell party hosted by Republican activists, Conway estimated that day's vagrancy arrests to be in the hundreds. Fullerton declined his invitation to attend.[56]

Declaring the city's Black orphans "able to work" but vagrant, Fullerton ordered the closure of New Orleans's two orphan asylums for nonwhite children and the apprenticeship of the orphaned children to planters, so that the orphans might "acquire industrious habits." Former slaveholders thronged the asylums, eager to obtain children. When the matron of one of the orphanages, freeborn Black woman Louise De Mortie, informed Fullerton that hers was a private institution beyond his power to close, Fullerton terminated the institution's bureau funding and confiscated the building within which the orphanage was housed. Yet the urgent danger of the orphans' removal and indenture provided the wives of New Orleans's freeborn Black activists with socially permissible entry points into the city's burgeoning civil rights struggle. Before their removal, the orphans of one of the institutions simply "disappeared":

smuggled, Fullerton presumed, into the households of sympathetic freeborn Black families. Meanwhile, thirty-three formerly free Black women—led by Paul Trévigne's wife, Marie Hortensia Léon Trévigne; Louis Charles Roudanez's wife, Louise Célie Saulay Roudanez; and Thomas Jennings's widow, Angelina Jennings—launched a protracted philanthropic campaign to save De Mortie's orphanage. Through months of charitable balls and national fundraising drives, the women secured the financial support to guarantee the institution's future. By their work, the institution would endure for another century, evolving into New Orleans's top high school for Black students under Jim Crow.[57]

The nation's newspapers closely followed Fullerton's actions in New Orleans. The nation's newspapers also looked to Jamaica, where on October 11, militiamen had opened fire on a parade of Black Jamaicans marching to protest the incarceration of a Black man for trespassing on an abandoned plantation, killing seven and triggering a broader peasant uprising. Colonial troops responded with vicious ferocity, killing some 400 Black Jamaicans. Another 254 Black Jamaicans were executed; another 600 were ordered flogged.[58] Events in Jamaica and New Orleans appeared side by side in the American press. To former slaveholders, this Morant Bay Rebellion, as it would become known, provided further proof that unregulated vagrancy led to anarchy.[59] To freedpeople and their allies, the uprisings suggested that unless freedpeople secured control of their own labor, they might become a class of landless paupers, left "on a naked rock in the midst of the Ocean" in the *New Orleans Tribune*'s words, controlled by planters.[60] Hoping to quell the brewing storm, bureau commissioner Otis Howard traveled to New Orleans, where in a public address to freedpeople on November 5 he favorably contrasted "the history of the French Islands," where "good wholesome rules" had ensured that "labor was undisturbed" and "prosperity" maintained, to that of another unmentionable island—implicitly, Jamaica—where "there became anarchy and everything went backwards." "I urge you not to be divided and agitated," Howard pleaded: return to your "former masters" and "be satisfied with what we have." Do not "push ahead any further." A reporter transcribing Howard's address recorded that the crowd drowned out his entreaties with "cries of no."[61]

The Black Codes

This was the crucible from which Louisiana's Black Code emerged. One week after Howard's speech, Governor Wells ordered an emergency session of the state legislature. The resulting body of laws, which Wells signed into law on December 21, bore imprints of Banks's labor system, planters' readings of events in the Caribbean, and antebellum efforts to coerce wage labor through vagrancy law. The legislature proposed a system of annual plantation contracts, while restricting plantation workers' ability to travel, access firearms, and change employers. The legislature debated various vagrancy bills but ultimately resolved that the antivagrancy articles contained within the state's crime law of 1855 remained sufficiently powerful and broad. Rather than pass a new vagrancy law, the legislature amended the 1855 law by adding indenture and up to twelve months' chain gang labor to the list of possible penalties for vagrancy.[62]

Though the details varied from state to state, the Black Codes passed between the winter of 1865 and spring of 1866 all shared a common vision of state coercive power with vagrancy law as its foundation.[63] Every Black Code included a new vagrancy law—excepting Tennessee and Arkansas, which joined Louisiana in judging their antebellum vagrancy laws sufficient. Every state, save North Carolina, authorized the hiring out of vagrants. Alabama, Georgia, South Carolina, Texas, and Virginia joined Louisiana in authorizing the creation of county chain gangs for vagrants. Virginia and Alabama authorized the construction of workhouses for vagrants in every county and town. In defining vagrancy, the codes varied. Mississippi's code defined as vagrant "all freedmen, free Negroes and mulattoes" who failed to contract and all "white persons" found "associating with freedmen, free Negroes or mulattoes on terms of equality." South Carolina's vagrancy law regulated the bonds tethering wife to husband, child to parent, ward to guardian, and apprentice, servant, and laborer to capital, underscoring legislators' conviction that the prevention of disorder lay in the maintenance of hierarchical relations between dependents and patriarchs. Most Black Codes, however, provided generic definitions of vagrancy that omitted any explicit mention of race.[64]

The Black Codes backfired, provoking vigorous northern opposition. Bureau commissioner Howard likened the vagrancy laws of Louisiana, Georgia, and Texas to "practical slavery." In Congress, Senator Henry Wilson of Massachusetts announced that "under the vagrant laws" of the South, freedpeople were being "sold into bondage." In January 1866, General-in-Chief Ulysses S. Grant instructed military commanders to prohibit the prosecution of Black persons "charged with offenses for which white persons are not prosecuted or punished in the same manner and degree." Twelve days later, General Alfred H. Terry overturned Virginia's vagrancy law, declaring it "slavery in all but its name." Military commanders began nullifying overtly discriminatory sections of the codes or mandating the laws' racially neutral enforcement. In New Orleans, General Absalom Baird, Fullerton's replacement as head of the Louisiana Freedmen's Bureau, rolled back his predecessor's counterreforms, blocked the forcible transportation of arrestees to the countryside, and allowed freedpeople to enter into contracts voluntarily, negotiate wages, or refuse to contract altogether.[65] The Civil Rights Act of 1866, passed by Congress in April over the president's veto, laid further groundwork for the nullification of racially prejudicial laws by affirming that freedpeople were citizens and that all citizens were entitled to equal protection under the law.[66]

Northern moderates had supported freedpeople's arrest and coercion on the assumption that the army's labor regulations were temporary expediencies, aligned to the spirit of northern poor laws, and intended to prepare freedpeople for their transition to fully free wage labor. They believed that the war had resolved the nation's great sectional schism of the past quarter-century: at long last free labor ideology had triumphed over proslavery thought. Yet these northerners now saw in the Black Codes the foundation for a permanent system of peonage, patently at odds with key elements of free labor. They perceived these laws as evidence that southern leadership had not accepted slavery's destruction and the terms of peace.[67]

In the North, southern vagrancy laws now seemed emblematic of a violently racist criminal justice system that pursued only the re-creation of slavery by another name. Republican lawmakers and leaders, including those who had previously endorsed and orchestrated freedpeople's arrest and coercion through vagrancy law, now denounced southern vagrancy laws as antithetical to freedom's true meaning.[68] The *New York Times*, which had printed full-throated endorsements of Banks's antivagrancy policies throughout 1864 and 1865, denounced the "odious vagrant law" of Virginia, "which sells both blacks and whites into servitude." Rejecting any effort "to *regulate* labor," the paper energetically denounced the poor law principles that it had espoused only months earlier: "LABOR, IN ORDER TO BE PROFITABLE AND SUCCESSFUL, MUST BE ENTIRELY FREE."[69]

Northern reversal on southern vagrancy law was laced with ironies. Northern reporting on the Black Codes routinely contained factual errors that overstated the laws' severity or made generalized references to southern "re-enslavement" that rendered vague the laws' actual provisions and enforcement.[70] Not only did many states' Black Codes resemble the coercive labor programs established under Union occupation, some states' Black Codes were on their face considerably *milder* than the Union army's contract system. Under Virginia's Black Code, for example, convicted vagrants could be hired out for a maximum of three months, rather than the one year that was standard under Union army labor regulations.[71] Banks's "Louisiana Plan" of 1863 and Louisiana's Black Code of 1865 were similar, not sharply distinct. More than anything else, northern ire revealed how much white northern public opinion had shifted during those interceding years.

Also obscured by northern reactions to the Black Codes was the degree to which deep preoccupation with "vagrants" was national, not regional, in scope. In denouncing the southern Black Codes as illegitimate and in claiming the freedom to choose one's own work and employer as fundamental rights, northerners disregarded the paradoxes of northern poor law, under which paupers were routinely denied the right to choose their employer or employ. Indeed, even as northerners denounced southern vagrancy law, an emergent "tramp scare" in the North, fueled by postwar demobilization and economic depression, was already beginning to precipitate the passage of new and draconian vagrancy laws. Arrest rates soon soared; northern newspapers began publishing vehement diatribes against vagrants; some moralists and social reformers predicted society's collapse.[72] North or South, panic over vagrancy encoded many of the same basic fears among landed elites regarding poverty, migration, and wage labor.

Many histories of the Reconstruction era unwittingly reproduce assumptions popularized by the northern press in 1865 and 1866: that southern vagrancy laws were exceptionally arbitrary and backward and were indicative of a society with underdeveloped legal traditions. Yet to a surprising degree, vagrancy enforcement patterns in New Orleans resembled antebellum enforcement patterns. In performing vagrancy arrests, Kennedy's police observed class distinctions, eschewing the vagrancy arrest of Black landowners and the well-to-do.[73] The persons seized by New Orleans police—orphans, laundresses, day laborers, pushcart vendors, sex workers, squatters, scavengers, and other landless persons whose flexible family relations, living arrangements, and employment conditions connoted dangerous mobility, autonomy, and uncontrollability—*were* guilty of vagrancy under established local criteria. Of course, nearly all the freedpeople who had fled into New Orleans could be construed as vagrant under those criteria. Yet the threat facing freedpeople was not the conjuring of an entirely arbitrary and novel criminal category so much as the incorporation of Blackness into a preexisting paradigm for conceptualizing deviance and regulating wage labor.

Nor had New Orleans authorities forgotten the menace posed by poor white vagrants. Perhaps the greatest irony of Louisiana's Black Code is that most arrests under the laws were likely of white men. In municipal elections in March 1866, as the Louisiana Freedmen's Bureau curtailed the seizure of freedpeople, New Orleans voters reelected the city's prewar mayor, the former Know-Nothing John Monroe. Monroe perceived that "the lawlessness of degraded white persons" was equal to that of "the blacks freed from restraints."[74] He conducted yet another purge of the New Orleans police, filling the department's ranks with his former Know-Nothing enforcers who had participated in nativist mob violence and engaged in the mass arrest of white immigrants as vagrants during the mid-1850s. Under Monroe's tenure, which lasted into 1867, foreign-born white persons constituted roughly two-thirds of all vagrancy arrests performed in New Orleans under Louisiana's Black Code.[75]

Federal nullification of explicitly discriminatory southern legislation did little to protect freedpeople from seizure under vagrancy statutes—northern or southern—that did not incorporate racially prejudicial language. In Louisiana, Georgia, North Carolina, Texas, and Virginia, the vagrancy laws of 1865 and 1866 made no mention of race and remained on the books. Florida simply amended its vagrancy law of 1865, replacing "persons of color" with the words "all persons without discrimination."[76] Other communities transitioned to municipal antivagrancy ordinances or prewar state laws. Police in Augusta, Georgia, for example, began seizing freedpeople under a broad antebellum antivagrancy municipal ordinance, opaquely referred to as "the eighteenth section" by newspapers, that made no explicit mention of race. During the 1870s, this municipal ordinance would account for a striking 60–70 percent of all arrests in Augusta. During that decade, Augusta law enforcement would remain so committed to performing vagrancy arrests that it would maintain a vagrancy arrest rate higher than the average arrest rate for *all* crimes in present-day US cities.[77]

Two police riots in May and July 1866 galvanized northern opposition to President Johnson's plan for southern self-Reconstruction. In Memphis on May 1, policemen dispersing an impromptu block party exchanged gunfire with Black soldiers. For two days thereafter, police and firemen rampaged through Black neighborhoods, killing forty-six Black residents and indiscriminately burning Black homes, churches, and schools. Three months later, in New Orleans, police and firemen opened fire on delegates and spectators attending an improvised constitutional convention that had convened for the purpose of extending voting rights to Black men. The massacre left more than 40 white and Black Republicans dead and more than 100 wounded. It was a wrenching blow to New Orleans's Black activist community. Lucien Jean-Pierre Capla, the well-respected freeborn shoe merchant who had been arrested in 1862 for aiding a fugitive slave, had brought his teenage son, Alfred, to observe the historic convention proceedings. Now he watched in horror as policemen murdered unarmed friends and proceeded to mutilate their bodies: "They shot them, and when they done that, they tramped upon them, and mashed their heads with their boots, and shot them after they were down," the shoe merchant later recalled. Capla was shot and beaten by the mob; Alfred was shot four times, stabbed three times, and suffered the obliteration of his right eye. Joseph Camps, a successful grocer and Paul Trévigne's first cousin, was stabbed in the back and suffered "extensive contusions of head and face." Victor Lacroix, a Union army veteran whose father, the prosperous real-estate developer François Lacroix, had co-organized the petition from January 1863 protesting prejudicial vagrancy policing, was killed, "cut from head to foot," his body "mutilated in the most shocking and barbarous manner." As news spread of these massacres in New Orleans and Memphis, political support for President Johnson collapsed and Congress seized the reins of Reconstruction policy.[78]

Climax of Revolution:
Louisiana's State Constitution of 1868

The Reconstruction Act of 1867, passed in March over President Johnson's veto, placed the states of the former Confederacy back under military control and conditioned the reestablishment of home rule on each state's ratification of a new state constitution, ratification of the Fourteenth Amendment, and extension of suffrage rights to Black men.[79] Elections for delegates to Louisiana's state constitutional convention were held in September 1867. Republicans swept the election, with men of African ancestry winning roughly half of the ninety-seven delegate seats. At least half of the Black convention delegates representing Orleans Parish—Arnold Bertonneau, Jean Baptiste Esnard, Henri Bonseigneur, P. B. S. Pinchback, Édouard Tinchant, and William Vigers—had co-organized or signed the petition of January 1863 protesting prejudicial vagrancy policing.[80]

Between November 1867 and March 1868, the convention drafted one of the most progressive state constitutions in the nation's history. In addition to producing Louisiana's first bill of rights, establishing an integrated public school system, protecting access to public accommodations, and requiring that all state officials swear their commitment to the civic and political equality of all men, the constitution enshrined a radical reimagining of state police power. It repealed the Black Codes; established due process rights; broadened habeas corpus rights; banned penal labor except upon conviction by jury; prohibited juvenile indenture without parental consent; required that all criminal convictions stem from "indictment or information" (effectively eliminating recorders' carte blanche power to preemptively incarcerate persons deemed to be likely future criminals); and guaranteed all convicted persons "the same pains and penalties," irrespective of race.[81]

Two weeks before elections in which Louisiana's interracial electorate would vote to ratify or reject the new constitution and elect a new state government, New Orleans Democrats staged a final, desperate scheme to retain political power by ordering police to arrest hundreds of Black men for vagrancy and release them on condition that they leave the city, in a ploy (Republicans alleged) to suppress Black voter turnout. While Republicans commenced hearings, 256 Black men, incarcerated in the City Workhouse after refusing to leave the city, sued for habeas corpus, demanding evidence of their vagrancy. The court dismissed the prisoners' writ: by Louisiana law, "evidence of Crime" remained irrelevant in vagrancy cases. Locally, the voter suppression scheme may have worked: the Democratic ticket maintained control in Orleans Parish by an average of 250 votes per seat.[82]

The ploy was not enough, however, to retain political control of Louisiana. The new constitution was ratified by a wide margin. Republican Henry Clay Warmoth, a moderate, was elected governor. Oscar Dunn was elected lieutenant governor, twenty years after his Police Jail imprisonment as soi-disant libre. The new Republican-controlled legislature dissolved the New Orleans police force and reorganized Orleans, Jefferson, and St. Bernard Parishes into the unified Metropolitan Police District, consisting of an interracial force and under the leadership of an interracial Board of Metropolitan Police Commissioners, chaired by Dunn.[83]

Louisiana's planter elite was in disbelief. Another profound shock awaited them: the new constitution had repealed Louisiana's Black Code without reenacting the antivagrancy articles of Louisiana's crime law of 1855. With the constitution's ratification, vagrancy ceased to be a prosecutable crime.[84]

"Give Us Back a Vagrant Law!"

That the constitution of 1868 had nullified all state vagrancy laws caught everyone by surprise, save the small cadre of radical convention delegates who had quietly incorporated the vaguely worded provision.[85] To Democrats and moderate Republicans alike, it was an act of madness. This endorsement of idleness was "a disgrace to any State that calls itself a civilized State," one Democratic congressman trumpeted. In the name of protecting freedpeople from police harassment, radicals had neutered the most indispensable policing power. They had decriminalized the "source of all crime": that clay from which is "moulded the peace-breaker, the petty thief, the prostitute and the daring burglar." The first rule of organized societies, that man must work for his bread, had been abolished. It was as though the convention had legalized cannibalism.[86]

Both Democrats and moderate Republicans soon asserted that the nullification had precipitated an apocalyptic mass migration of professional cutthroats, idlers, pirates, and thieves into Louisiana. Villains "rush such as the Vandals made upon Rome," wailed the *New Orleans Daily Crescent*. Policemen were "powerless," criminals "rob almost with impunity," the "lawless lazaroni render nothing safe." "Give us back a vagrant law, by which we can free ourselves from such unwelcome intruders," pleaded the *New-Orleans Times*. A new vagrancy law was "absolutely essential," agreed the *Daily Picayune*, "the most needed legislation that can be enacted." Moderate Republicans concurred. Calling vagrants "a fungus on society, which needs legislative surgery," Governor Warmoth demanded the immediate passage of a new vagrancy law. "There are no classes of laws which more imperatively demanded the serious and careful attention of legislators," pleaded the new superintendent of the Metropolitan Police. The superintendent recognized that the repeal had crippled the Republican regime's political legitimacy: "No government can hope to win the confidence and support of its citizens, while it fails to afford to them security."[87]

Yet Louisiana's warring political factions—conservative Democrats representing former slaveholder interests, "Workingmen's Democrats" representing poor white laborers, radical Republicans, and Governor Warmoth's moderate Republican faction—struggled vainly to agree on a new vagrancy law that was broad enough to furnish police with discretionary powers, narrow enough to protect laborers from arbitrary arrest, and constitutional under the new state constitution.[88] At least six vagrancy bills were introduced to the House and Senate in 1869 and 1870. Moderate Republicans reintroduced the text of Louisiana's 1855 law. Conservative Democrats clung to hopes for a massive statewide penal infrastructure for the punishment of vagrants, introducing bills for the constructions of a state workhouse and a diffuse network of parish workhouses. An alliance of radical Republicans and Workingmen's Democrats blocked every proposal.[89]

Opposition was spearheaded by Senator Curtis Pollard of Madison Parish, a Baptist minister and former slave whom the *Daily Picayune* described as "a black man, uncompromisingly so; and a Republican equally uncompromising." (A young Sarah Breedlove—later known to the world as Madam C. J. Walker, the renowned entrepreneur and wealthiest Black American woman of the Gilded Age—was a member of Pollard's congregation.) Pollard charged that vagrancy law was a ploy "to put a whole lot of darkies in jail." Conservative senators rebuked Pollard for assuming that all vagrancy laws were inherently racially prejudicial. Yet Pollard insisted that vagrancy laws would always disproportionately threaten freedpeople's liberty because so many freedpeople were forced to migrate in search of short-term employment. "A great many of our people are living about from one place to another," Pollard explained. "They work a little on plantations, some get a little pay, and some get nothing. Some get on steamboats to work, and when they get down to the city they can't get back again. . . . Where are we to go? We wander around from one place to another, and we can't help it." The problem was not innate Black dependency

or depravity, Pollard charged, but the structure of the labor market and the
federal government's failure to distribute land.[90]

A compromise was reached in March 1869. Radical Republicans and Workingmen's Democrats would consent to a new vagrancy bill, on condition that
three of the most vocal opponents—Black Republicans Pollard and P. B. S.
Pinchback and white Workingmen's Democrat George Braughn—drafted vagrancy's definition. The compromise embodied what the twentieth-century
activist and scholar W. E. B. Du Bois would deem Reconstruction's greatest
hope for lasting success: an interracial labor coalition, uniting freedpeople
and poor white workers, to counteract planter power.[91] Pollard, Pinchback,
and Braughn drafted a definition that restricted the vagrant to a person found
in possession of weapons, lockpicks, or other instruments that demonstrated
"probable intention" to commit an imminent felony. It was perhaps the narrow-
est definition of vagrancy ever conceived. To protect agricultural workers, the
law would apply only within the Metropolitan Police District. Furthermore,
the Board of Metropolitan Police Commissioners, chaired by Lieutenant Governor Dunn, would be tasked with reviewing each vagrancy arrest.[92] Over the
following year, the Metropolitan Police performed 843 vagrancy arrests under
this law, a vagrancy arrest rate less than one-tenth of New Orleans's vagrancy
arrest rate in 1850. Of those arrests, the board rejected nearly half. Others were
released on bond or after paying small fines.[93] The workhouse was virtually
empty: there were "ten or twelve" inmates in March 1870, down from more
than 300 in July 1868.[94]

William Cooley, a white conservative Unionist and the judge of New Orleans's Sixth District Court, argued that even this compromised vagrancy act
overreached. An iconoclast mistrusted by Democrats and Republicans alike,
Cooley claimed opposition to any unnecessary government encroachment into
a person's private affairs. He was no friend of the state's Black radical faction.
Indeed, as a delegate to the constitutional convention in 1868, he had rejected
and openly mocked that faction's efforts to add a guarantee of "public rights"
to the state constitution, deeming that guarantee an "absurd" violation of owners' right to exclude persons from their property. Yet Cooley also rejected the
principles of summary conviction and preemptive arrest, arguing that every
criminal defendant should have a basic right to jury trial and that all detentions
should stem from hard evidence linking the defendant to a specific crime.[95]
As convention delegate he had personally drafted the constitutional article
nullifying recorders' power of summary conviction, citing police abuse of the
white working poor.[96] In July 1870, Cooley ruled the new vagrancy law unconstitutional under Louisiana's new constitution, as it guaranteed jury trial and

required that prosecutions stem from indictments. "I don't believe that because a man is a thief he must be jerked up at a moment's warning by anybody or everybody and put in jail," Cooley argued, before invalidating the vagrancy conviction of a reputed professional burglar. "The individual who stands before me may be a scoundrel," but "a citizen is entitled to a trial."[97]

Moderate Republicans decried Cooley's refusal "to save society from the plague of thieves and vagrants" and drafted articles of impeachment, while Democrats lambasted Republicans for their inability to secure "preventative justice." Cooley remained intransigent. In January 1871, Governor Warmoth signed into law a bill that reenacted the antivagrancy articles of Louisiana's crime law of 1855: Cooley declared it unconstitutional and began releasing detainees convicted under that law. New Orleans's council passed a vagrancy ordinance: Cooley declared it unconstitutional as well. Courts with overlapping and legally murky jurisdictions issued contradictory rulings: New Orleans's Criminal Court affirmed Cooley's judgments while the Louisiana Seventh and Eighth District Courts sustained the constitutionality of the vagrancy law signed by Warmoth in 1871. Desperate to build their political legitimacy, the Metropolitans began staging highly publicized antivagrancy raids on gambling houses, bordellos, and criminal dens, arresting prominent criminals with flashy sobriquets including "Burnt Fingered Joe," "Big Mouth Hash," and "Bowlegged Donovan." Cooley approved every habeas corpus writ, vowing to continue "even if all the rogues in the country go unwipt of justice." Some of Cooley's releasees subsequently committed prominent burglaries and rapes, leading Republicans to wonder if the judge's true intent was to destroy the Republican regime from within. Cooley remained steadfast until 1873 when Robert Rhett Jr., editor of the *Daily Picayune* and scion of a leading architect of South Carolina's secession, shot the judge dead in a duel.[98]

From Louisiana's political struggles over vagrancy law emerged glimmers of Radical Reconstruction's possibilities: a dramatic reimagining of state police power, unprecedented rights for prisoners and criminal defendants, and signs of a potential interracial labor coalition. By the time of Cooley's death, each of those possibilities had faded. Louisiana's Republican Party was splintering into irreconcilable factionalism. Moderate Republicans had shunted radicals to the party's margins and terminated the state's printing contract with the *New Orleans Tribune*, contributing to that paper's collapse.[99] With the *Slaughterhouse* cases of 1873, the US Supreme Court ruled that the Fourteenth Amendment did not give the federal judiciary the power to overturn regulatory laws passed by the states unless those regulations were explicitly racially prejudicial. With the *Slaughterhouse* ruling, "The States have the same right they always had to make police regulations," explained one Republican senator, provided that those police regulations "operate equally upon men of all colors."[100] White para-military groups began launching coordinated terror campaigns—massacring upward of 150 Black men at Colfax, Louisiana, in April 1873; massacring two dozen freedmen and white Republicans in Coushatta, Louisiana, in June 1874; and staging successive coups d'état in New Orleans in September 1873 and September 1874—driving Black political operatives and white Republicans into hiding while draining national support for ongoing southern intervention.[101] Some radical leaders fled the state. Hounded by Klansmen, Curtis Pollard evacuated his congregation to Kansas.[102]

The constitutionality of vagrancy law in Louisiana would not be definitively resolved until May 1877: one month after the withdrawal of nearly all federal troops from Louisiana, the forced resignation of Louisiana's Republican governor, and the demise of Republican rule in Louisiana. Judge William Whitaker of Louisiana's Superior Criminal Court, beloved among Democrats for his spirited legal defense of the Colfax Massacre ringleaders, conceded that the "spirit" of the constitution of 1868 seemed opposed to summary conviction. Yet this vague sense of liberality was not enough to invalidate the incontrovertible, "ancient," and self-evident right of all states, upheld in the *Slaughterhouse* decision, to suppress idleness. Whitaker declared that the constitutionality of Louisiana's law of 1855, as amended in 1865 and reenacted in 1871, was "no longer an open question." The radicals had been removed from power. The interracial Metropolitan Police had been dissolved. Vagrancy law had been restored.[103] Finally, Louisiana could resume the essential work of disciplining idle labor.

CHAPTER 7

Aftershocks of Marronage

Labor Coercion in the Jim Crow City

I n May 1858, the slave Anaïse, arrested as a runaway, tricked Constance Bique Perrine, a freeborn Black woman arrested for public intoxication and disturbing the peace, into trading places while the two sat in police custody. Brought to the Police Jail courtyard, Perrine was stripped nude, "tightly pinioned and forcibly stretched upon" the whipping rack, and administered ten lashes as dozens of enslaved inmates were forced to watch.[1] A record of this routine punishment exists only because Perrine was a free woman, inadvertently tortured as though enslaved.

A half-century later, in August 1903, white woman Annie Dooley, arrested for disturbing the peace, was "stripped and laid across a barrel in one of the yards of the Police Jail and severely whipped by the Captain in the presence of the other prisoners, most colored," who were forced to watch.[2] A record of this routine punishment exists only because Dooley was a white woman, imprudently tortured as though a Black inmate.

These two women's stories of state torture, forced nudity, and strategic humiliation within the Police Jail courtyard underscore continuities of New Orleans's prison system that span the ruptures of the Civil War and Emancipation. Past histories have suggested that Emancipation precipitated "a rapid departure from southern penal traditions."[3] No such carceral revolution came to pass within the urban South, where expansive policing and coercive systems directed at Black and white workers already existed: instead of initiating an abrupt transition from privately inflicted violence to state-managed violence, urban leaders made adjustments and adaptations to preexisting policing and penal systems, including those originally developed for the control of the enslaved.

From Reconstruction's collapse in 1877 to the civil rights movement of the 1960s, Black wageworkers in New Orleans lived under the omnipresent threat of seizure, state torture, and redeployment on public works through the same police jail system that had once tortured their enslaved forebears. Within this reconceived carceral system, vagrancy law provided the key functional surrogate for the state's antebellum power to seize Black pedestrians as maroons. Viewed at the local level and from the longue durée, Reconstruction was but a brief interregnum within longer trends: before and after, menial laborers in New Orleans were required to carry passes, to undergo constant surveillance for their perceived "idleness," and to suffer recurrent redeployment on the public infrastructure that made private wealth accumulation possible.

Continuities notwithstanding, it would be misleading to discount all that *had* changed. With neither the funds nor the will to maintain the police force's relative size, postbellum city leaders proved unable to reestablish the degree of state surveillance and coercive pressure exerted by their antebellum predecessors. The postbellum prison system was far more chaotic and capricious than its antebellum predecessor, exposing inmates to indiscriminate violence and bodily injury but also offering inmates greater opportunity for resistance and escape. Even during the cruelest years of Jim Crow, arrest and incarceration rates among Black wageworkers in New Orleans were far *lower* than those previously suffered by enslaved residents. The history of southern state police power is narrated as a story of dramatic postbellum expansion and intensification in reaction to Emancipation. Yet told from the point of view of urban workers themselves, the history of southern state police power is one of dramatic and irreversible contraction.

Police Jail Redux

After assuming local and state control in 1877, Louisiana Democrats began undoing the reforms of their Republican predecessors. A new crime bill, passed in 1878 and known popularly as the "chain gang bill," reauthorized prisoners' deployment on public works.[4] A new state constitution, ratified in 1879, eliminated the most radical provisions of Louisiana's constitution of 1868—provisions establishing integrated public schooling and asserting equal "public rights"—while retaining *some* of the protections of that constitution's Bill of Rights.

Meanwhile, New Orleans lurched into a grave sanitation crisis. The abolition of the city's chain gangs in 1862 and again in 1868 had left the city without its traditional public works force. The city had pivoted to hired street cleaners, but with Reconstruction's collapse, massive tax cuts under the new Democratic leadership forced deep reductions to city services: in 1880 alone, the city slashed the number of hired sanitation workers from 338 to 101 men. Paved streets began reverting to muddied dirt. Garbage, human waste, and dead animals blocked gutters, sidewalks, and canals. While peer cities installed sewerage systems, most New Orleanians still relied on privies. Though the causes of yellow fever were not yet understood (many attributed the disease to impure swamp air), a devastating epidemic in 1878 left some 20,000 dead throughout the Mississippi River valley and impressed the urgency of the city's sanitation crisis on New Orleans's public officials and business leaders alike.[5]

In January 1881, the New Orleans City Council ordered "the conversion of the City Workhouse into a Police Jail." This "conversion" did not entail any significant changes to the prison building itself, which dated to 1842 and had previously served as both the City Police Jail and the City Workhouse. Instead, this ordinance eliminated indoor penal labor and reassigned prisoners to chain gang labor: in effect, this was a "conversion" from a cloistered penal labor system rationalized as a tool for the uplift of white inmates to a public penal labor system rationalized as a tool for the degradation of Black inmates. With passage of this ordinance, chain gangs resumed their work in city streets.[6]

Yet reforms instituted during Radical Reconstruction were not so easily undone. In September 1881, Judge Alfred Roman of the New Orleans Criminal Court—son of Governor André Roman, who had overseen the construction of the state's first penitentiary some fifty years earlier—ruled that New Orleans's chain gangs were unconstitutional because the state's constitution of 1879 had retained the provision from Louisiana's constitution of 1868 that prohibited the impressment of prisoners who had been summarily convicted without the benefit of jury trial. Once again, New Orleans's chain gang was abolished.[7]

The solution, reached in 1884, was to replace chain gangs with "voluntary" work gangs: for each day that Police Jail prisoners *consented* to outdoor penal labor, one day would be stricken from their sentences.[8] Shackles were discarded, and Police Jail inmates were again returned to city streets. This system of voluntary outdoor labor for misdemeanor offenders was quickly adopted throughout Louisiana and persists to this day.[9]

Police Jail gangs reoccupied the same economic niches as their antebellum counterparts: collecting trash, grading and paving streets, sweeping sidewalks, clearing gutters and sewage lines, raking public parks, scrubbing marketplace stalls, interring the bodies of paupers, and removing corpses amid disasters. They were a multipurpose janitorial and public works force, performing every conceivable task, large and small—erecting polling booths before elections, mounting a municipal park's new flagstaff, dragging water-damaged carpeting from a flooded courthouse—for the city's hospitals, asylums, libraries, police stations, fire stations, courtrooms, and public schools.[10] Virtually every city agency grew dependent on their labor. "If the asylums need the aid of a wood sawyer and a few darkies to saw and carry wood, the [Police Jail] captain calls up a couple of sawyers and pilers and sends them to the asylum," explained one official. "When there are squares to fix up, such as whitewashing and cleaning them out . . . the gangs are sent out." As during the antebellum era, incarcerated Black women were assigned to custodial work in the city's marketplaces and public institutions, while white and Black men built and repaired public infrastructure. Lawmakers barred white women from outdoor penal labor, ruling their public exposure too offensive. They cleaned the Police Jail and laundered inmates' uniforms.[11]

The new jail gangs were voluntary in name only. Prisoners who refused to work were beaten, whipped, denied food, placed in solitary confinement, and locked within sweatboxes—containers three feet in length by three feet in width, with three holes cut for ventilation—for hours and even days. "Hunger is a good way to bring them to subjugation," one jail superintendent advised. "If they won't work, they can't eat."[12]

But the removal of chains, combined with a chronic shortage of guards, provided jail gang workers with continual opportunities for escape and thus a degree of power to renegotiate their working conditions. The postbellum Police Jail was a sieve: on average, one prisoner fled their work crew every day. Between October 1907 and October 1909, a staggering 1,481 prisoners escaped, or nearly 10 percent of those admitted. By contrast, the Police Jail's antebellum escape rate had been closer to 0.5 percent.[13]

To stem the escapes, administrators were forced to adapt a carrot-and-stick approach, granting unprecedented concessions to compliant prisoners while viciously brutalizing recaptured escapees. For agreeing to complete unsupervised labor without escaping, trusted recidivists were offered special inducements: extra rations, liquor, favorable work assignments, and coveted "trustee" status (granting them supervisory powers over high-risk prisoners). In particular, and although New Orleans's judges and city council repeatedly decried and forbade the practice, trusted prisoners were allowed to return to their homes each night and to sleep within their own beds on condition that they voluntarily resubmit themselves to the prison in the morning.[14] Given these terms, local arrestees tended to attempt escape at far lower rates than jailed migrant workers from out of town, who thus were subjected to far greater surveillance. "When any of the home negroes are placed in the jail they make up their minds to serve out the term, for they know the captain can get them twelve hours after they skip out," explained one city official. "He knows the range and stamping ground of all of them. . . . There are a number of darkies that he practically owns."[15]

The result of these compromises was a perverse parody of a jail, where captivity was often negotiated, chain gangs lacked chains, and prisoners— endlessly attempting escapes and enduring recaptures, leaving for dinner and returning for breakfast—leaked out and in like water through a colander.

Measured in terms of its economic function within the city's economy, the postbellum Police Jail reproduced the roles of its antebellum counterpart. Yet measured in terms of the experiences of prisoners themselves, the postbellum Police Jail was an unregulated, unsupervised, and chaotic shadow of its former self. The destruction of slavery had divested the city of any financial interest in prisoners' safe return to their owners. Whereas this sometimes meant that prisoners exercised greater maneuverability and opportunity for resistance, it also placed prisoners at greater risk of bodily harm. The antebellum Police Jail had employed a full-time physician, the postbellum Police Jail did not.[16] Strict antebellum surveillance yielded to casual postbellum indifference. The tightly regulated and carefully structured violence of the antebellum institution—epitomized by the whipping rack—was replaced by a capricious medley of truncheons, whippings, and jail yard beatings.

Anecdotal evidence suggests that Black women were considerably more vulnerable to sexual assault within the postbellum jail. Before Emancipation, carceral impregnation had been common among state-owned convict slaves held in the state penitentiary but does not appear common among privately owned slaves held in police jails, suggesting, perhaps, that women held as private property were more protected from guard-on-inmate sexual violence because those guards were required to recognize slaveowners' exclusive claim of access to enslaved women's bodies. In contrast, rape within the postbellum institution was systematic and thorough. Dennis Mahoney, Police Jail superintendent from 1896 to 1900, treated the women's dormitory as his personal harem, encouraging jailors to select victims, particularly from among the imprisoned Black adolescents, on something approaching a nightly basis. This was disclosed openly after one inmate, described as a "pretty young mulattress of fifteen years," birthed a baby that was presumed to be Mahoney's biological child, prompting a brief public outcry. The superintendent received a two-week suspension without pay.[17]

Notably, Black women orchestrated virtually every prison revolt that rocked New Orleans's jail system during the early twentieth century. "They treat us like dogs! They beat us like dogs!" one woman shouted to reporters from her cell window in 1920, during a coordinated uprising of Black female inmates, while lowering her blouse to reveal bloody gashes along her shoulder blades. Black men joined the prison strike, in solidarity: "We boys made it up that we wouldn't work so long as they treated the women thataway," one explained. The following year, female jail gang workers beat their guard senseless with their brooms. When five Black men refused to leave their cell in solidarity, guards sprayed them with gasoline and lit them on fire.[18]

The experiences of Marie François, a Black teenager whom police identified as a Storyville sex worker, underscore the reorganized prison's violent anarchism. François was committed to the Police Jail for lewdness on May 6, 1898. Her age, her race, and the timing of her commitment mark her as a likely victim of the sexual violence overseen by Mahoney. One week after her commitment, François snuck out of the courthouse that her jail gang had been assigned to clean. Recommitted for lewdness one month later, she promptly re-escaped, this time as her gang washed marketplace stalls, only to be re-captured that following day. François again escaped that February. She was recommitted for lewdness and vulgar language in October 1899, only to *again* escape, also while washing marketplace stalls, and *again* be recaptured that November: five commitments and four escapes in eighteen months. François was back in the Police Jail when census takers entered in June 1900. Through-out, she presumably would have been whipped in the Police Jail courtyard for each escape and sexually assaulted by Superintendent Mahoney or one of his employees.[19]

For Black New Orleanians like Marie François, the experiences that defined enslavement—sexual violence, torture, forced labor, the violation of bodily autonomy—were intermittent traumas encountered by way of the prison, re-peatedly, throughout their lives. Historians have often imagined slavery and freedom as extremes within a multidimensional array of labor relations, with postbellum Black southerners inhabiting a range of points within this array.[20] Living under the Police Jail's shadow, members of New Orleans's Black working poor lived lives defined by abrupt leaps between opposite ends of this array, like a metronome's needle, as they were thrust back and forth between the relatively high degree of autonomy characteristic of urban wage work and brief yet tor-turous cycles of carceral neoslavery.

For white New Orleanians like Dennis Mahoney—a child of impoverished Irish immigrants who had risen through the ranks of New Orleans's Dem-ocratic Party machine as a paramilitary terrorist, fighting to overthrow Re-construction within the city's White League—the position of Police Jail super-intendent provided an opportunity to seize privileges once denied. Following Reconstruction's collapse, the governing coalition of elite businessmen and merchants in New Orleans was dethroned by a new political faction within the state Democratic Party, known popularly as "the Ring," that was backed by white working-class New Orleanians of recent immigrant roots. The Ring ruled through a rigidly managed patronage network: municipal jobs, lucrative contracts, and public moneys were distributed among ward club leaders who controlled white ethnic enclaves.[21] After 1878, most Police Jail employees were members of the Ring and recipients of this patronage. Every superintendent was either a first- or second-generation American raised in poverty.[22] Most had lived through the Know-Nothing terror of the 1850s, when police had arrested poor immigrants for vagrancy en masse: indeed, a man with the same name as Dennis Mahoney's father had been arrested for that crime by Know-Nothing policemen in 1855.[23] In no small measure, these were the sons of poor white vagrants.

Their rise to power highlights a line that divided the experiences of poor white from those of poor Black Americans: though they had once faced exclusion and discrimination, whiteness had opened potential avenues for economic and social advancement unavailable to the children of slaves. For these sons of poor white immigrants, that path from urban poverty to political patronage was drenched in racial terror. Four superintendents controlled the Police Jail between 1878 and 1900. All four had participated in massacres of Black New Orleanians or in violent coups d'état against the Republican regime during Reconstruction. Two were former policemen who bragged openly of their role in the New Orleans Massacre of 1866. Three were proud veterans of the city's White League.[24] Among these violence workers, racial terror and social mobility were entangled: anti-Black violence had facilitated their entry into politics, structured the organization of their ward clubs, and lubricated their political rise.[25]

Wardship over the Police Jail allowed these formerly poor white men to perform elements of the role of the Old South slaveholder. Each Police Jail superintendent imbibed this fantasy, treating prisoners as their de facto property by asserting symbolic and material mastery over prisoners' bodies, lives, and labor. Longtime superintendent Maurice Picheloup deployed prisoners as his personal workforce on private properties, in flagrant defiance of the city council. Superintendent Jim Waldron discouraged guards from beating Black prisoners without his consent, preferring to administer beatings himself, to impress upon even "the most stubborn blacks" that he alone controlled their bodies. Sexual violence was racially segregated under Peter Coyle's tenure: Black women reported their routine sexual assault within the women's dormitory, while a group of white women reported that they were forced to sleep in the guards' apartments.[26]

The prisoners of the postbellum South endured a diversity of penal labor systems and industries. Towns, cities, and counties typically organized misdemeanor offenders into chain gangs that paved streets, collected trash, cleaned public spaces, and performed other tasks essential to the maintenance of public infrastructure.[27] Other counties turned to debt peonage. Under this system, local courts handed indigent misdemeanor offenders over to white planters, who posted bond or paid the prisoners' fines and jail fees. These prisoners were forced to work for the planters as unpaid bonded laborers until their "debts" were repaid.[28] Both the chain gang system and the debt peonage system targeted poor southerners convicted of ambiguous and minor crimes: disorderliness, drunkenness, petty larceny, breach of the peace, and vagrancy.

Meanwhile, virtually every state convict in the South was subjected to convict lease between Reconstruction and the early twentieth century. Though convict lease had existed before the Civil War and was widely practiced across the nation, the death rates, violence, and ruthless exploitation typical of convict lease in the postbellum South were unequaled. Under postbellum southern convict lease, private corporations assumed full control of convicts' lives, labor, and maintenance. Prisoners were moved to temporary and unsafe workcamps; often, penitentiary buildings were entirely abandoned or demolished. From these workcamps, leased convicts mined coal, manufactured bricks and steel, harvested timber and turpentine, cultivated sugar and cotton, laid railroad track, and performed other backbreaking tasks in the service of private agricultural and industrial interests. Between 1869 and 1894, the lease to all of Louisiana's state convicts was owned by Samuel L. James, a civil engineer and Confederate veteran from Tennessee. James worked his convicts on Mississippi River levees, plantations, and railroad construction, amassing hundreds of thousands of dollars annually. In 1880, James moved some of his convicts to a massive cotton plantation he purchased in West Feliciana Parish, named Angola Plantation. Other convicts he subleased to various companies, or back to the state, as laborers on public works projects—draining swamps, building levees, laying railroad track—where annual mortality rates routinely surpassed 10 percent. Under James's regime, convicts were regularly whipped, beaten, and shot or lost limb or life to frostbite, disease, and exhaustion. When James died in 1894, the lease passed to his son, Samuel L. James Jr.[29]

A commonality shared by these chain gang, peonage, and convict lease systems was the degree to which antebellum chattel slavery—or perhaps slavery's ever-evolving meaning and contested memory—provided a central frame of reference that defined relations among guards, private employers of convicts, prison administrators, and the convicts themselves. The ways that antebellum slavery shaped postbellum penal practice were complex. Planters and industrialists such as Samuel James perceived in convict labor a way to re-create exploitative control over a captive labor force. Postbellum jailors implemented crowd-control and labor-extraction strategies borrowed from antebellum slave management. Penal reform advocates, including inmates themselves, compared these penal labor systems to antebellum chattel slavery as a discursive strategy. In turn, architects of the South's emergent Lost Cause mythology fretted that the horrific accounts of exploitation and brutalization emerging from southern convict camps hampered their efforts to propagate the fiction that paternalistic benevolence had governed antebellum relations between slave and master. All these extractive penal labor systems relied on racist logics that were themselves products of slavery.[30]

To this list of slavery-prison connections must be added the specific carceral institutions, bodies of institutional knowledge, and carceral technologies—including New Orleans's Police Jail, Louisiana's tradition of outdoor penal labor, and the municipal chain gang itself—whose genealogy can be traced directly to specialized penal systems developed for the subjugation of resistant enslaved people. The postbellum Police Jail represented both the restoration of an antebellum technology for controlling enslaved populations and a vessel for the reproduction of slavery's sexual violence, terrorism, economic exploitation, and racial humiliation. Marie François belonged to the first generation of Black southerners born after Emancipation. Dennis Mahoney was a first-generation American, raised poor and white on the fringes of slavocracy. When François wondered what the slavery of her parents' generation had been like, did her mind gravitate toward the Police Jail? When Superintendent Mahoney coveted the privileges of the old planter elite, did he imagine that he had found those privileges within his Police Jail?

Jim Crow, Progressivism, and Reform

As the nineteenth century yielded to the twentieth, two concurrent movements—the assemblage of Jim Crow and the prison reform movement of the Progressive Era—seemed poised to transform New Orleans's prison system. For many white progressives, these were parallel reform movements that seemed aligned: nominally, both developments promised a safer, healthier, tidier, less-corrupt society through increased governmental intervention and public-private partnership.[31]

Few southern leaders embodied the intersection of these movements quite like city councilmember and preeminent penal reformer James Zacharie. Scion of one of New Orleans's wealthiest banking families, Zacharie had fled to Europe during the Civil War to avoid the Confederate draft. Returning during Reconstruction, Zacharie had entered local politics while his older brother, Colonel Frank Zacharie, spearheaded Reconstruction's downfall as spokesman and chief legal counsel for the Louisiana White League. The elder Zacharie would go on to help orchestrate the disenfranchisement of Black Louisianans as adviser to Governor Murphy J. Foster and as Orleans Parish registrar of voters. Meanwhile, the younger Zacharie plunged his energies into urban reform: reorganizing New Orleans's streetcar system, investing in the city's public health infrastructure, overseeing the creation of public parks, and cofounding both the Louisiana Historical Society and the Louisiana State Museum.[32]

Prison reform was Zacharie's deepest passion. He cofounded the Louisiana Prison Reform Association in 1897 and was appointed to New Orleans's new prison regulatory agency, the Board of Commissioners of Prisons and Asylums, in 1898.[33] In that year, Zacharie resolved personally to redesign New Orleans's police jail system. He vowed to develop a new approach to urban jailing, one that would embody the most "advanced ideas of progress in civilization and in humanitarian works" and would inspire other cities.[34]

Like Edward Livingston before him, Zacharie sought to position himself as a leading carceral theorist as a groundswell of popular interest in penal reform surged throughout the state, southern region, and nation. Since the mid-nineteenth century, the vast majority of the nation's convicts, whether imprisoned within the South or elsewhere, had labored for private contractors under extractive, profit-seeking systems. Whereas most southern state convicts toiled in makeshift workcamps that were entirely owned and managed by convict lessees, most convicts outside of the South performed industrial labor within state-owned prison factories, occasionally for state-owned industries, though usually for the benefit of private corporations that had contracted with the state. Although prison conditions outside of the South were typically less brutal than living and working conditions within southern convict camps, penitentiaries in the North, Midwest, and West were still designed to maximize production and profit.[35]

Yet by the 1880s, popular opposition to profit-seeking convict labor was growing. Organized labor campaigned vigorously against contracted convict labor, charging that the competition drove down wages and "degraded" menial work. Muckraking journalists began publishing regular exposés of violence, neglect, and dysfunctionality within northern state penitentiaries and southern convict camps. Inmate rebellions against overwork and abuse grew larger and more frequent. Prison reformers, while not rejecting the efficacy of prison labor entirely, charged that the pursuit of profit had entirely displaced the mission of rehabilitation.

In the North, campaigns for the abolition of contracted prison labor emerged while analogous campaigns for the abolition of convict lease materialized in the South. In 1887, the federal government banned the leasing-out of federal prisoners and tried to remove federal prisoners from southern convict lease camps. By 1900, state legislatures in the North, Midwest, and West had begun abolishing contracted prison labor, laying the groundwork for the creation of the modern penal system.[36] Meanwhile, in the South, state legislatures began abolishing convict lease, removing convicts to state-owned and -operated prison plantations, several of which endure to this day.[37]

In the South, progressives' claim that the state could manage convicts better than private contractors dovetailed with claims that the state could legislate solutions to the region's "negro problem." Murphy J. Foster, elected governor of Louisiana in 1892, ran on a platform that included both projects. In 1898, a new state constitution abolished convict leasing in Louisiana, effective in 1901. The same constitution included voter disenfranchisement provisions—a poll tax, a literacy requirement, a property ownership requirement, and a grandfather clause—designed to eliminate the Black vote and significantly suppress the vote of poor white men who owned little or no property. Between 1897 and 1904, the number of registered white voters in Louisiana fell from more than 164,000 to fewer than 92,000. The number of registered Black voters fell from more than 130,000 to 1,342.[38] As Black and poor white Louisianians were purged from voter rolls, Louisiana purchased Angola Plantation from Samuel James's family, transforming it into Louisiana's new state penitentiary.[39] Today, Angola Penitentiary is the largest maximum-security prison in the United States. It remains an active plantation.

As Louisiana prepared to abolish convict lease, crush the Black vote, and restrict the poor white vote, James Zacharie began studying urban jail systems throughout the nation. He concluded that there existed a fundamental distinction between the northern and southern penal traditions, rooted, Zacharie believed, in the distinction between indoor and outdoor labor. According to Zacharie, prisons located outside of the South sought to impart marketable skills by training prisoners in mechanical arts. Southern prisons, by contrast, aimed only to suppress inmates' idleness, and inculcate industriousness, through outdoor penal labor, whether in agriculture or on public works projects. As he debated which model New Orleans should adopt, Zacharie discerned clear deficiencies in the northern approach. Most prisoners in New Orleans were confined on misdemeanor charges for terms too short for them to become "expert manufacturer[s]." The purchase of industrial machinery was a great burden to the taxpayer. Indoor penal labor contributed to jail overcrowding, thus increasing the risk of inmate violence, escape, and infectious disease. Most critically, indoor prison labor was unsuited for "our class of subjects" in the South— implicitly, Black prisoners—whom Zacharie deemed incapable of learning mechanical skills and suited only for outdoor, menial work. The southern system of "open-air exposure" for convicts was "the true solution" for Louisiana: more economical, safer, and better suited for the southern inmate.[40]

Dr. Frederick H. Wines, a nationally renowned penologist hired as a consultant by the Louisiana Prison Reform Association, instantly perceived that Zacharie's program of outdoor penal labor was the perfect penal system for the Black prisoner. "It is difficult to conceive of a more ideal method of dealing with prisoners, especially negro prisoners, than this," Wines lauded. "The negro is not fitted for indoor life. . . . There is no possibility," Wines argued, "of introducing into Southern prisons those forms of carrying on industries by machinery common in our [Northern] prisons." Wines confessed that within the annals of American penology, "the negro prisoner is a distinct problem." The pursuit of a "rational, scientific reformatory" system for "negro prisoners" had long eluded the nation's penologists: Louisiana, Wines extolled, had finally discovered the solution. At the subsequent annual conference of the National Prison Association, Wines announced to his colleagues that Louisiana's outdoor approach to Black inmates represented "a great step" forward in American penology of which "I have nothing but good to say." The Black prisoner has "no sense of degradation or disgrace," no "conscious ethical obligation," no capacity for "education . . . literary or industrial." In handling the Black prisoner, the only rational approach was to "put an end to idleness" and deny him the "privilege of loafing" by committing his body to that outdoor menial labor "to which he has always been accustomed."[41]

Reform in name only, Zacharie's vision fused a nationwide racist ideology with an indigenous penological tradition. Histories of the prison often define southern convict labor by its utter absence of any coherent penology. "The system," one scholar writes, "was not even driven by any penological philosophy at all."[42] But racially subjugationist thought is not the same thing as thoughtlessness. In rebuilding the Police Jail, New Orleans harnessed a century-old body of penological theory and practice within which outdoor penal labor was used to reaffirm Black inferiority, to broadcast demarcations between whiteness and Blackness, and to subject Black prisoners and onlookers to terrorizing humiliation, all while providing a captive labor force for economic modernization and infrastructure development.

Completed in 1904, the city's new Police Jail reproduced the basic architecture of its predecessor, garbed in new clothes: group cells, flanking an open-air courtyard, designed for little more than the overnight confinement of municipal work gangs.[43] Midway through construction, on learning that the prison would also house the indigent insane, Zacharie decided that the name "jail" was inappropriate and resolved to rename the prison the "House of Detention." Once the new building was complete, the former Police Jail building was transformed into a dog pound. A gas chamber was installed, where the city dogcatcher bragged that he could euthanize up to ninety vagrant dogs at a time.[44]

Within the new House of Detention courtyard, in place of the old whipping rack, the city constructed a "shower-bath box," consisting of a wooden rack, coffin-shaped, positioned beneath water barrels. Here, recaptured jail gang runaways and resistant prisoners were stripped entirely nude and strapped prone before jailors released a stream of water onto their faces, inducing the sensation of drowning. As the water began to pour, prisoners instinctively stopped struggling and refocused their attention toward stable breathing, leaving external observers with the impression that the water induced overriding calm: the shower-bath box appeared to render inmates disciplined, tranquil, tamed. Its effect on prisoners was "more than one can imagine," superintendent Maurice Picheloup reported glowingly. Picheloup noted that inmates' fear of the device was so great that it "seems to drive them wild" and "sometimes takes three or four strong men" to strap prisoners into position: they "fight and yell, fall on the floor and squirm like a snake, but we make them take their medicine." Along with the shower-bath box, discipline within the House of Detention relied on floggings with the cat-o'-nine-tails and sensory deprivation within the jail's unventilated and pitch-black solitary confinement cells.[45]

The basic story was similar throughout much of the urban South. Penal labor systems of antebellum origin, devised for the torture and redeployment of resistant enslaved people and "vagrant" white workers, evolved into the municipal carceral machinery of Jim Crow. In Richmond, Augusta, Louisville, and Nashville, antebellum workhouses and municipal chain gang systems, originally built for both white and Black prisoners, were revived during Reconstruction for the punishment of "vagrant" freedpeople and endured into the twentieth century.[46] In Memphis and St. Louis, antebellum workhouse systems, initially erected exclusively for "vagrant" white workers, were similarly repurposed during Reconstruction for the confinement of "vagrant" freedpeople and also endured.[47] In Union-occupied Charleston, the workhouse for white vagrants was integrated, then relocated to the building that had previously served as the slave workhouse; as in New Orleans, Charleston's two antebellum penal systems, designed for enslaved and poor white workers, were effectively merged into one.[48] In each of these cities, antebellum systems for coercing enslaved and poor white labor provided the template for labor coercion during Jim Crow.

New Orleans would rebuild the House of Detention in 1929 and again in 1965. Beneath successive facades of modernization, each new iteration of the institution reproduced the same underlying structure of its processor: group cells built for the overnight confinement of work gangs. Recreational, medical, educational, vocational, and religious facilities were minimal or nonexistent. Jail gangs, while playing a more marginal economic role than the antebellum chain gangs, would continue to contribute to the construction and maintenance of New Orleans's public infrastructure into the twenty-first century. From the 1880s to the 1960s, the number of outdoor penal laborers typically ranged from 60 to 200 on any given day. The prison measured output in "man-days" of labor: between 1897 and 1905, more than 32,000 man-days of labor were reported, on average, each year.[49] Few data emerged from the House of

Detention between 1915 and the early 1950s, but between 1953 and 1971, the jail reported completion of roughly 42,000 man-days of labor, on average, each year.[50] "Virtually every officeholder and civic group seem, sooner or later, to call on [Orleans Parish sheriff Charles] Foti for the loan of a few prisoners to do one chore or another," noted one reporter in 1981. In that decade, jail gangs painted "schools and churches," removed obstructions from storm drains, cleared trash from "the yacht harbor and the lakefront," cleaned parks and residential neighborhoods, gathered stray golf balls from the city's golf courses, performed janitorial services at city agencies, sold concessions at Jazz Fest, assembled bleachers for Mardi Gras, and provided security for tourists exploring the city's famed cemeteries.[51]

Rediscovering Vagrancy Law

In 1903, as New Orleans rebuilt the Police Jail, the South rediscovered vagrancy law. Since Reconstruction's collapse, southern enforcement of vagrancy laws had been sporadic and patchwork. Conservative newspapers complained that the laws were seldom enforced.[52] Organized labor fought the passage of new vagrancy laws, citing the threat posed to white workingmen.[53] Once the "tramp scare" of the 1870s had subsided, the nation's preoccupation with vagrancy law waned. Jurists increasingly challenged the laws' legitimacy, often citing the southern Black Codes as evidence: "If white men and women may be thus summarily disposed of at the north," reasoned the Maine Supreme Court in 1876, "of course black ones may be disposed of in the same way at the south." "What is the tortious element in the act of vagrancy?" conservative legal scholar Christopher Tiedeman probed in 1888. "A man has a legal right to live a life of absolute idleness, if he chooses." In New Orleans, where Democratic lawmakers had fought so bitterly for their right to arrest vagrants, the actual arrest rate fell to all-time lows. Police performed only 2.5 vagrancy arrests per 1,000 residents in 1879 and only 4.1 per 1,000 in 1900: in 1850, that rate had been greater than 50 per 1,000.[54]

Yet beginning in 1903, as southern states assembled their Jim Crow legislative packages, a mania for new vagrancy laws swept the South like brush fire. Whereas only three southern states had passed a new vagrancy law between 1880 and 1902, all but two passed new vagrancy laws between 1903 and 1909. The Louisiana legislature passed successive vagrancy laws in 1904, 1908, 1912, and 1918. "There is a growing disposition in the Southern States to enact vagrant laws that will induce or compel the idle and vicious to forsake their ways and become useful citizens," the *New Orleans Item* noted in 1903. The Memphis *Sentinel*, quoted in the *New Orleans Item*, agreed: "The sentiment is general throughout the South that the vagrant negroes must work or walk." Southern cities, large and small, declared all-out "wars on vagrants." Mississippi governor James Vardaman declared "a most vigorous campaign against the vagrant . . . in every community in the state."[55] Several of the South's new vagrancy laws were remarkably draconian. Under Alabama's criminal code of 1907, suspected vagrants were presumed guilty until proven innocent. The maximum penalties under Georgia's new law included a $1,000 fine and one year on the chain gang.[56]

Southern state legislatures passed new vagrancy laws alongside other legal mechanisms—anti-enticement laws, contract enforcement provisions, anti-emigrant-agent laws—that sought to help employers achieve a complete stranglehold over menial labor.[57] Of these diverse legal mechanisms, none was more widely used or more central to how elite white southerners construed Black criminality than vagrancy law. Southern lawmakers promised that by permanently quashing the vagrant, crime itself might be eliminated. Reconjuring arguments in circulation during the antebellum era, they identified the vagrant as the primary origin of every manner of economic dysfunction and crime. It was an undeniable "fact that nearly all the unspeakable negro crimes are committed by negro vagrants," proclaimed Mississippi congressman and House Minority Leader John Sharp Williams in 1907. The "real cause" of murder "could be traced to the non-enforcement of the vagrant law," one South Carolina judge echoed that following year. Mississippi governor James Vardaman attributed "75 percent" of *all crimes*, as well as *all* rapes, to vagrants. Vagrancy law was "a moral disinfectant" that would "greatly lessen the commission of burglary, murder and rape," argued one Mississippi judge—nothing was more important to the maintenance of "social order and purity." A South Carolina newspaper proclaimed that all presidential assassinations had been committed "by vagrants" ("with one exception," the newspaper added, in a nod to John Wilkes Booth). "They are thorough parasites, and their luxurious idleness is a great source of discontent," one Grenada, Mississippi, newspaper professed. "Our vagrants must go," wrote Alabama governor William Dorsey Jelks. "They bear upon us too heavily . . . a vast and growing army. . . . They are the people breaking the back of peace."[58]

After 1903, New Orleans's vagrancy arrest rate skyrocketed: from roughly 4.1 arrests per 1,000 in 1900 to more than 20 per 1,000 by 1914, and more than 45 per 1,000 by 1928 (graph 7.1). By the 1920s, New Orleans police performed more vagrancy arrests each year than the police departments of the nation's four largest cities—New York City, Chicago, Philadelphia, and Detroit, with a total population of more than 16 million—combined. Whereas the capture of fugitive slaves, mobile free Black workers, and poor white vagrants had captivated the attention of the antebellum policeman, now the New Orleans policeman

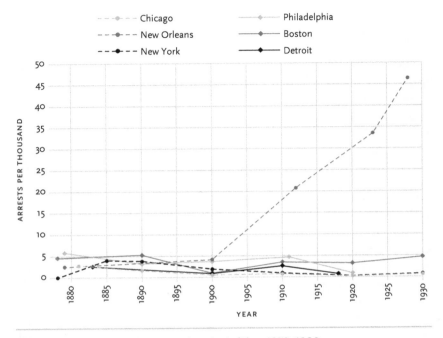

Graph 7.1. Vagrancy arrest rates in select cities, 1878–1930.

was fixated on seizing vagrants. Indeed, from the early twentieth century until the civil rights reforms of the 1960s, vagrancy arrests typically constituted no less than 20 to 40 percent *of all arrests* performed in the city each year.[59]

The reliance of twentieth-century police on vaguely worded vagrancy statutes was hardly exclusive to the South. In the West and Midwest, vagrancy laws were regularly used to regulate "hoboing" migrant farmhands and railroad workers.[60] In the North, as the labor movement grew, vagrancy laws were recruited to target union organizers, strikers, and Wobblies.[61] In cities throughout the nation, police relied on vagrancy laws to harass people who seemed unsavory or undesirable in lieu of charging them with any specific crime. The "underlying purpose" of vagrancy law "is to relieve the police of the necessity of proving that criminals have committed or are planning to commit specific crimes," affirmed New York's Law Revision Commission in 1935.[62]

Still, the scale of arrests in the South was unparalleled and nothing short of staggering. By the twentieth century, many American states and municipalities had folded their prohibitions on loitering, loafing, suspiciousness, idleness, and underemployment into various laws governing disorderly conduct,

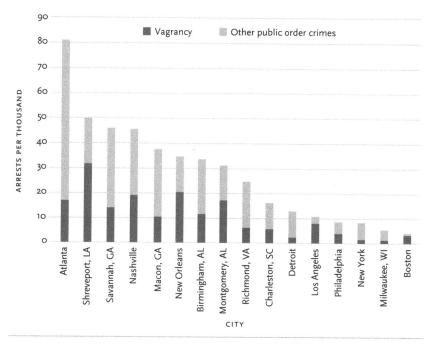

Graph 7.2. Average arrest rates for vagrancy and related public order crimes in select cities, 1900–1930.

disorderly persons, breaches of the peace, and disturbing the peace. When arrests under all these subjective and victimless public order offenses are read in tandem, the contrast between northern and southern police patterns becomes clear (graph 7.2).[63] Southern policemen of the Jim Crow era devoted immense and unequaled energies toward the summary seizure of those perceived to be underemployed or uncontrolled.

It would be tempting to interpret the South's high rates of summary seizure as evidence of a primitive, underdeveloped, and violently uncomplicated criminal justice system. Yet southern lawmakers' preoccupation with vagrancy also encoded a well-entrenched and fully articulated theory of social order derived from theories of state police power that were rooted in early modern Europe, embraced and repackaged by New World slaveholders, and revived by the architects of Jim Crow. This theory of social order held that certain workers were dependent and that crime stemmed from the disruption of static relations between dependents and masters. It read Blackness as evidence of dependency while proposing that governments could prevent crime by using state power to force dependents' submission. When rationalizing the coercion of landless menial laborers, southern white landowners of the Jim Crow era invoked a language of dependency and mastery that would have been familiar to their forebears a century earlier. Vagrants were persons without any "sort of relationship with the white man's life," Mississippi congressman John Sharp Williams argued: having "withdrawn from the white man," they had "reverted." Vagrants had forsaken "the whole some [*sic*] restraint of the white man," one Meridian, Mississippi, newspaper echoed: they had violated the Black worker's "natural" condition, "to be dependent upon his boss." Many white southerners attributed vagrancy to public education because education encouraged Black social mobility and thus drove a wedge between the Black farmworker and the white landowner. "Books have given us a larger portion of vagrants," suggested Alabama governor William Dorsey Jelks.[64]

Even though they explicitly racialized vagrancy as a Black crime, southern landowners' anxieties regarding masterless *white* laborers did not dissipate. Indeed, many repeatedly raised concerns, as had their forebears during Reconstruction, that overemphasis on Black vagrancy allowed too many white vagrants to slip through the cracks. They demanded that the new legal regime target the poor white worker as well as the Black. "Our lawmakers should devote at least as much attention to the white vagrant as to the negro race vagrant," demanded one Alabama newspaper in 1910. "A white vagrant is not entitled to any more consideration in the eyes of the law than a negro idler," agreed a Louisiana newspaper that same year. "There are more vagrant negroes than whites, but there are vagrant whites," a Tennessee newspaper echoed; the new vagrancy law must "be made comprehensive enough to cover" both populations. Florida had "a very good plan to prevent and handle the Negro vagrant," extolled the *Miami News*, "but what about the white vagrant? There are thousands of white men . . . who are not above the negro vagrant in anything but color. . . . Labor is in demand at all times."[65]

The Many Uses of Vagrancy Law in the Jim Crow South

Jim Crow vagrancy laws encoded the synthesis of two antebellum legal paradigms: a tradition of policing Black workers as maroons and a parallel tradition of policing poor white workers as vagrants. Enforcement patterns during Jim Crow reflected this dual heritage. Police used vagrancy law to regulate Black mobility, enforce de facto pass and curfew systems, and criminalize workers who appeared alienated from white mastery: traditions rooted in the antebellum regulation of marronage. Police also used vagrancy law to orchestrate the expulsions of unwanted peoples, to criminalize strikes and workers' strategic withholding of their labor, and to adjust the labor pool in response to shifting labor supply and demand: strategies whose legal ancestry traces to antebellum vagrancy law. In short, the marriage of these two legal traditions had birthed a remarkably nimble and multipurpose policing tool.

Events in the small town of Jennings, Louisiana, illustrate the laws' dynamism. In 1901, on a rice plantation outside of the sleepy hamlet, a farmer noticed bubbles of methane gas rising from his paddy fields. The first oil well was installed later that year; within two weeks, eleven oil companies had set up shop at Jennings. Waves of spectators and migrant workers followed. Thus began Louisiana's oil boom.[66]

Jennings's population doubled within the decade as oilfield workers poured into town. With boom times came the anxieties associated with strangers and fraying community ties. New municipal ordinances restricted the town's growing number of boardinghouses and saloons to Jennings's African American neighborhood, known as Pig Ankle. The fraying community ties snapped on July 9, 1906, when a Black migrant worker named Vivian Boutte shot and killed Deputy Sheriff Cam Coffin. Jennings's newspaper called it an unprovoked assassination but also noted that Jennings's oil workers, white and Black, had tried to hide Boutte afterward—suggesting, perhaps, that Boutte's peers knew something of the confrontation that the press refused to print. A posse found Boutte hiding in a Pig Ankle boardinghouse. After Boutte was taken into custody, a member of the posse shot Boutte in the back. He would die in a jail cell a week later.

Three nights later, Jennings's white residents rallied in the oil fields outside of town, readying themselves to hunt down and lynch the oil workers who had quartered Boutte and perhaps burn all of Pig Ankle to the ground. Pleading for moderation, Jennings's mayor proposed an alternative: purge Jennings of its Black vagrants. Thus commenced a thorough combing of Pig Ankle for every Black person who did not own property and was not related to a local landowner. All "idle and worthless negroes" were ejected from the town. Pig Ankle's boardinghouses were closed, and the renting of rooms to Black persons was prohibited. To save their property and perhaps their lives, a delegation of Black business owners volunteered to aid in the purge, asking only in return that Jennings's town council consider the appointment of a Black police officer.[67]

The antivagrant pogrom spread to the neighboring town of Lake Charles, where on July 14, hundreds of police, white men, and state militiamen "raided the coon section, and wherever they thought idle negroes harbored, and made them leave that night. Women as well as men were gathered up, some in their night clothes, and put on the night train and conducted as far as the parish line." The mob methodically searched "every house," gathering the city's Black residents and force-marching them "under guard of pistols" past "all of the big employers of labor" so that bosses could "identify their men" and prevent the expulsion of desirable employees. Nearly 5 percent of Lake Charles's Black population—described by newspapers as a "cargo of bad coons" that "none wanted"—was expelled that night. For days, Black women and men from Lake Charles, some still in their nightclothes, could be seen roaming Louisiana's countryside in search of a town that would take them.[68]

The expulsions continued spreading across Louisiana: soon the towns of Crowley, Opelousas, Alexandria, Colfax, Shreveport, Baton Rouge, Napoleonville, Monroe, Franklin, and New Iberia all announced the arrest and removal of their Black vagrants.[69] Police and city leaders likened the expulsions to a collective act of self-purification: "a general cleaning" of the town's foul material, a "city house cleaning party" of "scum," the "wiping out of this foul black pollution," a sanitizing of "parasitical negroes" and "black scum."[70] Racial violence, under the auspices of combatting vagrancy, was in the zeitgeist during the 1906 summer and autumn: that September, a newspaper campaign in Georgia to "Drive Out the Vagrants" helped jumpstart the Atlanta Massacre of 1906, in which dozens of Black residents were murdered. The chaos in Atlanta, in turn, was used to justify the subsequent expulsions of Black "vagrants" from towns throughout the South.[71] On September 25, Mississippi's governor ordered every law enforcement officer in the state to begin arresting and expelling vagrants, sparking mass arrests and expulsions throughout the state. In Washington, DC, a Tennessee industrialist met with President Theodore Roosevelt in the White House to propose the transformation of Panama into a penal colony for the South's Black vagrants. "Practically every southern city is preparing to wage war on the vagrants," the *Raleigh Times* reported.[72]

These antivagrancy pogroms on Black neighborhoods, all but forgotten today, were a recurrent ritual of the Jim Crow era. Like a long-lost cousin of lynching, these violent community events enforced white solidarity and defined community boundaries through performative spectacles of violence that affirmed Black Otherness.[73] Critics deemed the custom "selfish and unneighborly" because it pushed undesirables into neighboring communities. "It has got to the point that the city which does not take steps in that direction will find itself overrun with the negro vagrants migrating from the forbidden cities," one Louisiana newspaper complained in 1907.[74]

Other vagrancy mass arrests responded to immediate labor shortages and were executed for the explicit purpose of creating involuntary work crews for the maintenance of key public infrastructure. When the city of Miami lacked funds to hire trash collectors, police "promptly went out and rounded up a hatful of negro vagrants." When Monroe, Louisiana, needed street cleaners, police "[used] the vagrancy law" to conjure "a pretty fair gang of negroes." When the Automobile Club of America selected Savannah as the site of the next International Grand Prize Race, "Negro loafers and vagrants were rounded up by the scores" to build a new racecourse. When Greenville, Mississippi, sought to mitigate road dust, police performed vagrancy arrests and created a chain gang. When the Mississippi River rose during the great flood of 1927, communities throughout the river valley coordinated the vagrancy arrests of Black residents and their impressment as levee laborers.[75] In these instances, police acted as labor agents.

In contrast to these ad hoc creations of penal labor crews, many southern towns and cities executed regular vagrancy roundups every fall, in preparation for the labor-intensive harvest season, to drive down wages and push urban workers into the countryside. "It is now the season of the year," one Louisiana newspaper announced amid the start of the sugarcane harvest: time for the annual "'Round-up' of the Idle Coons." The sheriff of Earle, Arkansas, coordinated vagrancy mass arrests "about the same time every year," one Black resident noticed, "around crop time." Recalling his young adulthood in Depression era Mississippi, blues guitarist David "Honeyboy" Edwards remembered vagrancy mass arrests "once a year in the summer, when the farmer needed people real bad." A Savannah newspaper identified the "customary annual crusades in the cities against idle negroes" as critical to ensuring "ample" labor supply at cotton-picking time. The practice was so commonplace that some state governors went so far as to formally coordinate and announce the commencement of the annual vagrancy roundup. "Cotton is ripening. See that the 'vags' get busy," quipped the *Atlanta Constitution*.[76]

Although police and lawmakers framed these arrests as part of a broader battle against innate Black laziness, in truth, these seasonal arrests battled the basic laws of supply and demand. As during the antebellum era, harvest seasons were times of greatest economic activity throughout the South, resulting in higher-than-average wages in the cities where crops were loaded onto barges, steamships, and trains for transport. This economic cycle enticed rural wageworkers to "leave for the towns and cities to secure odd jobs," as one Louisiana newspaper complained, at the precise moment "when their services are most needed" in the countryside. By threatening wageworkers with vagrancy arrest, police sought to pressure them into remaining in the countryside and accepting plantation work at below-market rates. The practice "had a splendid effect" on the rural labor supply, according to one Louisiana planter writing amid the harvest of 1905: "The result was that on Monday morning the negroes were begging for work, and since that time there has been no trouble at all in getting labor."[77]

At other times, police performed vagrancy mass arrests at the behest of industry, particularly during both world wars as military enlistments depleted the South's supply of industrial workers. "The American Sugar Refinery needs 200 men. The New Orleans Railway and Light company needs 250 men for track work. Contractors in the city require 500 men," New Orleans police superintendent Frank Mooney telegraphed all stationhouse captains in 1919. "Round up all idle white and negro vagrants."[78] Often, police and jail managers coordinated with planters and industrialists directly. In 1917, New Orleans's House of Detention released convicted vagrants on condition that they accept employment on rural sugar plantations for fixed wages of between $1.50 and $1.75 per day.[79] In 1918, a coalition of executives from Louisiana's leading railroad, shipping, construction, fruit, and sugar companies personally drafted a new vagrancy ordinance for the city.[80] Similar vagrancy mass roundups, framed as essential to the war effort, were widespread throughout the South.[81]

Some vagrancy mass arrests selectively targeted Black women to drum up domestic workers. In 1907, responding to white residents' "loud complaint that kitchen labor is scarce," the sheriff of Birmingham announced targeted vagrancy arrests of Black women to "bring about a better supply of cooks." Following similar mass arrests of Black women in Jackson, Mississippi, a resident declared, "The servant problem has been largely solved. . . . Inquire of any housewife in Jackson and she will tell you that she has a dozen applications from negro women who want to cook, where she was fortunate to get ere a month heretofore."[82]

Vagrancy law was also critical to the breakup of strikes and the criminalization of workers' strategic withholding of their labor. Police used vagrancy law to end crippling roustabout strikes in New Orleans in 1900, 1901, and 1921, in Memphis in 1901, and in Natchez in 1904.[83] Employers in New Orleans regularly contacted police directly to request the vagrancy arrest of striking or rebellious employees. When factory workers at the Maestri Furniture Company struck for a meal break, Frank Maestri phoned New Orleans's police chief, who had the strikers arrested for vagrancy. When a farrier realized that his wallet was missing, he phoned the police, who arrested all the stable boys for vagrancy. When a white housewife suspected that the settings on her sewing machine had been adjusted, she asked policemen to arrest her Black maid, Obetie Thomas, for vagrancy. At the local precinct, policemen beat Thomas unconscious. Awakening on the jail cell floor, Thomas discovered that while she was unconscious, police had burned her genitals with cigarettes. Later, in an affidavit, Thomas testified that she was employed, that her husband was employed, that she maintained a stable home, that the couple had no debts, that they owned a Plymouth: how could police charge her with vagrancy?[84]

Like many bludgeons within the Jim Crow arsenal, vagrancy laws were often used to target poor white people as well as Black people, albeit in different ways and to wildly different degrees. The general tendency of New Orleans police was to presume that Black workers were vagrant until proven otherwise while presuming that white workers were employed unless their appearance or behavior indicated vagrancy.[85] Revealingly, white vagrancy arrestees in New Orleans tended to be transient outsiders, whereas Black vagrancy arrestees tended to be local residents. In a sampling of 452 vagrancy arrests performed in New Orleans during January and February of 1913, about two-thirds of vagrancy arrestees were Black, though Black residents constituted less than one-third of the city's population. Only 41 percent of white arrestees could provide a local address, compared to 76 percent of Black arrestees.[86]

In charging poor white persons with vagrancy, New Orleans policemen tended to target strangers to the city who seemed somehow shiftless, unkempt, suspicious, alien, or seedy. Joseph Herman, a foreign-born laborer, had migrated to New Orleans in April 1905, renting a room in Storyville, the city's red-light district (though in court, Herman claimed to have patronized a prostitute only "once"). During his first seven months in New Orleans, Herman was arrested for vagrancy "about five or six times," always while "loitering" or "walking along" in Storyville. Abraham Muskovitz, Louis Hager, and Abraham Klein—also foreign-born immigrants, each of whom had lived in New Orleans for only a few weeks or months—were similarly arrested for "loitering" on a Storyville streetcorner, though they claimed to be gainfully employed waiters at a local restaurant, discussing where they should buy drinks after work. "I came here for the Mardi Gras," claimed Charles Duke, a white migrant laborer from Vicksburg, who also claimed to have lived in Kansas City, Memphis, Little Rock, and Pueblo, Colorado. Police arrested Duke for vagrancy after spotting him in the company of a suspected burglar. Each of these white men was convicted and ordered to either pay a fine or work off his debt through a House of Detention work gang. They were typical of the poor white men seized in the city for vagrancy: itinerant, foreign, and possibly (though never conclusively) linked to seedy or illegal behaviors.[87] Occasionally, vagrancy mass arrests exclusively targeted white people: such as in Jackson in 1903, when the mayor perceived that the city was inundated with white gamblers and bootleggers, or in Montgomery in 1910, when public authorities concluded all the city's Black vagrants had already been seized.[88]

Vagrancy law provided the South with a remarkably flexible and multipurpose tool: useful for breaking up strikes, drumming up laborers, driving down wages, creating temporary penal labor crews, suppressing disruptive behaviors, and expelling undesirable populations, all while circumventing suspects' due process rights. Perhaps the greatest import of vagrancy laws lay in the mundane, atmospheric violence the laws exerted: an everyday, atmospheric, unyielding pressure placed on Black wageworkers to work harder, longer, and more diligently for less. Vagrancy law criminalized the Black worker who slowed down when employers demanded haste, dropped out of the labor market when employers demanded full employment, attended to frivolities such as gambling and drinking when employers demanded work. Police used vagrancy law to criminalize Black workers' perceived vices, distractions from "honest" work, and involvements in autonomous economic activities. In New Orleans, Voodoo practitioners were frequently policed through vagrancy law.[89] Vagrancy raids on Black bars were virtually a daily occurrence: for example, during an unremarkable week in 1913, police raided seven bars, arresting eighty-six Black patrons and two white patrons for idleness.[90]

Yet the overwhelming majority of vagrancy arrests were of "loitering" workers, predominantly Black men, found outdoors but idle during normal working hours. Inactivity was proof of guilt. Justifications for arrest, provided by policemen, attest to the state's constant persecution of perceived Black idleness:

"We noticed this negro hanging around."

"All he was doing . . . was standing on the sidewalk."

"She was not doing anything."

"He was not doing anything at all."[91]

In 1917, a reporter for the *New Orleans Item* transcribed a day in the life of patrolman Henry Borges. Suppressing perceived Black idleness consumed officer Borges's morning schedule:

7:40 a.m.	Inspected negro clubs . . . in search for loiterers.
9:30 a.m.	Arrested two negroes on a charge of loitering.
10:00 a.m.	Arrested another loitering negro.
10:30 a.m.	Judge Fogarty discharged negroes upon their statements that they were river-boat deck hands.
12:00 p.m.	To prevent trouble among the negro element, went to the river-front manufacturing district, where hundreds of negroes were streaming out of factories for their lunch.[92]

Sometimes the New Orleans Police Department hosted competitions to see which officer could arrest the most vagrants or how many vagrants the entire force could arrest within an allotted period. Sergeant John Dunn set a record in 1917 by arresting "twenty-two negroes" for vagrancy in under ten minutes. The police department's record, set in 1928, was 520 vagrancy arrests within twenty-four hours.[93]

For Black wageworkers of the Jim Crow South, this pervasive war on "idleness" overshadowed their lives. Black musicians were particularly vulnerable to vagrancy arrest because they lacked white employers and often traveled for work. "They would just pick you up [for vagrancy]," Delta blues guitarist Robert Lockwood Jr. recalled, late in life, of Mississippi police during the early twentieth century. "It was a law-breaking thing to not be in the field." "Every once in a while you'd get arrested for vagrancy. . . . I got pulled for that a number of times," blues guitarist David "Honeyboy" Edwards recalled of his young adulthood in the Delta region. "The police pick you up in the street during the day when everybody's working. . . . They give you four or five days, and that time was spent out in the fields, working the cotton."[94] Legendary New Orleans–based musicians Ferdinand "Jelly Roll Morton" LaMothe, George "Pops" Foster, and Danny Barker were each arrested for vagrancy numerous times. "Police had the power to arrest anyone who could not walk to the 'phone booth to call his or her employer and prove that they earned an honest livelihood," Barker recalled. At age nine, Louis Armstrong was arrested for vagrancy while scavenging scrap metal. At age thirteen, blues musician Willie Dixon spent thirty days in a Mississippi penal farm for vagrancy, where he was whipped. During one of his only two known recording sessions, blues pioneer Robert Johnson played on a borrowed guitar; the previous night, San Antonio police had smashed Johnson's regular guitar while arresting him for vagrancy. Blues guitarist Henry Williams died in jail while incarcerated for vagrancy. Early blues musicians William "Hambone Willie" Newbern, Willard "Ramblin'" Thomas, and Alonzo "Lonnie" Johnson each reworked their vagrancy arrests into blues standards. On occasion, New Orleans's House of Detention was featured in song. An early refrain of perhaps the very oldest jazz standard—"Funky Butt," by Buddy Bolden—recounts conviction by notoriously severe municipal recorder John Fogarty and labor on a House of Detention work gang:

I thought I heard Judge Fogarty say,
Thirty days in the market, take him away,
Give him a good broom to sweep with, take him away.

"Police put you in jail if they heard you singing that song," Sidney Bechet recalled. More than a half-century later, Jerry Jeff Walker wrote the folk rock standard "Mr. Bojangles" about his jailhouse encounter in New Orleans with a man imprisoned on vagrancy charges in 1965.[95]

Working-class Black southerners cultivated multiple strategies to reduce their risk of vagrancy arrest. The most effective tactic was to ally oneself with a propertied white sponsor. "You had to know the right people," James "Yank" Rachell recalled of Black life in Mississippi during the 1920s and 1930s. "If you had a big man there, nobody would bother his hands." "Honeyboy" Edwards recounted how the Greenwood, Mississippi, police chief regularly conscripted him to perform unpaid yardwork for his wife. For Edwards, this compulsory arrangement provided the benefit of protection: whenever police anywhere in the Delta arrested Edwards for vagrancy, that Greenwood police chief procured his release. "You got to have somebody to speak for you at that time," Edwards explained.[96]

Working-class Black southerners who were gainfully self-employed but who were nevertheless at high risk of arrest because they lacked a white employer often found supplemental wage work purely as protection from police. At age seventeen, and though already a successful cornet player, Louis Armstrong found a job hauling coal for the sole purpose of preventing vagrancy arrest. Initially, Jelly Roll Morton "only played piano as a sideline" because "you had to prove you were doing some kind of work or they'd put you in jail."[97]

These strategic manipulations of the master-servant relationship were unavailable to many itinerant migrants and autonomous day laborers living in large cities, forcing those workers to develop other strategies. Some hid during normal working hours. Mardi Gras Indian big chief Donald Harrison Sr. recalled that the Black men in his New Orleans neighborhood would gather daily to circulate information that might help them avoid vagrancy arrest: where police had been seen congregating, which street corners and bars had been raided, who was hiring. One way "Honeyboy" Edwards avoided "that vagrancy law" was to stay indoors "until 5:00 or 6:00 in the evening," coming outside only after plantation workers had been released from the fields; that way, police "don't know whether you been in the field or not." Black men often turned to Black women for protection. Whenever he arrived in a new town, Jelly Roll Morton would methodically bathe, change into a flashy suit, and flirt with local women until one invited him over for dinner, a routine developed so that "police would be unable to pick me up for vagrancy, because I had me a residence in that town." "Honeyboy" Edwards had "a girlfriend working for the white peoples, in service," who hid him when policemen prowled for workers. Willard "Ramblin'" Thomas alluded to the same protections provided by Black women in "No Job Blues," intoning of how "policeman came along and arrested me for vag" after he'd lost the protection of his "meal ticket woman."[98] Southern white newspapers routinely accused Black women of sheltering and provisioning vagrant Black men.[99]

To prove that they were not vagrant, New Orleans's working-class men, white and Black, typically carried verification of employment whenever they left their homes. "Most men carry cards" to prevent vagrancy arrest, New Orleans police superintendent Frank Mooney explained in 1918: "union cards, fraternal order cards, identification cards of one sort or the other." This semiformal rule endured well into the 1960s. Employers "had to give you a card that you worked" so that police wouldn't "bust you for 'no visible means of support,'" Harrison recalled of Black life in New Orleans during the 1950s. "You got a job, but you better have a work card or you're going to jail." Robert Hillary King, a future Black Panther Party organizer, always carried "check stubs proving I worked" to protect himself from vagrancy arrest. Nevertheless, King was jailed for vagrancy numerous times. For young Black men in King's neighborhood, vagrancy arrest almost seemed a rite of passage.[100]

Although arrests predominantly targeted the poor and propertyless, Black business owners could be seized during extreme labor shortages—again, particularly during both world wars—on the logic that they lacked a white employer. In Georgia in 1918, Maria Parker, owner of a hairdressing business with two employees, was arrested for vagrancy on the rationale that, among Black women, "washing and cooking" for white residents was the only valid form of employment. That same year, the owner of the only Black-owned restaurant in Franklin, Louisiana, was told that he and his sons would be arrested for vagrancy if they didn't immediately accept jobs at the local mill. The restaurant closed.[101]

Rethinking Continuity and Change

With Emancipation, former slaveholders imagined that an expansive web of workhouses and chain gangs, coupled with powerful vagrancy laws, could reestablish a stranglehold on labor and mitigate freedom's meaning. To a degree, that vision was realized. True, the patchwork of municipal, county, and state penal systems was never as coordinated or as totalizing as former slaveholders had hoped. But vagrancy law overshadowed the lives of the Black working poor and, to a lesser degree, the lives of the white working poor. Vagrancy arrest rates routinely ran extraordinarily high. The laws armed public authorities with a flexible and multipurpose tool for managing the labor supply, driving down wages, breaking up strikes, coordinating mass expulsions, and creating penal labor crews for the construction of public infrastructure. In New Orleans and elsewhere, Black workers were forced to carry passes, could be summarily seized and declared guilty without due process, and endured continuous surveillance for their perceived autonomy or alleged "idleness," much as their enslaved ancestors had been seized if distanced from putative owners. If convicted, they could be tortured and forced to labor through penal institutions first developed for the punishment of fugitives from slavery. In wartime, they could be forcibly removed to cotton and sugar plantations. For Black wage-workers, autonomy from white employ remained criminal.

Still, public authorities failed to reassert the level of coercive pressure exercised by their antebellum predecessors. Among Black New Orleanians, the vagrancy arrest rate peaked in 1961, at roughly 54 per 1,000.[102] That figure was prodigious: twice the national arrest rate among Black adults for *all* drug crimes during the height of the late twentieth-century War on Drugs.[103] At the same time, that rate was *far lower* than the peak antebellum rate at which the city had seized enslaved residents for marronage (close to 280 per 1,000 in 1830). Likewise, among white residents, the postbellum vagrancy arrest rate (29 per 1,000 in 1961) was lower than the antebellum vagrancy arrest rate among white residents (nearly 67 per 1,000 in 1850).[104]

The same trend holds true for incarceration rates. Between 1898 and 1915, Black persons were committed to the Police Jail and subsequent House of Detention at an approximate annual rate of 31 per 1,000, while white persons were committed at an approximate annual rate of 9 per 1,000 (the city's cumulative jail admissions rate, including commitments to Orleans Parish Prison, was roughly 53 per 1,000 among Black persons and 14 per 1,000 among white persons).[105] Antebellum incarceration rates were far higher: from 1820 to 1840, enslaved people (excluding the soi-disant libres) were committed to the Police Jail at an approximate annual rate of 261 per 1,000, whereas during a twelve-month period ending in June 1857, white persons were committed to the City Workhouse at a rate of roughly 36 per 1,000.[106] For both Black and white New Orleanians, Emancipation dramatically curtailed rates of seizure and penal conscription. Jim Crow New Orleans was a brutal police state where municipal officials routinely annexed the labor of the working poor for public and private use. And yet, this police state was a shadow of its former self.

In November 1967, two months after New Orleans voters elected Ernest "Dutch" Morial to be the first Black member of the Louisiana legislature since Reconstruction, he and Henry DeJoie, publisher of New Orleans's leading Black-owned newspaper, were arrested for vagrancy as the two friends chatted in front of Morial's home.[1] The vagrancy arrest of a Black legislator and a Black newspaper publisher, exactly one century after the days of Louisiana's Radical Republican legislature and the *New Orleans Tribune*, was a remarkable case of historical recurrence.

Morial and DeJoie were among the last generation of Black southerners seized for the crime of vagrancy. As the civil rights movement broadened the applicability of the Fourteenth Amendment, and as the vagrancy mass arrests of civil rights activists, antiwar protestors, and purported "hippies" drew national attention and criticism, an emergent legal consensus held that vagrancy laws were unconstitutionally vague and in violation of the Fourteenth Amendment's Due Process and Equal Protection Clauses. Between 1965 and 1969, appellate courts struck down or curtailed vagrancy state laws and city ordinances in Alabama, Colorado, Kentucky, Massachusetts, Nevada, New York, North Carolina, Ohio, and Washington, DC. As one lawyer observed in 1969, "Vagrancy laws are falling like ninepins."[2] On February 4, 1970, a federal judge ruled much of Louisiana's vagrancy law unconstitutional. Three weeks later, New Orleans's acting police superintendent halted all vagrancy arrests throughout the city. Police advocates denounced the order, charging that it left officers "handcuffed" and forecasting an apocalyptic crime wave.[3] No such crime wave struck: rates of reported property crimes and violent crimes, though already on the rise, held steady.[4] In 1972, the US Supreme Court ruled Florida's vagrancy law unconstitutional, effectively nullifying vagrancy laws throughout the nation.[5]

Ironically, the collapse of vagrancy law coincided not with the United States' retreat from incarceration but with the explosion of imprisonment rates throughout the nation. Between 1970 and 2000, the US incarceration rate increased by more than 400 percent. No city bore a greater brunt of mass incarceration than New Orleans, which by the year 2000 had the largest per capita jail population of any American city. Louisiana, in turn, had the highest incarceration rate of any US state and a higher incarceration rate than any country on the planet. New Orleans had become the world's imprisonment capital: "the most incarcerated city in the most incarcerated state in the most incarcerated country in the world."[6]

Driving forces within New Orleans mirrored national trends. In the 1970s, New Orleans's industrial sector collapsed, labor demand plummeted, and unemployment rates skyrocketed. Though part of national crises, these trends were amplified locally by the concurrent mechanization of the port of New Orleans—long the linchpin of the city's economy—and the subsequent oil bust of the 1980s. To stem the bleeding, city leaders tried pivoting to tourism. As unemployment and crime rates surged, voters embraced tough-on-crime prosecutors and policies that promised higher conviction rates, stiffer criminal penalties, and longer prison terms.[7]

Ultimately, it was the collapse of New Orleans's labor market in the 1970s—more than slavery's destruction, Reconstruction's collapse, or the rise of Jim Crow—that brought fundamental structural change to New Orleans's jail system. For 170 years, the state coercive systems deployed in New Orleans had remained remarkably consistent in the face of changing economic conditions. Through tectonic shifts in southern economy, politics, and society, New Orleans's criminal justice system had continuously doted upon the seizure, punishment, and redeployment of workers deemed dependent and underperforming, on the logic that suppressing dependents' idleness was equivalent to preventing crime. Each year, the combined total number of arrests for all property, violent, and financial crimes paled in comparison to arrests for vagrancy. The twentieth-century House of Detention had hardly deviated from the original mandate of the city's first nineteenth-century police jail of augmenting labor extraction; punishing resistant and underperforming workers be they enslaved, free, or freed; deploying penal laborers toward the construction of public infrastructure; and abetting the criminalization of workers' perceived "idleness."

This modus operandi had made sense when labor had been in high demand but no longer made sense within the labor surplus economy that emerged in the late twentieth century. With this new economic reality, New Orleans's jail system abandoned the production of disciplined workers and the maximization of their output for the prolonged warehousing of the unemployable and unwanted. Local, state, and federal officials increasingly relied on the House of Detention for the overflow confinement of state penitentiary inmates, federal inmates, federal immigration detainees, and pretrial detainees. Tent jails went up around the House of Detention and Parish Prison to cope with overcrowding. Work gangs became a marginal part of the jail's routine, leaving most inmates trapped within what amounted to continual lockdown, with as much as twenty-three hours per day spent locked within group cells. Effectively, collapsing labor demand transformed workhouse into warehouse.

Conditions within the Orleans Parish prison system were already far below national norms on the eve of the prison boom. Since the 1950s, the city's inmates had repeatedly tried drawing attention to their deteriorating living conditions by organizing work stoppages, hunger strikes, riots, and even acts of collective self-mutilation.[8] In 1970, a federal court placed the Orleans Parish prison system under a consent decree, ruling that conditions there "so shock the conscience as a matter of elemental decency and are so much more cruel than is necessary to achieve a legitimate penal aim that such confinement constitutes cruel and unusual punishment in violation of the Eighth and Fourteenth Amendments of the United States Constitution."[9]

Yet as the sheer number of inmates exploded, conditions collapsed entirely, and observers began to consistently cite the Orleans Parish prison system and its House of Detention as the single worst jail system and single worst jail, respectively, in the nation.[10] House of Detention inmates were routinely condemned to cells with as many as sixteen prisoners but only ten beds.[11] Sexual violence, inmate-on-inmate violence, and guard-on-inmate violence were endemic and flagrant. An investigation conducted by the Civil Rights Division of the US Department of Justice in 2008 found virtually no intake screening, no functioning inmate grievance system, rampant medical neglect, "grossly inadequate" suicide prevention practices, abysmally "inadequate" sanitation, and "disturbing evidence of officers openly engaging in retaliatory and abusive conduct."[12] A follow-up investigation in 2012 described "shockingly high rates of serious prisoner-on-prisoner violence," "persistent" officer misconduct, "widespread sexual assaults, including gang rapes," and a "pervasive atmosphere of fear."[13] The House of Detention lacked air conditioning. Meals, which prisoners were forced to consume within their cells, were delivered at inconsistent times and often consisted of food that was spoiled or still frozen. Sewage, rats, trash, feces, cockroaches, and broken plumbing were all widespread. With zigzagging corridors and a guard-to-inmate ratio of roughly one to seventy-five, supervision within the House of Detention was essentially nonexistent.[14] Little or no effort was made to separate violent from nonviolent offenders, pretrial detainees from convicts, or even cooperating witnesses from the prisoners against whom they were testifying.[15] Guards routinely instigated fights for their own entertainment. Suicidal inmates, if not ignored entirely, were left in five-point restraints, without any medical supervision, for hours and days.[16] Juvenile inmates reported unremitting physical and sexual abuse. Prison-rape victims learned that the jail system had no rape kits, no functional reporting system, and no testing or treatment for sexually transmitted infections.[17] "Prisoners face threats to their lives and safety on an almost daily basis, and struggle to secure even the most basic services," concluded the Southern Poverty Law Center.[18] "I have been threatened, beat up and stabbed multiple times. . . . No one responds when I ask for help. No one is safe in here," testified one pretrial House of Detention detainee.[19] "I have been raped, beat up by guards, jumped by prisoners, had my stuff stolen, and denied access to mental healthcare," another described.[20] "I have been in 11 different state prisons, 8 federal prisons, and 14 county jails," testified one Iraqi in federal immigration detention. "The House of Detention . . . was by far the worst."[21]

Extreme overcrowding had created new crises, but the root commitment to captivity and state violence was not new: indeed, the very same jail system that now led the nation in internments had once confined enslaved people at even higher rates (graph 8.1).[22] This moment marked New Orleans's second era of mass incarceration. Even as the city's incarceration rate peaked in the 1990s and 2000s and surpassed that of any other American city, that rate was no higher than that endured by enslaved people during the 1820s. New Orleans's antebellum arrest rates (161.5 per 1,000 in 1855) and police-to-population ratios (3.3 per 1,000 in 1854) were higher than or comparable to their modern corollaries (43.9 per 1,000 and 3.0 per 1,000, respectively, in 2016).[23] Though more research is needed, extant data from other cities suggest similar trends: antebellum incarceration rates, arrest rates, and police-to-population ratios of slaveholding cities far exceeded those of antebellum cities outside of the South and exceed or are comparable to those of major American cities in the twenty-first century.[24]

As Hurricane Katrina approached New Orleans in August 2005, Orleans Parish sheriff Marlin Gusman declined offers for aid in relocating prisoners inland, vowing instead "to keep our prisoners where they belong." As the city flooded, electricity and phone lines within the jail system failed. Guards abandoned their posts, condemning nearly 7,000 inmates to lockdown within their cells without food, drinking water, lighting, air conditioning, or medical care, for up to four days—for some, all while standing in chest-deep floodwater. More than 300 of the prisoners were juveniles. Nearly 90 percent were Black. Most were pretrial detainees. "They left us to die there," one survivor tersely put it. "Of all the nightmares during Hurricane Katrina, this must be one of the worst," concluded Human Rights Watch.[25]

Hurricane Katrina brought New Orleans's jail system under unprecedented global scrutiny. As community activists demanded reforms aimed at reducing the size of New Orleans's imprisoned population, the US Department of Justice entered into another consent decree, to improve jail conditions, with

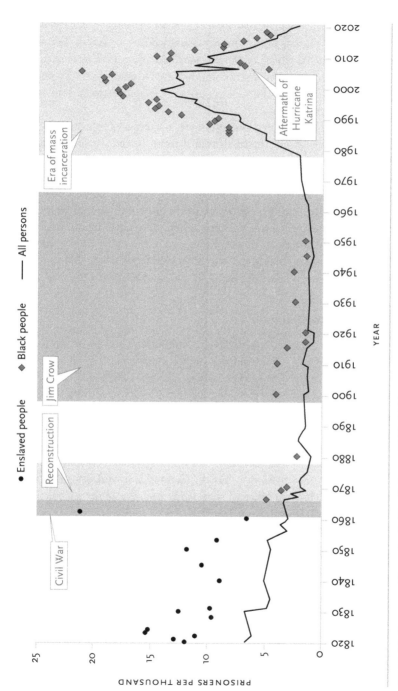

Graph 8.1. Incarceration rates in New Orleans, 1820–2020.

the city and sheriff. As pressure mounted, city officials began searching for a way to wash their hands of the embarrassingly decrepit, storm-damaged, and functionally vestigial House of Detention. FEMA's commitment of more than $50 million toward the reconstruction of New Orleans's jail system, and the subsequent construction of a new 1,438-bed facility between 2012 and 2015, provided such a means.[26]

The New Orleans House of Detention was permanently shuttered on May 3, 2012: just two days shy of the institution's 207th birthday. No one alive knew that the jail derived from a slave prison, had indirectly inspired the design of some of the world's first penitentiaries, and was among the oldest penal institutions in the United States. "The House of Detention is now a closed chapter in the history of the Sheriff's Office and the history of the city of New Orleans," Gusman told reporters as the last inmates shuffled onto the buses that would transport them to other jails dispersed throughout the state. When asked about the fate of the forsaken building, Gusman pleaded ignorance: "My suggestion is to implode it, watch it come down. . . . We want to keep it in the past."[27]

Slavery and the Prison

In May 2018, inmates at Louisiana State Penitentiary, still popularly referred to as Angola and still a productive forced-labor plantation, laid their bodies onto the ground and refused to work, charging that the conditions of their captivity were tantamount to "modern-day slavery." By August, similar protests had erupted in penal facilities throughout the nation, snowballing into the largest prison strike in US history. The demands released by the strike's inmate-leaders included "prison policies that recognize the humanity of imprisoned men and women," expanded "access to rehabilitation programs," access to Pell Grants, the right to vote, the creation of "proper channel[s] to address grievances," an "immediate end" to racial bias in sentencing and parole determinations, and "an immediate end to prison slavery."[28]

Perceptions of connections between slavery and the prison are nothing new: prisoners have compared themselves to slaves, or equated their condition to slavery, since the earliest days of the nation's first prison movement on the heels of the American Revolution. During the past half-century, scholars have explained this sense of connection by suggesting that after Emancipation, prisons replaced slavery as a labor control mechanism, instrument of racialized dehumanization, and tool for the maintenance of racial caste. This explanatory narrative proposes that "reverberations," "residues," and "echoes" of slavery permeate present-day prison systems. It draws a straight and unbroken line from the antebellum slave plantation to the present-day state penitentiary.

This book has sought to demonstrate that there are several lines from slavery to mass incarceration, though they are not all straight. Metaphors of "echoes" and "reverberations" homogenize and render vague a multitude of ways that slavery and the prison have fashioned one another's development. For the earliest American penal theorists writing in the eighteenth century, slavery provided a vital point of reference from which to develop ideas regarding freedom, captivity, labor, and pain. From the earliest days of the prison movement, slaveholders considered how they might adapt the prison for slave society, developing institutions and practices that remain with us today. For antebellum social reformers, prison reform provided a rich discursive field that contributed to the growth of the national abolitionist movement, structuring abolitionists' critiques of slavery. For former slaveholders in the aftermath of Emancipation, prisons enabled the creation of new systems of bonded labor or the reproduction of social relations endemic to the antebellum institution. In the twentieth century, prisoners in the South performed involuntary labor, often on former slave plantations, or were deployed on public infrastructure through chain gang systems that traced their ancestry to penal systems developed for the humiliation and subjugation of resistant enslaved people. A few of these prison plantations, and a handful of county chain gangs, persist to this day. Continuously, resistant inmates have compared themselves to slaves or insisted that their incarceration was tantamount to slavery as a discursive strategy. Throughout, the punishment of Black Americans has relied on inherited racial logics—that they are less qualified for freedom, more prone to criminality, less capable of personal growth and reflection, and less susceptible to physical pain—which are themselves products of slavery. In short, the historical relationships linking slavery and the prison are far more complex and multifaceted than any singular metaphor or moment of "replacement."

In his classic essay "Slavery and Freedom: The American Paradox," historian Edmund Morgan proposed that the idea of freedom relied on the institution of slavery. On one level, the financial boons of slave labor made possible the pursuit of American statehood. On another level, the racialization of freedom was an effective strategy for binding the interests of poorer white farmers to those of white plantation elites. On a deeper level still, Morgan contended that the American ideal of freedom—by itself, an abstract concept—relied on slavery for definition. Freedom was comprehensible only in juxtaposition to slavery; the two categories exist only as conceptual opposites. Without slavery, freedom could not exist.[29]

Perhaps it is time to broaden Morgan's classic formulation by noting how incarceration has historically provided, and continues to provide, Americans with a means of mediating relations between slavery and freedom. There is not one but two institutions—slavery and the prison—that have recurrently given meaning to freedom in American history by demarcating the limits of freedom. Indeed, the modern prison, as we today know it, *could only* have emerged from a slave society in the throes of Enlightenment liberalism. It is an institution born of a people committed to freedom but fearful of those they perceived as incapable of properly exercising it—a people curious as to the natures of compulsion and pain, fixated on the duality of freedom and captivity, and capable of imagining no better punishment than subjection to freedom's antithesis. Less a dichotomy, the American paradox is a trichotomy: slavery, freedom, and the prison, locked in interdependent evolution while providing one another with meanings.

Violence and the State

Between 1805 and the late twentieth century, the New Orleans Police Jail was reworked by a series of delineable human choices from Louisiana's premier "slave penitentiary" into the worst prison in the United States and the agonizing nucleus of the world's carceral capital. The road from slave prison to twenty-first-century prison was tumultuous. The Saint-Domingue Revolution, the cotton revolution, the late antebellum growth of wage labor, Emancipation, Reconstruction, the rise of Jim Crow, the twentieth-century civil rights movement, and the rise of mass incarceration in the late twentieth century each provoked significant reorganizations. If anything, this history reveals that prisons are remarkably malleable institutions, adaptable to a variety of historical changes.

Across two centuries of tumult and transformation, patterns pervade. Race has always played a central role in the development of police, prisons, and state power within Louisiana. White fears of Black resistance and unrest repeatedly steered major extensions of the state's governing capacity. State violence played a critical role in producing racial logics and delineating racial categories—even as, counterintuitively, the state repeatedly deployed profitable penal labor systems that blurred racial castes. Far from stymieing the development of coercive state power, slavery *drove* state building in Louisiana. Indeed, the histories of slavery and governance are so intertwined in Louisiana that neither can be fully disentangled from the other.

Nor can New Orleans's history of coercive violence be disentangled from the global circulation of ideas, technologies, and legal strategies. Neither primitive nor parochial, Louisiana's lawmakers repeatedly imported tools from the northeastern United States, Europe, and the Caribbean, adapting each innovation for the particular economic and political interests of slave and postslavery society. Ideas and tactics did not only flow into the slave South from outside: the chain gang, Edward Livingston's carceral vision, and the Union army's coercive labor system each reveal how innovations developed within New Orleans directly contributed to the global history of punishment. Slave societies are not peripheral to the broader histories of the prison or the development of the modern state but a fully integrated part of those histories.

The growth of coercive state power in New Orleans also underscores a strong and enduring commitment to government intervention in the lives of poorer Americans generally and poorer Black Americans in particular. Many Americans today embrace the conviction that anti-statism and opposition to state intervention in the individual's personal and economic affairs are deeply ingrained American traditions rooted in the nation's founding. The history of coercive state power in New Orleans points toward a radically different narrative by revealing a deep commitment to intrusive state intervention that is virtually as old as the nation itself. The United States may have a strong tradition of noninterference in the lives of the wealthy, white, and propertied, but that commitment to "small government" has not always been extended toward the poor, criminalized, and racially subordinated. The slave cities of the antebellum South marshaled large-scale public resources when inflicting coercive violence on certain residents: commitment to "big government," too, is a longstanding American tradition.

The most glaring continuity, of course, is the police jail system itself. The existence of direct institutional connections between slave prison and modern-day prison is disquieting, in part, because it disrupts many of our agreed-upon fictions regarding the nature of state power within our society. We imagine an objective boundary between the infliction of erratic and illegitimate violence, usually called "torture," and the state's infliction of well-ordered and legitimate penalties, usually referred to as "punishment." In the twenty-first century, we also tend to imagine slavery as typifying a certain irrational, premodern, and capriciously illegitimate violence—the very opposite of the rational, modern systems of institutionalized confinement that constitute state penalties today. The fabrication of this barrier between barbaric, premodern torture and rational, bureaucratized penal sanctions performs a vital role in the rationalization of modern state power.

Yet the police jail system violates these constructed barriers between slavery's world and our world, and between premodern "torture" and rational "punishment," in ways that force us to question the legitimacy of state penalties in our present. The infliction of violence on enslaved people—usually conceived of today as the very embodiment of illegitimate violence—influenced the development of modern prisons. The binary between barbaric "torture" and civilized "punishment" is compromised when we consider that infliction of violence on enslaved people could also be state sanctioned, institutionalized, bureaucratized, and structured by laws and norms. We are forced to confront the discomforting truth that there is no intrinsic boundary between "torture" and "punishment," or, rather, that the distinction between "torture" and "punishment" lies not in the inherent nature of the violence inflicted but in the degree to which that violence has been accepted as legitimate.

Few today would deny that the state's infliction of penalties is essential to the public good and that those penalties should be structured by legal systems, institutions, and norms. But we should see the state's use of force with clear eyes, girding ourselves against the tacit pressure to embrace unquestionably the legitimacy of the punitive systems that governments develop. Today, the scale at which the United States incarcerates its citizens is an unprecedented event in world history: if nothing else, that outcome is abnormal.

In the years since the House of Detention's closure, New Orleans has become a national focal point in the movement to end mass incarceration. Dedicated grassroots activists have helped push through reforms aimed at reducing jail time for low-level offenders, including lowering bond fees, decriminalizing marijuana, and employing pretrial diversion policies that encourage the issuance of summonses rather than jail time for persons charged with misdemeanors. As a result, the city's jail population has fallen to the lowest levels in a half-century.[30] New Orleans's second age of mass incarceration may be nearing its end.

Still, we are not saved. Louisiana's incarceration rate remains among the highest in the United States. The US incarceration rate, though the lowest in thirty years, remains the highest in the world.[31] Inmate abuse, trauma, neglect, extreme overcrowding, dehumanization, and extreme racial inequity are all endemic. Whether we label these conditions "torture" or "punishment," we remain a society committed to the infliction of state violence, particularly on those among us who are poor or Black, at an unimaginable and unequaled scale. No society on earth is more committed, it would seem, to inflicting penalties on its members.

Someday, New Orleans may enter a third age of mass incarceration. Different historical circumstances will define that moment, although the outcomes may look familiar. We will not avoid that future unless we address the base origins of our wounds: extreme wealth inequality, traditions of Black criminalization, and the unresolved tensions of our historical commitments to slavery and freedom.

ACKNOWLEDGMENTS

The debts I have accumulated while writing this book are incalculable, but I will try.

I started this project while pursuing my doctorate within the History Department of Tulane University. Early research for this project was made possible by generous financial support from the New Orleans Center for the Gulf South at Tulane University, Tulane University's School of Liberal Arts, Tulane University's History Department, and the Louisiana Chapter of the Colonial Dames of America. A Mellon/ACLS Dissertation Completion Fellowship from the American Council of Learned Societies allowed me to devote one full year of graduate school to writing, truly an invaluable experience. After I joined the LSU faculty, additional research was supported by a Manship Summer Research Fellowship.

This book would not have been possible without the help and knowledge of skilled archivists at the Historic New Orleans Collection, the Xavier University of Louisiana Library, Hill Memorial Library at Louisiana State University, the New Orleans Notarial Archives Research Center, the Earl K. Long Library at the University of New Orleans, the Amistad Research Center, the New-York Historical Society, the Rhode Island Historical Society, the Maine Historical Society, the Huntington Library, the St. Tammany Parish Clerk of Court's Office, the Washington, DC, branch of the National Archives, and the Library of Congress. In particular, I owe great debts to the staff of the City Archives at the New Orleans Public Library—Christina Bryant, Amanda Fallis, Stephen Kuehling, Yvonne Loiselle, Andrew Mullins, Greg Osborn, Cheryl Picou, and Brittanny Silva—for their boundless expertise and patience with me. I humbly ask their forgiveness for my interminable questions, and document requests, over the years.

While at Tulane, I was the beneficiary of supportive, challenging, committed teachers. I am especially grateful for my four committee members—R. Blakeslee Gilpin, Rosanne Adderley, Emily Clark, and Randy Sparks—for modeling the highest caliber of scholarship, teaching, empathy, and intellectual engagement. I am also indebted to Yigit Akin, Guadalupe García, Karissa Haugeberg, Andy Horowitz, Walter Isaacson, Kris Lane, Jana Lipman, Elisabeth McMahon, Marline Otte, and Justin Wolfe for their counsel and support at this project's various stages. A special thanks to Blake and Andy for workshopping passages, reading grant application drafts, listening to ideas, and providing continual encouragement—their mentorship has made me the historian I am today.

As I began soliciting feedback on early chapter drafts, meetings, emails, and chance encounters with colleagues yielded invaluable criticisms and advice. I am particularly grateful for the critical feedback that I received from Edward Baptist, Mary Ellen Curtin, Louis Ferleger, Michael Fitzgerald, Eric Foner, Thavolia Glymph, Jean Hébrard,

Walter Johnson, Kelly Kennington, Linda Kerber, Kate Masur, Hamish Maxwell-Stewart, Michael Pfeifer, Larry Powell, Marcus Rediker, and Rachel Shelden: the care with which they reviewed my work bespeaks both their generosity and their devotion to the profession. I thank Kelly Birch and Camille Pachot for helping me locate and translate key documents. I thank Mary Howell for giving me the opportunity to see the inside of New Orleans's House of Detention in 2020. I am especially grateful for Rebecca Scott's feedback and encouragement: her writing and wisdom continue to guide and inspire me. I also owe a special thanks to Edward Ball for so beautifully modeling the transformation of dissociated historical documents into cogent narrative.

At LSU, I have been truly blessed to work with so many dedicated and supportive colleagues. I owe particular thanks to Gaines Foster and Aaron Sheehan-Dean for reading drafts, sharpening sentences, hearing ideas, and providing continuous encouragement. Shortly after I joined LSU, Aaron and Gaines organized a workshop of my manuscript, truly the greatest gift a budding scholar can receive. I thank Leslie Harris, Mary Niall Mitchell, and Joshua Rothman for the wealth of insightful suggestions and invaluable criticism that they provided.

I am tremendously grateful for the guidance and support I received from everyone at UNC Press. I owe a great thanks to my editor, Debbie Gershenowitz, as well as the manuscript's two readers, Jeff Forret and Adam Malka. Special thanks to Laura Dooley and Valerie Burton for their hypervigilant copyediting. Thanks to all of them, the journey from manuscript to book has been a genuine joy.

My commitment to the study of history was sparked by Harry Williams of Carleton College: I thank him for first teaching me how to critically question, analyze, argue, imagine, write, revise, and think. The underlying roots of this project trace to the time I spent teaching in New Orleans schools: I don't know how to put into words the sense of debt that I feel to all the students, families, and teachers I worked with at Walter L. Cohen High School and at Arthur Ashe Charter School.

This book would not have been possible without the love and support of family. I am grateful for my parents, Chuck Bardes and Barbara Kilpatrick, and my grandmothers, Judy Leopold Bardes and Geraldine Frick Kilpatrick, in more ways than can be expressed. I thank my parents for teaching me that art and empathy are life's greatest forces. I owe a huge thanks to my mother-in-law, Theresa Enters, for the many hours of childcare (and thus, writing time) that she provided. My dad gave every chapter a thorough line editing: as with so many of my debts owed to him, this one is too great to be repaid.

Key ideas were honed through conversations with my dear friends Forrest Collins, Aron Michalski, and Mary Ellen Stitt; with my father, Chuck Bardes; and with my wife, Lindsay Bardes. I thank each of them for their patient listening, thoughtfulness, and friendship. Finally, I am grateful for my children, Malcolm and Lila, for reminding me of the importance of challenging power.

NOTES

Abbreviations

CHMS   Charles F. Heartman Manuscripts of Slavery Collection, Xavier University of Louisiana, New Orleans.

HNOC   Historic New Orleans Collection, New Orleans, LA.

LARC   Louisiana Research Center, Tulane University, New Orleans.

LLVC   Louisiana and Lower Mississippi Valley Collections, Louisiana State University Libraries, Baton Rouge.

LOC   Library of Congress, Washington, DC.

LR-CA   Letters Received, ser. 1920, Civil Affairs, Records of Subordinate Offices, Department of the Gulf and Louisiana (P)., Record Group 393, Pt. 1, National Archives and Records Administration, Washington, DC.

LR-HR   Letters Received, ser. 1756, Correspondence, General Records, Headquarters Records, Department of the Gulf and Louisiana (P)., Record Group 393, Pt. 1, National Archives and Records Administration, Washington, DC.

LRO-PM   Letters Received (Originals), 2 vols. (309 and 306/684), ser. 1844, General Records, Provost Marshal, Records of Staff Officers, Department of the Gulf and Louisiana (P)., Record Group 393, Pt. 1, National Archives and Records Administration, Washington, DC.

LR-PM   Letters Received, ser. 1845, General Records, Provost Marshal, Records of Staff Officers, Department of the Gulf and Louisiana (P)., Record Group 393, Pt. 1, National Archives and Records Administration, Washington, DC.

LR-SCP   Letters Received by the Provost Marshal General, ser. 1515, St. Charles Parish, Provost Marshal Field Organizations of the Civil War, Record Group 393, Pt. 4, National Archives and Records Administration, Washington, DC.

LRS-SMP   Letters Received and Sent by the Provost Marshal General, ser. 1519, St. Mary Parish, Provost Marshal Field Organizations of the Civil War, Record Group 393, Pt. 4, National Archives and Records Administration, Washington, DC.

MM-CDV   Mayors' Messages (Translations), Conseil de Ville, City Council Records, City Archives and Special Collections, New Orleans Public Library, New Orleans, LA.

MMR   Monthly Morning Reports of the Police Jail, ser. 1675, Chief of Police,
               New Orleans, LA, Towns and Posts, Provost Marshal Field Organiza-
               tions of the Civil War, Record Group 393, Pt. 4, National Archives and
               Records Administration, Washington, DC.

MR-PM   Miscellaneous Records, ser. 1896, General Records, Provost Marshal,
               Records of Staff Officers, Department of the Gulf and Louisiana (P).,
               Record Group 393, Pt. 1, National Archives and Records Administra-
               tion, Washington, DC.

NOPL   City Archives and Special Collections, New Orleans Public Library, New
               Orleans, LA.

OI-OP   Orders Issued by the Provost Marshal, ser. 1498, Orleans Parish, Provost
               Marshal Field Organizations of the Civil War, Record Group 393, Pt. 4,
               National Archives and Records Administration, Washington, DC.

OP-CDV   Official Proceedings (Translations), Conseil de Ville, City Council
               Records, City Archives and Special Collections, New Orleans Public
               Library, New Orleans, LA.

OR-CDV   Ordinances and Resolutions (Translations), Conseil de Ville, City Coun-
               cil Records, City Archives and Special Collections, New Orleans Public
               Library, New Orleans, LA.

OR-OP   Orders Received by the Provost Marshal, ser. 1499, Orleans Parish, Pro-
               vost Marshal Field Organizations of the Civil War, Record Group 393,
               Pt. 4, National Archives and Records Administration, Washington, DC.

PMG-LA   Letters Received by the Provost Marshal General, ser. 1390, State of
               Louisiana, Provost Marshal Field Organizations of the Civil War, Rec-
               ord Group 393, Pt. 4, National Archives and Records Administration,
               Washington, DC.

PM-JJBP   Letters Received by the Provost Marshal General, ser. 1516, St. James
               and St. John the Baptist Parishes, Provost Marshal Field Organizations
               of the Civil War, Record Group 393, Pt. 4, National Archives and Rec-
               ords Administration, Washington, DC.

PM-JP   Letters Received by the Provost Marshal General, ser. 1482, Jefferson
               Parish, Provost Marshal Field Organizations of the Civil War, Record
               Group 393, Pt. 4, National Archives and Records Administration,
               Washington, DC.

PM-OP   Letters Received by the Provost Marshal General, ser. 1497, Orleans
               Parish, Provost Marshal Field Organizations of the Civil War, Record
               Group 393, Pt. 4, National Archives and Records Administration,
               Washington, DC.

RIHS   Rhode Island Historical Society, Providence.

SCLC   Supreme Court of Louisiana Collection, University of New Orleans,
               New Orleans.

SFLC   Slavery and Freedom in Louisiana Collection, Xavier University of
               Louisiana, New Orleans.

The following sources are shortened as indicated below and cited by year.

Atlanta Police Annual Report: Atlanta Police Department. [. . .] *Annual Report of the Chief of Police of the City of Atlanta, Georgia for the Year Ending* [. . .]. Atlanta, 1901–26.

Boston Police Annual Report: Boston Police Department. [. . .] *Annual Report of the Police Commissioner for the City of Boston for the Year Ending* [. . .]. Boston: Wright and Potter, 1891–1926.

Charities and Corrections Report: Louisiana State Board of Charities and Corrections. [. . .] *Report of the Louisiana State Board of Charities and Corrections.* New Orleans, 1906, and Baton Rouge, 1908–10.

Charleston Yearbook: Charleston Municipal Government. *Year Book* [. . .] *City of Charleston* [. . .]. Charleston, SC, 1880–1921.

Chicago Police Annual Report: Chicago Police Department. *Police* [. . .] *Annual Report* [. . .] *Year Ending* [. . .]. Chicago, 1881–1931.

Detroit Police Annual Report: Detroit Police Department. [. . .] *Annual Report* [. . .] *to the Common Council of the City of Detroit* [. . .]. Detroit, 1883–1911.

Los Angeles Police Annual Report: Los Angeles Police Department. *Annual Report of the Police Department of the City of Los Angeles, California* [. . .]. [Los Angeles, 1913–31].

Louisiana Acts: Louisiana Legislature. *Acts* [. . .] *of the Legislature of the State of Louisiana.* New Orleans, 1812–59, Baton Rouge, 1859–1918.

Milwaukee Police Annual Report: Milwaukee Police Department. *Annual Report* [. . .]. Milwaukee, 1906–31.

Nashville Annual Report: Nashville City Government. *Annual Report of Departments of the City of Nashville for the Fiscal Year* [. . .]. Nashville, TN, 1905–16.

New Orleans Police Annual Report: New Orleans Department of Police. *Annual Report.* New Orleans: Department of Police, 1947–.

New York Police Annual Report: New York Police Department. [. . .] *Annual Report* [. . .]. New York, 1886–1931.

Philadelphia Common Council Journal: Philadelphia Common Council. *Journal of the Common Council of* [. . .] *Philadelphia* [. . .] *with an Appendix.* Philadelphia, 1856–60.

Philadelphia Mayor's Message: Philadelphia Mayor's Office. [. . .] *Annual Message of* [. . .] *Mayor of the City Philadelphia* [. . .]. Philadelphia, 1857–1923.

Police Commissioners Annual Report: New Orleans Board of Police Commissioners. *Annual Report of the Board of Commissioners of the Police Department and the Supt. of Police Force of the City of New Orleans for the Year* [. . .]. New Orleans, 1909–16.

Prisons and Asylums Annual Report: New Orleans Board of Commissioners of Prisons and Asylums. [. . .] *Annual Report of the Board of Commissioners of Prisons and Asylums* [. . .]. New Orleans, 1901–18.

Richmond Mayor's Message: Richmond Mayor's Office. *Annual Message* [. . .] *of the Mayor* [. . .]. Richmond, VA, 1909–19.

Savannah Mayor's Message: Savannah Mayor's Office. *Annual* [. . .] *Reports of the City Officers of the City of Savannah, Georgia* [. . .] *Year Ending* [. . .]. Savannah, GA, 1899–1916.

State Engineer Annual Report: Louisiana State Engineer. *Annual Report of the State Engineer, to the Legislature of the State of Louisiana.* New Orleans, 1843–58.

The following sources are shortened as indicated below and cited by legislature number and session number.

Louisiana House Journal: Louisiana Legislature. House. *Journal of the House of Representatives* [. . .] *of the State of Louisiana.* New Orleans, 1812–80.

Louisiana Senate Journal: Louisiana Legislature. Senate. *Journal of the Senate of the State of Louisiana* [. . .]. New Orleans, 1820–80.

Introduction

1. *New Orleans States,* August 19, 23, 24, 26, 27, 1943; *Times-Picayune* (New Orleans), August 19, 20, 26, 27, 31, September 3, 1943; *Louisiana Weekly* (New Orleans), August 28, September 4, 1943. The 1940 census enumerated 49,931 Black male New Orleans residents over the age of fourteen; *Sixteenth Census of the United States, 1940, Population,* vol. 2, pt. 3, p. 426. On work-or-fight laws, see Chamberlain, *Victory at Home;* and Shenk, *Work or Fight.*

2. Daniel E. Byrd to "U.S. Department of Justice, Civil Liberties Section," August 27, 1943, file 50-32, in Daniel, *Peonage Files,* reel 11.

3. *Negro Star* (Wichita), September 17, 1943; *Plaindealer* (Kansas City), September 24, 1943; *Dallas Morning News,* October 2, 1943; *Morning Star* (Wilmington, NC), June 29, 1943; *Marion (NC) Progress,* July 1, 1943; *New York Times,* July 30, 1943; *New Orleans States,* September 8, 1843.

4. Important works on mass incarceration include Alexander, *New Jim Crow;* Chase, *We Are Not Slaves;* Davis, *Are Prisons Obsolete?;* Garland, *Mass Imprisonment;* Gottschalk, *Prison and the Gallows;* Schoenfeld, *Building the Prison State;* Thompson, *Blood in the Water;* Thompson, "Why Mass Incarceration Matters"; and Wacquant, *Punishing the Poor.*

5. Sawyer and Wagner, "Mass Incarceration."

6. Forman, *Locking Up Our Own;* Harcourt, *Illusion of Order;* Hinton, *From the War on Poverty to the War on Crime;* Murakawa, *First Civil Right;* Pfaff, *Locked In;* Simon, *Governing through Crime.*

7. Childs, *Slaves of the State;* Hernández, *City of Inmates;* Muhammad, *Condemnation of Blackness;* Thompson, "From Researching the Past to Reimagining the Future"; Wacquant, "From Slavery to Mass Incarceration."

8. For the second quarter of 2021, the Bureau of Justice Statistics (BJS) reported 713 Black people incarcerated within Orleans Parish; 17,097 Black people held in state or federal detention throughout Louisiana; and 378,000 Black people in state or federal detention throughout the United States—yielding incarceration rates of 3.4, 11.7, and 9.2 per thousand, respectively. In 1820, the enslaved incarceration rate in Orleans

Parish was roughly 12.0 per thousand. For BJS figures, see Vera Institute of Justice, "Incarceration Trends." For overall population figures, see US Bureau of the Census, "Census Bureau Data." For antebellum incarceration rates, see graph 8.1.

9. Dubber, *Police Power*; Neocleous, *Fabrication of Social Order*; Novak, *People's Welfare*; Wagner, *Disturbing the Peace*.

10. Foucault, *Discipline and Punish*; Hirsch, *Rise of the Penitentiary*; Ignatieff, *Just Measure of Pain*; Kirchheimer and Rusche, *Punishment and Social Structure*; Manion, *Liberty's Prisoners*; McKelvey, *American Prisons*; McLennan, *Crisis of Imprisonment*; Melossi and Pavarini, *Prison and the Factory*; Meranze, *Laboratories of Virtue*; Rothman, *Discovery of the Asylum*; Rubin, *Deviant Prison*. On this scholarship's tendency to omit race, see Gibson, "Global Perspectives on the Birth of the Prison."

11. Fogelson, *Big City Police*; Lane, *Policing the City*; Miller, *Cops and Bobbies*; Mitrani, *Rise of the Chicago Police Department*; Monkkonen, *Police in Urban America*; Steinberg, *Transformation of Criminal Justice*. On policing in the slave South, see Hadden, *Slave Patrols*; Malka, *Men of Mobtown*; and Rousey, *Policing the Southern City*.

12. Ayers, *Vengeance and Justice*; Blackmon, *Slavery by Another Name*; Carleton, *Politics and Punishment*; Childs, *Slaves of the State*; Curtin, *Black Prisoners and Their World*; Haley, *No Mercy Here*; LeFlouria, *Chained in Silence*; Lichtenstein, *Twice the Work of Free Labor*; Mancini, *One Dies, Get Another*; Oshinsky, *Worse Than Slavery*; Perkinson, *Texas Tough*; Shapiro, *New South Rebellion*.

13. For imprisonment as slavery's "surrogate," "replacement," or "continuation," see, in addition to the preceding note, Gilmore, "Slavery and Prison"; Hinton and Cook, "Mass Criminalization of Black Americans"; Stevenson, "Why American Prisons Owe Their Cruelty to Slavery"; Thompson, "From Researching the Past to Reimagining the Future"; and Wacquant, "From Slavery to Mass Incarceration." On prisoners' own deployment of the slavery-prison comparison as a discursive strategy, see Chase, *We Are Not Slaves*. For "two ancestral lines," see Perkinson, *Texas Tough*, 8.

14. Adamson, "Punishment after Slavery," 555, 557; Rice, "'This Province, So Meanly and Thinly Inhabited,'" 19. Also see Ayers, *Vengeance and Justice*, 61; Campbell, *Crime and Punishment in African American History*, 44–49; Clavin, "'The Floor Was Stained with the Blood of a Slave,'" 264; Colvin, *Penitentiaries, Reformatories, and Chain Gangs*, 249; Dale, *Criminal Justice in the United States*, 36–39; Friedman, *Crime and Punishment in American History*, 88; Gottschalk, *Prison and the Gallows*, 48; Hindus, *Prison and Plantation*; and McNair, *Criminal Injustice*, 163–65.

15. Colvin, *Penitentiaries*, chap. 11; Paton, *No Bond but the Law*; Scott, *Refashioning Futures*, 86–87. For southern law enforcement as "premodern," see Hinton and Cook, "Mass Criminalization," 263; and Reichel, "Southern Slave Patrols as a Transitional Police Type."

16. Foundational works within the Marxist approach are Kirchheimer and Rusche, *Punishment and Social Structure*; and Melossi and Pavarini, *Prison and the Factory*. Foundational works within the "revisionist" school are Foucault, *Discipline and Punish*; Ignatieff, *Just Measure of Pain*; and Rothman, *Discovery of the Asylum*.

17. On southern honor culture, fiscal conservatism, and opposition to centralized power, see Ayers, *Vengeance and Justice*; Bardaglio, *Reconstructing the Household*, chap. 1; Cash, *Mind of the South*, 33; Egnal, *Divergent Paths*; Escott, *Many Excellent*

People, 23–24; Fox-Genovese and Genovese, *Mind of the Master Class*; Genovese, *Political Economy of Slavery*; Genovese, *Slaveholder's Dilemma*; Greenberg, *Honor and Slavery*; and Wyatt-Brown, *Southern Honor*, chap. 14. On these themes as related to southern lawlessness and the laxity of southern legal systems, see Brown, "Southern Violence"; Franklin, *Militant South*; Hindus, *Prison and Plantation*; and Sydnor, "Southerners and the Laws."

18. Wade, *Slavery in the Cities*, chap. 7; Haunton, "Law and Order in Savannah"; Johnson, *Slavery's Metropolis*, chap. 4; Jones, *Born a Child of Freedom*, 76–77; Jordan, "Police Power and Public Safety in Antebellum Charleston"; Malka, *Men of Mobtown*; McGoldrick, "Policing of Slavery in New Orleans"; Rousey, *Policing the Southern City*. Other important studies of the urban slavery in the United States include Berlin and Harris, *Slavery in New York*; Fields, *Slavery and Freedom on the Middle Ground*; Goldin, *Urban Slavery in the American South*; Rockman, *Scraping By*; and Takagi, *Rearing Wolves to Our Own Destruction*. On urban policing in Latin America and Caribbean slave society, see Algranti, "Slave Crimes"; Brown, "'A Black Mark on Our Legislation'"; Fuentes, *Dispossessed Lives*; Holloway, *Policing Rio de Janeiro*; Hünefeldt, *Paying the Price of Freedom*; Mattos, *Laborers and Enslaved Workers*, chap. 3; and Welch, *Slave Society in the City*.

19. Rashauna Johnson proposes that "confined cosmopolitanism"—defined by ubiquitous surveillance, regulated geographies, and slaveholders' exploitation of urban slaves' relative mobility—better categorizes enslaved peoples' urban experiences. Johnson, *Slavery's Metropolis*, esp. 3–7.

20. On the essentialization of the South as rural, see Towers, "Southern Path to Modern Cities." On southern essentialism generally, see Ayers, "What We Talk about When We Talk about the South"; Edwards, "Southern History as U.S. History"; Kolchin, *Sphinx on the American Land*; and Ring, *Problem South*.

21. Wood, "Prisons, Workhouses, and the Control of Slave Labour." Works on slave incarceration in Latin America and the Caribbean include Beattie, *Punishment in Paradise*; Harris, *Punishing the Black Body*; and Paton, *No Bond but the Law*. Works disputing the assumption that enslaved people were entirely excluded from US prisons include Birch and Buchanan, "Penalty of a Tyrant's Law"; Derbes, "'Secret Horrors'"; Forret, "Before Angola"; Forret, *Williams' Gang*, chap. 11; Johnson, *Slavery's Metropolis*, chap. 4; and Walker, *No More, No More*, 28–34. Other studies note US slaveholders' reliance on prisons, in passing: Dusinberre, *Them Dark Days*, 125–31; Glymph, *Out of the House of Bondage*, 50–51.

22. Compare, for example, New Orleans and New York City during the 1850s. New York City established its first full-time, professionalized police department in 1845. In 1855, New York City maintained 17 police officers for every 10,000 residents. In 1854, that police force had performed 49,237 arrests, or roughly 780 arrests per 10,000 (assuming constant population growth between decimal censuses). By contrast, New Orleans established its first full-time, professionalized police department four decades before New York City, in 1805. In 1854, New Orleans maintained 33 police officers for every 10,000 residents (nearly twice that of New York). New Orleans police performed 23,259 arrests in that year, or roughly 1,700 arrests for every 10,000 residents (more than twice that of New York), a figure that excludes arrests performed by the slave patrols and private civilians that were legally empowered to seize suspect slaves and free

Black people. For these figures, see *New York Herald*, March 9, 1855; Rousey, *Policing the Southern City*, 24; and monthly arrest reports printed in the *New Orleans Daily Crescent*.

23. For example, in 1858, the Charleston slave workhouse received 2,171 admittances, while the average workhouse population was 91, yielding roughly 144 admittances and 6.1 prisoners per 1,000 enslaved urban residents. In 2010, the Charleston County jail system received 32,136 admissions, while the average jail population was 1,686, yielding 91.7 admittances and 4.8 prisoners per 1,000 urban residents. Monthly workhouse reports were printed in the *Charleston Daily Courier*. For twenty-first-century figures, see Vera Institute of Justice, "Incarceration Trends."

24. Works disputing Old South "premodernity" include Barnes, Schoen, and Towers, *Old South's Modern Worlds*; Majewski, *Modernizing a Slave Economy*; Marrs, *Railroads in the Old South*; and Smith, *Mastered by the Clock*. Works disputing southern statelessness include Ambrose, "Statism in the Old South"; Edwards, *People and Their Peace*; Karp, *This Vast Southern Empire*; and Quintana, *Making a Slave State*. Studies rejecting the notion of an underdeveloped southern legal culture include Bardaglio, *Reconstructing the Household*; Gross, *Double Character*; Morris, *Southern Slavery and the Law*; and Welch, *Black Litigants*.

25. Muhammad, *Condemnation of Blackness*, 5.

26. Thompson, "Blinded by a 'Barbaric' South."

27. Garland, *Punishment and Modern Society*, chap. 11, esp. 252.

28. On New Orleans's colonial and early American history, see Clark, *New Orleans*; Dawdy, *Building the Devil's Empire*; Dessens, *Creole City*; Faber, *Building the Land of Dreams*; Ingersoll, *Mammon and Manon*; Powell, *Accidental City*; and Vidal, *Caribbean New Orleans*. On the region's antebellum transformation, see Johnson, *River of Dark Dreams*; Rothman, *Flush Times and Fever Dreams*; and Rothman, *Slave Country*. For immigration figures, see Logsdon, "Immigration through the Port of New Orleans," 105–24; and Spletstoser, "Back Door to the Land of Plenty." On the region's Indigenous histories, see Usner, *American Indians in Early New Orleans*.

29. Balogh, *Government out of Sight*; Evans, Rueschemeyer, and Skocpol, *Bringing the State Back In*; John, "Ruling Passions"; Mehrotra, "Bridge Between"; Novak, "Myth of the 'Weak' American State"; Novak, *People's Welfare*. For surveys of the "new" history of capitalism, and relations between state governance and economic development, see Beckert and Desan, introduction to *American Capitalism*, 1–32; Novak, Sawyer, and Sparrow, "Beyond Stateless Democracy"; Rockman, "What Makes the History of Capitalism Newsworthy?"; Sklansky, "Elusive Sovereign"; and Sugrue, "Reconfiguration of Political History." On the relation of public and private governance in particular, see Hartog, *Public Property and Private Power*; Novak, "Public-Private Governance"; Wang, "Dogs and the Making of the American State"; and Wilson, *Business of Civil War*.

30. Baptist, *Half Has Never Been Told*; Beckert, *Empire of Cotton*; Beckert and Berry, *Price for Their Pound of Flesh*; Johnson, *River of Dark Dreams*; Rockman, *Scraping By*; Rockman, *Slavery's Capitalism*; Rosenthal, *Accounting for Slavery*; Schermerhorn, *Business of Slavery*; Williams, *Capitalism and Slavery*.

31. See especially Hall, "Public Slaves and State Engineers"; Hall, "Slaves of the State"; Quintana, *Making a Slave State*; and Rockman, *Scraping By*.

32. Kirchheimer and Rusche, *Punishment and Social Structure*; Melossi and Pavarini, *Prison and the Factory*.

33. Adamson, "Punishment after Slavery"; Adamson, "Toward a Marxist Penology"; Lichtenstein, *Twice the Work of Free Labor*, 11; Shelden, "Convict Leasing."

34. Rockman, *Scraping By*, esp. 7–8.

35. Foucault, *Discipline and Punish*; Ignatieff, *Just Measure of Pain*; Rothman, *Discovery of the Asylum*.

36. Bernault, "Shadow of Rule," 79; Paton, *No Bond but the Law*, 11–13; Sen, "Separate Punishment," 82.

37. Davis, "Racialized Punishment and Prison Abolition," 362–62; Hernandez, *City of Inmates*, 8–10; Mancini, *One Dies, Get Another*, 75.

38. Lichtenstein, *Twice the Work of Free Labor*, 11; Reichel, "Southern Slave Patrols."

39. For "acceptance of their subjection" as a core objective of slave prisons, see Paton, *No Bond but the Law*, 21.

40. *Belmont Chronicle* (St. Clairsville, OH), January 1, 1857; *Emancipator and Weekly Chronicle* (Boston), April 23, 1845; *Richmond Daily Dispatch*, April 29, 1854; Watkins, *Struggles for Freedom*, 22; *Richmond Daily Dispatch*, April 29, 1854; Samuel Gridley Howe to Horace Mann, December 23–26, 1841, in Richards, *Letters and Journals*, 112–15.

41. My thinking here is indebted to recent studies of colonial prison development—and in particular, Diana Paton's *No Bond but the Law* (2004). Aguirre, *Criminals of Lima and Their Worlds*; Botsman, *Punishment and Power in the Making of Modern Japan*; Branch, "Imprisonment and Colonialism in Kenya"; Dikötter, *Crime, Punishment and the Prison in China*; Sherman, "Tensions of Colonial Punishment."

42. Foucault, *Discipline and Punish*; Garland, *Punishment and Modern Society*; Waquant, "From Slavery to Mass Incarceration," 42, 54–60.

43. Bernault, "Shadow of Rule," 73–76; Brown, *Dark Matters*; Dawdy, "Burden of Louis Congo"; Hartman, *Scenes of Subjection*.

44. On power and resistant counterpower, see Foucault, *Power/Knowledge*; Foucault, *History of Sexuality*, 1:95–96; and Scott, *Domination and the Arts of Resistance*.

45. On resistant mobility and capitalist economic development in the Atlantic world, see Linebaugh and Rediker, *Many-Headed Hydra*; Mattos, *Laborers and Enslaved Workers*, chap. 3; Rockman, *Scraping By*; Scott, *Common Wind*; Van der Linden, *Workers of the World*; Van Rossum and Kamp, *Desertion in the Early Modern World*; and Van Rossum, Rediker, and Chakraborty, *Global History of Runaways*. On slave marronage, see Bolton, *Fugitivism*; Diouf, *Slavery's Exiles*; Franklin and Schweninger, *Runaway Slaves*; and Pargas, *Fugitive Slaves and Spaces of Freedom*. On urban marronage, see Franklin and Schweninger, *Runaway Slaves*, chap. 6; Marshall, "'They Are Supposed to Be Lurking about the City'"; Mitchell, "Lurking but Working"; and Pargas, *Freedom Seekers*, chap. 2.

46. Bardaglio, *Reconstructing the Household*; Bercaw, *Gendered Freedoms*; Downs, *Declarations of Dependence*; Edwards, *Gendered Strife and Confusion*, esp. 77; Fox-Genovese, *Within the Plantation Household*; McCurry, *Masters of Small Worlds*. On master-servant law, see Linder, *Employment Relationship in Anglo-American Law*; Orren, *Belated Feudalism*; Shammas, *History of Household Government*; Stanley,

From Bondage to Contract; Steinfeld, *Coercion, Contract, and Free Labor*; Steinfeld, *Invention of Free Labor*; and Tomlins, *Law, Labor, and Ideology.*

47. Bodin, *Six Books of the Commonwealth*, chaps. 2–5; Dubber, *Police Power*, 81; Ghachem, *Old Regime and the Haitian Revolution*, 29–76, 127–28; Rousseau, "Discourse on Political Economy"; Tucker, "Sources of Louisiana's Law of Persons."

48. "Book 1: Of Persons," in *Digest of the Civil Laws Now in Force*, 8–93.

49. Blackstone, *Commentaries on the Laws of England*, 4:162; Dubber, *Police Power*, chaps. 1–4, esp. 50–62; Neocleous, *Fabrication of Social Order*, 16–21; Steinfeld, *Invention of Free Labor*, chap. 2.

50. Scholars have debated when master-servant theory lost its currency within American law. For its part, Louisiana did not drop Book 1 of its civil code until 1990; Devlin, "Reconsidering the Louisiana Doctrine," 1529.

51. Du Bois, *Black Reconstruction in America*, 700.

52. Rockman, *Scraping By*, 4.

Chapter 1

1. Ayers, *Vengeance and Justice*, 61; Davis, "Racialized Punishment and Prison Abolition"; Friedman, *Crime and Punishment in American History*, 88.

2. Cobb, *Inquiry into the Law of Negro Slavery*, 1:266; William Pugh to C. W. Rudyard, May 26, 1863, box 5, MR-PM.

3. Here, "police" would have referred to the act of regulating society rather than the force tasked with enforcing laws; on the word's etymology, see Dubber, *Police Power*, 64–69. The precise origin of *Geôle de police* is elusive; neither that name nor any Spanish corollary appears on French or Spanish colonial documents. The name may derive from *prison de police*, an archaic term commonly used in eighteenth-century France to describe the lockups that held disorderly persons arrested by patrols: see, for example, Manuel, *La police de Paris dévoilée*, 1:343. For Spanish colonial records of the city's penal complex, see "Detalle de los reparos, y de los Augmentos que se debe hacer à la Carcel de esta Ciudad por disposición del Illustro Cabildo," February 28, 1799, Miscellaneous Spanish and French Records of New Orleans, NOPL.

4. For the growth of Louisiana's police jail system, see "An Act in Relation to Runaway Slaves in this State," approved March 17, 1826, in *Louisiana Acts, 1826*, pp. 90–95; "An Act to Amend an Act, Entitled 'An Act Relative to Runaway Slaves in this State,'" approved January 16, 1827, in *Louisiana Acts, 1827*, pp. 30–33; "An Act Supplementary to Several Acts Relative to Runaway Slaves, in this State," approved March 9, 1833, in *Louisiana Acts, 1833*, pp. 51–52; "An Act to Incorporate the Town of Donaldsonville," approved April 22, 1846, in *Louisiana Acts, 1846*, § 15, pp. 15–19; "An Act Establishing the Jail at Plaquemines, in the Parish of Iberville, a Depot for Runaway Slaves," approved April 7, 1847, and "An Act Establishing the Jail of the Parish of St. Tammany, a Depot for Runaway Slaves," approved April 19, 1847, both in *Louisiana Acts, 1847*, pp. 79, 98; "An Act Providing for Runaway Slaves and Establishing a General Depot for the Same," approved March 19, 1857, in *Louisiana Acts, 1857*, pp. 172–75; and *Daily Picayune* (New Orleans), November 30, 1848. For Mississippi, see "An Act, Respecting Runaway Slaves," approved January 29, 1829, in Hutchinson, *Code of Mississippi*,

531–22; Davis, *Black Experience in Natchez*, 120, 122; and Taylor, *Brokered Justice*, 7. For Tennessee, see Lewis Shanks, John Trigg, and F. P. Stanton to the Tennessee General Assembly, November 29, 1841, Legislative Petitions, State of Tennessee, Tennessee State Library and Archives, Nashville (microfilm edition), reel 16; "An Act to Authorize the Mayor and Alderman of any Incorporated Town in the State, to Employ Runaway Slaves Committed to the Jail of any County, for the Public Improvement of said Town," approved January 20, 1844, in *Acts Passed at the First Session of the Twenty-Fifth General Assembly of the State of Tennessee, 1843–44*, p. 161; and Lovett, *African-American History of Nashville*, 44.

5. Into the 1840s, travelers to Louisiana noted the expression while stating their own lack of prior familiarity with the term. Outside of Louisiana, Mississippi, travelers' accounts to those regions, and reprints of documents from the British Caribbean, the term "chain gang" does not appear anywhere in the United States before the 1840s. The *Oxford English Dictionary* also dates the term's emergence to the 1840s; *OED Online*, "chain, n.," www.oed.com/view/Entry/30197. For travelers expressing unfamiliarity with the term, see especially Brown, *Slave Life in Georgia*, 123; Ingraham, *South-West*, 2:185; and "Slave-Auction." For formal use of "chain gang," see *Louisiana Courier* (New Orleans), October 31, 1829.

6. For southern postbellum penal labor as lacking "any penological philosophy at all," see Colvin, *Penitentiaries, Reformatories, and Chain Gangs*, 249.

7. For chain gangs as "worse" than slavery, see Terrell, "Peonage in the United States."

8. Literature on the Haitian Revolution is extensive and growing. Good starting places include Dubois, *Avengers of the New World*; Fick, *Making of Haiti*; James, *Black Jacobins*; and Popkin, *You are All Free*.

9. On fear of revolutionary Black contamination in the United States, see Frey, *Water from the Rock*; Geggus, *Impact of the Haitian Revolution*; Horne, *Confronting Black Jacobins*; Hunt, *Haiti's Influence on Antebellum America*; and Scott, *Common Wind*.

10. William Claiborne to Thomas Jefferson, September 18, 1804, in Carter and Bloom, *Territorial Papers*, 9:298; John Watkins to William Claiborne, February 2, 1804, in Rowland, *Official Letter Books*, 2:9; Pitot, *Observations on the Colony*, 30; meetings of June 6 and 30, 1804, both in bk. 1, and meetings of September 7 and 28, 1805, both in bk. 2, all in vol. 1, OP-CDV; Lachance, "Politics of Fear"; Le Glaunec, "Slave Migrations and Slave Control."

11. On this elite, see especially Faber, *Building the Land of Dreams*, 6–7, 76–79, 104–6. Also see Ingersoll, *Mammon and Manon*; Vidal, *Caribbean New Orleans*.

12. Meetings of June 6 and 30, 1804, both in bk. 1, and meetings of September 7 and 28, 1805, both in bk. 2, all in vol. 1, OP-CDV. On these revolutionary fears, also see Dubois, *Avengers of the New World*, 52–55; and Fick, *Making of Haiti*, 42–45.

13. Geggus, "Enigma of Jamaica in the 1790s," 279; Geggus, "Slavery, War, and Revolution."

14. Clark, *New Orleans*, 219–20; Rothman, *Slave Country*, 26–29, 46–47, 75–76.

15. Faber, *Building the Land of Dreams*, 7–10, 118–54.

16. Berquin-Duvallon, *Travels in Louisiana*, 24, 32, 35–36; Pitot, *Observations on the Colony*, 110, 112; Robin, *Voyage to Louisiana*, 31.

17. *National Intelligencer, and Washington Advertiser*, August 8, 24, September 5,

1804; William Claiborne to James Madison, March 10, 16, June 3, July 1, 26, 1804, all in Rowland, *Official Letter Books*, 2:25–26, 42–48, 190–91, 233–34, 270–72; Vernet, *Strangers on their Native Soil*, 65.

18. Thomas Paine to "French Inhabitants of Louisiana," September 22, 1804, in *Complete Religious and Theological Works*, 321, 324.

19. William Claiborne to Thomas Jefferson, September 18 and November 25, 1804, both in Carter and Bloom, *Territorial Papers*, 9:298, 340; Horne, *Confronting Black Jacobins*, chap. 4; Le Glaunec, "Slave Migrations and Slave Control."

20. Meetings of November 30, 1803, and June 30, 1804, both in bk. 1, vol. 1, OP-CDV.

21. Lachance, "1809 Immigration."

22. Meeting of August 16, 1804, bk. 1, and meeting of February 15, 1806, bk. 3, both in vol. 1, OP-CDV; John Pintard to Albert Gallatin, September 14, 1808, and James Brown to John Breckinridge, September 17, 1805, both in Carter and Bloom, *Territorial Papers*, 9:53, 510; James Watkins to Conseil de Ville, January 24, 1806, in vol. 1, MM-CDV; [Amendment to Ordinance Regarding Strangers], December 12, 1807, folder 29, and Conseil de Ville to James Mather, July 20, 1809, folder 34, both in box 16, subser. A, ser. 4, Rosemond E. and Emile Kuntz Collection, LARC; William Claiborne to Capt. Nichols, July 25, 1804, and William Claiborne to James Pitot, August 10, 1804, both in Rowland, *Official Letter Books*, 1:365–66; 301–3; Pitot, *Observations on the Colony*, 27, 29.

23. John Watkins to John Graham, September 6, 1805, and John Graham to William Claiborne, September 16, 1805, both in Carter and Bloom, *Territorial Papers*, 9:500–504, 504–6; meetings of September 7 and 28, 1805, both in bk. 2, vol. 1, OP-CDV; John Watkins to Conseil de Ville, September 4 and 28, 1805, both in vol. 1, MM-CDV.

24. Ingersoll, *Mammon and Manon*, 299–300; Lachance, "Politics of Fear," 169–76, 196; Le Glaunec, "Slave Migrations and Slave Control," 213–18; Le Glaunec, "'Writing' the Runaways." For "Kongolization," see Roberts, "Slaves and Slavery in Louisiana," chap. 3.

25. William Claiborne to "Commandants of Districts," [March 1804], and William Claiborne to Julien Poydrass, August 6, 1804, both in Rowland, *Official Letter Books*, 2:71–75, 294; meetings of March 17, May 19, and August 18 and 25, 1804, all in bk. 1, vol. 1, OP-CDV; Le Glaunec, "Slave Migrations and Slave Control," 220–21, 224–35; Hall, *Africans in Colonial Louisiana*, 372.

26. City leaders and early police regulations explicitly prioritized the pursuit of maroons and vagrants, for example, Pitot, *Observations on the Colony*, 27; meeting of May 5, 1811, bk. 3, vol. 2, OP-CDV; and "An Ordinance Concerning the Appointment and Duties of Different Police Officers for the City and Suburbs of New-Orleans," approved June 2, 1808, in *Police Code*, 278–84.

27. "Ordinance Concerning the Establishment of a Paid Guard for the City, the Faubourgs and the Banlieue of New Orleans," approved May 18, 1805, and "Resolution of the City Council stating that the Slaves Detained at the Police Gaol Shall be Put on the Chain Gang and Employed in the City Works," approved May 22, 1805, both in vol. 1, subser. 1, OR-CDV. Convict labor was not entirely new to Louisiana. During the Spanish colonial period, a squad of six convicts had cleaned city streets, while officials had sporadically forced free Black men, slaves, and convicts to strengthen faltering levees; see Din and Harkins, *New Orleans Cabildo*, 80, 230–31, 242. The costly new police

department would be abolished and reorganized repeatedly over the proceeding years; Rousey, *Policing the Southern City*, 16–18.

28. Alderson, "Charleston's Rumored Slave Revolt"; Egerton, *Gabriel's Rebellion*; Marks, *Black Freedom in the Age of Slavery*, chap. 2.

29. "An Act to Establish a Guard in the City of Richmond," approved January 22, 1801, in *Collection of All Such Acts of the General Assembly of Virginia*, 2:174–75; "An Act to Authorize and Empower the Mayor and Aldermen of the City of Savannah, to Assess and Levy a Tax for the Purpose of Establishing a Regular Watch in the Said City," approved December 2, 1805, in *Compilation of the Laws of the State of Georgia*, 243–44; "City Guard," approved October 17, 1806, in *Digest of the Ordinances of the City Council of Charleston*, 104–16; Cantwell, *History of the Charleston Police Force*, 3; Rousey, *Policing the Southern City*, chap. 1; Washington, "Efforts to Prevent Negro Revolts." Charleston reformed its city watch and constabulary repeatedly between 1783 and 1806, leading to several different proposed dates for the formation of Charleston's first "modern" police—an inconsistency dependent, largely, on different ways of defining the advent of "modern" policing. For the defining characteristics of "modern" policing, see Johnston, *Policing Britain*, 12; and Wright, *Policing*, 9.

30. "An Act on Vagabonds and Suspicious Persons," approved June 7, 1806, "An Act to Prevent the Introduction of Free People of Color from Hispaniola, and the other French Islands of America into the Territory of Orleans," approved June 7, 1806, and "Black Code. An Act Prescribing the Rules and Conduct to be Observed with Respect to Negroes and Other Slaves of This Territory," approved June 7, 1806, all in *Acts Passed at the First Session of the First Legislature of the Territory of Orleans*, 106–23, 126–31, 150–91. On the heritage of Louisiana's 1806 slave code, see Faber, *Building the Land of Dreams*, 235.

31. "Motion de M. P. Bertonnière," November 9, 1808, folder 3, box 8, ser. 2, New Orleans Municipal Papers, LARC (translation by author).

32. Resolution of May 22, 1805, vol. 1, subser. 1, OR-CDV; Nicholas Girod to Conseil de Ville, May 8, 1813, and James Mather to Conseil de Ville, April 25, 1812, both in vol. 5, MM-CDV. For police jail regulations, see "Règlement pour la Prison de Police," approved August 31, 1807, folder 4, box 2, New Orleans Collection, New-York Historical Society, New York; "Ordinance Concerning the Police Prisons for the Detention of Slaves in the Cases Therein Mentioned," approved October 8, 1817, and "Ordinance to Regulate the Service of Slaves Employed in the City Works and to Allow a Remuneration to The Owners Who Shall Put on the Chain Gang One or More Slaves, to be Employed in the Said Works," approved November 10, 1817, both in vol. 2, subser. 1, OR-CDV.

33. Beccaria, *Essay on Crimes and Punishment*, 44; Thomas Jefferson to Edmund Pendleton, August 26, 1776, in Boyd et al., *Papers of Thomas Jefferson*, 1:503–6; Thomas Jefferson, "A Bill for Proportioning Crimes and Punishments," in Peterson, *Thomas Jefferson*, 349–50; Foucault, *Discipline and Punish*, 73–114; Hirsch, *Rise of the Penitentiary*, 45–46, 85, 170n122; Manion, *Liberty's Prisoners*, 18–21; Masur, *Rites of Execution*, 78–81; McLennan, *Crisis of Imprisonment*, 32–34; Meranze, *Laboratories of Virtue*, chap. 2, esp. 55, 62, 63; Rice, "'This Province, So Meanly and Thinly Inhabited.'"

34. Jefferson, *Memoirs*, 1:39; Rush, *Containing an Enquiry into the Influence of*

Physical Causes upon the Moral Faculty, 20–21, 32; Foucault, *Discipline and Punish*, 73–114; Hirsch, *Rise of the Penitentiary*, 45–46, 85, 170; Manion, *Liberty's Prisoners*, 18–21; Meranze, *Laboratories of Virtue*, chap. 2, esp. 55, 62–63.

35. Pitot, *James Pitot*.

36. Moreau de Saint-Méry, *Description topographique*, 1:397–98; François de Neuf-château, *Lettre*, 5 (translations by author).

37. François de Neufchâteau, *Lettre*, 7–9 (translation by author); Joseph-Gabriel, "Mobility and the Enunciation of Freedom," 218–20.

38. On ties between Philadelphia and Cap-Français, see Clark, *Strange History of the American Quadroon*, chap. 1.

39. Ignatieff, *Just Measure of Pain*, 11–14; Jütte, *Poverty and Deviance*; Spierenburg, "Body and the State," 68–72; Wagner, *Poorhouse*, 10.

40. See, for example, "An Act to enable the Mayor, Recorder, Aldermen, and Common Council-men of The Free Borough and Town of Elizabeth, to build a Poor-House, Work-House, and House of Correction within the said Borough, and to make Rules, Orders and Ordinances for the governing of the same, and to repair the Gaols for the same Borough," approved 1754, in *Acts of the General Assembly of the Province of New-Jersey*, 2:25–31; "An Act for Establishing Public Workhouses in the Several Parishes in this Island," approved December 16, 1791, in *Laws of Jamaica*, 2:486–93; and Byrd, "First Charles Town Workhouse."

41. Brackett, *Negro in Maryland*, 122–23; Dorsey, *Hirelings*, 85; Navin, "New England Yankee Discovers Southern History," 186–87; Paton, *No Bond but the Law*, 23–24, 27; Smalls, "Behind Workhouse Walls," 23–25; Smith, "Black Women Who Stole Themselves," 149–50, 154n12.

42. Paton, *No Bond but the Law*.

43. Great Britain Colonial Office, *Papers Relating to the West Indies*, 83. By the 1820s the term "chain gang" had reached Tasmania, suggesting the term's circulation throughout the British Empire; *Hobart (Australia) Town Gazette*, June 10, 17, August 26, 1826.

44. James Mather to Conseil de Ville, December 2, 1807, vol. 2, MM-CDV.

45. In particular, see article 12 of New Orleans's Police Jail regulations of 1817, which closely paraphrased article 7 of Charleston's workhouse regulations of 1807. "Ordinance Concerning the Police Prisons for the Detention of Slaves in the Cases Therein Mentioned," approved October 8, 1817, vol. 2, subser. 1, OR-CDV; "Work-House," approved August 8, 1807, in *Digest of the Ordinances of the Council of Charleston*, 254–63.

46. Francisco Hernandez to Conseil de Ville, September 25, 1812, folder 3, box 8, and William Church and A. Lavitt, affidavit, December 27, 1822, folder 1, box 9, both in CHMS; *State of Louisiana vs. Jim, a Slave of George Holloway*, filed June 3, 1826, docket no. 289, in folder 8, box 18, Stray Court Records, NOPL; *Bruce v. Stone et al.*, docket no. 2,389, 5 La. 1 (1832), SCLC.

47. Coleridge, *Six Months in the West Indies*, 117–18, 257; Cooper, *Facts Illustrative of the Condition of the Negro Slaves*, 176–77, 201, 243, 274; Karasch, *Slave Life in Rio de Janeiro*, 118–21; Laurence, *Tobago in Wartime*, 113–15; Paton, *No Bond but the Law*, 21, 40, 207n11, 208n22; Schultz, *Tropical Versailles*, 123–25; Walker, *No More, No More*, 30–31, 168n45; Whiteley, *Three Months in Jamaica*, 12–13.

48. In addition to the preceding notes, see Bibb, *Narrative of the Life and Adventures*, 91–93; Campbell, *Slavery on Trial*, 71–72; "An Act Respecting Runaway Slaves," approved January 29, 1829, in Hutchinson, *Code of Mississippi*, 531–32; J. Stoddard Johnston, "City Government and City Institutions," in Johnston, *Memorial History of Louisville*, 1:341; "An Act to Remove the Quarters of the Work-House and for Other Purposes," approved December 22, 1859, in Raines, *Compilation of the General Laws of the City of Nashville*, 143–44; "An Act to Incorporate the City of Louisville," approved February 13, 1828, § 13, in Strattan and Vaughn, *Collection of the State and Municipal Laws, in Force, and Applicable to the City of Louisville*, 47–63; and *Republican Banner* (Nashville), December 3, 1841, November 24, 1843. Nashville's slave chain gang initially consisted of several dozen convict slaves from Virginia and Maryland purchased by the municipality in 1831. They were maintained by the workhouse keeper during the night and delivered daily in chains to the street overseer. Local fugitive slaves were subsequently added to this street force, likely after the Tennessee legislature authorized the practice in 1844. A Nashville workhouse manifest from 1862 identifies twenty prisoners (a figure that excludes approximately sixty municipality-owned convict slaves), of which eleven (all men) were assigned to labor and six were "placed for safekeeping." John Q. Dodd to Andrew Johnson, August 12, 1862, in Graf, Haskins, and Bergeron, *Papers of Andrew Johnson*, 5:609–10; Lovett, *African-American History of Nashville*, 20, 44.

49. Schafer, "'Guaranteed against the Vices and Maladies Prescribed by Law.'"

50. Din, *Spaniards, Planters, and Slaves*, 178–80, 196; Powell, *Accidental City*, 224–25, 233; Spear, *Race, Sex, and Social Order*, 59–75, 104–7; White, *Voices of the Enslaved*, 45, 221.

51. For an example of this paper trail's relevance in court proceedings, see *Bertin v. Phillips*, docket no. 5728, 1 La. Ann. 173 (1846), SCLC.

52. Robin, *Voyage to Louisiana*, 30–32.

53. Din, *Spaniards, Planters, and Slaves*, 54, 147, 170–72, 200; Hall, *Africans in Colonial Louisiana*, 127; Padgett, "Decree for Louisiana Issued by the Baron of Carondelet"; Vidal, *Caribbean New Orleans*, 314–15.

54. On tensions between state and slaveholders in the formation of slave law, see Campbell, *Slavery on Trial*, 34–35, 58–59; Morris, *Southern Slavery and the Law*, 50–51, 174–78, 190–92; and Paton, *No Bond but the Law*, 2–3, 19–20.

55. The council had previously instituted, then discontinued, a similar payment system in 1808. "Motion de M. P. Bertonnière," November 9, 1808, folder 3, box 8, Ser. 2, Municipal Papers, LARC; James Mather to Conseil de Ville, December 29, 1810, folder 34, box 5, Wisdom Collection, LARC; Meeting of March 13, 1813, bk. 3, vol. 2, OP-CDV; James Mather to Conseil de Ville, December 2, 1807, vol. 2, and April 25, 1812, vol. 5, and Nicholas Girod to Conseil de Ville, July 1, 1815, vol. 6, all in MM-CDV.

56. Joseph Chardon to Conseil de Ville, December 16, 1815, folder 4, Slavery in Louisiana Collection, HNOC.

57. "Ordinance Concerning the Police Prisons for the Detention of Slaves in the Cases Therein Mentioned," approved October 8, 1817, and "Ordinance to Regulate the Service of Slaves Employed in the City Works and to Allow a Remuneration to The Owners Who Shall Put on the Chain Gang One or More Slaves, to be Employed in the Said Works," approved November 10, 1817, both in vol. 2, subser. 1, and Resolution of June 7,

1820, vol. 5, subser. 2, all in OR-CDV; Nicholas Girod to Conseil de Ville, May 8, 1813, vol. 5, MM-CDV; meeting of June 3, 1820, bk. 3, and meeting of September 22, 1821, bk. 4, both in vol. 3, OP-CDV; meeting of May 28, 1813, folder 71, box 16, subser. A, ser. 4, Kuntz Collection, LARC; *Chase v. City of New Orleans, Mayor et al.*, docket no. 2876, 9 La. 343 (1836), SCLC.

58. *George Lewis v. City of New Orleans*, docket no. 4679, 12 La. Ann. 190 (1857), SCLC. Also see *Stewart v. Municipality No. 2 (New Orleans) et al.*, docket no. 3043, 9 La. Ann. 461 (1854), and *Henry Fassman v. City of New Orleans*, docket no. 5304, unreported case (1858), both in SCLC.

59. French, *History of Policing America*, 34–35; Reichel, "Southern Slave Patrols as a Transitional Police Type"; Waxman, "How the U.S. Got Its Police Force."

60. Stuart, *Three Years in North America*, 2:236; Tasistro, *Random Shots and Southern Breezes*, 2:135; Olmsted, *Journey in the Seaboard Slave States*, 20, 404.

61. *Louisiana Advertiser* (New Orleans), February 14, 17, 18, 21, 1834; Rousey, *Policing the Southern City*, 32–33.

62. Report of the City Guard, January 6–7, 1810, folder 2, box 8, CHMS; Rousey, *Policing the Southern City*, 17–25.

63. The New Orleans force consisted of fifty-three policemen in February 1814, equivalent to twenty-five police per 10,000 residents (assuming constant population growth between decimal census). Dennis Rousey provides similar figures for subsequent years. In 2019, the average urban police-to-population ratio in the United States was twenty-nine law enforcement employees (including civilian employees without arresting powers) per 10,000 residents. "État de Prêt de la Garde de Ville pour le mois de Février, [1814]," folder 4, box 7, Wisdom Collection, LARC; Rousey, *Policing the Southern City*, 24; Federal Bureau of Investigation, "Full-Time Law Enforcement Employees."

64. Charles Patton and Lewis Rochelle, affidavits, September 11, 1810, folder 2, box 8, CHMS; James Pierpont to "Recorder of Aldermen of the City of New Orleans," June 29, 1821, and James Pierpont and Joseph Peralta, affidavits, July 3, 1821, both in folder 1, box 9, CHMS; *Louisiana Advertiser* (New Orleans), February 17, 21, 1834.

65. Policemen's birthplaces were identified by cross-referencing police payrolls from 1814 and 1816 against sacramental records. Among thirty-three officers whose birthplaces could be identified with confidence, twenty (60.6 percent) were named as Saint-Domingue natives in sacramental records. The actual concentration of refugees on the police force was doubtless higher: many of the officers identified as French natives (six men, or 18.2 percent) may also have been refugees who had emigrated from France to Saint-Domingue before the island's revolution. "État de Prêt de la Garde de Ville pour le mois de Février [1814]," folder 4, "État de Prêt de la Garde de Ville pour le mois de Septembre, 1814," folder 24, and "État de Prêt de la Garde de Ville pour le mois de Mai, 1816," folder 39, all in box 7, Wisdom Collection, LARC; Woods, *Sacramental Records*, 10:25, 126, 188, 234, 237, 262, 11:44, 99, 133, 203, 205, 225, 305, 12:301, 13:265, 295, 366, 14:33, 53, 273, 275, 15:43, 191, 348, 16:374, 17:41, 234, 18:1, 234, 19:83, 228, 241.

66. In Saint-Domingue, militia service had been mandatory for all free men between the ages of fifteen and fifty-five. The colony maintained a complex hierarchy of militia companies, segregated by class and racial categorization (though by law all commissioned officers were white). Garrigus, *Before Haiti*; King, *Blue Coat or Powdered Wig*.

67. Meeting of March 17, 1804, bk. 1, vol. 1, OP-CDV; Rousey, *Policing the Southern City*, 27, 29, 59. For a free Black policeman who was also a Saint-Domingue refugee, see Constant Michel; Woods, *Sacramental Records*, 11:305.

68. James Brown to John Breckinridge, September 17, 1805, in Carter and Bloom, *Territorial Papers*, 9:506–13; *Louisiana Advertiser* (New Orleans), February 14, 17, 18, 21, 1834.

69. William Claiborne to "Commandants of Districts," [March 1804], in Rowland, *Official Letter Books*, 2:71–75; Ordinance of September 10, 1814, folder 23, box 7, Wisdom Collection, LARC; A Resident, *New Orleans as It Is*, 71.

70. Benwell, *Englishman's Travels in America*; Hearn, "*Gombo Zhèbes*," 16n1 (translation by author); Brown, *Slave Life in Georgia*, 104–5.

71. Dessens, *From Saint-Domingue to New Orleans*, 72, 75–76. On the city's rapid growth, see Faber, *Building the Land of Dreams*; and Ingersoll, *Mammon and Manon*. For figures cited here, see Baptist, *Half Has Never Been Told*, 3; Clark, *New Orleans*, 305; and "Trade and Commerce of New Orleans."

72. For the three rejected plans, see Joseph Pilié, *Plan des augmentations, et altérations projetées aux prisons de celle* [*sic*] *ville*, May 1, 1830, Joseph Pilié, [Plans for the Ground Floor of Parish Prison], August 2, 1832, and Joseph Pilié, [Plans for "Prison for the negroes" and "prison for white people"], February 19, 1833, all in Louisiana Map Collection, NOPL.

73. Pennsylvania's Eastern State Penitentiary, considered large when completed in 1829, was built to hold 250 inmates. Rubin, *Deviant Prison*, 23.

74. Denis Prieur to Conseil de Ville, April 8, 1833, vol. 15, MM-CDV; "Contrat de bâtisse entre Messieurs Gobet et Larochette et la municipalité no 1," act no. 103, filed October 17, 1836, notary Felix de Armas, Notarial Archives Research Center, New Orleans, LA; A. Guerties et al., grand jury report, January 23, 1838, folder 9, box 11, Municipal Papers, LARC; *Daily Picayune* (New Orleans), May 9, 1849; *Historical Epitome of the State of Louisiana*, 328–29.

75. Admittance data provided here have been constructed by using compilations of daily reports from the City Police Jail for 1820–24, 1828, and 1830–31 (containing records of 18,169 admittances), daily reports from the Third Municipality Police Jail for 1838 and 1839 (947 admittances), twenty-eight monthly reports from the Second Municipality Police Jail for 1843–45 (1,858 admittances), the admittance ledger of the Third Municipality Police Jail, May 1846 to August 1851 (4,403 admittances), and the admittance ledger, dated November 1835 to August 1841, of the Police Jail designed by Pilié, which served as the City Police Jail until January 1837, and as the First Municipality Police Jail thereafter (13,921 admittances). For these sources, see Daily Reports (6 vols.) and Register of Slaves Entering the Police Jail, both in Police Jail Records, and Daily Reports (2 vols.), Police Jail of the Third Municipality Records, all in NOPL; Daily Reports, boxes 10–12, [Second Municipality Monthly Reports], folder 3, box 19, and Record Book of the Third Municipality Police Jail, box 21, all in CHMS; [Second Municipality Monthly Reports], folders 12–14, ser. 5A, box 1, SFLC.

76. In 1820, when the census reported 7,355 enslaved people in Orleans Parish, approximately 1,525 prisoners were committed to the Police Jail, of which approximately 1,400 were enslaved and approximately 125 were free Black itinerant workers jailed

on the pretext that they were maroons (on this practice, see chapter 3). In 1830, when the census reported 9,397 enslaved people, the Police Jail received 3,028 imprisoned enslaved people and 516 free Black prisoners. The 1840 census reported 23,448 enslaved people; however, only records of the First Municipality Police Jail survive for that year (showing 1,629 imprisoned enslaved people and 143 free Black prisoners). Using admittance data from 1836, the closest year with complete citywide data (3,184 imprisoned enslaved people and 495 free Black prisoners), yields a slave incarceration rate of 13.5. Alternatively, a rough estimate for 1840 can be reconstructed by combining existent First Municipality data for 1840 with Second and Third Municipality data for nearby years. Second Municipality monthly reports of prisoners retained and released, complete for twelve months between September 1843 and October 1845, reveal approximately 1,365 annual admittances of imprisoned enslaved people and 175 annual admittances of free Black prisoners. The Third Municipality Police Jail received approximately 1,020 imprisoned enslaved people and 330 free Black prisoners in 1838 and 1839—or, approximately 510 enslaved and 170 free Black prisoners annually. Cumulatively, these figures suggest a rough estimate for 1840 of 3,500 admittances of imprisoned enslaved people and 500 admittances of free Black prisoners, yielding a slave admittance rate of 14.9, comparable to (though somewhat higher than) the figure yielded by using data from 1836. Thus, the slave admittance rate in 1840 likely fell between 13.5 and 14.9—or nearly 14—admittances per 100 residents.

77. Data in graph 1.1 derive from daily reports of the City Police Jail for 1820–31 and the Register of Slaves Entering the Police Jail for 1836. Some daily reports, representing forty-one days in total, are missing: seven days in 1820, twenty-three in 1821, six in 1822, and five in 1824. Data for these missing days have been substituted with the daily admittance average for the given year, as indicated by existent reports. Daily Reports (6 vols.) and Register of Slaves Entering the Police Jail, both in Police Jail Records, and Daily Reports (2 vols.), Police Jail of the Third Municipality Records, all in NOPL; Daily Reports, boxes 10–12, [Second Municipality Monthly Reports], folder 3, box 19, and Record Book of the Third Municipality Police Jail, box 21, all in CHMS; [Second Municipality Monthly Reports], folders 12–14, ser. 5A, box 1, SFLC.

78. Police Jail records do not differentiate between local and out-of-parish prisoners. However, in a sampling of 192 enslaved prisoners confined in the First Municipality in January 1839—a month of peak steamboat traffic, when the share of out-of-state runaways would have been particularly high—176 (91.7 percent) were listed as the property of masters with surnames that appear in New Orleans's 1842 city directory, while virtually all the remaining slaves were listed under surnames resembling phonetic misspellings of local surnames. A surviving jail register from Savannah, Georgia, [also] differentiate[s] between local and nonlocal prisoners: it identifies 82.8 percent of the [ensl]aved prisoners entered between April 30, 1809, and May 16, 1815, as the property [of Sav]annah residents. Register of Slaves Entering the Police Jail, Police Jail Records, [New-Orleans] Directory for 1842; Jail Register, Jail Registers and Jail Prisoner [Po]lice Department Records, City of Savannah Research Library and Municipal [Archives, a]vailable at ancestry.com.

[79. Thes]e calculations assume constant population growth between decimal cen[suses. From Ap]ril 30, 1809, to May 16, 1815, Savannah's jail recorded 3,971 admittances, of which 3,822 admittances were of imprisoned enslaved people and 149 admittances were of free Black prisoners. Future researchers should note that the actual number of names in this register is far greater than 3,971, as jailors periodically conducted counts of all inmates in the jail, redundantly reentering the names of current prisoners into the admissions book without explicitly distinguishing lists of current prisoners from names of new admittances. Jail Register, Jail Registers and Jail Prisoner Books, Police Department Records, City of Savannah Research Library and Municipal Archives, available at ancestry.com.

80. Between March 1840 and May 1844, and again between October 1855 and April 1862, monthly reports of Charleston's slave workhouse were printed—though not for every month—in the *Charleston Daily Courier*, the *Southern Patriot* (Charleston), or the *Charleston Mercury*. Complete admittance data survive for the years 1843, 1856, 1857, and 1858, while data for all but two months survive for both 1842 and 1859 (data for those four missing months were supplanted with averages of immediately preceding and proceeding months). During those years, Charleston's average per capita incarceration rate was 15.5 per hundred enslaved residents. This calculation fails to account for the presence of free Black prisoners jailed as slaves.

81. Monthly and annual reports of persons jailed by police appeared in the Richmond *Dispatch* between 1854 and 1860. Complete data survive for 1854 and 1856, while near-complete data survive for 1855, 1857, 1858, and 1859 (again, missing monthly data were supplanted with averages of the immediately preceding and proceeding months). As with data for Charleston, this figure does not account for the presence of free Black people jailed as slaves.

82. Memphis Police Blotter, 1858–1860, Shelby County Archives, Memphis, TN, https://search.register.shelby.tn.us/memphis_blotter/.

83. Only one surviving ledger, representing the Third Municipality from May 13, 1846, to March 27, 1851, includes the reasons for which prisoners were committed. Roughly three-fourths of admittances recorded in this register were for marronage and other illicit mobility crimes (see graph 1.3). A similar figure is suggested by the ledger of the First Municipality Police Jail, November 1, 1835, to August 18, 1841. Although this register does not include reasons for admittance, it records that 74.5 percent of enslaved admittances were made by police, by a neighborhood watch, or by private individuals who were not the prisoners' owners and who were likely acting as slave catchers, suggesting that roughly three-fourths of inmates were committed for openly visible public order offenses. Record Book of the Third Municipality Police Jail, box 21, CHMS; Register of Slaves Entering the Police Jail, Police Jail Records, NOPL.

84. Brown to "Master of the Work House," March 1, 1856, J. A. Alston to "Master of the Workhouse," February 9, 1856, L. M. to "Master of the Work house," February 1856, A. V. Dawson to "Master of the Work House," May 3, 1856, and Rob Rowan Withers, February 18, 1856, all in HM 48564, Duncan McKercher Papers, Huntington Library, San Marino, CA.

85. *State of Louisiana vs. Jim, a Slave of George Holloway*, filed June 3, 182 no. 289, in folder 8, box 18, and *State vs. Church, a Slave*, filed May 7, 1825 273, in folder 35, box 10, both in Stray Court Records, NOPL; *Daily Pi* Orleans), February 17, 1843; Rachel O'Connor to Mary Weeks, June 5,

Mistress of Evergreen Plantation, 98–200; *St. Landry Whig* (Opelousas, LA), November 28, 1844, April 24, 1845. On Louisiana's slave tribunal system, see Schafer, "'Under the Present Mode of Trial.'"

86. *Louis Doubrère, f.m.c., v. Grillier's Syndic*, docket no. 860, 2 Mart. (N.S.) 171 (1824), SCLC; "Marie to the District Court, West Baton Rouge Parish, Louisiana, 1848," in Schweninger, *Southern Debate over Slavery*, 2:49–51; Nathaniel Jenkins, petition, filed May 19, 1821, First Judicial District Court of New Orleans, New Orleans Public Library (PAR no. 20882118), Tyrone Middleton, petition, filed February 2, 1846, Catahoula Parish Courthouse, Harrisonburg, LA (PAR no. 20884604), and A. T. Margraf, petition, filed March 7, 1855, Fifth Judicial District Court, New Orleans Public Library (PAR no. 20885508), all in *Race, Slavery, and Free Blacks*, ser. 2, pt. F, reels 3, 12, 17; Bremer, *Homes of the New World*, 2:210–11; Brown, *My Southern Home*, 220.

87. Anderson, *Life and Narrative*, 21; A Resident, *New Orleans as It Is*, 71; Brown, *My Southern Home*, 119–20.

88. Graph 1.2 omits a negligible number of admittances (sixteen persons, or 0.1 percent) committed from other sources (in most cases, the hospital). Data in graph 1.2 derive from Register of Slaves Entering the Police Jail, Police Jail Records, NOPL.

89. *Constance Bique Perrine v. City of New Orleans, Edward Planchard, appellant and als.*, docket no. 6036, 15 La. Ann. 133 (1860), SCLC.

90. In contrast to other police jail records, notation within the Third Municipality ledger is inconsistent. The Third Municipality was the poorest of the three, and its government had a warranted reputation for sloppiness. Here I have excluded data of all prisoners for whom jailors omitted any owner's name, many of whom—though it is impossible to know how many—were free Black prisoners confined as slaves. I have also omitted data from 193 commitments for whom jailors did not provide any reason for commitment. "Safekeeping" includes sixty-two persons listed as "free of charges" or "not a runaway." "Other" includes commitments for unspecified crimes (such as "violating ordinances" or "for punishment"), court commitments, and commitments for miscellaneous crimes (for example, "cruelty to horse") that defy division into other categories. Data in graph 1.3 derive from Record Book of the Third Municipality Police Jail, box 21, CHMS.

91. "Liste des prisonniers détenus à la Geôle de Police du 22 Septembre 1825 au 31 Mai 1840 (non employés aux travaux)," and "Liste de Nègres de Chaine détenus à la Geôle de Police employés aux Travaux Publics de le Municipalité No 1 du 6 Janvier 1836 au 31 Mai 1840," both in Registers of Chained Slaves Employed in the Public Works, vol. 4, Police Jail Records, NOPL; Report of Prisoners Remaining in the Police Jail of the Second Municipality, October 1, 1843, folder 3, box 19, and "List of Slaves Remaining in the Police Jail the 11th Day of May 1846," in Record Book of the Third Municipality Police Jail, box 21, both in CHMS. Data in graph 1.4 derive from Register of Slaves Entering the Police Jail, Police Jail Records, NOPL.

92. Registers of Chained Slaves Employed in the Public Works, vol. 1, Police Jail Records, NOPL. Chain gang receipts from 1822 to 1828 suggest a similar ratio of days worked to days incarcerated. "Mandat de Payement . . . Salaire de Nègre de Chaîne"], 1822, 1825, 1828, folders 3, 5, 6, box 7, CHMS.

93. Savannah abandoned its slave workhouse in the early nineteenth century, moving

inmates into a segregated wing of the city prison. Smalls, "Behind Workhouse Walls"; Strickland, *All for Liberty*; Wood, "Prisons, Workhouses, and the Control of Slave Labour."

94. For Louisville, see "Charter of the City of Louisville," approved February 13, 1828, in Strattan and Vaughan, *Collection of the State and Municipal Laws*, 47–63; and Bibb, *Narrative of the Life*, 91–93. For Nashville, see "An Act to Remove the Quarters of the Work-House and for Other Purposes," approved December 22, 1859, "An Act to Amend the Revenue Laws of the City of Nashville," approved April 24, 1856, § 12, and "An Act to Regulate Slaves and Free Persons of Color within the City of Nashville," approved May 7, 1850, all in Raines, *Compilation of the General Laws of the City of Nashville*, 143–44, 178–80, 223–26. For St. Louis, see "An Ordinance in Relation to Negroes and Mulattoes," approved July 8, 1846, § 7, and "An Ordinance in Relation to the Work House," approved August 12, 1846, both in Drake, *Revised Ordinances of the City of Saint Louis*, 229–30, 306–11. Construction of Augusta's workhouse, though not completed until 1866, was initially intended for slaves, suspect free Black people, and vagrant white people; see *Daily Chronicle and Sentinel* (Augusta), May 7, 18, June 15, 1859.

95. *Mississippi Free Trader* (Natchez), November 5, 1838; *Voice of Freedom* (Montpelier, VT), November 16, 1843; Watkins, *Struggles for Freedom*, 22; American Anti-Slavery Society, "Slave Market of America."

96. Corey, *History of the Richmond Theological Seminary*, 49–50; Finley, "'Cash to Corinna.'"

97. Prison Discipline Society, *Sixteenth Annual Report*, 63–74.

98. "An Act Concerning the Penitentiary," approved February 10, 1845, in *Acts of the General Assembly of the Commonwealth of Kentucky*, 83–84; Sneed, *Report on the History and Mode of Management of the Kentucky Penitentiary*, 343, 366, 377, 383, 422, 437, 448–49; Thompson, *Prison Life and Reflections*, 315.

99. Anderson, *Life and Narrative*, 11, 17, 23–24, 44; Douglass, *Narrative of the Life*, 91–93; Jacobs, *Incidents in the Life of a Slave Girl*, 23, 25, 37, 62, 95, 101, 108, 154–57, 160, 176.

100. James Bolton, interview, in Works Progress Administration, *Slave Narratives*, vol. 4, pt. 1, pp. 92–104.

101. *Lafourche Gazette* (Donaldson, LA), May 20, 1826; *Louisiana State Gazette* (New Orleans), June 20, 1826; *New Orleans Argus*, November 9, 1828; *New Orleans Daily Crescent*, December 1, 1848.

102. Anonymous to Arthur Tappan, 1833, in Ames, *"Liberty,"* 136; M. Gillis to St. John R. Liddell, October 22, 1856, folder 80, box 12, Moses and St. John Richard Liddell Family Papers, LLVC; Rachel O'Connor to Mary Weeks, April 9 and May 6, 1833, and June 5, 1836, all in Webb, *Mistress of Evergreen Plantation*, 97–99, 102–3, 198–200; Follett, *Sugar Masters*, 144; entry of January 15, 1823, Registers of Chained Slaves Employed in the Public Works, vol. 2, Police Jail Records, NOPL.

103. "An Act in Relation to Runaway Slaves in this State," approved March 17, 1826, in *Louisiana Acts, 1826*, pp. 90–95; "An Act to Amend an Act, Entitled 'An Act Relative to Runaway Slaves in this State,'" approved January 16, 1827, in *Louisiana Acts, 1827*, pp. 30–33; "An Act Supplementary to Several Acts Relative to Runaway Slaves, in this

State," approved March 9, 1833, in *Louisiana Acts, 1833*, pp. 51–52; "An Act to Incorporate the Town of Donaldsonville," approved April 22, 1846, in *Louisiana Acts, 1846*, § 15, pp. 15–19; "An Act Establishing the Jail at Plaquemines, in the Parish of Iberville, a Depot for Runaway Slaves," approved April 7, 1847, and "An Act Establishing the Jail of the Parish of St. Tammany, a Depot for Runaway Slaves," approved April 19, 1847, both in *Louisiana Acts, 1847*, pp. 79, 98.

104. By 1852, Baton Rouge newspapers published monthly chain gang account statements. Court records from 1862 show that the St. Tammany Parish jail, a former slave depot, maintained chain gang labor regimes, printed forms, and fee structures identical to that of the New Orleans facility, suggesting the existence of an administrative bureaucracy for the maintenance of chain gangs. *Baton Rouge Gazette*, December 26, 1840, April 1, 1848; *State vs. Jeff, Billy and Joseph*, filed September 29, 1862, folder 4, box 6, Justice Court, Archives Department, St. Tammany Parish Clerk of Court's Office, Covington, LA.

105. "An Act Relative to Slaves and Free Colored Persons," approved March 15, 1855, § 80, in *Louisiana Acts, 1855*, pp. 377–91; "An Act Providing for Runaway Slaves and Establishing a General Depot for the Same," approved March 19, 1857, in *Louisiana Acts, 1857*, pp. 172–75.

106. R. Parkinson to "President and Board of Council," February 25, March 4 and 18, April 1 and 29, May 13, and December 11, 1841, all in Reports by Police Officers of Work and Repairs, vol. 3, Police Department, City of Lafayette, NOPL. There is some evidence that smaller Mississippi towns also used ad hoc slave penal labor: see "An Act to Prescribe the Duties of Jailors in Relation to Runaway Slaves, and to Fix the Penalty for Violating the Same," approved March 5, 1846, in Hutchinson, *Code of Mississippi*, 541; *Garrett v. Hamblin*, 11 Smed. and M. (Miss.) 219, (1848); and Sydnor, *Slavery in Mississippi*, 124.

107. Howe, "Scene in a Slave Prison"; Trent, *Manliest Man*. On the eroticization of pain in reformist literature, see Halttunen, "Humanitarianism and the Pornography of Pain."

108. Howe, "Scene in a Slave Prison," 179–80.

109. For inmates' uniforms, see Perrilliat to Louis Philippe de Roffignac, January 1823, folder 3, ser. 5A, box 1, SFLC.

110. Paton, *No Bond but the Law*, 21.

111. "Contrat de bâtisse entre Messieurs Gobet et Larochette et la municipalité no 1," act no. 103, filed October 17, 1836, notary Felix de Armas, and "Réparations de la Geôle de Police," act no. 63, filed February 25, 1847, notary Joseph Cuvillier, both in Notarial Archives Research Center, New Orleans; A. Guerties et al., grand jury report, January 23, 1838, folder 9, box 11, Municipal Papers, LARC.

112. A Resident, *New Orleans as It Is*, 71–72.

113. Meeting of June 20, 1848, Journal of Minutes and Proceedings, vol. 5, Second Municipality Council Records, NOPL; Girod to Conseil de Ville, May 8, 1813, vol. 5, MM-CDV.

114. Anderson, *Life and Narrative*, 21–22; Brown, *My Southern Home*, 118; Watkins, *Struggles for Freedom*, 22; *Constance Bique Perrine v. City of New Orleans, Edward Planchard, appellant and als.*, docket no. 6036, 15 La. Ann. 133 (1860), SCLC.

115. *Green-Mountain Freeman* (Montpelier, VT), May 6, 1847; *Anti-Slavery Bugle* (New Lisbon, OH), August 18, 1849; *Emancipator* (New York), September 20, 1838.

116. Adams, *Manuel Pereira*, 130; Anderson, *Life and Narrative*, 23; Brown, *My Southern Home*, 118; Watkins, *Struggles for Freedom*, 22; *Emancipator and Weekly Chronicle* (Boston), April 23, 1845; *Belmont Chronicle* (St. Clairsville, OH), January 1, 1857; Samuel Gridley Howe to Horace Mann, December 23–26, 1841, in Richards, *Letters and Journals*, 112–15.

117. Anderson, *Life and Narrative*, 21; Benwell, *Englishman's Travels*, 114–15; Brown, *My Southern Home*, 118; Howe, "Scene in a Slave Prison," 177–80; Watkins, *Struggles for Freedom*, 22; *Daily Picayune* (New Orleans), June 13, September 6, 1845.

118. James Mather to Conseil de Ville, April 25, 1812, vol. 5, MM-CDV; *Daily Picayune* (New Orleans), January 25, 1843.

119. Daybooks of Public Works Performed, 4 vols., and Recapitulations of Employment on the Public Works, 2 vols., both in First Municipality Surveyor's Office Records, and Daily Reports of Superintendent of Laborers and Carts and Overseers of Chain Gangs, Street Commissioner's Office Records, all in NOPL.

120. *North Star* (Rochester, NY), February 2, 1849; Latrobe, *Impressions Respecting New Orleans*, 57; A Resident, *New Orleans as It Is*, 72; *Daily Picayune* (New Orleans), March 1, 1867.

121. Daybooks of Public Works Performed, 4 vols., and Recapitulations of Employment on the Public Works, 2 vols., both in First Municipality Surveyor's Office Records, and Daily Reports of Superintendent of Laborers and Carts and Overseers of Chain Gangs, Street Commissioner's Office Records, all in NOPL; meetings of June 3, 1820, bk. 2, vol. 3, June 19, 1824, bk. 1, vol. 4, and January 14 and November 4, 1826, bk. 1, vol. 5, all in OP-CDV; J. Dillie to Denis Prieur, May 19, 1828, folder 1, box 8, CHMS; *New Orleans Argus*, July 18, 1829; *Daily Picayune* (New Orleans), January 25, 1843, June 23, 1852, *New Orleans Daily Creole*, October 30, 1856; *New Orleans Daily Crescent*, September 17, 1852, March 31, 1856.

122. *Farmers' Cabinet* (Amherst, MA), December 7, 1832; "Plague in the South-West," 619; *Daily Picayune* (New Orleans), August 9, 1853; *Planters' Banner* (Franklin, LA), August 18, 1853.

123. Marx, *Capital*, 352.

124. Meeting of July 11, 1815, vol. 2, bk. 5, OP-CDV, NOPL; "Ordinance to Regulate the Service of Slaves Employed in the City Works and to Allow a Remuneration to the Owners who Shall Put on the Chain Gang One or More Slaves, to be Employed in the Said Works," approved November 10, 1817, vol. 2, subser. 1, OR-CDV. Data presented in graph 1.5 derive from 1,049 chain gang receipts and 244 prisoners listed in a ledger of the First District chain gang. "Mandat de Payement . . . Salaire de Nègre de Chaîne," 1814, 1818, folders 2–12, box 13, Municipal Papers, and "Mandat de Payement . . . Salaire de Nègre de Chaîne," 1814, 1819, boxes 16 and 17, subser. A, ser. 4, Kuntz Collection, both in LARC; "Mandat de Payement . . . Salaire de Nègre de Chaîne," 1822, 1825, 1828, folders 1–7, box 7, CHMS; [Second Municipality Vouchers], 1843–1845, folders 8, 10, 13, box 1, ser. 6A, SFLC; [Second Municipality Vouchers], 1843–1845, folder 7, box 7, CHMS; [First District Chain Gang Register, 1852–1854], enclosed in MMR.

125. *North Star* (Rochester, NY), February 2, 1849; Anderson, *Life and Narrative*, 21.

126. Brown, *Slave Life in Georgia*, 123; John Hatfield, testimonial, in Drew, *North-Side View of Slavery*, 363–66.

127. Ingraham, *South-West*, 2:185; *New-Orleans Commercial Times*, June 7, 1848.

128. *New-York Evening Post*, April 22, 1826; *Daily Picayune* (New Orleans), April 9, 1844; September 17, 1846; *Emancipator and Weekly Chronicle* (Boston), March 5, 1845; *Herald of Freedom* (Concord, NH), May 16, 1845; *Anti-Slavery Bugle* (Salem, OH), March 3, 1855; *George Lewis v. City of New Orleans*, docket no. 4679, 12 La. Ann. 190, (1857), SCLC.

129. *New Orleans Daily Crescent*, November 18, 1854; Pavie and Klier, *Pavie in the Borderlands*, 221.

130. *Constance Bique Perrine v. City of New Orleans, Edward Planchard, appellant and als.*, docket no. 6036, 15 La. Ann. 133 (1860), SCLC.

131. Latrobe, *Impressions Respecting New Orleans*, 57–58; Ingraham, *South-West*, 2:185; Caroline Hale to Mary Hale and Alice L. March, March 14, 1844, Caroline Hale Letter, LARC; Charles Trudeau to James Mather, November 28, 1807, folder 41, box 4, Wisdom Collection, LARC.

132. Meeting of June 3, 1820, bk. 3, vol. 3, OP-CDV; ordinance of June 7, 1820, vol. 5, subser. 2, OR-CDV.

133. Entry of September 3, 1842, Daybooks of Public Works Performed, vol. 4, First Municipality Surveyor's Office Records, NOPL.

134. *New Orleans Daily Crescent*, January 24, 1850; Johnson, *William Johnson's Natchez*.

135. Barrow, *Plantation Life in the Florida Parishes*, 169, 178, 277.

136. Tally-Ho Plantation overseer quoted in Follett, *Sugar Masters*, 144; Anonymous to Arthur Tappan, 1833, in Ames, *"Liberty,"* 136.

137. Calculations exclude all committals for which place of origin, or committing party, were omitted. Jail Register, Jail Registers and Jail Prisoner Books, Police Department Records, City of Savannah Research Library and Municipal Archives, available at ancestry.com.

138. See especially *Daily Picayune* (New Orleans), June 10, 1845.

139. On violence and the household, see especially Glymph, *Out of the House of Bondage*.

140. Douglass, *My Bondage and My Freedom*, 147–48; Benwell, *Englishman's Travels*, 114; A Resident, *New Orleans as It Is*, 71; Hall, *Travels in North America*, 3:167; Hughes, *Thirty Years a Slave*, 9; Bodichon, "Slavery in the South," 179; Jacques Telesphore Roman to Célina Roman, March 15, 1841, folder 3, box 1, Roman Family Papers, LARC; Hindus, *Prison and Plantation*, 149; Wade, *Slavery in the Cities*, 95.

141. Follett, *Sugar Masters*, 176–78; Greenberg, *Masters and Statesmen*, 20–22; Gross, *Double Character*, 105–11; Jones, *Born a Child of Freedom*, 77.

142. In the First Municipality register, the average prison term among enslaved men (n = 7,708) was 19.9 days; among enslaved women (n = 4,388), the average prison term was 28.2 days. These figures exclude 134 commitments without a release date. A total of 2,510 committals were made by prisoners' owners, of which women constituted 1,094 (43.6 percent). In the Third Municipality register, women constituted 1,300 of the 4,000 enslaved commitments (32.5 percent) but 226 of the 548 enslaved commitments for

"safekeeping" (41.2 percent) and 11 of the 27 enslaved commitments "for punishment" (40.7 percent). For these calculations, inmates' genders were inferred by their given names. Committals of persons with illegible or unisex given names—145 commitments listed in the First Municipality register, and 56 commitments listed in the Third Municipality register—are excluded from these figures. Register of Slaves Entering the Police Jail, Police Jail Records, NOPL; Record Book of the Third Municipality Police Jail, box 21, CHMS.

143. Anderson, *Life and Narrative*, 22; Brown, *Slave Life in Georgia*, 123; Jacobs, *Incidents in the Life*, 62, 154–57.

144. Glymph, *Out of the House of Bondage*, 54–59.

145. For example, among ten unclaimed enslaved prisoners sold at auction in 1845, six were women. Augustin François de Macarty to Conseil de Ville, September 30, 1815, vol. 6, MM-CDV; "Liste des Esclaves marrons détenus à la Geôle de Police Première Municipalité," September 18, 1844, folder 3, box 19, CHMS; "Les Esclaves dont les Noms suivent, vendus à l'encan le 30 Août 1845, Doivent à la Geôle de Police 1re Municipalité," [1845], "Liste des prisonniers détenus à la Geôle de Police du 22 Septembre 1825 au 31 Mai 1840 (non employés aux travaux)," and "Liste de Nègres de Chaine détenus à la Geôle de Police employés aux Travaux Publics de le Municipalité No 1 du 6 Janvier 1836 au 31 Mai 1840," all in Registers of Chained Slaves Employed in the Public Works, vol. 4, Police Jail Records, NOPL; entry of August 18, 1838, Register of Slaves Entering the Police Jail, Police Jail Records, NOPL; Charles Duron et al., grand jury report, February 4, 1842, in Minute Book, vol. 4, Criminal Court of the First District Records, NOPL.

146. Foucault, *Discipline and Punish*, 261. On performance and race, see Gross, *What Blood Won't Tell*, esp. 48–72; Hale, *Making Whiteness*, 199–239; Hartman, *Scenes of Subjection*; Johnson, "Slave Trader"; and Wood, *Lynching and Spectacle*.

147. Entry of June 20, 1848, Journal of Minutes and Proceedings, vol. 5, Second Municipality Council Records, NOPL; Benwell, *Englishman's Travels*, 114.

148. Bloom, *Against Empathy*.

149. Goodell, *American Slave Code*, 287.

Chapter 2

1. Ayers, *Vengeance and Justice*, 46–48; Hirsch, *Rise of the Penitentiary*, 71–72, 74, 77–78, 199–200n42; Manion, *Liberty's Prisoners*, 9–10, 63–64; Smith, *Prison and the American Imagination*, 41–44, 50, 73.

2. On "racial modernity" in the United States, see Kantrowitz, *More Than Freedom*, esp. 24–27; Roediger, *Wages of Whiteness*; Saxton, *Rise and Fall of the White Republic*; and Stewart, "Emergence of Racial Modernity."

3. For the preliminary draft of Livingston's penal code, see Livingston, *Report Made to the General Assembly*. For the finalized codes, see Livingston, *System of Penal Law, for the State of Louisiana*.

4. "Offenses committed by slaves, form the subject of a separate code, they are not included in any of the provisions of this." Livingston, *Report Made to the General Assembly*, 128.

5. Foucault, *Discipline and Punish*; Ignatieff, *Just Measure of Pain*; Manion,

Liberty's Prisoners; Melossi and Pavarini, *Prison and the Factory*; Meranze, *Laboratories of Virtue*; Rothman, *Discovery of the Asylum*.

6. "Rapport," February 26–28, July 15–17, and November 30–December 1, 1820, all in Daily Reports, vol. 1, Police Jail Records, NOPL; "Rapport," January 13–15, March 21–22, March 24–25, June 15–16, July 7–8, August 24–25, November 13–14, and December 10–11, 1821, all in box 10, and July 3–5 and July 12–13, 1822, both in box 11, all in CHMS.

7. For a progressive "modernizing narrative," see Muhammad, *Condemnation of Blackness*, 5. Also see Kamerling, *Capital and Convict*; and Thompson, "Blinded by a 'Barbaric' South." The essentialization of southern and northern penal traditions dates at least to the antebellum period. Writing in 1833, the noted German American jurist Francis Lieber asserted that Livingston's progressive penal philosophy was patently uninfluenced by Livingston's "residence in Louisiana" and "of a decided Anglo-American character." Beaumont and Tocqueville, *On the Penitentiary System*, 9–10.

8. Ayers, *Vengeance and Justice*, 61. On the penitentiary movement in the South, also see Carleton, *Politics and Punishment*, chap. 1; Perkins, *Texas Tough*, chap. 2; and Ward and Rogers, *Alabama's Response to the Penitentiary Movement*.

9. Edward Livingston, "Introductory Report to the Code of Crimes and Punishments," introduced to the Louisiana legislature in 1826 and reproduced in Livingston, *System of Penal Law, for the State of Louisiana*, 113–96, esp. 146.

10. On punishments, racial difference, and cultural production, see Browne, *Dark Matters*; Dawdy, "Burden of Louis Congo"; Pierce and Rao, "Discipline and the Other Body," 4–7, 21; Garland, *Punishment and Modern Society*; Hartman, *Scenes of Subjection*; Paton, *No Bond but the Law*, esp. 27–28.

11. Hunt, *Memoir of Mrs. Edward Livingston*.

12. On the uncontrolled diffusion of Enlightenment humanitarianism, see Campbell, *Slavery on Trial*, esp. 4–5; and Johnson, "Inconsistency, Contradiction, and Complete Confusion."

13. Ayers, *Vengeance and Justice*, 34; Lewis, *From Newgate to Dannemora*, 65–70; McLennan, *Crisis of Imprisonment*, 53–57; Johnston, *Forms of Constraint*, 69–79.

14. Benjamin Levy et al., grand jury report, January 9, 1832, in Minute Book, vol. 1, and Charles Papet et al., grand jury report, June 23, 1834, in Minute Book, vol. 2, both in Criminal Court of the First District Records, NOPL; *Louisiana House Journal*, 10th leg., 1st sess., pp. 98–99; Thomas Robertson, governor's annual message, in *Louisiana House Journal*, 5th leg. 1st sess., pp. 30–34, esp. 32; *Louisiana Courier* (New Orleans), February 18, 1822.

15. Beaumont and Tocqueville, *On the Penitentiary System*, 13.

16. Charles Papet et al., grand jury report, June 23, 1834, in Minute Book, vol. 2, Criminal Court of the First District Records, NOPL; Henry Johnson, governor's annual message, in *Louisiana House Journal*, 7th leg., 2nd sess., p. 9; Thomas Robertson, governor's annual message, in *Louisiana House Journal*, 5th leg., 1st sess., December 18, 1820, p. 23; Jacques Dupre, governor's annual message, in *Louisiana House Journal*, 5th leg., 1st sess., p. 12; Denis Prieur to Conseil de Ville, April 5, 1833, vol. 15, MM-CDV.

17. Faber, *Building the Land of Dreams*, 175–76, 204, 325, 388n8; Flory, "Edward Livingston's Place in Louisiana Law"; Hatcher, *Edward Livingston*; Hunt, *Life of Edward Livingston*; Lyons, "Louisiana and the Livingston Criminal Codes," 249.

18. Livingston, *Introductory Report to the Code of Prison Discipline*, 12, 16.

19. Hirsch, *Rise of the Penitentiary*, 13, 16, 24, 27, 37, 43; Manion, *Liberty's Prisoners*, 34; Montgomery, *Citizen Worker*, 83–89; Rodgers, *Work Ethic in Industrial America*, 11–12, 94, 123, 194, 223–24; Rothman, *Discovery of the Asylum*, 103.

20. Livingston, *Introductory Report to the Code of Prison Discipline*, 16, 49; Livingston and Vaux, *Letter from Edward Livingston*, 13; Livingston, *Introductory Report to the Code of Procedure*, 11.

21. Livingston, *Introductory Report to the Code of Procedure*, 53, 56; Lyons, "Louisiana and the Livingston Codes," 255.

22. Livingston, *Introductory Report to the Code of Prison Discipline*, 26, 29; Livingston, *Introductory Report to the Code of Procedure*, 56.

23. Livingston did not evade the topic of slavery, simply the experiences or punishments of enslaved people themselves. His writings discuss punishments aimed at free persons convicted of slave stealing, and the procedures by which legally free persons illegally held in slavery should seek redress, in detail. See, for example, "System of Penal Law for the United States," 51, 103, and "Code of Procedure to be Observed in Executing the Laws of the United States," 19–20, 25, 110, 112, 167, both in Livingston, *System of Penal Law for the United States of America*.

24. Livingston, "Introductory Report to the Code of Crimes and Punishments," 146.

25. Livingston and Vaux, *Letter from Edward Livingston*, 10.

26. Davis, *Problem of Slavery in the Age of Revolution*, 241–42, 254, 382, 456, 464; Hirsch, *Rise of the Penitentiary*, 76–77, 106–9; Manion, *Liberty's Prisoners*, 9–10, 63–64; Meranze, *Laboratories of Virtue*, 1; Paton, *No Bond but the Law*, 5–6.

27. Ayers, *Vengeance and Justice*, 46–49; *Alexandria Gazette*, June 5, 1840; Sawyer, *Southern Institutes*, 234–35; Holmes, "Ancient Slavery, Part 1"; Smith, *Prison and the American Imagination*, 41–44, 50, 73.

28. Livingston and Vaux, *Letter from Edward Livingston*, 6, 13–14.

29. Henderson, *Correction and Prevention*, 1:151–57; Hunt, *Life of Edward Livingston*, 278, 404–5, 278; Lyons, "Louisiana and the Livingston Criminal Codes," 258, 261; Mouledous, "Pioneers in Criminology," 288; Jeremy Bentham to Edward Livingston, February 23, 1830, in Bowring, *Works of Jeremy Bentham*, 9:35–36.

30. Livingston, *System of Penal Law for the United States of America*; Mackey, "Edward Livingston and the Origins of the Movement to Abolish Capital Punishment," 159.

31. Vaux, *Letter on the Penitentiary System of Pennsylvania*, 10; Smith, *Defense of the System*, 23–24; Rothman, *Discovery of the Asylum*, 85–86.

32. Blake McKelvey calls Livingston the first "dean" of Jacksonian-era rehabilitative penology; McKelvey, *American Prisons*, 37–38. Other scholars, observing similarities between solitary confinement and Quakers' mode of silent worship, have assumed that Philadelphia's Quaker community inspired Pennsylvania's separate system, though the latest study rejects this attribution; Rubin, *Deviant Prison*.

33. Vaux, *Notices of the Original*, 56; Beaumont and Tocqueville, *On the Penitentiary System*, 9; Smith, *Defense of the System*, 94; Livingston and Vaux, *Letter from Edward Livingston*, 10–11; *National Gazette and Literary Register* (Philadelphia), July 20, 1825, March 29, December 5, 1826. The concept of voluntary penal labor was already in circulation in Philadelphia, predating Livingston's influence; see Rubin, *Deviant Prison*, 23.

34. For examples of Livingston's influence on European penology, see Combe, *Remarks on the Principles of Criminal Legislation*, 13, 81–85; Ducpétiaux, *Des progrès et de l'état actuel de la réforme pénitentiaire*, 1:127–34, 216–18; Faucher, *De la réforme des prisons*, 64, 72, 85; Julius, "Die Aussichten zur Gefängniß"; Oskar, *Über Strafe und Strafanstalten*, 42–43. On Europe's adaptation of the separate system, see Barnes, *Evolution of Penology in Pennsylvania*, 173–76; Cary, "France Looks to Pennsylvania"; and McKelvey, *American Prisons*, 38.

35. McLennan, *Crisis of Imprisonment*, 63–64.

36. *New Orleans Bee*, October 28, 1827; Report [of the Committee to Examine Public Prisons], January 23, 1828, in *Louisiana House Journal*, 8th leg., 1st sess., p. 22; Alexander, *Transatlantic Sketches*, 2:17.

37. Dawdy, "Burden of Louis Congo," 63, 70–71.

38. Livingston, *System of Penal Law, for the State of Louisiana*, 146.

39. Louis Philippe de Roffignac to Conseil de Ville, October 27, 1827, in vol. 12, MM-CDV; ordinance of December 1, 1828, vol. 13, subser. 2, OR-CDV; Report [of the Committee to Examine Public Prisons], January 23, 1828, in *Louisiana House Journal*, 8th leg., 1st sess., p. 22.

40. *Louisiana Courier* (New Orleans), April 6, 11, 13, 17, 1829.

41. Pierre Derbigny to Conseil de Ville, April 10, 1829, vol. 3, Letters, Petitions and Reports, Conseil de Ville Records, NOPL.

42. *Creole* (Donaldsonville, LA), reprinted in *Louisiana Courier* (New Orleans), April 22, 1829; Jean Boze to Henri de Ste-Gême, March 10, 1830, folder 160, Ste-Gême Family Papers, HNOC.

43. Pierre Derbigny to Conseil de Ville, April 11, 1829, in *Louisiana Courier* (New Orleans), April 11, 1829; *New York American*, May 7, 1829.

44. Carleton, *Politics and Punishment*, chap. 1.

45. J. B. Lepretre et al., grand jury report, July 8, 1837, and A. Querties et al., grand jury report, January 25, 1838, both in folder 9, box 11, New Orleans Municipal Papers, LARC.

46. Stern, *Race and Education in New Orleans*, chap. 1.

47. "Rules for the internal regulation of the work house," [1842], in Proceedings of the Board of Inspectors of the Workhouse, House of Refuge, and Prison of the First Municipality, vol. 1, subser. 4, OR-CDV; *Daily Picayune* (New Orleans), February 5, May 10, 1842, October 27, 1843.

48. The original House of Refuge was only for boys and served only the Second Municipality. In 1852, the House of Refuge was designated for use by the entire city. A separate House of Refuge for girls was completed in 1854. Ordinance No. 1104, approved April 29, 1845, and Ordinance No. 33, approved May 17, 1852, both in Henderson, *Synopsis of Ordinances*, n.p.; Ordinance No. 1,340, approved February 23, 1854, in Leovy and Luzenberg, *Laws and General Ordinances of the City of New Orleans*, 194. For the House of Refuge's mission and methods, see House of Refuge Minute Book, vol. 1, NOPL; *Report of the Board of Commissioners of the House of Refuge*, 4; *Memorial of the Board of Commissioners of the House of Refuge*; and Walker, *City Digest*, 29. On the House of Refuge movement, see Pisciotta, "Treatment on Trial"; and Rothman, *Discovery of the Asylum*, 77, 209–40, 257–64.

49. Chaillé, *Memoir of the Insane Asylum*, 3.

50. Emerson, "Man the Reformer," 146.

51. Grimes, *Institutional Care*, 123–25; Rothman, *Discovery of the Asylum*, 130, 180, 209.

52. Entry of December 13, 1842, Journal of Minutes and Proceedings, vol. 2, Second Municipality Council Records, NOPL; grand jury report, March 14, 1835, in Minute Book, vol. 2, Criminal Court of the First District Records, NOPL; *Daily Picayune* (New Orleans), March 27, 1842; André Roman, governor's annual message, in *Louisiana Senate Journal*, 10th leg., 3rd sess., p. 7.

53. Hunt, *Life of Edward Livingston*, 432.

54. Grand jury report, March 14, 1835, in Minute Book, vol. 2, Criminal Court of the First District Records, NOPL; *New Orleans Bee*, July 13, 1837; *New Orleans Daily Crescent*, May 1, 1848.

55. On the "nearly identical language and formats" of escaped slave and escaped convict advertisements, see Manion, *Liberty's Prisoners*, 25. For examples, see *Louisiana State Gazette* (New Orleans), August 13, 1926; and *Louisiana Advertiser* (New Orleans), July 11, 1827.

56. *Louisiana Senate Journal*, 17th leg., 1st sess., pp. 4–5; Thomas Bailly Blanchard et al., October 3, 1842, in Minute Book, vol. 4, Criminal Court of the First District Records, NOPL; *Daily Picayune* (New Orleans), July 20, 1848.

57. On Saint-Domingue's *maréchaussée*, see Garrigus, *Before Haiti*; and King, *Blue Coat or Powdered Wig*. On Louisiana's free Black militias, see Hanger, *Bounded Lives, Bounded Places*; and Vidal, *Caribbean New Orleans*, 422–42.

58. Meeting of March 17, 1804, bk. 1, vol. 1, OP-CDV, NOPL; Bell, *Revolution, Romanticism, and the Afro-Creole Protest Tradition*, 79; Rousey, *Policing the Southern City*, 28–29.

59. Rousey, *Policing the Southern City*, 34, 50, 83–85, 100.

60. "Report of the Committee on the Penitentiary," March 18, 1840, in *Louisiana House Journal*, 14th leg., 2nd sess., p. 110; *New Orleans Weekly Delta*, May 10, 1847.

61. *Daily Delta* (New Orleans), February 13, 1853; *New Orleans Daily Crescent*, March 31, 1856; Record of Work Performed by the Workhouse, 2 vols., Workhouse Records, NOPL; House of Refuge, in Minute Book, vol. 1, House of Refuge Records, NOPL.

62. Record of Work Performed by the Workhouse, 2 vols., Workhouse Records, NOPL.

63. *Daily Picayune* (New Orleans), February 26, March 25, 1842.

64. *Daily Picayune* (New Orleans), March 13, 1841, November 24, 1843, December 12, 1844.

65. Thomas Bailly Blanchard et al., grand jury report, October 3, 1842, in Minute Book, vol. 4, Criminal Court of the First District Records, NOPL; Report of the Board of Inspectors of the Work House and Public Prisons of Municipality No. 2, December 13, 1842, in Journal of Minutes and Proceedings, vol. 2, Second Municipality Council Records, NOPL; *Daily Picayune* (New Orleans), May 10, December 4, 7, 14, 1842, February 8, 1846, July 12, 26, 1848.

66. Hypolite Lanoue to Board of Managers of the Prison Discipline Society, May 28,

1839, in *Fourteenth Annual Report of the Board of Managers of the Prison Discipline Society*, 103.

67. Hines, *Life and Adventures*, 151–52.

68. See especially A. Guerties et al., grand jury report, January 23, 1838, folder 9, box 11, Municipal Papers, LARC.

69. R. Brenan et al., grand jury report, August 7, 1845, in Minute Book, vol. 6, Criminal Court of the First District Records, NOPL; *Daily Picayune* (New Orleans), May 17, June 10, 12, 13, 14, 15, September 4, 5, 6, 1845; *Jeffersonian Republican* (New Orleans), June 14, 1845.

70. Entry of June 20, 1848, Journal of Minutes and Proceedings, vol. 5, Second Municipality Council Records, NOPL; *New Orleans Daily Crescent*, May 10, June 28, 1848; *New-Orleans Commercial Times*, June 7, 13, 27, 28, 1848.

71. Schafer, *Slavery, the Civil Law, and the Supreme Court*, 122, 124–25.

72. "Crimes and Offences Committed by Slaves and Free Colored Persons," §§ 1–7, 9, in Phillips, *Statutes of the State of Louisiana*, 52–55; Schafer, "Slaves and Crime," 56.

73. On the social functions of public executions, see Foucault, *Discipline and Punish*, esp. 94; Meranze, *Laboratories of Virtue*, 37–48; and Spierenburg, *Spectacle of Suffering*, 184–85. On slave executions, see Brown, "'A Black Mark on Our Legislation'"; Jones, *Born a Child of Freedom*, 23, 41, 92, 187; and McNair, "Slave Women, Capital Crime, and Criminal Justice."

74. *Daily Picayune* (New Orleans), July 19, 1837, August 8, 1841, February 28, 1842, March 29, 1846, September 22, 1855; Jean Boze to Henri de Ste-Gême, June 4–15, 1831, April 21–27, 1832, March 23–28, 1833, May 13–31, 1835, August 11–December 3, 1835, and April 1–May 5, 1837, folders 187, 203, 220, 253, 258, and 275, all in Ste-Gême Family Papers, HNOC; Castellanos, *New Orleans as It Was*, chap. 9; Thrasher, *On to New Orleans!*, 64–65.

75. *Daily Picayune* (New Orleans), February 26, 28, 1842, December 14, 1843, July 3, 1852; *St. Landry Whig* (Opelousas, LA), May 1, 1845; *Daily Comet* (Baton Rouge), June 2, September 30, 1855.

76. Entries of January 20 and 22, 1845, Official Proceedings, vol. 2, First Municipality Council Records, NOPL; Kendall, "Notes on the Criminal History of New Orleans," 149–50.

77. In a compromise, the legislature in 1852 granted slave tribunals discretionary power to order public slave executions on a case-by-case basis. "An Act to amend the Black Code," approved April 6, 1843, §§ 5–7, in *Louisiana Acts, 1843*, pp. 91–93; "An Act Relative to Trials of Slaves," approved June 1, 1846, in *Louisiana Acts, 1846*, pp. 114–16; *State of Louisiana v. Lewis, a Slave*, docket no. 584, 3 La. Ann. 398 (1848), SCLC; Schafer, "Slaves and Crime," 59, 60.

78. "Crimes and Offenses," approved June 7, 1806, § 12, in *Acts Passed at the First Session of the First Legislature of the Territory of Orleans*, 190–213; "An Act Relative to Trials of Slaves," approved June 1, 1846, § 10, in *Louisiana Acts, 1846*, pp. 114–16; Schafer, "Slaves and Crime," 58–59.

79. Pardons of condemned enslaved people were not uncommon: see *Report of the Board of Directors of the Penitentiary of the State of Louisiana*, 4.

80. Schafer, "Slaves and Crime," 59–60.

81. *Daily Picayune* (New Orleans), June 10, 23, 1838, August 1, 1846, September 22, 1855.

82. *Daily Picayune* (New Orleans), January 15, February 21, 1845, March 29, 28, 1846; *Jeffersonian Republican* (New Orleans), January 16, 1845; Castellanos, *New Orleans as It Was*, chap. 9.

83. Livingston, *Argument of Edward Livingston*; Davis, "Movement to Abolish Capital Punishment," 31–34, 36–37, 41–42; Jones, *Against the Gallows*, 18–19, 28–29, 32, 180, 186; Masur, *Rites of Execution*, 97–98, 143.

84. Johnson, "Inconsistency, Contradiction, and Complete Confusion," 406.

85. On slave incarceration within the Louisiana State Penitentiary, see Derbes, "'Secret Horrors'"; Fisher-Giorlando, "Women in the Walls"; Forret, "Before Angola"; Forret, *Williams' Gang*, chap. 11.

86. In graph 2.1, data for October 1, 1846, were calculated by using reports of inmates released, died, pardoned, transferred, admitted, and remaining over the year, as printed in the annual report for 1847. The penitentiary clerk made calculation errors in his figures for January 1, 1852, and January 2, 1854, resulting in minor inconsistencies between the clerk's overall headcount and the number of inmates listed on the published roster. For 1836 and 1837, see *Historical Epitome of the State of Louisiana*, 261. For 1838, see *Thirteenth Annual Report of the Board of Managers of the Prison Discipline Society*, 63. For 1839, see *Report on the Penitentiary* [1840]. For 1840, see "List of Convicts Remaining in the Louisiana Penitentiary," December 31, 1840, in *Louisiana House Journal*, 15th leg., 1st sess., n.p. For January 1843, see *Louisiana House Journal*, 17th leg., 1st sess., p. 40. For December 1843, see "Report of the Standing Committee on The State Penitentiary, made at the Second Session of the Sixteenth Legislature," in *Louisiana Senate Journal*, 16th leg., 2nd sess., appendix F, xlvi–xlviii. For 1844, see *Report on the Penitentiary, by a Joint Committee of the Senate and House of Representatives*, n.p. For 1845, see *Third Report of the Prison Association of New York*, 2:347. For 1846 and 1847, see *Report of the Board of Directors of the Penitentiary of the State of Louisiana*, 10–12. For 1848, see *Report [to His Excellency Isaac Johnson]*, n.p. For 1849, see *Report of the Board of Directors on the State Penitentiary*, 5. For 1850, see *Seventh Census of the United States*, reel 229, Baton Rouge, East Baton Rouge Parish, Louisiana, pp. 361–66, and reel 242, slave schedule, East Baton Rouge Parish, Louisiana, pp. 321–22. For 1851 and 1852, see *Report of the Board of Directors, on the State Penitentiary to the Governor of Louisiana*, 7. For 1853, see *Report of the Board of Directors of the Penitentiary of the State of Louisiana*, 4. For 1854, see *Annual Report of the Board of Directors, Clerk and Officers of the Louisiana State Penitentiary*, 2–7. For January 1855, see *Annual Report of the Board of Directors of the Louisiana Penitentiary*, 13–18. For December 1855 and 1856, see *Message of Robert C. Wickliffe*, 55–62. For 1857, see *Report of the Board of Control of the Louisiana Penitentiary, January 1858*, pp. 59–64. For 1858, see *Report of the Board of Control of the Louisiana Penitentiary*, 45–57. For 1859, see *Rapport du bureau de contrôle du pénitencier de la Louisiane*, 39–51. For 1860, see *Report of the Board of Control of the Louisiana Penitentiary*, 49–56. For 1861, see *Baton Rouge Tri-Weekly Gazette and Comet*, December 7, 1861.

87. *Southron* (Jackson, MS), January 27, 1842, January 31, 1844; "Slaves," §§ 14–20, in Gould, *Digest of the Statutes of Arkansas*, 1027–29; "An Act Concerning the

Penitentiary," § 5, approved February 10, 1845, in *Acts of the General Assembly of the Commonwealth of Kentucky*, 83–84; "An Act Providing for the Disposition of Runaway Slaves," approved April 8, 1861, in *Laws of the Eighth Legislature of the State of Texas*, 49–51; Brackett, *Negro in Maryland*, 123–26; Birch and Buchanan, "Penalty of a Tyrant's Law," 29; Dorsey, *Hirelings*, 85–86; Flanigan, "Criminal Law of Slavery and Freedom," 21–23; Highsaw, *Growth of State Administration in Mississippi*, 26; Sneed, *Report on the History and Mode of Management of the Kentucky Penitentiary*, 343, 366, 377, 383, 422, 437, 448–49; Sydnor, *Slavery in Mississippi*, 123; Taylor, *Negro Slavery in Arkansas*, 214–15; Thompson, *Prison Life and Reflections*, 315.

88. *Daily Dispatch* (Richmond), April 29, 1854. On the workhouse revolt, see Strickland, *All for Liberty*.

89. André Roman, governor's annual message, January 4, 1841, in *Louisiana House Journal*, 15th leg., 1st sess., p. 6; "Report of The Committee on the Penitentiary," March 18, 1840, in *Louisiana House Journal*, 14th leg., 2nd sess., p. 111; J. Perkins and James McCalep, "Report of the Committee Appointed by the Board of Inspectors," January 7, 1841, in *Louisiana House Journal*, 15th leg., 1st sess., p. 4.

90. William Freret to General Council, May 14, 1840, vol. 16, MM-CDV; "Report of The Committee on the Penitentiary," March 18, 1840, in *Louisiana House Journal*, 14th leg., 2nd sess., p. 111; "Report of the Committee Appointed by the Board of Inspectors," January 7, 1841, in *Louisiana House Journal*, 15th leg., 1st sess., p. 4; Alexandre Mouton, governor's annual message, January 1, 1844, in *Louisiana Senate Journal*, 16th leg., 2nd sess., p. 3.

91. Hall, "Slaves of the State"; Hall, "Public Slaves and State Engineers"; Forret, *Williams' Gang*, 258; Thompson, "Circuits of Containment," 160.

92. "An Act providing for the Manner of Employing the Colored Male Convicts in the Penitentiary, and for other Purposes," approved March 26, 1842, in *Louisiana Acts, 1842*, pp. 518–23; "An Act Amendatory of the Several Acts Relative to the Penitentiary," approved March 27, 1843, in *Louisiana Acts, 1843*, pp. 68–69; *State Engineer Annual Report, 1843*, pp. 16–19, 21–22; Alexandre Mouton, governor's annual message, January 1, 1844, in *Louisiana Senate Journal*, 16th leg., 2nd sess., p. 3.

93. Ayers, *Vengeance and Justice*, 66–67; Kamerling, *Capital and Convict*; McLennan, *Crisis of Imprisonment*, 53, 64–67.

94. Although James McHatton would hold the penitentiary lease through to the Civil War, a chain of other businessmen—including George Ward, Samuel Hart, and McHatton's brother, Charles McHatton—would replace Pratt as co-lessees. Carleton, *Politics and Punishment*, 9–12.

95. *Baton Rouge Gazette*, December 9, 1843; *Opelousas (LA) Patriot*, May 26, 1855; Carleton, *Politics and Punishment*, 10.

96. *Baton Rouge Gazette*, April 30, May 7, 1842; Martin Penn, "Report of the State Engineer," in *Louisiana House Journal*, 16th leg., 2nd sess., pp. ii–iii; *Report on the Penitentiary, by a Joint Committee of the Senate and House of Representatives*, n.p.; Forret, *Williams' Gang*, 271.

97. "An Act to Provide for the Return of the Colored Convicts to the Penitentiary, and for other Purposes," approved March 8, 1845, in *Louisiana Acts, 1845*, pp. 28–29.

98. *Report of the Board of Directors of the Louisiana Penitentiary*, 4.

99. *Report [of the Committee Appointed to Investigate the Discrepancies between the Accounts of the Lessees of the Penitentiary]*, 9–10.

100. Hines, *Life and Adventures*, 152.

101. Hines, *Life and Adventures*, 152; *New Orleans Weekly Delta*, August 15, 1852; *Weekly Comet* (Baton Rouge), October 29, 1854; *Daily Picayune* (New Orleans), July 8, 1856; *Baton Rouge Tri-Weekly Gazette and Comet*, July 1, 1857.

102. *Daily Picayune* (New Orleans), October 8, 1840; *Annual Report of the Board of Directors, Clerk and Officers of the Louisiana Penitentiary*, 7; *Message of Robert C. Wickliffe*, 22; *Daily Gazette and Comet* (Baton Rouge), May 28, 1857.

103. *Report of the Board of Control of the Louisiana Penitentiary*, 6–7, 11.

104. *Baton Rouge Gazette*, March 13, 1852; *New Orleans Weekly Delta*, March 12, 1857; "The Prisoners in the Parish Prison" to Benjamin Butler, May 6, 1862, box 11, Benjamin F. Butler Papers, LOC.

105. *New Orleans Daily Crescent*, May 12, 1856, October 17, 1857; *New Orleans Daily Creole*, July 24, October 9, 1856.

106. *Daily Picayune* (New Orleans), September 19, 20, 1856; *New Orleans Daily Crescent*, September 20, 1856.

107. *Daily Picayune* (New Orleans), July 7, 1857, July 10, 1859; *New Orleans Daily Crescent*, October 17, 1857.

108. Richter, "Slavery in Baton Rouge," 135.

109. "An Act Relative to Slaves and Free Colored Persons," approved March 15, 1855, §§ 80, 85, in *Louisiana Acts, 1855*, pp. 377–91.

110. *State Engineer Annual Report, 1858*, pp. 8–9, 24; *Annual Report of the Auditor of Public Accounts*, 57–58; "Joint Resolution for a Special Committee to Examine the Jails and Lock-Ups in New Orleans, to See whether the Law is Complied with in Relation to Runaway Negroes," approved March 19, 1861, in *Louisiana Acts, 1861*, p. 134.

111. *Report of the Board of Directors of the Louisiana Penitentiary*, 4.

112. "An Act Providing for the Disposal of Such Slaves as are or may be Born in the Penitentiary, the Issue of Convicts," approved December 11, 1848, in *Louisiana Acts, 1848*, pp. 3–4; Derbes, "'Secret Horrors.'"

113. Thompson, "Blinded by a 'Barbaric' South."

114. Johnson, "Inconsistency, Contradiction, and Complete Confusion."

Chapter 3

1. Entry of December 24–25, 1840, Reports of the Captain, vol. 1, Day Police and Night Watch of the Second Municipality, NOPL; Jacob Barker and Roland Hazard, memos, March 12, 12–13, and n.d., 1841, folder 81, and Rufus Kinsman to Jacob Barker, June 18, 1841, folder 82, both in box 24, Rowland G. and Caroline (Newbold) Hazard Papers, RIHS. For Kinsman's family in Boston, see *Fourth Census of the United States*, reel 53, Ward 6, Boston, Massachusetts, p. 142.

2. Bolster, *Black Jacks*; Byrd, *Captives and Voyagers*; Dawson, *Undercurrents of Power*; Gilroy, *Black Atlantic*, 4, 12–17; Linebaugh and Rediker, *Many-Headed Hydra*; Schoeppner, *Moral Contagion*; Scott, *Common Wind*.

3. Jones, *Birthright Citizens*, 50–58; Pryor, *Colored Travelers*.

4. On the Negro Seamen Acts, see especially Bolster, *Black Jacks*; Hamer, "Great Britain, the United States, and the Negro Seamen Acts"; Schoeppner, *Moral Contagion*; Wilson, *Freedom at Risk*, 58–63; and Wong, *Neither Fugitive nor Free*, chap. 4. On the criminalization of Black travel more broadly, see Berlin, *Slaves without Masters*, 79–198; and Wolf, *Race and Liberty in the New Nation*, 115–20, 130–43.

5. Bolster, *Black Jacks*, 198; Tansey, "Out-of-State Free Blacks," 370, 381.

6. Chalhoub, "Illegal Enslavement"; Fiske, *Solomon Northup's Kindred*; Wells, *Kidnapping Club*; Wilson, *Freedom at Risk*.

7. For "reform and rehabilitation" as enslaved people's "acceptance of their subjugation," within the context of slave prisons, see Paton, *No Bond but the Law*, 21.

8. *Daily Picayune* (New Orleans), February 17, 1852; Barker and Hazard, memo, March 12, 1841, folder 81, box 24, Hazard Papers, RIHS.

9. For "property-ness," see Scott, "Paper Thin."

10. On Powell's efforts, see William Powell to [American Seamen's Friend Society], April 15, 1862, folder 6, box 1, Records of the American Seamen's Friend Society, G. W. Blunt White Library, Mystic Seaport Museum, Mystic, CT; and Foner, "William P. Powell." For Powell's study, see *National Anti-Slavery Standard* (New York), September 10, 17, 24, October 1, 8, 15, 22, 29, 1846.

11. W. Jeffry Bolster concludes that southern jails incarcerated, at most, 10,000 free Black sailors cumulatively under the Negro Seamen Acts. Michael Schoeppner estimates that the total figure was closer to 20,000. Both estimates only consider arrests under the Negro Seamen Acts, excluding arrests of sailors on the legal fiction that they were fugitive enslaved people (which, at least for New Orleans, doubtless constituted a considerably larger number of arrests). Bolster, *Black Jacks*, 206, 231, 289n39; Schoeppner, *Moral Contagion*, 221–30; Tansey, "Out-of-State Free Blacks," 379.

12. On the category's use elsewhere in the French Atlantic world, see Canelas, "Escravidão e liberdade no Caribe francês," 169–70, 178–79; Elisabeth, "French Antilles," 145; Vaughn, *Creating the Creole Island*, 152, 154.

13. Data in graph 3.1 derive from compilations of daily reports from the City Police Jail for 1820–24, 1828, and 1830–31 (containing records of 2,577 SDL committals), daily reports from the Third Municipality Police Jail for 1838 and 1839 (232 SDL committals), twenty-eight monthly reports from the Second Municipality Police Jail for 1843–45 (containing 228 committals of persons who were either identified as free or who were explicitly identified as riverboat workers or sailors), and the admittance ledger, dated November 1835 to August 1841, of a facility that served as the City Police Jail until January 1837 and as the First Municipality Police Jail thereafter (1,625 SDL committals). Some daily reports, covering forty-one days in total, are missing: seven days in 1820, twenty-three in 1821, six in 1822, and five in 1824. Data for these missing days have been substituted with the daily admittance average for the given year, as indicated by existent reports.

Complete citywide data do not survive for any year after the city's splinter into three municipalities in 1836; however, existent records of the city's three police jails suggest the continued incarceration of at least 500 "free" prisoners annually. The "Register of Slaves Entering the Police Jail" records 8,322 admittances in the First Municipality for the years 1837–40, of which 885 (10.6 percent) were SDL (an annual average of

221 SDL admittances). The Second Municipality produced separate monthly reports of all prisoners released and of all prisoners retained. While twenty-eight monthly reports survive, concurrent pairs of reports—and thus, a complete admittance record—survive for only twelve nonconsecutive months: August, September, and December 1843, January 1844, and February–June and August–October 1845. In those twelve months, 1,539 admittances were made, of which 174 (11.3 percent) were identified as free. In the Third Municipality, daily reports survive for 230 days in 1838 and 289 days in 1839. These reports record 947 admittances, of which 232 (24.5 percent) were SDL (an approximate annual average of 160). Taken together, these records suggest roughly 220 annual SDL admittances in the First Municipality, 170 in the Second, and 160 in the Third (or, 550 persons) during the early 1840s. Daily Reports, 6 vols., and Register of Slaves Entering the Police Jail, both in Police Jail Records, and Daily Reports, 2 vols., Police Jail of the Third Municipality Records, all in NOPL; Daily Reports, boxes 10–12, [Second Municipality Monthly Reports], folder 3, box 19, and Record Book of the Third Municipality Police Jail, box 21, all in CHMS; [Second Municipality Monthly Reports], folders 12–14, ser. 5A, box 1, SFLC.

14. "Pretends to be free" and "claims to be free" appeared regularly in runaway slave advertisements. "Runaway [committed] for want of his free papers" appears throughout the runaway slave book of Richmond's jail: see Record Book, Richmond, Virginia City Sergeant Papers, in Stampp, *Records of Ante-Bellum Southern Plantations*, reel 45. "He is informed he is a slave" appears repeatedly in records from Vicksburg's jail: see, for example, John Gibbs, petition, filed March 9, 1836, High Court of Errors and Appeals, Warren County, Mississippi (Par no. 21083601), and Richard Coleman, petition, filed January 30, 1837, Criminal Court, Warren County, Mississippi (Par no. 21083705), both in *Race, Slavery, and Free Blacks*, ser. 2, pt. A, reel 15.

15. Y. Lockett et al., Report ["on Workhouses and Prisons"], March 15, 1842, in Journals of Minutes and Proceedings, vol. 1, Second Municipality Council Records, NOPL.

16. Among the 1,625 SDL prisoners entered into the "Register of Slaves Entering the Police Jail," 1,493 (91.9 percent) were listed with surnames. Among the 12,297 prisoners identified as having owners, only 392 prisoners (3.2 percent) were listed with surnames.

17. See the cases of Mary Noël (a victim of kidnapping) and Felix (mistakenly seized during a raid on a gathering of slaves and free persons), neither of whom were labeled "SDL." *Mary Noël, alias Nounoutte, vs. Clement Ramos*, filed August 2, 1839, docket no. 27, and *Petition of Felix f.m.c. praying for an Habeas Corpus*, filed February 15, 1839, docket no. 23, both in Habeas Corpus Records, First Judicial District Court Records, NOPL; entries of December 24, 1838, and July 18, 1839, Register of Slaves Entering the Police Jail, Police Jail Records, NOPL.

18. Register of Slaves Entering the Police Jail, Police Jail Records, NOPL.

19. Among the 1,946 admittances made to the First Municipality Police Jail in 1839, thirteen died in captivity and nine escaped. Seven and five, respectively, were SDL. Register of Slaves Entering the Police Jail, Police Jail Records, NOPL.

20. From 1838 to 1840, the First Municipality Police Jail averaged 46 SDL monthly admittances between July and November. In December, the jail averaged 103 SDL admittances. Register of Slaves Entering the Police Jail, Police Jail Records, NOPL.

21. Among the 13,921 committals recorded in the "Register of Slaves Entering the Police Jail," 13,672 had gender-specific first names or were described using gender-specific pronouns. Among 1,529 SDL committals of discernable gender, 177 committals (11.6 percent) were of women. Among 12,149 committals of enslaved prisoners of discernable gender, 4,401 (36.2 percent) were of women. Among white people imprisoned for vagrancy, sailors and migrant workers were typically designated "loafers" in workhouse records. In the Third Municipality, roughly 89 percent of the vagrant "loafers" sent to the workhouse between 1844 and 1851 were male. Register of Slaves Entering the Police Jail, Police Jail Records, and Register of Persons Committed to the Third Municipality Workhouse, Workhouse of the Third Municipality Records, both in NOPL.

22. [Second Municipality Monthly Reports], folder 3, box 19, CHMS; [Second Municipality Monthly Reports], folders 12–14, ser. 5A, box 1, SFLC.

23. Among 1,625 SDL prisoners listed in the "Register of Slaves Entering the Police Jail," 1,507 (92.7 percent) were admitted by criminal justice authorities (compared to 54.9 percent among prisoners with owners). The remainder were committed by civilians; none were committed by persons claiming to be their owners.

24. Ely, *Israel on the Appomattox*, esp. 259–60; Maris-Wolf, *Family Bonds*, 3–4, 72, 108; Von Daacke, *Freedom Has a Face*; Wegmann, "To Fashion Ourselves Citizens"; Wolf, *Almost Free*; Wolf, *Race and Liberty*, 138–52. For articulations of this distinction by white Louisianians, see *Daily Picayune* (New Orleans), February 25, 1858, January 18, September 4, 7, 1859; and *Report of the Attorney General*, 11.

25. Before the 1990s, scholarship tended to characterize New Orleans as a "three-caste society," consisting of three discrete racial groups. Recent scholarship tends to reject these groupings' immutability, emphasizing fluidity and contestation in the construction of race: see Aslakson, *Making Race in the Courtroom*; Clark, *Strange History of the American Quadroon*; Scott, "Asserting Citizenship and Refusing Stigma"; Scott and Hébrard, *Freedom Papers*; Spear, *Race, Sex, and Social Order*; and Thompson, *Exiles at Home*. On the population's wealth relative to white people's, see Lachance, "Limits of Privilege."

26. For the relevant Louisiana case law, see Aslakson, *Making Race in the Courtroom*, 180–82; and Schafer, *Slavery, the Civil Law, and the Supreme Court*, 19–21. In 1862, a coalition of free Black property holders asserted that they had not felt compelled to carry freedom papers on their person under the antebellum regime: see Manuel Moreau et al. to George F. Shepley, [1863], file 2, box 7, George F. Shepley Papers, Maine Historical Society, Portland.

27. *State of Louisiana v. Levy et al.*, docket no. 1414, 5 La. Ann. 64 (1850), SCLC.

28. On dynamics between free Black "Creoles" and free Black residents of Anglo-American heritage, see Logsdon and Cossé Bell, "Americanization of Black New Orleans."

29. Meeting of August 16, 1804, vol. 1, OP-CDV; "Resolution of the City Council Relative to Colored Persons Calling Themselves Free," approved July 24, 1805, "Ordinance Concerning Strangers," approved February 21, 1806, and "Resolution of the City Council Concerning Strangers," approved January 7, 1807, all in vol. 1, subser. 1, OR-CDV; "An Act to Prevent the Introduction of Free People of Color from Hispaniola, and the

other French Islands of America into the Territory of Orleans," approved June 7, 1806, in *Acts Passed at the First Session of the First Legislature of the Territory of Orleans*, 126–31.

30. Canelas, "Escravidão e liberdade no Caribe francês," 169–70; Elisabeth, "French Antilles," 145; Louis, "Les libres de couleur en Martinique," 153–55; Moitt, *Women and Slavery*, chap. 8.

31. On these mounting anxieties, see Scott, *Common Wind*, chap. 3.

32. Ordinance of July 21, 1767, "Arrêt du Conseil de Port-au-Prince, qui confisque au profit du Roi un Mulâtre se disant Libre," approved February 7, 1770, and "Arrêt du Conseil de Port-au-Prince, touchant les Actes qui concernent les Gens de couleur se disant libres," approved January 9, 1778, all in Moreau de Saint-Méry, *Loix et constitutions des colonies françaises*, 5:93–94, 290, 807–8; "Ordonnance de MM. les Général et Intendant concernant les soi-disant libres et les libertés non-registrées," approved September 10, 1789, in Durand-Molard, *Code le la Martinique*, 4:157–59; Ballet, *La Guadeloupe*, 3:44; Canelas, "Escravidão e liberdade no Caribe francês," 178–79.

33. Scott, "Paper Thin."

34. William C. C. Claiborne to Robert Smith, May 20, 1809, and James Mather to William C. C. Claiborne, July 18, 1809, both in Rowland, *Official Letter Books* 4:363–66, 387–89; Aslakson, *Making Race in the Courtroom*, 29–30; Scott, "Paper Thin."

35. Jacques Lamothe to Nicholas Girod, March 3, April 4, May 3, June 2, July 5 and 19, and August 3, 1814, all in folder 5, box 18, CHMS.

36. For 1820, 359 existent daily reports record 122 committals of SDL prisoners. Daily Reports, vol. 1, Police Jail Records, NOPL.

37. Louis Philippe de Roffignac to Conseil de Ville, July 14, 1821, bk. 4, vol. 3, MM-CDV.

38. Between April and August, at least 160 SDL committals were made to the Police Jail, up from fifty-six, during those months, in 1820. Daily Reports, box 10, CHMS.

39. Linebaugh and Rediker, *Many-Headed Hydra*; Scott, *Common Wind*.

40. *New York v. Miln*, 36 US 102 (1837); *Prigg v. Pennsylvania*, 41 US 539 (1842); *Moore v. People of the State of Illinois*, 55 US 13 (1852); Manion, *Liberty's Prisoners*, 25–26; O'Brassill-Kulfan, *Vagrants and Vagabonds*, 91–93; Schoeppner, *Moral Contagion*, 104–7; Wagner, 38.

41. *Daily Picayune* (New Orleans), June 20, 1852, September 18, 1859; C. W. Jacobs to Thomas J. Keating, January 10, 1859, in *Easton (MD) Gazette*, March 5, 1859; Hirota, *Expelling the Poor*, 54–55, 73.

42. On Blackness and the "taint" of dependency, see Edwards, *Gendered Strife and Confusion*, 77.

43. *New-Orleans Commercial Bulletin*, April 29, 1841; *Daily Picayune* (New Orleans), August 22, 1841; *New Orleans Daily Crescent*, September 16, 1841, November 14, 1860; *Daily Advocate* (Baton Rouge), April 5, 1859.

44. *Liberator* (Boston), January 15, 1831.

45. *Liberator* (Boston), June 7, 1834.

46. Brown, *Description of William Wells Brown's Original Panoramic Views*, 14.

47. William P. Powell, "Coloured Seamen—Their Character and Condition. No. III.— (Continued). Statistics of coloured seamen imprisoned in Southern and foreign ports,"

National Anti-Slavery Standard (New York), October 8, 1846; Chalhoub, "Illegal Enslavement," 88–115.

48. Walker, *David Walker's Appeal*, 33.

49. Record Book, Richmond, Virginia, City Sergeant Papers, in Stampp, *Records of Ante-Bellum Southern Plantations*, reel 45.

50. Hynson, *Absconders, Runaways, and Other Fugitives*, 116–26.

51. Count includes eight inmates who were not explicitly identified as free but who were released on their own recognizance. Hynson, *District of Columbia Runaway and Fugitive Slave Cases*, 3–88.

52. "An Act Concerning Free Negroes, Mulattoes, and Slaves," approved May 31, 1827, in Sheahan, *Corporation Laws of the City of Washington*, 244–48; "An Ordinance to Re-Organize the Work House Department, to Establish a Mart for the Public Sale of Slaves, and for Other Purposes," in *Charleston Courier*, January 1, 1840.

53. *National Intelligencer and Washington Advertiser*, March 9, 1807.

54. *National Intelligencer and Washington Advertiser*, August 24, 1807.

55. *Alexandria (VA) Gazette*, August 16, 1841.

56. *City Gazette and Daily Advertiser* (Charleston), January 9, 1812.

57. *Weekly Standard* (Raleigh, NC), May 16, 1860.

58. *Emancipator* (New York), July 26, 1838.

59. *Mississippi State Gazette* (Natchez), July 17, 1824.

60. For example, *City Gazette and Commercial Daily Advertiser* (Charleston), November 4, 1822; and *Ariel* (Natchez), February 13, 1826.

61. Bolster, *Black Jacks*, esp. 2, 74, 102–30, 235–36; Buchanan, *Black Life on the Mississippi*; Cecelski, *Waterman's Song*, 140–41; Johnson, *River of Dark Dreams*, 143.

62. Bolster, *Black Jacks*, 1–2; Cecelski, *Waterman's Song*, chap. 5; Jacobs, *Incidents in the Life of a Slave Girl*, 169–72; Johnson, *River of Dark Dreams*, 135–47; Northrup, *Twelve Years a Slave*, 80; Parker, *His Promised Land*, 39; Schafer, *Slavery, the Civil Law, and the Supreme Court*, 113–14; "Narrative of Tom Wilson" in Ripley, *Black Abolitionist Papers*, 1:431; *True American* (New Orleans), March 9, 1839; *New-Orleans Commercial Bulletin*, April 29, 1841; *Weekly Picayune* (New Orleans), January 24, 1842.

63. *Emancipator and Free American* (Boston), December 1, 1842; Charles Deliole et al. to [Rowland Hazard], April 1, 1841, folder 82, box 24, Hazard Papers, RIHS; *Daily Picayune* (New Orleans), May 3, 1852, June 10, 1855. On the visual coding of strangers, see Halttunen, *Confidence Men and Painted Women*, 33–55.

64. Joseph Thompson, testimonial, November 20, 1833, in appendix to Child, *Despotism of Freedom*, 70.

65. In addition to arrest books, see Chambers, *Trials and Confessions*, 56.

66. Among 1,625 SDL committals recorded in one register, 1,092 (67.2 percent) were arrested after dark, compared to only 51.3 percent of enslaved committals. Register of Slaves Entering the Police Jail, Police Jail Records, NOPL; *Daily Picayune* (New Orleans), May 18, 1838; William Henry Bissell, affidavit, February 19, 1857, Freedom Papers of New Orleans, NOPL.

67. Edwards, *People and Their Peace*, chap. 4; Gross, *Double Character*; Gross, *What Blood Won't Tell*; Johnson, "Death Rites as Birthrights"; Kennington, *In the Shadow of*

Dredd Scott, 134–41; Maris-Wolf, *Family Bonds*; Welch, *Black Litigants*, 60–81; Wolf, *Race and Liberty*, 138–52.

68. *Emancipator and Free American* (Boston), December 1, 1842.

69. Charles Duron et al., grand jury report, February 4, 1842, in Minute Book, vol. 4, Criminal Court of the First District Records, NOPL. Also see the autobiography of James Thomas, wherein the well-traveled free Black barber describes the importance of traveling with "some reputable [white] person or persons to Identify the applicant as free, as a measure of protection." Thomas, *From Tennessee Slave to St. Louis Entrepreneur*, 134.

70. William Freeman, affidavit, June 15, 1836, in *Race, Slavery, and Free Blacks*, ser. 2, pt. C, reel 15; James Barbadoes, testimonial, November 20, 1833, in appendix to Child, *Despotism of Freedom*, 71; *David King, f.c.m., praying for a writ of habeas corpus*, filed May 16, 1848, docket no. 2266, First District Court Records, NOPL; *Daily Picayune* (New Orleans), June 4, 1840; Chambers, *Trials and Confessions*, 56.

71. Kinsman to Barker, June 18, 1841, folder 82, box 24, Hazard Papers, RIHS; Jacob Barker to Samuel H. Jenks, August 19, 1837, in *Report on the Deliverance of Citizens*, 14–15; *Daily Picayune* (New Orleans), June 11, 1840; William Freret to Second Municipality Council, June 16, 1840, printed in *Daily Picayune* (New Orleans), June 18, 1840.

72. Lewis Madison, certificate, March 5, 1841, LLMVC.

73. *Mathias Freeman, a free man of color, vs. Dominique Bélaumé, Keeper of the Police Prison*, filed May 20, 1822, docket no. 4686, First Judicial District Court Records, NOPL.

74. Barker and Hazard, memos, March 12 and 15, 1841, folder 81, box 24, Hazard Papers, RIHS. Years earlier, a free Black Virginian named Henry Goings—seemingly, the same person jailed in New Orleans in 1841—had helped an enslaved man escape to freedom. Goings, *Rambles of a Runaway*, 38.

75. Thomas Lloyd, affidavit, May 11, 1825, folder 1, box 9, CHMS.

76. Robert Moore and Thomas Hawkins, affidavit, June 26, 1819, folder 4, box 8, CHMS; Barker and Hazard, memos, March 12 and 14, 1841, both in folder 81, box 24, Hazard Papers, RIHS.

77. John Roberts to William P. Powell, [1846?], in Powell, "Coloured Seamen," *National Anti-Slavery Standard* (New York), October 8, 1846; David William and Luther Morehouse, affidavit, November 26, 1818, folder 4, box 8, CHMS; John Faulkner, affidavit, May 21, 1813, folder 3, box 8, CHMS; *Daily Picayune* (New Orleans), May 18, 1838.

78. Bissell, affidavit, February 19, 1857, and Thomas Moffett, affidavit, February 20, 1857, both in Freedom Papers of New Orleans Collection, NOPL; Charles Robertson, affidavit, July 7, 1825, folder 1, box 9, CHMS; *Daily Picayune* (New Orleans), May 3, 1852, June 10, 1855.

79. Segal, "Lincoln, Benjamin Jonas and the Black Code."

80. *Daily Picayune* (New Orleans), June 10, 1840; Barker and Hazard, memo, n.d., folder 81, box 24, Hazard Papers, RIHS; *Charles T. Clark, f.m.c. praying a writ of Habeas Corpus*, filed August 16, 1848, docket no. 1487, Fifth District Court Records, NOPL.

81. Entry of June 8–9, 1838, Recorder's Book, vol. 2, Third Municipality Guard Records, NOPL; entry of August 18–19, 1840, Reports of the Captain, vol. 1, Day Police and Night Watch of the Second Municipality Records, NOPL; entry of June 3, 1846, Record

Book of the Third Municipality Police Jail, box 21, CHMS; Barker and Hazard, memo, March 12–13, 1841, folder 81, box 24, Hazard Papers, RIHS; Duron et al., grand jury report, February 4, 1842, in Minute Book, vol. 4, Criminal Court of the First District Records, NOPL. For the routes of the *Cordelia*, see *New York Herald*, August 6, October 24, November 10, 1853.

82. During its brief tenure, this private security force performed 214 SDL committals, of which 183 occurred at night. Roughly one-third of these SDL commitments were of persons with francophone names of obvious native "Creole" extraction (Celestin Destrehan, François Porée, Manuel Forneret, Jean Bapitste Valmour, etc.). This private security force also appears to have occasionally raided free Black community gatherings: for example, on June 19, 1836, this private police committed twenty-six free men with francophone surnames, including members of prominent local families, after an apparent raid and mass arrest. For the arrests of Roudanez, Trévigne, and Dunn, see entry of May 15–16, 1837, Report of the Captain of the Guard, vol. 1, First Municipality Guard Records, NOPL; Report of the Night Police, October 4, 1848, in Reports of the Captain, vol. 6, Third Municipality Guard Records, NOPL; entries of March 22, 1836, and June 8, 1840, Register of Slaves Entering the Police Jail, Police Jail Records, NOPL; entry of October 3, 1848, Record Book of the Third Municipality Police Jail, box 21, CHMS; and *Daily Picayune* (New Orleans), June 10, 1840. On the privatized police, see [Resolution Recognizing the Sixth Ward Night Watch], approved July 18, 1835, in *Digest of the Ordinances, Resolutions, By-Laws, and Regulations of the Corporation of New Orleans*, 103.

83. Deliole et al. to [Hazard], April 1, 1841, folder 82, box 24, Hazard Papers, RIHS.

84. John Hatfield, testimonial, in Drew, *North-Side View of Slavery*, 363–66.

85. Barbadoes, testimonial, November 20, 1833, in appendix to Child, *Despotism of Freedom*, 71.

86. *Charleston Mercury*, June 23, 1824; Schoeppner, *Moral Contagion*, 577–79.

87. "Imprisonment of Coloured Seamen"; Schoeppner, *Moral Contagion*, 136; Horne, *Negro Comrades of the Crown*, 142.

88. Carpenter, *Imprisonment and Enslavement of British Coloured Seamen*, 6.

89. "Imprisonment of Coloured Seamen," 38; *Elkinson v. Deliesseline*, 8 Fed. Cas. 593 (1823).

90. On jailors' control of writing utensils, and sailors resorting to blood, see Barbadoes, testimonial, November 20, 1833, in appendix to Child, *Despotism of Freedom*, 71; *Emancipator and Free American* (Boston), December 1, 1842; Charles Challander et al. to Jacob Barker, April 6, 1841, copied in Jacob Barker to Samuel Willetts, April 12, 1841, folder 82, box 24, Hazard Papers, RIHS; and Chambers, *Trials and Confessions*, 56.

91. Challander et al. to Barker, April 6, 1841, copied in Barker to Willetts, April 12, 1841, folder 82, box 24, Hazard Papers, RIHS.

92. Deliole et al. to [Hazard], April 1, 1841, folder 82, box 24, Hazard Papers, RIHS.

93. "An Act in Relation to Runaway Slaves in this State," approved March 17, 1826, in *Louisiana Acts, 1826*, pp. 90–95.

94. Barker to Willetts, April 12, 1841, folder 82, box 24, Hazard Papers, RIHS; *Emancipator and Free American* (Boston), December 1, 1842; Barker to Jenks, August 19, 1837, in *Report on the Deliverance of Citizens*, 16.

95. Deliole et al. to [Hazard], April 1, 1841, folder 82, box 24, Hazard Papers, RIHS.

96. *Emancipator and Free American* (Boston), December 1, 1842; Barker to Jenks, August 19, 1837, in *Report on the Deliverance of Citizens*, 14–15; Bissell, affidavit, February 19, 1857; *Daily Picayune* (New Orleans), October 6, 1860; A. Walden to Rowland Hazard, August 1, 1840, folder 82, box 24, Hazard Papers, RIHS.

97. Robert Anderson to William Powell, March 7, 1843, in Powell, "Coloured Seamen," *National Anti-Slavery Standard* (New York), October 8, 1846; *Daily Picayune* (New Orleans), December 11, 1844; Barker, *Incidents in the Life of Jacob Barker*, 222; Barker to Jenks, August 19, 1837, in *Report on the Deliverance of Citizens*, 17; Duron et al., grand jury report, February 4, 1842, in Minute Book, vol. 4, Criminal Court of the First District Records, NOPL; *Charles T. Clark, f.m.c. praying a writ of Habeas Corpus*, filed August 16, 1848, docket no. 1487, Fifth District Court Records, NOPL.

98. Barker and Hazard, memo, March 14, 1841, folder 81, box 24, Hazard Papers, RIHS.

99. Barker to Jenks, August 19, 1837, in *Report on the Deliverance of Citizens*, 14.

100. Data in graph 3.2 derive from Register of Slaves Entering the Police Jail, Police Jail Records, NOPL. For jail fees, see [Second Municipality Monthly Reports], folder 3, box 19, CHMS.

101. Powell, "Coloured Seamen," *National Anti-Slavery Standard* (New York), October 8, 1846; *Louisiana Courier* (New Orleans), October 19, 1843; Bolster, *Black Jacks*, 206.

102. Powell, "Coloured Seamen," *National Anti-Slavery Standard* (New York), October 8, 1846; entry of June 10, 1840, Register of Slaves Entering the Police Jail, Police Jail Records, NOPL.

103. Wong, *Neither Fugitive nor Free*, 189.

104. Entry of January 1, 1838, Register of Slaves Entering the Police Jail, Police Jail Records, NOPL; Barker and Hazard, memo, n.d., folder 81, box 24, Hazard Papers, RIHS; "Liste des Esclaves marrons détenus à la Geôle de Police Première Municipalité," [1845], folder 3, box 19, CHMS; "Les Esclaves dont les Noms suivent, vendus à l'encan le 30 Août 1845, Doivent à la Geôle de Police 1re Municipalité," [1845], in Register of Chained Slaves Employed in Public Works, vol. 4, Police Jail Records, NOPL; *Louisiana Courier* (New Orleans), August 28, 1845; Joseph Montegut to First Municipality Council, September 1, 1845, Mayors' Messages to the First Municipality Council, vol. 4, First Municipality Council Records, NOPL; [Second Municipality Monthly Reports], September 1845, folder 3, box 19, CHMS.

105. On "protective networks" of "fictive kin," see Johnson, "Death Rites as Birthrights," 235.

106. Thompson, affidavit, November 20, 1833, and Barbadoes, testimonial, November 20, 1833, both in appendix to Child, *Despotism of Freedom*, 70, 71; Price, *Slavery in America*, 274.

107. William Hess and George Cain, affidavit, November 23, 1819, folder 4, box 8, CHMS.

108. *North Star* (Rochester, NY), February 2, 1849.

109. *Mathias Freeman, a free man of color, vs. Dominique Bélaumé, Keeper of the*

Police Prison, filed May 20, 1822, docket no. 4686, First Judicial District Court Records, NOPL; Pedro Thomasin and Predro Esnandez, affidavit, April 11, 1812, and Faulkner, affidavit, May 21, 1813, both in folder 3, Richard Hovendon and Henry King, affidavit, May 27, 1816, and Hess and Cain, affidavit, November 23, 1819, both in folder 4, all in box 8, CHMS; Thomas Shields to [Nicholas Girod], November 9, 1821, folder 1, box 9, CHMS; Chambers, *Trials and Confessions*, 56.

110. Deliole et al. to [Hazard], April 1, 1841, and Challander et al. to Barker, April 6, 1841, both in folder 82, box 24, Hazard Papers, RIHS. Most of these men's birthplaces are enumerated in Barker and Hazard, memos, March 12–15, 1841, folder 81, box 24, Hazard Papers, RIHS.

111. Anderson, *Life and Narrative*, 13.

112. Ingraham, *South-West*, 2:111.

113. Brown, *Description of William Wells Brown's Original Panoramic Views*, 13.

114. Both consuls are mentioned in Barker and Hazard, memo, March 12–15, 1841, folder 81, box 24, Hazard Papers, RIHS.

115. *Daily Picayune* (New Orleans), April 30, June 10, 11, 17, 21, 1840.

116. *Daily Picayune* (New Orleans), April 19, 20, 21, 1859; *Weekly Picayune* (New Orleans), April 27, 1859; *New Orleans Daily Crescent*, April 19, 20, 21, 1859; William Mure et al. to Summers, April 18, 1859, in *New Orleans Daily Crescent*, April 20, 1859.

117. *Liberator* (Boston), June 7, 1834.

118. *Louisiana Courier* (New Orleans), January 6, 1845; Henry Hubbard to George N. Briggs, [January 1845], printed in *Boston Courier*, February 10, 1845; Resolution, approved March 8, 1845, in *Louisiana Acts, 1845*, pp. 79–80; "An Act to Provide for the Punishment of Persons Disturbing the Peace of this State, in Relation to Slaves and Free Persons of Color," approved December 18, 1844, in *Acts of the General Assembly of the State of South-Carolina*, 292–93; Schoeppner, *Moral Contagion*, 145–56; Wong, *Neither Fugitive nor Free*, 187–88.

119. *Proceedings of the United States Senate*, 34.

120. *Weekly Picayune* (New Orleans), April 13, 1840; *New York Herald*, February 6, 1857; Bolster, *Black Jacks*, 208–10; Wong, *Neither Fugitive nor Free*, 188.

121. Barker and Hazard, memos, March 12 and 14, and n.d., 1841, folder 81, box 24, Hazard Papers, RIHS; Faulkner, affidavit, May 21, 1813, folder 3, box 8, CHMS.

122. Bolster, *Black Jacks*, 210–11.

123. Marianne Edwards to Maria Edwards, July 11, 1859, Marianne Edwards to Charles Edwards, December 1, 1859, both in folder 2, Marianne Edwards to Maria Edwards, January 25, 1860, folder 3, all in Edwards (Marianne) Letters, LLMVC.

124. Theophilus L. Adams, affidavits, November 9, 1821, and July 22, 1824, both in folder 1, box 9, CHMS.

125. Jacob Barker to James Birney, August 5 and 23, 1845, in Dumond, *Letters of James Gillespie Birney*, 2:957, 964; *Daily Picayune* (New Orleans), April 22, June 30, September 11, 1845.

126. Hilt, "Rogue Finance"; Barker, *Incidents in the Life of Jacob Barker*, 4–6, 154–77.

127. Barker, *Incidents in the Life of Jacob Barker*, 220–22; Barker to Jenks, August 19, 1837, in *Report on the Deliverance of Citizens*, 14–15; Barker to Birney, October 2, 1845,

in Dumond, *Letters of James Gillespie Birney*, 2:975; Barker, *Mr. Jacob Barker's Speech*, 5.

128. Barker to Jenks, August 19, 1837, in *Report on the Deliverance of Citizens*, 14–15; Barker, *Rebellion*, 9–12.

129. Bammell and Robinson, *Life and Services*, 8–9; Robinson, *Hazard Family*, 77, 120, 122.

130. Barker to Jenks, August 19, 1837, in *Report on the Deliverance of Citizens*, 14–17.

131. Barker and Hazard, memo, March 15, 1841, folder 81, box 24, Hazard Papers, RIHS.

132. Robinson, *Hazard Family*, 77, 120, 122; Bammell and Robinson, *Life and Services*, 8–9.

133. Kinsman to Barker, June 18, 1841, folder 82, box 24, Hazard Papers, RIHS.

134. Jacob Barker to Elisha Potter, December 30, 1841, printed in *Emancipator and Free American* (Boston), December 1, 1842.

135. Entry of October 21, 1842, Register of Chained Slaves Employed in Public Works, vol. 4, and entry of February 17, 1840, Register of Slaves Entering the Police Jail, both in Police Jail Records, NOPL; Duron et al., grand jury report, February 4, 1842, in Minute Book, vol. 4, Criminal Court of the First District Records, NOPL.

136. [Second Municipality Monthly Reports], 1843–1845, folder 3, box 19, CHMS; [Second Municipality Monthly Reports], 1843–1845, folders 12–14, ser. 5A, box 1, SFLC.

137. Barker, *Rebellion*, 10; Barker, *Incidents in the Life*, 222.

138. [Jacob Barker], editorial, in *New Orleans Bee*, April 30, 1841. Marginalia written on a clipping of the editorial identifies Barker as the author; folder 80, box 24, Hazard Papers, RIHS.

139. *New-Orleans Commercial Bulletin*, April 28, 29, 1841; untitled clipping, [April–May 1841], folder 80, box 24, Hazard Papers, RIHS; *William R. Augustin and Amos Simons Detained in Confinement Praying for a Habeas Corpus*, filed March 17, 1841, docket no. 3779, in General Docket, vol. 2, Commercial Court Records, NOPL.

140. Duron et al., grand jury report, February 4, 1842, in Minute Book, vol. 4, Criminal Court of the First District Records, NOPL; Barker to Jenks, August 19, 1837, in *Report on the Deliverance of Citizens*, 14–15.

141. Barker and Hazard, memo, March 14, 1841, folder 81, box 24, Hazard Papers, RIHS.

142. [Jacob Barker], editorial, in *New Orleans Bee*, April 30, 1841.

143. *Louisiana Advertiser* (New Orleans), reprinted in *Emancipator* (New York), August 5, 1841.

144. Duron et al., grand jury report, February 4, 1842, in Minute Book, vol. 4, and George C. Brower et al., grand jury report, May 8, 1845, in Minute Book, vol. 6, both in Criminal Court of the First District Records, NOPL.

145. *New-Orleans Commercial Bulletin*, July 23, 1841; *Daily Picayune* (New Orleans), July 23, 24, 27, 29, August 4, 12, 19, 22, September 16, 1841; *Baton Rouge Gazette*, August 28, 1841; *Vicksburg (MS) Daily Whig*, July 27, 29, 1841; *Vicksburg (MS) Tri-Weekly Sentinel*, July 27, 1841; *Wetumpka (AL) Argus*, August 4, 1841; *Weekly Mississippian* (Jackson), July 30, 1841; *Liberty (MS) Advocate*, July 28, 1841; *Mississippi Free Trader*

(Natchez), July 27, 29, 1841; *Lexington (MS) Union*, August 21, 1841; *New-York Daily Tribune*, August 2, 1841.

146. *Daily Missouri Republican* (St. Louis), August 5, 1841.

147. In 1845, Barker aided an imprisoned sailor on condition that his involvement would remain secret: see Barker to Birney, October 2, 1845, in Dumond, *Letters of James Gillespie Birney*, 2:975.

148. Kerr-Ritchie, *Rites of August First*.

149. *New-Orleans Commercial Bulletin*, April 29, 1841.

150. "An Act to Prevent Free Persons of Color from Entering This State, and for Other Purposes," approved March 16, 1830, in *Louisiana Acts, 1830*, pp. 90–95; Schafer, *Becoming Free, Remaining Free*, 130–31.

151. *Daily Picayune* (New Orleans), June 5, 1841; *Southern Banner* (Holly Springs, MS), August 13, 1841; *Lexington (MS) Union*, August 21, 1841. For "contraventionist" arrests and mass arrests, also see the *Daily Picayune* (New Orleans) of July 1, 10, 18, 23, 24, 28, August 1, September 15, November 20, 1841, February 25, 28, May 12, 1842.

152. Barker and Hazard, memo, n.d., folder 81, box 24, Hazard Papers, RIHS; *Daily Picayune* (New Orleans), July 28, August 1, 1841.

153. Barker and Hazard, memos, March 12 and 14, 1841, folder 81, box 24, Hazard Papers, RIHS; *State vs. William Wilson, free man of color*, December 4, 1841, in Minute Book, vol. 4, Criminal Court of the First District Records, NOPL; "An Act Amendatory of the Several Acts Relative to the Penitentiary," approved March 27, 1843, in *Louisiana Acts, 1843*, pp. 68–69; *State of Louisiana vs. Simon Brown, f.m.c.*, filed February 3, 1842, Records of the State vs. Free Persons of Color, Third Municipality Recorder's Office, NOPL; "Report of the Standing Committee on The State Penitentiary, made at the Second Session of the Sixteenth Legislature," in *Louisiana Senate Journal*, 16th leg., 2nd sess., appendix F, xliii.

154. "An Act More Effectually to Prevent Free Persons of Color from Entering into this State, and for Other Purposes," approved March 16, 1842, in *Louisiana Acts, 1842*, pp. 308–19; "An Act to Amend an Act Approved the Sixteenth March, 1842, Entitled 'An Act More Effectually to Prevent Free Persons of Color from Entering into this State, and for Other Purposes,'" approved March 22, 1843, in *Louisiana Acts, 1843*, pp. 45–46; "An Act to Amend an Act, Entitled 'An Act, the More Effectively to Prohibit Free Negroes and Persons of Color, from Entering into and Remaining in this State,' approved 2d. February, 1839," approved December 4, 1841, in *Acts Passed at the Annual Session of the General Assembly, of the State of Alabama*, 11–12; "An Act to Prohibit the Emigration and Settlement of Free Negroes, or Free Persons of Color, into this State," approved January 20, 1843, in *Acts Passed at the Fourth Session of the General Assembly of the State of Arkansas*, 61–64; "An Act to Prevent the Future Migration of Free Negroes or Mulattoes to this Territory, and for Other Purposes," approved March 5, 1842, in *Acts and Resolutions of the Legislative Council of the Territory of Florida*, 34–35; "An Act to Amend the Several Acts of this State in Relation to Free Negroes and Mulattoes," approved February 26, 1842, in *Laws of the State of Mississippi; Passed at a Regular Biennial Session of the Legislature*, 65–71; "An Act More Effectually to Prevent Free Persons of Color from Entering into this State, and for other Purposes," approved February 23,

1843, in *Laws of the State of Missouri*, 66–68; "An Act to Amend the Laws Now in Force in Relation to Free Persons of Color," approved February 4, 1842, in *Acts Passed at the First Session of the Twenty-Fourth General Assembly of the State of Tennessee*, 229–30.

155. The surveyor received 804 prisoners on or before March 16, 1842, identifying 104 as SDL. Among the subsequent 2,663 entries, only 34 were identified as SDL or free. Register of Chained Slaves Employed in Public Works, Police Jail Records, NOPL.

156. Daily Reports, 2 vols., Police Jail of the Third Municipality Records, NOPL; Record Book of the Third Municipality Police Jail, box 21, CHMS.

157. *Louisiana Courier* (New Orleans), May 14, 1845; *Daily National Intelligencer* (Washington, DC), May 2, 1845; *New Orleans Daily Crescent*, May 1, 1848.

158. *Daily Picayune* (New Orleans), October 17, 1858, December 2, 1859.

159. *New Orleans Daily Crescent*, September 5, 1859; *Daily Picayune* (New Orleans), August 16, 1851, June 7, 1852.

160. *State of Louisiana vs. Julia Arbuckle, f.w.c.*, filed August 13, 1849, Records of the State vs. Free Persons of Color, Third Municipality Recorder's Office, NOPL; *Daily Picayune* (New Orleans), August 25, November 6, 1857, November 13, 1860, May 30, 1863; *New Orleans Daily Crescent*, May 20, 29, 1856; *State v. Arbuckle, f.w.c.*, filed December 7 1860, docket no. 14740, First District Court Records, NOPL.

161. *Daily Picayune* (New Orleans), August 8, 1851; Schafer, *Brothels, Depravity, and Abandoned Women*, 137. For more on Sarah Conner, see Finley, *Intimate Economy*, chap. 3.

162. Henry Williams, petition, filed March 15, 1843, folder 2, box 9, CHMS.

163. *Louisiana vs. Hannah Cornelius, f.w.c.*, filed June 14, 1861, docket no. 15325, First District Court Records, NOPL.

164. "Liste des prisoniers détenus à la Geôle de Police," May 31, 1840, and entries of June 15, 1841, and January 3 and October 21, 1842, all in Register of Chained Slaves Employed in Public Works, Police Jail Records, NOPL; Joseph Montegut to First Municipality Council, August 5, 1844, in Messages from the Mayor to the First Municipality Council, vol. 2, First Municipality Council Records, NOPL; *Louisiana vs. Mary Ann Martin, f.w.c.*, filed June 5, 1846, docket no. 299, First District Court Records, NOPL; *Daily Picayune* (New Orleans), January 23, 1845, October 15, 1846.

165. Barker and Hazard, memo, March 12–13, 1841, folder 81, box 24, Hazard Papers, RIHS; Duron et al., grand jury report, February 4, 1842, in Minute Book, vol. 4, Criminal Court of the First District Records, NOPL; Report of Prisoners Remaining in the Police Jail of the Second Municipality for August 1843, folder 9, ser. 5A, box 1, SFLC; entry of June 3, 1846, Record Book of the Third Municipality Police Jail, box 21, CHMS; *State vs. Augustin Smith, f.c.m.*, March 10, 1845, *State vs. Augustus Smith, free man of color*, March 30, 1846, and *State vs. Augustus Smith, free colored person*, March 31, 1846, all in Minute Book, vol. 6, and *State vs Augustus Smith, free colored person*, April 22, 1846, in Minute Book, vol. 7, all in Criminal Court of the First District Records, NOPL; *Augustus Smith f.m.c. praying for a writ of Habeas Corpus*, filed May 19, 1848, docket no. 2279, First District Court Records, NOPL; *Daily Picayune* (New Orleans), March 4, 1852.

166. *Daily Picayune* (New Orleans), October 24, 1847.

167. *Daily Picayune* (New Orleans), September 3, 1848, October 19, 1850; *New Orleans Daily Crescent*, February 15, 1849.

168. *Daily Picayune* (New Orleans), November 11, 1859; *Report of the Attorney General*, 11–12.

169. Thomas, *From Tennessee Slave to St. Louis Entrepreneur*, 113–14.

170. Bell, *Revolution, Romanticism, and the Afro-Creole Protest Tradition*, 84–88; Reinders, *End of an Era*, 24; Schafer, *Slavery, the Civil Law, and the Supreme Court*, 179; Sterkx, *Free Negro in Ante-Bellum Louisiana*, 297–315; Thompson, *Exiles at Home*, 81–87; West, *Family or Freedom*, 37–39. On escalating persecution in the South generally, see Berlin, *Slaves without Masters*, 343–80; and De la Fuente and Gross, *Becoming Free, Becoming Black*, 132–218.

171. "An Ordinance to Regulate the Service of Slaves Confined in the Police Jail," approved December 10, 1855, in *New Orleans Daily Crescent*, December 11, 1855; "Prisoners in the Parish Prison" to Benjamin Butler, May 6, 1862, box 11, Butler Papers, LOC; Greenwood et al., *Report of the Grand Jury of the Parish of Orleans*, 9. Richard Tansey finds that among 461 arrests performed in the Third District between October 1859 and February 1862 for being in Louisiana illegally, only 135 (30 percent) were sent to Parish Prison, as the law prescribed. Tansey was unable to account for the discrepancy; it seems likely that the missing remainder were sent to the Police Jail. Tansey, "Out-of-State Free Blacks," 379.

172. "An Act Relative to Free Persons of Color Coming into the State from other States or Foreign Countries," approved March 15, 1859, in *Louisiana Acts, 1859*, pp. 70–72.

173. *Opelousas (LA) Patriot*, February 5, March 19, 1859; Sterkx, *Free Negro*, 297–302.

174. *State v. Harrison, a Slave*, docket no. 4464, 1 La. Ann. 722 (1856), SCLC; *Report of the Attorney General*, 11; *Daily Picayune* (New Orleans), February 25, 1858, July 15, September 5, 7, 1859.

175. *Daily Picayune* (New Orleans), October 21, 1860; *New Orleans Daily Crescent*, March 1, 1861; *Daily True Delta* (New Orleans), May 10, 1861; Tansey, "Out-of-State Free Blacks," 376–77.

176. *Daily Picayune* (New Orleans), August 26, September 1, 5, 1859; Everett, "Free Persons of Color in New Orleans," 104.

177. *Daily Picayune* (New Orleans), October 21, 1860.

178. West, *Family or Freedom*, 47–51.

179. "An Act to Prevent Free Persons of Color, Commonly Known as Free Negroes, from Being Brought or Coming to the State of Georgia," approved December 17, 1859, and "An Act to Define and Punish Vagrancy in Free Persons of Color, and for Other Purposes," both in *Acts of the General Assembly of the State of Georgia*, 68–69, 69–70; *Evening Star* (Washington, DC), February 14, 1860.

180. James Marsh Johnson to Henry Ellison, August 20, 1860, in Johnson and Roark, *No Chariot Let Down*, 85–99.

181. *Daily Delta* (New Orleans), November 28, 29, 1860, January 1, 1861; *Daily True Delta* (New Orleans), November 28, 29, 30, 1860; *New Orleans Daily Crescent*, November 29, December 31, 1860, May 30, August 24, 1861; *Daily Picayune* (New Orleans), May 30, 1861, January 31, 1862; *New-Orleans Times*, June 5, 1866; *Catalogue of the*

Officers and Students of Harvard University, 13; *Seventh Census of the United States*, reel 235, Ward 1, Municipality 1, Orleans Parish, Louisiana, p. 72; *Eighth Census of the United States*, reel 417, Ward 3, Orleans Parish, Louisiana, p. 198; *Thomas Jinnings, f.m.c., last Will and Testament*, filed February 13, 1862, docket no. 18806, Second District Court Records, NOPL; Riffel, *New Orleans Register of Free People of Color*, 92, 160.

Chapter 4

1. *Daily Picayune* (New Orleans), January 29, 1852; Jean Boze to Henri de Ste-Gême, July 8–September 3, 1831, folder 188, Ste-Gême Family Papers, HNOC (translation by author); *Daily Comet* (Baton Rouge), December 1, 1855; *Southern Sentinel* (Plaquemine, LA), January 16, 1850.

2. For Louisiana's antebellum vagrancy laws, see "An Act on Vagabonds and Suspicious Persons," approved June 7, 1806, in *Acts Passed at the First Session of the First Legislature of the Territory of Orleans*, 106–23; "An Act Supplementary to the Act Entitled 'An Act on Vagabonds and Suspicious Persons,'" approved March 16, 1818, in *Louisiana Acts, 1818*, pp. 110–14; "An Act to Establish Work Houses and Houses of Refuge by the Several Municipalities of the City of New Orleans, and for Other Purposes," approved March 5, 1841, in *Louisiana Acts, 1841*, pp. 46–48; and "An Act Relative to Crimes and Offenses," approved March 15, 1855, §§ 120–27, in *Louisiana Acts, 1855*, pp. 130–50.

3. On vagrancy law in nineteenth-century America, see Adler, "Vagging the Demons"; Clement, "Transformation of the Wandering Poor"; Beier and Ocobock, *Cast Out*; Kerber, *No Constitutional Right to Be Ladies*, chap. 2; Montgomery, *Citizen Worker*, esp. chaps. 1, 2; O'Brassill-Kulfan, *Vagrants and Vagabonds*; Rodgers, *Work Ethic in Industrial America*, chaps. 7, 8; Schmidt, *Free to Work*, chap. 2; and Stanley, *From Bondage to Contract*, chap. 3. On labor law in nineteenth-century America, see Linder, *Employment Relationship in Anglo-American Law*; Orren, *Belated Feudalism*; Steinfeld, *Invention of Free Labor*; and Tomlins, *Law, Labor, and Ideology*.

4. Recent exceptions, emphasizing southern preoccupation with vagrancy law, are Brown, "Vagabond's Tale"; and Merritt, *Masterless Men*, chap. 6.

5. Data presented in graphs 4.1 and 4.2 are based on averages of yearly arrest rates for available years between 1849 and 1860. All calculations assume constant population growth between decimal censuses. Calculations include arrests for suspiciousness, loitering, and begging, offenses that typically fell under the umbrella of vagrancy law but that some police reports disaggregated. For Baltimore, see *Sun* (Baltimore), January 1, 1853; and "Report of the Board of Police," 24, 26, 27, in *Report of the Board of Police of the City of Baltimore*. For Boston, see *Emancipator and Republican* (Boston), January 3, 1850; and *Boston Daily Atlas*, January 20, 1852, January 10, 1854, January 9, 1855, January 20, 1857. For Buffalo, see *Buffalo Commercial Advertiser*, July 21, 1857; and *Morning Express and Illustrated Buffalo Express*, January 11, 1859, January 10, 1860. For Brooklyn, see *Brooklyn Daily Eagle*, January 18, 1854; *New York Times*, January 17, 1855; *New York Herald*, January 2, 1860; and *Brooklyn Times Union*, March 7, 1861. For Cincinnati, see *Cincinnati Daily Press*, January 9, 1860, January 19, 1861. For Memphis, see Memphis Police Blotter, 1858–1860, Shelby County Archives, Memphis, TN, https://search.register.shelby.tn.us/memphis_blotter/. For New Orleans, see "General

Statement of Police Operations of the City of New Orleans for the Year Commencing on the First July 1849, and Ending on the 30th June 1850," in entry of December 9, 1850, Official Proceedings, vol. 6, First Municipality Council Records, NOPL, and monthly arrest reports, published in the *New Orleans Daily Crescent*, for 1854, 1855, 1858, 1859, and 1860 (database in possession of author; data for September 1859 and January and June 1860 were not published and have been supplemented with the averages of the figures for the immediately preceding and subsequent months). For New York City, see *New York Herald*, January 22, 1852, March 9, 1855, January 2, 1860; *Weekly Lancaster (OH) Gazette*, September 21, 1854; *New York Times*, November 17, 1858; and *Communication from the Governor, Transmitting the Annual Report of the Metropolitan Police*, 101–3. For Philadelphia, see appendix to *Philadelphia Common Council Journal, 1856*, p. 391; *Philadelphia Mayor's Message, 1856*, p. 45; appendix to *Philadelphia Common Council Journal, 1858*, p. 578; *Philadelphia Mayor's Message, 1859*, p. 114; appendix to *Philadelphia Common Council Journal, 1860*, p. 412; and *Philadelphia Mayor's Message, 1861*, p. 227. For St. Louis, see *Daily Missouri Republican* (St. Louis), January 3, 1859; *Daily Missouri Democrat* (St. Louis), January 1, 1861; and monthly reports printed in the *Daily Missouri Republican* (St. Louis) and *Daily Missouri Democrat* (St. Louis) for the year 1859 (database in possession of author; data for September and December 1859 were not published and have been supplemented with the averages of the figures for the immediately preceding and subsequent months).

6. In 1848, London police recorded 8,557 arrests of vagrants and suspicious persons, equal to roughly 3.2 arrests per 1,000. Fletcher, "Account of the Police of the Metropolis," 260.

7. Existent arrest reports from Charleston and Richmond do not disaggregate arrests for vagrancy from other arrests for city misdemeanors. For the total number of arrests in Richmond, see monthly reports printed in the Richmond *Dispatch* between 1854 and 1859 (database in possession of author; data for eleven months are missing and have been supplemented with the averages of the figures for the immediately preceding and subsequent months). For Charleston, see monthly reports printed in the *Charleston Daily Courier* between 1856 and 1858 (database in possession of author). For all other figures, see preceding notes.

8. Bardaglio, *Reconstructing the Household*; Bercaw, *Gendered Freedoms*; Downs, *Declarations of Dependence*; Edwards, *Gendered Strife and Confusion*; Edwards, *People and Their Peace*; McCurry, *Masters of Small Worlds*; Shammas, *History of Household Governance*.

9. De Koster and Reinke, "Policing Minorities," 272–74; Dubber, *Police Power*; Neocleous, *Fabrication of Social Order*.

10. Brown, "Vagabond's Tale," 800–805; Merritt, *Masterless Men*, 1–37; Lockley, *Lines in the Sand*, ix–xiv.

11. Owsley, *Plain Folk of the Old South*, 133.

12. Fredrickson, *Black Image in the White Mind*, 61–68.

13. Bolton, *Poor Whites of the Antebellum South*, 5, 192n9; Cecil-Fronsman, *Common Whites*, 15–16; Harris, *Plain Folk and Gentry*, 77; Linden, "Economic Democracy in the Slave South," 178–79; McCurry, *Masters of Small Worlds*, 71. On the persecution of landless poor white people in the South, see also Brown, "Vagabond's Tale"; Forret,

Race Relations at the Margins, chap. 1; Isenberg, *White Trash*, chap. 6; and Merritt, *Masterless Men*.

14. Beier, *Masterless Men*; Chambliss, "Sociological Analysis of the Law of Vagrancy"; Ocobock, introduction to *Cast Out*, 6–11.

15. Hamilton, *Farmer Refuted*, 24.

16. Livingston, *System of Penal Law, for the State of Louisiana*, 243, 319.

17. John Larue, judgment, in *State vs. John Clayton, praying for habeas corpus*, filed November 11, 1850, docket no. 5548, First District Court Records, NOPL.

18. Tiedeman, *Treatise on the Limitations of Police Power*, 1:116–17, 120; Novak, *People's Welfare*, 167–71; Dubber, *Police Power*, esp. 50–62, chap. 4; Neocleous, *Fabrication of Social Order*, 16–21; Wagner, *Disturbing the Peace*, 37–42.

19. Nicolas Chauvin de la Frenière to the Superior Council, September 3, 1763, Records of the Superior Council of Louisiana (translations), Louisiana State Historical Center, New Orleans; entry of September 21, 1808, bk. 1, vol. 2, OP-CDV; "Native Kentuckian," editorial, in *Louisiana Advertiser* (New Orleans), May 16, 1820; Hardy, "Transportation of Convicts to Colonial Louisiana."

20. Halttunen, *Confidence Men and Painted Women*; Laurie, *Artisans into Workers*, chap. 1; Montgomery, *Citizen Worker*, 13; Rothman, *Discovery of the Asylum*, chap. 3; Schmidt, *Free to Work*, 59; Stanley, *From Bondage to Contract*, chap. 3.

21. On slavery's urban decline, see Goldin, *Urban Slavery in the American South*; Fields, *Slavery and Freedom on the Middle Ground*, chap. 3; Takagi, *Rearing Wolves to Our Own Destruction*, chap. 4; Thompson, *Working on the Dock of the Bay*, chap. 4; Wade, *Slavery in the Cities*, chap. 9.

22. "Yellow Fever in Charleston in 1852," 143; Schechter, "Free and Slave Labor," 168; Berlin and Gutman, "Natives and Immigrants"; Miller, "Enemy Within."

23. Linden, "Economic Democracy in the Slave South," 155–56; Merritt, *Masterless Men*, 14; Shugg, *Origins of Class Struggle*, 24, 319–20; Towers, *Urban South*.

24. Fertel, *Imagining the Creole City*, 58; Kendall, *History of New Orleans*, 3:161; Marler, *Merchants' Capital*, 23; Wyche, "Union Defends the Confederacy," 273–74. For these men's slave ownership, see *Sixth Census of the United States*, reel 133, Municipality 2, Orleans Parish, Louisiana, pp. 47A–B; *Seventh Census of the United States*, reel 245, slave schedule, Orleans Parish, Louisiana, p. 407; *Eighth Census of the United States, 1860*, reel 429, slave schedule, Orleans Parish, Louisiana, p. 20.

25. *Nott's Case*, 11 Me. 208 (1834).

26. *New York Herald*, March 30, 31, 1855; Hill, *Their Sisters' Keepers*, 109–44, esp. 118.

27. Schmidt, *Free to Work*, chap. 2; Stanley, *Bondage to Contract*, chap. 3.

28. Schmidt, *Free to Work*, chap. 2, esp. 53.

29. Katz, *Shadow of the Poorhouse*, 20; Bellows, "Tempering the Wind," 181; Franklin, "Public Welfare in the South," 385; Ely, "'There Are Few Subjects in Political Economy of Greater Difficulty'"; Green, *This Business of Relief*, esp. 43–45; Lockley, *Welfare and Charity*. On the brief life of New Orleans's almshouse—finally built through private philanthropy in 1858, though accidentally burned by the Union army in 1865—see *New Orleans Daily Crescent*, February 18, 1850, October 23, 1858; *New-Orleans Times*, October 6, 1865; and *General Message of Mayor C. M. Waterman*, 45–48.

30. J. Stoddard Johnston, "City Government and City Institutions," in *Memorial*

History of Louisville, 1:341; "An Ordinance in Relation to the Work House," approved September 5, 1843, in *Revised Ordinances of the City of Saint Louis*, 478–85; Green, *This Business of Relief*, 60–61; *Charleston Daily Courier*, March 6, July 3, 1856; "Workhouse," in *Digest of the Ordinances of the City Council of Memphis*, 186–88; Rôbert, *Nashville City Guide Book*, 37; *Daily Chronicle and Sentinel* (Augusta, GA), April 5, 1859; Tripp, *Yankee Town, Southern City*, 40, 283n86; "An Act for the Better Preservation of Order on and about the Fish Wharf," approved March 21, 1842, printed in *Alexandria (VA) Gazette*, March 23, 1842; "An Act to Establish and Regulate the Work-House," approved September 13, 1855, in Raines, *Compilation of the General Laws of the City of Nashville*, 141; Rockman, *Scraping By*, 198–213; *Daily Gazette and Comet* (Baton Rouge), September 8, 1852; Doss, *Cotton City*, 142, 171.

31. In 1844, the First Municipality Workhouse recorded 658 admittances, while the Second Municipality Workhouse reported 774 admittances. In 1845, the Third Municipality Workhouse recorded 856 admittances. In 2017, Chicago reported 53,290 jail admissions (2.0 imprisonments per hundred residents) and Los Angeles reported 128,531 jail admissions (3.3 per hundred), while in 2019, New York City reported 34,389 jail admissions (0.4 per hundred). Register of Vagrants Entering the Workhouse, Workhouse of the First Municipality Records, entry of January 14, 1845, Journal of Minutes and Proceedings, vol. 3, Second Municipality Council Records, and Register of Persons Committed to the Third Municipality Workhouse, Workhouse of the Third Municipality Records, all in NOPL; *New Orleans Daily Crescent*, October 17, 1857; Scrivener et al., *New York City Jail Population in 2019*, 1; *Care First, Jails Last*, 17; "Jail: Admissions Are Down."

32. *Daily Picayune* (New Orleans), March 21, April 13, June 29, December 1, 1842, January 27, February 8, 17, 1846, November 12, 1850, July 23, 1851; *New Orleans Daily Crescent*, April 17, July 18, October 18, 1850, March 31, 1851; *State vs. John Clayton, praying for habeas corpus*, filed November 11, 1850, docket no. 5548, First District Court Records, NOPL.

33. *New York v. Miln*, 36 US 102 (1837); *Prigg v. Pennsylvania*, 41 US 539 (1842); *New Orleans Daily Crescent*, March 31, April 7, 1851. On how "vagrancy laws provided the legal justification for the imprisonment of runaways," see Manion, *Liberty's Prisoners*, 25–26.

34. "An Act Relative to Crimes and Offenses," approved March 15, 1855, §§ 120–27, in *Louisiana Acts, 1855*, pp. 130–50.

35. *Daily Picayune* (New Orleans), May 27, 1851, December 26, 1856. A search of the First District Court docket books confirms the absence of any subsequent habeas corpus suits; General Dockets, vols. 2–3, First District Court Records, NOPL.

36. La. Const. of 1868, art. 7.

37. These or similar subcategories were common elsewhere: see *New York Herald*, March 30, 1855; Freund, *Police Power*, 97–98, 100, 244, 246; and Neocleous, *Fabrication of Social Order*, 67, 75. For data presented in graph 4.3, see Register of Persons Committed to the Third Municipality Workhouse, Workhouse of the Third Municipality Records, NOPL. This sample represents 209 prisoners committed between January 1, 1850, and April 30, 1851 (the only period during which jailors consistently recorded vagrants' subtypes). This sample excludes all repeat offenders whose first

commitment occurred before January 1850, since in cases involving recidivists, jailors merely reentered the reference number associated with the inmate's previous admittance rather than creating a new entry (and thus never recorded the inmate's subtype if the first commitment had occurred before January 1850).

38. *New Orleans Daily Crescent*, October 18, 1850. On illegitimate power relations, see Halttunen, *Confidence Men and Painted Women*, esp. 24.

39. On disorder and the disruption of feminine dependency, see Bynum, *Unruly Women*, chap. 4. On vagrancy law and prostitution, see Butler, *Daughters of Joy*, 28; Freund, *Police Power*, 97–98, 224–46; Hill, *Their Sisters' Keepers*; Hobson, *Uneasy Virtue*, 33; Schafer, *Brothels, Depravity, and Abandoned Women*, 27, 121, 145; Stansell, *City of Women*, 5, 6, 50, 194, 205–6; and Williams, *Vogues and Villainy*, 58. On vagrancy and the policing of persons who might self-identify as LGBTQ in the twenty-first century, see Eskridge, *Dishonorable Passions*, 58–59, 93, 97, 223; Goluboff, *Vagrant Nation*, 164–76; and Manion, *Female Husbands*, 3, 25–29, 42–43, 140–42, 154, 170, 185–88, 199, 250–51.

40. *Daily Picayune* (New Orleans), April 22, 1840, June 29, 1842, April 18, 26, 1849, September 30, 1850, February 16, 1857; *New Orleans Daily Crescent*, November 20, 1851; *Jeffersonian* (New Orleans), January 12, 1846.

41. *Daily Picayune* (New Orleans), April 13, 1842, January 28, 29, 1849, April 23, 1853; *Weekly Picayune* (New Orleans), March 21, 1842.

42. *Weekly Picayune* (New Orleans), March 21, 1842; *Daily Picayune* (New Orleans), November 12, 1850; *State of Louisiana v. Ben Rose and John Blunk*, filed November 27, 1846, docket no. 522, *James McLean and Oliver Hunt Praying for writ of Habeas Corpus*, filed April 15, 1848, docket no. 2142, and *State vs. John Clayton, praying for habeas corpus*, filed November 11, 1850, docket no. 5548, all in First District Court Records, NOPL.

43. Record of Work Performed by the Workhouse, 2 vols., Workhouse Records, NOPL; Minute Book, vol. 1, House of Refuge Records, NOPL.

44. See especially *Daily Picayune* (New Orleans), October 5, 1856.

45. *Daily Picayune* (New Orleans), October 15, 1840, May 13, 1846, February 11, 1850, February 4, 1852.

46. Graph 4.4 reflects 530 commitments made between March 1, 1846, and April 30, 1851. This sample excludes all commitments made from June 15, 1847, to June 3, 1848 (those entries are missing). This sample also excludes 7 commitments of persons identified generically as natives of "America" or "North America," 5 commitments of persons whose birthplaces are illegible, and all commitments of recidivists whose first commitment occurred either before March 1846 or during the missing period from June 15, 1847, to June 3, 1848. Register of Persons Committed to the Third Municipality Workhouse, Workhouse of the Third Municipality Records, NOPL.

47. Census records suggest the same racial trend. Census takers in 1850 recorded fifty-four prisoners in the First Municipality Workhouse; five were Black, and all five were Louisiana natives. In the Third Municipality Workhouse, census takers identified forty-four prisoners; none were identified as Black (the Second Municipality Workhouse was empty when census takers visited due to a recent court order). *Seventh Census of the United States*, reel 236, Ward 5, Municipality 1, Orleans Parish, Louisiana,

pp. 234B–35A; *Seventh Census of the United States*, reel 238, Ward 3, Municipality 3, Orleans Parish, Louisiana, pp. 234A–34B. Whiteness also appears ubiquitous among vagrants tried during the 1820s: see Decisions of the Mayor in Criminal Cases, 2 vols., Office of the Mayor Records, NOPL. Keri Leigh Merritt also finds that virtually all persons arrested for vagrancy in Georgia were white; Merritt, *Masterless Men*, 32, 35–36, 214, chap. 6, esp. 183–84.

48. For vagrants describing themselves as locals, or for police identification of arrestees as "notorious" or "well known" (suggesting localism), see *Daily Picayune* (New Orleans), January 31, February 15, April 10, September 27, 1849, April 2, 1850; *New Orleans Daily Crescent*, October 7, 1848; *New Orleans Daily Crescent*, January 29, 1852; and *Theodore George and Horatio Forrest Praying for a writ of Habeas Corpus*, filed January 22, 1852, docket no. 4953, Fourth District Court Records, NOPL.

49. *Daily Picayune* (New Orleans), April 2, 1850; *New Orleans Daily Crescent*, October 7, 1848; *Seventh Census of the United States*, reel 238, Ward 4, Municipality 3, Orleans Parish, Louisiana, p. 452 [456]; Gardner, *Gardner's New Orleans Directory*, 475; *Ninth Census of the United States*, reel 521, Ward 5, Orleans Parish, Louisiana, p. 143.

50. *Daily Picayune* (New Orleans), February 11, 1850; *Seventh Census of the United States*, reel 236, Ward 6, Municipality 1, Orleans Parish, Louisiana, p. 569.

51. The Prudhommes' domestic movements are inferable by the birthplaces of their children. *New Orleans Daily Crescent*, October 13, 1848, November 14, 1850; *Daily Picayune* (New Orleans), December 29, 1852, December 3, 1856; *Seventh Census of the United States*, reel 238, Ward 3, Municipality 3, Orleans Parish, Louisiana, p. 337; *Eighth Census of the United States*, reel 419, Ward 6, Orleans Parish, Louisiana, p. 177; *Passenger Lists of Vessels Arriving at New Orleans*, reel 21, p. 157.

52. *Daily Picayune* (New Orleans), March 26, 1854; *Daily Comet* (Baton Rouge), December 1, 1855.

53. Bolton, *Poor Whites of the Antebellum South*, 5, 71; Bolton, "Edward Isham and Poor White Labor," 23; Bonner, "Profile of a Late Antebellum Community"; Forret, *Race Relations at the Margins*, 12; Grivno, *Gleanings of Freedom*, 152–63; Harris, *Plain Folk and Gentry*, 88–90; McDonnell, "Work, Culture, and Society in the Slave South"; Rockman, *Scraping By*, 46; Wright, "'Economic Democracy.'"

54. Among 137 commitments of "loafers" made to the Third Municipality Workhouse between January 1, 1850, and April 30, 1851, only 12 commitments were of women. Register of Persons Committed to the Third Municipality Workhouse, Workhouse of the Third Municipality Records, NOPL.

55. *Daily Picayune* (New Orleans), February 16, 1847; *Daily True Delta* (New Orleans), December 13, 1857.

56. *Daily Picayune* (New Orleans), September 30, 1840, March 13, 1870.

57. *Daily Picayune* (New Orleans), May 19, 1848, January 16, 1849, April 4, 5, 1850, June 9, August 14, 1851, November 18, 1857; *Daily True Delta* (New Orleans), January 7, 1858; *State of Louisiana v. Ben Rose and John Blunk*, filed November 27, 1846, docket no. 522, First District Court Records, NOPL.

58. Data in graph 4.5 is based on 522 commitments for vagrancy between March 1, 1846, and April 30, 1851. Sample excludes 6 commitments of prisoners whose occupations were illegible, all commitments made between June 15, 1847, and June 3, 1848,

and all commitments of recidivists whose first commitment occurred before March 1846 or during the aforementioned missing window. Register of Persons Committed to the Third Municipality Workhouse, Workhouse of the Third Municipality Records, NOPL.

59. *Daily Picayune* (New Orleans), May 31, 1850, February 14, 1856; Towers, *Urban South*, 44.

60. *Daily Picayune* (New Orleans), January 8, 1864.

61. Arnesen, *Waterfront Workers of New Orleans*, 271–72n24; Engerman and Goldin, "Seasonality in Nineteenth-Century Labor Markets," 99; Margo, *Wages and Labor Markets*, 42; Rockman, *Scraping By*, esp. 158.

62. Reinders, *End of an Era*, 21; Shugg, *Origins of Class Struggle*, 113, 116–17; Towers, *Urban South*, 44.

63. *Philadelphia Inquirer*, November 20, 1847; Houston, *Texas and the Gulf of Mexico*, 1:138; *Daily Picayune* (New Orleans), December 1, 1839, November 16, 1842, August 14, 1858, October 7, 1860; *New-York Spectator*, June 12, 1851; Haskel and M'Culloch, *M'Culloch's Universal Gazetteer*, 2:453; Norman, *Norman's New Orleans and Environs*, 81; Arnesen, *Waterfront Workers*, 41; Clark, *New Orleans*, 313.

64. For estimates, see *Daily Picayune* (New Orleans), February 9, 1840, May 13, November 16, 1842, August 4, 1851, March 26, 1854; *New Orleans Daily Crescent*, October 18, 1850, September 27, October 20, 1860; Buckingham, *Slave States of America*, 2:343; Farshey, "Louisiana: Geology and Hydrography," 500; McChesney, "Notes by the Way," 227; and Osborne, *Guide to the West Indies*, 312.

65. Russell, *North America*, 253.

66. *Charleston Courier*, January 20, 1852; Silver, "New Look at Old South Urbanization."

67. *Daily Picayune* (New Orleans), December 1, 1839, November 16, 1842, August 14, 1858, Louis Philippe de Roffignac to Conseil de Ville, December 29, 1827, vol. 12, MM-CDV; *New Orleans Daily Crescent*, October 17, 1857.

68. Blackmar, *Manhattan for Rent*, 170; Clement, "Transformation of the Wandering Poor," 58; Phillips, "Poverty, Unemployment, and the Administration of the Criminal Law."

69. Data presented in graph 4.6 derive from seventy-four monthly arrest reports provided by New Orleans's chief of police and printed in New Orleans's newspapers (most commonly, the *New Orleans Daily Crescent*) between October 1852 and April 1862. Data include reported arrests for "vagrancy" and for being "dangerous and suspicious," often enumerated separately on arrest reports, though both under the umbrella of the state's vagrancy law. Sample excludes monthly reports for April 1861 and for all subsequent months, when vagrancy arrests plummeted due to the outbreak of the Civil War. Sample also excludes monthly reports of April, May, and June 1855, immediately after the Know-Nothings seized control of the city government in the March municipal elections, when police conducted a major antivagrancy purge, averaging more than 500 vagrancy arrests per month, in an effort to drive immigrants from the city.

70. *State vs. John Clayton, praying for habeas corpus*, filed November 11, 1850, docket no. 5548, First District Court Records, NOPL; *Daily Picayune* (New Orleans),

November 12, 1850; *Daily Picayune* (New Orleans), December 1, 1839, February 9, 1840, November 16, 1842, March 26, 1854; *New Orleans Daily Crescent*, October 18, 1850.

71. Chambers, *Trials and Confessions*, 47–63, esp. 57.

72. Katz, *Shadow of the Poorhouse*, 5, 6; Clement, "Transformation of the Wandering Poor," 58; Engerman and Goldin, "Seasonality in Nineteenth-Century Labor Markets"; Friedman and Percival, *Roots of Justice*, 84; Margo, *Wages and Labor Markets*, 43, 82.

73. Gudmestad, *Steamboats and the Rise of the Cotton Kingdom*, 54; Haites, Mak, and Walton, *Western River Transportation*, 162; Kotar and Gessler, *Steamboat Era*, 219.

74. Eder, "Bavarian's Journey," 498; Holmes, *Account of the United States*, 282–83; Niehaus, *Irish in New Orleans*, 137; Vandal, "Nineteenth-Century Municipal Response," 30–59.

75. *Daily Picayune* (New Orleans), March 28, 1849, April 17, 1850; *Seventh Census of the United States*, reel 234, Representative District 3, Orleans Parish, Louisiana, p. 372; *Seventh Census of the United States*, reel 238, Ward 4, Municipality 3, Orleans Parish, Louisiana, p. 463.

76. Philadelphia officials also observed that migrant agricultural workers "travel South" in winter. O'Brassill-Kulfan, *Vagrants and Vagabonds*, 40.

77. Conway, "New Orleans as a Port of Immigration," 5–10; Logsdon, "Immigration through the Port of New Orleans"; Spletstoser, "Back Door to the Land of Plenty," chap. 3, esp. 63. For seasonal immigration patterns, see *Quarterly Abstracts of Passenger Lists of Vessels Arriving at New Orleans*.

78. Eder, "Bavarian's Journey," 495; Holmes, *Account of the United States*, 282; Conway, "New Orleans as a Port of Immigration," 106–7.

79. Gleeson, *Irish in the South*, 28.

80. Gaschet De Lisle et al., grand jury report, August 3, 1843, in Minute Book, vol. 5, Criminal Court of the First District Records, NOPL; Neuman, *Strangers to the Constitution*, 30; "An Act Supplementary to the Act Entitled 'An Act on Vagabonds and Suspicious Persons,'" approved March 16, 1818, §§ 2, 3, in *Louisiana Acts, 1818*, pp. 110–14.

81. Murray, *Lands of the Slave and the Free*, 148.

82. Register of Persons Committed to the Third Municipality Workhouse, Workhouse of the Third Municipality Records, NOPL; *Daily Picayune* (New Orleans), May 4, 1845.

83. *Daily Picayune* (New Orleans), May 4, 1845.

84. Rousey, *Policing the Southern City*, 55–60; James Brown to John Breckinridge, September 17, 1805, in Carter and Bloom, *Territorial Papers*, 9:506–13.

85. Among forty-nine vagrant women who entered the Third Municipality Workhouse between January 1, 1850, and April 30, 1851, jailors identified thirty-three (67.3 percent) as "lewd and abandoned," twelve (24.5 percent) as "loafers," and four (8.2 percent) as "dangerous and suspicious." Register of Persons Committed to the Third Municipality Workhouse, Workhouse of the Third Municipality Records, NOPL. In addition, among 21,561 vagrancy arrests reported in city newspapers between June 1852 and March 1861, 3,077 (14.3 percent) were of women.

86. Hill, *Their Sisters' Keepers*, esp. 109–44; Schafer, *Brothels, Depravity, and Abandoned Women*, 27, 121, 145; Stansell, *City of Women*, esp. 173.

87. *Daily Picayune* (New Orleans), October 12, 1845, March 31, 1849, May 19, 1851,

August 28, 1852, May 24, 1853; *New Orleans Daily Crescent*, October 2, 1848, October 25, 1855. Red-light district raids also appear throughout Reports of the Capitan, vol. 5, Day Police and Night Watch of the Second Municipality Records, NOPL.

88. Entries of October 26, 1851, and November 29, 1851, both in Reports of the Capitan, vol. 5, Day Police and Night Watch of the Second Municipality Records, NOPL; *Daily Picayune* (New Orleans), October 2, 1854, December 2, 1857, February 22, 1859; *New Orleans Daily Crescent*, July 16, 1856.

89. *Daily Picayune* (New Orleans), April 29, 1849, March 14, 1851, June 26, 1855, February 16, 1856, August 17, October 31, 1858; entry of September 26, 1851, Reports of the Captain, vol. 5, Day Police and Night Watch of the Second Municipality Records, NOPL; entry of January 14, 1855, Reports of Arrests, vol. 8, Third District, Department of Police Records, NOPL.

90. *Report of the Board of Commissioners of the House of Refuge*, 9–11; Everest, *Everest's Journey*, 111; Minute Book, vol. 1, House of Refuge Records, NOPL.

91. *Mary Jane Owen for her minor Son, John Dudley Owen, alias Irvin, praying for a writ of Habeas Corpus*, filed March 9, 1849, docket no. 2019, Second District Court Records, NOPL; *Mary Cassidy praying for a Writ of Habeas Corpus Petition*, filed August 17 1852, docket no. 5518, Fourth District Court Records, NOPL; entries of December 3, 1856 and May 23, 1858, in Minute Book, vol. 1, House of Refuge Records, NOPL.

92. *Report of the Board of Commissioners of the House of Refuge*, 4; *Daily Picayune* (New Orleans), January 4, 1850.

93. Entries of March 3, May 12 and 23, June 16, and August 12, 1858, all in Minute Book, vol. 1, House of Refuge Records, NOPL.

94. Entries of August 12, 1857, and May 12 and September 1, 1858, Minute Book, vol. 1, House of Refuge Records, NOPL.

95. See, for example, the case of Theodore George and Horatio Forrest, who protested that they were "dwellers in this city" with "house + family." The judge rejected their petition, concluding that residency did not preclude vagrancy. *Theodore George and Horatio Forrest Praying for a writ of Habeas Corpus*, filed January 22, 1852, docket no. 4953, Fourth District Court Records, NOPL. For other "dangerous and suspicious" vagrants who owned property, see *New Orleans Daily Crescent*, January 29, 1852; *Daily Picayune* (New Orleans), February 5, 1852; *State of Louisiana v. William Cintis*, filed February 10, 1847, docket no. 679, and *State of Louisiana vs. Thomas O'Hara*, filed February 18, 1847, docket no. 681, both in First District Court Records, NOPL.

96. *New Orleans Daily Crescent*, October 18, 1850.

97. *Daily Picayune* (New Orleans), April 8, 1846, July 1, 1849, June 20, 1850, May 19, November 17, 1852, February 11, 1855, March 22, October 12, 1857, June 19, 1859, January 30, 1861; *Southerner* (New Orleans), August 19, 1847; *New Orleans Daily Crescent*, September 30, 1848; *Seventh Census of the United States*, reel 237, Ward 4, Municipality 2, Orleans Parish, Louisiana, p. 35.

98. *Edgefield (SC) Advertiser*, July 9, 1856.

99. *Abbeville (SC) Banner*, May 10, 1851; Hieke, *Jewish Identity in the Reconstruction South*, 44.

100. *Vicksburg (MS) Daily Whig*, July 30, 1835; *Alabama Intelligencer and State Rights Expositor* (Tuscaloosa), September 19, 1835; *National Banner and Nashville*

Whig, January 8, 1836. On the Murrell Excitement, see Johnson, *River of Dark Dreams*, chap. 2; and Rothman, *Flush Times and Fever Dreams*.

101. *Georgian* (Savannah), reprinted in *Macon Telegraph*, April 9, 1839.

102. *Abbeville (SC) Banner*, May 10, 1851; *Columbus (GA) Enquirer*, November 25, 1840, September 11, 1844; *Yazoo Democrat* (Yazoo City, MS), August 6, 1859; Olmsted, *Journey in the Back Country*, 73, 75, 137, 219, 449–50; Cecil-Fronsman, *Common Whites*, 108–9; Harris, *Plain Folk and Gentry*, 68–72.

103. Cobb, *Inquiry into the Law of Negro Slavery* 1:ccxiii; Forsyth, "North and the South," 374; Fitzhugh, *Sociology for the South*, 253; Hammond, "Mudsill Speech," 121–23.

104. Fitzhugh, *Sociology for the South*, 253–55; Finkelman, *Defending Slavery*, 25–26, 32–33; Genovese, *Slaveholders' Dilemma*, 33–40; Tise, *Proslavery*, 106, 110–11, 120–23; Faust, *Ideology of Slavery*.

105. Fitzhugh, *Sociology for the South*, 282; Fitzhugh, *Cannibals All!*, 282–83; Holmes, "Slavery and Freedom"; Glickstein, *Concepts of Free Labor*, chap. 6.

106. For example, Cobb, *Inquiry into the Laws of Negro Slavery*, 1:ccxiii.

107. Simms, *Slavery in America*, 73; *Southern Sentinel* (Plaquemine, LA), August 29, 1857; Foner, *Politics and Ideology*, 104.

108. Fitzhugh, *Sociology for the South*, 105; Genovese, *World the Slaveholders Made*, 195; "Southern Convention at Vicksburg," 209–10.

109. On this contradictory inheritance, see Steinfeld, "Property and Suffrage," 338.

110. Brown, "Vagabond's Tale," 838–40; Montgomery, *Citizen Worker*, 21–22; Neuman, *Strangers to the Constitution*, 23–24; Smith, *Civic Ideas*, 214–25; Steinfeld, "Property and Suffrage"; O'Brassill-Kulfan, *Vagrants and Vagabonds*, 26–29.

111. Defining the vagrant for the purpose of his political exclusion proved difficult. Convention delegates feared that partisan judges might hold mass tribunals before elections, convicting political rivals' supporters of vagrancy en masse. A fixed residency requirement was also deemed untenable because many of Louisiana's businessmen and planters were themselves of a "migratory disposition" and seasonally resided out of state. The convention ultimately settled upon a two-year residency requirement alongside a grandfather clause protecting the suffrage rights of anyone able to vote under the previous constitution. *Daily Picayune* (New Orleans), February 6, 1840, January 15, 1841; Ker, *Proceedings and Debates of the Convention of Louisiana*, 99–101, 855; Glenn, *New Constitution of the State of Louisiana*, 5–6.

112. Ker, *Proceedings and Debates*, 926.

113. On Know-Nothings in the South, see Broussard, "Some Determinants of Know Nothing Electoral Strength in the South"; Carriere, "Political Leadership of the Louisiana Know Nothing Party"; Hall, "Glorious Assemblage"; Overdyke, *Know-Nothing Party in the South*; and Towers, *Urban South*, 94–95, 112, 117–25.

114. *Daily Comet* (Baton Rouge), December 1, 1855; *New Orleans Daily Crescent*, February 18, 1856.

115. *New Orleans Daily Crescent*, October 19, 1855, October 25, 1856, October 31, 1857.

116. *Daily Picayune* (New Orleans), November 30, 1855; *New Orleans Daily Crescent*, October 19, 1855; *South-Western* (Shreveport), January 24, 1855; *American Patriot* (Clinton, LA), September 8, 1855; entry of February 12, 1855, Journal of Minutes and Proceedings, vol. 6, Board of Assistant Aldermen, Common Council Records, NOPL.

117. The police force flipped from 38 percent native-born to 78 percent. Carriere, *Know Nothings in Louisiana*, 41.

118. *Thibodaux (LA) Minerva*, November 3, 24, 1855 (translations by author); *Opelousas (LA) Patriot*, March 3, 1855; *New Orleans Daily Crescent*, October 19, 1855.

119. *Daily Picayune* (New Orleans), October 10, 1856; Kemble, *Journal of a Residence on a Georgian Plantation*, 146; Hundley, *Social Relations in Our Southern States*, 254, 257; Brown, "Vagabond's Tale," 819–20; Wray, *Not Quite White*, chap. 3; Isenberg, *White Trash*, chap. 6.

120. Leps, *Apprehending the Criminal*, 25–31.

121. *National Era* (Washington, DC), December 24, 1857; James Denver to Jacob Thompson, November 30, 1857, in *Report of the Commissioner of Indian Affairs . . . for the Year 1857*, p. 5; Douglas Cooper to Elias Rector, October 14, 1858, and O. P. Stark to Douglas Cooper, October 4, 1868, both in *Report of the Commissioner of Indian Affairs . . . for the Year 1858*, pp. 156–58.

122. "Destiny of the Slave States," 282; Knox, *Historical Account of St. Thomas*, 123; "West India Islands"; Wright, "Free Negroes in Hayti"; Wright, "Free Negroes in Jamaica"; Wright; "Free Negro Rule"; Guterl, *American Mediterranean*, 117–19; O'Brassill-Kulfan, *Vagrants and Vagabonds*, 102–3; Wagner, *Disturbing the Peace*, 37.

123. Hall, *Two-Fold Slavery*, 42, 66; *Anti-Slavery Bugle* (New Lisbon, OH), March 6, 1846; Wright, "'Horrors of St. Domingo,'" 281–84; Nott, *Slavery, and the Remedy*, xxvii–xxviii, xxxv–xxxvi, 89–90, 111; Abraham Lincoln, Annual Message to Congress, December 1, 1862, in Lapsley, *Writings of Abraham Lincoln*, 6:200; Owen, McKaye, and Howe, *Preliminary Report Touching the Condition and Management of Emancipated Refugees*, 22–23. On the perceived failure of British emancipation policy to stem vagrancy, also see Holt, "Essence of the Contract."

124. Hernández, *City of Inmates*, 36–39; O'Brassill-Kulfan, "'Vagrant Negroes'"; Merritt, *Masterless Men*, 183–84.

125. See "An Act to Prevent Free Persons of Color, Commonly Known as Free Negroes, from Being Brought or Coming to the State of Georgia," approved December 17, 1859, and "An Act to Define and Punish Vagrancy in Free Persons of Color," approved December 17, 1859, both in *Acts of the General Assembly of the State of Georgia*, 68–70. For a similar re-racialization of vagrancy in Maryland, see C. W. Jacobs to Thomas J. Keating, January 10, 1859, in *Easton (MD) Gazette*, March 5, 1859; and *Evening Star* (Washington, DC), February 14, 1860.

126. *Civilian and Galveston (TX) Gazette*, April 16, 1842.

127. Morris, "Labor Controls in Maryland," 387.

128. Lipscomb and Jacobs, "Magistrates and Freeholders Court," 62.

129. "Joint Resolution for the Punishment of Vagrants," approved January 10, 1839, in *Telegraph and Texas Register* (Houston), January 19, 1839.

130. *Hudson River Chronicle* (Ossining, NY), March 24, 1840; *Daily Chronicle and Sentinel* (Augusta, GA), May 9, 1840; *Daily Picayune* (New Orleans), March 25, 1851; *Columbian Register* (New Haven, CT), September 6, 1851; *National Era* (Washington, DC), September 22, 1853; Merritt, *Masterless Men*, 241; Morris, "White Bondage in Ante-Bellum South Carolina," 199; Williams, *Vogues and Villainy*, 58. The sale of vagrants triggered national political controversy during both the 1840 and the 1848

presidential elections: see, for example, *White Slavery!! Or, Selling White Men for Debt!*; *Daily National Intelligencer* (Washington, DC), July 25, 1840; *Portland (ME) Advertiser*, October 13, 1840; *Jeffersonian Republican* (Stroudsburg, PA), November 2, 1848; *State Gazette* (Trenton, NJ), July 25, 1848; and *Burlington (VT) Free Press*, July 14, 1848.

131. "Rules for the Internal Regulation of the Work House," [1842?], Proceedings of the Board of Inspectors of the Workhouse, House of Refuge, and Prison of the First Municipality, enclosed within vol. 1, subser. 4, OR-CDV; "An Ordinance for the Government of the Work House, House of Refuge and Prison of Municipality No. 1," approved March 16, 1842, Ordinances and Resolutions, vol. 1, subser. 2, First Municipality Council Records, NOPL; entry of March 15, 1842, and "Report of the Board of Inspectors of the Work House and Public Prisons of Municipality No. Two," December 13, 1842, both in Journal of Minutes and Proceedings, vol. 2, and Resolution No. 400, approved June 9, 1842, Ordinances and Resolutions, vol. 4, subser. 1, all in Second Municipality Council Records, NOPL; entry of May 16, 1854, Journal of Minutes and Proceedings, vol. 3, Board of Aldermen, Common Council Records, NOPL; Norman, *Norman's New Orleans and Environs*, 130–32; *New Orleans Daily Crescent*, February 3, 1849; *Daily Picayune* (New Orleans), May 3, 1850, April 3, 1853, May 1, 1854; "An Ordinance Relating to Work-House," approved June 2, 1852, in *Daily Picayune* (New Orleans), June 3, 1852.

132. *Daily Delta* (New Orleans), April 19, 21, 1854; *New Orleans Daily Crescent*, May 3, 1854; *Daily Picayune* (New Orleans), January 17, February 28, October 3, November 21, December 5, 1855; entry of February 27, 1855, Journal of Minutes and Proceedings, vol. 6, Board of Assistant Aldermen, Common Council Records, NOPL; Leovy, *Laws and General Ordinances of the City of New Orleans*, 41.

133. *Daily Chronicle and Sentinel* (Augusta, GA), May 7, 18, June 15, 1859.

134. Bibb, *Narrative of the Life and Adventures*, 91–93; "An Act to Incorporate the City of Louisville," approved February 13, 1828, § 13, in Strattan and Vaughan, *Collection of the State and Municipal Laws, in Force, and Applicable to the City of Louisville*, 47–63, esp. 59.

135. *Transcriptions of Parish Records of Louisiana*, no. 26, ser. 1, vol. 3, p. 17; Robert F. W. Allston to Benjamin Allston, September 6, 1860, in Allston, *South Carolina Rice Plantation*, 165; *New Orleans Bee*, September 9, 1835; *National Anti-Slavery Standard* (New York), September 20, 1849; *Keowee Courier* (Pickens Court House, SC), September 15, 1860; Hadden, *Slave Patrols*, 90, 114; Reichel, "Southern Slave Patrols as a Transitional Police Type," 61.

136. *Daily Picayune* (New Orleans), October 4, 1858; Olmsted, *Journey in the Seaboard Slaves States*, 674; Olmsted, *Cotton Kingdom*, 356.

137. *Edgefield (SC) Advertiser*, July 9, 1856; Merritt, *Masterless Men*, 87, 201–2; *Abbeville (SC) Banner*, May 10, 1851; *New Orleans Daily Crescent*, December 19, 1856. Also see *Western Democrat* (Charlotte, NC), January 27, 1857; Greenberg, *Honor and Slavery*, 81, 102, 144; and Lockley, *Lines in the Sand*, 129.

138. Northrup, *Twelve Years a Slave*, 264–65.

139. *New Orleans Bee*, July 14, September 7, 1835; *True American* (New Orleans), August 31, 1835; *Baltimore Gazette and Daily Advertiser*, September 15, 1835; *Commercial Advertiser* (New York), October 21, 1835; *New-York Evening Post*, August 8, 1835.

140. *Daily Picayune* (New Orleans), August 4, September 16, 1841; *Lexington (MS) Union*, August 21, 1841; *Concordia Intelligencer* (Vidalia, LA), reprinted in *Daily Picayune* (New Orleans), August 22, 1841; *Baton Rouge Gazette*, August 28, 1841.

141. *New Orleans Daily Crescent*, December 19, 1856; *New York Herald*, December 11, 1856.

Chapter 5

1. Capers, *Occupied City*; Hearn, *Capture of New Orleans*.

2. *Daily Picayune* (New Orleans), August 5, 6, 1862; *Daily Delta* (New Orleans), August 5, 6, 1862; *Sun* (Baltimore), August 19, 1862; *Crisis* (Columbus, OH), August 27, 1862; *New Orleans Bee*, August 5, 1862, reprinted in *New York Times*, August 17, 1862; entry of August 3, 1862, Reports of Arrests, vol. 11, Third District, Department of Police Records, NOPL; entry of August 4, 1862, Admissions Book, vol. 30, Charity Hospital Records, NOPL.

3. *Daily Picayune* (New Orleans), August 6, 1862. For insurrectionary panic, see, for example, *Shreveport Semi-Weekly News*, September 16, 1862; *Richmond Enquirer*, August 29, 1862; *Memphis Daily Appeal*, August 29, 1862; and *Daily Delta* (New Orleans), August 16, 1862.

4. *Daily Delta* (New Orleans), August 5, 1862.

5. Sprague, *History of the 13th infantry Regiment*, 65–67; Horace Greeley to Abraham Lincoln, August 19, 1862, in *New-York Daily Tribune*, August 20, 1862; Abraham Lincoln to Horace Greeley, August 22, 1862, in Basler, *Collected Works of Abraham Lincoln*, 5:388–89.

6. E. F. Brasier to R. B. Irvin, February 17, 1863, box 1, LR-CA; Registers of Black Persons, 11 vols., Subordinate Office (Plantation Department), in *Records of the Field Offices for the State of Louisiana*, reels 27–29.

7. McCrary, *Abraham Lincoln and Reconstruction*, 271–72. On the "Louisiana Experiment," see also Berlin et al., *Freedom*, ser. 1, vol. 3; Gerteis, *From Contraband to Freedman*; Ripley, *Slaves and Freedmen*; and Tunnell, *Crucible of Reconstruction*.

8. On the Federal government's antivagrancy policies during Emancipation, see Bardes, "Redefining Vagrancy"; Farmer-Kaiser, "'Are They Not in Some Sorts Vagrants?'"; Farmer-Kaiser, "'Because They Are Women,'" 173–74; Farmer-Kaiser, *Freedwomen and the Freedmen's Bureau*; Kerber, *No Constitutional Right to Be Ladies*, chap. 2; Schmidt, *Free to Work*, chaps. 3–4; and Schwalm, *Hard Fight for We*, esp. 249–60.

9. Frank H. Peck to John W. Phelps, June 15, 1862, copied in John W. Phelps, Report of Service, January 16, 1873, reel 4, *U.S. Army Generals' Reports*, reel 4 (hereinafter cited as Phelps, Report of Service).

10. *New York Times*, June 23, 1862; C. H. Conant to Jonas French, October 7, 1862, box 2, PMG-LA; E. F. Jones to C. Strong, May 10, 1862, box 11, and Benjamin Butler to Edwin Stanton, May 25, 1862, box 12, both in Butler Papers, LOC; Dewey, *Memorial of Lt. Daniel Perkins Dewey*, 48; Parton, *General Butler in New Orleans*, 580.

11. For self-emancipation see Williams, *I Freed Myself*.

12. Between 1860 and 1870, the Black population of New Orleans grew from 24,074 (both free and enslaved) to 50,456 persons. Gibson and Jung, "Historical Census Statistics," table 19.

13. On freedpeople's urban migration, see Foner, *Reconstruction*, 81–82; Hunter, *To 'Joy My Freedom*, 24–25; Litwack, *Been in the Storm So Long*, 310–22; and Sternhell, *Routes of War*, 170. On the search for lost kin, see Williams, *Help Me to Find My People*.

14. Peck to Phelps, June 15, 1862, copied in Phelps, Report of Service; George Hanks, testimony, in Berlin et al., *Freedom*, ser. 1, 3:517–21, esp. 518; W[illiam] Mithoff to Benjamin Butler, May 21, 1862, box 12, Butler Papers, LOC; Beecher, *Record of the 114th Regiment*, 131, 185–86; Stevens, *History of the Fiftieth Regiment of Infantry*, 70.

15. "Proclamation of General Butler," May 1, 1862, in Marshall, *Private and Official Correspondence*, 1:434, 436; Butler to Stanton, May 25, 1862, box 12, Butler Papers, LOC; *New York Times*, June 23, 1862. On this humanitarian crisis, see Downs, *Sick from Freedom*, 38, 56–57; Manning, *Troubled Refuge*; and Taylor, *Embattled Freedom*.

16. On these anxieties, see especially Montgomery, *Citizen Worker*; Rodgers, *Work Ethic in Industrial America*, esp. chaps. 7–8; Schmidt, *Free to Work*; and Stanley, *From Bondage to Contract*, chap. 3.

17. Butler to Stanton, May 25, 1862, and Mithoff to Butler, May 21, 1862, both in box 12, Butler Papers, LOC; *New York Times*, December 7, 1862.

18. General Orders No. 14, October 17, 1862, in Berlin et al., *Freedom*, ser. 1, 3:380–82, esp. 380.

19. Butler to Stanton, May 25, 1862, box 12, Butler Papers, LOC; General Order No. 32, May 27, 1862, Special Order No. 45, May 27, 1862, and General Order No. 44, June 21, 1862, all in *War of the Rebellion*, ser. 1, 15:445–46, 492; Benjamin Butler to John W. Phelps, May 12, 1862, copied in Phelps, Report of Service; Benjamin Butler to John W. Phelps, May 9, 1862, and Benjamin Butler to John W. Phelps, May 23, 1862, both in *War of the Rebellion*, ser. 1, 15:442, 443–44.

20. On French's background, see *Boston Evening Transcript*, October 27, 1854; and Jackson, "Keeping Law and Order in New Orleans under General Butler," 56–58. On the arrests of fugitives, see "J. P. M." [S. H. Stafford] to Benjamin Butler, July 18, 1862, and S. H. Stafford to Benjamin Butler, July 21, 1862, both in box 14, Butler Papers, LOC; George Hepworth and Edwin Wheelock to Nathaniel Banks, April 9, 1863, box 26, Nathaniel Banks Papers, LOC; William Gray to Nathaniel Banks, n.d. [January 1863] and January 17, 1863, both in box 2, and F. V. Stewart to Nathaniel Banks, February 9 and 13, 1863, both in box 4, all in LR-CA; W[illiam] H. G[ray] to Harris Cowdry, February 9, 1863, printed in *Liberator* (Boston), March 6, 1863; and Edmond Forstall to Jonas French, January 7, 1863, box 3, PMG-LA.

21. Gerteis, *From Contraband to Freedman*, 11–18; Masur, "'Rare Phenomenon of Philological Vegetation.'"

22. Edward Page to James Bowen, February 16, 1863, box 2, LR-PM.

23. Berlin et al., *Freedom*, ser. 1, 1:194.

24. For these orders, see Butler to Phelps, May 12, 1862, copied in Phelps, Report of Service; and Butler to Phelps, May 9 and 23, 1862, and Butler to Stanton, May 25 and June 18, 1862, all in *War of the Rebellion*, ser. 1, 15:439–42, esp. 440–41, 442, 443–44, 486. For antislavery officers' refusals to impress or return the fugitives, see Page to Bowen, February 16, 1863, box 2, LR-PM; John W. Phelps to Robert S. Davis, July 31, 1862, copied in Phelps, Report of Service; Peter Haggerty to John W. Phelps, May 28, 1862, in Berlin et al., *Freedom* ser. 1, 1:208–9; Benjamin Butler to Edwin Stanton, June 18, 1862, in *War of the Rebellion*, ser. 1, 15:485–86; John W. Phelps to Benjamin

Butler, August 2, 1862, copied in Phelps, Report of Service; and Berlin et al., *Freedom*, ser. 1, 1:187–99, esp. 194.

25. Célina Roman to Henri Roman, January 3, 1863, folder 1, box 2, Roman Family Papers, LARC; "Report of 75 Black Boys Transferred on the 6th Nov 1862 by order of Genl Butler + the amt due on Each to the Police Jail," [November] 1862, enclosed in Henry C. Deming to George C. Strong, November 18, 1862, and "Statement of Blacks transferred by order of Genl Butler from the Police Jail + the amts due on Each to the City Police Jail," [November] 1862, enclosed in Julian Neville to Henry C. Deming, November 17, 1862, both in LR-HR; *Daily Delta* (New Orleans), November 29, 1862. On overcrowded jail conditions, see *Daily True Delta* (New Orleans), January 28, 1863; Mary Graham to Nathaniel Banks, January 28, 1863, and George Hanks to Nathaniel Banks, April 8, 1863, both in box 2, LR-CA; Conant to French, October 7, 1862, box 3, and J. H. M. Connick to Jonas French, May 24, 1862, box 4, both in PMG-LA; "J. P. M." [Stafford] to Butler, July 18, 1862, and Stafford to Butler, July 21, 1862, both in box 14, Butler Papers, LOC; and Phelps to Butler, August 2, 1862, copied in Phelps, Report of Service.

26. Anonymous to Jonas French, July 26, 1862, and Charles B. Child to [Jonas French], September 18, 1862, both in box 3, PMG-LA; I. V. Burnside to Nathaniel Banks, February 21, 1863, box 1, C. C. Morgan [Cyprian Clamorgan] to Nathaniel Banks, January 21, 1863, box 3, and Stewart to Banks, February 9, 1863, and Gorgener Roman to Nathaniel Banks, February 23, 1863, both in box 4, all in LR-CA; Le Grand, *Journal of Julia Le Grand*, 56–57, 282–83, 287–91.

27. Charles W. Drew to James Bowen, April 7, 1863, box 1, and Ephraim L. Patterson to James Bowen, July 8, 1863, box 2, both in LR-PM; Rachel Cosley to Nathaniel Banks, February 22, 1863, box 1, and Hanks to Banks, April 8, 1863, box 2, both in LR-CA; Child to [French], September 18, 1862, box 3, PMG-LA. On the Knapp family, see "Obituary [for Frederick H. Knapp]."

28. For "dependence not as an insult but a strategy," see Downs, *Declarations of Dependence*, 2.

29. G. Keating to Nathaniel Banks, December 30, 1862, enclosed in Jacob Barker to George Shepley, December 6, 1862, box 1, LR-CA. Similarly, see Stewart to Banks, February 9, 1863, box 4, LR-CA; G[ray] to Cowdry, February 9, 1863, in *Liberator* (Boston), March 6, 1863; and *Daily Picayune* (New Orleans), October 2, 1862.

30. Gray to Banks, January n.d., 1863, and January 17, 1863, both in box 2, LR-CA; G[ray] to Cowdry, February 9, 1863, printed in *Liberator* (Boston), March 6, 1863; William Gray, compiled military service record.

31. G[ray] to Cowdry, February 9, 1863, in *Liberator* (Boston), March 6, 1863; Stewart to Banks, February 9 and 13, 1863, both in box 4, LR-CA; Hepworth and Wheelock to Banks, April 9 and 10, 1863, both in box 26, Banks Papers, LOC; Keating to Banks, December 30, 1862, enclosed in Barker to Shepley, December 6, 1862, box 1, and Graham to Banks, January 28, 1863, box 2, both in LR-CA; C. Antoinine to Jonas French, November 21, 1862, box 3, PMG-LA.

32. "Report of 75 Black Boys Transferred on the 6th Nov 1862 by order of Genl Butler + the amt due on Each to the Police Jail," [November] 1862, enclosed in Deming to Strong, November 18, 1862, and "Statement of Blacks transferred by order of Genl

Butler from the Police Jail + the amts due on Each to the City Police Jail," [November] 1862, enclosed in Neville to Deming, November 17, 1862, both in LR-HR; George C. Strong, General Orders No. 99, November 21, 1862, in *War of the Rebellion*, ser. 1, 15:602.

33. *New-York Daily Tribune*, August 13, 1862.

34. In 1866, Capla and his son would both be gravely injured during the New Orleans massacre. Entry of August 14, 1862, Reports of Arrests, vol. 11, Third District, Department of Police Records, NOPL; *Report of the Select Committee on the New Orleans Riots*, 15, 119–23.

35. R. K. T. to anonymous, in *New-York Daily Tribune*, February 5, 1863; Wallace A. Brice to Nathaniel Banks, January 30, 1863, box 1, LR-CA; Ochs, *Black Patriot and a White Priest*, 74–75, 185–87; C. C. Morgan [Cyprian Clamorgan] to Nathaniel Banks, January 19 and 21, 1863, both in box 3, LR-CA; Winch, *Clamorgans*.

36. Hollandsworth, *Louisiana Native Guards*, chap. 2; Ochs, *Black Patriot and a White Priest*, 83–86.

37. Thomas Cahill, order, September [1862], General Orders No. 14, October 17, 1862, General Orders No. 88, November 1, 1862, and General Orders No. 91, November 9, 1862, all in Berlin et al., *Freedom*, ser. 1, 3:377–80, 380–82, 382–83, 385–88.

38. General Orders No. 12, January 29, 1863, printed in *Daily Delta* (New Orleans), February 7, 1863. Further details were hashed out in a later circular, dated February 6, 1863, and copied in Berlin et al., *Freedom*, ser. 1, 3:419.

39. General Orders No. 23, February 3, 1864, in Berlin et al., *Freedom*, ser. 1, 3:512–17, esp. 515.

40. The best general account of Banks's plan is Berlin et al., *Freedom*, ser. 1, vol. 3. Also see Gerteis, *From Contraband to Freedman*; Messner, *Freedmen and the Ideology of Free Labor*; Ripley, *Slaves and Freedmen*; and Schmidt, *Free to Work*, chap. 3.

41. Rodrigue, *Reconstruction in the Cane Fields*, 39–40.

42. Harrington, *Fighting Politician*, 23–25; Hirota, *Expelling the Poor*, 126–28, 216; Mulkern, *Know-Nothing Party in Massachusetts*.

43. *Daily Picayune* (New Orleans), January 31, 1863; Abbott, *Cotton and Capital*, 149–50; *New York Times*, February 14, 1863; Abraham Lincoln to Nathaniel Banks, November 5, 1863, box 29, Nathaniel Banks to Mary Banks, January 30, 1863, box 5, and Issachar Zacharie to Nathaniel Banks, January–February 1863, box 26, all in Banks Papers, LOC; "Justice" to Nathaniel Banks, April 3, 1863, LR-HR; Page to Bowen, February 16, 1863, box 2, LR-PM.

44. Schmidt, *Free to Work*, 53.

45. On gradualism versus immediatism in antislavery thought, see Davis, "Emergence of Immediatism in British and American Antislavery Thought"; Macleod, "From Gradualism to Immediatism"; and Newman, *Transformation of American Abolitionism*. On the perceived "failure" of British emancipation policy, see especially Holt, "Essence of the Contract." For gradual emancipation schemes that cited prior Caribbean emancipations, see Hall, *Two-Fold Slavery*, 42, 66; *Anti-Slavery Bugle* (New Lisbon, OH), March 6, 1846; Wright, "'The Horrors of St. Domingo,'" 281–84; Nott, *Slavery, and the Remedy*, 89–90, 111; Abraham Lincoln, Annual Message to Congress, December 1, 1862, in Lapsley, *Writings of Abraham Lincoln*, 6:179–212, esp. 200; and Owen,

McKaye, and Howe, *Preliminary Report Touching the Condition and Management of Emancipated Refugees*, 22–23.

46. *New York Times*, February 14, 1863; "Slaves in Louisiana"; Schmidt, *Free to Work*, 106–7.

47. Bock, *Radical Pacifists in Antebellum America*, chap. 4.

48. *Liberator* (Boston), January 16, February 27, March 20, April 3, 1863; *National Anti-Slavery Standard* (New York), March 14, 1863. One notable exception was William Lloyd Garrison, who expressed cautious support for aspects of Banks's program; Schmidt, *Free to Work*, 107, 110.

49. *Chicago Tribune*, February 19, 1862.

50. Moses Townsley to Nathaniel Banks, January 15, 1863, box 4, Jonas French to James Smith, enclosed within Morgan [Clamorgan] to Banks, January 19, 1863, box 3, and Rachel Cosley to Nathaniel Banks, February 22, 1863, box 1, all in LR-CA; George Hepworth and Edwin Wheelock to Nathaniel Banks, April 9, 1863, box 26, Banks Papers, LOC.

51. Nathan McKinney to Nathaniel Banks, February 2, 1863, box 3, LR-CA; Nathan M. Kinny [*sic*], compiled military service record, corpl., 7 La. Inf. (Col'd.), in *Compiled Military Service Records of Volunteer Union Soldiers Who Served with the U.S. Colored Troops*, reel 114; *Ninth Census of the United States*, reel 529, Ward 3, St. James Parish, Louisiana, p. 15.

52. Isaac White et al. to Nathaniel Banks, February 23, 1863, and Nancy Young to Nathaniel Banks, January 12, 1863, both in box 4, LR-CA.

53. *Seventh Census of the United States*, reel 245, slave schedule, Orleans Parish, Louisiana, p. 403; *Eighth Census of the United States*, reel 416, Ward 2, Orleans Parish, Louisiana, p. 454; Blassingame, *Black New Orleans*, 74; Foner and Lewis, *Black Worker*, 1:318. For the family's landholdings, see *Marie Rose Malbernac vs. Jean Bonseigneur et als.*, filed April 17, 1874, docket no. 37078, Second District Court Records, NOPL.

54. Previously, Henri Bonseigneur had killed Marie-Thérèse Blanchard's son, Paul Armand Bonseigneur, in a duel (the courts exonerated Henri of any wrongdoing). *Daily Picayune* (New Orleans), June 9, 10, 18, 1857, January 24, 1858; *Daily True Delta* (New Orleans), January 24, 1858; Nérestant Bonseigneur, death certificate, filed August 7, 1855, and Armand Bonseigneur, death certificate, filed December 17, 1860, both in Death Certificates, vols. 14 and 22, New Orleans (LA) Board of Health Records, NOPL.

55. Hollandsworth, *Louisiana Native Guards*; Bergeron, "Louisiana's Free Men of Color in Gray," 106–7.

56. Ochs, *Black Patriot and a White Priest*, 90–93, 112–13; Hollandsworth, *Louisiana Native Guards*, 30–32.

57. Conspicuously, policemen identified several arrestees as "f.m.c." (free man of color) in arrest reports even while arresting them for being outdoors without passes: see entry of January 20–21, 1863, Reports of Arrests, vol. 11, Third District, Department of Police Records, NOPL.

58. Schell, "Old Slave Laws"; *Liberator* (Boston), February 13, 1863. For the reporters' identities, see *Daily Delta* (New Orleans), December 16, 1862; and Andrews, *North Reports the Civil War*, 754.

59. *New York Times*, February 11, 1863; [Albert Hills], editorial, January 23, 1863, in *Liberator* (Boston), February 13, 1863; *New-York Daily Tribune*, February 5, 1863.

60. Schell, "Old Slave Laws," 369, 370, 381; *New York Times*, February 11, 1863; [Hills], editorial, January 23, 1863, in *Liberator* (Boston), February 13, 1863; *Daily Delta* (New Orleans), January 22, 1863; *Daily Picayune* (New Orleans), January 22, 1863; *New Orleans Bee*, January 22, 1863; G[ray] to Cowdry, February 9, 1863, in *Liberator* (Boston), March 6, 1863.

61. Issachar Zacharie to Nathaniel Banks, January–February 1863, box 26, Banks Papers, LOC; *Daily Picayune* (New Orleans), January 22, February 8, 1863.

62. The *Daily Delta* noted considerable "excitement among the colored population" and "a good deal of talk." *Daily Delta* (New Orleans), January 22, 1863.

63. Contrary to the petitioners' claims, some signatories—Jordan B. Noble, for example—had been born enslaved. A handful of signatories (such as P. B. S. Pinchback) had a formerly enslaved parent. The petition is undated, though John R. Hamilton of the *New York Times* predicted that it would be submitted to the government on January 30. Manuel Moreau et al. to George F. Shepley, [January 1863], folder 2, box 7, George F. Shepley Papers, Maine Historical Society, Portland; *New York Times*, February 11, 1863.

64. On these individuals, see Gehman, "Visible Means of Support," 213–14, 217; Bell, *Revolution, Romanticism, and the Afro-Creole Protest Tradition*, 223–28; and Foner, *Reconstruction*, 63.

65. The only three exceptions, who signed by mark—J. D. St. Herman, Similien Brulée, and Jacques Meffre Rouzan—were War of 1812 veterans.

66. The Tinchant-Gonzales family is the subject of Scott and Hébrard, *Freedom Papers*.

67. Works highlighting the importance of Louisiana's Black activist tradition to the national civil rights movement and emphasizing continuity between Reconstruction-era battles and the civil rights movement of the twentieth century include Fairclough, *Race and Democracy*, esp. 2; Luxenberg, *Separate*; Scott, "Atlantic World"; and Scott, "Public Rights." For antebellum free Black people and the "making of modern citizenship," see Jones, *Birthright Citizens*; and Novak, *New Democracy*, 44–54.

68. On *L'Union* and the *Tribune*, see Abbott, *For Free Press and Equal Rights*; Connor, "Reconstruction Rebels"; and Houzeau, *My Passage at the New Orleans Tribune*. On the political activism of New Orleans's formerly free Black community, see Blassingame, *Black New Orleans*; Bell, *Revolution*; and Rankin, "Origins of Black Leadership."

69. On public rights, see Scott, "Atlantic World"; Scott, "Discerning a Dignitary Offense"; Scott, "Public Rights"; Scott and Hébrard, *Freedom Papers*, 129–32; and La. Const. of 1868, arts. 2 and 13.

70. James Bowen to C. W. Kilbourn, March 5, 1863, and Jasper Miller to A. W. Miller, April 4, 1863, both in PM-OP; Special Order No. 120, July 9, 1863, vol. 309, LRO-PM.

71. Mott, *Between the Ocean and the Lakes*, 461; Fauconnet, *Ruined by This Miserable War*, 4–5; Alec Alexander Hypolité Atocha to Nathaniel Banks, March 18, 1863, box 26, Banks Papers, LOC; *Daily Picayune* (New Orleans), March 20, 1863.

72. James Bowen to C. W. Kilbourn, March 5, 14, and 18, 1863, all in OR-OP; C. W. Kilbourn to Chapman, March 5, 1863, C. W. Kilbourn, order, March 11, 1863, and C. W. Kilbourn to O'Brien, March 7, 1863, all in OI-OP; George Hanks to James Bowen, March 16, 1863, James Duane to C. W. Kilbourn, March 16, 1863, and C. W. Kilbourn to Perault, March 20, 1863, all in PM-OP; James Miller to James Bowen, March 12, 1863, box 1, LR-PM.

73. P. F. Mancosas to Nathaniel Banks, August 7, 1863, LR-HR; *Daily Picayune* (New Orleans), August 6, 1863; C. T. Buddeck to Nathaniel Banks, August 5, 1863, box 1, A. Lavissour to Nathaniel Banks, August 10, 1863, and George Hanks to Nathaniel Banks, August 15, 1863, both in box 2, and J[oseph] L'Official et al. to [Don Albert] Pardee, [November 1863], box 3, all in LR-CA; Enoch Foster to Henry Pierson, August 3, 1863, box 1, and H. M. Porter to James Bowen, August 8, 1863, box 2, both in LR-PM; George Hanks to R. B. Irwin, July 11, 1863, box 27, Banks Papers, LOC; *L'Union* (New Orleans), August 20, 1863.

74. Orders No. 9, March 11, 1864, in *War of the Rebellion*, ser. 3, 4:166–70; A. S. Hitchcock to Hall, August 25, 1864, in Berlin et al., *Freedom*, ser. 1, 3:316–18, esp. 317; General Orders No. 75, July 17, 1863, printed in *Memphis Bulletin*, July 29, 1863; A. W. Kelly, order, March 19, 1864, in Berlin et al., *Freedom*, ser. 1, 3:814–15, esp. 815; Cohen, *At Freedom's Edge*, 8–11.

75. H. C. Forbes to [Edward Hatch], [June 1865], enclosed in Edward Hatch to W. D. Whipple, June 22, 1865, in *War of the Rebellion*, ser. 1, vol. 49, pt. 2, pp. 1024–25; Henry Hotze to Felix Ducaigne, August 21, 1863, in *War of the Rebellion*, ser. 2, 3:866–68.

76. James Bowen to Nathaniel Banks, March 1864, and George Hanks to Nathaniel Banks, March 28, 1864, both in box 32, and Hanks to Irwin, July 11, 1863, box 27, all in Banks Papers, LOC; Hanks to Banks, April 8 and August 15, 1863, both in box 2, LR-CA; Thomas Conway to George Hanks, April 25, 1864, LR-SMP; Le Grand, *Journal of Julia Le Grand*, 230.

77. Le Grand, *Journal of Julia Le Grand*, 229–30; *Daily Picayune* (New Orleans), March 27, 29, 1864; *Daily True Delta* (New Orleans), July 1, 7, 8, 1864; George Bell to Stephen Hoyt, February 13, 1864, folder 71, box 4, Civil War Collection, LARC; Eugene Tindale to James Bowen, April 25, 1864, box 2, MR-PM.

78. A. H. Davis to Laura [Davis], April 26, 1863, in McGregor, *History of the Fifteenth Regiment*, 279.

79. *Daily Picayune* (New Orleans), August 18, October 11, 1863; *Daily True Delta* (New Orleans), October 11, 1863.

80. John Ela to James Bowen, June 11, 1863, box 3, LR-PM.

81. A. J. H. Dunganne to James Bowen, April 30, 1863, box 1, Robert Rennie to George Hanks, September 7, 1863, and Ephraim Patterson to James Bowen, July 8, 1863, both in box 2, and James Ennis, E[udaldo] G. Pintado, and Duparty to A. P. Dansty, June 1864, box 3, all in LR-PM.

82. William Bragg to T. E. Chickering, July 31, 1864, box 3, LR-PM.

83. Page to Bowen, February 16, 1863, box 2, LR-PM.

84. Berlin et al., *Freedom*, ser. 1, 3:365; La. Const. of 1864, art. 1.

85. General Orders No. 23, February 3, 1864, in Berlin et al., *Freedom*, ser. 1, 3:512–17, esp. 515.

86. G[ray] to Cowdry, February 9, 1863, printed in *Liberator* (Boston), March 6, 1863.

87. E[dmund] Russel to James Bowen, March 6, 1863, box 2, LR-PM.

88. Drew to Bowen, April 7, 1863, box 1, LR-PM; James Bowen to C. W. Kilbourn, March 18, 1863, OR-OP; *L'Union* (New Orleans), August 20, 1863; Nathaniel Banks to "Commander of Enrollment for the Corps d'Afrique," September 2, 1863, box 28, Banks Papers, LOC.

89. Farmer-Kaiser, *Freedwomen and the Freedmen's Bureau*, 81–91; Farmer-Kaiser, "'Are They Not in Some Sorts Vagrants?'"; Kerber, *No Constitutional Right*, chap. 2; Glymph, *Out of the House of Bondage*, chap. 5; Schwalm, *Hard Fight for We*.

90. George Darling to George Hanks, July 18, 1864, box 34, Banks Papers, LOC.

91. George Hanks to James Bowen, April 13, 1864, endorsement in Thomas Conway to George Hanks, April 13, 1864, box 32, Banks Papers, LOC.

92. R. B. Brown to I. L. Carey, April 6, 1864, LR-SCP; Albert Stearns to "Comm[an]d-[in]g Officer of [the St. Mary Parish] Provost Guard," July 11, 1864, and Albert Stearns to Simon James, May 4, 1864, both in LRS-SMP.

93. S. B. Bevans to George Hanks, August 2, 1864, endorsement in S. B. Bevans to Edward Canby, August 2, 1864, box 5, and Thomas Sherman to George Drake, August 17, 1864, box 8, both in LR-CA.

94. Henry Norvall et al. to James Bowen, April 5, 1863, enclosed in Charles C. Nott to James Bowen, April 5, 1863, box 3, LR-CA.

95. John Lee to Couzins, March 2, 1864, in Berlin et al., *Freedom*, ser. 1, 3:528–29.

96. Conway to Hanks, April 13, 1864, box 32, and George Hanks to James T. Tucker, May 27, 1864, box 33, both in Banks Papers, LOC; *New-York Daily Tribune*, April 8, 1887; *Times-Democrat* (New Orleans), April 16, 1864; *New York Times*, April 24, 1864; Messner, *Freedmen and the Ideology of Free Labor*, 66–68; Bell, "'Une Chimère,'" 150.

97. *Liberator* (Boston), April 8, 1863, March 25, May 27, 1864, February 10, 1865; *National Anti-Slavery Standard* (New York), February 21, 1863.

98. Douglass, "What the Black Man Wants"; *Liberator* (Boston), April 29, 1864.

99. Mahood, *General Wadsworth*, 204.

100. *Report of the Secretary of War, Communicating . . . the Final Report of the American Freedmen's Inquiry Commission*, 13–14, 110.

101. McKaye, *Mastership and Its Fruits*, 26–27; Gerteis, *From Contraband to Freedman*, 77–78; Schmidt, *Free to Work*, 107–9.

102. Schmidt, *Free to Work*, 110–11.

103. George Hanks to Nathaniel Banks, October 6, 1864, box 35, [Hanks], circular, March 26, 1864, enclosed within Hanks to Banks, March 28, 1864, box 32, and Banks, *Emancipated Labor in Louisiana* [1864], box 82, all in Banks Papers, LOC; Thomas Conway to George B. Drake, October 3, 1864, LA-CR.

104. Gerteis, *From Contraband to Freedman*, 80–81.

105. Thomas Conway to James Andrew, August 25, 1864, box 34, Banks Papers, LOC; Bell, "'Une Chimère,'" 149; Thomas Conway, testimony, January 28, 1865, in Berlin et al., *Freedom*, ser. 1, 3:575–81, esp. 576.

106. *New Orleans Tribune*, August 18, 1864; Thomas Porée et al. to Nathaniel Banks, August 17, 1864, box 7, LR-CA.

107. On the Louisiana Freedmen's Bureau, see Bell, "'Une Chimère'"; Rodrigue, "Freedmen's Bureau"; and White, *Freedmen's Bureau in Louisiana*.

108. Thomas Conway to George B. Drake, March 29, 1865, box 10, LR-CA.

Chapter 6

1. Tobias Gibson to Benjamin Flanders, December 1, 1864, in *Message of the President of the United States . . . in Relation to the States of the Union Lately in Rebellion*, 85–87. For Gibson's net worth, see *New York Herald*, February 18, 1863.

2. *New Orleans Tribune*, August 1, 1865 (French edition, translation by author); John Morton [*sic*], affidavit, in *New-York Daily Tribune*, July 29, 1865; Clinton Fisk to Thomas Conway, July 3, 1865, and Thomas Conway to Hugh Kennedy, July 7, 1865, both enclosed in Hugh Kennedy to Andrew Johnson, July 21, 1865, all in *Andrew Johnson Papers*, ser. 1, reel 16; McFeely, *Yankee Stepfather*, 166–69. On the visual coding of vagrants, see Wagner, *Disturbing the Peace*, 37.

3. On former slaveholders' vision for postbellum coercion and social order, see especially Carter, *When the War Was Over*; Cohen, *At Freedom's Edge*, esp. chap. 2; and Wilson, *Black Codes*.

4. A variety of conflicting origins for the Black Codes have been proposed, to wit: they represented the re-creation of antebellum plantation controls, the revival of antebellum laws directed at free Black people, the mutilation of northern free labor ideology, or the resurrection of forgotten and vestigial colonial laws. See Carter, *When the War Was Over*, 216–19; Foner, *Nothing but Freedom*, 49–52; O'Brassill-Kulfan, "'Vagrant Negroes'"; Ranney, *In the Wake of Slavery*, 5; and Summers, *Ordeal of the Reunion*, 73, 76. Keri Leigh Merritt suggests that antebellum policing practices aimed at poor white people—antebellum vagrancy laws, in particular—provided a template for postbellum policing practices aimed at freedpeople; Merritt, *Masterless Men*, 36, 180–81.

5. Works emphasizing the influence of Caribbean emancipations on US Emancipation include Carter, *When the War Was Over*, 218–19; Clavin, *Toussaint Louverture and the American Civil War*; Eudell, *Political Languages of Emancipation*; Guterl, *American Mediterranean*; and Rugemer, *Problem of Emancipation*. On the ubiquity of post-emancipation vagrancy laws, see Kloosterboer, *Involuntary Servitude*, 191–203; and Woodward, *Future of the Past*, 153.

6. Wagner, *Disturbing the Peace*, 37.

7. McKaye, *Mastership and Its Fruits*, 4–5; Litwack, *Been in the Storm So Long*, 305; Edward Hatch to W. D. Whipple, June 22, 1865, in *War of the Rebellion*, ser. 1, pt. 2, pp. 1024–25; Sternhell, *Routes of War*, chap. 4.

8. Gibson and Jung, "Historical Census Statistics," table 19.

9. Olmsted, *Journey in the Seaboard Slave States*, 677; White, *Freedmen's Bureau in Louisiana*, 103. On freedpeople's urban migration and its motivations, see Cohen, *At Freedom's Edge*, 119; Foner, *Reconstruction*, 81–82; Hunter, *To 'Joy My Freedom*, 24–25; Litwack, *Been in the Storm So Long*, 310–22; Rabinowitz, *Race Relations in the Urban South*, 118–24; Rodrigue, *Reconstruction in the Cane Fields*, 71; Sternhell, *Routes of War*, 168–71; and Williams, *Help Me to Find My People*, esp. 150.

10. Roberts, *Freedom as Marronage*.

11. Litwack, *Been in the Storm So Long*, 297, 311; Sternhell, *Routes of War*, 168–71, esp. 169; Henry Adams, testimony, March 13, 1880, in *Report and Testimony of the Select Committee . . . to Investigate the Causes of the Removal of the Negroes*, 191.

12. Edward Beckwith to John Crosby, box 9, May 16, 1865, LR-CA; *New-Orleans Times*, October 30, 1866; *Daily Picayune* (New Orleans), August 8, 1865.

13. Mary Johnson, interview, in *Slave Narratives*, vol. 16, 2:219–22, esp. 222; Registers of Complaints, vol. 1, in *Records of the Field Offices for the State of Louisiana*, reel 7. On urban wage work after Emancipation, see especially Hunter, *To 'Joy My Freedom*.

14. Dennett, *South as It Is*, 364; *Tri-Weekly Advocate* (Baton Rouge), October 24, 1865; *New-Orleans Times*, August 27, October 12, 18, 1865, February 15, 1867; *New York Times*, December 3, 1865.

15. "Loi concernant la culture" in Christophe, *Code Henry*, 7:5, 28; *Rural Code of Haiti*, 84–89; Wright, "'Horrors of St. Domingo,'" 282; Barclay, *Practical View*, unpaginated preface; Dubois, *Haiti*, 66; Matibag, *Haitian-Dominican Counterpoint*, 102; Smith, *Liberty, Fraternity, Exile*, 39–43.

16. Taylor, *Paper on the Proposed Emancipation of Slaves*, 67, 74; *Mirror of Parliament*, 4:3531; Green, "James Stephen and British West India Policy," 41–42; Handler and Bilby, *Enacting Power*; Harris, *Punishing the Black Body*, chap. 3; Holt, *Problem of Freedom*, 185–86; Levy, *Emancipation, Sugar, and Federalism*, 73, 92; Lightfoot, *Troubling Freedom*, 99, 185–88; Paton, *Cultural Politics of Obeah*, 10, 13, 121–25, 142–43, 161–76, 191, 194, 206, 247; Paton, *No Bond but the Law*.

17. *Recueil de la législation nouvelle*, 8–9, 17; "Décret relatif à la répression de la mendicité et du vagabondage aux colonies," approved April 27, 1848, and "Arrêté du ministre de la marine concernant les ateliers de discipline pour la répression du vagabondage et de la mendicité aux colonies," approved April 27, 1848, both in *Recueil complet des actes du gouvernement provisoire*, 330–31, 474–79; Pluskota, "Freedom of Movement," 106.

18. Pluskota, "Freedom of Movement," 106–7.

19. Gigault de Crisenoy, *Études sur la situation économique*, 51–55; Renard, "Labour Relations in Martinique and Guadeloupe," 44–48; Chester, *Transatlantic Sketches*, 26, 154.

20. *Debates in the Convention for the Revision and Amendment of the Constitution*, 604–5; *New-Orleans Times*, July 3, 1865; *New Orleans Tribune*, October 7, 1865; *New Orleans Bee*, October 6, 11, 1865; *Standard* (Clarksville, TX), November 25, 1865; Fauconnet, *Ruined by This Miserable War*, 124.

21. Sitterson, *Sugar Country*, 231.

22. Fitzhugh, "Freedmen," 491; Fitzhugh, "Virginia," 184.

23. Foner, *Nothing but Freedom*, 52; *New-Orleans Times*, July 29, 1865; *South-Western* (Shreveport), October 24, 1866; *Memphis Bulletin*, May 30, 1865; B. F. Moore, W. S. Mason, and R. S. Donnell, "Report of the Committee Appointed to Prepare and Report to the Legislature a System of Laws upon the Subject of Freedmen, &c.," January 22, 1866, in *Message of the President of the United States . . . in Regard to Provisional Governors of States*, 48–55, esp. 50.

24. Foner, *Reconstruction*, 182–83; Lowrey, "Political Career of James Madison Wells"; Tunnell, *Crucible of Reconstruction*, chap. 5; *New Orleans Tribune*, June 20, 1865.

25. Hollandsworth, *Absolute Massacre*, 31; Foner, *Reconstruction*, 182–83; Lowrey, "Political Career of James Madison Wells"; Tunnell, *Crucible of Reconstruction*, 96.

26. John Burke, order, June 12, 1865, printed in *New-Orleans Times*, June 13, 1865; Glendy Burke, order, June 23, 1865, printed in *Daily Picayune* (New Orleans), June 28, 1865; Conway, *Freedmen of Louisiana*, 6; *Daily Picayune* (New Orleans), July 4,

August 1, 13, 1865; Thomas Conway, testimony, February 22, 1866, in *Report of the Joint Committee on Reconstruction*, 78–86.

27. *New Orleans Tribune*, July 20, 26, 1865; *Daily Picayune* (New Orleans), August 12, 1865; Andrew Morse to Thomas Conway, August 18, 1865, Letters and Endorsements Sent, Provost Marshal General of Freedmen, in *Records of the Field Offices for the State of Louisiana*, reel 6; Conway, *Freedmen of Louisiana*, 6.

28. Hugh Kennedy to Edward Canby, July 22, 1865, enclosed in Hugh Kennedy to Andrew Johnson, July 29, 1865, in *Andrew Johnson Papers*, ser. 1, reel 16; Frank Bagley to Thomas Conway, August 10, 1865, and James Madison Wells to Edward Canby, August 7, 1865, both in Registered Letters and Telegrams Received, Assistant Commissioner for the State of Louisiana, *Records of the Assistant Commissioner for the State of Louisiana*, reels 7, 10; *Daily Picayune* (New Orleans), August 1, 1865; *New-Orleans Times*, August 16, 1865.

29. Charles Dusuau et al. to R. B. Brown, January 1, 1864, PM-JP; "Regulations for the Patrol of the Parish of St. John the Baptist Left Bank," [n.d.], PM-JJBP; Albrecht and Plagge to Nathaniel Banks, January 31, 1864, box 31, Banks Papers, LOC; W. B. Stickney to Thomas Conway, August 1, 1865, in *Message of the President . . . in Relation to the States of the Union Lately in Rebellion*, 87–90, esp. 89; "Freedmen of St. James Parish" to [Thomas Conway], December 25, 1865, in Registered Letters and Telegrams Received, Assistant Commissioner for the State of Louisiana, *Records of the Assistant Commissioner for the State of Louisiana*, reel 10; *Baton Rouge Tri-Weekly Gazette and Comet*, August 10, 1865; *New Orleans Tribune*, August 20, 1865; *Transcriptions of Parish Records of Louisiana*, no. 26, ser. 1, 3:17, 4:60.

30. "An Ordinance Relative to the Police of Recently Emancipated Negroes or Freedmen within Corporate Limits of the Town of Opelousas," approved July 3, 1865, "An Ordinance Relative to the Police of Negroes Recently Emancipated within the Parish of St. Landry," approved [July?] 1865, and "Proceedings of the Mayor and Council of the Town of Franklin," approved July 28, 1865, all in *Message of the President . . . in Relation to the States of the Union Lately in Rebellion*, 92–96; *New Orleans Tribune*, July 30, 1865.

31. San Antonio *Herald* quoted in the *New-Orleans Times*, July 21, 1865; *Alabama Beacon* (Greensboro), January 26, 1866; *Montgomery Advertiser*, December 29, 1865; *Athens (AL) Weekly Post*, January 13, 1866; *Clark County Democrat* (Grove Hill, AL), July 26, 1866; *Livingston (AL) Journal*, July 28, 1866; *Jacksonville (AL) Republican*, October 27, 1866; *Tuskegee (AL) News*, November 22, 1866.

32. Fitzgerald, *Urban Emancipation*, 44, 36, 71–72; Durham, *Reluctant Partners*, 159; *Chronicle and Sentinel* (Augusta, GA), June 30, November 17, 1865; *Macon Daily Telegraph*, June 15, July 20, 1865; *Daily Constitutionalist* (Augusta, GA), March 21, May 24, June 16, July 27, 1865; *New-York Daily Tribune*, January 1, 1867.

33. *New Orleans Tribune*, July 16, 1865; Ash, *Massacre in Memphis*, 23; Fields Cook et al. to Andrew Johnson, June 10, 1865, printed in *New-York Daily Tribune*, June 17, 1865; "An Appeal from the Negroes of Richmond for Protection," 1865, Anthony Motley to Clinton Fisk, September 28, 1865, and Edward Lovell to W. H. Morgan, September 4, 1865, all in Hahn et al., *Freedom*, ser. 3, 1:206–7, 270–72, esp. 207; *New-Orleans Times*, September 10, 1865; *Tri-Weekly Telegraph* (Houston), August 21, 23, 1865; Durham,

Reluctant Partners, 159; Kerber, *No Constitutional Right to Be Ladies*, 63; Litwack, *Been in the Storm So Long*, 35–36, 44.

34. Goetsch, *Lost Nashville*, 26; *Daily Dispatch* (Richmond), August 21, November 29, 1866.

35. The Louisiana legislature authorized the creation of chain gangs for vagrants in March 1867, and New Orleans's municipal council ordered the institution's deployment in June: see *Daily Picayune* (New Orleans), April 6, 1867; and "An Ordinance Relative to Vagrants Committed to Workhouse in the City of New Orleans," approved June 15, 1867, printed in *New-Orleans Times*, June 18, 1867.

36. *New-Orleans Times*, February 15, 19, 25, 1867; *Daily Picayune* (New Orleans), January 5, March 1, 1867.

37. *Nationalist* (Mobile), March 22, August 2, 1866; *New Orleans Tribune*, July 22, 1865; Trowbridge, *The South*, 436; *Alton (LA) Democrat*, reprinted in *Daily Picayune* (New Orleans), August 15, 1867.

38. *Richmond Whig*, reprinted in *Louisville Daily Journal*, June 23, 1865; *Daily Constitutional Union* (Washington, DC), June 12, 1865; *New-York Daily Tribune*, June 17, 1865; O'Brien, "Reconstruction in Richmond," 274–75; Jinny [*sic*] Scott, statement, June 8, 1865, and Richard Adams, statement, June 8, 1865, both in Statements Relating to the Abuses of Freedmen in Richmond, June 1865, *Records of the Assistant Commissioner for the State of Virginia*, reel 59; William Kreutzer to Albert Ordway, June 7, 1865, John Oliver to Alfred Terry, August 23, 1865, and "Release for Ned Scott[,] col[ore]d," September 9, 1865, all in *Union Provost Marshals' File of Papers Relating to Individual Civilians*, reel 240.

39. Albert Brooks, statement, June 9 and 10, 1865, Edward Davenport, statement, June 9, 1865, and Alexander Davis to O. Brown, June 9, 1865, all in Statements Relating to the Abuses of Freedmen in Richmond, June 1865, in *Records of the Assistant Commissioner for the State of Virginia*, reel 59; Anthony Motley to Clinton Fisk, September 28, 1865, in Hahn et al., *Freedom*, ser. 3, 1:271–72.

40. Cook et al. to Johnson, June 10, 1865, in *New-York Daily Tribune*, June 17, 1865; William McLaurin, testimony, May 1866, in *Message from the President of the United States . . . Relative to Refugees, Freedmen and Abandoned Lands*, 42.

41. *Nashville Daily Union and American*, October 16, 17, 1866; *Public Ledger* (Nashville), October 17, 1866; *Daily Memphis Avalanche*, November 23, 1866.

42. *Daily Dispatch* (Richmond), December 12, 13, 1866, February 20, 1867.

43. Fitzgerald, *Urban Emancipation*, 61, 89.

44. Thomas Scott et al., Report [of Colored Citizens in Petersburg], June 6, 1865, printed in *New-York Daily Tribune*, June 15, 1865; *Proceedings of the Convention of the Colored People of VA*, 3; Foner, *Reconstruction*, 103.

45. Bell, *Revolution, Romanticism, and the Afro-Creole Protest Tradition*, chap. 7, esp. 224–26. On slavery's relation to race prejudice, see, for example, *L'Union* (New Orleans), October 25, 1862.

46. Blassingame, *Black New Orleans*, 56–57; Foner, *Reconstruction*, 62–65; Houzeau, *My Passage at the New Orleans Tribune*, 82; Reid, *After the War*, 244.

47. Paschal Randolph is misidentified as "J. P. Randolph" in the December 3, 1864, issue of the *New Orleans Tribune*. *New Orleans Tribune*, December 3, 29, 1864,

January 15, 1865; Foner, *Reconstruction*, 62–65; Blasingame, *Black New Orleans*, 56–57; Belz, "Origins of Negro Suffrage"; Thompson, *Exiles at Home*, chap. 5, esp. 215, 226–33.

48. *New Orleans Tribune*, February 7, March 30, April 9, July 22, April 9, October 7, 1865. Also see the proscription, made in *L'Union*, that "'Liberty' is not the signal of anarchy and laziness" ("Liberté" n'est pas le signal de l'anarchie et de la paresse); *L'Union* (New Orleans), November 15, 1862.

49. *New Orleans Tribune*, January 10, February 24, March 14, 21, April 11, May 2, June 3, July 20, 1865; Bell, "'Une Chimère,'" 148.

50. *New Orleans Tribune*, July 20, August 1, 1865; Fisk to Conway, July 3, 1865, in *Andrew Johnson Papers*, ser. 1, reel 16.

51. *New Orleans Tribune*, March 18, 1865; Conway to Kennedy, July 7 and 10, 1865, both in Letters and Telegrams Sent, vol. 1, *Records of the Assistant Commissioner for the State of Louisiana*, reel 1; Houzeau, *My Passage*, 51; Bell, "'Une Chimère,'" 150–51; Bell, *Revolution, Romanticism, and the Afro-Creole Protest Tradition*, 252–58; Foner, *Reconstruction*, 143, 158; Ripley, *Slaves and Freedmen*, 204.

52. Commitments to the New Orleans workhouse plummeted, from 362 in July to 68, virtually all of them white, in September. *New Orleans Tribune*, July 18, 1865; *New-Orleans Times*, August 29, October 30, 1865; Conway, *Freedmen of Louisiana*, 6.

53. James Madison Wells to Andrew Johnson, July 29, 1865, in Graf, Haskins, and Bergeron, *Papers of Andrew Johnson*, 8:503–4.

54. Andrew Johnson, "Speech at Knoxville," April 16, 1864, in Graf, Haskins, and Bergeron, *Papers of Andrew Johnson*, 6:673–79, esp. 675; Andrew Johnson, testimony, November 23, 1863, in Berlin et al., *Freedom*, ser. 1, 2:411–15, esp. 414; Zipf, *Forced Apprenticeship in North Carolina*, 8.

55. Bell, "'Une Chimère,'" 151–52.

56. Joseph Fullerton to John Burke, October 28, 1865, in Letters and Telegrams Sent, vol. 1, *Records of the Assistant Commissioner for the State of Louisiana*, reel 1; *New Orleans Tribune*, October 28, 29, 1865; *New-Orleans Times*, October 27, 28, 29, 1865; *Daily Picayune* (New Orleans), October 28, 29, 1865; Fullerton, *Report of the Administration of Freedmen's Affairs*, 5.

57. The school's prestigious twentieth-century alumni include noted composers, poets, athletes, and the civil rights activist, Atlanta mayor, and United Nations ambassador Andrew Young. *New York Times*, October 24, December 31, 1865; Louise De Mortie to D. G. Fenno, October 27, 1865, Registered Letters and Telegrams Received, *Records of the Assistant Commissioner for the State of Louisiana*, reel 7; *New Orleans Tribune*, November 4, 23, December 5, 7, 17, 22, 23, 24, 31, 1865; Carolyn M. Jones, "Louise De Mortie (1833–1867): Lecturer, Missionary, Fund-Raiser," in Smith, *Notable Black American Women*, 2:173–76; *Gilbert Academy and Agricultural College*, 52; Rogers, *Righteous Lives*, 6, 51, 53, 63; 121. For the women's names, see Picard, "Racing Jules Lion," 30; *New-Orleans Times*, June 5, 1866; and *Republican* (New Orleans), January 11, 1876.

58. Heuman, *"Killing Time"*; Holt, *Problem of Freedom*, chaps. 7–8; Rugemer, *Problem of Emancipation*, 273, 291–301.

59. See, in particular, *Daily Picayune* (New Orleans), November 4, 1865.

60. *New Orleans Tribune*, November 10, 24, December 13, 1865.

61. *New-Orleans Times*, November 7, 1865.

62. *Daily Picayune* (New Orleans), November 12, 1865. Governor Wells refused to sign the act establishing yearlong contracts, which never became law.

63. On the Black Codes, see especially Carter, *When the War Was Over*, 187–91, 216–31; and Wilson, *Black Codes*.

64. Cohen, *At Freedom's Edge*, 31, 33. For the Mississippi and South Carolina laws, see "An Act to Confer Civil Rights on Freedmen, and for Other Purposes," approved November 25, 1865, in *Laws of the State of Mississippi . . . 1865*, pp. 82–86; and "An Act to Establish and Regulate the Domestic Relations of Persons of Color, and to Amend the Law in Relation to Paupers and Vagrancy," approved December 21, 1865, in *Acts of the General Assembly of the State of South Carolina*, 291–304.

65. Rodrigue, *Reconstruction*, 70–71; Scott, *Degrees of Freedom*, 38.

66. Cohen, *At Freedom's Edge*, 34; Foner, *Reconstruction*, 209; Wilson, *Black Codes*, 118; Hahn et al., *Freedom*, ser. 3, 1:59; Nieman, *To Set the Law in Motion*, 76–80; Hayden et al., *Freedom*, ser. 3, 2:72–76, 500.

67. Carter, *When the War Was Over*, 226–28.

68. Benjamin Butler to Thaddeus Stevens, November 20, 1865, box 2, Thaddeus Stevens Papers, LOC. Also see Michael Hahn's evolving position on vagrancy in Hahn, *What Is Unconditional Unionism?*, 10; and Hahn, *Ex-Governor Hahn on Louisiana Legislation Relating to Freedmen*, 2.

69. *New York Times*, January 25, March 11, 1866.

70. Wilson, *Black Codes*, 116–19.

71. "An Act Providing for the Punishment of Vagrants," approved January 15, 1866, in *Acts of the General Assembly of the State of Virginia*, 91–93.

72. Cresswell, *Tramp in America*, 19, 92–97; Rodgers, *Work Ethic in Industrial America*, chap. 8; Schmidt, *Free to Work*, 208–35; Stanley, *From Bondage to Contract*, chap. 3.

73. The *Tribune* noted that only the "humblest citizens" were subjected to arrest. *New Orleans Tribune*, July 20, 26, August 6, 1865.

74. *New Orleans Daily Crescent*, October 3, 1866; Thomas Adams to [John Monroe], April 12, 1866, Reports of Various Departments to the City Council, NOPL.

75. Bardes, "Redefining Vagrancy," 101.

76. Cohen, *At Freedom's Edge*, 35.

77. *Daily Chronicle and Sentinel* (Augusta, GA), October 10, 1874; *Chronicle and Constitutionalist* (Augusta, GA), April 5, 1878; *Augusta City Code*, 92–93. Under this ordinance, Augusta police made 1,339 arrests in a twelve-month period between 1873 and 1874 and 907 arrests in a twelve-month period between 1877 and 1878, yielding vagrancy arrest rates of roughly 76 and 45 per 1,000, assuming constant population growth between decimal censuses. The average present-day arrest rate in metropolitan counties is 42 per 1,000; Neusteter and O'Toole, *Every Three Seconds*, 9.

78. On these massacres, see Ash, *Massacre in Memphis*; Egerton, *Wars of Reconstruction*, chap. 5, esp. 207–10; and Hollandsworth, *Absolute Massacre*. On the experiences of Camps, Lacroix, and Capla, see C. Delery, coroner's report, n.d., and Lucien Jean-Pierre Capla, testimony, December 24, 1866, both in *Report of the Select Committee on the New Orleans Riots*, 12–15, 119–23; Bell, *Romanticism, and the Afro-Creole Protest Tradition*, 261; Reed, *Life of A. P. Dostie*, 338. For Camps's relation to Trévigne, see Neidenbach, *Life and Legacy of Marie Couvent*, 330n52, 338.

79. The act excepted Tennessee, which had already ratified the Fourteenth Amendment. On the law's passage and immediate ramifications see Foner, *Reconstruction*, 271–91.

80. Hume and Gough, *Blacks, Carpetbaggers, and Scalawags*, 161. For a full listing of delegates, see *Constitution Adopted by the State Constitutional Convention of the State of Louisiana*, 21–22.

81. La. Const. of 1868, arts. 2, 3, 6, 8, 9, 10, 87, 128, 130, and 149.

82. *Republican* (New Orleans), April 7, 15, 18, 1868; *Zach Taylor et al. vs. Julius A. Noble, Warden of the City Workhouse*, filed April 14, 1868, docket no. 19950, Fifth District Court Records, NOPL; *Daily Picayune* (New Orleans), April 21, 1868.

83. For election results, see Vincent, *Black Legislators in Louisiana*, 69. On the Metropolitans, see Rousey, *Policing the Southern City*, 124–58.

84. *Republican* (New Orleans), August 9, 1868.

85. William Cooley, a white Unionist delegate from Pointe Coupée Parish, later claimed to have been aware: see *Republican* (New Orleans), June 29, 1870.

86. *Debates of the House of Representatives of the State of Louisiana*, 867; *Daily Picayune* (New Orleans), November 11, 1870.

87. *New Orleans Daily Crescent*, March 7, 1869; *Daily Picayune* (New Orleans), January 23, 26, February 13, 16, 1869; *New-Orleans Times*, February 11, 1870; *Annual Message of Governor H. C. Warmoth*, 10; *Annual Report of the Attorney General*, 6.

88. Little is known regarding the short-lived Louisiana Workingmen's Party. The conservative *Daily Picayune* charged that the party was merely an "electioneering trick," designed to ferret votes away from the Democratic Party and toward carpetbag rule—suggesting that the party's base included white workers, whose support the Democrats coveted. However, political ward clubs self-styled as Workingmen's Democrats actively participated in mob violence directed against freedpeople during the elections of 1868, suggesting that the Workingmen were not allied with the radicals, as the *Daily Picayune* had claimed. For the party's formation, see *Daily Picayune* (New Orleans), April 12, 16, 17, 1868. The party is briefly discussed in Arnesen, *Waterfront Workers of New Orleans*, 10–11, 261n26; and Jones, "Biographical Sketches of Members of the 1868 Louisiana State Senate," 91, 91–92n184, 99, 100. On Louisiana politics during Reconstruction generally, see Vincent, *Black Legislators*; Nystrom, *New Orleans after the Civil War*; and Tunnell, *Crucible of Reconstruction*.

89. *Louisiana Senate Journal, 1869*, pp. 82, 228, 234; *New Orleans Daily Crescent*, October 13, 1868, January 28, 1869; *Daily Picayune* (New Orleans), February 6, 27, 1869; *Weekly Advocate* (Baton Rouge), February 6, 1869.

90. Jones, "Biographical Sketches," 78; *New Orleans Daily Crescent*, October 13, 1868; Bundles, *On Her Own Ground*; Foner, *Freedom's Lawmakers*, 172; Vincent, *Black Legislators*, chap. 5.

91. Du Bois, *Black Reconstruction in America*.

92. *Official Journal of the Proceedings of the Senate*, 228; Jones, "Biographical Sketches," 100–102; Vincent, *Black Legislators*, 108–9; "An Act Relative to Vagrants in the Metropolitan Police District," approved March 6, 1869, in *Louisiana Acts, 1869*, 87–89.

93. Between July 1, 1849, and June 30, 1850, New Orleans performed 5,979 vagrancy arrests out of a free population of 101,392, an arrest rate of 59 per 1,000 persons. In

1870, the population of the Metropolitan Police District (Orleans, Jefferson, and St. Bernard Parishes) was 212,738, yielding an arrest rate of 4 per 1,000. "General Statement of Police Operations of the City of New Orleans for the Year Commencing on the First July 1849, and Ending on the 30th June 1850," in entry of December 9, 1850, Official Proceedings, vol. 6, First Municipality Council Records, NOPL; *Annual Report of the Board of Metropolitan Police . . . for the Year Ending September 30, 1870,* p. 43.

94. *Republican* (New Orleans), July 5, 1868; *New-Orleans Times,* March 10, 1870; *New Orleans Daily Crescent,* April 4, 1869.

95. Historical sources contradictorily identify Cooley as a Democrat, scallywag, or Republican. Even Cooley's contemporaries expressed uncertainty as to his true allegiance. In truth, his record defied rigid political affiliation: Governor Wells (a Democrat) appointed him to the court in 1866, Republicans supported his nomination as a delegate to the state constitutional convention in 1867, and he ran on the Democratic ticket in 1868. *New Orleans Daily Crescent,* March 24, 1866; *Republican* (New Orleans), April 15, 1868; *Daily Picayune* (New Orleans), April 15, 1868, January 21, 1872; Labbé and Lurie, *Slaughterhouse Cases,* 82–83, 111; Scott and Hébrard, *Freedom Papers,* 130–32.

96. *Official Journal of the Proceedings of the Convention,* 255; *Daily Picayune* (New Orleans), February 28, 1868; *Republican* (New Orleans), June 29, 1870.

97. *Daily Picayune* (New Orleans), July 14, 1870, January 21, 1872; *Republican* (New Orleans), April 27, June 29, July 3, 7, 8, October 1, December 16, 1870.

98. *Daily Picayune* (New Orleans), September 29, 1870, June 28, 1871, February 3, 1873; *Republican* (New Orleans), January 14, 1871; *New-Orleans Times,* March 2, 1875; *New Orleans Bulletin,* June 17, 1874. Also see *Daily Picayune* (New Orleans), May 20, 21, September 20, 1870, January 5, 6, 7, 11, 17, 29, February 10, March 8, July 15, November 28, 1871; *Republican* (New Orleans), October 25, November 1, December 16, 1870; *Louisianian* (New Orleans), March 23, 1871; Vincent, *Black Legislators,* 110; and *New York Times,* July 8, 1873. Between these mass arrests and mass releases, the number of workhouse inmates oscillated violently: 40 inmates in October 1870, nearly 200 inmates in July 1873, only 8 inmates in January 1875; *Republican* (New Orleans), October 4, 1870; *Daily Picayune* (New Orleans), July 6, 1873; *New Orleans Bulletin,* January 3, 1875.

99. On Louisiana factionalism, see Bell, *Romanticism, and the Afro-Creole Protest Tradition,* 274–79; Nystrom, *New Orleans after the Civil War,* esp. 82–159; Tunnell, *Crucible of Reconstruction,* chap. 8; and Vincent, *Black Legislatures,* esp. chaps. 6–8. On the collapse of the *New Orleans Tribune* see Rankin, introduction to *My Passage at the New Orleans Tribune,* 47–57.

100. Labbé and Lurie, *Slaughterhouse Cases;* Ross, "Justice Miller's Reconstruction," esp. 673; *The Slaughter-House Cases,* 83 US 36 (1873).

101. On white violence and Reconstruction's demise, see Trelease, *White Terror;* Egerton, *Wars of Reconstruction;* and Emberton, *Beyond Redemption.* On these massacres in particular, see Goldman, *Reconstruction and Black Suffrage,* 42–51; Keith, *Colfax Massacre;* Lane, *Day Freedom Died;* and Lemann, *Redemption.*

102. *Supplemental Report . . . on the Conduct of the Late Elections,* 235–36; Curtis Pollard, affidavit, March 19, 1879, in *Report and Testimony of the Select Committee . . . to Investigate the Causes of the Removal of the Negroes,* 3:47–48.

103. *New Orleans Daily Democrat*, May 22, 1877. On Redemption in Louisiana, see Nystrom, *New Orleans after the Civil War*, esp. 140–85; and Tunnell, *Crucible of Reconstruction*, esp. chap. 9. On the Metropolitans' dissolution, see Rousey, *Policing the Southern City*, 157–58. Although recent scholarship has disputed the assignment of a singular date to Reconstruction's collapse, the departure of federal troops from New Orleans on April 24, 1877, was met with great fanfare, and read as a watershed moment, within Louisiana: see *Daily Picayune* (New Orleans), April 25, 1877.

Chapter 7

1. *Constance Bique Perrine v. City of New Orleans, Edward Planchard, appellant and als.*, filed January 27, 1859, docket no. 6036, SCLC.
2. Michel Reyman to Paul Capdevielle, August 31, 1903, in Outgoing Correspondence, Department of Police and Public Buildings, NOPL.
3. Lichtenstein, *Twice the Work of Free Labor*, 19.
4. "An Act Relative to Crimes and Offenses; Authorizing Judges, in Certain Cases, to Sentence Convicts to Work on the Public Works and Roads, or in Workhouses; and Delegating the Power to Parochial and Municipal Authorities Necessary to Enforce the Same," approved February 23, 1878, in *Louisiana Acts, 1878*, pp. 63–64.
5. *Daily Picayune* (New Orleans), January 4, 1880, January 27, 1881; Waring and Cable, *History and President Condition of New Orleans*, 77–82; Espinosa, *Epidemic Invasions*, 7, 14–15, 32–33, 51–57; Sullivan and Strach, "Statebuilding through Corruption"; Willoughby, *Yellow Fever*.
6. *Daily Picayune* (New Orleans), January 4, 1880; "An Ordinance to Establish a Police Jail in the City of New Orleans, to Provide for the Management Thereof, and for Other Purposes in Connection with the Same," printed in *Daily Picayune* (New Orleans), January 27, 1881.
7. La. Const. of 1868, art. 87; La. Const. of 1879, art. 7; *Daily Picayune* (New Orleans), September 7, November 6, 1881.
8. *Daily Picayune* (New Orleans), August 1, November 1, 1884.
9. For example, see Leslie Williams, "Ellis May Not Serve Entire Year in Jail," *Times-Picayune* (New Orleans), January 19, 1991.
10. John Murphy to Dennis Mahoney, May 9 and 23, 1898, and Joinville Bercegeay to Dennis Mahoney, September 13, 1898, all in Outgoing Correspondence, Department of Police and Public Buildings, NOPL.
11. *Daily Picayune* (New Orleans), April 2, 1885, September 17, 1887, May 13, 1895; K. K. Blackmar, "House of Detention as I Saw It," *Daily Picayune* (New Orleans), March 9, 1913. For penal labor statistics, see monthly reports in Outgoing Correspondence, and Daily Reports for the Parish Prison and Police Jail, both in Department of Police and Public Buildings Records, NOPL.
12. *Daily Picayune* (New Orleans), August 1, November 1, 1884, September 25, 26, 1888, March 6, 1890; Blackmar, "House of Detention as I Saw It."
13. The escape rate in the city's First Municipality Police Jail was 5 per 1,000 between 1837 and 1839. *Daily Picayune* (New Orleans), October 25, 1888; *Charities and Corrections Report, 1906–1907*, pp. 19, 21; Register of Slaves Entering the Police Jail, Police Jail Records, NOPL.

14. *Daily Picayune* (New Orleans), July 17, 1888, September 16, 1893, January 8, April 8, 1908; *Daily Item* (New Orleans), July 30, 1894, March 4, 22, 1926. Reports of prisoners leaving for the night, on condition that they voluntarily return, persisted into the twenty-first century: see Curry, "Video Shows New Orleans Prisoners Allegedly Taking Drugs, Walking City Streets."

15. *Daily Picayune* (New Orleans), May 13, 1895.

16. The employment of a jail physician was first noted, a new development, in 1909. *New Orleans Item*, September 21, 1909.

17. *Times-Democrat* (New Orleans), March 15, 25, 1898; Joseph-Gaudet, *He Leadeth Me*, 40–43.

18. *New Orleans Item*, March 19, 1920; *Daily Picayune* (New Orleans), March 19, 20, 21, 1920, April 27, September 28, October 7, 1921, April 10, 1927; *New Orleans States*, September 28, 1921. On resistance and sexual violence among postbellum prisoners, see LeFlouria, "'Under the Sting of the Lash.'"

19. [Escape and Recapture Reports], May 13, July 7, 16, November 6, 1898, February 27, and November 6, 1899, all in Outgoing Correspondence, Department of Police and Public Buildings, NOPL; *Daily Picayune* (New Orleans), March 15, June 8, November 1, 1898; *Twelfth Census of the United States*, reel 571, Enumeration District 25, Ward 3, Orleans Parish, Louisiana, p. 16.

20. Cooper, Holt, and Scott, *Beyond Slavery*, 5–11, 153.

21. Haas, *Political Leadership in a Southern City*.

22. Between 1878 and 1900, the jail's successive superintendents (excluding interim appointees) were George Murphy, Bartholomew Moran, James Waldron, and Dennis Mahoney. For these men's backgrounds and political affiliations, see *Daily Picayune* (New Orleans), August 23, 1896, December 15, 1903, August 23, 1913; *Times-Democrat* (New Orleans), September 24, 1913; and *New Orleans Item*, April 15, 1903.

23. *Eighth Census of the United States*, reel 415, Ward 1, Orleans Parish, Louisiana, pp. 42–43; *Daily Picayune* (New Orleans), September 4, 1855.

24. Notably, obituaries for all four men identify them as members of the same volunteer fire brigade: on the relation between New Orleans's volunteer fire brigades and White League formation, see Ball, *Life of a Klansman*.

25. For "violence workers," see Frantz, "Violent Lives of William Faucett."

26. *Times-Democrat* (New Orleans), September 23, 1888, December 15, 1903; *Daily Picayune* (New Orleans), May 13, 1895, January 7, 1909, April 23, 1920.

27. On misdemeanor chain gangs, see especially LeFlouria, *Chained in Silence*, chap. 5.

28. Blackmon, *Slavery by Another Name*; Cohen, "Negro Involuntary Servitude in the South."

29. Carleton, *Politics and Punishment*, chaps. 2–3; Cardon, "'Less than Mayhem.'" On convict lease generally, see Curtin, *Black Prisoners and Their World*; Haley, *No Mercy Here*; LeFlouria, *Chained in Silence*; Lichtenstein, *Twice the Work of Free Labor*; Mancini, *One Dies, Get Another*; Oshinsky, *Worse than Slavery*; Perkinson, *Texas Tough*; and Shapiro, *New South Rebellion*.

30. Scholarship have offered a variety of frameworks for interpreting the relationship of postbellum penal labor to antebellum chattel slavery. Works emphasizing symbolic and cultural connections, or the re-creation of antebellum social patterns, include

Adams, *Wounds of Returning*, chap. 5; Childs, *Slaves of the State*; Davis, *Are Prisons Obsolete?*; Davis, "Incarcerated Women"; and Gilmore, "Slavery and Prison." On prisoners' own deployment of the slavery-prison comparison as a discursive strategy, see especially Chase, *We Are Not Slaves*. For postbellum convict labor as the reproduction of slavery or as a new form of slavery, see Blackmon, *Slavery by Another Name*; Lichtenstein, *Twice the Work of Free Labor*; and Oshinsky, *Worse Than Slavery*. For a pointed criticism of this literature's tendency to overstate continuity and blur distinctions between exploitative labor systems, see Scott, "Scandal of Thirteentherism." For tensions between exploitative convict labor and Lost Cause ideology, see Ayers, *Vengeance and Justice*, 208; Cable, *Silent South*; Woodward, *Origins of the New South*, 215; and *Daily Picayune* (New Orleans), June 23, 1883.

31. On the intersection of Progressive reform and Jim Crow, see Gilmore, *Gender and Jim Crow*; McGerr, *Fierce Discontent*, chap. 6; and Southern, *Progressive Era and Race*.

32. *Daily Picayune* (New Orleans), February 13, 1906; *Times-Democrat* (New Orleans), January 7, 1910; Fortier, *Louisiana*, 2:119, 491, 642; Frank C. Zacharie, testimony, January 5, 1875, in *Report of the Select Committee on That Portion of the President's Message Relating to the Condition of the South*, 221–25.

33. *Daily Picayune* (New Orleans), April 29, 1897, September 9, 1898.

34. Zacharie, *Police Jails and Reformatories*, 3.

35. Kamerling, *Capital and Convict*; McLennan, *Crisis of Imprisonment*, 88–90.

36. McLennan, *Crisis of Imprisonment*, chap. 4.

37. Carleton, "Movement to End the Convict Lease System in Louisiana"; Holmes, "James K. Vardaman and Prison Reform in Mississippi"; Lichtenstein, "Good Roads and Chain Gangs in the Progressive South"; Zimmerman, "Penal Reform Movement in the South."

38. Carleton, *Politics and Punishment*, chap. 3; Hair, *Bourbonism and Agrarian Protest*, chap. 11; Taylor, *Louisiana*, 140–43; Webb, "History of Negro Voting in Louisiana."

39. Carleton, *Politics and Punishment*, 92.

40. Zacharie, *Police Jails and Reformatories*, 3–4.

41. Wines, *Report upon the Penal and Other State Institutions*, 7–8; Wines, "Prisons of Louisiana," 154, 156.

42. Colvin, *Penitentiaries, Reformatories, and Chain Gangs*, 249. For the charge that convict labor scholarship tends to emphasize political economy over racial ideology, see Childs, *Slaves of the State*, esp. 9.

43. [House of Detention Architectural Schematics], n.d., Louisiana Map Collection, NOPL.

44. *Times-Democrat* (New Orleans), October 1, 1900; *New Orleans Item*, September 1, 1901, February 15, 1903.

45. *New Orleans Item*, October 4, 1907, January 2, August 10, 1909; *Daily Picayune* (New Orleans), August 11, 1909; Blackmar, "House of Detention as I Saw It."

46. *Nashville Tennessean*, June 20, 1901; *Richmond Times*, March 17, 1900; Dunbar, *Code of the City of Augusta Georgia*, 164; Gravatte and Logan, "Louisville City Workhouse."

47. Ritter, *Inventing America's First Immigration Crisis*, 116, 118–19; Bouscaren, "What's the Workhouse?"; Walk, *Memphis and Shelby County Government Buildings*; *Nashville Tennessean*, November 28, 1925.

48. Butler, "Charleston's House of Corrections." Of the workhouse systems named here, only Charleston's workhouse system, abandoned in 1886, failed to survive into the twentieth century.

49. In addition to preceding note, see Daily Reports for Parish Prison and Police Jail, 1895–1903, and Daily Reports of Parish Prison and the House of Detention, 1903–1907, both in NOPL.

50. For figures, see annual reports produced by the New Orleans Department of Police, each entitled *Annual Report*, for the years 1953 to 1971.

51. Charlie East, "The Forgotten Men: How Do They Manage Survival on Skid Row in N.O.?," *Times-Picayune* (New Orleans), December 9, 1972; Joe Massa, "Prison Labor Saves Money for City," *Times-Picayune* (New Orleans), May 20, 1980; Bill Grady, "Ex-Inmate Tells of Affair That Led to Shooting," *Times-Picayune* (New Orleans), January 25, 1989; Keith Woods and Susan Finch, "Inmates Often Work for Private Citizens," *Times-Picayune* (New Orleans), January 25, 1989; Walt Philbin, "Foti Inmate Held in Rape at Jazzfest," *Times-Picayune* (New Orleans), May 2, 1989; Walt Philbin, "Foti Believes in Lending a Hand, Especially When It's a Prisoner's," *Times-Picayune/States-Item* (New Orleans), November 30, 1981; Sexton, Miller, and Jacobsen, *Operating Jail Industries*, 3.

52. *State Ledger* (Jackson, MS), February 6, 1884; *West Alabamian* (Carrollton), September 24, 1884; *Knoxville Daily Journal*, April 25, 1890; *Atlanta Constitution*, January 9, 1893; *Birmingham Daily News*, July 17, 1894; *Tampa Tribune*, June 20, 1895.

53. For Democratic opposition within Louisiana, see *New Orleans Daily Democrat*, May 13, 1879; George Cronan et al., petition to the legislature, February 9, 1880, in *Louisiana House Journal*, reg. sess., 1880, pp. 108–10; *State ex rel. Lewis v. Arnauld*, 50 La. Ann. 1, 22 South 886 (1898). For similar opposition beyond Louisiana, see, for example, *Fort Worth Daily Gazette*, June 22, 1894; and *Norfolk Landmark*, May 24, 1894.

54. *City of Portland v. City of Bangor*, 65 Me. 120 (1876); Tiedeman, *Treatise on the Limitations of Police Power*, 2:118; Cohen, *At Freedom's Edge*, 240–41; Novak, *People's Welfare*, 170–71; *New Orleans Item*, January 6, 1880; *Bulletin of the Department of Labor*, 839.

55. Cohen, *At Freedom's Edge*, 240–41; "An Act to Empower the Several Municipal Corporations throughout the State to Adopt Ordinances Declaring Certain Persons Vagrants and Punishing Them as Such," approved July 7, 1904, in *Louisiana Acts, 1904*, pp. 368–69; "An Act Requiring all Able-Bodied Male Persons, between the Ages of Seventeen and Fifty-Five Years, Inclusive, to be Regularly or Continuously Engaged in Some Lawful, Useful and Recognized Business," approved July 9, 1918, in *Louisiana Acts, 1918*, pp. 237–38; *New Orleans Item*, August 10, 1903; *Columbus (MS) Commercial*, March 14, 1905; *Greenville (SC) News*, January 3, 1903; *Fayette (AL) Banner*, July 7, 1904; *Chattanooga News*, September 12, 1903; *Arkansas Democrat* (Little Rock), October 1, 1903; *Birmingham News*, March 22, 1904; *Natchez Democrat*, October 16, 1903; *Nashville Banner*, July 17, 1905.

56. Mayfield, *Code of Alabama*, 1:955–56; *Laws of the Various States Relating to Vagrancy*, 55.

57. Cohen, *At Freedom's Edge*, chap. 8.

58. Williams, "Negro and the South," 149; *Edgefield (SC) Advertiser*, May 20, 1908; *Columbus (MS) Commercial*, March 14, 1905; *Greenville (MS) Times*, January 19, 1907; *Grenada (MS) Sentinel*, July 6, 1901; Jelks, "Acuteness of the Negro Question," 392–93.

59. *Police Commissioners Annual Report, 1914*, pp. 21–22; *Police Commissioners Annual Report, 1915*, pp. 21–23; *Daily Picayune* (New Orleans), April 11, 1923, April 22, 1924, May 1, 1925; *New Orleans Item*, February 5, 1928. Also see annual reports produced by the New Orleans Department of Police, each entitled *Annual Report*, for the years 1947 to 1968. For data in graph 7.1, see note 63 of this chapter.

60. Higbie, "Between Romance and Degradation"; Schneider, "Omaha Vagrants and the Character of Western Hobo Labor," 225–72.

61. Goluboff, *Vagrant Nation*, chap. 1.

62. Quoted in Goluboff, *Vagrant Nation*, 57.

63. All per capita arrest rates in graphs 7.1 and 7.2 assume constant population growth between decimal censuses. Wherever possible, averages presented in graph 7.2 derive from data for every fifth year. For some cities, data from every fifth year were not available; wherever possible, missing data were supplanted by using data from the closest available year. Arrests for vagrancy include arrests for all crimes that customarily fall under the auspices of vagrancy law but that some cities' police departments enumerated separately, including idleness, suspicious persons, loitering, lounging, loafing, begging, and mendicancy. Arrests for related public order offenses include arrests for disorderly persons, breach of the peace, and disturbing the peace. I have excluded data for any year or city in which disorderly conduct arrests and public intoxication arrests were counted together. For all data for the year 1900 (excepting data for Macon, Georgia, and Birmingham, Alabama), see *Bulletin of the Department of Labor*, 839. For all other figures for Atlanta, see *Atlanta Police Annual Report, 1900*, pp. 17–18; *Atlanta Police Annual Report, 1905*, pp. 14–15; *Atlanta Police Annual Report, 1910*, pp. 27–28; *Atlanta Police Annual Report, 1915*, pp. 22–23; *Atlanta Police Annual Report, 1920*, pp. 22–23; *Atlanta Police Annual Report, 1925*, p. 16; and *Atlanta Police Annual Report, 1930*, pp. 9–10. For Birmingham, see *Birmingham News*, May 14, 1902, January 24, 1911, January 5, 1914. For Boston, see *Boston Police Annual Report, 1890*, pp. 43–45, 47; *Boston Police Annual Report, 1905*, pp. 52–53, 56–57; *Boston Police Annual Report, 1910*, pp. 112–13, 116–17; *Boston Police Annual Report, 1915*, pp. 52–53, 54, 56, 60; *Boston Police Annual Report, 1920*, pp. 70–71, 73–74, 76–77; *Boston Police Annual Report, 1925*, pp. 70, 72, 75, 76; and *Boston Police Annual Report, 1930*, pp. 66–67, 69, 71. For Charleston, see *Charleston Yearbook, 1900*, p. 148; *Charleston Yearbook, 1905*, p. 202; *Charleston Yearbook, 1910*, pp. 133–34; *Charleston Yearbook, 1915*, p. 219; and *Charleston Yearbook, 1920*, p. 285. For Chicago, see *Chicago Police Annual Report, 1880*, p. 22; *Chicago Police Annual Report, 1890*, p. 59; *Chicago Police Annual Report, 1910*, p. 20; *Chicago Police Annual Report, 1920*, p. 27; and *Chicago Police Annual Report, 1930*, p. 25. For Detroit, see *Detroit Police Annual Report, 1882*, p. 41; *Detroit Police Annual Report, 1905–1906*, pp. 73–74; *Detroit Police Annual Report, 1910–11*, pp. 52–53; and *Detroit Police Annual Report, 1917–18*, p. 19. For Los Angeles, see *Los Angeles Times*, November 12, 1882; *Los Angeles Herald*, December 7, 1890; *Los Angeles Police Annual Report, 1911–12*, pp. 17–19; *Los Angeles Police Annual Report, 1920–21*, pp. 48–51; and *Los Angeles Police Annual Report, 1930–31*, p. 39. For Macon, see *Macon Daily Telegraph*, January 11, 1902, January 2, 1907, December 23, 1910, January 2, 1916. For Milwaukee, see *Milwaukee Police Annual Report, 1906*, p. 16; *Milwaukee Police Annual Report, 1910*, p. 18; *Milwaukee Police Annual Report, 1915*, p. 21; *Milwaukee Police Annual Report, 1920*, p. 20; *Milwaukee Police Annual Report, 1925*, n.p.; and *Milwaukee*

Police Annual Report, 1930, pp. 15–16. For Montgomery, see *Annual Message of Mayor W. M. Teague*, 109–11; and *Montgomery Advertiser*, February 26, 1918, January 16, 1921. For Nashville, see *Nashville Tennessean*, January 26, 1923; *First Annual Report of the Metropolitan Police Department City of Nashville, Tennessee for the Year Ending December 31st, 1915*; *Nashville Annual Report, 1904*, pp. 116–17; *Nashville Annual Report, 1907*, pp. 97–98; and *Nashville Annual Report, 1910*, pp. 96–97, 156–57. For New Orleans, see *New Orleans Item*, January 6, 1880; *Daily Picayune* (New Orleans), April 3, 1915; *Police Commissioners Annual Report, 1914*, pp. 22–23; *Daily Picayune* (New Orleans), April 22, 1924; *New Orleans Item-Tribune*, August 28, 1927; and *Enforcement of Prohibition Laws*, 4:535. For New York City, see *New York City Record*, August 30, 1906, March 28, 1911; *New York Police Annual Report, 1885*, pp. 19–21; *New York Police Annual Report, 1890*, pp. 28–31; *New York Police Annual Report, 1915*, pp. 15, 17–18; *New York Police Annual Report, 1921*, pp. 346, 348; *New York Police Annual Report, 1925*, pp. 52, 54; and *New York Police Annual Report, 1930*, p. 25. For Philadelphia, see *Philadelphia Mayor's Message, 1878*, p. 7; *Philadelphia Mayor's Message, 1891*, p. 28; *Philadelphia Mayor's Message, 1906*, pp. 1:38–39, *Philadelphia Mayor's Message, 1913*, pp. 1:107–8; *Philadelphia Mayor's Message, 1915*, pp. 1:52–53; and *Philadelphia Mayor's Message, 1922*, pp. 38–40. For Richmond, see *Richmond News Leader*, February 26, 1931; *Richmond Mayor's Message, 1908*, p. 17; *Richmond Mayor's Message, 1915*, pp. 16–17; and *Richmond Mayor's Message, 1918*, pp. 19–20. For Savannah, see *Savannah Mayor's Message, 1905*, p. 36; *Savannah Mayor's Message, 1910*, pp. 66–67; and *Savannah Mayor's Message, 1915*, pp. 164–64. For Shreveport, see *Shreveport Times*, September 27, 1903, January 4, 1922, January 1, 1928; and *Shreveport Journal*, January 13, 1913.

64. Williams, "Negro and the South," 149; *Okolona (MS) Messenger*, August 19, 1903; Jelks, "Acuteness of the Negro Question," 391.

65. *New Iberia (LA) Enterprise and Independent Observer*, December 10, 1910; *Herald* (Columbia, TN), November 25, 1904; *Daily Picayune* (New Orleans), October 5, 1906; *New Orleans Item*, March 7, 1912; *Interior Journal* (Stanford, KY), July 7, 1908; *Miami News*, June 21, 1905.

66. Riser, "History of Jennings," chap. 3.

67. *Jennings (LA) Daily Times-Record*, July 10, 1906; *Rice Belt Journal* (Welsh, LA), July 13, 1906; *Crowley (LA) Post-Signal*, July 12, 1929; *New Orleans Item*, July 11, 14, 1906; *Daily Picayune* (New Orleans), July 11, 13, 14, 1906.

68. *St. Landry Clarion* (Opelousas, LA), July 21, 28, 1906; *Daily Picayune* (New Orleans), July 16, 1906; *Lafayette (LA) Advertiser*, August 8, 1906; *Shreveport Times*, July 16, 1906; *Alexandria (LA) Town Talk*, July 17, 1906; *Jennings (LA) Daily Times-Record*, July 18, 1906; *Crowley (LA) Daily Signal*, July 16, 1906. For racial demographics, see *Times-Democrat* (New Orleans), May 9, 1902.

69. *St. Landry Clarion* (Opelousas, LA), July 21, 28, October 13, 1906; *Rice Belt Journal* (Welsh, LA), August 24, 1906; *Times-Democrat* (New Orleans), October 21, 1906; *Shreveport Times*, December 4, 1906; *Semi-Weekly Times-Democrat* (New Orleans), October 19, 1906; *Shreveport Journal*, August 3, 1906; *St. Mary Banner* (Franklin, LA), October 13, November 3, 1906; *New Iberia (LA) Enterprise and Independent Observer*, September 1, 1906; *Daily Picayune* (New Orleans), October 25, November 5, 1906.

70. *Daily Picayune* (New Orleans), July 11, 1906; *Shreveport Times*, July 16, 1906; *Crowley (LA) Daily Signal*, July 16, 1906; *Daily Picayune* (New Orleans), July 16, 1906.

71.*Atlanta Constitution*, August 26, 1906; Godshalk, *Veiled Visions*, 76, 82, 40–41, 48; *Wilmington (NC) Messenger*, October 5, 25, 1906; *Montgomery Times*, September 27, 1906; *Birmingham News*, September 28, 1906; *Weekly Tribune* (Tampa), September 27, 1906.

72.*Sea Coast Echo* (Bay St. Louis, MS), September 29, 1906; *Jackson (MS) Daily News*, October 11, 1906; *Natchez Democrat*, October 7, 1906; *Vicksburg (MS) Evening Post*, October 16, 1906; *Raleigh Times*, September 28, 1906; *Daily Picayune* (New Orleans), October 23, November 14, 1906.

73. On the acculturative functions of lynchings, see Garland, "Penal Excess and Surplus Meaning"; Hale, *Making Whiteness*, 199–239.

74.*Lafayette (LA) Advertiser*, July 25, 1906; *St. Landry Clarion* (Opelousas, LA), August 31, 1907; *Commercial* (Union City, TN), July 2, 1909; *Daily Picayune* (New Orleans), July 31, 1913; *New Orleans States*, April 5, 1918; *Columbus (MS) Dispatch*, February 13, 1908.

75. Cohen, "Negro Involuntary Servitude," 51–52; *St. Martinsville (LA) Messenger*, September 19, 1903; *Daily Picayune* (New Orleans), November 15, 23, December 28, 1888, April 28, 1915, April 22, 1927; Barry, *Rising Tide*, 316.

76.*St. Landry Clarion* (Opelousas, LA), October 28, 1905; L. L. Barham, affidavit, October 22, 1906, in Daniel, *Peonage Files*, reel 19; Edwards, Martison, and Frank, *World Don't Owe Me Nothing*, 47, 49; Trynka, *Portrait of the Blues*, 33; *Daily Picayune* (New Orleans), December 8, 1907, September 13, 1915; *St. Mary Banner* (Franklin, LA), December 9, 1911; Cohen, "Negro Involuntary Servitude," 50.

77.*Southern Sentinel* (Winnfield, LA), December 6, 1907; *St. Landry Clarion* (Opelousas, LA), August 13, 19, 1905.

78. Frank T. Mooney to "Precinct Commanders," April 20, 1918, in *New Orleans Item*, April 21, 1918.

79.*New Orleans Item*, November 7, 8, 1917; *New Orleans States*, August 22, November 9, 1917; *Times-Picayune* (New Orleans), November 8, 1917.

80. *Times-Picayune* (New Orleans), October 29, 1918; *New Orleans Item*, October 28, 29, 1918; *New Orleans States*, October 22, 1918.

81. "Work or Fight" Subject File in Boehm, Meier, and Fox, *Papers of the NAACP*, pt. 10, reel 23; Chamberlain, *Victory at Home*; Shenk, *"Work or Fight!"*

82.*Birmingham News*, August 29, 1907; *Fort Worth Star-Telegram*, May 7, 1904; *St. Landry Clarion* (Opelousas, LA), August 19, 1905; *Hattiesburg (MS) News*, June 6, 1910; Walter White, "Arkansas," [1918?], p. 3, and Walter White, "Report of Conditions Found in Investigation of 'Work or Fight' Laws in Southern States: Georgia," [1918?], p. 4, both in "Work or Fight" Subject File, in Boehm, Meier, and Fox, *Papers of the NAACP*, pt. 10, reel 23.

83. *Times-Democrat* (New Orleans), October 30, 1900, November 8, 1901, October 12, 1904; *New Orleans Item*, November 6, 1901, May 24, 1921.

84.*City of New Orleans vs. Joseph Steele et als.*, filed May 30, 1905, docket no. 34,040, and *City of New Orleans vs. Willie Garner, Lenard Perry, and Oscar Jones*, filed April 2, 1906, docket no. 34651, both in Criminal District Court Records, NOPL; Obetie Thomas, affidavit, May 17, 1949, folder 22, box 15, A. P. Tureaud Papers, Amistad Research Center, New Orleans, LA.

85. Morial, *Witness to Change*, 114–15; *Times-Picayune* (New Orleans), January 20, 21, 1968.

86. Entries of January 21–February 3, 1913, Arrest Records, New Orleans, LA Police Department Records, NOPL.

87. *City of New Orleans vs. Joseph Herman*, filed March 27, 1906, docket no. 34632, *City of New Orleans vs. Abe Muskovitz, Abe Klein and Louis Hager*, filed December 5, 1904, docket no. 33734, *State of Louisiana vs. Charles Duke and George Hendon*, filed March 18, 1904, docket no. 33384, all in Criminal District Court Records, NOPL.

88. *Jackson (MS) Daily News*, October 13, 1903; *Montgomery Advertiser*, January 7, 1910.

89. *Times-Democrat* (New Orleans), September 21, 1894; *Daily Picayune* (New Orleans), November 30, 1908, September 9, 1912, November 19, 1913; *City of New Orleans vs. Anita LeRoy*, filed April 3, 1906, docket no. 34652, Criminal District Court Records, NOPL.

90. Arrest Records, January 26–February 1, 1913, New Orleans Police Department, NOPL; Shapiro and Hentoff, *Hear Me Talkin' to Ya*, 6.

91. *City of New Orleans v. Levi Jones*, filed June 5, 1906, docket no. 34,759, *City of New Orleans vs. Walter Scott*, filed April 18, 1908, docket no. 36174, and *City of New Orleans vs. Mabel Robbins*, filed August 22, 1905, docket no. 34226, all in Criminal District Court Records, NOPL.

92. *New Orleans Item*, December 9, 1917.

93. *New Orleans Item*, October 7, 1917; *New Orleans States*, January 28, 1928.

94. Trynka, *Portrait of the Blues*, 33–35; Edwards, Martison and Frank, *World Don't Owe Me Nothing*, 47.

95. *Daily Picayune* (New Orleans), October 22, 1910; Russell, *"Oh, Mister Jelly,"* 48; Foster and Stoddard, *Pops Foster*, 33, Shapiro and Hentoff, *Hear Me Talkin' to Ya*, 5–6; Gussow, *Seems Like Murder Here*, 51; Weissman, *Blues*, 58; Bastin, *Red River Blues*, 103; Cohn and Aldin, *Nothing but the Blues*, 75; Thomas, "No Job Blues"; Johnson, "Broken Levee Blues"; Hobson, *Creating Jazz Counterpoint*, 21; Krist, *Empire of Sin*, 137; Walker, *Gypsy Songman*.

96. Trynka, *Portrait of the Blues*, 35; Edwards, Martinson, and Frank, *World Don't Owe Me Nothing*, 47.

97. Kennedy, *Big Chief Harrison*, 81; Armstrong, *Satchmo*, 92–93, 141; Foster and Stoddard, *Pops Foster*, 33.

98. Kennedy, *Big Chief Harrison*, 81; Edwards, Martinson, and Frank, *World Don't Owe Me Nothing*, 47; "'Honeyboy,' the Last Link to Delta Blues"; Lomax, *Mister Jelly Roll*, 116–18; Foster and Stoddard, *Pops Foster*, 33; Trynka, *Portrait of the Blues*, 33; Thomas, "No Job Blues."

99. *Magnolia (MS) Gazette*, reprinted in *People's Journal* (Pickens, SC), October 10, 1901; *Grenada (MS) Sentinel*, July 6, 1901; *Southern Sentinel* (Winnfield, LA), December 6, 1907; *Manning (SC) Times*, August 26, 1903; *Weekly Messenger* (St. Martinsville, LA), September 19, 1903; *Asheville (NC) Citizen-Times*, August 7, 1903.

100. *New Orleans Item*, October 29, 1918; Kennedy, *Big Chief Harrison*, 81; King, *From the Bottom of the Heap*, 131–32; Shapiro and Hentoff, *Hear Me Talkin' to Ya*, 5.

101. Walter White, "Louisiana," December 16, 1818, and Walter White, "Report of

Conditions Found in Investigation of 'Work or Fight' Laws in Southern States: Georgia," [1918?], p. 4, both in "Work or Fight" Subject File, Boehm, Meier, and Fox, *Papers of the NAACP*, pt. 10, reel 23.

102. In 1961, police performed 12,720 arrests of Black adults for vagrancy or being suspicious, out of a total Black population (assuming constant growth between decimal censuses) of 236,893. Among white people, police performed 11,363 vagrancy and suspicion arrests, out of a population of 385,677. *New Orleans Police Annual Report, 1961*, n.p.

103. Among Black adults, the drug arrest rate peaked in 1989 at 2 per 1,000. The drug arrest rate in large urban areas was 6.9 per 1,000 in 1986. Castellano and Uchida, "Local Drug Enforcement, Prosecutors and Case Attrition," 136; "Decades of Disparity."

104. In 1830, the Police Jail received 3,544 enslaved people, of which roughly three-fourths (roughly 2,650 persons) had been arrested for marronage, out of a total enslaved population of 9,397. Between July 1, 1849, and June 30, 1850, police performed 5,979 vagrancy arrests, virtually all of which were of white persons, out of a population in 1850 of 89,495 white persons. Register of Slaves Entering the Police Jail, Police Jail Records; "General Statement of Police Operations of the City of New Orleans for the Year Commencing on the First July 1849, and Ending on the 30th June 1850," December 9, 1850, Official Proceedings, vol. 6, First Municipality Council Records, both in NOPL.

105. New Orleans's Police Jail and the subsequent House of Detention received roughly 2,600 Black inmates and 2,200 white inmates, annually, between 1898 and 1915. Overall, New Orleans's entire jail system averaged receipt of 4,500 Black inmates and 3,300 white inmates, yearly, between 1900 and 1910. Figures assume constant population growth between decimal censuses. For the years 1898 and 1899, see Frank Bishop to James Zacharie, July 5, 1900, in Outgoing Correspondence, Department of Police and Public Buildings, NOPL. For 1900–1901, 1902–3, 1906–10, and 1914–15, see *Prisons and Asylums Annual Report, 1900–1901*, pp. 5–6; *Prisons and Asylums Annual Report, 1902–1903*, pp. 5–6; *Prisons and Asylums Annual Report, 1906–1907*, pp. 10, 13; *Prisons and Asylums Annual Report, 1907–1908*, pp. 7, 12; *Prisons and Asylums Annual Report, 1908–1909*, pp. 16, 21; *Prisons and Asylums Annual Report, 1909–1910*, pp. 9, 12; and *Prisons and Asylums Annual Report, 1914–15*, p. 14. For 1904–5, see *Charities and Corrections Report, 1905*, p. 23.

106. For antebellum police jail admittance totals, see graph 1.1. For the workhouse figure, see *New Orleans Daily Crescent*, October 17, 1857.

Epilogue

1. Morial, *Witness to Change*, 114–15; *Times-Picayune* (New Orleans), January 20, 21, 1968.

2. Goluboff, *Vagrant Nation*, esp. 222.

3. *Scott v. Dist. Atty., Jefferson Parish, St. of La.*, 309 F. Supp. 833 (E.D. La. 1970); *Times-Picayune* (New Orleans), February 13, 26, March 9, 1970.

4. Asher, "Historical Statistics."

5. *Papachristou v. City of Jacksonville*, 405 US 156 (1972).

6. Kang-Brown, Hinds, Heiss, and Lu, *New Dynamics of Mass Incarceration*, 8;

Harrison and Karberg, "Prison and Jail Inmates at Midyear 2002," 10; Mock, "New Orleans Continues on a Path of Decarceration."

7. Campanella, "New Orleans," 6–11; Pelot-Hobbs, "Louisiana's Turn to Mass Incarceration"; Ross, "New Orleans as a Rust Belt City?"; Souther, *New Orleans on Parade*, chap. 7.

8. *Times-Picayune* (New Orleans), July 27, 1954, May 23, 1956, August 13, 1966, October 5, 1971, September 6, 1981; *Morning Advocate* (Baton Rouge), October 21, 1964, January 6, 1971; *State Times Advocate* (Baton Rouge), October 2, 8, 1971.

9. *Hamilton v. Schriro*, 338 F. Supp. 1016 (E.D. La. 1970).

10. *Times-Picayune* (New Orleans), August 15, 1969; Zollman, "Conditions Said Improved at Orleans Parish Prison," *Sunday Advocate* (Baton Rouge), March 21, 1976; Hedges, "Suit Details the Beatings of Detainees in Louisiana," *New York Times*, January 2, 2001; Ridgeway and Casella, "America's 10 Worst Prisons"; Peters, "Drug Abuse, Moldy Walls, an Inmate with a Gun."

11. *Broken Promises*, 12; Mazza, *Report on Sexual Victimization in Prisons and Jails*, 76; Leonard Lewis, affidavit, April 1, 2012, in Declarations II, in *Jones v. Gusman*.

12. Loretta King to Marlin Gusman, September 11, 2009, in *Jones v. Gusman*.

13. Jonathan Smith to Marlin Gusman, April 23, 2012, in *Jones v. Gusman*.

14. King to Gusman, September 11, 2009, in *Jones v. Gusman*; *Broken Promises*, 26.

15. Leonard Lewis, affidavit, April 1, 2012, in *Jones v. Gusman*.

16. King to Gusman, September 11, 2009, in *Jones v. Gusman*.

17. *Abandoned and Abused*, 15.

18. Houppert, *Chasing Gideon*, 143.

19. Lewis, affidavit, April 1, 2012, in *Jones v. Gusman*.

20. Mark Walker, affidavit, March 30, 2020, in *Jones v. Gusman*.

21. Chris Hedges, "Suit Details the Beatings of Detainees in Louisiana," *New York Times*, January 2, 2001.

22. For each year (see graph 8.1), I have estimated incarceration rates in one of two ways: by using a count of the total number of prisoners on a single day (often referred to in historic records as the number of prisoners on hand, or POH) or by using the average daily population (ADP) for that entire year. For years that both figures were available, I've relied on ADP figures. Calculated by Orleans Parish correctional authorities, ADP figures were published by the local press, in grand jury reports, in municipal or state government reports, or by the US Department of Justice's Bureau of Justice Statistics (BJS). On occasion, different sources provided different ADP figures for the same year—or local correctional authorities performed POH counts for different jails on different days, or they reported an ADP count for some jails but a POH count for other jails. For the purpose of estimating incarceration rates, these variations are so small as to be statistically insignificant, with the notable exception of ADP figures for the two years following Hurricane Katrina, which are highly variable (for those years, I've relied on BJS figures).

For the purposes of this graph, "enslaved" refers to prisoners that jailors identified as legally owned chattel (excluding prisoners that jailors identified as "soi-disant libres," or prisoners for whom census takers omitted any owner's name on the slave census). Historically and presently, Orleans Parish correctional authorities have racialized prisoners as either "white" or "negro" (updated to "African American" and "black" in the late twentieth century): thus, all population counts for Black prisoners doubtless include persons who considered themselves neither white nor Black.

To minimize the impact of seasonal fluctuation, most POH figures used here are mid-year counts. Police Jail POH counts for 1820, 1824, 1828, 1830, 1831, and 1840, First Municipality Police Jail counts for 1841, 1850, and 1853, and Second Municipality Police Jail counts for 1853 fail to distinguish enslaved prisoners from free Black prisoners jailed as slaves. To account for the presence of free Black prisoners, which would otherwise inflate the total count, I have used other Police Jail manifests to estimate their number, which I then subtracted from the total inmate count: 3 percent of inmates from the 1820 count, 13 percent from all counts for years 1824–40, and 4 percent from the 1850 and 1853 counts. For 1820, see *Fourth Census of the United States*, reel 32, New Orleans, Louisiana, p. 110. For 1821, see Daily Report, June 1–2, 1821, box 10, CHMS. For 1822, see Daily Report, June 1–3, 1822, box 11, CHMS; and *Courrier de la Louisiane* (New Orleans), February 18, 1822. For 1823, see Daily Report, June 1–2, 1823, Daily Reports, vol. 2, Police Jail Records, NOPL. For 1824, see Daily Report, June 1–2, 1824, box 12, CHMS. For 1828, see Daily Report, June 1–2, 1828, Daily Reports, vol. 3, Police Jail Records, NOPL. For 1830, see *Fifth Census of the United States*, reel 45, New Orleans, Louisiana, p. 248. For 1831, see Daily Report, June 1–2, 1831, Daily Reports, vol. 5, Police Jail Records, NOPL; and *Louisiana House Journal*, 10th leg., 1st sess., February 22, 1831, pp. 98–99. For 1834, missing Police Jail data have been substituted with data from June 1, 1836: see Charles Papet et al., grand jury report, June 23, 1834, in Minute Book, vol. 2, Criminal Court of the First District Records, NOPL; and Register of Slaves Entering the Police Jail, June 1, 1836, Police Jail Records, NOPL. For 1840, data for the Third Municipality Police Jail could not be located in the 1840 census and were substituted with the Third Municipality inmate count on June 1, 1839: see *Sixth Census of the United States*, reel 132, Municipality 1, Orleans Parish, Louisiana, pp. 255–56; *Sixth Census of the United States*, reel 133, Municipality 2, Orleans Parish, Louisiana, pp. 83–84; and Daily Report, June 1–2, 1839, Daily Reports, vol. 2, Third Municipality Police Jail Records, NOPL. Data for 1845 are a composite estimate, combining the First Municipality Police Jail count of June 1, 1841, the Second Municipality count of June 1, 1845, and the Third Municipality count of May 11, 1846: entry of May 31, 1841, Register of Slaves Entering the Police Jail, Police Jail Records, NOPL; "Report of Blacks Remaining in the Police Jail of Municipality No. Two," May 31, 1845, folder 3, box 19, CHMS; and "List of Slaves Remaining in the Police Jail the 11th Day of May 1846," in Record Book of the Third Municipality Police Jail, box 21, CHMS. For 1850, see *Seventh Census of the United States*, reel 245, slave schedule, Orleans Parish, Louisiana, pp. 111–13, 345; *Seventh Census of the United States*, reel 236, Ward 5, Municipality 1, Orleans Parish, Louisiana, pp. 234B–35A; *Seventh Census of the United States*, reel 238, Ward 3, Municipality 3, Orleans Parish, Louisiana, pp. 234A–34B; and *Seventh Census of the United States*, reel 236, Ward 5, Municipality 1, Orleans Parish, Louisiana, pp. 238A–40B [442–47]. For 1853, data for the Second Municipality Workhouse, Second Municipality Police Jail, and Third Municipality Police Jail were missing. Data for the Second Municipality Workhouse and Third Municipality Police Jail were substituted with an inmate count conducted in April 1852, while data for the Second Municipality Police Jail were substituted with data from the 1850 census: see *Daily Picayune* (New Orleans), May 2, 1852, March 3, 1853; and *Seventh Census of the United States*, reel 245, slave schedule, Orleans Parish, Louisiana, p. 345. For 1856, see *Report of the Grand Jury of the Parish of Orleans*, 9, 11. For 1858, see *Daily Picayune* (New Orleans), April 5, 1858. For 1859, see *Daily Picayune* (New Orleans), July 10, 1859. For 1860, see *Eighth Census of the United States*, reel 417, Ward 3, Orleans Parish, Louisiana, pp. 527–34; *Eighth Census of the United States*, reel 418, Ward 5, Orleans Parish, Louisiana, pp. 935–37; and *Eighth Census of the United States*, reel 429, Ward 5, Orleans Parish, Louisiana, pp. 11–12. For 1862, see "Report of 75 Black Boys Transferred on the 6th Nov 1862 by order of Genl Butler + the amt due on Each to the Police Jail," [November] 1862, enclosed in Henry C. Deming to George C. Strong, November 18, 1862, and "Statement of Blacks transferred by order of Genl Butler from the Police Jail + the amts due on Each to the City Police Jail," [November] 1862, enclosed in Julian Neville to Henry C. Deming, November 17, 1862, both in LR-HR; and *Daily Delta* (New Orleans), November 28, 1862. Throughout 1865, prison populations fluctuated wildly as the government regularly removed workhouse prisoners en masse. As such, data for 1865 are an average of three sources: *New-Orleans Times*, January 10, April 17, 1865; and *Daily Picayune* (New Orleans), July 11, 1865. For 1866, see *New Orleans Daily Crescent*, July 4, 1866. For 1867, see *Daily Picayune* (New Orleans), June 28, 1867. For 1868, see *Republican* (New Orleans), July 5, 1868. For 1869, see *Daily Picayune* (New Orleans), October 2, 1869. For 1870, see *Ninth Census of the United States*, reel 520, Ward 3, Orleans Parish, Louisiana, pp. 557B–58B; and *Ninth Census of the United States*, reel 521, Ward 5, Orleans Parish, Louisiana, pp. 107A–9B. For 1872, see *Daily Picayune* (New Orleans), March 24, 1872. For 1873, see *Daily Picayune* (New Orleans), July 6, 1873. For 1875, see *New Orleans Bulletin*, January 3, 1875. For 1880, see *Daily Picayune* (New Orleans), January 4, 1880; and *Tenth Census of the United States*, Enumeration District 36, Orleans Parish, Louisiana, reel 461, pp. 246B–48B. Data for 1882 are an ADP count for January 1 to November 15: *Daily Picayune* (New Orleans), December 8, 1882. For 1885, see *Daily Picayune* (New Orleans), December 2, 1885. For 1886, see *Daily Picayune* (New Orleans), May 2, 1886. For 1888, see *Daily Picayune* (New Orleans), September 26, 1888. For 1889, see *Daily Picayune* (New Orleans), June 9, 1889. For 1900, see *Twelfth Census of the United States*, Enumeration District 153, Ward 3, Orleans Parish, Louisiana, reel 571, pp. 1A–5A, 14B–16B. For 1901, see *Police Commissioners Annual Report, 1901*, pp. 5–6. For 1905, see *Charities and Corrections Report, 1905*, p. 23. For 1906 and 1907, see *Charities and Corrections Report, 1906–1907*, pp. 16, 19. For 1908 and 1909, see *Charities and Corrections Report, 1908–1909*, pp. 16, 21. For 1910, see *Thirteenth Census of the United States*, Enumeration District 32, Ward 3, Orleans Parish, Louisiana, reel 520, pp. 1A–5A; and *Thirteenth Census of the United States*, Enumeration District 47, Ward 3, Orleans Parish, Louisiana, reel 520, pp. 12B–14B. For 1915, see *Police Commissioners Annual Report, 1915*, pp. 12, 14. For 1917, see *Prisons and Asylums Annual Report, 1917*, pp. 7, 9. For 1920, see *Fourteenth Census of the United States*, reel 618, Ward 3, Enumeration District 36, Orleans Parish, Louisiana, pp. 1A–3A; *Fourteenth Census of the United States*, reel 619, Ward 3, Enumeration District 51, Orleans Parish, Louisiana, pp. 1A–1B. For 1921, see *New Orleans States*, February 19, 1921. For 1930, see *Fifteenth Census of the United States*, reel 802, Enumeration District 30, New Orleans, Louisiana, pp. 22A–24B; and *Fifteenth Census of the United States*, reel 802, Enumeration District 44, New Orleans, Louisiana, pp. 1A–5B. For 1940, see *Sixteenth Census of the United States*, reel 1,416, Enumeration District 36, Orleans Parish, Louisiana, pp. 1A–6A, 61A–66B. For 1945, see *Daily Picayune* (New Orleans), March 6, 1945. For 1949, see *New Orleans Item*, September 11, 1950. For 1950, see *Seventeenth Census of the United States*, Enumeration District 26–99, pp. 1–14; and *Seventeenth Census of the United States*, Enumeration District 36–97, pp. 21–26. For 1951, see *New Orleans States*, August 15, 1951. For 1954, see *New Orleans States*, October 19, 1954. For 1962, see *Times-Picayune* (New Orleans), January 1, 1963. For 1965, see *Times-Picayune* (New Orleans), January 1, 1965. For 1970, see *Local Jails*, 64. For 1977, see *Crime in Louisiana, 1977*, pp. 80, 86. For 1978, see *Census of Jails, 1978*, p. 37. For 1982, *Jail Inmates 1982*, p. 3. For 1983, see *Census of Jails, 1983*, p. 3:33. For 1985, see *Jail Inmates 1987*, p. 33. For 1988 and 1994, see Perkins et al., *Census of Jails*, 7. For 1989 and 1990, see Jankowski, *Correctional Populations in the United States, 1990*, p. 12. For 1991 and 1992, see *Jail Inmates 1992*, p. 4. For 1995, see *Prison and Jail Inmates, 1995*, p. 12. For 1996, 1997, and 1998, see Gilliard, *Prison and Jail Inmates at Midyear 1998*, p. 8. For 1999, 2000, and 2001, see Beck, Karberg, and Harrison, *Prison and Jail Inmates at Midyear 2001*, p. 11. For 2002, 2003, and 2004, see Beck and Harrison, *Prison and Jail Inmates at Midyear 2004*, p. 10. For 2005, see Minton and Sabol, *Jail Inmates at Midyear 2007*, p. 4. For 2006, 2007, and 2008, see Minton and Sabol, *Jail Inmates at Midyear 2008*, p. 7. For 2009 and 2010, see Minton, *Jail Inmates at Midyear 2010*, p. 10. For 2012, 2013, and 2014, see Austin and Peyton, *Orleans Prison Population Projection Update*, 10. For 2011–18, see "Incarceration Trends." For 2020, see "Jail Population Snapshot."

23. Police logged 23,019 arrests in 1855, as reported in monthly reports printed in the *New Orleans Daily Crescent*. For other figures see Rousey, *Policing the Southern City*, 24; and "Orleans Parish Criminal Justice System Accountability Report."

24. As noted in chapter 1, existent jail records from Memphis, Savannah, and Charleston suggest slave incarceration rates of between fifteen and twenty-six admissions per hundred enslaved residents. In 2015, the jail admissions rates for these cities' respective counties fell between 0.8 and 2.9 per hundred. For twenty-first-century jail admissions figures, see "Incarceration Trends." For a city-by-city comparison of antebellum police-to-population ratios, see Rousey, *Policing the Southern City*, 24. Antebellum arrest rates for Memphis, Charleston, and Richmond fell between 5.9 and 15 per hundred (see graph 4.2); in 2015, those cities' arrest rates fell between 1.7 and 5.1 per hundred. For twenty-first-century arrest rates and police-to-population ratios, see "Police Scorecard"; and Neusteter and O'Toole, *Every Three Seconds*.

25. *Abandoned and Abused*, 13, 20, 29; "New Orleans: Prisoners Abandoned to Floodwaters."

26. Shleifstein, "'FEMA's $7.7 Million Will Help Build New Prison Administration Center in New Orleans"; Johnson, Laisne, and Wool, "Criminal Justice."

27. Monteverde, "Orleans Parish Sheriff Marlin Gusman Formally Ends Jail Stays at House of Detention"; "Last Inmate Leaves House of Detention."

28. Covert, "Louisiana's Prisoners Demand an End to 'Modern-Day Slavery'"; Lopez, "America's Prisoners Are Going on Strike in at Least 17 States."

29. Morgan, "Slavery and Freedom."

30. Johnson, Laisne, and Wool, "Criminal Justice."

31. Carson, *Prisoners in 2020*, 13, 15–16.

BIBLIOGRAPHY

Manuscript and Archival Collections

Baton Rouge, LA
   Special Collections, Hill Memorial Library, Louisiana State University
      Edwards (Marianne) Letters
      Lewis Madison, Certificate, March 5, 1841
      Moses and St. John Richard Liddell Family Papers
Covington, LA
   St. Tammany Parish Clerk of Court's Office
      Justice Court Records, Archives Department
Memphis, TN
   Shelby County Archives
Mystic, CT
   G. W. Blunt White Library, Mystic Seaport Museum
      Records of the American Seamen's Friend Society
Nashville, TN
   Tennessee State Library and Archives
      Legislative Petitions, State of Tennessee
New Orleans, LA
   Amistad Research Center, Tulane University
      A. P. Tureaud Papers
   Archives and Special Collections, Earl K. Long Library, University of New Orleans
      Supreme Court of Louisiana Collection
   Archives and Special Collections, Xavier University of Louisiana
      Charles F. Heartman Manuscripts of Slavery Collection
      Slavery and Freedom in Louisiana Collection
   Historic New Orleans Collection
      Slavery in Louisiana Collection
      Ste-Gême Family Papers
   Louisiana Division/City Archives and Special Collections, New Orleans
               Public Library
      Charity Hospital Records
      City Archives Pamphlet Collection
      Daily Report of Parish Prison and Police Jail, Prisoners and Supplies on Hand
      Daily Report of Parish Prison and the House of Detention
      Department of Police and Public Buildings
      Freedom Papers of New Orleans Collection

Miscellaneous Spanish and French Records of New Orleans
New Orleans (LA) Board of Health Records
Orleans Parish Civil and Criminal Courts
    Civil District Court Records
    Commercial Court Records
    Criminal Court of the First District Records
    Criminal District Court Records
    Fifth District Court Records
    First District Court Records
    First Judicial District Court Records
    Fourth District Court Records
    Miscellaneous Criminal Courts in New Orleans
    Parish Court Records
    Second District Court Records
    "Stray" Court Records
Records of Correctional Institutions
    House of Refuge Records
    Police Jail of the Third Municipality Records
    Police Jail Records
    Workhouse of the First Municipality Records
    Workhouse of the Third Municipality Records
    Workhouse Records
Records of Police Departments
    Arrest Records
Records of the City Councils
    Board of Aldermen Records
    Board of Assistant Aldermen Records
    Common Council Records
    Conseil de Ville Records
    First Municipality Council Records
    General Council Records
    Second Municipality Council Records
Records of the Office of the Mayor
Records Relating to Legal and Judicial Matters
    Third Municipality Recorder's Office
Records Relating to Public Property and Public Works
    First Municipality Surveyor's Office Records
    Street Commissioner's Office Records
Records Relating to Public Property, Public Works and Public Buildings
        in New Orleans
Records Relating to the Public Safety of New Orleans
    Records of Police Departments
Louisiana Research Collection, Tulane University
    Civil War Collection
    John Minor Wisdom Collection
    Names of Prisoners Sent to State Prison at Baton Rouge Penitentiary

New Orleans Municipal Papers
Roman Family Papers
Rosemond E. and Emile Kuntz Collection
Louisiana State Historical Center
Records of the Superior Council of Louisiana
New Orleans Notarial Archives Research Center
New York, NY
New-York Historical Society
New Orleans Collection
Portland, ME
Maine Historical Society
George F. Shepley Papers
Providence, RI
Rhode Island Historical Society
Rowland G. and Caroline (Newbold) Hazard Papers
San Marino, CA
Huntington Library, Art Collections, and Botanical Gardens
Duncan McKercher Papers
Savannah, GA
City of Savannah Research Library and Municipal Archives
Police Department Records
Washington, DC
Library of Congress
Benjamin F. Butler Papers
Nathaniel P. Banks Papers
Thaddeus Stevens Papers
National Archives and Records Administration
Record Group 393: Records of the US Army Continental Commands,
    1821–1920
Part I. Department of the Gulf and Louisiana
    Headquarters Records
        General Records. Correspondence
    Records of Staff Officers
        Provost Marshal. General Records
    Records of Subordinate Offices
        Civil Affairs
Part IV. Provost Marshal Field Organizations of the Civil War
    State of Louisiana, 1862–63. Parishes
        Jefferson, 1862–65
        Orleans, 1862–66
        St. Charles, 1863–65
        St. James and St. John Baptiste, 1863–65
        St. Mary's, 1863–65
    Town and Posts
        New Orleans, LA, 1862–68. Chief of Police

Newspapers and Periodicals

Abbeville (SC) Banner
Alabama Beacon (Greensboro)
Alabama Intelligencer and State Rights Expositor (Tuscaloosa)
Alexandria (VA) Gazette
Alexandria (LA) Town Talk
Alton (LA) Democrat
American Patriot (Clinton, LA)
Anti-Slavery Bugle (New Lisbon, OH)
Ariel (Natchez)
Arkansas Democrat (Little Rock)
Asheville (NC) Citizen-Times
Athens (AL) Weekly Post
Atlanta Constitution
Baltimore Gazette and Daily Advertiser
Baton Rouge Gazette
Baton Rouge Tri-Weekly Gazette and Comet
Birmingham Daily News
Birmingham News
Boston Courier
Boston Daily Atlas
Boston Evening Transcript
Brooklyn Daily Eagle
Brooklyn Times Union
Buffalo Commercial Advertiser
Burlington (VT) Free Press
Charleston Courier
Charleston Daily Courier
Charleston Mercury
Chattanooga News
Chicago Tribune
Chronicle and Constitutionalist (Augusta, GA)
Chronicle and Sentinel (Augusta, GA)
Cincinnati Daily Press
City Gazette and Commercial Daily Advertiser (Charleston)
City Gazette and Daily Advertiser (Charleston)
Civilian and Galveston (TX) Gazette
Clark County Democrat (Grove Hill, AL)
Columbian Register (New Haven, CT)
Columbus (GA) Enquirer

Columbus (MS) Commercial
Columbus (MS) Dispatch
Commercial (Union City, TN)
Commercial Advertiser (New York)
Concordia Intelligencer (Vidalia, LA)
Crisis (Columbus, OH)
Crowley (LA) Post-Signal
Daily Advocate (Baton Rouge)
Daily Chronicle and Sentinel (Augusta, GA)
Daily Comet (Baton Rouge)
Daily Constitutionalist (Augusta, GA)
Daily Constitutional Union (Washington, DC)
Daily Delta (New Orleans)
Daily Dispatch (Richmond)
Daily Gazette and Comet (Baton Rouge)
Daily Memphis Avalanche
Daily Missouri Democrat (St. Louis)
Daily Missouri Republican (St. Louis)
Daily National Intelligencer (Washington, DC)
Daily Picayune (New Orleans)
Daily True Delta (New Orleans)
Dallas Morning News
Easton (MD) Gazette
Edgefield (SC) Advertiser
Emancipator (New York)
Emancipator and Free American (Boston)
Emancipator and Republican (Boston)
Emancipator and Weekly Chronicle (Boston)
Evening Star (Washington, DC)
Farmers' Cabinet (Amherst, MA)
Fayette (AL) Banner
Fort Worth Daily Gazette
Fort Worth Star-Telegram
Georgian (Savannah)
Green-Mountain Freeman (Montpelier, VT)
Greenville (MS) Times
Greenville (SC) News
Grenada (MS) Sentinel

Hattiesburg (MS) News
Herald (Columbia, TN)
Herald of Freedom (Concord, NH)
Hobart (Australia) Town Gazette
Hudson River Chronicle (Ossining, NY)
Interior Journal (Stanford, KY)
Jackson (MS) Daily News
Jacksonville (AL) Republican
Jeffersonian Republican (New Orleans)
Jeffersonian Republican (Stroudsburg, PA)
Jennings (LA) Daily Times-Record
Keowee Courier (Pickens Court House, SC)
Knoxville Daily Journal
Lafayette (LA) Advertiser
Lafourche Gazette (Donaldson, LA)
Lexington (MS) Union
Liberator (Boston)
Liberty (MS) Advocate
Livingston (AL) Journal
Los Angeles Herald
Los Angeles Times
Louisiana Advertiser (New Orleans)
Louisiana Courier (New Orleans)
Louisiana State Gazette (New Orleans)
Louisiana Weekly (New Orleans)
Louisianian (New Orleans)
Louisville Daily Journal
L'Union (New Orleans)
Macon Daily Telegraph
Macon Telegraph
Magnolia (MS) Gazette
Manning (SC) Times
Marion (NC) Progress
Memphis Daily Appeal
Miami News
Mississippi Free Trader (Natchez)
Mississippi State Gazette (Natchez)
Moniteur de la Louisiane (New Orleans)
Montgomery Advertiser
Montgomery Times
Morning Advocate (Baton Rouge)
Morning Express and Illustrated Buffalo Express
Morning Star (Wilmington, NC)

Nashville Banner
Nashville Daily Union and American
Nashville Tennessean
National Anti-Slavery Standard (New York)
National Banner and Nashville Whig
National Era (Washington, DC)
National Gazette and Literary Register (Philadelphia)
National Intelligencer and Washington Advertiser
Nationalist (Mobile)
Negro Star (Wichita)
New Iberia (LA) Enterprise and Independent Observer
New Orleans Argus
New Orleans Bee
New Orleans Bulletin
New-Orleans Commercial Bulletin
New-Orleans Commercial Times
New Orleans Daily Creole
New Orleans Daily Crescent
New Orleans Daily Democrat
New Orleans Item
New Orleans Item-Tribune
New Orleans States
New-Orleans Times
New Orleans Tribune
New Orleans Weekly Delta
New York American
New York City Record
New-York Daily Tribune
New-York Evening Post
New York Herald
New-York Spectator
New York Times
Norfolk (VA) Landmark
North Star (Rochester, NY)
Okolona (MS) Messenger
People's Journal (Pickens, SC)
Philadelphia Inquirer
Plaindealer (Kansas City)
Planters' Banner (Franklin, LA)
Portland (ME) Advertiser
Public Ledger (Nashville)
Raleigh Times

Republican (New Orleans)
Republican Banner (Nashville)
Rice Belt Journal (Welsh, LA)
Richmond Enquirer
Richmond Times
Sea Coast Echo (Bay St. Louis, MS)
Semi-Weekly Times-Democrat (New Orleans)
Shreveport Journal
Shreveport Semi-Weekly News
Shreveport Times
Southern Banner (Holly Springs, MS)
Southerner (New Orleans)
Southern Sentinel (Plaquemine, LA)
Southern Sentinel (Winnfield, LA)
Southron (Jackson, MS)
South-Western (Shreveport)
St. Landry Clarion (Opelousas, LA)
St. Landry Whig (Opelousas, LA)
St. Mary Banner (Franklin, LA)
Standard (Clarksville, TX)
State Gazette (Trenton, NJ)
State Ledger (Jackson, MS)
State Times Advocate (Baton Rouge)
Sun (Baltimore)
Sunday Advocate (Baton Rouge)

Tampa Tribune
Telegraph and Texas Register (Houston)
Thibodaux (LA) Minerva
Times-Democrat (New Orleans)
Times-Picayune (New Orleans)
Tri-Weekly Advocate (Baton Rouge)
Tri-Weekly Telegraph (Houston)
True American (New Orleans)
Tuskegee (AL) News
Vicksburg (MS) Daily Whig
Vicksburg (MS) Evening Post
Vicksburg (MS) Tri-Weekly Sentinel
Weekly Comet (Baton Rouge)
Weekly Lancaster (OH) Gazette
Weekly Messenger (St. Martinsville, LA)
Weekly Mississippian (Jackson)
Weekly Picayune (New Orleans)
Weekly Standard (Raleigh, NC)
Weekly Tribune (Tampa)
West Alabamian (Carrollton)
Western Democrat (Charlotte, NC)
Wetumpka (AL) Argus
Wilmington (NC) Messenger
Voice of Freedom (Montpelier, VT)
Yazoo Democrat (Yazoo City, MS)

Other Published Sources

Abbott, Richard H. *Cotton and Capital: Boston Businessmen and Antislavery Reform, 1854–1868.* Amherst: University of Massachusetts Press, 1991.
———. *For Free Press and Equal Rights: Republican Newspapers in the Reconstruction South.* Edited by John W. Quist. Athens: University of Georgia Press, 2004.
Adams, Francis Colburn. *Manuel Pereira; or, The Sovereign Rule of South Carolina. With Views of Southern Laws, Life, and Hospitality.* Washington, DC: Buell and Blanchard, 1853.
Adams, Jessica. *Wounds of Returning: Race, Memory, and Property on the Post-slavery Plantation.* Chapel Hill: University of North Carolina Press, 2007.
Adamson, Christopher. "Punishment after Slavery: Southern State Penal Systems, 1865–1890." *Social Problems* 30, no. 5 (June 1983): 555–69.
———. "Toward a Marxist Penology: Captive Criminal Populations as Economic Threats and Resources." *Social Problems* 31, no. 4 (April 1984): 435–58.
Adler, Jeffrey S. "Vagging the Demons and Scoundrels: Vagrancy and the Growth of St. Louis, 1830–1861." *Journal of Urban History* 13, no. 1 (November 1986): 3–30.
Aguirre, Carlos. *The Criminals of Lima and Their Worlds: The Prison Experience, 1850–1935.* Durham, NC: Duke University Press, 2005.

Alabama Legislature. *Acts Passed at the Annual Session of the General Assembly, of the State of Alabama, Begun and Held in the City of Tuscaloosa, on the First Monday in November, 1841.* Tuscaloosa, AL: Hale and Phelan, 1841.

Alderson, Robert. "Charleston's Rumored Slave Revolt of 1783." In *The Impact of the Haitian Revolution in the Atlantic World*, edited by David Geggus, 93–111. Columbia: University of South Carolina Press, 2001.

Alexander, James Edward. *Transatlantic Sketches: Comprising Visits to the Most Interesting Scenes in North and South America, and the West Indies.* 2 vols. London: Richard Bentley, 1833.

Alexander, Michelle. *The New Jim Crow: Mass Incarceration in the Age of Colorblindness.* New York: New Press, 2010.

Algranti, Leila Mezan. "Slave Crimes: The Use of Police Power to Control the Slave Population of Rio de Janeiro." *Luso-Brazilian Review* 25, no. 1 (Summer 1988): 27–49.

Allston, Robert F. W. *The South Carolina Rice Plantation as Revealed in the Papers of Robert F. W. Allston.* Edited by J. H. Easterby. Columbia: University of South Carolina Press, 1994 [1945].

Ambrose, Douglas. "Statism in the Old South: A Reconsideration." In *Slavery, Secession, and Southern History*, edited by Robert Louis Paquette and Louis A. Ferleger, 101–25. Charlottesville: University Press of Virginia, 2000.

American Anti-Slavery Society. "Slave Market of America." Broadside, 1836. Rare Book and Special Collections Division, Library of Congress. www.loc.gov/resource /ppmsca.19705/.

American Civil Liberties Union. *Abandoned and Abused: Complete Report.* August 2006. www.aclu.org/report/abandoned-abused-complete-report.

———. *Broken Promises: Two Years after Katrina.* August 2007. www.aclu.org/sites /default/files/field_document/brokenpromises_20070820.pdf.

Ames, Julius Rubens. *"Liberty": The Image and Superscription on Every Coin in the United States of America.* [New York: American Anti-Slavery Society], 1837.

Anderson, William J. *Life and Narrative of William J. Anderson, Twenty-Four Years a Slave; Sold Eight Times! In Jail Sixty Times!! Whipped Three Hundred Times!!! or The Dark Deeds of American Slavery Revealed. Containing Scriptural Views of the Origin of the Black and of the White Man. Also, a Simple and Easy Plan to Abolish Slavery in the United States. Together with an Account of the Services of Colored Men in the Revolutionary War—Day and Date, and Interesting Facts.* Chicago: Daily Tribune Book and Job Printing Office, 1857.

Andrews, J. Cutler. *The North Reports the Civil War.* Pittsburgh, PA: University of Pittsburgh Press, 1955.

Archbold, Carol A., Carol M. Huynh, and Thomas J. Mrozla. *Policing: The Essentials.* Thousand Oaks, CA: Sage, 2022.

Arkansas Legislature. *Acts Passed at the Fourth Session of the General Assembly of the State of Arkansas: Which Was Begun and Held at the Capitol in the City of Little Rock, on Monday, the Sixth Day of November, One Thousand Eight Hundred and Forty-Two, and Ended on Saturday, the Fourth Day of February, One Thousand Eight Hundred and Forty-Three.* Little Rock, AR: Eli Colby, 1843.

Armstrong, Louis. *Satchmo: My Life in New Orleans.* New York: Prentice-Hall, 1954.

Arnesen, Eric. *Waterfront Workers of New Orleans: Race, Class, and Politics, 1863–1923*. Urbana: University of Illinois Press, 1991.

Ash, Stephen V. *A Massacre in Memphis: The Race Riot That Shook the Nation One Year after the Civil War*. New York: Hill and Wang, 2013.

Asher, Jeff. "Historical Statistics." NOLA Crime News. May 19, 2020. https://nola crimenews.com/statistics/historical-statistics/.

Aslakson, Kenneth. *Making Race in the Courtroom: The Legal Construction of Three Races in New Orleans*. New York: New York University Press, 2014.

Atlanta Police Department. [. . .] *Annual Report of the Chief of Police of the City of Atlanta, Georgia for the Year Ending* [. . .]. Atlanta, 1901–26.

Augusta Municipal Government. *The Augusta City Code: Comprising the Ordinances, Resolutions, and Rules Relating to the City of Augusta, Georgia*. Augusta, GA: Chronicle and Sentinel, 1872.

Austin, James, and Johnette Peyton. *Orleans Prison Population Projection Update*. Denver, CO: JFA Institute, 2015. https://nola.gov/getattachment/Criminal-Justice -Coordination/Reports/Orleans-Parish-Prison-Population-Projection-2015.pdf.

Ayers, Edward. *Vengeance and Justice: Crime and Punishment in the Nineteenth-Century American South*. New York: Oxford University Press, 1984.

———. "What We Talk about When We Talk about the South." In *All Over the Map: Rethinking American Region*, edited by Edward Ayers, Patricia Nelson Limerick, Stephen Nissenbaum, and Peter Onuf, 62–82. Baltimore: Johns Hopkins University Press, 1995.

Ball, Edward. *Life of a Klansman: A Family History in White Supremacy*. New York: Picador, 2021.

Ballet, Jules. *La Guadeloupe : renseignements sur l'histoire, la flore, la faune, la géologie, la minéralogie, l'agriculture, le commerce, l'industrie, la législation*. 4 vols. Basse-Terre, Guadeloupe: 1890–99.

Balogh, Brian. *A Government out of Sight: The Mystery of National Authority in Nineteenth-Century America*. New York: Cambridge University Press, 2009.

Baltimore Board of Police Commissioners. *Report of the Board of Police of the City of Baltimore. In Extra Session, 1861*. Frederick, MD: E. S. Riley, 1861.

Baptist, Edward E. *The Half Has Never Been Told: Slavery and the Making of American Capitalism*. New York: Basic Books, 2014.

Barclay, Alexander. *A Practical View of the Present State of Slavery in the West Indies; or, An Examination of Mr. Stephen's "Slavery of the British West India Colonies": Containing More Particularly an Account of the Actual Condition of the Negroes in Jamaica: from Observations on the Decrease of the Slaves Since the Abolition of the Slave Trade, and on the Probable Effects of Legislative Emancipation: Also, Strictures on the Edinburgh Review, and on the Pamphlets of Mr. Cooper and Mr. Bickell*. London: Smith, Elder, 1827.

Bardaglio, Peter Winthrop. *Reconstructing the Household: Families, Sex, and the Law in the Nineteenth-Century South*. Chapel Hill: University of North Carolina Press, 1995.

Bardes, John K. "The Notorious Bras Coupé: A Slave Rebellion Replayed in Memory, History, and Anxiety." *American Quarterly* 72, no. 1 (March 2020): 1–23.

——. "Redefining Vagrancy: Policing Freedom and Disorder in Reconstruction New Orleans, 1862–1868." *Journal of Southern History* 84, no. 1 (February 2018): 69–112.

Barker, Jacob. *Incidents in the Life of Jacob Barker, of New Orleans, Louisiana: With Historical Facts, His Financial Transactions with the Government and His Course on Important Political Questions, from 1800 to 1855*. Washington, 1855.

——. *Mr. Jacob Barker's Speech, in the Case of Barker vs. Barker, in the Parish Court*. New Orleans, [1843].

——. *The Rebellion: Its Consequences, and the Congressional Committee, Denominated the Reconstruction Committee, with Their Action*. New Orleans, 1866.

Barnes, Harry Elmer. *The Evolution of Penology in Pennsylvania*. Indianapolis, IN: Bobbs-Merrill, 1968 [1927].

Barnes, L. Diane, Brian Schoen, and Frank Towers, eds. *The Old South's Modern Worlds: Slavery, Region, and Nation in the Age of Progress*. New York: Oxford University Press, 2011.

Barrow, Bennet H. *Plantation Life in the Florida Parishes of Louisiana, 1836–1846, as Reflected in the Diary of Bennet H. Barrow*. Edited by Edwin Adams Davis. New York: AMS Press, 1967.

Barrow, John Henry, ed. *The Mirror of Parliament, for the Second Session of the Fourteenth Parliament of Great Britain and Ireland, in the Second and Third Years of the Reign of Queen Victoria, Appointed to Meet February 5, and from Thence Continued till August 27, 1839*. 6 vols. London: Longman, Orme, Brown, Green, and Longmans, John Murray, and J. Richards, 1839.

Barry, John. *Rising Tide: The Great Mississippi Flood of 1927 and How It Changed America*. New York: Simon and Schuster, 1997.

Bastin, Bruce. *Red River Blues: The Blues Tradition in the Southeast*. Urbana: University of Illinois Press, 1995.

Beattie, Peter M. *Punishment in Paradise: Race, Slavery, Human Rights, and a Nineteenth-Century Brazilian Penal Colony*. Durham, NC: Duke University Press, 2015.

Beaumont, Gustave de, and Alexis de Tocqueville. *On the Penitentiary System in the United States, and Its Application in France; with an Appendix on Penal Colonies, and also, Statistical Notes*. Translated by Francis Lieber. Philadelphia: Carey, Lea and Blanchard, 1833.

Beccaria, Cesare. *An Essay on Crimes and Punishment Translated from the Italian with a Commentary attributed to Mons. Voltaire, Translated from the French*. 4th ed. London: E. Newbery. 1785 [1775].

Beckert, Sven. *Empire of Cotton: A Global History*. New York: Alfred A. Knopf, 2014.

Beckert, Sven, and Christine Desan, eds. *American Capitalism: New Histories*. New York: Columbia University Press, 2018.

Beckert, Sven, and Seth Rockman, eds. *Slavery's Capitalism: A New History of American Economic Development*. Philadelphia: University of Pennsylvania Press, 2016.

Beecher, Harris H. *Record of the 114th Regiment, N.Y.S.V.: Where It Went, What It Saw, and What It Did*. Norwich, NY: J. F. Hubbard, 1866.

Beier, A. L. *Masterless Men: The Vagrancy Problem in England, 1560–1640*. New York: Methuen, 1985.

Beier, A. L., and Paul Ocobock, eds. *Cast Out: Vagrancy and Homelessness in Global and Historical Perspective*. Athens: Ohio University Press, 2008.

Belden, Simeon. *Annual Report of the Attorney General to the General Assembyy* [*sic*] *of the State of Louisiana, February, 1869*. New Orleans, 1869.

Bell, Caryn Cossé. "'Une Chimère': The Freedmen's Bureau in Creole New Orleans." In *The Freedmen's Bureau and Reconstruction: Reconsiderations*, edited by Paul A. Cimbala and Randall M. Miller, 140–60. New York: Fordham University Press, 1990.

———. *Revolution, Romanticism, and the Afro-Creole Protest Tradition in Louisiana, 1718–1868*. Baton Rouge: Louisiana State University Press, 1997.

Bell, James T. *Report of Departments of the City of Nashville for the Fiscal Year Ending October 1, 1888*. Nashville: Brandon Lithograph and Printing, 1888.

Bellows, Barbara L. "Tempering the Wind: The Southern Response to Urban Poverty, 1850–1865." PhD diss., University of South Carolina, 1983.

Belz, Herman. "Origins of Negro Suffrage during the Civil War." *Southern Studies* 17, no. 2 (Summer 1978): 115–30.

Bentham, Jeremy. *The Works of Jeremy Bentham*. Edited by John Bowring. 11 vols. Edinburgh: William Tait, 1838–43.

Bercaw, Nancy. *Gendered Freedoms: Race, Rights, and the Politics of Household in the Delta, 1861–1875*. Gainesville: University Press of Florida, 2003.

Bergeron, Arthur W., Jr. "Louisiana's Free Men of Color in Gray." In *Louisianans in the Civil War*, edited by Lawrence Hewitt and Arthur Bergeron, 100–119. Columbia: University of Missouri Press, 2002.

Berlin, Ira. *Slaves without Masters: The Free Negro in the Antebellum South*. New York: Pantheon, 1974.

Berlin, Ira, and Herbert G. Gutman. "Natives and Immigrants, Free Men and Slaves: Urban Workingmen in the Antebellum American South." *American Historical Review* 88, no. 5 (December 1983): 1175–200.

Berlin, Ira, and Leslie M. Harris. *Slavery in New York*. New York: New Press, 2005.

Berlin, Ira, Joseph P. Reidy, and Leslie S. Rowland, eds. *Freedom: A Documentary History of Emancipation, 1861–1867*. Ser. 2: *The Black Military Experience*. New York: Cambridge University Press, 1982.

Berlin, Ira, et al., eds. *Freedom: A Documentary History of Emancipation, 1861–1867*. Ser. 1, Vol. 1: *The Destruction of Slavery*. New York: Cambridge University Press, 1985.

———. *Freedom: A Documentary History of Emancipation, 1861–1867*. Ser. 1, Vol. 2: *The Wartime Genesis of Free Labor: The Upper South*. New York: Cambridge University Press, 1993.

———. *Freedom: A Documentary History of Emancipation, 1861–1867*. Ser. 1, Vol. 3: *The Wartime Genesis of Free Labor: The Lower South*. New York: Cambridge University Press, 1990.

Bernault, Florence. "The Shadow of Rule: Colonial Power and Modern Punishment in Africa." In *Cultures of Confinement: A History of the Prison in Africa, Asia, and Latin America*, edited by Frank Dikötter and Ian Brown, 55–94. Ithaca, NY: Cornell University Press, 2007.

Berquin-Duvallon, Pierre-Louis. *Travels in Louisiana and the Floridas, in the Year, 1802, Giving a Correct Picture of Those Countries.* Translated by John Davis. New York: I. Riley, 1806.

Berry, Daina Ramey. *The Price for Their Pound of Flesh: The Value of the Enslaved from Womb to Grave, in the Building of a Nation.* Boston: Penguin Random House, 2017.

Birch, Kelly, and Thomas C. Buchanan. "The Penalty of a Tyrant's Law: Landscapes of Incarceration during the Second Slavery." *Slavery and Abolition* 34, no. 1 (March 2013): 22–38.

Blackmon, Douglas A. *Slavery by Another Name: The Re-Enslavement of Black Americans from the Civil War to World War II.* New York: Anchor Books, 2009.

Blassingame, John. *Black New Orleans, 1860–1880.* Chicago: University of Chicago Press, 1973.

Bloom, Paul. *Against Empathy: The Case for Rational Compassion.* New York: HarperCollins, 2016.

Board of Managers of the Prison Discipline Society. *Fourteenth Annual Report of the Board of Managers of the Prison Discipline Society.* Boston, 1839.

——. *Sixteenth Annual Report of the Board of Managers of the Prison Discipline Society.* Boston, 1841.

Bodichon, Barbara L. S. "Slavery in the South." *English Woman's Journal* 8, no. 45 (1861): 179–87.

Bodin, Jean. *Six Books of the Commonwealth.* Translated by M. J. Tooley. Oxford: Alden, 1955 [1606].

Boehm, Randolph, August Meier, and Mark Fox, eds. *Papers of the NAACP.* Microfilm edition. 1,292 reels. Frederick, MD: University Publications of America, 1981.

Bolster, W. Jeffrey. *Black Jacks: African American Seamen in the Age of Sail.* Cambridge. MA: Harvard University Press, 1997.

Bolton, Charles C. "Edward Isham and Poor White Labor in the Old South." In *The Confessions of Edward Isham: A Poor White Life of the Old South*, edited by Charles C. Bolton and Scott P. Culclasure, 19–31. Athens: University of Georgia Press, 1998.

——. *Fugitivism: Escaping Slavery in the Lower Mississippi Valley, 1820–1860.* Fayetteville: University of Arkansas Press, 2019.

——. *Poor Whites of the Antebellum South: Tenants and Laborers in Central North Carolina and Northeast Mississippi.* Durham, NC: Duke University Press, 1994.

Bolton, Charles C., and Scott Culclasure, eds. *The Confessions of Edward Isham: A Poor White Life of the Old South.* Athens: University of Georgia Press, 1998.

Bonner, James C. "Profile of a Late Antebellum Community." *American Historical Review* 49, no. 4 (July 1944): 663–80.

Boston Police Department. [. . .] *Annual Report of the Police Commissioner for the City of Boston for the Year Ending* [. . .]. Boston: Wright and Potter, 1891–1926.

Botsman, Daniel V. *Punishment and Power in the Making of Modern Japan.* Princeton, NJ: Princeton University Press, 2004.

Bouscaren, Durrie. "What's the Workhouse? Here's What You Need to Know about St Louis' Medium Security Institution." St. Louis Public Radio, July 26, 2017.

https://news.stlpublicradio.org/government-politics-issues/2017-07-26/whats-the
-workhouse-heres-what-you-need-to-know-about-st-louis-medium-security
-institution#stream/0.

Brackett, Jeffrey R. *The Negro in Maryland: A Study of the Institution of Slavery.*
Baltimore: John Murphy, 1889.

Branch, Daniel. "Imprisonment and Colonialism in Kenya, c. 1930–1952: Escaping
the Carceral Archipelago." *International Journal of African Historical Studies* 38,
no. 2 (2005): 239–65.

Bremer, Fredrika. *Homes of the New World: Impressions of America.* 2 vols. Translated by Mary Howitt. New York, 1853.

Broussard, James. "Some Determinants of Know Nothing Electoral Strength in the
South, 1856." *Louisiana History* 7, no. 1 (Winter 1966): 5–20.

Brown, Alexandra K. "'A Black Mark on Our Legislation': Slavery, Punishment, and
the Politics of Death in Nineteenth-Century Brazil." *Luso-Brazilian Review* 37
(Winter 2000): 95–121.

Brown, David. "A Vagabond's Tale: Poor Whites, Herrenvolk Democracy, and the
Value of Whiteness in the Late Antebellum South." *Journal of Southern History* 79,
no. 4 (November 2013): 799–840.

Brown, John. *Slave Life in Georgia: A Narrative of the Life, Sufferings, and Escape
of John Brown, a Fugitive Slave, Now in England.* Edited by L. A. Chamerovzow.
London, 1855.

Brown, Richard Maxwell. "Southern Violence—Regional Problem or National
Nemesis? Legal Attitudes toward Southern Homicide in Historical Perspective."
Vanderbilt Law Review 32, no. 1 (January 1979): 219–33.

Brown, Simone. *Dark Matters: On the Surveillance of Blackness.* Durham, NC: Duke
University Press, 2015.

Brown, William Wells. *A Description of William Wells Brown's Original Panoramic
Views of the Scenes in the Life of an American Slave, from His Birth in Slavery to
His Death or His Escape to His First Home of Freedom on British Soil.* London:
Charles Gilpin, 1849.

———. *My Southern Home; or, The South and Its People.* Boston: A. G. Brown, 1880.

Buchanan, Thomas. *Black Life on the Mississippi: Slaves, Free Blacks, and the Western Steamboat World.* Chapel Hill: University of North Carolina Press, 2004.

Buckingham, James Silk. *The Slave States of America.* 2 vols. London: Fisher, Son,
1842.

Bundles, A'Lelia. *On Her Own Ground: The Life and Times of Madam C. J. Walker.*
New York: Scribner, 2001.

Bureau of Refugees, Freedmen, and Abandoned Lands. *Records of the Assistant Commissioner for the State of Louisiana, Bureau of Refugees, Freedmen, and Abandoned Lands, 1865–1869.* Microfilm edition. 36 reels. Washington, DC: National
Archives Microfilm Publications, 1979.

———. *Records of the Assistant Commissioner for the State of Virginia, Bureau of
Refugees, Freedmen, and Abandoned Lands, 1865–1869.* Microfilm edition. 67
reels. Washington, DC: National Archives Microfilm Publications, 1988.

——. *Records of the Field Offices for the State of Louisiana, Bureau of Refugees, Freedmen, and Abandoned Lands, 1863–1872.* Microfilm edition. 111 reels. Washington, DC: National Archives Microfilm Publications, 2004.

Burns, Robert Elliott. *I Am a Fugitive from a Georgia Chain Gang!* New York: Vanguard, 1932.

Butler, Anne M. *Daughters of Joy, Sisters of Misery: Prostitutes in the American West, 1865–90.* Urbana: University of Illinois Press, 1985.

Butler, Benjamin. *Private and Official Correspondence of Gen. Benjamin F. Butler, during the Period of the Civil War.* Edited by Jessie Ames Marshall. 5 vols. Norwood, MA: Plimpton, 1917.

Butler, Nic. "Charleston's House of Corrections." The Charleston Archive, November 21, 2010. https://ccplarchive.wordpress.com/2010/11/21/hoc/.

Bynum, Victoria E. *Unruly Women: The Politics of Social and Sexual Control in the Old South.* Chapel Hill: University of North Carolina Press, 1992.

Byrd, Alexander X. *Captives and Voyagers: Black Migrants across the Eighteenth-Century British Atlantic World.* Baton Rouge: Louisiana State University Press, 2008.

Byrd, Michael D. "The First Charles Town Workhouse, 1738–1775: A Deterrent to White Pauperism?" *South Carolina Historical Magazine* 110, no. 1/2 (January–April 2009): 35–52.

Cable, George Washington. *The Silent South Together with the Freedman's Case in Equity and the Convict Lease System.* New York: Charles Scribner's Sons, 1895.

Campanella, Richard. "New Orleans: A Timeline of Economic History." In *New Orleans: New Opportunities.* New Orleans: New Orleans Business Alliance, 2012.

Campbell, James M. *Crime and Punishment in African American History.* New York: Palgrave Macmillan, 2013.

——. *Slavery on Trial: Race, Class, and Criminal Justice in Antebellum Richmond, Virginia.* Gainesville: University Press of Florida, 2007.

Canelas, Letícia Gregório. "Escravidão e liberdade no Caribe francês: A Alforria na Martinica sob uma perspectiva de gênero, raça e classe (1830–1848)." PhD diss., Universidade Estadual de Campinas, 2017.

Cantwell, Edward P. *A History of the Charleston Police Force from the Incorporation of the City, 1783 to 1908.* Charleston, SC: J. J. Furlong, [1908].

Capers, Gerald M. *Occupied City: New Orleans under the Federals, 1862–1865.* Lexington: University of Kentucky Press, 1980.

Cardon, Nathan. "'Less than Mayhem': Louisiana's Convict Lease, 1865–1901." *Louisiana History* 58, no. 4 (Fall 2017): 417–41.

Carleton, Mark T. "The Movement to End the Convict Lease System in Louisiana." *Louisiana Studies* 8, no. 3 (Fall 1969): 211–23.

——. *Politics and Punishment: The History of the Louisiana State Penal System.* Baton Rouge: Louisiana State University Press, 1984.

Carpenter, Russell Lant. *Imprisonment and Enslavement of British Coloured Seamen; Illustrated in the Case of John Glasgow.* Leeds, UK: 1853.

Carrey, Émile, ed. *Recueil complet des actes du gouvernement provisoire (février, mars, avril, mai 1848) avec des notes explicatives, des tables chronologiques et une table alphabétique, analytique et raisonnée des matières.* Paris: Auguste Durane, 1848.

Carriere, Marius M., Jr. *The Know Nothings in Louisiana.* Jackson: University Press of Mississippi, 2018.

———. "Political Leadership of the Louisiana Know Nothing Party." *Louisiana History* 21, no. 2 (Spring 1980): 183–95.

Carter, Clarence E., and John Porter Bloom, eds. *The Territorial Papers of the United States.* 28 vols. Washington, DC: Government Printing Office, 1934–75.

Carter, Dan T. *When the War Was Over: The Failure of Self-Reconstruction in the South, 1865–1867.* Baton Rouge: Louisiana State University Press, 1984.

Cary, John H. "France Looks to Pennsylvania: The Eastern Penitentiary as a Symbol of Reform." *Pennsylvania Magazine of History and Biography* 82, no. 2 (April 1958): 186–203.

Cash, W. J. *The Mind of the South.* New York: Alfred A. Knopf, 1941.

Castellano, Thomas C., and Craig D. Uchida. "Local Drug Enforcement, Prosecutors and Case Attrition: Theoretical Perspectives for the Drug War." *American Journal of Police* 9, no. 1 (1990): 133–62.

Castellanos, Henry C. *New Orleans as It Was: Episodes of Louisiana Life.* New Orleans: L. Graham and Son, 1895.

Cecelski, David S. *The Waterman's Song: Slavery and Freedom in Maritime North Carolina.* Chapel Hill: University of North Carolina Press, 2001.

Cecil-Fronsman, Bill. *Common Whites: Class and Culture in Antebellum North Carolina.* Lexington: University Press of Kentucky, 1992.

Chaillé, Stanford Emerson. *A Memoir of the Insane Asylum of the State of Louisiana, at Jackson.* Baton Rouge: J. M. Taylor, 1858.

Chalhoub, Sidney. "Illegal Enslavement and the Precariousness of Freedom in Nineteenth-Century Brazil." In *Assumed Identities: The Meanings of Race in the Atlantic World*, edited by John Garrigus and Christopher Morris, 88–115. College Station: Texas A&M University Press, 2010.

Chamberlain, Charles D. *Victory at Home: Manpower and Race in the American South during World War II.* Athens: University of Georgia Press, 2003.

Chambers, A. B., ed. *The Revised Ordinances of the City of Saint Louis, Revised and Digested by the Fifth City Council during the First Session, Begun and Held in the City of St. Louis, on the Second Monday of May, A.D. 1843. With the Constitutions of the United States and the State of Missouri, and the City Charter.* St. Louis: Chambers and Knapp, 1843.

———. *Trials and Confessions of Madison Henderson, alias Blanchard, Alfred Amos Warrick, James W. Seward, and Charles Brown, Murderers of Jesse Baker and Jacob Weaver, as Given by Themselves; and a Likeness of Each, Taken in Jail Shortly after Their Arrest.* St. Louis: Chambers and Knapp, 1841.

Chambliss, William J. "A Sociological Analysis of the Law of Vagrancy." *Social Problems* 12, no. 1 (July 1964): 67–77.

The Charleston Archive. "Records of the Commissioners of the House of Corrections,

1868–1885." The Charleston Archive, November 16, 2010. https://ccplarchive
.wordpress.com/collections/.

Charleston City Council. *Digest of the Ordinances of the City Council of Charleston, from the Year 1783 to July 1818, to Which Are Annexed, Extracts from the Acts of the Legislature Which Relate to the City of Charleston.* Charleston, SC: Archibald E. Miller, 1818.

Charleston Municipal Government. *Year Book* [. . .] *City of Charleston* [. . .]. Charleston, SC: 1880–1921.

Chase, Robert T. *We Are Not Slaves: State Violence, Coerced Labor, and Prisoners' Rights in Postwar America.* Chapel Hill: University of North Carolina Press, 2020.

Chester, Greville John. *Transatlantic Sketches in the West Indies, South America, Canada and the United States.* London, 1869.

Chicago Police Department. *Police* [. . .] *Annual Report* [. . .] *Year Ending* [. . .]. Chicago: 1881–1931.

Childs, Dennis. *Slaves of the State: Black Incarceration from the Chain Gang to the Penitentiary.* Minneapolis: University of Minnesota Press, 2015.

Christophe, Henri. *Code Henry.* Cap-Henry [Haiti]: P. Roux, 1812.

Cimbala, Paul A., and Randall M. Miller, eds. *The Freedmen's Bureau and Reconstruction: Reconsiderations.* New York: Fordham University Press, 1990.

"Civil War Records of William H. Gray." Acton Memorial Library, December 19, 2014. www.actonmemoriallibrary.org/civilwar/records/gray_william_h.html.

Claiborne, William C. C. *Official Letter Books of W. C. C. Claiborne, 1801–1816*, edited by Dunbar Rowland. 6 vols. Jackson, MS: State Department of Archives and History, 1917.

Clark, Emily. "The Ceremonial Public Sphere: The New Orleans Free Black Militia, 1736–1804." Paper presented at "Performances, Archives and Repertories in the Francophone Circum-Atlantic World Conference." New Orleans, October 19–20, 2017.

———. *The Strange History of the American Quadroon: Free Women of Color in the Revolutionary Atlantic World.* Chapel Hill: University of North Carolina Press, 2013.

Clark, John G. *New Orleans, 1718–1812: An Economic History.* Baton Rouge: Louisiana State University Press, 1970.

Clavin, Matthew J. *Aiming for Pensacola: Fugitive Slaves on the Atlantic and Southern Frontiers.* Cambridge, MA: Harvard University Press, 2015.

———. "'The Floor Was Stained with the Blood of a Slave': Crime and Punishment in the Old South." In *Buried Lives: Incarcerated in Early America*, edited by Michele Lise Tarter and Richard Bell, 259–81. Athens: University of Georgia Press, 2012.

———. *Toussaint Louverture and the American Civil War: The Promise and Peril of a Second Haitian Revolution.* Philadelphia: University of Pennsylvania Press, 2010.

Clayton, Augustin Smith. *A Compilation of the Laws of the State of Georgia, Passed by the Legislature since the Political Year 1800, to the Year 1810, Inclusive.* Augusta, GA: Adams and Duyckinck, 1812.

Clement, Priscilla Ferguson. "The Transformation of the Wandering Poor in Nineteenth-Century Philadelphia." In *Walking to Work: Tramps in America,*

1790–1935, edited by Eric H. Monkkonen, 59–66. Lincoln: University of Nebraska Press, 1984.

Cobb, Thomas R. R. *An Inquiry into the Law of Negro Slavery in the United States of America. To Which Is Prefixed, a Historical Sketch of Slavery.* 2 vols. Philadelphia: T. and J. W. Johnson, 1858.

Cohen, William. *At Freedom's Edge: Black Mobility and the Southern White Quest for Racial Control, 1861–1915.* Baton Rouge: Louisiana State University Press, 1991.

———. "Negro Involuntary Servitude in the South, 1865–1940: A Preliminary Analysis." *Journal of Southern History* 42, no. 1 (February 1976): 31–60.

Cohn, Lawrence, and Mary Katherine Aldin. *Nothing but the Blues: The Music and the Musicians.* New York: Abbeville, 1993.

Colvin, Mark. *Penitentiaries, Reformatories, and Chain Gangs: Social Theory and the History of Punishment in Nineteenth-Century America.* New York: St. Martin's, 1997.

Combe, George. *Remarks on the Principles of Criminal Legislation, and the Practice of Prison Discipline.* London: Simpkin, Marshall, 1854.

Commission pour l'abolition de l'esclavage. *Recueil de la législation nouvelle.* Basse-Terre, Guadeloupe, 1848.

Connor, William P. "Reconstruction Rebels: The New Orleans Tribune in Post-War Louisiana." *Louisiana History* 21, no. 2 (Spring 1980): 159–81.

Conway, Alan A. "New Orleans as a Port of Immigration, 1820–1860." MA thesis, University of London, 1949.

Conway, Thomas W. *The Freedmen of Louisiana. Final Report of the Bureau of Free Labor, Department of the Gulf, to Major General E .R. S. Canby, Commanding.* New Orleans: Times Book and Job Office, 1865.

Cooper, David J., and Thomas McCord, eds. *The Statutes at Large of Souh Carolina.* 10 vols. Columbia, 1837–41.

Cooper, Frederick, Thomas Cleveland Holt, and Rebecca J. Scott. *Beyond Slavery: Explorations of Race, Labor, and Citizenship in Postemancipation Societies.* Chapel Hill: University of North Carolina Press, 2000.

Cooper, Thomas. *Facts Illustrative of the Condition of the Negro Slaves in Jamaica: With Notes and an Appendix.* London, 1824.

Corey, Charles H. *A History of the Richmond Theological Seminary, with Reminiscences of the Thirty Years' Work among the Colored People of the South.* Richmond: J. W. Randolph, 1895.

Coronel, Justina. "Board of Aldermen President Hopes to Close 'the Workhouse' and Use That Money to Help Neighborhoods and Reduce Recidivism." FirstCoast News, June 30, 2020. www.firstcoastnews.com/article/news/local/board-of-alderman-president-the-workhouse-st-louis/63-15773fd4-9e4b-4cb7-a590-16a65b60a7b3.

Correctional Association of New York. *Report of the Prison Discipline Committee for 1846.* New York, [1847].

Covert, Bryce. "Louisiana's Prisoners Demand an End to 'Modern-Day Slavery.'" The Appeal, June 8, 2018. https://theappeal.org/louisiana-prisoners-demand-an-end-to-modern-day-slavery/.

Cresswell, Tim. *The Tramp in America.* London: Reaktion, 2001.

Curry, Colleen. "Video Shows New Orleans Prisoners Allegedly Taking Drugs, Walking City Streets." ABC News, April 3, 2013. https://abcnews.go.com/US/video-shows-orleans-prisoners-allegedly-taking-drugs-walking/story?id=18871262.

Curtin, Mary Ellen. *Black Prisoners and Their World, Alabama, 1865–1900*. Charlottesville: University Press of Virginia, 2000.

Dale, Elizabeth. *Criminal Justice in the United States, 1789–1939*. New York: Cambridge University Press, 2011.

Daniel, Pete, ed. *Peonage Files of the U.S. Department of Justice, 1901–1945*. Microfilm edition, 26 reels. Frederick, Md: University Publications of America, 1989.

———. *The Shadow of Slavery: Peonage in the South, 1901–1969*. Urbana: University of Illinois Press, 1972.

Davis, Angela Y. *Are Prisons Obsolete?* New York: Seven Stories, 2003.

———. "Incarcerated Women: Transformative Strategies." *Black Renaissance/Renaissance Noire* 1, no. 1 (Fall 1996): 20–34.

———. "Racialized Punishment and Prison Abolition." In *A Companion to African-American Philosophy*, edited by Tommy L. Lott and John P. Pittman, 360–69. Malden, MA: Blackwell, 2003.

Davis, David Brion. "The Emergence of Immediatism in British and American Antislavery Thought." *Mississippi Valley Historical Review* 49, no. 2 (September 1962): 209–30.

———. "The Movement to Abolish Capital Punishment in America, 1787–1861." *American Historical Review* 63, no. 1 (October 1957): 23–46.

———. *The Problem of Slavery in The Age of Revolution, 1770–1823*. Ithaca, NY: Cornell University Press, 1975.

Davis, Ronald L. F. *The Black Experience in Natchez, 1720–1880*. Denver, CO: US Dept. of the Interior, National Park Service, 1993.

Dawdy, Shannon Lee. *Building the Devil's Empire: French Colonial New Orleans*. Chicago: University of Chicago Press, 2008.

———. "The Burden of Louis Congo and the Evolution of Savagery in Colonial Louisiana." In *Discipline and the Other Body: Correction, Corporeality, Colonialism*, edited by Steven Pierce and Anupama Rao, 61–89. Durham, NC: Duke University Press, 2006.

Dawson, Kevin. *Undercurrents of Power: Aquatic Culture in the African Diaspora*. Philadelphia: University of Pennsylvania Press, 2018.

De Koster, Margo, and Herbert Reinke. "Policing Minorities." In *The Oxford Handbook of the History of Crime and Criminal Justice*, edited by Paul Knepper and Anja Johansen, 268–85. New York: Oxford University Press, 2016.

De la Fuente, Alejandro, and Ariela J. Gross. *Becoming Free, Becoming Black: Race, Freedom and Law in Cuba, Virginia, and Louisiana*. New York: Cambridge University Press, 2020.

Dennett, John Richard. *The South as It Is, 1865–1866*. Edited by Caroline E. Janney. Tuscaloosa: University of Alabama Press, 2010.

Derbes, Brett Josef. "'Secret Horrors': Enslaved Women and Children in the Louisiana State Penitentiary, 1833–1862." *Journal of African American History* 98, no. 2 (Spring 2013): 277–90.

Dessens, Nathalie. *Creole City: A Chronicle of Early American New Orleans*. Gainesville: University Press of Florida, 2015.

———. *From Saint-Domingue to New Orleans: Migration and Influences*. Gainesville: University Press of Florida, 2010.

"Destiny of the Slave States." *DeBow's Review* 17, no. 3 (September 1854): 280–84.

Detroit Police Department. [. . .] *Annual Report* [. . .] *to the Common Council of the City of Detroit* [. . .]. Detroit, 1883–1911.

De Vito, Christian G., and Alex Lichtenstein. "Writing a Global History of Convict Labour." *International Review of Social History* 58, no. 2 (August 2013): 285–325.

Devlin, John. "Reconsidering the Louisiana Doctrine of Employment at Will: On the Misinterpretation of Article 2747 and the Civilian Case for Requiring Good Faith in Termination of Employment." *Tulane Law Review* 69, no. 6 (1995): 1513–99.

Dewey, Daniel Perkins. *A Memorial of Lt. Daniel Perkins Dewey, of the Twenty-Fifth Regiment, Connecticut Volunteers*. Edited by Caroline Lloyd. Hartford, CT: Case, Lockwood, 1864.

A Digest of the Ordinances, Resolutions, By-Laws and Regulations of the Corporation of New Orleans: And a Collection of the Laws of the Legislature Relative to the Said City. New Orleans: Gaston Brusle, 1836.

Dikötter, Frank. *Crime, Punishment and the Prison in China*. New York: Columbia University Press, 2002.

Dikötter, Frank, and Ian Brown, eds. *Cultures of Confinement: A History of the Prison in Africa, Asia and Latin America*. Ithaca, NY: Cornell University Press, 2007.

Din, Gilbert C. *Spaniards, Planters, and Slaves: The Spanish Regulation of Slavery in Louisiana, 1763–1803*. College Station: Texas A&M University Press, 1999.

Din, Gilbert C., and John E. Harkins. *The New Orleans Cabildo: Colonial Louisiana's First City Government, 1769–1803*. Baton Rouge: Louisiana State University Press, 1996.

Diouf, Sylviane A. *Slavery's Exiles: The Story of the American Maroons*. New York: New York University Press, 2014.

Donoghue, John, and Evelyn P. Jennings, eds. *Building the Atlantic Empires: Unfree Labor and Imperial States in the Political Economy of Capitalism, ca. 1500–1914*. Boston: Brill, 2016.

Dorsey, Jennifer Hull. *Hirelings: African American Workers and Free Labor in Early Maryland*. Ithaca, NY: Cornell University Press, 2011.

Doss, Harriett E. Amos. *Cotton City: Urban Development in Antebellum Mobile*. Tuscaloosa: University of Alabama Press, 1985.

Douglass, Frederick. *My Bondage and My Freedom*. New York: Miller, Orton and Mulligan, 1855.

———. *Narrative of the Life of Frederick Douglass, an American Slave. Written by Himself.* Boston: Anti-Slavery Office, 1845.

———. "What the Black Man Wants." In *The Equality of All Men before the Law, Claimed and Defended in Speeches by Hon. William D. Kelley, Wendell Phillips, and Frederick Douglas*. Boston, 1865.

Downs, Gregory P. *Declarations of Dependence: The Long Reconstruction of Popular Politics in the South, 1861–1908*. Chapel Hill: University of North Carolina Press, 2011.

Downs, Jim. *Sick from Freedom: African American Illness and Suffering during the Civil War and Reconstruction*. New York: Oxford University Press, 2012.

Drake, Charles D., ed. *The Revised Ordinances of the City of Saint Louis, Revised and Digested by the Eighth City Council, in the Year 1846; with the Constitution of the United States and of the State of Missouri; the Various Charters of, and Laws Applicable to, the Town and City of Saint Louis; and a List of the Trustees of the Town, and of the Officers of the City, of Saint Louis, from 1810 to 1846, Inclusive*. St. Louis: Keemle and Field, 1846.

Drew, Benjamin, ed. *A North-Side View of Slavery: The Refugee: or the Narratives of Fugitive Slaves in Canada. Related by Themselves, with an Account of the History and Condition of the Colored Population of Upper Canada*. Boston: John P. Jewett, 1856.

Dubber, Markus Dirk. "Histories of Crime and Criminal Justice and the Historical Analysis of Criminal Law." In *The Oxford Handbook of the History of Crime and Criminal Justice*, edited by Paul Knepper and Anja Johansen, 597–612. New York: Oxford University Press, 2016.

———. *The Police Power: Patriarchy and the Foundations of American Government*. New York: Columbia University Press, 2005.

Dubois, Laurent. *Avengers of the New World: The Story of the Haitian Revolution*. Cambridge, MA: Harvard University Press, 2009.

———. *Haiti: The Aftershocks of History*. New York: Henry Holt, 2012.

Du Bois, W. E. B. *Black Reconstruction in America, 1860–1880*. New York: Free Press, 1992 [1935].

Ducpétiaux, Edouard. *Des progrès et de l'état actuel de la réforme pénitentiaire et des institutions préventives, aux États-Unis, en France, en Suisse, en Angleterre et en Belgique*. 3 vols. Brussels: Société Belge de Librairie, 1837–38.

Dunbar, C. E. *Code of the City of Augusta Georgia*. Augusta, GA: Wolfe and Lombard, 1909.

Dupree, L. J., ed. *A Digest of the Ordinances of the City Council of Memphis, from the Year 1826 to 1857, Together with All Acts of the Legislature of Tennessee Which Relate Exclusively to the City of Memphis, with an Appendix*. Memphis, TN: Memphis Bulletin, 1857.

Durand-Molard, ed. *Code de la Martinique*. 5 vols. St. Pierre, Martinique: Jean-Baptiste Thounens, fils, 1807–14.

Durham, Walter T. *Reluctant Partners: Nashville and the Union, July 1, 1863, to June 30, 1865*. Nashville: University of Tennessee Press, 1987.

Dusinberre, William. *Them Dark Days: Slavery in the American Rice Swamps*. New York: Oxford University Press, 1996.

Eder, Joseph. "A Bavarian's Journey to New Orleans and Nacogdoches in 1853–1854." Edited by Karl J. R. Arndt. *Louisiana Historical Quarterly* 23, no. 2 (April 1940): 485–500.

Edwards, David Honeyboy, Janis Martison, and Michael Robert Frank. *The World Don't Owe Me Nothing: The Life and Times of Delta Bluesman Honeyboy Edwards*. Chicago: Chicago Review Press, 1997.

Edwards, Laura F. *Gendered Strife and Confusion: The Political Language of Reconstruction*. Urbana: University of Illinois Press, 1997.

——. *The People and Their Peace: Legal Culture and the Transformation of Inequality in the Post-Revolutionary South*. Chapel Hill: University of North Carolina Press, 2009.

——. "Southern History as U.S. History." *Journal of Southern History* 75, no. 3 (February 2009): 533–64.

Egerton, Douglas R. *Gabriel's Rebellion: The Virginia Slave Conspiracies of 1800 and 1802*. Chapel Hill: University of North Carolina Press, 1993.

——. *The Wars of Reconstruction: The Brief, Violent History of America's Most Progressive Era*. New York: Bloomsbury, 2014.

Egnal, Marc. *Divergent Paths: How Culture and Institutions Have Shaped North American Growth*. New York: Oxford University Press, 1996.

Elisabeth, Léo. "The French Antilles." In *Neither Slave nor Free: The Freedmen of African Descent in the Slave Societies of the New World*, edited by David W. Cohen and Jack P. Greene, 134–71. Baltimore: Johns Hopkins University Press, 1972.

Ely, James W. "'There Are Few Subjects in Political Economy of Greater Difficulty': The Poor Laws of the Antebellum South." *American Bar Foundation Research Journal* 10, no. 4 (Fall 1985): 849–79.

Ely, Melvin Patrick. *Israel on the Appomattox: A Southern Experiment in Black Freedom from the 1790s through the Civil War*. New York: Vintage Books, 2004.

Emberton, Carole. *Beyond Redemption: Race, Violence and the American South after the Civil War*. Chicago: University of Chicago Press, 2013.

Emerson, Ralph Waldo. "Man the Reformer." In *The Collected Works of Ralph Waldo Emerson*, Vol. 1: *Nature, Address, and Lectures*, edited by Robert E. Spiller and Alfred R. Ferguson, 141–59. Cambridge, MA: Harvard University Press, 1971.

Engerman, Stanley, and Claudia Goldin. "Seasonality in Nineteenth-Century Labor Markets." In *American Economic Development in Historical Perspective*, edited by Thomas Joseph Weiss and Donald Schaefer, 99–126. Stanford, CA: Stanford University Press, 1994.

Escott, Paul D. *Many Excellent People: Power and Privilege in North Carolina, 1850–1900*. Chapel Hill: University of North Carolina Press, 1985.

Eskridge, William N. *Dishonorable Passions: Sodomy Laws in America, 1861–2003*. New York: Viking, 2008.

Espinosa, Mariola. *Epidemic Invasions: Yellow Fever and the Limits of Cuban Independence, 1878–1930*. Chicago: University of Chicago Press, 2009.

Eudell, Demetrius Lynn. *The Political Languages of Emancipation in the British Caribbean and the U.S. South*. Chapel Hill: University of North Carolina Press, 2002.

Evans, Peter B., Dietrich Rueschemeyer, and Theda Skocpol, eds. *Bringing the State Back In*. New York: Cambridge University Press, 1985.

Everest, Robert. *Everest's Journey through the United States and Parts of Canada*. Carlisle, MA: Applewood Books, 2007 [1855].

Everett, Donald E. "Demands of the New Orleans Free Colored Population for Political Equality, 1862–1865." *Louisiana Historical Quarterly* 38, no. 2 (April 1955): 43–64.

——. "Free Persons of Color in New Orleans, 1803–1865." PhD diss., Tulane University, 1952.

Faber, Eberhard L. *Building the Land of Dreams: New Orleans and the Transformation of Early America*. Princeton, NJ: Princeton University Press, 2015.

Fairclough, Adam. *Race and Democracy: The Civil Rights Struggle in Louisiana, 1915–1972*. Athens: University of Georgia Press, 2008 [1995].

Farmer-Kaiser, Mary J. "'Are They Not in Some Sorts Vagrants?': Gender and the Efforts of the Freedmen's Bureau to Combat Vagrancy in the Reconstruction South." *Georgia Historical Quarterly* 88, no. 1 (Spring 2004): 25–49.

———. "'Because They Are Women': Gender and the Virginia Freedmen's Bureau's War on Dependency." In *The Freedmen's Bureau and Reconstruction: Reconsiderations*, edited by Paul A. Cimbala and Randall M. Miller, 161–92. New York: Fordham University Press, 1999.

———. *Freedwomen and the Freedmen's Bureau: Race, Gender, and Public Policy in the Age of Emancipation*. New York: Fordham University Press, 2010.

Farshey, C. G. "Louisiana: Geology and Hydrography." *DeBow's Review* 8, no. 5 (May 1850): 495–500.

Faucher, Léon. *De la réforme des prisons*. Paris: Angé, 1838.

Fauconnet, Charles Prosper. *Ruined by This Miserable War: The Dispatches of Charles Prosper Fauconnet, a French Diplomat in New Orleans, 1863–1868*. Edited by Carl A. Brasseaux and Katherine Carmines Mooney. Knoxville: University of Tennessee Press, 2012.

Faust, Drew Gilpin. *The Ideology of Slavery: Proslavery Thought in the Antebellum South, 1830–1860*. Baton Rouge: Louisiana State University Press, 1981.

Fertel, Rien. *Imagining the Creole City: The Rise of Literary Culture in Nineteenth-Century New Orleans*. Baton Rouge: Louisiana State University Press, 2014.

Fick, Carolyn E. *The Making of Haiti: The Saint Domingue Revolution from Below*. Knoxville: University of Tennessee Press, 1990.

Fields, Barbara Jeanne. *Slavery and Freedom on the Middle Ground: Maryland during the Nineteenth Century*. New Haven, CT: Yale University Press, 1985.

Finkelman, Paul. *Defending Slavery: Proslavery Thought in the Old South: A Brief History with Documents*. Boston: Bedford/St. Martin's, 2003.

Finley, Alexandra. "'Cash to Corinna': Domestic Labor and Sexual Economy in the 'Fancy Trade.'" *Journal of American History* 104, no. 2 (September 2017): 410–30.

———. *An Intimate Economy: Enslaved Women, Work, and America's Domestic Slave Trade*. Chapel Hill: University of North Carolina Press, 2020.

Fisher-Giorlando, Marianne. "Women in the Walls: The Imprisonment of Women at the Baton Rouge Penitentiary, 1835–1862." In *The Wall Is Strong: Corrections in Louisiana*, edited by Burk Foster, Wilbert Rideau, and Douglas A. Dennis, 16–25. Lafayette: Center for Louisiana Studies, University of Southwestern Louisiana, 1995.

Fiske, David. *Solomon Northup's Kindred: The Kidnapping of Free Citizens before the Civil War*. Santa Barbara, CA: Praeger, 2016.

Fitzgerald, Michael W. *Urban Emancipation: Popular Politics in Reconstruction Mobile, 1860–1890*. Baton Rouge: Louisiana State University Press, 2002.

Fitzhugh, Brundage W. *Civilizing Torture: An American Tradition*. Cambridge, MA: Harvard University Press, 2018.

Fitzhugh, George. *Cannibals All! Or, Slaves without Masters*. Richmond, VA: A. Morris, 1857.

——. "The Freedmen." *DeBow's Review* 2, no. 5 (November 1866): 489–93.

——. *Sociology for the South; or, The Failure of Free Society*. Richmond, VA: A. Morris, 1854.

——. "Virginia: Her Past, Present and Future." *DeBow's Review* 1, no. 2 (February 1866): 178–84.

Flanigan, Daniel J. "The Criminal Law of Slavery and Freedom." PhD diss., Rice University, 1973.

Fletcher, Joseph. "Account of the Police of the Metropolis." *Journal of the Statistical Society of London* 13, no. 3 (1850): 221–67.

Florida Legislature. *Acts and Resolutions of the Legislative Council of the Territory of Florida, Passed at Its Twentieth Session*. Tallahassee, FL: C. E. Bartlett, 1842.

Flory, Ira, Jr. "Edward Livingston's Place in Louisiana Law." *Louisiana Historical Quarterly* 19, no. 3 (April 1936): 328–89.

Fogelson, Robert M. *Big City Police*. Cambridge, MA: Harvard University Press, 1977.

Follett, Richard J. *The Sugar Masters: Planters and Slaves in Louisiana's Cane World, 1820–1860*. Baton Rouge: Louisiana State University Press, 2005.

Foner, Eric. *Freedom's Lawmakers: A Directory of Black Officeholders during Reconstruction*. New York: Oxford University Press, 1993.

——. *Free Soil, Free Labor, Free Men: The Ideology of the Republican Party before the Civil War*. New York: Oxford University Press, 1995 [1970].

——. *Nothing but Freedom: Emancipation and Its Legacy*. Baton Rouge: Louisiana State University Press, 1983.

——. *Politics and Ideology in the Age of the Civil War*. New York: Oxford University Press, 1980.

——. *Reconstruction: America's Unfinished Revolution, 1863–1877*. New York: Harper and Row, 1988.

Foner, Laura. "The Free People of Color in Louisiana and St. Domingue: A Comparative Portrait of Two Three-Caste Slave Societies." *Journal of Social History* 3, no. 4 (Summer 1970): 406–30.

Foner, Philip S. "William P. Powell: Militant Champion of Black Seamen." In *Essays in Afro-American History*, edited by Philip S. Foner, 88–111. Philadelphia: Temple University Press, 1978.

Foner, Philip S., and Ronald L. Lewis, eds. *The Black Worker: A Documentary History from Colonial Times to the Present*. 8 vols. Philadelphia: Temple University Press, 1978–84.

Forman, James, Jr. *Locking Up Our Own: Crime and Punishment in Black America*. New York: Farrar, Straus and Giroux, 2017.

Forret, Jeff. "Before Angola: Enslaved Prisoners in the Louisiana State Penitentiary." *Louisiana History* 54, no. 2 (2013): 133–71.

——. *Race Relations at the Margins: Slaves and Poor Whites in the Antebellum Southern Countryside*. Baton Rouge: Louisiana State University Press, 2006.

——. *Slave against Slave: Plantation Violence in the Old South*. Baton Rouge: Louisiana State University Press, 2015.

——. *Williams' Gang: A Notorious Slave Trader and His Cargo of Black Convicts.* New York: Cambridge University Press, 2020.

Forsyth, John. "The North and the South." *DeBow's Review* 17, no. 4 (October 1854): 361–79.

Fortier, Alcee. *Louisiana: Comprising Sketches of Parishes, Towns, Events, Institutions, and Persons, Arranged in Cyclopedic Form.* 3 vols. Atlanta, GA: Century Historical Association, 1914.

Foster, George M., and Tom Stoddard. *Pops Foster: The Autobiography of a New Orleans Jazzman as Told to Tom Stoddard.* Berkeley: University of California Press, 1971.

Foucault, Michel. *Discipline and Punish: The Birth of the Prison.* Translated by Alan Sheridan. New York: Vintage Books, 1977.

——. *The History of Sexuality.* Vol. 1: *An Introduction.* Translated by Robert Hurley. New York: Pantheon Books, 1978.

——. "Nietzsche, Genealogy, History." Translated by Donald Bouchard and Sherry Simon. In *The Foucault Reader,* edited by Paul Rabinow, 76–100. New York: Pantheon Books, 1984.

——. *Power/Knowledge: Selected Interviews and Other Writings, 1972–1977.* Translated by Colon Gordon et al. New York: Pantheon Books, 1980.

Fox-Genovese, Elizabeth. *Within the Plantation Household: Black and White Women of the Old South.* Chapel Hill: University of North Carolina Press, 1988.

Fox-Genovese, Elizabeth, and Eugene Genovese. *The Mind of the Master Class: History and Faith in the Southern Slaveholders' Worldview.* New York: Cambridge University Press, 2005.

François de Neufchâteau, Nicolas-Louis. *Lettre de M. François de Neufchâteau au conseil souverain du cap à M. le P. Dup. : sur quelques réformes à faire dans la législation criminelle : suivie de lettres de M. le P. Dup.* Cap-Français [Haiti], 1787.

Franklin, John Hope. *The Militant South, 1800–1861.* Cambridge, MA: Belknap Press of Harvard University Press, 1956.

——. "Public Welfare in the South during the Reconstruction Era, 1865–80." *Social Service Review* 44, no. 4 (December 1970): 379–92.

Franklin, John Hope, and Loren Schweninger. *Runaway Slaves: Rebels on the Plantation.* New York: Oxford University Press, 1999.

Franklin, Mitchell. "Concerning the Historic Importance of Edward Livingston." *Tulane Law Review* 11, no. 2 (February 1937): 163–212.

Fraser, Nancy, and Linda Gordon. "A Genealogy of Dependency: Tracing a Keyword of the U.S. Welfare State." *Signs* 19, no. 2 (Winter 1994): 309–36.

Fredrickson, George M. *The Black Image in the White Mind: The Debate on Afro-American Character and Destiny, 1817–1914.* New York: Harper and Row, 1971.

French, Laurence Armand. *The History of Policing America: From Militias and Military to the Law Enforcement of Today.* New York: Rowman and Littlefield, 2018.

Freund, Ernst. *The Police Power: Public Policy and Constitutional Rights.* Chicago: Callaghan, 1904.

Frey, Sylvia. *Water from the Rock: Black Resistance in a Revolutionary Age.* Princeton, NJ: Princeton University Press, 1991.

Friedman, Lawrence M. *Crime and Punishment in American History.* New York: Basic Books, 1993.

Friedman, Lawrence M., and Robert V. Percival. *The Roots of Justice: Crime and Punishment in Alameda County, California, 1870–1910.* Chapel Hill: University of North Carolina Press, 1981.

Fuentes, Marisa J. *Dispossessed Lives: Enslaved Women, Violence, and the Archive.* Philadelphia: University of Pennsylvania Press, 2016.

Fullerton, Joseph Scott. *Report of the Administration of Freedmen's Affairs in Louisiana, by J. S. Fullerton, Bvt. Brig. Gen. Vols. While Temporarily Acting as Assistant Commissioner of the Bureau of Refugees, Freedmen, and Abandoned Lands for That State.* Washington, DC, 1865.

Gardner, Charles. *Gardner's New Orleans Directory, for 1861, including Jefferson City, Gretna, Carrollton, Algiers, and McDonogh, with a New Map of the City, a Street and Levee Guide, Business Directory, an Appendix of Much Useful Information, and a Planters Directory Containing the Names of the Cotton and Sugar Planters of Louisiana, Mississippi, Arkansas and Texas.* New Orleans: Charles Gardner, 1861.

Garland, David. *The Culture of Control: Crime and Social Control in Contemporary Society.* Chicago: University of Chicago Press, 2001.

———. "Penal Excess and Surplus Meaning: Public Torture Lynchings in Twentieth-Century America." *Law and Society Review* 39, no. 4 (December 2005): 793–834.

———. *Punishment and Modern Society: A Study in Social Theory.* Chicago: University of Chicago Press, 1993.

Garrigus, John D. *Before Haiti: Race and Citizenship in French Saint-Domingue.* New York: Palgrave Macmillan, 2006.

Gaspar, David Barry, and David Patrick Geggus, eds. *A Turbulent Time: The French Revolution and the Greater Caribbean.* Bloomington: Indiana University Press, 1997.

Geggus, David Patrick. "The Enigma of Jamaica in the 1790s: New Light on the Causes of Slaves Rebellions." *William and Mary Quarterly,* 3rd ser., 44, no. 2 (April 1987): 274–99.

———, ed. *The Impact of the Haitian Revolution in the Atlantic World.* Columbia: University of South Carolina Press, 2001.

———. "Slavery, War, and Revolution in the Greater Caribbean, 1789–1815." In *A Turbulent Time: The French Revolution and the Greater Caribbean,* edited by David Barry Gaspar and David Patrick Geggus, 1–50. Bloomington: Indiana University Press, 1997.

Gehman, Mary. "Visible Means of Support: Businesses, Professions, and Trades of Free People of Color." In *Creole: The History and Legacy of Louisiana's Free People of Color,* edited by Sybil Klein, 208–22. Baton Rouge: Louisiana State University Press, 2000.

Genovese, Eugene D. *The Political Economy of Slavery: Studies in the Economy and Society of the Slave South.* Middletown, CT: Wesleyan University Press, 1989 [1961].

———. *The Slaveholders' Dilemma: Freedom and Progress in Southern Conservative Thought, 1820–1860.* Columbia: University of South Carolina Press, 1992.

——. *The World the Slaveholders Made: Two Essays in Interpretation*. Middletown, CT: Wesleyan University Press, 1988 [1969].

Georgia Legislature. *Acts of the General Assembly of the State of Georgia, Passed in Milledgeville, at an Annual Session in November and December, 1859*. Milledgeville, GA: Boughton, Nisbet and Barnes, 1860.

Gerteis, Louis S. *From Contraband to Freedman: Federal Policy toward Southern Blacks, 1861–1865*. Westport, CT: Greenwood, 1973.

Ghachem, Malick W. *The Old Regime and the Haitian Revolution*. New York: Cambridge University Press, 2012.

Gibson, Mary. "Global Perspectives on the Birth of the Prison." *American Historical Review* 116, no. 6 (October 2011): 1040–63.

Gigault de Crisenoy, Jules-Étienne. *Études sur la situation économique des Antilles françaises*. Paris: Guillaumin, 1860.

Gikandi, Simon. *Slavery and the Culture of Taste*. Princeton, NJ: Princeton University Press, 2011.

Gilmore, Glenda Elizabeth. *Gender and Jim Crow: Women and the Politics of White Supremacy in North Carolina, 1896–1920*. Chapel Hill: University of North Carolina Press, 1996.

Gilmore, Kim. "Slavery and Prison: Understanding the Connections." *Social Justice* 27, no. 3 (Fall 2000): 195–205.

Gilroy, Paul. *The Black Atlantic: Modernity and Double Consciousness*. Cambridge, MA: Harvard University Press, 1993.

Gleeson, David T. *The Irish in the South, 1815–1877*. Chapel Hill: University of South Carolina Press, 2001.

Glenn, Samuel S. F., ed. *The New Constitution of the State of Louisiana: Adopted in Convention on the Fourteenth of May, 1845, and Ratified by the People of the State on the Fifth of November, 1845, and Ratified by the People of the State on the Fifth of November, 1845; with a Comparative View of the Old and New Constitutions of the State; and a Copious Index*. New Orleans, 1845.

Glickstein, Jonathan A. *Concepts of Free Labor in Antebellum America*. New Haven, CT: Yale University Press, 1991.

Glymph, Thavolia. *Out of the House of Bondage: The Transformation of the Plantation Household*. New York: Cambridge University Press, 2008.

Godshalk, David Fort. *Veiled Visions: The 1906 Atlanta Race Riot and the Reshaping of American Race Relations*. Chapel Hill: University of North Carolina Press, 2006.

Goetsch, Elizabeth K. *Lost Nashville*. Charleston, SC: History Press, 2018.

Goings, Henry. *Rambles of a Runaway from Southern Slavery*. Edited by Calvin Schermerhorn, Michael Plunkett, and Edward Gaynor. Charlottesville: University of Virginia Press, 2012.

Goldin, Claudia Dale. *Urban Slavery in the American South, 1820–1860: A Quantitative History*. Chicago: University of Chicago Press, 1976.

Goldman, Robert M. *Reconstruction and Black Suffrage: Losing the Vote in Reese and Cruikshank*. Lawrence: University Press of Kansas, 2001.

Goluboff, Risa. *Vagrant Nation: Police Power, Constitutional Change, and the Making of the 1960s*. New York: Oxford University Press, 2016.

Gonzalez, Johnhenry. *Maroon Nation: A History of Revolutionary Haiti*. New Haven, CT: Yale University Press, 2019.

Goodell, William. *The American Slave Code in Theory and Practice: Its Distinctive Features Shown by Its Statutes, Judicial Decisions, and Illustrative Facts*. London: Clarke, Beeton, 1853.

Gottschalk, Marie. *The Prison and the Gallows: The Politics of Mass Incarceration in America*. Cambridge: Cambridge University Press, 2006.

Gould, Josiah, ed. *A Digest of the Statutes of Arkansas, Embracing All Laws of a General and Permanent Character in Force at the Close of the Session of the General Assembly of 1856: Together with Notes of the Decisions of the Supreme Court upon the Statutes, and an Appendix Containing Forms for Justices of the Peace*. Little Rock, AR: Johnson and Yerkes, 1858.

Graf, Leroy P., Ralph W. Haskins, and Paul Bergeron, eds. *The Papers of Andrew Johnson*. 16 vols. Knoxville: University of Tennessee Press, 1967–2000.

Gravatte, Jay, and Shawn Logan. "Louisville City Workhouse." Kentucky Historic Institutions. September 23, 2020. https://kyhi.org/louisville-city-workhouse/.

Great Britain. Colonial Office. *Papers Relating to the West Indies: Ordered, by the House of Commons, to be Printed 12th July, 1815*. London, 1815.

Green, Elna C. *This Business of Relief: Confronting Poverty in a Southern City, 1740–1940*. Athens: University of Georgia Press, 2003.

Green, William A. "James Stephen and British West India Policy, 1834–1847." *Caribbean Studies* 13, no. 4 (January 1974): 33–56.

Greenberg, Kenneth S. *Honor and Slavery: Lies, Duels, Noses, Masks, Dressing as a Woman, Gifts, Strangers, Humanitarianism, Death, Slave Rebellions, the Proslavery Argument, Baseball, Hunting, and Gambling in the Old South*. Princeton, NJ: Princeton University Press, 1996.

———. *Masters and Statesmen: The Political Culture of American Slavery*. Baltimore: Johns Hopkins University Press, 1985.

Greenwood, Moses, et al. *Report of the Grand Jury of the Parish of Orleans. By Order of the First District Court. New Orleans, 1856*. New Orleans: Louisiana Courier, 1856.

Grimes, John Maurice. *Institutional Care of Mental Patients in the United States*. Chicago, 1934.

Grivno, Max. *Gleanings of Freedom: Free and Slave Labor along the Mason-Dixon Line, 1790–1860*. Urbana: University of Chicago Press, 2011.

Gross, Ariela Julie. *Double Character: Slavery and Mastery in the Antebellum Southern Courtroom*. Princeton, NJ: Princeton University Press, 2000.

———. *What Blood Won't Tell: A History of Race on Trial in America*. Cambridge, MA: Harvard University Press, 2008.

Gudmestad, Robert H. *Steamboats and the Rise of the Cotton Kingdom*. Baton Rouge: Louisiana State University Press, 2011.

Gussow, Adam. *Seems Like Murder Here: Southern Violence and the Blues Tradition*. Chicago: University of Chicago Press, 2002.

Guterl, Matthew Pratt. *American Mediterranean: Southern Slaveholders in the Age of Emancipation*. Cambridge, MA: Harvard University Press, 2008.

Haas, Edward F. *Political Leadership in a Southern City: New Orleans in the Progressive Era, 1896–1902*. Ruston, LA: McGinty, 1988.

Hadden, Sally. *Slave Patrols: Law and Violence in Virginia and the Carolinas*. Cambridge, MA: Harvard University Press, 2001.

Hahn, Michael. *Ex-Governor Hahn on Louisiana Legislation relating to Freedmen*. Washington, DC: W. H. Moore, 1866.

———. *What Is Unconditional Unionism?* New Orleans: New Orleans Era, 1863.

Hahn, Steven, et al., eds. *Freedom: A Documentary History of Emancipation, 1861–1867*. Ser. 3, Vol. 1: *Land and Labor, 1865*. New York: Cambridge University Press, 2008.

Hair, William Ivy. *Bourbonism and Agrarian Protest: Louisiana Politics, 1877–1900*. Baton Rouge: Louisiana State University Press, 1969.

Haites, Erik F., James Mak, and Gary M. Walton. *Western River Transportation*. Baltimore: Johns Hopkins University Press, 1975.

Hale, Grace Elizabeth. *Making Whiteness: The Culture of Segregation in the South, 1890–1940*. New York: Vintage Books, 1998.

Haley, Sarah. *No Mercy Here: Gender, Punishment, and the Making of Jim Crow Modernity*. Chapel Hill: University of North Carolina Press, 2016.

Hall, Aaron. "Public Slaves and State Engineers: Modern Statecraft on Louisiana's Waterways, 1833–1861." *Journal of Southern History* 85, no. 3 (August 2019): 531–76.

———. "Slaves of the State: Infrastructure and Governance through Slavery in the Antebellum South." *Journal of American History* 106, no. 1 (June 2019): 19–46.

Hall, Basil. *Travels in North America in the Years 1827 and 1828*. 3 vols. Edinburgh: Cadell, 1830.

Hall, Gwendolyn Midlo. *Africans in Colonial Louisiana: The Development of Afro-Creole Culture in the Eighteenth Century*. Baton Rouge: Louisiana State University Press, 1992.

Hall, Marshall. *The Two-Fold Slavery of the United States; with a Project of Self-Emancipation*. London, 1854.

Hall, Ryan M. "A Glorious Assemblage: The Rise of the Know Nothing Party in Louisiana." MA thesis, Louisiana State University, 2015.

Halttunen, Karen. *Confidence Men and Painted Women: A Study of Middle-Class Culture in America, 1830–1870*. New Haven, CT: Yale University Press, 1982.

———. "Humanitarianism and the Pornography of Pain in Anglo-American Culture." *American Historical Review* 100, no. 2 (April 1995): 303–34.

Hamer, Philip M. "Great Britain, the United States, and the Negro Seamen Acts, 1822–1848." *Journal of Southern History* 1, no. 1 (February 1935): 3–28.

Hamilton, Alexander. *The Farmer Refuted*. New York: James Rivington, 1775.

Hammond, James Henry. "Mudsill Speech." In *Slavery Defended: The Views of the Old South*, edited by Eric McKitrick, 121–23. Englewood Cliffs, NJ: Prentice-Hall, 1963.

Handler, Jerome S., and Kenneth M. Bilby. *Enacting Power: The Criminalization of Obeah in the Anglophone Caribbean, 1760–2011*. Jamaica, Barbados, Trinidad and Tobago, 2012.

Hanger, Kimberly S. *Bounded Lives, Bounded Places: Free Black Society in Colonial New Orleans, 1769–1803*. Durham, NC: Duke University Press, 1997.

Harcourt, Bernard E. *The Illusion of Order: The False Promise of Broken Windows Policing*. Cambridge, MA: Harvard University Press, 2001.

Hardy, James D. "The Transportation of Convicts to Colonial Louisiana." *Louisiana History* 7, no. 2 (Spring 1966): 208–12.

Harris, Dawn P. *Punishing the Black Body: Making Social and Racial Structures in Barbados and Jamaica*. Athens: University of Georgia Press, 2017.

Harris, J. William. *Plain Folk and Gentry in a Slave Society: White Liberty and Black Slavery in Augusta's Hinterlands*. Middletown, CT: Wesleyan University Press, 1985.

Harris, Leslie M. *In the Shadow of Slavery: African Americans in New York City, 1626–1863*. Chicago: University of Chicago Press, 2003.

Hartman, Saidiya V. *Scenes of Subjection: Terror, Slavery, and Self-Making in Nineteenth-Century America*. New York: Oxford University Press, 1997.

Hartog, Hendrick. *Public Property and Private Power: The Corporation of the City of New York in American Law, 1730–1870*. Chapel Hill: University of North Carolina Press, 1983.

Harvard University. *A Catalogue of the Officers and Students of Harvard University, for the Academic Year 1841–42*. Cambridge, MA, 1841.

Haskel, Daniel, and J. R. M'Culloch. *M'Cullochs Universal Gazetteer: A Dictionary, Geographical, Statistical, and Historical, of the Various Countries, Places, and Principal Natural Objects in the World*. 2 vols. New York: Harper and Brothers, 1855.

Hatcher, William B. *Edward Livingston, Jeffersonian Republican and Jacksonian Democrat*. Baton Rouge: Louisiana State University Press, 1940.

Haunton, Richard H. "Law and Order in Savannah, 1850–1860." *Georgia Historical Quarterly* 56, no. 1 (Spring 1972): 1–24.

Hayden, René, Anthony E. Kaye, Kate Masur, Steven F. Miller, Susan E. O'Donovan, Leslie S. Rowland, and Stephen A. West, eds. *Freedom: A Documentary History of Emancipation, 1861–1867*. Ser. 3, Vol. 2: *Land and Labor, 1866–1867*. New York: Cambridge University Press, 2013.

Hearn, Chester G. *The Capture of New Orleans, 1862*. Baton Rouge: Louisiana State University Press, 1995.

Henderson, Charles. *Correction and Prevention: Four Volumes Prepared for the Eighth International Prison Congress*. 4 vols. New York, 1910.

Henderson, Violet L., comp. *Synopsis of Ordinances*. New Orleans: City of New Orleans Archives Department, 1938.

Hernández, Kelly Lytle. *City of Inmates: Conquest, Rebellion, and the Rise of Human Caging in Los Angeles, 1771–1965*. Chapel Hill: University of North Carolina Press, 2017.

Heuman, Gad. *"The Killing Time": The Morant Bay Rebellion in Jamaica*. Knoxville: University of Tennessee Press, 1994.

Hieke, Anton. *Jewish Identity in the Reconstruction South: Ambivalence and Adaptation*. Berlin: De Gruyter, 2013.

Higbie, Frank Tobias. "Between Romance and Degradation: Navigating the Meanings of Vagrancy in North America, 1870–1940." In *Cast Out: Vagrancy and*

Homelessness in Global and Historical Perspective, edited by A.L. Beier and Paul Ocobock, 250–69. Athens: Ohio University Press, 2008.

Highsaw, Robert B. *The Growth of State Administration in Mississippi*. University: University of Mississippi, 1950.

Higman, B. W. *Slave Populations of the British Caribbean, 1807–1834*. Baltimore: Johns Hopkins University Press, 1984.

Hild, Matthew, and Keri Leigh Merritt, eds. *Reconsidering Southern Labor History: Race, Class, and Power*. Gainesville: University Press of Florida, 2018.

Hill, Marilynn Wood. *Their Sisters' Keepers: Prostitution in New York City, 1830–1870*. Berkeley: University of California Press, 1993.

Hilt, Eric. "Rogue Finance: The Life and Fire Insurance Company and the Panic of 1826." *Business History Review* 83, no. 1 (Spring 2009): 87–112.

Hindus, Michael Stephen. *Prison and Plantation: Crime, Justice, and Authority in Massachusetts and South Carolina, 1767–1878*. Chapel Hill: University of North Carolina Press, 1980.

Hines, David Theo. *The Life and Adventures of Dr. David T. Hines: A Narrative of Thrilling Interest and Most Stirring Scenes of His Eventful Life*. Charleston, SC, 1852.

Hinton, Elizabeth. *From the War on Poverty to the War on Crime: The Making of Mass Incarceration in America*. Cambridge, MA: Harvard University Press, 2016.

Hinton, Elizabeth, and DeAnza Cook. "The Mass Criminalization of Black Americans: A Historical Overview." *Annual Review of Criminology* 4, no. 1 (January 2021): 261–86.

Hirota, Hidetaka. *Expelling the Poor: Atlantic Seaboard States and the Nineteenth-Century Origins of American Immigration Policy*. New York: Oxford University Press, 2017.

Hirsch, Adam Jay. *The Rise of the Penitentiary: Prisons and Punishment in Early America*. New Haven, CT: Yale University Press,1992.

Hirsch, Arnold R., and Joseph Logsdon, eds. *Creole New Orleans: Race and Americanization*. Baton Rouge: Louisiana State University Press, 1992. *Historical Epitome of the State of Louisiana, with an Historical Notice of New-Orleans, Views and Descriptions of Public Buildings, &c, &c*. New Orleans, 1840.

Hobson, Barbara Meil. *Uneasy Virtue: The Politics of Prostitution and the American Reform Tradition*. New York: Basic Books, 1987.

Hobson, Vic. *Creating Jazz Counterpoint: New Orleans, Barbershop Harmony, and the Blues*. Jackson: University Press of Mississippi, 2014.

Hogue, James K. *Uncivil War: Five New Orleans Street Battles and the Rise and Fall of Radical Reconstruction*. Baton Rouge: Louisiana State University Press, 2006.

Hollandsworth, James G. *An Absolute Massacre: The New Orleans Race Riot of July 30, 1866*. Baton Rouge: Louisiana State University Press, 2001.

———. *The Louisiana Native Guards: The Black Military Experience during the Civil War*. Baton Rouge: Louisiana State University Press, 1995.

Holloway, Thomas H. *Policing Rio de Janeiro: Repression and Resistance in a 19th-Century City*. Stanford, CA: Stanford University Press, 1993.

Holmes, George Frederick. "Ancient Slavery, Part 1." *DeBow's Review* 19, no. 5 (November 1855): 559–78.

————. "Slavery and Freedom." *Southern Quarterly Review* 1, no. 1 (April 1856): 62–65.

Holmes, Isaac. *An Account of the United States of America*. London: Caxton Press, 1823.

Holmes, William F. "James K. Vardaman and Prison Reform in Mississippi." *Journal of Mississippi History* 27, no. 3 (August 1965): 229–48.

Holt, Thomas. "The Essence of the Contract: The Articulation of Race, Gender, and Political Economy in British Emancipation Policy, 1838–1866." In *Beyond Slavery: Explorations of Race, Labor, and Citizenship in Postemancipation Societies*, edited by Frederick Cooper, Thomas Cleveland Holt, and Rebecca J. Scott, 33–60. Chapel Hill: University of North Carolina Press, 2000.

————. *The Problem of Freedom: Race, Labor, and Politics in Jamaica and Britain, 1832–1938*. Baltimore: Johns Hopkins University Press, 1992.

"'Honeyboy,' the Last Link to Delta Blues." NPR, August 30, 2011. Radio transcript. www.npr.org/transcripts/92453606.

Honora, Jari Christopher Louis. "'Cast Your Eyes upon a Loyal Population': Lincoln and the Louisiana's Free People of Color." *La Créole: A Journal of Creole History and Genealogy* 2, no. 1 (October 2009): 1–8.

Horne, Gerald. *Confronting Black Jacobins: The United States, the Haitian Revolution, and the Origins of the Dominican Republic*. New York: Monthly Review, 2015.

————. *Negro Comrades of the Crown: African Americans and the British Empire Fight the U.S. before Emancipation*. New York: New York University Press, 2012.

Houppert, Karen. *Chasing Gideon: The Elusive Quest for Poor People's Justice*. New York: New Press, 2013.

Houston, Matilda. *Texas and the Gulf of Mexico; or, Yachting in the New World*. 2 vols. London: John Murray, 1844.

Houzeau, Jean-Charles. *My Passage at the New Orleans Tribune: A Memoir of the Civil War Era*. Edited by David C. Rankin and translated by Gerard F. Denault. Baton Rouge: Louisiana State University Press, 1984.

Howe, Samuel Gridley. *Letters and Journals of Samuel Gridley Howe*, edited by Laura E. Richards. Boston: Dana Estes and Company, 1909.

————. "Scene in a Slave Prison." In *The Liberty Bell*, 175–80. Boston: Oliver Johnson, 1843.

Hughes, Henry. *Treatise on Sociology, Theoretical and Practical*. Philadelphia: Lippincott, Grambo, 1854.

Hughes, Louis. *Thirty Years a Slave: From Bondage to Freedom*. Milwaukee: South Side, 1897.

Human Rights Watch. "Decades of Disparity: Drug Arrests and Race in the United States." Human Rights Watch, March 2, 2009. www.hrw.org/report/2009/03/02/decades-disparity/drug-arrests-and-race-united-states#.

————. "New Orleans: Prisoners Abandoned to Floodwaters." Human Rights Watch, September 21, 2005. www.hrw.org/news/2005/09/21/new-orleans-prisoners-abandoned-floodwaters#.

Hume, Richard L., and Jerry B. Gough. *Blacks, Carpetbaggers, and Scalawags: The Constitutional Conventions of Radical Reconstruction*. Baton Rouge: Louisiana State University Press, 2008.

Hünefeldt, Christine. *Paying the Price of Freedom: Family and Labor among Lima's*

Slaves, 1800–1854. Translated by Alexandra Stern. Berkeley: University of California Press, 1994.

Hunt, Alfred N. *Haiti's Influence on Antebellum America: Slumbering Volcano in the Caribbean*. Baton Rouge: Louisiana State University Press, 1988.

Hunt, Charles Havens. *Life of Edward Livingston*. New York: D. Appleton, 1864.

Hunt, Louise Livingston. *Memoir of Mrs. Edward Livingston with Letters Hitherto Unpublished*. New York: Harper and Brothers, 1886.

Hunter, Tera. *To 'Joy My Freedom: Southern Black Women's Lives and Labors after the Civil War*. Cambridge, MA: Harvard University Press, 1997.

Hutchinson, Anderson. *Code of Mississippi: Being an Analytical Compilation of the Public and General Statutes of the Territory and State, with Tabular References to the Local and Private Acts, from 1798 to 1848*. Jackson, MS: Price and Fall, 1848.

Hynson, Jerry M., ed. *Absconders, Runaways, and other Fugitives in the Baltimore City and County Jail, 1831–1864*. Westminster, MD: Heritage Books, 2004.

———. *District of Columbia Runaway and Fugitive Slaves Cases, 1848–1863*. Westminster, MD: Heritage Books, 2012.

Ignatieff, Michael. *A Just Measure of Pain: The Penitentiary in the Industrial Revolution, 1750–1850*. New York: Pantheon Books, 1978.

"Imprisonment of Coloured Seamen." *Anti-Slavery Reporter* 5, no. 3 (February 1857): 37–38.

"Incarceration Trends: County Demographics: Orleans Parish, LA." Vera Institute of Justice, 2020. https://trends.vera.org/rates/orleans-parish-la.

Ingersoll, Thomas N. *Mammon and Manon in Early New Orleans: The First Slave Society in the Deep South, 1718–1819*. Knoxville: University of Tennessee Press, 1999.

Ingraham, Joseph Holt. *The South-West, by a Yankee*. 2 vols. New York: Harper and Brothers, 1835.

Isenberg, Nancy. *White Trash: The 400-Year Untold History of Class in America*. New York: Viking, 2016.

Jackson, Joy J. "Keeping Law and Order in New Orleans under General Butler, 1862." *Louisiana History* 34, no. 1 (Winter 1993): 51–67.

Jacobs, Harriet A. *Incidents in the Life of a Slave Girl, Written by Herself*. Edited by Lydia Maria Francis Child. Boston, 1861.

"Jail: Admissions Are Down." Cook County Justice Audit, 2022. https://cookcounty.justiceaudit.org/what-drives-the-jail-population/.

James, C. R. L. *The Black Jacobins: Toussaint L'Ouverture and the San Domingo Revolution*. New York: Vintage Books, 1963 [1938].

Jefferson, Thomas. *Memoirs, Correspondence, and Private Papers of Thomas Jefferson, Late President of the United States*. Edited by Thomas Jefferson Randolph. 4 vols. London: Henry Colburn and Richard Bentley, 1829.

———. *The Papers of Thomas Jefferson*. Edited by Julian P. Boyd et al. 42 vols. to date. Princeton, NJ: Princeton University Press, 1950–.

———. *Thomas Jefferson: Writings*. Edited by Merrill Peterson. New York: Library of America, 1984.

Jelks, William Dorsey. "The Acuteness of the Negro Question: A Suggested Remedy." *North American Review* 184, no. 609 (February 1907): 38–95.

John, Richard R. "Ruling Passions: Political Economy in Nineteenth-Century America." *Journal of Policy History* 18, no. 1 (January 2006): 1–20.

Johnson, Andrew, et al. *Andrew Johnson Papers*. Washington, DC: Library of Congress, 1960. Microfilm edition, 55 reels.

Johnson, Calvin, Mathilde Laisne, and Jon Wool. "Criminal Justice: Changing Course on Incarceration." Nonprofit Knowledge Works, June 2015. www.data centerresearch.org/reports_analysis/criminal-justice-changing-course-on -incarceration/.

Johnson, Jessica Marie. "Death Rites as Birthrights in Atlantic New Orleans: Kinship and Race in the Case of María Teresa v. Perine Dauphine." *Slavery and Abolition* 36, no. 2 (July 2015): 233–56.

Johnson, Lonnie. "Broken Levee Blues." In *Complete Recorded Works, 1925–1932, in Chronological Order*. Vol. 4: *9 March 1928 to 8 May 1929*. Compact disc. Document Records, 1991.

Johnson, Michael P., and James L. Roark, eds. *No Chariot Let Down: Charleston's Free People of Color on the Eve of the Civil War*. Chapel Hill: University of North Carolina Press, 1984.

Johnson, Rashauna. *Slavery's Metropolis: Unfree Labor in New Orleans during the Age of Revolutions*. New York: Cambridge University Press, 2016.

Johnson, Walter. "Inconsistency, Contradiction, and Complete Confusion: The Everyday Life of the Law of Slavery." *Law and Social Inquiry* 22, no. 2 (Spring 1997): 405–33.

——. *River of Dark Dreams: Slavery and Empire in the Cotton Kingdom*. Cambridge, MA: Harvard University Press, 2013.

——. "The Slave Trader, The White Slave, and the Politics of Racial Determination in the 1850s." *Journal of American History* 87, no. 1 (June 2000): 13–38.

Johnson, William. *William Johnson's Natchez: The Ante-Bellum Diary of a Free Negro*. Edited by William Ransom Hogan and Edwin Adams Davis. Baton Rouge: Louisiana State University Press, 1979.

Johnston, Les. *Policing Britain: Risk, Security and Governance*. Harlow, UK: Longman, 2000.

Johnston, Norman. *Forms of Constraint: A History of Prison Architecture*. Urbana: University of Illinois Press, 2000.

Jones, Howard J. "Biographical Sketches of Members of the 1868 Louisiana State Senate." *Louisiana History* 19, no. 1 (Winter 1978): 65–110.

Jones, Martha S. *Birthright Citizens: A History of Race and Rights in Antebellum America*. New York: Cambridge University Press, 2018.

Jones, Norrece T. *Born a Child of Freedom, Yet a Slave: Mechanisms of Control and Strategies of Resistance in Antebellum South Carolina*. Middletown, CT: Wesleyan University Press, 1990.

Jones, Paul Christian. *Against the Gallows: Antebellum American Writers and the Movement to Abolish Capital Punishment*. Iowa City: University of Iowa Press, 2011.

Jones v. Gusman. Civil Rights Litigation Clearinghouse, 2022. https://clearinghouse .net/case/12097/.

Jordan, Laylon Wayne. "Police Power and Public Safety in Antebellum Charleston: The Emergence of a New Police, 1800–1860." *South Atlantic Urban Studies* 3 (1979): 122–40.

Joseph-Gabriel, Annette. "Mobility and the Enunciation of Freedom in Urban Saint-Domingue." *Eighteenth-Century Studies* 50, no. 2 (Winter 2017): 213–29.

Joseph-Gaudet, Frances. *He Leadeth Me*. New Orleans: Louisiana Printing, 1913.

Julius, Nikolaus Heinrich. "Die Aussichten zur Gefängniß: Verbesserung im Königreiche Niederland." In *Jahrbücher der Gefängnisskunde und Besserungsanstalten*. Frankfurt, 1843.

Jütte, Robert. *Poverty and Deviance in Early Modern Europe*. New York: Cambridge University Press, 1994.

Kamerling, Henry. *Capital and Convict: Race, Region, and Punishment in Post–Civil War America*. Charlottesville: University of Virginia Press, 2017.

Kang-Brown, Jacob, Oliver Hinds, Jasmine Heiss, and Olive Lu. *The New Dynamics of Mass Incarceration*. New York: Vera Institute of Justice, 2018.

Kantrowitz, Stephen David. *More Than Freedom: Fighting for Black Citizenship in a White Republic, 1829–1889*. New York: Penguin, 2012.

Karasch, Mary C. *Slave Life in Rio de Janeiro, 1808–1850*. Princeton, NJ: Princeton University Press, 1987.

Kastor, Peter J., and François Weil, eds. *Empires of the Imagination: Transatlantic Histories of the Louisiana Purchase*. Charlottesville: University of Virginia Press, 2009.

Katz, Michael B. *The Shadow of the Poorhouse: A Social History of Welfare in America*. New York: Basic Books, 1986.

Kein, Sybil, and Consuela Provost, eds. *Creole: The History and Legacy of Louisiana's Free People of Color*. Baton Rouge: Louisiana State University Press, 2000.

Keith, LeeAnna. *The Colfax Massacre: The Untold Story of Black Power, White Terror, and the Death of Reconstruction*. New York: Oxford University Press, 2008.

Kemble, Frances Anne. *Journal of a Residence on a Georgian Plantation in 1838–1839*. New York: Harper and Brothers, 1864.

Kendall, John Smith. *History of New Orleans*. 3 vols. Chicago: Lewis, 1922.

———. "Notes on the Criminal History of New Orleans." *Louisiana Historical Quarterly* 34 (July 1951): 147–75.

Kennedy, Al. *Big Chief Harrison and the Mardi Gras Indians*. Gretna, LA: Pelican, 2010.

Kennington, Kelly M. *In the Shadow of Dred Scott: St. Louis Freedom Suits and the Legal Culture of Slavery in Antebellum America*. Athens: University of Georgia Press, 2017.

Kentucky Legislature. *Acts of the General Assembly of the Commonwealth of Kentucky: Passed at December Session, 1844*. Frankfort, KY: A. G. Hodges, 1845.

Ker, Robert J. *Proceedings and Debates of the Convention of Louisiana: Which Assembled at the City of New Orleans January 14, 1844*. New Orleans: Besancon, Ferguson, 1845.

Kerber, Linda K. *No Constitutional Right to Be Ladies: Women and the Obligations of Citizenship*. New York: Hill and Wang, 1998.

Kerr, Derek N. *Crime and Criminal Justice in Spanish Louisiana, 1770–1803: Petty Felony, Slave Defiance, and Frontier Villainy*. New York: Garland, 1993.

Kerr-Ritchie, Jeffrey R. *Rites of August First: Emancipation Day in the Black Atlantic World*. Baton Rouge: Louisiana State University Press, 2007.

King, Robert Hillary. *From the Bottom of the Heap: The Autobiography of Black Panther Robert Hillary King*. Oakland, CA: PM, 2009.

King, Stewart R. *Blue Coat or Powdered Wig: Free People of Color in Pre-Revolutionary Saint Domingue*. Athens: University of Georgia Press, 2001.

Kirchheimer, Otto, and Georg Rusche. *Punishment and Social Structure*. New York: Columbia University Press, 1939.

Kloosterboer, Wilhelmina. *Involuntary Labour since the Abolition of Slavery: A Survey of Compulsory Labour throughout the World*. Leiden: E. J. Brill, 1960.

Knepper, Paul, and Anja Johansen, eds. *The Oxford Handbook of the History of Crime and Criminal Justice*. New York: Oxford University Press, 2016.

Knox, John P. *A Historical Account of St. Thomas, W.I.: With its Rise and Progress in Commerce, Missions and Churches, Climate and Its Adaptation to Invalids, Geological Structure, Natural History, and Botany: And Incidental Notices of St. Croix and St. Johns, Slave Insurrections in These Islands, Emancipation and Present Condition of the Laboring Classes*. New York: Charles Scribner, 1852.

Kolchin, Peter. *A Sphinx on the American Land: The Nineteenth-Century South in Comparative Perspective*. Baton Rouge: Louisiana State University Press, 2003.

Kotar, S. L., and J. E. Gessler. *The Steamboat Era: A History of Fulton's Folly on American Rivers, 1807–1860*. Jefferson, NC: McFarland, 2009.

Krist, Gary. *Empire of Sin: A Story of Sex, Jazz, Murder, and the Battle for Modern New Orleans*. New York: Broadway Books, 2014.

Kusmer, Kenneth L. *Down and Out, on the Road: The Homeless in American History*. New York: Oxford University Press, 2002.

Labbé, Ronald M., and Jonathan Lurie. *The Slaughterhouse Cases: Regulation, Reconstruction, and the Fourteenth Amendment*. Lawrence: University Press of Kansas 2003.

Lachance, Paul F. "The 1809 Immigration of Saint-Domingue Refugees to New Orleans: Reception, Integration, and Impact." *Louisiana History* 29, no. 2 (Spring 1988): 109–41.

———. "The Formation of a Three-Caste Society: Evidence from Wills in Antebellum New Orleans." *Social Science History* 18, no. 2 (Summer 1994): 211–42.

———. "The Limits of Privilege: Where Free Persons of Colour Stood in the Hierarchy of Wealth in Antebellum New Orleans." In *Against the Odds: Free Blacks in the Slave Societies of the Americas*, edited by Jane G. Landers, 65–84. London: Frank Cass, 1996.

———. "The Politics of Fear: French Louisianans and the Slave Trade, 1786–1809." *Plantation Society in the Americas* 1, no. 2 (June 1979): 162–97.

Landers, Jane G., ed. *Against the Odds: Free Blacks in the Slave Societies of the Americas*. London: Frank Cass, 1996.

Lane, Charles. *The Day Freedom Died: The Colfax Massacre, the Supreme Court, and the Betrayal of Reconstruction.* New York: Henry Holt, 2008.

Lane, Roger. *Policing the City: Boston, 1822–1885.* Cambridge, MA: Harvard University Press, 1967.

"Last Inmate Leaves House of Detention." WDSU News, May 4, 2012. www.wdsu.com /article/last-inmate-leaves-house-of-detention/3356845.

Latrobe, Benjamin. *Impressions Respecting New Orleans: Diary and Sketches, 1818–1820.* Edited by Samuel Wilson Jr. New York: Columbia University Press, 1951.

Laurence, K. O. *Tobago in Wartime, 1793–1815.* Barbados: Press University of the West Indies, 1995.

Laurie, Bruce. *Artisans into Workers: Labor in Nineteenth-Century America.* New York: Hill and Wang, 1989.

The Laws of Jamaica: Comprehending All the Acts in Force, Passed between First-Year of the Reign of King George the Third, and the Thirty-Second Year of the Reign of King George the Third, Inclusive. To Which Is Prefixed, a Table of the Titles of the Public and Private Acts Passed during That Time. Carefully Revised and Corrected from the Original Records; and Published under the Direction of Commissioners Appointed for That Purpose by 30 Geo. III cap XX. and 32 Geo. III. Cap. Xxix. 2nd ed. Vol. 2. St. Jago de la Vega, Jamaica: 1802.

LeFlouria, Talitha L. *Chained in Silence: Black Women and Convict Labor in the New South.* Chapel Hill: University of North Carolina Press, 2015.

———. "'Under the Sting of the Lash': Gendered Violence, Terror, and Resistance in the South's Convict Camps." *Journal of African American History* 110, no. 3 (Summer 2015): 366–84.

Le Glaunec, Jean-Pierre. "Slave Migrations and Slave Control in New Orleans." In *Empires of the Imagination: Transatlantic Histories of the Louisiana Purchase,* edited by Peter J. Kastor and François Weil, 204–38. Charlottesville: University of Virginia Press, 2009.

———. "'Writing' the Runaways: Descriptions, Inscriptions and Narrations in the Runaway Slave 'Advertisements' of *Le Moniteur de la Louisiane,* 1802–1814." In "L'Amérique : des colonies aux républiques." Special issue, *Cahiers Charles V,* no. 39 (December 2005): 205–36.

Le Grand, Julia. *The Journal of Julia Le Grand, New Orleans, 1862–1863.* Edited by Kate Mason Rowland and Morris L. Croxall. Richmond, VA: Everett Waddey, 1911.

Lemann, Nicholas. *Redemption: The Last Battle of the Civil War.* New York: Farrar, Straus and Giroux, 2006.

Leovy, Henry J. *Laws and General Ordinances of the City of New Orleans, Together with the Acts of the Legislature, Decisions of the Supreme Court, and Constitutional Provisions, Relating to the City Government.* New Orleans, 1857.

Leovy, Henry J., and C. H. Luzenberg, eds. *The Laws and General Ordinances of the City of New Orleans: Together with the Acts of the Legislature, Decisions of the Supreme Court, and Constitutional Provisions, relating to the City Government: Revised and Digested, Pursuant to an Order of the Common Council.* New Orleans: Simmons, 1870.

Leps, Marie-Christine. *Apprehending the Criminal: The Production of Deviance in Nineteenth-Century Discourse*. Durham, NC: Duke University Press, 1992.

"The Levee—Third Municipality, New Orleans." *Frank Leslie's Illustrated Newspaper* 1, no. 21 (May 1856): 328.

Levy, Claude. *Emancipation, Sugar, and Federalism: Barbados and the West Indies, 1833–1876*. Gainesville: University Press of Florida, 1980.

Lewis, W. David. *From Newgate to Dannemora: The Rise of the Penitentiary in New York, 1796–1848*. Ithaca, NY: Cornell University Press, 1965.

Lichtenstein, Alex. "Good Roads and Chain Gangs in the Progressive South: 'The Negro Convict Is a Slave.'" *Journal of Southern History* 59, no. 1 (February 1993): 85–110.

——. *Twice the Work of Free Labor: The Political Economy of Convict Labor in the New South*. New York: Verso, 1996.

Lightfoot, Natasha. *Troubling Freedom: Antigua and the Aftermath of British Emancipation*. Durham, NC: Duke University Press, 2015.

Lincoln, Abraham. *The Collected Works of Abraham Lincoln*. Edited by Roy P. Basler, Marion Dolores Pratt, and Lloyd A. Dunlap. 9 vols. New Brunswick, NJ: Rutgers University Press, 1953–55.

——. *The Writings of Abraham Lincoln*. Edited by Arthur Brooks Lapsley. 8 vols. New York: G. P. Putnam's Sons, 1888–1906.

Linden, Fabian. "Economic Democracy in the Slave South: An Appraisal of Some Recent Views." *Journal of Negro History* 31, no. 2 (April 1946): 140–89.

Linder, Marc. *The Employment Relationship in Anglo-American Law: A Historical Perspective*. New York: Greenwood, 1989.

Linebaugh, Peter, and Marcus Rediker. *The Many-Headed Hydra: Sailors, Slaves, Commoners, and the Hidden History of the Revolutionary Atlantic*. Boston: Beacon, 2000.

Lipscomb, Terry W., and Theresa Jacobs. "The Magistrates and Freeholders Court." *South Carolina Historical Magazine* 77, no. 1 (January 1976): 62–65.

Litwack, Leon. *Been in the Storm So Long: The Aftermath of Slavery*. New York: Alfred A. Knopf, 1979.

Livingston, Edward. *Argument of Edward Livingston, against Capital Punishment*. New York: Burns and Baner, 1847.

——. *Introductory Report to the Code of Prison Discipline: Explanatory of the Principles on Which the Code Is Founded, Being Part of the System of Penal Law, Prepared for the State of Louisiana*. Philadelphia: Carey, Lea and Cary, 1827.

——. *Introductory Report to the Code of Procedure of Reform and Prison Discipline*. New Orleans: B. Levy, 1826.

——. *Introductory Report to the Code of Reform and Prison Discipline: Explanatory of the Principles on Which the Code Is Founded, Being Part of the System of Penal Law, Prepared for the State of Louisiana*. Philadelphia: Carey, Lea and Carey, 1827.

——. *Report Made to the General Assembly of the State of Louisiana, on the Plan of a Penal Code for the Said State*. New Orleans: Benjamin Levy, 1822.

——. *A System of Penal Law for the United States of America: Consisting of a Code of*

Crimes and Punishments; a Code of Procedure in Criminal Cases; a Code of Prison Discipline; and a Book of Definitions. Washington, DC: Gales and Seaton, 1828.

———. *A System of Penal Law, for the State of Louisiana: Consisting of a Code of Crimes and Punishments, a Code of Procedure, a Code of Evidence, a Code of Reform and Prison Discipline, a Book of Definitions, Prepared under the Authority of a Law of the Said State*. Philadelphia: James Kay, Jun. and Brother, 1833.

Livingston, Edward, and Roberts Vaux. *Letter from Edward Livingston, Esq. to Roberts Vaux, on the Advantages of the Pennsylvania System of Prison Discipline, for the Application of Which the New Penitentiary Has Been Constructed near Philadelphia, &c. &c.* Philadelphia: Jesper Harding, 1828.

Lockley, Timothy James. *Lines in the Sand: Race and Class in Lowcountry Georgia, 1750–1860*. Athens: University of Georgia Press, 2001.

———. *Welfare and Charity in the Antebellum South*. Gainesville: University Press of Florida, 2007.

Logsdon, Joseph. "Immigration through the Port of New Orleans." In *Forgotten Doors: The Other Ports of Entry to the United States*, edited by Mark Stolarik, 105–24. Philadelphia: Balch Institute, 1988.

Logsdon, Joseph, and Caryn Cossé Bell. "The Americanization of Black New Orleans, 1850–1900." In *Creole New Orleans: Race and Americanization*, edited by Arnold R. Hirsch and Joseph Logsdon, 201–61. Baton Rouge: Louisiana State University Press, 1992.

Lomax, Alan. *Mister Jelly Roll: The Fortunes of Jelly Roll Morton, New Orleans Creole and "Inventor of Jazz."* Berkeley: University of California Press, 2001 [1950].

Lopez, German. "America's Prisoners Are Going on Strike in at Least 17 States." Vox Media, August 22, 2018. www.vox.com/2018/8/17/17664048/national-prison-strike-2018.

Los Angeles County Alternatives to Incarceration Work Group. *Care First, Jails Last: Health and Racial Justice Strategies for Safer Communities*. Los Angeles: Los Angeles County, 2020. https://lacalternatives.org/wp-content/uploads/2020/03/ATI_Full_Report_single_pages.pdf.

Los Angeles Police Department. *Annual Report of the Police Department of the City of Los Angeles, California [. . .]* . [Los Angeles, 1913–31].

Louis, Abel Alexis. "Les libres de couleur en Martinique des origines à 1815 : l'entredeux d'un groupe social dans la tourmente coloniale." PhD diss., Université des Antilles et de la Guyane, 2011.

Louisiana Attorney General. *Report of the Attorney General to the Legislature of the State of Louisiana*. New Orleans: John Claiborne, 1857.

Louisiana Auditor of Public Accounts. *Annual Report of the Auditor of Public Accounts, to the Legislature of the State of Louisiana*. Baton Rouge: J. M. Taylor, 1861.

Louisiana Commission on Law Enforcement, Louisiana Criminal Justice Information System. *Crime in Louisiana, 1977: An Annual Report on the Problems of Crime and the Action of the Criminal Justice System in Louisiana*. Baton Rouge, 1978.

Louisiana Legislature. *Acts of the General Assembly of Louisiana, Regulating Labor. Extra Session, 1865*. New Orleans: J. O. Nixon, 1866.

———. *Acts* [. . .] *of the Legislature of the State of Louisiana.* New Orleans, 1812–59, Baton Rouge, 1859–1918.

———. *Report [of the Committee Appointed to Investigate the Discrepancies between the Accounts of the Lessees of the Penitentiary].* [New Orleans, 1854].

———. *Report on the Penitentiary, by a Joint Committee of the Senate and House of Representatives.* New Orleans: Magne and Weisse: 1845.

———. *Supplemental Report of Joint Committee of the General Assembly of Louisiana on the Conduct of the Late Elections, and the Condition of Peace and Good Order in the State.* New Orleans: A. L. Lee, 1869.

Louisiana Legislature. House. *Debates of the House of Representatives of the State of Louisiana, Session of 1869.* New Orleans: A. L. Lee, 1869.

———. *Journal of the House of Representatives* [. . .] *of the State of Louisiana.* New Orleans, 1812–80.

———. *Report on the Penitentiary.* [New Orleans, 1840].

Louisiana Legislature. Senate. *Journal of the Senate of the State of Louisiana* [. . .]. New Orleans, 1820–80.

Louisiana State Board of Charities and Corrections. [. . .] *Report of the Louisiana State Board of Charities and Corrections.* New Orleans, 1906, and Baton Rouge, 1908–10.

Louisiana State Constitutional Convention. *Constitution Adopted by the State Constitutional Convention of the State of Louisiana, March 7, 1868.* New Orleans: Republican Office, 1868.

———. *Constitution of the State of Louisiana Adopted in Convention at the City of New Orleans, the Twenty-Third Day of July, A.D. 1879.* New Orleans: Jas. H. Cosgrove, 1879.

———. *Debates in the Convention for the Revision and Amendment of the Constitution of the State of Louisiana, Assembled at Liberty Hall, New Orleans, April 6, 1864.* New Orleans, 1864.

———. *Official Journal of the Proceedings of the Convention: For Framing a Constitution for the State of Louisiana.* New Orleans: J. B. Roudanez, 1868.

Louisiana State Engineer. *Annual Report [for 1842] of the State Engineer, to the Legislature of the State of Louisiana.* New Orleans, 1843.

———. *Annual Report [for 1858] of the State Engineer to the Legislature of the State of Louisiana.* Baton Rouge: J. M. Taylor, 1859.

———. *Annual Report of the Chief Engineer of the Board of Public Works, for the Year Ending December 31, 1860, to the Legislature of the State of Louisiana.* Baton Rouge: J. M. Taylor, 1861.

———. *Annual Report of the State Engineer, to the Legislature of the State of Louisiana.* New Orleans, 1843–58.

Louisiana State Penitentiary. *Annual Report of the Board of Directors, Clerk and Officers of the Louisiana State Penitentiary, at Baton Rouge, for the Year Ending December 31, 1854.* New Orleans: Emile La Sère, 1855.

———. *Annual Report of the Board of Directors of the Louisiana Penitentiary, to the Governor of the State of Louisiana, January, 1856.* New Orleans: John Claiborne, 1856.

———. *Rapport du bureau de contrôle du pénitencier de la Louisiane, à la legislature de l'état de la Louisiane*. Baton Rouge: J. M. Taylor, 1860.

———. *Report [to his Excellency Isaac Johnson]*. [New Orleans, 1848?].

———. *Report of the Board of Control of the Louisiana Penitentiary*. Baton Rouge: J. M. Taylor, 1859.

———. *Report of the Board of Control of the Louisiana Penitentiary, January, 1858*. Baton Rouge: Daily Advocate, 1858.

———. *Report of the Board of Control of the Louisiana Penitentiary, to the General Assembly. January, 1861*. Baton Rouge: J. M. Taylor, 1861.

———. *Report of the Board of Directors of the Penitentiary of the State of Louisiana*. New Orleans: Emile La Sère, 1854.

———. *Report of the Board of Directors of the Penitentiary of the State of Louisiana*. New Orleans: Louisiana Courier, 1848.

———. *Report of the Board of Directors of the Penitentiary of the State of Louisiana*. New Orleans: Emile La Sere, 1853.

———. *Report of the Board of Directors on the State Penitentiary*. New Orleans, 1849.

———. *Report of the Board of Directors, on the State Penitentiary to the Governor of Louisiana*. [New Orleans]: Bee, 1852.

Lovett, Bobby L. *The African-American History of Nashville, Tennessee, 1780–1930: Elites and Dilemmas*. Fayetteville: University of Arkansas Press, 1999.

Lowe, Richard G., and Randolph B. Campbell. *Planters and Plain Folk: Agriculture in Antebellum Texas*. Dallas: Southern Methodist University Press, 1987.

Lowrey, Walter. "The Political Career of James Madison Wells." *Louisiana Historical Quarterly* 31, no. 4 (October 1948): 995–1034.

Luxenberg, Steve. *Separate: The Story of Plessy v. Ferguson and America's Journey from Slavery to Segregation*. New York: W. W. Norton, 2019.

Lyons, Grant. "Louisiana and the Livingston Criminal Codes." *Louisiana History* 15, no. 3 (Summer 1974): 243–72.

Mackey, Philip English. "Edward Livingston and the Origins of the Movement to Abolish Capital Punishment in America." *Louisiana History* 16, no. 2 (Spring 1975): 145–66.

Macleod, Duncan. "From Gradualism to Immediatism: Another Look." *Slavery and Abolition* 3, no. 2 (September 1982): 140–52.

Mahood, Wayne. *General Wadsworth: The Life and Wars of Brevet General James S. Wadsworth*. Cambridge, MA: Da Capo, 2003.

Majewski, John D. *Modernizing a Slave Economy: The Economic Vision of the Confederate Nation*. Chapel Hill: University of North Carolina Press, 2009.

Malka, Adam. *The Men of Mobtown: Policing Baltimore in the Age of Slavery and Emancipation*. Chapel Hill: University of North Carolina Press, 2018.

Mancini, Matthew J. *One Dies, Get Another: Convict Leasing in the American South, 1866–1928*. Columbia: University of South Carolina Press, 1996.

Manion, Jen. *Female Husbands: A Trans History*. New York: Cambridge University Press, 2020.

———. *Liberty's Prisoners: Carceral Culture in Early America*. Philadelphia: University of Pennsylvania Press, 2015.

Manning, Chandra. *Troubled Refuge: Struggling for Freedom in the Civil War*. New York: Vintage Books, 2017.

Manuel, Louis-Pierre. *La police de Paris dévoilée. Avec gravure et tableaux*. 2 vols. Paris: J. B. Garnery, [1793].

Margo, Robert A. *Wages and Labor Markets in the United States, 1820–1860*. Chicago: University of Chicago Press, 2000.

Maris-Wolf, Ted. *Family Bonds: Free Blacks and Re-Enslavement Law in Antebellum Virginia*. Chapel Hill: University of North Carolina Press, 2015.

Marks, John Garrison. *Black Freedom in the Age of Slavery: Race, Status, and Identity in the Urban Americas*. Columbia: University of South Carolina Press, 2020.

Marler, Scott P. *The Merchants' Capital: New Orleans and the Political Economy of the Nineteenth-Century South*. New York: Cambridge University Press, 2012.

Marrs, Aaron W. *Railroads in the Old South: Pursuing Progress in a Slave Society*. Baltimore: Johns Hopkins University Press, 2009.

Marshall, Amani T. "'They Are Supposed to Be Lurking about the City': Enslaved Women Runaways in Antebellum Charleston." *South Carolina Historical Magazine* 115, no. 3 (July 2014): 188–212.

Marx, Karl. *Capital: An Abridged Edition*. Edited by David McLellan. Oxford: Oxford University Press, 1995.

Masur, Kate. "'A Rare Phenomenon of Philological Vegetation': The Word 'Contraband' and the Meanings of Emancipation in the United States." *Journal of American History* 93, no. 4 (March 2007): 1050–84.

Masur, Louis P. *Rites of Execution: Capital Punishment and the Transformation of American Culture, 1776–1865*. New York: Oxford University Press, 1989.

Matibag, Eugenio. *Haitian-Dominican Counterpoint: Nation, State, and Race in Hispaniola*. New York: Palgrave, 2003.

Mattos, Marcelo Badaró. *Laborers and Enslaved Workers: Experiences in Common in the Making of Rio de Janeiro's Working Class, 1850–1920*. Translated by Renata Meirelles. New York: Berghahn Books, 2017.

Mayfield, James J., ed. *The Code of Alabama: Adopted by Act of the Legislature of Alabama*. 3 vols. Nashville, TN: Marshall and Bruce, 1907.

McChesney, W. R. "Notes by the Way." *Millennial Harbinger* 4, no. 4 (April 1847): 226–29.

McCrary, Peyton. *Abraham Lincoln and Reconstruction: the Louisiana Experiment*. Princeton, NJ: Princeton University Press, 1978.

McCurry, Stephanie. *Masters of Small Worlds: Yeoman Households, Gender Relations, and the Political Culture of the Antebellum South Carolina Low Country*. New York: Oxford University Press, 1995.

McDonnell, Lawrence T. "Work, Culture, and Society in the Slave South, 1790–1861." In *Black and White: Cultural Interaction in the Antebellum South*, edited by Ted Ownby, 125–48. Jackson: University Press of Mississippi, 1993.

McFeely, William S. *Yankee Stepfather: General O. O. Howard and the Freedmen*. New York W. W. Norton, 1994 [1968].

McGerr, Michael. *A Fierce Discontent: The Rise and Fall of the Progressive Movement in America, 1870–1920*. New York: Free Press, 2003.

McGoldrick, Stacy K. "The Policing of Slavery in New Orleans, 1852–1860." *Journal of Historical Sociology* 14, no. 2 (December 2001): 397–417.

McGregor, Charles. *History of the Fifteenth Regiment, New Hampshire Volunteers: 1862–1863*. [New Hampshire]: Fifteenth Regiment Association, 1900.

McKaye, James. *The Emancipated Slave, Face to Face with His Old Master*. New York: Wm. C. Bryant, 1864.

———. *The Mastership and Its Fruits: The Emancipated Slave Face to Face with His Old Master. A Supplemental Report to Hon. Edwin M. Stanton, Secretary of War*. New York: Wm. C. Bryant, 1864.

McKelvey, Blake. *American Prisons: A History of Good Intentions*. Montclair, NJ: Patterson Smith, 1997.

McLennan, Rebecca M. *The Crisis of Imprisonment: Protest, Politics, and the Making of the American Penal State, 1776–1941*. New York: Cambridge University Press, 2008.

McNair, Glenn. *Criminal Injustice: Slaves and Free Blacks in Georgia's Criminal Justice System*. Charlottesville: University of Virginia Press, 2009.

———. "Slave Women, Capital Crime, and Criminal Justice in Georgia." *Georgia Historical Quarterly* 93, no. 2 (Summer 2009): 135–58.

Mehrotra, Ajay K. "A Bridge Between: Law and the New Intellectual Histories of Capitalism." *Buffalo Law Review* 64, no. 1 (January 2016): 1–22.

Melossi, Dario, and Massimo Pavarini. *The Prison and the Factory: Origins of the Penitentiary System*. Translated by Glynis Cousin. London: Macmillan, 1981.

Meranze, Michael. *Laboratories of Virtue: Punishment, Revolution, and Authority in Philadelphia, 1760–1835*. Chapel Hill: University of South Carolina Press, 2012.

Merritt, Keri Leigh. *Masterless Men: Poor Whites and Slavery in the Antebellum South*. New York: Cambridge University Press, 2017.

Messner, William F. *Freedmen and the Ideology of Free Labor: Louisiana, 1862–1865*. Lafayette: Center for Louisiana Studies, 1978.

Metropolitan Crime Commission. "Orleans Parish Criminal Justice System Accountability Report, May 2017: 2013–2016 Arrests and Felony Case Outcomes." Metrocrime.org, 2017. http://metrocrime.org/wp-content/uploads/2019/04/NO-CJS -Accountability-Report-May-2017.pdf.

Michigan State Library. Legislative Reference Department. *Laws of the Various States relating to Vagrancy*. Rev. ed. Lansing, MI, 1916.

Miller, Randall M. "The Enemy Within: Some Effects of Foreign Immigrants on Antebellum Southern Cities." *Southern Studies* 24, no. 1 (Spring 1985): 43–53.

Miller, Wilbur R. *Cops and Bobbies: Police Authority in New York and London, 1830–1870*. Chicago: University of Chicago Press, 1977.

Milwaukee Police Department. *Annual Report* [. . .]. Milwaukee, 1906–31.

Mississippi Legislature. *Laws of the State of Mississippi; Passed at a Regular Biennial Session of the Legislature, Held in the City of Jackson in January and February A.D. 1842*. Jackson, MS: C. M. Price and G. R. Fall, 1842.

———. *Laws of the State of Mississippi, Passed at a Regular Session of the Mississippi Legislature, Held in the City of Jackson, October, November and December, 1865*. Jackson, MS: J. J. Shannon, State Printers, 1866.

Missouri Legislature. *Laws of the State of Missouri, Passed at the First Session of the Twelfth General Assembly, Begun and Held at the City of Jefferson, on Monday, the Twenty-First Day of November, Eighteen Hundred and Forty-Two, and Ended Tuesday, the Twenty-Eighth Day of February, Eighteen Hundred and Forty-Three.* Jefferson, MO: Allen Hammond, 1843.

Mitchell, Mary Niall. "Lurking but Working: City Maroons in Antebellum New Orleans." In *A Global History of Runaways: Workers, Mobility, and Capitalism, 1600–1850*, edited by Matthias Van Rossum, Marcus Rediker, and Titas Chakraborty, 199–215. Oakland: University of California Press, 2019.

Mitrani, Sam. *The Rise of the Chicago Police Department: Class and Conflict, 1850–1894.* Urbana: University of Illinois Press, 2013.

Mock, Brentin. "New Orleans Continues on a Path of Decarceration." Bloomberg CityLab, April 15, 2016. www.bloomberg.com/news/articles/2016-04-15/new-orleans-receives-macarthur-foundation-grant-to-decrease-jail-population.

Moitt, Bernard. *Women and Slavery in the French Antilles, 1635–1848.* Bloomington: Indiana University Press, 2001.

Monkkonen, Eric H. *Police in Urban America, 1860–1920.* New York: Cambridge University Press, 1981.

Monteverde, Danny. "Orleans Parish Sheriff Marlin Gusman Formally Ends Jail Stays at House of Detention." NOLA.com, May 5, 2012. www.nola.com/news/crime_police/article_34d95e64-e0b5-5114-ba4c-eca8230fooob.html.

Montgomery, David. *Citizen Worker: The Experience of Workers in the United States with Democracy and the Free Market during the Nineteenth Century.* New York: Cambridge University Press, 1993.

Montgomery Mayor's Office. *Annual Message of Mayor W. M. Teague Together with Annual Reports of City Officers for the Fiscal Year Ending September 30, 1906.* Montgomery, AL: Brown Printing, 1906.

Moreau de Saint-Méry, Médéric Louis Élie. *Description topographique, physique, civile, politique et historique de la partie française de l'isle Saint-Domingue. Avec des observations générales sur sa population, sur le caractère et les moeurs de ses divers habitans ; sur son climat, sa culture, ses productions, son administration, &c. &c* [. . .]. 2 vols. Philadelphia, 1796.

———. *Loix et constitutions des colonies françoises de l'Amérique sous le vent.* 6 vols. Paris, 1784–90.

Morgan, Edmund S. *American Slavery, American Freedom: The Ordeal of Colonial Virginia.* New York: W. W. Norton, 1975.

———. "Slavery and Freedom: The American Paradox." *Journal of American History* 59, no. 1 (June 1972): 5–29.

Morial, Sybil. *Witness to Change: From Jim Crow to Political Empowerment.* Durham, NC: John F. Blair, 2015.

Morris, Norval, and David Rothman, eds. *The Oxford History of the Prison: The Practice of Punishment in Western Society.* New York: Oxford University Press, 1995.

Morris, Richard B. "Labor Controls in Maryland in the Nineteenth Century." *Journal of Southern History* 14, no. 3 (August 1948): 385–400.

———. *Southern Slavery and the Law, 1619–1860.* Chapel Hill: University of North Carolina Press, 1996.

———. "White Bondage in Ante-Bellum South Carolina." *South Carolina Historical and Genealogical Magazine* 49, no. 4 (October 1948): 191–207.

Mott, Edward Harold. *Between the Ocean and the Lakes: The Story of Erie.* New York: John S. Collins, 1901.

Mouledous, Joseph C. "Pioneers in Criminology: Edward Livingston (1764–1836)." *Journal of Criminal Law, Criminology, and Police Science* 54, no. 3 (September 1963): 288–95.

Muhammad, Khalil Gibran. *The Condemnation of Blackness: Race, Crime, and the Making of Modern Urban America.* Cambridge, MA: Harvard University Press, 2010.

Mulkern, John R. *The Know-Nothing Party in Massachusetts: The Rise and Fall of a People's Movement.* Boston: Northeastern University Press, 1990.

Müller, Viola Franziska. "Runaway Slaves in Antebellum Baltimore: An Urban Form of Marronage?" *International Review of Social History* 65, special issue no. 28 (March 2020): 169–95.

Murakawa, Naomi. *The First Civil Right: How Liberals Built Prison America.* New York: Oxford University Press, 2014.

Murray, Henry Anthony. *Lands of the Slave and the Free; or, Cuba, the United States, and Canada.* London: G. Routledge, 1857 [1855].

Myers, Martha A. *Race, Labor, and Punishment in the New South.* Columbus: Ohio State University Press, 1998.

Nashville City Government. *Annual Report of Departments of the City of Nashville for the Fiscal Year [. . .].* Nashville, TN, 1905–16.

Nashville Police Department. *First Annual Report of the Metropolitan Police Department City of Nashville, Tennessee for the Year Ending December 31st, 1915.* Nashville, TN, 1916.

Navin, John J. "A New England Yankee Discovers Southern History." In *Becoming Southern Writers: Essays in Honor of Charles Joyner*, edited by Orville Vernon Burton and Eldred E. Prince, 184–91. Columbia: University of South Carolina Press, 2016.

Neidenbach, Elizabeth Clark. "The Life and Legacy of Marie Couvent: Social Networks, Property Ownership, and the Making of a Free People of Color Community in New Orleans." PhD diss., College of William and Mary, 2015.

Neocleous, Mark. *The Fabrication of Social Order: A Critical Theory of Police Power.* Sterling, VA: Pluto, 2000.

Neuman, Gerald L. *Strangers to the Constitution: Immigrants, Borders, and Fundamental Law.* Princeton, NJ: Princeton University Press, 2010.

Neusteter, S. Rebecca, and Megan O'Toole. *Every Three Seconds: Unlocking Police Data on Arrests.* New York, 2019. https://dataspace.princeton.edu/handle/88435/dsp011r66j4081.

Nevill, Samuel, ed. *The Acts of the General Assembly of the Province of New-Jersey: From the Year 1753, Being the Twenty-sixth of the Reign of King George the Second,*

Where the First Volume Ends, to the Year 1761, Being the First of King George the Third. 2 vols. Philadelphia, 1752, and Woodbridge, NJ, 1761.

New England Freedmen's Society. *Second Annual Report of the New England Freedmen's Aid Society.* Boston: New England Freedmen's Aid Society, 1864.

Newman, Richard S. *The Transformation of American Abolitionism: Fighting Slavery in the Early Republic.* Chapel Hill: University of North Carolina Press, 2002.

New Orleans Board of Commissioners of Prisons and Asylums. [. . .] *Annual Report of the Board of Commissioners of Prisons and Asylums* [. . .]. New Orleans, 1901–18.

New Orleans Board of Police Commissioners. *Annual Report of the Board of Commissioners of the Police Department and the Supt. of Police Force of the City of New Orleans for the Year* [. . .]. New Orleans, 1909–16.

New Orleans City Council Criminal Justice Committee. "Jail Population Snapshot." City of New Orleans, 2022. https://council.nola.gov/committees/criminal -justice-committee/.

New Orleans Conseil de Ville. *A Digest of the Ordinances, Resolutions, By-Laws, and Regulations of the Corporation of New Orleans.* New Orleans: Gaston Brusle, 1836.

New Orleans Department of Police. *Annual Report.* New Orleans: Department of Police, 1947–.

New-Orleans Directory for 1842: Comprising the Names, Residences and Occupations of the Merchants, Business Men, Professional Gentlemen and Citizens of New-Orleans, Lafayette, Algiers and Gretna. New Orleans: Pitts and Clark, 1842.

New Orleans House of Refuge. *Memorial of the Board of Commissioners of the House of Refuge, to the Common Council of New Orleans.* New Orleans, 1859.

———. *Report of the Board of Commissioners of the House of Refuge to the Common Council.* New Orleans: Alexander Levy, 1857.

New Orleans Metropolitan Police. *Annual Report of the Board of Metropolitan Police to the Governor of Louisiana for the Year Ending September 30, 1870.* New Orleans: A. L. Lee, 1871.

New Orleans Municipal Government. *Police Code, or Collection of the Ordinances of Police Made by the City Council of New-Orleans. To Which Is Prefixed the Act for Incorporating Said City with the Acts Supplementary Thereto.* New Orleans: J. Renard, 1808.

New Orleans Second Municipality Council. *Digest of the Ordinances and Resolutions of the Second Municipality of New-Orleans.* New Orleans: F. Cook and A. Levy, 1840.

New York City Metropolitan Police. *Communication from the Governor, Transmitting the Annual Report of the Metropolitan Police.* New York, 1861.

New York Police Department. [. . .] *Annual Report* [. . .]. New York, 1886–1931.

Niehaus, Earl F. *The Irish in New Orleans, 1800–1860.* Baton Rouge: Louisiana State University Press, 1965.

Nieman, Donald G. *To Set the Law in Motion: The Freedmen's Bureau and the Legal Rights of Blacks, 1865–1868.* Millwood, NY: KTO Press, 1979.

Norman, Benjamin Moore. *Norman's New Orleans and Environs: Containing a Brief Historical Sketch of the Territory and State of Louisiana and the City of New Orleans, from the Earliest Period to the Present Time: Presenting a Complete Guide to All Subjects of General Interest in the Southern Metropolis; with a Correct and Improved Plan of the City, Pictorial Illustrations of Public Buildings, etc.* New Orleans: B. M. Norman, 1845.

Northup, Solomon. *Twelve Years a Slave: Narrative of Solomon Northrup, a Citizen of New-York, Kidnapped in Washington City in 1841, and Rescued in 1853.* Edited by David Wilson. New York, 1855.

Nott, Samuel. *Slavery, and the Remedy; or, Principles and Suggestions for a Remedial Code.* 5th ed. New York, 1857.

Novak, Daniel. *The Wheel of Servitude: Black Forced Labor after Slavery.* Lexington: University Press of Kentucky, 1978.

Novak, William J. "The Myth of the 'Weak' American State." *American Historical Review* 113, no. 3 (June 2008): 752–72.

———. *New Democracy: The Creation of the Modern American State.* Cambridge, MA: Harvard University Press, 2022.

———. *The People's Welfare: Law and Regulation in Nineteenth-Century America.* Chapel Hill: University of North Carolina Press, 1996.

———. "Public-Private Governance: A Historical Introduction." In *Government by Contract: Outsourcing and American Democracy*, edited by Jody Freeman and Martha Minow, 23–40. Cambridge, MA: Harvard University Press, 2009.

Novak, William J., Stephen W. Sawyer, and James T. Sparrow. "Beyond Stateless Democracy." *Tocqueville Review/Revue Tocqueville* 36, no. 1 (Spring 2015): 21–41.

Nystrom, Justin A. *New Orleans after the Civil War: Race, Politics, and a New Birth of Freedom.* Baltimore: Johns Hopkins University Press, 2010.

"Obituary." *Missouri Dental Journal: A Monthly Record of Dental Science and Art* 15, no. 9 (1883): 287–88.

O'Brassill-Kulfan, Kristin. "'Vagrant Negroes': The Policing of Labor and Mobility in the Upper South in the Early Republic." In *Reconsidering Southern Labor History: Race, Class, and Power*, edited by Matthew Hild and Keri Leigh Merritt, 32–46. Gainesville: University Press of Florida, 2018.

———. *Vagrants and Vagabonds: Poverty and Mobility in the Early American Republic.* New York: New York University Press, 2019.

O'Brien, John T. "Reconstruction in Richmond: White Restoration and Black Protest, April–June 1865." *Virginia Magazine of History and Biography* 89, no. 3 (July 1981): 259–81.

Ochs, Stephen J. *A Black Patriot and a White Priest: André Cailloux and Claude Paschal Maistre in Civil War New Orleans.* Baton Rouge: Louisiana State University Press, 2000.

Ocobock, Paul. "Introduction: Vagrancy and Homelessness in Global and Historical Perspective." In *Cast Out: Vagrancy and Homelessness in Global and Historical Perspective*, edited by A. L. Beier and Paul Ocobock, 1–34. Athens: Ohio University Press, 2008.

O'Connor, Rachel. *Mistress of Evergreen Plantation: Rachel O'Connor's Legacy of Letters, 1823–1845.* Edited by Alice Bayne Windham Webb. Albany: State University of New York Press, 1983.

O'Donovan, Susan Eva. "Universities of Social and Political Change: Slaves in Jail in

Antebellum America." In *Buried Lives: Incarcerated in Early America*, edited by Michele Lise Tarter and Richard Bell, 124–48. Athens: University of Georgia Press, 2012.

Olmsted, Frederick Law. *The Cotton Kingdom: A Traveller's Observations on Cotton and Slavery in the American Slave States. Based upon Three Former Volumes of Journeys and Investigations by the Same Author*. 2 vols. New York: Mason Brothers, 1861.

———. *A Journey in the Back Country*. New York: Mason Brothers, 1863.

———. *A Journey in the Seaboard Slave States; with Remarks on Their Economy*. New York: Dix and Edwards, 1856.

Orleans Territorial Legislature. *Acts Passed at the First Session of the First Legislature of the Territory of Orleans*. New Orleans, 1807.

———. *A Digest of the Civil Laws Now in Force in the Territory of Orleans, with Alterations and Amendments Adapted to Its Present System of Government*. New Orleans: Bradford and Anderson, 1808.

Orren, Karen. *Belated Feudalism: Labor, the Law, and Liberal Development in the United States*. New York: Cambridge University Press, 1991.

Oshinsky, David M. *Worse Than Slavery: Parchman Farm and the Ordeal of Jim Crow Justice*. New York: Free Press, 1996.

Oskar. *Über Strafe und Strafanstalten*. Leipzig, 1841.

Overdyke, W. Darrell. *The Know-Nothing Party in the South*. Baton Rouge: Louisiana State University Press, 1950.

Owen, Robert Dale, James McKaye, and Samuel G. Howe. *Preliminary Report Touching the Condition and Management of Emancipated Refugees; Made to the Secretary of War, by the American Freedmen's Inquiry Commission, June 30, 1863*. New York: John F. Trow, 1863.

Owsley, Frank Lawrence. *Plain Folk of the Old South*. Baton Rouge: Louisiana State University Press, 1949.

Padgett, James A. "A Decree for Louisiana Issued by the Baron of Carondelet, June 1, 1795." *Louisiana Historical Quarterly* 20, no. 3 (July 1937): 590–605.

Paine, Thomas. *The Complete Religious and Theological Works of Thomas Paine*. New York: Peter Eckler, 1922.

Pargas, Damian Alan. *Freedom Seekers: Fugitive Slaves in North America*. New York: Cambridge University Press, 2022.

———, ed. *Fugitive Slaves and Spaces of Freedom in North America*. Gainesville: University Press of Florida, 2018.

Parker, John. *His Promised Land: The Autobiography of John P. Parker, Former Slave and Conductor on the Underground Railroad*. Edited by Stuart Seely Sprague. New York: W. W. Norton, 1996.

Parton, James. *General Butler in New Orleans*. New York: Mason Brothers, 1864.

Paton, Diana. *The Cultural Politics of Obeah: Religion, Colonialism and Modernity in the Caribbean World*. New York: Cambridge University Press, 2015.

———. *No Bond but the Law: Punishment, Race and Gender in Jamaican State Formation, 1780–1870*. Durham, NC: Duke University Press, 2004.

Pavie, Théodore, and Betje Black Klier. *Pavie in the Borderlands: The Journey of Théodore Pavie to Louisiana and Texas, 1829–1830, Including Portions of His* Souvenirs atlantiques. Baton Rouge: Louisiana State University Press, 2000.

Pelot-Hobbs, Lydia. "Louisiana's Turn to Mass Incarceration: The Building of a Carceral State." American Association of Geographers, February 1, 2018. http://news.aag.org/2018/02/louisianas-turn-to-mass-incarceration-the-building-of-a-carceral-state/.

Pennsylvania Constitutional Convention. *Proceedings and Debates of the Convention of the Commonwealth of Pennsylvania.* 2 vols. Harrisburg, PA: Packer, Barrett, and Parker, 1838.

Pennsylvania Legislature. Senate. *Journal of the Senate of the Commonwealth of Pennsylvania, Which Commenced at Harrisburg, the Fifth Day of December, in the Year of our Lord, One Thousand Eight Hundred and Twenty, and of the Independence of the United States of America, the Forty-Fifth.* Harrisburg, PA: William F. Buyers, 1820.

Perkinson, Robert. *Texas Tough: The Rise of America's Prison Empire.* New York: Metropolitan Books, 2010.

Peters, Justin. "Drug Abuse, Moldy Walls, an Inmate with a Gun; Is Orleans Parish Prison the Worst City Jail in America?" Slate, April 5, 2013. https://slate.com/news-and-politics/2013/04/orleans-parish-prison-marlin-gusman-does-new-orleans-have-the-worst-city-jail-in-america.html.

Pfaff, John F. *Locked In: The True Causes of Mass Incarceration and Grow to Achieve Real Reform.* New York: Basic Books, 2017.

Philadelphia Common Council. *Journal of the Common Council of* [. . .] *Philadelphia* [. . .] *with an Appendix.* Philadelphia, 1856–60.

Philadelphia Mayor's Office. [. . .] *Annual Message of* [. . .] *Mayor of the City Philadelphia* [. . .]. Philadelphia, 1857–1923.

Phillips, Jim. "Poverty, Unemployment, and the Administration of the Criminal Law: Vagrancy Laws in Halifax, 1864–1890." In *Essays in the History of Canadian Law: Nova Scotia,* edited by Philip Girard and Jim Phillips, 128–62. Toronto: University of Toronto Press, 2012.

Phillips, U. B. *The Statutes of the State of Louisiana.* New Orleans: Emile La Sere, 1855.

Picard, Sara M. "Racing Jules Lion." *Louisiana History* 58, no. 1 (Winter 2017): 5–37.

Pierce, Steven, and Anupama Rao. "Discipline and the Other Body: Humanitarianism, Violence, and the Colonial Exception." In *Discipline and the Other Body: Correction, Corporeality, Colonialism,* edited by Steven Pierce and Anupama Rao, 1–35. Durham: Duke University Press, 2006.

——, eds. *Discipline and the Other Body: Correction, Corporeality, Colonialism.* Durham, NC: Duke University Press, 2006.

Pisciotta, Alexander. "Treatment on Trial: The Rhetoric and Reality of the New York House of Refuge, 1857–1935." *American Journal of Legal History* 29, no. 2 (April 1985): 151–81.

Pitot, Henry Clement. *James Pitot: A Documentary Study.* New Orleans: Bocage Books, 1988 [1968].

Pitot, James. *Observations on the Colony of Louisiana, from 1796 to 1802.* Edited by Robert D. Bush. Baton Rouge: Louisiana State University Press, 1979.

"The Plague in the South-West: The Great Yellow Fever Epidemic in 1853." *DeBow's Review* 15, no. 6 (1853): 595–635.

Pluskota, Marion. "Freedom of Movement, Access to the Urban Centres, and Abolition of Slavery in the French Caribbean." *International Review of Social History* 65, special issue no. 28 (April 2020): 93–115.

"Police Scorecard." Police Scorecard Project. April 18, 2023. https://policescorecard .org.

Popkin, Jeremy D. *You Are All Free: The Haitian Revolution and the Abolition of Slavery.* New York: Cambridge University Press, 2010.

Powell, Lawrence N. *The Accidental City: Improvising New Orleans.* Cambridge, MA: Harvard University Press, 2012.

Powers, Gershom. *Letter of Gershom Powers, Esq. in Answer to a Letter of the Hon. Edward Livingston, in Relation to the Auburn State Prison.* Albany, NY: Croswell and Van Benthuysen, 1829.

Price, Thomas. *Slavery in America: With Notices of the Present State of Slavery and the Slave Trade throughout the World.* London: G. Wightman, 1837.

Prison Association of New York. *Third Report of the Prison Association of New York: Including the Institution and By-Laws, Act of Incorporation, and a List of Officers and Members. In Two Parts.* New York: Burns and Baner, 1847.

Prison Discipline Society. *Fourteenth Annual Report of the Board of Managers of the Prison Discipline Society.* Boston: Prison Discipline Society, 1839.

——. *Sixteenth Annual Report of the Board of Managers of the Prison Discipline Society.* Boston: Samuel N. Dickinson, 1841.

——. *Thirteenth Annual Report of the Board of Managers of the Prison Discipline Society.* Boston: Prison Discipline Society, 1838.

Proceedings of the Convention of the Colored People of VA., Held in the City of Alexandria, Aug. 2, 3, 4, 5, 1865. Alexandria, VA: Cowing and Gillis, 1865.

Pryor, Elizabeth Stordeur. *Colored Travelers: Mobility and the Fight for Citizenship before the Civil War.* Chapel Hill: University of North Carolina Press, 2016.

Quintana, Ryan A. *Making a Slave State: Political Development in Early South Carolina.* Chapel Hill: University of North Carolina Press, 2018.

Rabinowitz, Howard N. *Race Relations in the Urban South, 1865–1990.* New York: Oxford University Press, 1978.

Raines, James E., ed. *A Compilation of the General Laws of the City of Nashville: Together with the Charters of the City, Granted by the States of North Carolina and Tennessee, and a List of the Chief Officers of the Municipal Government of Nashville in Each Year, from 1806 to 1860.* Nashville, TN: J. O. Griffith, 1860.

Rankin, David C. "The Origins of Black Leadership in New Orleans during Reconstruction." *Journal of Southern History* 40, no. 3 (August 1974): 417–40.

Ranney, Joseph. *In the Wake of Slavery: Civil War, Civil Rights, and the Reconstruction of Southern Law.* Westport, CT: Praeger, 2006.

Reed, Emily Hazen. *Life of A. P. Dostie; or, The Conflict in New Orleans.* New York: William P. Tomlinson, 1868.

Reichel, Philip L. "Southern Slave Patrols as a Transitional Police Type." *American Journal of Police* 7, no. 2 (1988): 51–78.

Reid, Whitelaw. *After the War: A Southern Tour; May 1, 1865, to May 1, 1866.* London: Sampson Low, Son, and Marston, 1866.

Reinders, Robert C. "The Decline of the New Orleans Free Negro in the Decade before the Civil War." *Journal of Mississippi History* 24, no. 2 (January 1962): 88–98.

———. *End of an Era: New Orleans, 1850–1860.* New Orleans: Pelican, 1964.

Renard, Rosamunde. "Labour Relations in Martinique and Guadeloupe, 1848–1870." *Journal of Caribbean History* 26, no. 1 (1992): 37–61.

A Resident. *New Orleans as It Is: Its Manners and Customs—Morals—Fashionable Life—Profanation of the Sabbath—Prostitution—Licentiousness—Slave Markets and Slavery, &c., &c., &c.* Utica, NY: DeWitt C. Grove, 1849.

Rice, Jim. "'This Province, So Meanly and Thinly Inhabited': Punishing Maryland's Criminals, 1681–1850." *Journal of the Early Republic* 19, no. 1 (Spring 1999): 15–42.

Richmond Mayor's Office. *Annual Message [. . .] of the Mayor [. . .].* Richmond, VA, 1909–19.

Richter, William L. "Slavery in Baton Rouge, 1820–1860." *Louisiana History* 10, no. 2 (April 1969): 125–45.

Ridgeway, James, and Jean Casella. "America's 10 Worst Prisons: NOLA." *Mother Jones*, May 6, 2013. www.motherjones.com/politics/2013/05/10-worst-prisons -america-orleans-parish-opp/.

Riffel, Judy, ed. *New Orleans Register of Free People of Color, 1840–1864.* Baton Rouge: Comité des Archives de la Louisiane, 2008.

Ring, Natalie J. *The Problem South: Region, Empire, and the New Liberal State, 1880–1930.* Athens: University of Georgia Press, 2012.

Ripley, C. Peter, ed. *The Black Abolitionist Papers.* 5 vols. Chapel Hill: University of North Carolina Press, 1985–1992.

———. *Slaves and Freedmen in Civil War Louisiana.* Baton Rouge: Louisiana State University Press, 1976.

Riser, Henry LeRoy. "The History of Jennings, Louisiana." PhD diss., Louisiana State University, 1948.

Ritter, Luke. *Inventing America's First Immigration Crisis: Political Nativism in the Antebellum West.* New York: Fordham University Press, 2020.

Rôbert, Charles Edwin, ed. *Nashville City Guide Book, Issued under Authority of the Board of Directors, Centennial Commission.* Nashville, TN: Wheeler Brothers, 1880.

Roberts, Kevin David. "Slaves and Slavery in Louisiana: The Evolution of Atlantic World Identities, 1791–1831." PhD diss., University of Texas at Austin, 2003.

Roberts, Neil. *Freedom as Marronage.* Chicago: University of Chicago Press, 2015.

Robin, Charles-César. *Voyage to Louisiana, 1803–1805.* Translated by Stuart O. Landry Jr. New Orleans: Pelican, 1966.

Robinson, Caroline E. *The Hazard Family of Rhode Island, 1863–1894.* Boston, 1895.

Rockman, Seth. *Scraping By: Wage Labor, Slavery, and Survival in Early Baltimore.* Baltimore: Johns Hopkins University Press, 2009.

———. "What Makes the History of Capitalism Newsworthy?" *Journal of the Early Republic* 34, no. 3 (Fall 2014): 439–66.

Rodgers, Daniel T. *The Work Ethic in Industrial America, 1850–1920*. Chicago: University of Chicago Press, 1978.

Rodrigue, John C. "The Freedmen's Bureau and Wage Labor in the Louisiana Sugar Region." In *Freedmen's Bureau and Reconstruction: Reconsiderations*, edited by Paul A. Cimbala and Randall M. Miller, 193–218. New York: Fordham University Press, 1999.

——. *Reconstruction in the Cane Fields: From Slavery to Free Labor in Louisiana's Sugar Parishes, 1862–1880*. Baton Rouge: Louisiana State University Press, 2001.

Roediger, David R. *The Wages of Whiteness: Race and the Making of the American Working Class*. Rev. ed. New York: Verso, 2007.

Rogers, Kim Lacy. *Righteous Lives: Narratives of the New Orleans Civil Rights Movement*. New York: New York University Press, 1993.

Rosenthal, Caitlin. *Accounting for Slavery: Masters and Management*. Cambridge, MA: Harvard University Press, 2018.

Ross, Michael A. "Justice Miller's Reconstruction: The Slaughter-House Cases, Health Codes, and Civil Rights in New Orleans, 1861–1873." *Journal of Southern History* 64, no. 4 (November 1998): 649–76.

Ross, Robert J. S. "New Orleans as a Rust Belt City?" Metropolitics, July 6, 2011. https://metropolitiques.eu/New-Orleans-as-a-Rust-Belt-City.html.

Rothman, Adam. *Slave Country: American Expansion and the Origins of the Deep South*. Cambridge, MA: Harvard University Press, 2005.

Rothman, David J. *The Discovery of the Asylum: Social Order and Disorder in the New Republic*. Boston: Little, Brown, 1971.

Rothman, Joshua D. *Flush Times and Fever Dreams: A Story of Capitalism and Slavery in the Age of Jackson*. Athens: University of Georgia Press, 2012.

Rousey, Dennis Charles. *Policing the Southern City: New Orleans, 1805–1889*. Baton Rouge: Louisiana State University Press, 1996.

Rousseau, Jean-Jacques. "Discourse on Political Economy." In *On the Social Contract: Discourse on the Origin of Inequality; Discourse on Political Economy*, 163–90. Translated by Donald A. Cress. Indianapolis: Hackett Publishing Company, 1983.

Rubin, Ashley. *The Deviant Prison: Philadelphia's Eastern State Penitentiary and the Origins of America's Modern Penal System, 1829–1913*. New York: Cambridge University Press, 2021.

Rugemer, Edward Bartlett. *The Problem of Emancipation: The Caribbean Roots of the American Civil War*. Baton Rouge: Louisiana State University Press, 2008.

The Rural Code of Haiti; in French and English. With a Prefatory Letter to the Right. Hon. the Earl Bathurst, K.G. London: McMillan, 1827.

Rush, Benjamin. *An Oration, Delivered before the American Philosophical Society: Held in Philadelphia on the 27th of February, 1786; Containing an Enquiry into the Influence of Physical Causes upon the Moral Faculty*. Philadelphia: Charles Cist, 1786.

Russell, Bill. *"Oh, Mister Jelly": A Jelly Roll Morton Scrapbook*. Copenhagen: JazzMedia, 1999.

Russell, Robert. *North America, Its Agriculture and Climate: Containing Observations on the Agriculture and Climate of Canada, the United States, and the Island of Cuba*. Edinburgh: Adam and Charles Black, 1857.

Savannah Mayor's Office. *Annual* [. . .] *Reports of the City Officers of the City of Savannah, Georgia* [. . .] *Year Ending* [. . .]. Savannah, GA, 1899–1916.

Sawyer, George S. *Southern Institutes; or, An Inquiry into the Origin and Early Prevalence of Slavery and the Slave-Trade: With an Analysis of the Laws, History, and Government of the Institution in the Principal Nations, Ancient and Modern, from the Earliest Ages down to the Present Time. With Notes and Comments in Defence of the Southern Institutions.* Philadelphia: J. B. Lippincott, 1858.

Sawyer, Wendy, and Peter Wagner. "Mass Incarceration: The Whole Pie 2020." Prison Policy Initiative, March 24, 2020. www.prisonpolicy.org/reports/pie2020 .html.

Saxton, Alexander. *The Rise and Fall of the White Republic: Class Politics and Mass Culture in Nineteenth-Century America.* New York: Verso, 1990.

Schafer, Judith K. *Becoming Free, Remaining Free: Manumission and Enslavement in New Orleans, 1846–1862.* Baton Rouge: Louisiana State University Press, 2003.

———. *Brothels, Depravity, and Abandoned Women: Illegal Sex in Antebellum New Orleans.* Baton Rouge: Louisiana State University Press, 2009.

———. "'Guaranteed against the Vices and Maladies Prescribed by Law': Consumer Protection, the Law of Slave Sales, and the Supreme Court in Antebellum Louisiana." *American Journal of Legal History* 31, no. 4 (October 1987): 306–22.

———. *Slavery, the Civil Law, and the Supreme Court of Louisiana.* Baton Rouge: Louisiana State University Press, 1994.

———. "Slaves and Crime: New Orleans, 1846–1862." In *Local Matters: Race, Crime, and Justice in the Nineteenth-Century South*, edited by Christopher Waldrep and Donald G. Nieman, 125–54. Athens: University of Georgia Press, 2001.

———. "'Under the Present Mode of Trial, Improper Verdicts Are Very Often Given': Criminal Procedure in the Trials of Slaves in Antebellum Louisiana." *Cardozo Law Review* 18, no. 4 (1996): 635–77.

Schechter, Patricia A. "Free and Slave Labor in the Old South: The Tredegar Ironworkers' Strike of 1847." *Labor History* 35, no. 2 (Spring 1994): 165–86.

Schell, Francis H. "The Old Slave Laws." *Frank Leslie's Illustrated Newspaper* 15, no. 388 (March 1863): 369–70, 381.

Schermerhorn, Calvin. *The Business of Slavery and the Rise of American Capitalism, 1815–1860.* New Haven, CT: Yale University Press, 2015.

Schmidt, James. *Free to Work: Labor Law, Emancipation, and Reconstruction, 1815–1880.* Athens: University of Georgia Press, 1998.

Schneider, John C. "Omaha Vagrants and the Character of Western Hobo Labor, 1887–1913." *Nebraska History* 63, no. 2 (Summer 1982): 225–72.

Schoenfeld, Heather. *Building the Prison State: Race and the Politics of Mass Incarceration.* Chicago: University of Chicago Press, 2018.

Schoeppner, Michael. *Moral Contagion: Black Atlantic Sailors, Citizenship, and Diplomacy in Antebellum America.* New York: Oxford University Press, 2019.

Schultz, Kirsten. *Tropical Versailles: Empire, Monarchy, and the Portuguese Royal Court in Rio de Janeiro, 1808–1821.* New York: Routledge, 2001.

Schwalm, Leslie A. *A Hard Fight for We: Women's Transition from Slavery to Freedom in South Carolina.* Urbana: University of Illinois Press, 1997.

Schweninger, Loren, ed. *Race, Slavery, and Free Blacks.* Series I: *Petitions to*

Southern State Legislatures, 1777–1867. Microfilm edition, 23 reels. Bethesda, MD: University Publications of America, 1999.

———. *Race, Slavery, and Free Blacks.* Series II: *Petitions to Southern County Courts, 1775–1867: Part A, Georgia (1796–1867), Florida (1821–1867), Alabama (1821–1867), Mississippi (1822–1867).* Microfilm edition, 21 reels. Bethesda, MD: University Publications of America, 2003.

———. *Race, Slavery, and Free Blacks.* Series II: *Petitions to Southern County Courts, 1775–1867: Part C, Virginia (1775–1867) and Kentucky (1790–1864).* Microfilm edition, 22 reels. Bethesda, MD: University Publications of America, 2005.

———. *Race, Slavery, and Free Blacks.* Series II: *Petitions to Southern Legislatures, 1777–1867: Part F, Parish Courts (Louisiana 1795–1863).* Microfilm edition, 18 reels. Bethesda, MD: University Publications of America, 1998.

———. *The Southern Debate over Slavery.* Vol. 2: *Petitions to Southern County Courts, 1775–1867.* Urbana: University of Illinois Press, 2008.

Scott, Daryl Michael. "The Scandal of Thirteentherism." *Liberties* 2, no. 2 (Winter 2021): 273–93.

Scott, David. *Refashioning Futures: Criticism after Postcoloniality.* Princeton, NJ: Princeton University Press, 1999.

Scott, James C. *Domination and the Arts of Resistance: Hidden Transcripts.* New Haven, CT: Yale University Press, 1990.

Scott, Julius Sherrard. *The Common Wind: Afro-American Currents in the Age of the Haitian Revolution.* New York: Verso, 2018.

Scott, Rebecca J. "Asserting Citizenship and Refusing Stigma: New Orleans Equal-Rights Activists Interpret 1803 and 1848." In *New Orleans and Saint-Louis, Senegal: Mirror Cities in the Atlantic World*, edited by Emily Clark, Ibrahima Thioub, and Cecil Vidal, 146–67. Baton Rouge: Louisiana State University Press, 2019.

———. "The Atlantic World and the Road to 'Plessy v. Ferguson.'" *Journal of American History* 94, no. 3 (December 2007): 726–33.

———. *Degrees of Freedom: Louisiana and Cuba after Slavery.* Cambridge, MA: Harvard University Press, 2005.

———. "Discerning a Dignitary Offense: The Concept of Equal 'Public Rights' during Reconstruction." *Law and History Review* 38, no. 3 (August 2020): 519–53.

———. "Paper Thin: Freedom and Re-Enslavement in the Diaspora of the Haitian Revolution." *Law and History Review* 29, no. 4 (November 2011): 1061–87.

———. "Public Rights, Social Equality, and the Conceptual Roots of the *Plessy* Challenge." *Michigan Law Review* 106, no. 5 (March 2008): 777–804.

Scott, Rebecca, and Jean Hébrard. *Freedom Papers: An Atlantic Odyssey in the Age of Emancipation.* Cambridge, MA: Harvard University Press, 2012.

Scrivener, Luke, Shannon Tomascak, Erica Bond, and Preeti Chauhan. *New York City Jail Population in 2019.* New York: Data Collaborative for Justice at John Jay College, 2021. https://datacollaborativeforjustice.org/wp-content/uploads/2021/07/2021_07_09_DOC_Full_Brief_FINAL.pdf.

Segal, Charles M. "Lincoln, Benjamin Jonas and the Black Code." *Journal of the Illinois State Historical Society* 46, no. 3 (Fall 1953): 277–82.

Sellin, Johan Thorsten. *Slavery and the Penal System.* New York: Elsevier, 1976.

Sen, Satadru. "A Separate Punishment: Juvenile Offenders in Colonial India." *Journal of Asian Studies* 63, no. 1 (February 2004): 81–104.

Shammas, Carole. *A History of Household Government in America*. Charlottesville: University of Virginia Press, 2002.

Shapiro, Karin A. *A New South Rebellion: The Battle against Convict Labor in the Tennessee Coalfields, 1871–1896*. Chapel Hill: University of North Carolina Press, 1998.

Shapiro, Nat, and Nat Hentoff, eds. *Hear Me Talkin' to Ya: The Story of Jazz as Told by the Men Who Made It*. New York: Dover, 2012.

Sheahan, James W., ed. *Corporation Laws of the City of Washington, to the End of the Fiftieth Council, (To June 3d, 1853, Inclusive), Revised and Compiled by James W. Sheahan, under the Direction of a Joint Committee, Consisting of the Mayor and One Member of the Board of Aldermen and One Member of the Board of Common Council: and, also the Acts of Incorporation and Other Acts of Congress, with an Appendix, to Which Are Added the General Laws Enacted from June 3, 1853, to June 1, 1860, Embracing the 51st, 52d, 53d, 54th, 55th, and 57th Councils. Prepared and Published by Order of the Corporation of Washington*. Washington, DC: Robert A. Waters, 1860.

Shelden, Randall G. "Convict Leasing: An Application of the Rusche-Kirchheimer Thesis to Penal Changes in Tennessee, 1830–1915." In *Crime and Capitalism: Readings in Marxist Criminology*, edited by David F. Greenberg, 612–20. Palo Alto, CA: Mayfield, 1981.

Shenk, Gerald E. *"Work or Fight!": Race, Gender, and the Draft in World War One*. New York: Palgrave MacMillan, 2005.

Sherman, Taylor C. "Tensions of Colonial Punishment: Perspectives on Recent Developments in the Study of Coercive Networks in Asia, Africa and the Caribbean." *History Compass* 7, no. 3 (May 2009): 659–77.

Shleifstein, Mark. "FEMA's $7.7 Million Will Help Build New Prison Administration Center in New Orleans." NOLA.com, July 7, 2011. www.nola.com/news/crime _police/article_98bb7631-096d-539c-a9d2-2590624e18f2.html.

Shugg, Roger W. *Origins of Class Struggle in Louisiana: A Social History of White Farmers and Laborers during Slavery and after, 1840–1875*. Baton Rouge: Louisiana State University Press, 1968.

Silver, Christopher. "A New Look at Old South Urbanization: The Irish Worker in Charleston, South Carolina, 1840–1860." *South Atlantic Urban Studies* 3 (1979): 149–51.

Simon, Jonathan. *Governing through Crime: How the War on Crime Transformed American Democracy and Created a Culture of Fear*. New York: Oxford University Press, 2009.

Sims, William Gilmore. *Slavery in America: Being a Brief Review of Miss Martineau on That Subject*. Richmond, VA: Thomas W. White, 1838.

Sitterson, Joseph Carlyle. *Sugar Country: The Cane Sugar Industry in the South, 1753–1950*. Lexington: University of Kentucky Press, 1953.

Sklansky, Jeffrey. "The Elusive Sovereign: New Intellectual and Social Histories of Capitalism." *Modern Intellectual History* 9, no. 1 (April 2012): 233–48.

"A Slave-Auction." *Christian Miscellany, and Family Visiter* [sic] 1 (February 1846): 54–55.

"Slaves in Louisiana." *Harper's Weekly* 7, no. 320 (February 1863): 114.

Smalls, Samanthis Quantrellis. "Behind Workhouse Walls: The Public Regulation of Slavery in Charleston, 1730–1850." PhD diss., Duke University, 2015.

Smith, Billy G. "Black Women Who Stole Themselves." In *Inequality in Early America*, edited by Carla Gardina Pestana and Sharon V. Salinger, 134–59. Hanover, NH: University Press of New England, 1999.

Smith, Caleb. *The Prison and the American Imagination.* New Haven, CT: Yale University Press, 2009.

Smith, Carney Jessie, ed. *Notable Black American Women.* 2 vols. Detroit, MI: Gale Research, 1992–96.

Smith, George W. *A Defense of the System of Solitary Confinement of Prisoners Adopted by the State of Pennsylvania, with Remarks on the Origins, Progress and Extension of This Species of Prison Discipline.* Philadelphia: E. G. Dorsey, 1833 [1829].

Smith, Mark M. *Debating Slavery: Economy and Society in the Antebellum American South.* New York: Cambridge University Press, 1998.

———. *Mastered by the Clock: Time, Slavery, and Freedom in the American South.* Chapel Hill: University of North Carolina Press, 1997.

Smith, Matthew J. *Liberty, Fraternity, Exile: Haiti and Jamaica after Emancipation.* Chapel Hill: University of North Carolina Press, 2014.

Sneed, William C. *A Report on the History and Mode of Management of the Kentucky Penitentiary, from Its Origin, in 1798, to March 1, 1860.* Frankfort, KY: Yeoman Office, 1860.

South Carolina Legislature. *Acts of the General Assembly of the State of South Carolina, Passed at the Sessions of 1864–65. Printed by Order of the Legislature, in Conformity with the Statutes at Large, and Designed to Form a Part of the Thirteenth Volume, Commencing with the Acts of 1861.* Columbia, SC: Julian A. Selby, 1866.

———. *Acts of the General Assembly of the State of South-Carolina, Passed in December, 1844.* Columbia, SC: A. H. Pemberton, 1845.

Souther, J. Mark. *New Orleans on Parade: Tourism and the Transformation of the Crescent City.* Baton Rouge: Louisiana State University Press, 2006.

Southern, David W. *The Progressive Era and Race: Reaction and Reform, 1900–1917.* Wheeling, WV: Harlan Davidson, 2005.

"Southern Convention at Vicksburg, Part 2." *DeBow's Review* 27, no. 2 (August 1859): 205–20.

Spear, Jennifer. *Race, Sex, and Social Order in Early New Orleans.* Baltimore: Johns Hopkins University Press, 2009.

Spierenburg, Pieter. "The Body and the State: Early Modern Europe." In *The Oxford History of the Prison: The Practice of Punishment in Western Society*, edited by Norval Morris and David Rothman, 49–78. New York: Oxford University Press, 1995.

———. *The Prison Experience: Disciplinary Institutions and Their Inmates in Early Modern Europe.* Amsterdam: Amsterdam University Press, 1991.

——. *The Spectacle of Suffering: Executions and the Evolution of Repression, from a Preindustrial Metropolis to the European Experience.* Cambridge, MA: Harvard University Press, 1984.

Spletstoser, Frederick M. "Back Door to the Land of Plenty: New Orleans as an Immigrant Port, 1820–1860." 2 vols. PhD diss., Louisiana State University, 1978.

Stampp, Kenneth, ed. *Records of Ante-Bellum Southern Plantations from the Revolution through the Civil War. Series M: Selections from the Virginia Historical Society, Part 4: Central Piedmont Virginia.* Microfilm edition, 59 reels. Frederick, MD: University Publications of America, 1996.

Stanley, Amy Dru. *From Bondage to Contract: Wage Labor, Marriage, and the Market in the Age of Slave Emancipation.* New York: Cambridge University Press, 1998.

Stansell, Christine. *City of Women: Sex and Class in New York, 1789–1860.* New York: Alfred A. Knopf, 1986.

Steinberg, Allen. *The Transformation of Criminal Justice: Philadelphia, 1800–1880.* Chapel Hill: University of North Carolina Press, 1989.

Steinfeld, Robert J. *Coercion, Contract, and Free Labor in the Nineteenth Century.* New York: Cambridge University Press, 2001.

——. *The Invention of Free Labor: The Employment Relation in English and American Law and Culture, 1350–1870.* Chapel Hill: University of North Carolina Press, 1991.

——. "Property and Suffrage in the Early American Republic." *Stanford Law Review* 41, no. 2 (January 1989): 335–76.

Sterkx, Herman E. *The Free Negro in Ante-Bellum Louisiana.* Rutherford, NJ: Farleigh Dickinson University Press, 1972.

Stern, Walter C. *Race and Education in New Orleans: Creating the Segregated City, 1764–1960.* Baton Rouge: Louisiana State University Press, 2018.

Sternhell, Yael A. *Routes of War: The World of Movement in the Confederate South.* Cambridge, MA: Harvard University Press, 2012.

Stevens, William B. *History of the Fiftieth Regiment of Infantry, Massachusetts Volunteer Militia, in the Late War of the Rebellion.* Boston: Griffith-Stillings, 1907.

Stevenson, Bryan. "Why American Prisons Owe Their Cruelty to Slavery." *New York Times Magazine,* August 14, 2019. www.nytimes.com/interactive/2019/08/14/magazine/prison-industrial-complex-slavery-racism.html.

Stewart, James Brewer. "The Emergence of Racial Modernity and the Rise of the White North, 1790–1840." *Journal of the Early Republic* 18, no. 2 (June 1998): 181–217.

Strattan, Oliver H., and John M. Vaughan, eds. *A Collection of the State and Municipal Laws, in Force, and Applicable to the City of Louisville, KY. Prepared and Digested, under an Order from the General Council of Said City, by Oliver H. Strattan and John M. Vaughan, City Clerks. Which Includes the State Constitution and City Charter, with Notes of Reference.* Louisville, KY: C. Settle, 1857.

Strickland, Jeff. *All for Liberty: The Charleston Workhouse Slave Rebellion of 1849.* New York: Cambridge University Press, 2021.

Strother, David Hunter. *A Virginia Yankee in the Civil War: The Diaries of David Hunter Strother.* Edited by Cecil D. Eby. Chapel Hill: University of North Carolina Press, 1998.

Stuart, James. *Three Years in North America*. 2 vols. Edinburgh: Robert Cadell, 1833.

Sugrue, Thomas J. "Preface: The Reconfiguration of Political History." *Tocqueville Review/Revue Tocqueville* 36, no. 1 (Spring 2015): 11–20.

Sullivan, Kathleen S., and Patricia Strach. "Statebuilding through Corruption: Graft and Trash in Pittsburgh and New Orleans." In *Statebuilding from the Margins: Between Reconstruction and the New Deal*, edited by Carol Nackenoff and Julie Novkov, 95–117. Philadelphia: University of Pennsylvania Press, 2014.

Summers, Mark W. *The Ordeal of the Reunion: A New History of Reconstruction*. Chapel Hill: University of North Carolina Press, 2014.

Sydnor, Charles Sackett. *Slavery in Mississippi*. New York: D. Appleton-Century, 1933.

———. "Southerners and the Laws." *Journal of Southern History* 6, no. 1 (February 1940): 3–23.

Takagi, Midori. *Rearing Wolves to Our Own Destruction: Slavery in Richmond, Virginia, 1782–1865*. Charlottesville: University Press of Virginia, 1999.

Tanenhaus, David S. "The Elusive Juvenile Court: Its Origins, Practices, and Re-Inventions." In *The Oxford Handbook of Juvenile Crime and Juvenile Justice*, edited by Barry C. Feld and Donna M. Bishop, 419–44. New York: Oxford University Press, 2012.

Tansey, Richard. "Out-of-State Free Blacks in Late Antebellum New Orleans." *Louisiana History* 22, no. 4 (Fall 1981): 369–86.

Tarter, Michele Lise, and Richard Bell, eds. *Buried Lives: Incarcerated in Early America*. Athens: University of Georgia Press, 2012.

Tasistro, Louis. *Random Shots and Southern Breezes, Containing Critical Remarks on the Southern States and Southern Institutions, with Semi-Serious Observations on Men and Manners*. 2 vols. New York: Harper and Brothers, 1842.

Taylor, Amy Murrell. *Embattled Freedom: Journeys through the Civil War's Slave Refugee Camps*. Chapel Hill: University of North Carolina Press, 2018.

Taylor, Henry. *West Indies; Paper on the Proposed Emancipation of Slaves Presenting the Advantages and Disadvantages of a Number of Plans for Effecting the Abolition of Slavery*. London: W. Clowes, 1838.

Taylor, Joe Gray. *Louisiana: A Bicentennial History*. New York: W. W. Norton, 1976.

———. *Negro Slavery in Louisiana*. Baton Rouge: Louisiana Historical Association, 1963.

Taylor, Orville W. *Negro Slavery in Arkansas*. Fayetteville: University of Arkansas Press, 2000 [1958].

Taylor, William Banks. *Brokered Justice: Race, Politics, and Mississippi Prisons, 1798–1992*. Columbus: Ohio State University Press, 1993.

Tennessee Legislature. *Acts Passed at the First Session of the Twenty-Fifth General Assembly of the State of Tennessee, 1843–44*. [Knoxville, TN]: L. Gifford and E. G. Eastman, 1844.

———. *Acts Passed at the First Session of the Twenty-Fourth General Assembly of the State of Tennessee, 1841–42*. Murfreesborough, TN: D. Cameron, 1842.

Terrell, Mary Church. "Peonage in the United States: The Convict Lease System and the Chain Gangs." *Nineteenth Century* 62, no. 8 (August 1907): 306–22.

Texas Legislature. *Laws of the Eighth Legislature of the State of Texas. Extra Session.* Austin: John Marshall, 1861.

Thomas, James. *From Tennessee Slave to St. Louis Entrepreneur: The Autobiography of James Thomas.* Edited by Loren Schweninger. Columbia: University of Missouri Press, 1984.

Thomas, Willard. "No Job Blues." In *I'm Going Where the Water Drinks Like Wine: 18 Unsung Bluesmen Rarities, 1923–29.* Compact disc. Quartermass, 2010.

Thompson, Darla Jean. "Circuits of Containment: Iron Collars, Incarceration and the Infrastructure of Slavery." PhD diss., Cornell University, 2014.

Thompson, George. *Prison Life and Reflections; or, A Narrative of the Arrest, Trial, Conviction, Imprisonment, Treatment, Observations, Reflections, and Deliverance of Work, Burr, and Thomson, Who Suffered an Unjust and Cruel Imprisonment in Missouri Penitentiary, for Attempting to Aid Some Slaves to Liberty.* New York: S. W. Benedict, 1848.

Thompson, Heather Ann. "Blinded by a 'Barbaric' South: Prison Horrors, Inmate Abuse, and the Ironic History of American Penal Reform." In *The Myth of Southern Exceptionalism*, edited by Matthew D. Lassiter and Joseph Crespino, 74–95. New York: Oxford University Press, 2010.

———. *Blood in the Water: The Attica Prison Uprising of 1971 and Its Legacy.* New York: Pantheon, 2016.

———. "From Researching the Past to Reimagining the Future: Locating the Carceral Crisis, and the Key to Its End, in the Long 20th Century." In *The Punitive Turn: Race, Prisons, Justice, and Inequality*, edited by Deborah E. McDowell, Claudrena N. Harold, and Juan Battle, 45–72. Charlottesville: University of Virginia Press, 2013.

———. "Why Mass Incarceration Matters: Rethinking Crisis, Decline, and Transformation in Postwar American History." *Journal of American History* 97, no. 3 (December 2010): 703–34.

Thompson, Michael D. *Working on the Dock of the Bay: Labor and Enterprise in an Antebellum Southern Port.* Columbia: University of South Carolina Press, 2015.

Thompson, Shirley Elizabeth. *Exiles at Home: The Struggle to Become American in Creole New Orleans.* Cambridge, MA: Harvard University Press, 2009.

Thrasher, Albert. *On to New Orleans! Louisiana's Heroic 1811 Slave Revolt: A Brief History and Documents Relating to the Rising of Slaves in January 1811, in the Territory of New Orleans.* New Orleans: Cypress, 1995.

Tiedeman, Christopher G. *A Treatise on the Limitations of Police Power in the United States: Considered from Both a Civil and Criminal Standpoint.* 2 vols. St. Louis, MO: 1886.

Tise, Larry E. *Proslavery: A History of the Defense of Slavery in America, 1701–1840.* Athens: University of Georgia Press, 1987.

Tomlins, Christopher L. *Law, Labor, and Ideology in the Early American Republic.* New York: Cambridge University Press, 1993.

Towers, Frank. "The Southern Path to Modern Cities: Urbanization in the Slave States." In *The Old South's Modern Worlds: Slavery, Region, and Nation in the Age of Progress*, edited by L. Diane Barnes, Brian Schoen, and Frank Towers, 145–65. New York: Oxford University Press, 2011.

——. *The Urban South and the Coming of the Civil War*. Charlottesville: University of Virginia Press, 2004.

"Trade and Commerce of New Orleans." *Merchants' Magazine* 13, no. 4 (October 1845): 369–75.

Tregle, Joseph. *Louisiana in the Age of Jackson: A Clash of Cultures and Personalities*. Baton Rouge: Louisiana State University Press, 1999.

Trelease, Allen W. *White Terror: The Ku Klux Klan Conspiracy and Southern Reconstruction*. New York: Harper and Row, 1971.

Trent, James W. *The Manliest Man: Samuel G. Howe and the Contours of Nineteenth-Century American Reform*. Amherst: University of Massachusetts Press, 2012.

Tripp, Steven Elliot. *Yankee Town, Southern City: Race and Class Relations in Civil War Lynchburg*. New York: New York University Press, 1997.

Trowbridge, John Townsend. *The South: A Tour of Its Battlefields and Ruined Cities: A Journey through the Desolated States, and Talks with the People: Being a Description of the Present State of the Country—Its Agriculture—Railroads—Business and Finances—Giving an Account of Confederate Misrule, and of the Sufferings, Necessities and Mistakes, Political Views, Social Condition and Prospects, of the Aristocracy, Middle Class, Poor Whites and Negroes. Including Visits to Patriot Graves and Rebel Prisons—and Embracing Special Notes on the Free Labor System—Education and Moral Elevation of the Freedmen—Also, on Plans of Reconstruction and Inducements to Emigration. From Personal Observations and Experience during Months of Southern Travel*. Hartford, CT: L. Stebbins, 1866.

Trynka, Paul. *Portrait of the Blues*. Cambridge, MA: Da Capo, 1997.

Tucker, Thomas W. "Sources of Louisiana's Law of Persons: Blackstone, Domat, and the French Codes." *Tulane Law Review* 44, no. 2 (February 1970): 264–95.

Tunnell, Ted. *Crucible of Reconstruction: War, Radicalism, and Race in Louisiana, 1862–1877*. Baton Rouge: Louisiana State University Press, 1984.

US Bureau of Customs. *Passenger Lists of Vessels Arriving at New Orleans, Louisiana, 1820–1902*. Microfilm edition, 93 reels. Washington, DC: National Archives Microfilm Publications, 1969.

——. *Quarterly Abstracts of Passenger Lists of Vessels Arriving at New Orleans, Louisiana, 1820–1875*. Microfilm edition, 17 reels. Washington, DC: National Archives Microfilm Publications, 1969.

US Bureau of the Census. "Census Bureau Data." United States Bureau of the Census. Accessed September 19, 2023. https://data.census.gov/.

——. *Eighth Census of the United States, 1860*. Microfilm edition, 1,438 reels. Washington, DC: National Archives and Records Administration, n.d.

——. *Fifteenth Census of the United States, 1930*. Microfilm edition, 2,668 reels. Washington, DC: National Archives and Records Administration, n.d.

——. *Fifth Census of the United States, 1830*. Microfilm edition, 201 reels. Washington, DC: National Archives and Records Administration, n.d.

——. *Fourth Census of the United States, 1820*. Microfilm edition, 142 reels. Washington, DC: National Archives and Records Administration, n.d.

——. "Historical Census Statistics on Population Totals by Race, 1790 to 1990, and by Hispanic Origin, 1970 to 1990, for Large Cities and Other Urban Places in the

United States." By Campbell Gibson and Kay Jung. Washington, DC: US Census Bureau, 2005.

——. *Ninth Census of the United States, 1870.* Microfilm edition, 1,748 reels. Washington, DC: National Archives and Records Administration, n.d.

——. *Seventeenth Census of the United States, 1950.* Microfilm edition, 6,373 reels. Washington, DC: National Archives and Records Administration, 1952. https:// 1950Census.archives.gov/search.

——. *Seventh Census of the United States, 1850.* Microfilm edition, 1,009 reels. Washington, DC: National Archives and Records Administration, n.d.

——. *Sixteenth Census of the United States, 1940.* Microfilm edition, 4,643 reels. Washington, DC: National Archives and Records Administration, n.d.

——. *Sixteenth Census of the United States: 1940, Population.* Vol. 2: *Characteristics of the Population, Part 3: Kansas–Michigan.* Washington, DC: Government Printing Office, 1943.

——. *Sixth Census of the United States, 1840.* Microfilm edition, 580 reels. Washington, DC: National Archives and Records Administration, n.d.

——. *Tenth Census of the United States, 1880.* Microfilm edition, 1,454 reels. Washington, DC: National Archives and Records Administration, n.d.

——. *Twelfth Census of the United States, 1900.* Microfilm edition, 1,854 reels. Washington, DC: National Archives and Records Administration, n.d.

US Congress. House. *Message from the President of the United States, in Answer to a Resolution of the House of 21st Instant, Relative to Refugees, Freedmen and Abandoned Lands.* 39th Cong., 1st Sess., 1866. H.R. Exec. Doc. No. 120, serial 1263. Washington, DC: Government Printing Office, 1866.

——. *Report of the Joint Committee on Reconstruction, Part IV: Florida, Louisiana, and Texas.* 39th Cong., 1st Sess., 1866. H.R. Rep. No. 30, serial 1273. Washington, DC: Government Printing Office, 1866.

——. *Report of the Select Committee on That Portion of the President's Message Relating to the Condition of the South. Testimony Taken by the Committee.* 43rd Cong., 2nd sess., 1875. Washington, DC: Government Printing Office, 1875.

——. *Report of the Select Committee on the New Orleans Riots.* 39th Cong., 2nd sess., 1867. H. Rep. 16, serial 1304. Washington, DC: Government Printing Office, 1867.

——. *Riot at Norfolk. Letter from the Secretary of War, in Answer to a Resolution of the House of December 10, Calling for Information Relative to the Riot at Norfolk.* 39th Cong., 2nd sess., 1867. H.R. Exec. Doc. No. 72, serial 1293. Washington, DC: Government Printing Office, 1867.

US Congress. Senate. *Message of the President of the United States, Communicating, in Compliance with a Resolutions of the Senate of the 5th of January and 27th of February Last, Information in Regard to Provisional Governors of States.* 39th Cong., 1st sess., 1866. S. Exec. Doc. No. 26, serial 1237–26. Washington, DC: Government Printing Office, 1866.

——. *Message of the President of the United States, Communicating, in Compliance with a Resolution of the Senate of the 12th Instant, Information in Relation to the States of the Union Lately in Rebellion, Accompanied by a Report of Carl Schurz on the States of South Carolina, Georgia, Alabama, Mississippi, and Louisiana;*

also a Report of Lieutenant General Grant, on the Same Subject. 39th Cong., 1st
    sess., 1865. S. Exec. Doc. No. 2, serial 1237. Washington, DC: Government Printing
    Office, 1865.

———. *Message of the President of the United States, in Compliance with a Resolution
    of the Senate of the 8th of January Last, Calling for Information in Relation to
    Violations of the Act Entitled "An Act to Protect All Persons in the United States in
    Their Civil Rights and Furnish the Means of Their Vindication," Such Informa-
    tion as in the Possession of the Departments on the Subject, and the Steps Taken
    to Enforce the Law*. 39th Cong., 2nd sess., 1867. S. Exec. Doc. No. 29, serial 1277.
    Washington, DC: Government Printing Office, 1867.

———. *Proceedings of the United States Senate, on the Fugitive Slave Bill: The Aboli-
    tion of the Slave-Trade in the District of Columbia, and the Imprisonment of Free
    Colored Seamen in the Southern Ports: With the Speeches of Messrs Davis, Win-
    throp and Others*. Washington DC: T. R. Marvin, 1850.

———. *Report and Testimony of the Select Committee of the United States Senate to
    Investigate the Causes of the Removal of the Negroes from the Southern States to the
    Northern States: In Three Parts*. 46th Cong., 2nd sess., 1880. S. Rep. No. 693, serial
    1899. Washington, DC: Government Printing Office, 1880.

———. *Report of the Secretary of War, Communicating, in Compliance with a Resolu-
    tion of the Senate of the 26th of May, a Copy of the Preliminary Report, and also of
    the Final Report of the American Freedmen's Inquiry Commission*. 38th Cong., 1st
    sess., 1864. Washington, DC: Government Printing Office, 1864.

US Department of Justice. Bureau of Justice Statistics. *Census of Jails and Annual
    Survey of Jails: Jail and Jail Inmates 1993–94*. By Craig A. Perkins et al. Washing-
    ton, DC: Government Printing Office, 1995.

———. *Census of Jails, 1978*. Vol. 3: *Data for Individual Jails in the South*. Washing-
    ton, DC: Government Printing Office, 1981.

———. *Census of Local Jails, 1988*. Vol. 4: *Data for Individual Jails in the South*.
    Washington, DC: Bureau of Justice Statistics, 1988.

———. *Correctional Populations in the United States, 1990*. By Louis W. Jankowski.
    Washington, DC: Government Printing Office, 1992.

———. *Jail Inmates at Midyear 2007*. By Todd D. Minton and William J. Sabol. Wash-
    ington, DC: Government Printing Office, 2008.

———. *Jail Inmates at Midyear 2008—Statistical Tables*. By Todd D. Minton and
    William J. Sabol. Washington, DC: Government Printing Office, 2009.

———. *Jail Inmates at Midyear 2010*. By Todd D. Minton. Washington, DC: Govern-
    ment Printing Office, 2011.

———. *Jail Inmates 1982*. Washington, DC: US Department of Justice, 1983.

———. *Jail Inmates 1987*. Washington, DC: Government Printing Office, 1988.

———. *Jail Inmates 1992*. By Darrell K. Gilliard, Allen J. Beck, and Thomas P. Bon-
    czar. Washington, DC: Government Printing Office, 1993.

———. *Local Jails: A Report Presenting Data for Individual County and City Jails
    from the 1970 National Jail Census*. Washington, DC: Government Printing Office,
    1973.

———. *Prison and Jail Inmates, 1995*. By Darrell K. Gilliard and Allen J. Beck. Wash-
    ington, DC: Government Printing Office, 1996.

——. *Prison and Jail Inmates at Midyear 1998.* By Darrell K. Gilliard. Washington, DC: Government Printing Office, 1999.

——. *Prison and Jail Inmates at Midyear 2001.* By Allen J. Beck, Jennifer C. Karberg, and Paige M. Harrison. Washington, DC: Government Printing Office, 2002.

——. *Prison and Jail Inmates at Midyear 2002.* By Page M. Harrison and Jennifer C. Karberg. Washington, DC: Government Printing Office, 2003.

——. *Prison and Jail Inmates at Midyear 2004.* By Allen J. Beck and Paige M. Harrison. Washington, DC: Government Printing Office, 2005.

——. *Prisoners in 2020—Statistical Tables.* By E. Ann Carson. Washington, DC: Government Printing Office, 2021.

US Department of Justice. Federal Bureau of Investigation, Criminal Justice Information Services Division. "Crime in the United States 2019." Uniform Crime Reporting Program, Fall 2020. https://ucr.fbi.gov/crime-in-the-u.s/2019/crime-in-the-u.s.-2019/topic-pages/about-cius.

——. "Full-Time Law Enforcement Employees, by Religion and Geographic Division by Population Group, Number, and Rate per 1,000 Inhabitants, 2019." Uniform Crime Reporting Program, 2020. https://ucr.fbi.gov/crime-in-the-u.s/2019/crime-in-the-u.s.-2019/topic-pages/tables/table-70.

US Department of Justice. National Commission on Law Observance and Enforcement. *Enforcement of the Prohibition Laws: Official Records of the National Commission on Law Observance and Enforcement Pertaining to Its Investigation of the Facts as to the Enforcement, the Benefits, and the Abuses under the Prohibition Laws, both before and since the Adoption of the Eighteenth Amendment to the Constitution.* 14 vols., 71st Cong., 3rd sess., 1931. Washington DC: Government Printing Office, 1931.

US Department of Justice. National Institute of Justice. *Operating Jail Industries: A Resource Manual.* By George E. Sexton, Rod Miller, and Victor J. Jacobsen. Washington, DC: Government Printing Office, 1990.

US Department of Justice. Review Panel on Prison Rape. *Report on Sexual Victimization in Prisons and Jails.* Edited by G. J. Mazza. Washington, DC: US Department of Justice, 2012. www.ojp.gov/sites/g/files/xyckuh241/files/media/document/prea_finalreport_2012.pdf.

US Department of Labor. *Bulletin of the Department of Labor.* No. 36. Washington, DC: Government Printing Office, 1901.

US Department of War. *Compiled Military Service Records of Volunteer Union Soldiers Who Served with the U.S. Colored Troops, 2nd through 7th Colored Infantry including 3d Tennessee Volunteers (African Descent), 6th Louisiana Infantry (African Descent), and 7th Louisiana Infantry (African Descent).* Microfilm edition, 116 reels. Washington, DC: National Archives and Records Administration, n.d.

——. *Union Provost Marshals' File of Papers relating to Individual Civilians, 1861–1867.* Microfilm edition, 300 reels. Washington, DC: National Archives Microfilm Publications, n.d.

——. *U.S. Army Generals' Reports of Civil War Service 1864–1887.* Microfilm edition, 8 reels. Washington, DC: National Archives Microfilm Publications, 1981.

——. *The War of the Rebellion: A Compilation of the Official Records of the Union and Confederate Armies*. 128 vols. Washington, DC: Government Printing Office, 1880–1901.

Usner, Daniel H., Jr. *American Indians in Early New Orleans: From Calumet to Raquette*. Baton Rouge: University of Louisiana Press, 2018.

US Office of Indian Affairs. *Report of the Commissioner of Indian Affairs, Accompanying the Annual Report of the Secretary of the Interior, for the Year 1857*. Washington, DC: William A. Harris, 1858.

———. *Report of the Commissioner of Indian Affairs, Accompanying the Annual Report of the Secretary of the Interior, for the Year 1858*. Washington, DC: William A. Harris, 1859.

Vandal, Gilles. "The Nineteenth-Century Municipal Response to the Problem of Poverty: New Orleans Free Lodgers, 1850–1890, as a Case Study." *Journal of Urban History* 19 (November 1992): 30–59.

Van der Linden, Marcel. *Workers of the World: Essays toward a Global Labor History*. Leiden: Brill, 2008.

Van Rossum, Matthias, and Jeanette Kamp, eds. *Desertion in the Early Modern World: A Comparative History*. New York: Bloomsbury Academic, 2016.

Van Rossum, Matthias, Marcus Rediker, and Titas Chakraborty, eds. *A Global History of Runaways: Workers, Mobility, and Capitalism, 1600–1850*. Oakland: University of California Press, 2019.

Vaughn, Megan. *Creating the Creole Island: Slavery in Eighteenth-Century Mauritius*. Durham, NC: Duke University Press, 2005.

Vaux, Roberts. *Letter on the Penitentiary System of Pennsylvania. Addressed to William Roscoe, Esquire, of Toxteth Park, near Liverpool*. Philadelphia: Jesper Harding, 1827.

———. *Notices of the Original, and Successive Efforts, to Improve the Discipline of the Prison at Philadelphia, and to Reform the Criminal Code of Pennsylvania: With a Few Observations on the Penitentiary System*. Philadelphia: Kimber and Sharpless, 1826.

Veneziani, Bruno. "The Evolution of the Contract of Employment." In *The Making of Labour Law in Europe: A Comparative Study of Nine Countries up to 1945*, edited by Bob Hepple, 99–128. New York: Mansell, 1986.

Vera Institute of Justice. "Incarceration Trends." Vera Institute of Justice, 2023. https://trends.vera.org/.

Vernet, Julien. *Strangers on Their Native Soil: Opposition to the United States' Governance in Louisiana's Orleans Territory, 1803–1809*. Jackson: University Press of Mississippi, 2013.

Vidal, Cécile. *Caribbean New Orleans: Empire, Race, and the Making of a Slave Society*. Chapel Hill: University of North Carolina Press, 2019.

Vincent, Charles. *Black Legislators in Louisiana during Reconstruction*. Baton Rouge: Louisiana State University Press, 1976.

Virginia Legislature. *A Collection of All Such Acts of the General Assembly of Virginia of a Public and Permanent Nature as Have Passed since the Session of 1801*, 2 vols. Richmond, VA: Samuel Pleasants, Jr., 1803–8.

Von Daacke, Kirt. *Freedom Has a Face: Race, Identity, and Community in Jefferson's Virginia*. Charlottesville: University of Virginia Press, 2012.

Wacquant, Loïc. "From Slavery to Mass Incarceration: Rethinking the 'Race Question' in the US." *New Left Review* 13, no. 3 (January–February 2002): 41–60.

———. *Punishing the Poor: The Neoliberal Government of Social insecurity.* Durham, NC: Duke University Press, 2009.

Wade, Richard C. *Slavery in the Cities: The South, 1820–1860.* New York: Oxford University Press, 1964.

Wagner, Bryan. *Disturbing the Peace: Black Culture and the Police Power after Slavery.* Cambridge, MA: Harvard University Press, 2009.

Wagner, David. *The Poorhouse: America's Forgotten Institution.* New York: Rowman and Littlefield, 2005.

Waldrep, Christopher. *Roots of Disorder: Race and Criminal Justice in the American South, 1817–80.* Urbana: University of Illinois Press, 1998.

Waldrep, Christopher, and Donald G. Nieman, eds. *Local Matters: Race, Crime, and Justice in the Nineteenth-Century South.* Athens: University of Georgia Press, 2001.

Walk, Joe. *Memphis and Shelby County Government Buildings: County Courthouses, Jails and Workhouses: The Early Years: 1820–1880.* Memphis, TN: Published by the author, 2000 [1996].

Walker, Alexander. *City Digest: Including a Sketch of the Political History of New Orleans.* New Orleans, 1852.

Walker, Daniel E. *No More, No More: Slavery and Cultural Resistance in Havana and New Orleans.* Minneapolis: University of Minnesota Press, 2004.

Walker, David. *David Walker's Appeal, in Four Articles, Together with a Preamble, to the Coloured Citizens of the World, but in Particular, and Very Expressly, to Those of the United States of America.* Boston: Published by the author, 1830.

Walker, Jerry Jeff. *Gypsy Songman.* Versailles, KY: Woodford, 2000.

Walker, Samuel. *Popular Justice: A History of American Criminal Justice.* New York: Oxford University Press, 1980.

Wang, Jessica. "Dogs and the Making of the American State: Voluntary Association, State Power, and the Politics of Animal Control in New York City, 1850–1920." *Journal of American History* 98 (March 2012): 998–1024.

Ward, Robert David, and William Warren Rogers. *Alabama's Response to the Penitentiary Movement, 1829–1865.* Gainesville: University Press of Florida, 2003.

Waring, George E., and George Washington Cable. *History and President Condition of New Orleans, Louisiana, and Report on the City of Austin, Texas.* Washington, DC: Government Printing Office, 1881.

Warmoth, Henry Clay. *Annual Message of Governor H.C. Warmoth to the General Assembly of Louisiana, January 4, 1869.* New Orleans, 1869.

———. *War, Politics, and Reconstruction: Stormy Days in Louisiana.* New York: MacMillan, 1930.

Washington, Austin D. "Efforts to Prevent Negro Revolts in Early Savannah." *Savannah State College Bulletin* 21 (December 1967): 39–42.

Waterman, Charles M. *General Message of Mayor C. M. Waterman, to the Common Council of the City of New Orleans, October 1st, 1857.* New Orleans: Bulletin Office, 1857.

Watkins, James. *Struggles for Freedom; or, The Life of James Watkins, Formerly a*

Slave in Maryland, U.S.; in Which Is Detailed a Graphic Account of His Extraor-
dinary Escape from Slavery, Notices of the Fugitive Slave Law, the Sentiments of
American Divines on the Subject of Slavery, etc., etc. Manchester, UK: A. Haywood, 1860.

Waxman, Olivia B. "How the U.S. Got Its Police Force." *Time*, May 29, 2017. https://
time.com/4779112/police-history-origins/.

Webb, Allie Bayne Windham. "A History of Negro Voting in Louisiana, 1877–1906."
PhD diss, Louisiana State University, 1962.

Wegmann, Andrew N. "To Fashion Ourselves Citizens: Colonization, Belonging, and
the Problem of Nationhood in the Atlantic South, 1829–1859." In *Race and Nation*
in the Age of Emancipation, edited by Whitney Nell Steward and John Garrison
Marks, 35–52. Athens: University of Georgia Press, 2018.

Weissman, Dick. *Blues: The Basics.* New York: Routledge, 2005.

Welch, Kimberly M. *Black Litigants in the Antebellum American South.* Chapel Hill:
University of North Carolina Press, 2018.

Welch, Pedro L. V. *Slave Society in the City: Bridgetown, Barbados, 1680–1834.*
Oxford: James Currey, 2004.

Wells, Jonathan Daniel. *The Kidnapping Club: Wall Street, Slavery, and Resistance*
on the Eve of the Civil War. New York: Bold Type Books, 2020.

———. *The Origins of the Southern Middle Class, 1800–1861.* Chapel Hill: University of
North Carolina Press, 2004.

Wells, Jonathan Daniel, and Jennifer R. Green, eds. *The Southern Middle Class in the*
Long Nineteenth Century. Baton Rouge: Louisiana State University Press, 2011.

West, Emily. *Family or Freedom: People of Color in the Antebellum South.* Lexington:
University Press of Kentucky, 2012.

"The West India Islands." *DeBow's Review* 5, no. 6 (June 1848): 455–500.

White, Howard A. *The Freedmen's Bureau in Louisiana.* Baton Rouge: Louisiana
State University Press, 1970.

White, Sophie. *Voices of the Enslaved: Love, Labor and Longing in French Louisi-*
ana. Chapel Hill: University of North Carolina Press, 2019.

Whiteley, Henry. *Three Months in Jamaica, in 1832: Comprising a Residence of*
Seven Weeks on a Sugar Plantation. London: J. Hatchard and Son, 1833.

"White Slavery!! Or, Selling White Men for Debt!" [Lexington, KY], 1840.

Wickliffe, Robert C. *Message of Robert C. Wickliffe, Governor of the State of Louisi-*
ana. Together with an Appendix, Containing the Report of the Penitentiary Agents
for the Year 1856. Baton Rouge: Office of the Daily Advocate, 1857.

Williams, David. *I Freed Myself: African American Self-Emancipation in the Civil*
War Era. New York: Cambridge University Press, 2014.

Williams, Eric Eustace. *Capitalism and Slavery.* Chapel Hill: University of North
Carolina Press, 1944.

Williams, Heather Andrea. *Help Me to Find My People: The African American Search*
for Family Lost in Slavery. Chapel Hill: University of North Carolina Press, 2012.

Williams, Jack Kenny. *Vogues and Villainy: Crime and Retribution in Ante-Bellum*
South Carolina. Columbia: University of South Carolina Press, 1959.

Williams, John Sharp. "The Negro and the South." *Metropolitan Magazine* 27, no. 2
(November 1907): 137–41.

Willoughby, Umi Engineer. *Yellow Fever, Race, and Ecology in Nineteenth-Century New Orleans*. Baton Rouge: Louisiana State University Press, 2017.

Wilson, Carol. *Freedom at Rick: The Kidnapping of Free Blacks in America, 1780–1865*. Lexington: University Press of Kentucky, 1994.

Wilson, Mark R. *The Business of Civil War: Military Mobilization and the State, 1861–1865*. Baltimore: Johns Hopkins University Press, 2006.

Wilson, Theodore Brantner. *The Black Codes of the South*. Tuscaloosa: University of Alabama Press, 1965.

Winch, Julie. *The Clamorgans: One Family's History of Race in America*. New York: Hill and Wang, 2011.

Wines, Frederick H. "The Prisons of Louisiana." In *Proceedings of the Annual Congress of the National Prison Association of the United States*, 154–59. Indianapolis, IN: William B. Burford, 1906.

——. *Report upon the Penal and Other State Institutions and upon the Jails of Thirty-Nine Parishes, Made by Dr. Frederick H. Wines, Penologist, of Springfield, Illinois, Late Secretary of Board of Prisons of State of Illinois, to Prison Reform Association of Louisiana for Information and Use of the Board of Charities and Corrections*. [New Orleans], 1906.

Wolf, Eva Sheppard. *Almost Free: A Story about Family and Race in Antebellum Virginia*. Athens: University of Georgia Press, 2012.

——. *Race and Liberty in the New Nation: Emancipation in Virginia from the Revolution to Nat Turner's Rebellion*. Baton Rouge: Louisiana State University Press, 2006.

Wong, Eddie. *Neither Fugitive nor Free: Atlantic Slavery, Freedom Suits, and the Legal Culture of Travel*. New York: New York University Press, 2009.

Wood, Amy Louise. *Lynching and Spectacle: Witnessing Racial Violence in America, 1980–1940*. Chapel Hill: University of North Carolina Press, 2009.

Wood, Betty. "Prisons, Workhouses, and the Control of Slave Labour in Low Country Georgia, 1763–1815." *Slavery and Abolition* 8, no. 3 (December 1987): 247–71.

Woods, Earl C., ed. *Sacramental Records of the Roman Catholic Church of the Archdiocese of New Orleans*. 19 vols. to date. New Orleans: Archdiocese of New Orleans, 1987–.

Woodward, C. Vann. *The Future of the Past*. New York: Oxford University Press, 1989.

——. *Origins of the New South, 1877–1913: A History of the South*. Baton Rouge: Louisiana State University Press, 1966.

Works Progress Administration. *Slave Narratives: A Folk History of Slavery in the United States from Interviews with Former Slaves*. 17 vols. Washington, DC: Library of Congress, 1941.

Works Progress Administration of Louisiana. Historical Records Survey. *Transcriptions of Parish Records of Louisiana*. No. 26: *Jefferson Parish (Gretna)*. Ser. 1: *Police Jury Minutes*. 16 vols. New Orleans, 1939–40.

Wray, Matt. *Not Quite White: White Trash and the Boundaries of Whiteness*. Durham, NC: Duke University Press, 2006.

Wright, Alan. *Policing: An Introduction to Concepts and Practice*. Portland, ME: Willan, 2002.

Wright, Elizur. "'The Horrors of St. Domingo.'" *Quarterly Anti-Slavery Magazine* 1, no. 3 (April 1836): 241–307.

Wright, Gavin. "'Economic Democracy' and the Concentration of Agricultural Wealth in the Cotton South, 1850–1860." *Agricultural History* 44, no. 1 (January 1970): 63–93.

Wright, W. W. "Free Negroes in Hayti." *DeBow's Review* 27, no. 5 (November 1859): 526–49.

——. "Free Negroes in Jamaica." *DeBow's Review* 28, no. 1 (July 1860): 87–100.

——. "Free Negro Rule." *DeBow's Review* 28, no. 4 (October 1860): 440–60.

Wyatt-Brown, Bertram. *Southern Honor: Ethics and Behavior in the Old South*. New York: Oxford University Press, 1982.

Wyche, Billy H. "The Union Defends the Confederacy: The Fighting Printers of New Orleans." *Louisiana History* 35, no. 3 (Summer 1994): 271–84.

"Yellow Fever in Charleston in 1852." *Southern Quarterly Review* 7, no. 13 (January 1853): 140–78.

Zacharie, James S. *Police Jails and Reformatories of the Northern and Western States, Their Operations and Systems Compared, Especially with Reference to Louisiana*. New Orleans: Picayune Job Print, 1901.

Zimmerman, Jane. "The Penal Reform Movement in the South during the Progressive Era." *Journal of Southern History* 17, no. 4 (November 1951): 462–92.

Zipf, Karin L. *Labor of Innocents: Forced Apprenticeship in North Carolina, 1715–1919*. Baton Rouge: Louisiana State University Press, 2005.

INDEX

Printed in the USA
CPSIA information can be obtained
at www.ICGtesting.com
CBHW021133270324
5932CB00003B/85